CINEMATIC IMMUNITY

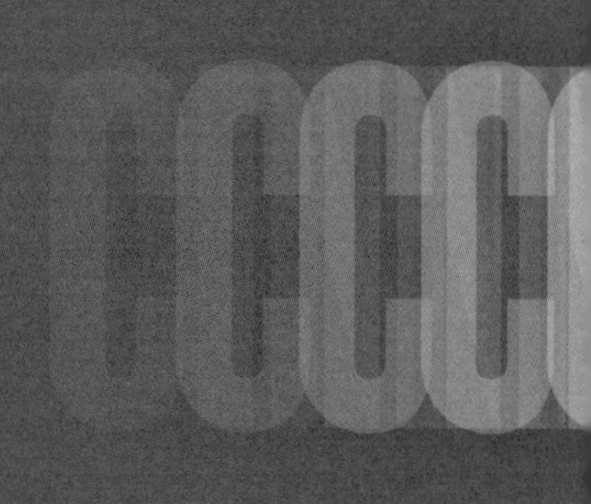

AN ORAL HISTORY OF NEW YORK FILMMAKING AS TOLD BY THE CREWS THAT GOT THE SHOT

CINEMATIC IMMUNITY

MICHAEL LEE NIRENBERG

fh

Cinematic Immunity:
An Oral History of New York Filmmaking
As Told by the Crews that Got the Shot

By Michael Lee Nirenberg

ISBN: 9781627311717

Designed by Bill Smith

Feral House

1240 W. Sims Way

Port Townsend, WA 98368

www.feralhouse.com

info@feralhouse.com

Cover Photo courtesy of MGM and the Margaret Herrick Library of the Academy of Motion Picture Arts and Sciences.

To the movie veterans who've exited the stage. I was lucky to have interviewed Steven Felder, Billy Kane, Kevin Ladson, Chris Markunas, as well as my friends Phil Kennedy and Kjeld Tidemand before they passed. If you have someone who worked in this crazy business, document their stories for us.

To Jessie, Oliver, and Vivian—I hope this book helps frame my problems integrating back into our consensus reality.

Table of Contents

Introduction

We really do know what we're doing. It only looks as if we don't. Serious work is going on even when it seems as if we're just standing around. For everyone else, I'll try and tell you as best as I can how movies are made. It's a complex technical and emotional process. It's art. It's commerce. It's heartbreaking and it's fun. It's a great way to live. —Sidney Lumet, *Making Movies*, 1995

Shooting any sequence, indeed an entire film, is like knitting—one stitch at a time. To an outsider, it can seem tedious.
—William Friedkin, *The Friedkin Connection*, 2013

"Cinematic immunity," generally is anytime rules, regulations, laws, or common practices are flouted, ignored, broken, or let slide, allowing a film crew, collectively or individually, to do or get away with actions no one else could. It often applies retroactively when the film unit is caught out of bounds, past allotted time, even breaking laws, with the casually confident assumption that it is always easier to ask forgiveness than to get permission; especially when one already has "cinematic immunity."

As a personal example, I once got pulled over for speeding, reckless driving and for an illegal turn which was reduced to a warning because the cops recognized me as an actor who played a detective on one of their favorite shows. I didn't say anything. . . . Didn't have to. That's "cinematic immunity."
—Dean Taucher, *MOVIES TV MAYHEM*, 2023

AS NEW YEAR'S EVE 2015 turned into 2016, I was working on whatever programming NBC was turning out in *Saturday Night Live*'s famous Studio 8H at Rockefeller Plaza. I don't remember much about the job, but a fellow scenic artist, Linda Covello, told me her "favorite old man story." As I remember it—there was a janitor who was working on

The Jackie Gleason Show, and, as it was nearing show time, he was sweeping up and then suddenly drops dead. The producers had his body dragged behind the set until after wrap.

"Fuck it, he's dropped dead. The show must go on."

That anecdote resonated with me because it embodies so much of what I love about this business—the dark humor, but also the oral folklore movie people pass down, which is largely unknown outside the business. Despite the glut of information that purportedly tells us how movies are made, the dead janitor story gets at the essence of this thing, beyond the technical, the budgetary, and the glamorous. Best of all, I have no way of knowing if it's true, and I don't care.

The East Coast movie industry emerged prior to Hollywood. It nearly died several times since the late 1800s and had to be resuscitated over and over again. Today, streaming tech companies dominate TV and movie production hubs on the East Coast, but throughout the 1960s and into the 1990s New York was home to a small, freewheeling community of motion picture technicians. That era was a wild, pre-gentrified, dangerous New York that no longer exists. This book looks at half a century—from 1954's *On the Waterfront* through the 9/11 industrywide shutdown—nearly fifty years commonly thought of as the Golden Age of New York filmmaking.

New York's film crews had funny, outrageous characters, with outsized talents whose personalities sometimes dwarfed what was onscreen. We're going to learn how they got the shots and some of the decisions that led to what eventually went up on the screen. "Cinematic immunity" is an industry term for the invincibility crews feel on a film set, wherever that set is located. Having spent most of my waking adult life on movie sets, I've come to think that this invincibility comes with creating our own superseding reality. A movie is a traveling circus. We show up with a fleet of trucks and bring electric generators, grip trucks to rig anything together, prop trucks that store all manner of objects, and then the people: set dressers, carpenters, and scenic artists create towns where none existed, turn modern places into period and hundred-year-old locales modern. We create fake ruins, futuristic cityscapes, car crashes, and explosions. We set up catering and craft service (all-day coffee and food), and there's even a set medic. This work unlocks parts of the City and its outskirts that are closed off to the public—rural pastures to sewers to multimillion dollar penthouses to crackhouses. Nearly every neighborhood evokes a sense memory in me.

I have worked as a scenic artist in television and movies in New York City since 2007, and alongside many of the people featured in this book. Despite the fact that we argue about every choice and decision, there is a general camaraderie over our shared experience. We're splintered up into departments, hierarchies, and pecking orders. It's not a family or a gang, but sometimes it behaves like one. People wander in and out of projects with relative ease depending on the timing and who's doing the hiring. You can work with someone every day for six months and then not see that person again for decades, if ever again. It's not all nice either. There is shit-talking, backbiting, and pettiness as you'd see among any other group of co-workers. I'm as guilty as anyone else.

During the quarantine, I started recording the folklore, relentlessly seeking out as many first-hand accounts as possible. This book is the result of hundreds of hours of conversations. It consists of 150 original interviews done (mostly) from October 2020 to October 2022, featuring never-heard-before, deep behind-the-scenes stories about classic (and not so classic) films and television shows, including *Midnight Cowboy, The Exorcist, The Great Gatsby, The Warriors, The French Connection, The Godfather, The Wiz, The Taking of Pelham 123, Annie Hall, Cruising, Wolfen, Do the Right Thing, Mississippi Burning, New Jack City, Malcolm X, The Sopranos,* and more.

The first two years of this project were spent tracking down cinematographers, camera assistants, gaffers, best boys, makeup artists, assistant directors, scenic artists, costume designers, art directors, production designers, grips, props, set dressers, wardrobe assistants, production assistants, and others who worked on New York City film crews. It's still only a fraction of the thousands of names you see in the film credits, not counting commercials, after-school specials, music videos, etc.

At the time of this writing, five people interviewed for this book have passed away. Film history is lost with every passing. Entire books have been written about many of these movies. Film scholars and historians debate which movies are important and what they mean. I don't care about any of that. This book is about how some of these movies and TV shows were made. This is a primary text.

Behind-the-scenes documentaries and books almost exclusively feature "above the line" talent—actors, producers, directors, and writers. All the biographies and behind-the-scenes documentaries tell one side of what happened. What was the director's vision behind the film? The acting process? The fights with studios and millionaire squabbles? Sometimes you hear from the cinematographer or production designer, but that's it. My kind guess is that these omissions are attributable to the difficulty in getting access to these people. Most of my interviewees are not public figures and are hard to get hold of. I'm inside the business, and it was incredibly difficult for me to track down and get people talking. Yet, when you're working on the set, nobody shuts up!

Celebrities and the idea of celebrity come up frequently throughout these interviews. Even the most hardened film veterans remain charmed by the stardust. They may not admit it, but you hear it in their voices. Another reason you never hear from the technicians is that it's an industry first. The studio celebrity machine needs to keep the viewer at a distance in order to keep selling glamour. My intention is not to demystify celebrity but to shift your perspective to reveal a wider frame. The worst "behind the scenes" material reads like a fan-club book. Celebrities are mentioned throughout this book, but only because the action often swirls around them. It's a complicated relationship.

There's so much more just beyond the spotlight—union politics, labor strikes, dangerous locations, difficult shots, volatile directors, pranks, friendships, rivalries, bad behavior, technical feats, overlapping family businesses, and long hours are what working technicians face every day in order to get the shot no matter what.

Why is this important? Why should you, dear reader, care about the names beneath the bold names? If you're interested in movies—really interested—then you probably wonder about the mechanics of it. How do we capture the magic? Why doesn't it work sometimes? Nobody knows. But I can give you a better account of what craftspeople did when they caught it and when they didn't.

Despite the nostalgia, many people have shared the ugly stuff—the substance abuse that went too far, the casual and outright racism, sexism, and homophobia. The industry during the years covered here was woefully short on employing people of color and women. Every effort has been made to seek those people out for interviews in an attempt to diversify the voices and experiences. As the New York business becomes more corporate, there has been an analogous shift toward greater gender and racial diversity. Bigotry is no longer tolerated. The Business constantly evolves alongside the broader culture both positively and sometimes negatively.

Because these interviews were largely done while quarantined or partially quarantined during the Covid-19 pandemic era, this collection of stories, reminiscences, ruminations, disses, zingers, and filmmaking lessons can be read as a love letter to a New York City that is gone. This book is about the City even when its film crews move into other cities to work, which is why there's a chapter on *Raising Arizona* [1987], despite its being filmed in Scottsdale, Arizona. It's still a New York film crew, and with it comes that energy.

I didn't go to film school, but I'm told that it doesn't prepare you for working in the film industry. I went to art school, which certainly doesn't prepare you for the art world. What happens between the institutions and the business itself? I hope this book fills some of those gaps. Many people were kind enough to give me their time. I hope they are not too disappointed in me having left this or that person out.

SHARON ILSON-BURKE (KEY MAKEUP ARTIST): I guess what I liked at the beginning and what I still like is the whole experience of filmmaking. That was the thing, and it's still kind of organic too. It's like every film, every TV show is its own animal. It becomes its own thing. You can't really compare jobs; it's like apples and oranges.

CHRIS SOLDO (FIRST ASSISTANT DIRECTOR): Filmmaking isn't antiseptic. Filmmaking is sloppy and challenging and difficult and full of, adjustments, and mishaps due to just being in the real world. Not to say you can't make a good studio movie, but it's just something for me about the energy about working on New York City streets that is just sort of unparalleled.

ANGELO DIGIACOMO (FIRST CAMERA ASSISTANT): One morning we were finishing up, and it was I think a Sunday morning, and the sun was up already and people were starting to stir. We were around Central Park again, and one of the other [camera] assistants went to get his car, and they had a car accident in the middle of 59th Street because he was making a U-turn to get to his equipment or something. People think they have cinematic immunity. That was very much the attitude in New York at the time.

How to Read This Book

THIS BOOK CAN BE USED as a reference for movies you've seen or something to reach for after you finish one, or it can be swallowed whole. You may not want to read the chapters about the films you don't like or care about, but there's a reason they're included. Often, the making of the film is better than the film itself.

Beware—spoilers throughout. They are only mentioned in passing to support someone's story. Keep this book around, and when you're done watching *Do the Right Thing* [1989], read the eyewitness stories about how certain things did or didn't go off.

A word should be said about the use of the words "they" and "them." In the film worker vernacular, it is often the common pronoun for "the studio" or "the producers." At various times throughout the process, the crews work in concert with the producers, but never with the studio. Crews and studios have a historically adversarial relationship. Sometimes when the interviewees say "producers" they mean the studio executives or financiers. Other times they mean the people there on site actually doing the daily producing work—budgets, hiring, firing, and coordinating the actions of the various departments. I tried to clarify this context throughout. Producer can mean anything. A great producer is invaluable to a show and paid accordingly.

The interviews lean heavily on the art department and camera people. To a lesser extent grips and electrics. Those are the departments I generally know best and have worked with more intimately over the years. Documentary or oral history work depends on who you happen to connect with at the moment you're working. I could have spent a lifetime tracking down the thousands of people who worked in those years. None of these chapters is the final word on any of the films, TV shows, commercials, or anything. Archival material was only used if it supported the primary sources. This is a population sampling, because a definitive history is a database, not a book.

This book is about mainstream union-made movies and TV because it's the business I fell into. The era in New York that this book consists of had an enormous amount of low-budget, independent, and art cinema that warrants its own oral history. My apologies in advance for not having covered your favorite New York movies. My rationale behind excising *Taxi Driver* is simply that the crew stories I got just didn't have enough insights or add anything to what we already know, or maybe it's just that the right crew members that worked it wouldn't talk to me. I will always hold some low-simmering resentment toward them, as should you dear reader.

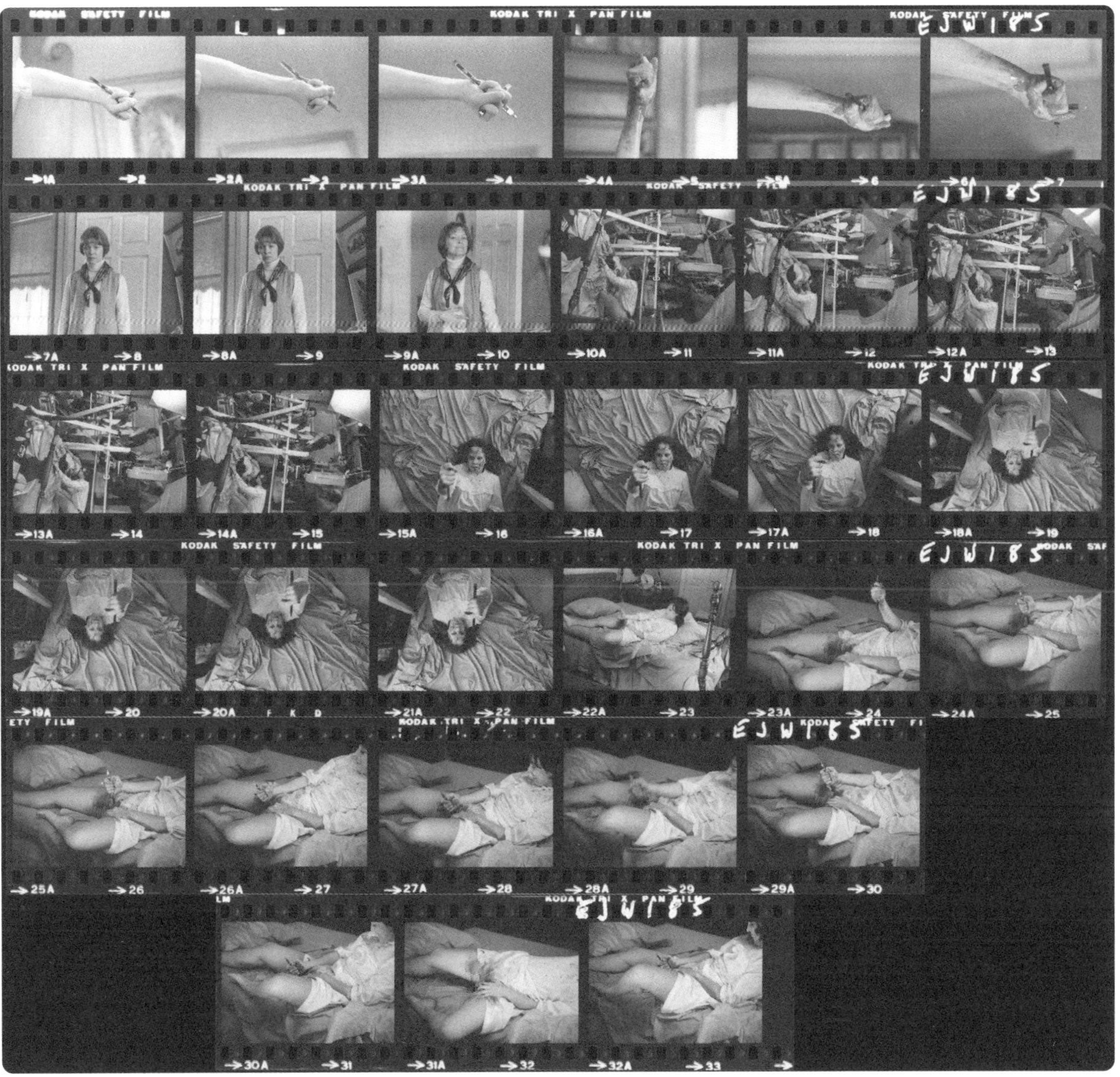

People had multiple jobs in the business, and many of these people moved up to the top of their profession. I tried to keep the interviewee's job title consistent with the time period that the chapter is in.

The Business loves its jargon. All of the terms mentioned should be in the glossary.

Lastly, it was common at this time for a film to be mostly shot elsewhere and then in New York for exteriors or whatever. In these cases, I interviewed the person who did the New York portion of the filming to keep the focus on these people doing what they did during this time.

The Exorcist contact sheet by Josh Weiner. Image courtesy of the Margaret Herrick Library, Academy of Motion Picture Arts and Sciences.

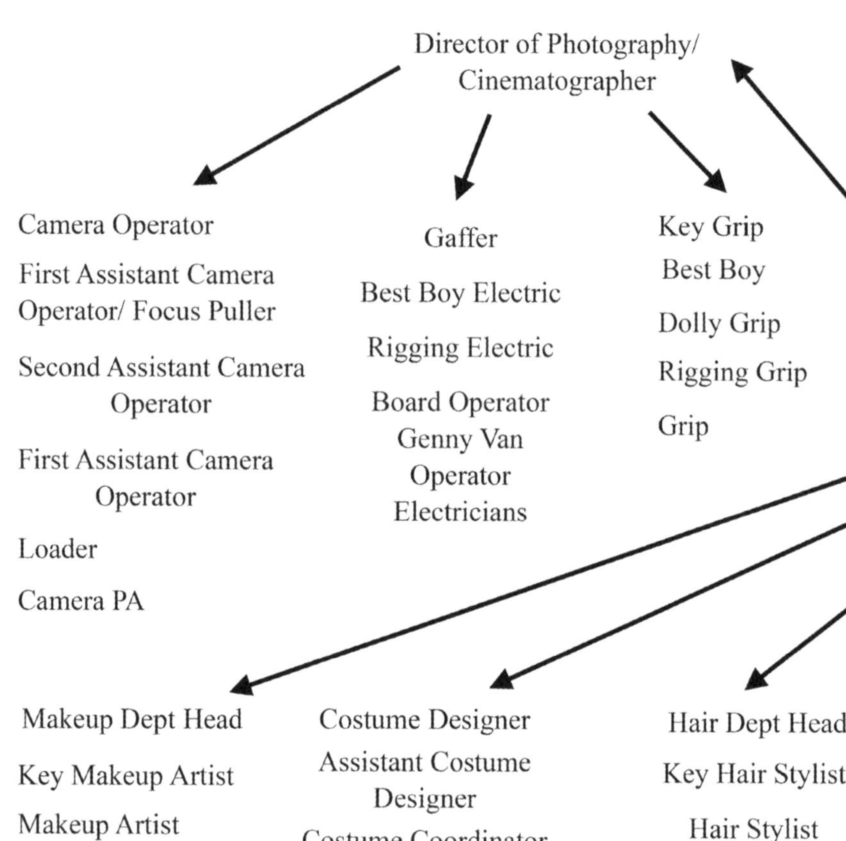

Department Chart

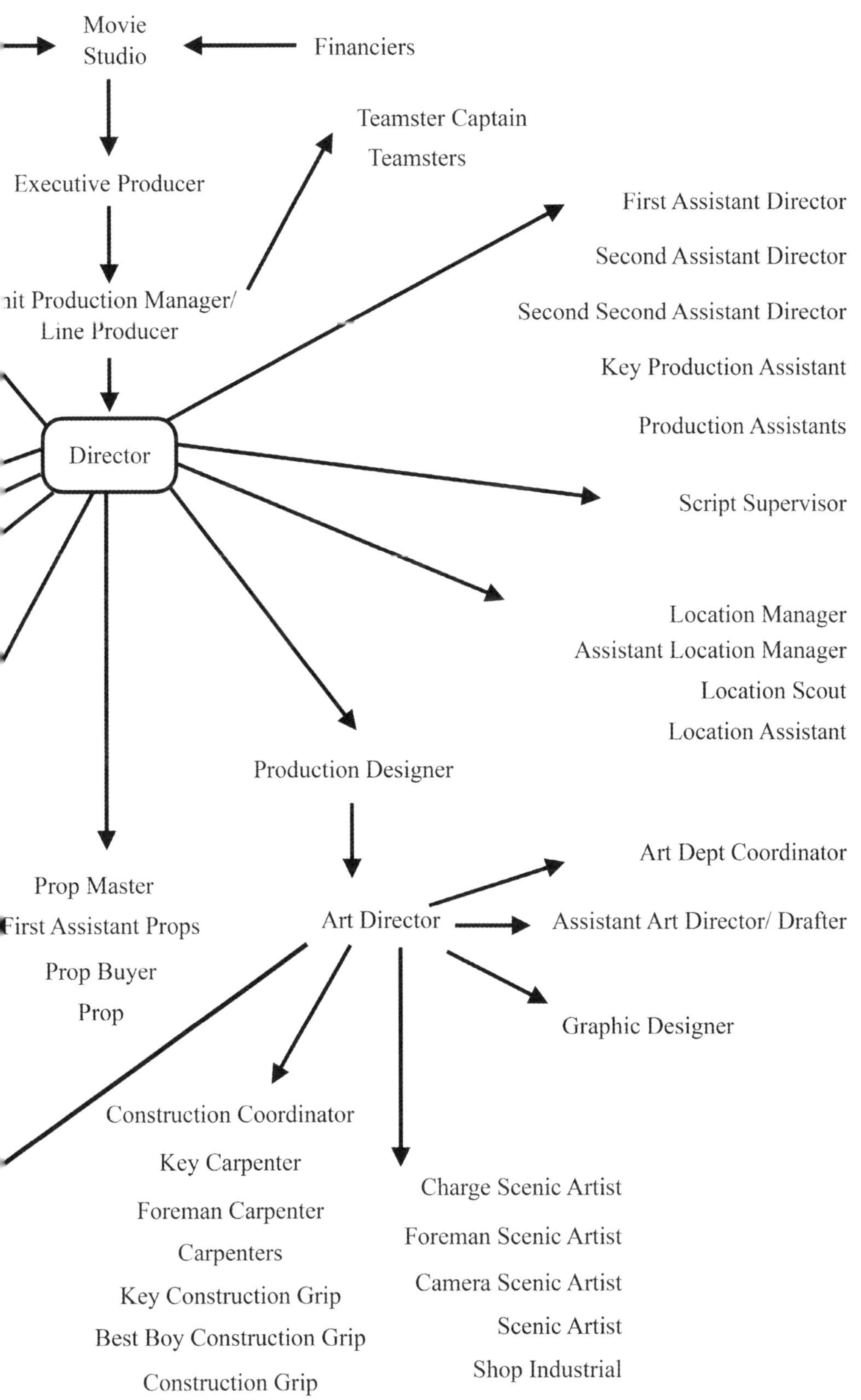
Movie
Studio
Financiers
Teamster Captain
Teamsters
Executive Producer
First Assistant Director
Second Assistant Director
Second Second Assistant Director
Key Production Assistant
Production Assistants
Line Producer
Director
Script Supervisor
Location Manager
Assistant Location Manager
Location Scout
Location Assistant
Production Designer
Art Dept Coordinator
Prop Master
Art Director
Assistant Art Director/ Drafter
Prop Buyer
Prop
Graphic Designer
Construction Coordinator
Key Carpenter
Foreman Carpenter
Carpenters
Key Construction Grip
Best Boy Construction Grip
Construction Grip
Charge Scenic Artist
Foreman Scenic Artist
Camera Scenic Artist
Scenic Artist
Shop Industrial

New York City's Film & TV Production Unions

Directors Guild of America (DGA)
director
first assistant director
second assistant director

Writers Guild of America (WGA)
writers

Screen Actors Guild
actors
background actors (extras)

Teamsters Local 817
captains
drivers
locations managers
locations assistants

International Alliance of Stage and Theatrical Employees (IATSE)
All the locals below negotiate their deals together via IATSE. There are others, but for the purpose of this book these are the ones that are pertinent to our story:

Local 52 Motion Picture Mechanics
prop master
props
set decorator
lead set dresser
set dressers
construction coordinators
carpenters
construction grips
gaffers
electric best boys
electricians
sound mixers
sound utility
boom operators
set medics

Local 161 Script Supervisors, Production Coordinators, Travel Coordinators, Accountants

script supervisors
production office coordinators
accountants

Local 600 International Cinematographers Guild

directors of photography
camera operators
assistant camera operators
loaders
digital imaging technicians
still photographers

Local 764 Theatrical Wardrobe Union

wardrobe workers
child actor guardians

Local 798 Makeup Artists

makeup artists
hairstylists

Local 829 United Scenic Artists

production designers
costume designers
art directors
graphic artists
scenic artists
digital artists
art department coordinators

National Association of Broadcast Employees and Technicians (NABET)

NABET was the union that competed with IATSE for music videos, commercials, television, and smaller-budget films. NABET covered all of the jobs that are listed in the above categories, aside from the ones covered by DGA, SAG, and WGA. NABET was absorbed by the IATSE locals in 1990. It still exists today in network TV stations, local news, network news, and elsewhere.

Cast of Characters

PEOPLE MOVED UP, DOWN, AND IN AND OUT OF POSITIONS OVER THE COURSE OF THEIR CAREERS. THE JOB TITLES LISTED BELOW REFLECT WHAT EACH PERSON DID DURING THE ERA IN WHICH THIS BOOK TAKES PLACE OR THEIR ROLE ON THE SPECIFC FILM.

Richard Adee • prop master, set decorator, special effects

Troy Adee • set dresser

Peter Abraham • camera operator

Marlene Arvan • assistant director

Ira Brenner • camera operator

Kelly Britt • electrician

Michael F. Burke • electrician, gaffer

Jonathan Burkhart • assistant camera operator, producer

Joe Burns • assistant director, production assistant

Al Cerullo • helicopter pilot

Joe Cirillo • actor, producer, security

Dan Davis • production designer, art director

Jerry DeCarlo • hair stylist

Craig DiBona • camera operator, director of photography

Angelo DiGiacomo • assistant camera operator

Henry Duys • carpenter

Russell Engels • gaffer

Steven Felder (d. 2023) • assistant director, producer

Dave Franzoni • best boy, electrician, gaffer

Steve Gamiello • leadman, props, set dresser

Tony Gamiello • set dresser, special effects

Stephen Geiger • scenic artist

Jeff Glave • charge scenic artist

Daniel Grosso • leadman, set dresser

Barbara Hause • costume designer, wardrobe assistant, wardrobe supervisor

Jonathan Herron • camera operator, director, director of photography

Alec Hirschfeld • camera operator, cinematographer

Larry Hoff • boom operator, sound mixer

Sharon Ilson-Burke • makeup artist

Steven J. Jordan • art director, production designer, set decorator

Randy Jurgensen • actor, production services, security, technical consultant

Mark Kamine • executive producer, location manager, unit production manager

Bill Kane (d. 2021) • prop master

John Kasarda • assistant art director, production designer

Lloyd Kaufman • location executive, unit production manager, director

Susan Kaufman • set decorator, art director

Phil Kennedy (d. 2024) • scenic artist

Steven Kirshoff • special effects coordinator

Richard Koszarski • New York film historian

Leland Krane • cinematographer, camera operator

Gordon Krause • carpenter

Kevin Ladson (d. 2025) • prop master

Mitchell Lillian • key grip

John Lowry • key grip

William Lowry • grip, union representative

Kim Maitland • boom operator, sound recordist

Tod Maitland • boom operator, sound mixer

Chris Markunas (d. 2023) • carpenter, shop foreman

Gary Martone • key grip

John Mazzoni • grip

Ray Mendez • entomologist, insect-wrangler

Danny Michael • sound mixer

Beverly Miller • Local 829 president, scenic artist

Octavio Molina • prop master, set dresser

Gary Muller • assistant camera operator

Jane Musky • production designer

Don Nace • charge scenic artist

Cathy Nasch • scenic artist, union representative

Elen Orson • camera assistant and operator, editor

David W. Paone • assistant camera operator

John S. Paul • scenic artist

Martha Pinson • script supervisor

Ingrid Price • wardrobe supervisor

Tom Priestley, Jr. • camera operator, director of photography

Chris Quilles • key grip

Benny Rappa • scenic artist

Joseph Reidy • first assistant director

Bill Reynolds • prop master, set decorator

Bruno Robotti • charge scenic artist

Bradley Rubenstein • scenic artist

Maggie Ryan • scenic artist

Bradley Rubenstein • scenic artist

Steve Saklad • art director, production designer

Cassandra Saulter • makeup artist, scenic artist

Chris Soldo • assistant director

Tony Starbuck • boom operator, set dresser, sound mixer

Frank Stettner • sound mixer

Michael Tadross • assistant director, assistant production manager, producer

Dean Taucher • assistant art director, production designer, scenic artist

Bill Ward • electrician, gaffer

Barry Wetcher • still photographer

Tom Whelan • location manager, producer, unit production manager

Bernadette Wise-Tuteur • carpenter

Michael Zansky • charge scenic artist

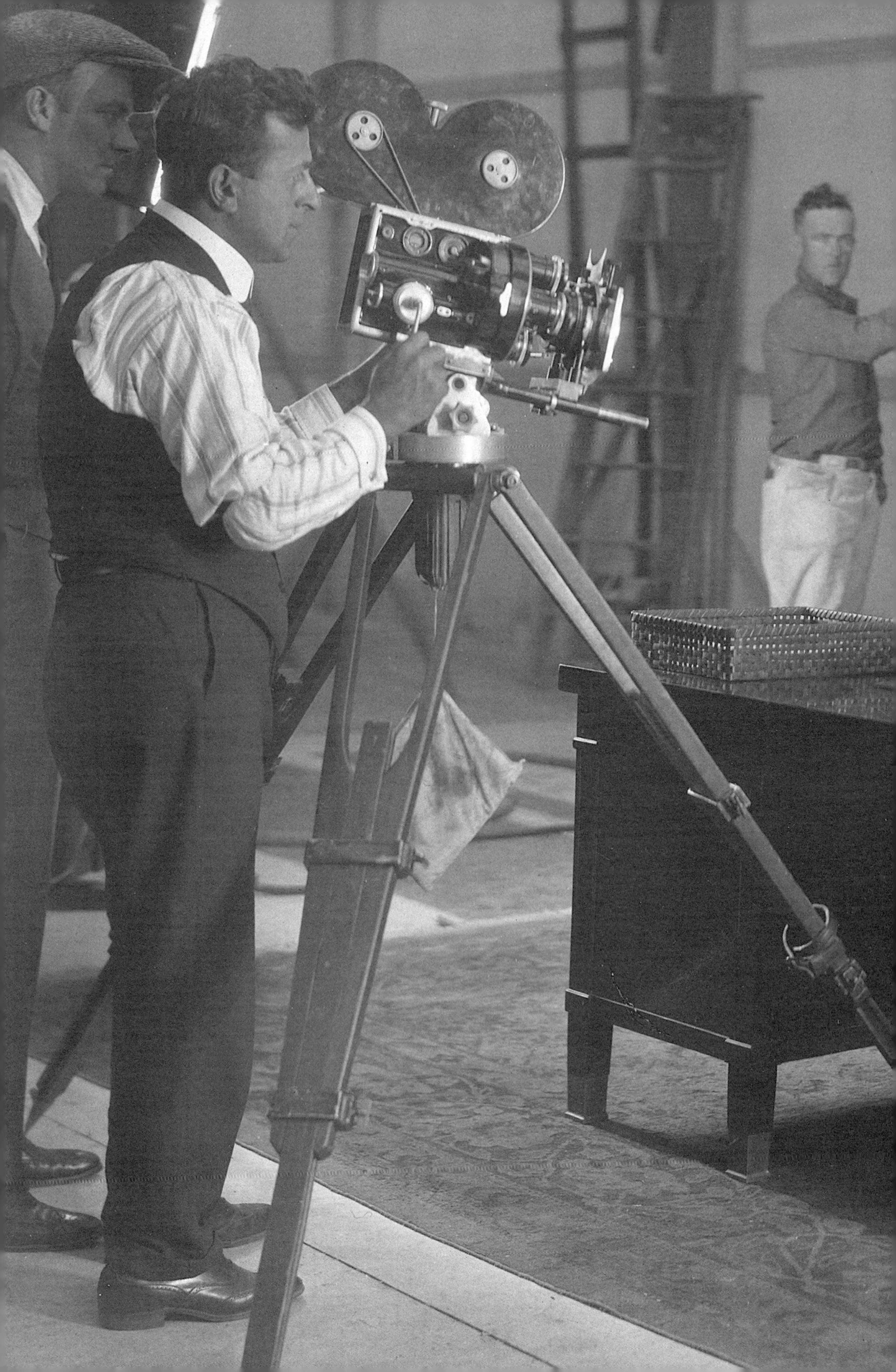

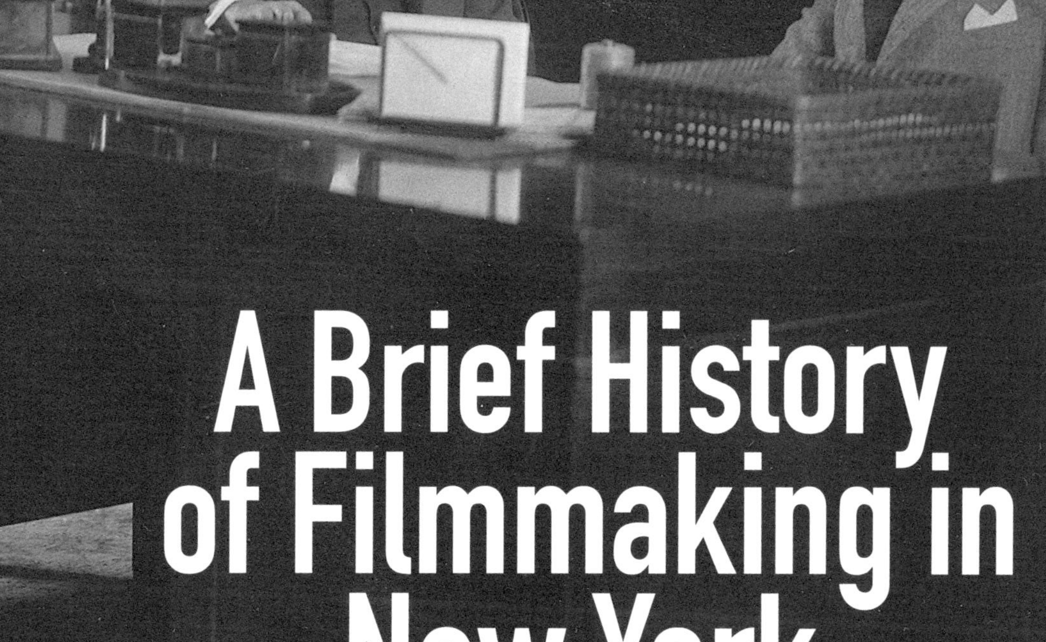

A Brief History of Filmmaking in New York

William C. Marshall operating camera. Jesse Lasky and Adolph Zukor in unidentified film

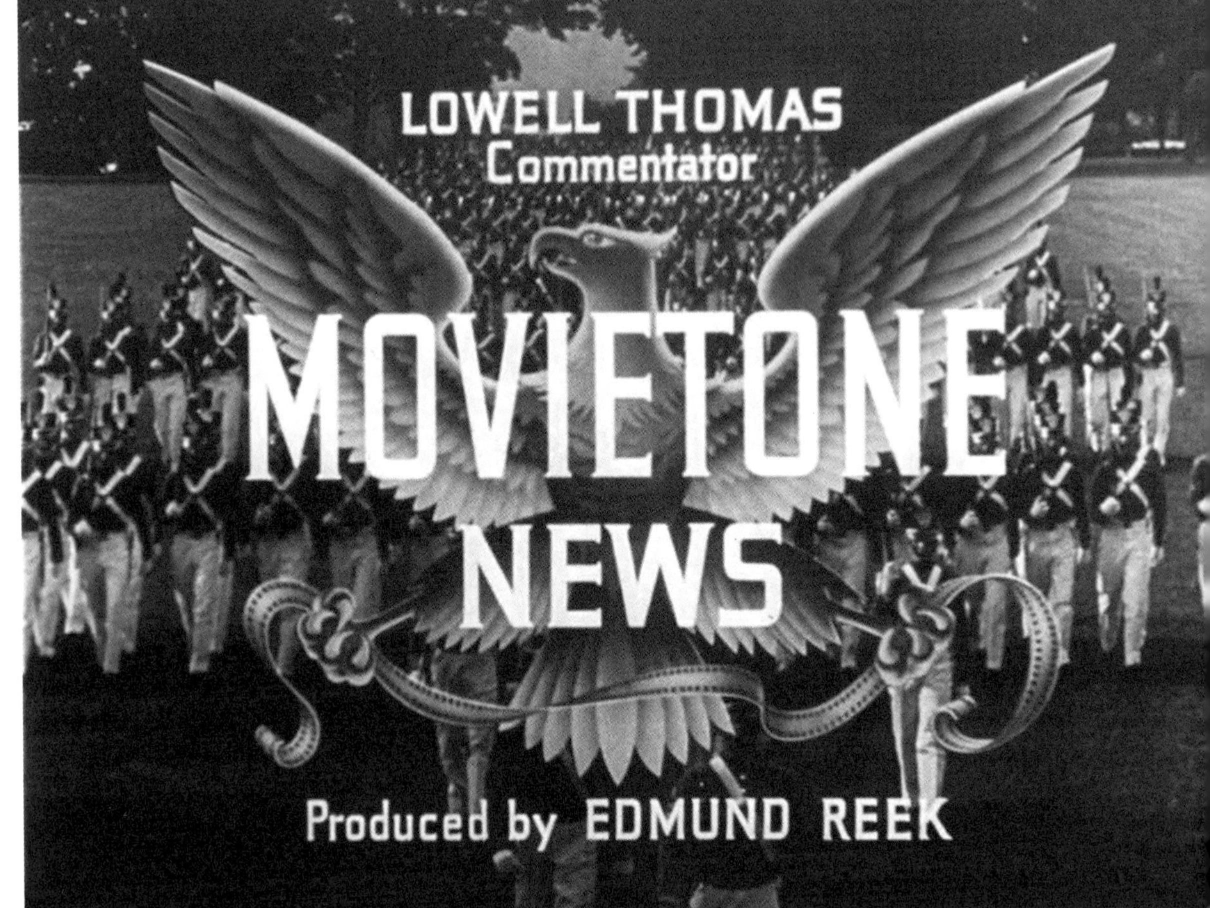

Opening logo for Fox Movietone news.

RICHARD KOSZARSKI (FILM HISTORIAN): Edison develops his technology in New Jersey. They move it right away to New York because they need an institutional center or place that's close to talent. In the beginning, all of the movies, all American movies, are made in or around New York. There are some in Chicago and down in Philadelphia, but gradually as the industry ramps up they want to establish a factory site.

Now, the land was cheaper out on the West Coast. They could work throughout the winter and so on. They try Florida, they try Arizona, and basically they wind up building these studio facilities in Southern California.

BRUNO ROBOTTI (CHARGE SCENIC ARTIST): Actually, between 1915 and 1920, right after the First World War, the movie industry started in Fort Lee, New Jersey.

TOM PRIESTLEY, JR. (CAMERA OPERATOR, DIRECTOR OF PHOTOGRAPHY): My grandfather was a master carpenter at the Warner Brothers Studios in Fort Lee, New Jersey, around 1916, 1917. He was then asked by the people at Warner Brothers to come out to Hollywood. He took a train right out there and got off the train. And someone walked up to him with a telegram and said, "Are you Sylvester Priestley?" And he said, "Yes."

It said that his wife, my grandmother, was very ill, and they thought she was going to die. He got back on a train and went back to New York. He never went back to California again. But he used to make covered wagons in New Jersey and ship them out to California.

RICHARD KOSZARSKI: If they're going to make a Western, or if they're going to make biblical spectacles, Paramount is going to do that on the West Coast. On the other hand, if they're going to do films that are making use of Broadway talent that they've put under contract, those people prefer to work in the East. And if they've hired Broadway talent, then they've probably also bought the Broadway shows that made them interested in that talent. So suddenly they wind up with a profile, a practical profile of the interests that attracted the producers who were based in the East.

Why did they maintain this studio? I mean, my conclusion was that Adolph Zukor and especially Jesse Lasky [both founders of Paramount Pictures] wanted to have a working studio close by the home office, because all the executive operations always stayed in the East. So, Adolph Zukor is sitting in the Paramount building on Times Square, but he doesn't want the factory and everybody working there to be three days away on the other side of the continent. He wants to be able to keep an eye on some of the pulse of Paramount's output.

The creative people wanted to work in New York. So, Paramount built this studio in 1920. And so did Fox. Fox built their studio on the West Side of Manhattan at the same time for the same reasons. It was a bumpy ride after that. Sometimes the production of features in New York wasn't going very well. By 1924, 40% of the films released by Paramount were made in the East. That's a lot. But then suddenly a very, very rapid decline.

There are lots of reasons to explain this very rapid decline. Possibly there was pressure from the West Coast, which was still making most of the films. They said, "Well, why do we need this redundant studio? It's just giving us extra overhead. We really could do everything here." So Paramount shuts down their feature film production in the East by 1927. Nineteen-twenty-seven of course, is also the year that

Warner Brothers makes *The Jazz Singer* [1927] and what appeared to be the death of New York cinema.

TONY GAMIELLO (SET DRESSER, SPECIAL EFFECTS): I guess it was the mid-thirties things started changing. Everything moved to Hollywood. A lot of the silent films in the twenties that my grandfather worked on, a lot of them were destroyed because back then the nitrate film didn't last. And if you didn't keep them with temperature control and humidity control, they would either disintegrate or burst into flames. Some of them they even recycled. And it wasn't until later on that they transferred everything to Kodak safety film. They estimate that about half of the films that were shot before 1950 were lost.

RICHARD KOSZARSKI: In the early twenties they didn't have the sort of union problems that they did in the East, because California was not as unionized as New York City. So that's why they had built up their factories on the West Coast. The labor costs are less and so on.

TONY GAMIELLO: When my grandfather was working at Paramount, I remember [him] telling us there were times when they would work fifteen, twenty hours [per day]. They'd sleep on the stage for a few hours and go back to work. He'd leave for work on Monday and come home on Saturday or Friday night or whatever. That's why they had the unions because of the hours they were working. Because to them [the studios], they're renting the stage so whether they shoot eight hours or twenty hours, it's the same cost for that stage. So they want to work as many hours as they can, but that's what the unions pushed and that's what they got eventually back then, they got double time and triple time.

BRUNO ROBOTTI: During the Depression scenic artists really worked a lot, because the government put everybody to work and they painted murals and did the decorating in all the government buildings all over the country. Then, at the end of the forties, TV really came into play, and it grew because [of] it being a new method, a new form of entertainment. Broadway was also really big at that time, and so that created a lot of work for us. The union became pretty active, especially on TV.

RICHARD KOSZARSKI: After World War I, you have studios that had abandoned New York and New Jersey coming back, especially to New York City. First, just so that they could work with the actors and the talent here, it became easier to work outdoors with sound equipment and put the sights and sounds of New York City to work as part of the spectacle.

BILLY WARD (GAFFER): My father went over to newsreels. Newsreel covered all the different stories of the day. John Tillman used to be an on-air reporter at the time on WPIX every evening and he would just do the stories of the day. They hung out in a place over in Fox's over there on 54th and 10th, and they'd get a story and pack up, go out, and cover the stories. You needed an electrician in those days. Everything had to be lit.

So, it was kind of a nice job in a way. I don't think he made a lot of money to do it. And he would be on call all hours of the day. Even if we had company, he had to shoot out and cover the story. In those days, every channel had its own crews.

TONY GAMIELLO: Then a while later my grandfather joined Fox Movietone News and he would go on the newsreels, because back then every movie theater would show a newsreel, maybe a short, B film, and then there's a feature film.

STEVEN GAMIELLO (PROP, SET DRESSER, LEADMAN): He was on the crew covering *Hindenburg* when it blew up.

TONY GAMIELLO: Not only that, but my grandfather had a new car, so they gave him the film after they shot that historic footage.

STEVEN GAMIELLO: He had the fastest car on the crew, so he was given the film with a police escort to take it into the lab on West 54th street.

TONY GAMIELLO: With the police escort, he raced it down the highway over to the GW [George Washington] Bridge to the lab so they could print it and then make X number of copies to send to theaters all over the country.

BILLY WARD: I went to work with him [father] one time. As a matter of fact, we went up to Sugar Ray Robinson's house up in the Bronx. I think it was Mother's Day or something, or Easter. He knew I liked sports, but in the middle of that he gets a call. He's got to go to Brooklyn; some kid shot his mother or something.

So now I'm in the car and he's got to go cover the story. He locked all the doors, left me in the car, and underneath the el there. I didn't realize how dangerous it was. I was a kid. He didn't expect that to happen. That was in 1954 because he had the 1954 Nash.

When he would go buy a car, he had all these lights that had to go in the trunk. We would go into a showroom, and he would go right to the car and say, "Open up the trunk." He always looked at all the trunks. He needed something to carry all the lights.

TONY GAMIELLO: Back then, the newsreel crews were usually four people. You had your announcer, your cameraman, your soundman, and your lighting man. Yeah, he'd [father] be called away. And there were times when he wouldn't come home for days; the hours were rough.

STEVEN GAMIELLO: He was covering the Beatles when they landed at JFK in February '64.

TONY GAMIELLO: Later my father joined NBC News. He was with NBC News for over twenty years. When he went to NBC News, he covered the Cuban missile crisis.

STEVEN GAMIELLO: I know he worked with NBC News a lot. In fact, I remember one time ABC News came on and news anchor Frank Reynolds came on, and he was a news anchor, and my grandfather exploded, "That son of a bitch still owes me five dollars!"

DEAN TAUCHER (PRODUCTION DESIGNER): Guys like Gene Powell—who was a great guy, an incredibly talented artist, could do any finish, and was very methodical, very patient, and very good at showing people how to do something, and taking them along—he had been a prisoner of the Germans during the

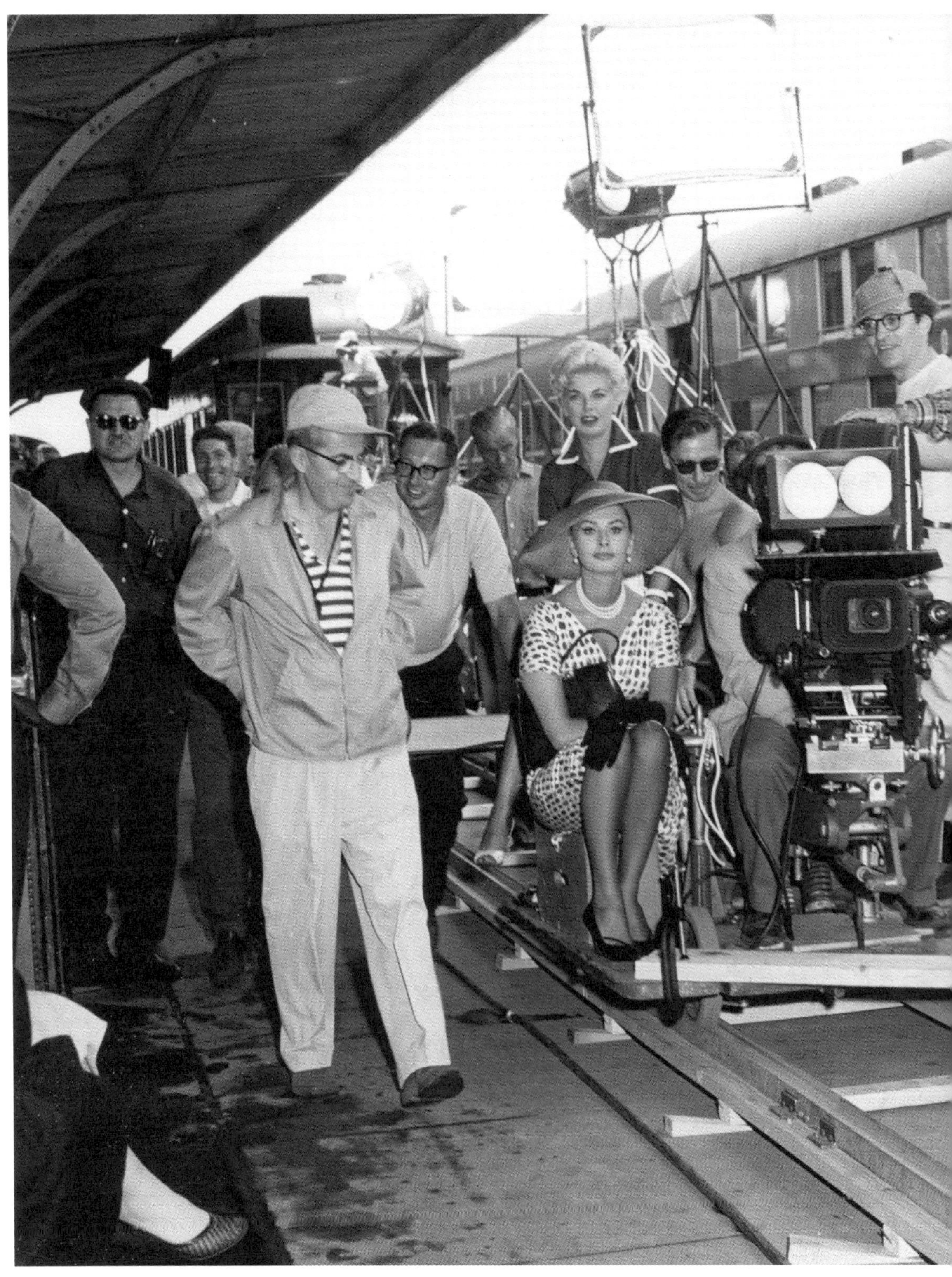

Boris Kaufman, Barbara Nichols, Sophia Loren, and Sidney Lumet, filming *That Kind of Woman* (1959). Photo courtesy of the Margaret Herrick Library, Academy of Motion Picture Arts and Sciences.

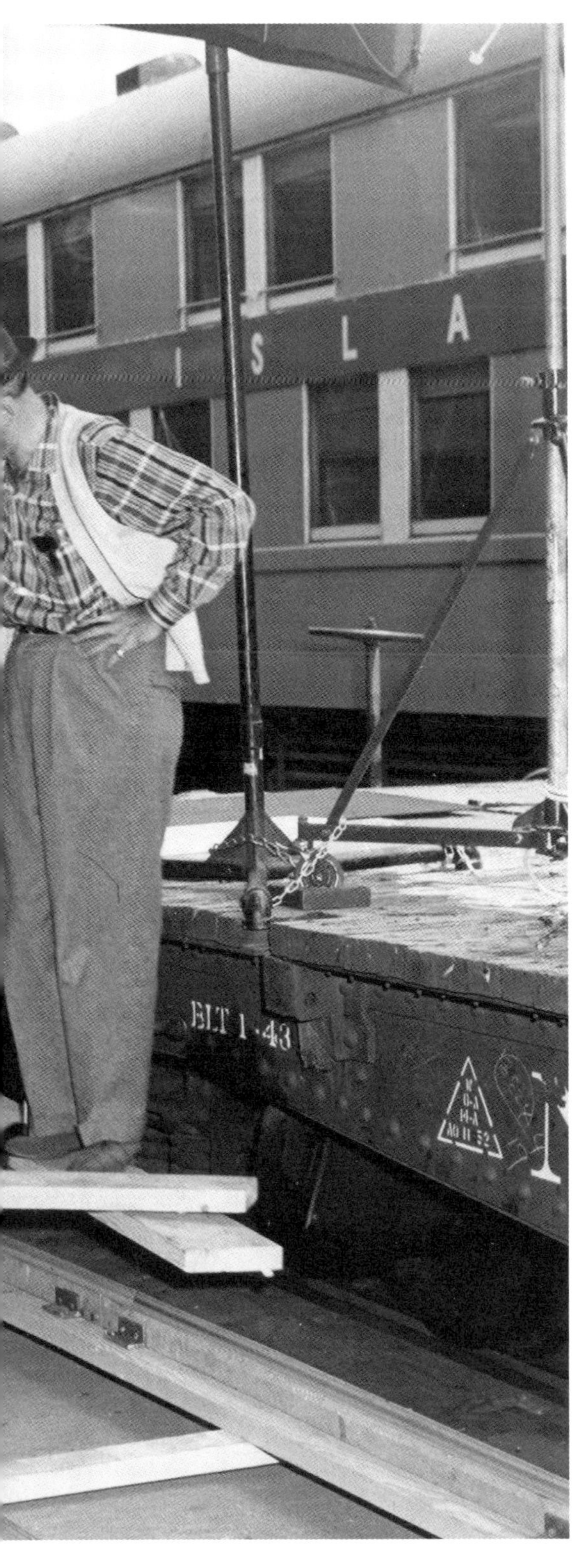

Second World War in the Battle of the Bulge and literally he watched people, American soldiers, starved to death who would trade their food for cigarettes, and I think he was down to skin and bones when the Americans relieved the camp. He had almost died.

Consequently, any chaos that was happening on the set was meaningless to Gene. He was chain-smoking and whistling and happy as a clam. The whole attitude of most of those guys, including the production managers who are all that generation too was, "Fuck, we're still alive. So we're having some fun. There was this just shared understanding that we're living a fucking dream, and nobody looked too hard. The job always got done, but nobody was looking too hard at overtime and lunch hours and this or that because they were all just thrilled to be alive, and had won, and this was play time for them.

RICHARD KOSZARSKI: After World War II, they realize that they're missing something by having everything on the West Coast, and the people on the West Coast said, "We can build anything you want. We can build Paris. We can build Monte Carlo. We can build London. We've got standing streets, from big towns, little towns. We don't need to do that"—but in fact that's not true. In fact, audiences do sense a difference.

On the Waterfront

(1954)

ELEN ORSON (EDITOR, CAMERA OPERATOR): In the fifties and the early sixties it was a very different country. Something started to change, because in New York there were a lot of European filmmakers who had been soldiers in the war, and they came out of Europe to get away from all of that and they brought with them a sort of a social-consciousness element that hadn't previously existed.

RICHARD KOSZARSKI (HISTORIAN): For *On the Waterfront* [1954) the director of photography was Boris Kaufman. And Boris Kaufman was artistically central to the development of the visual style of New York films in the fifties and sixties. He did *On the Waterfront, Twelve Angry Men* [1957], *The Pawnbroker* [1964], and all those films. And when the decision was made, "We're going to shoot *On the Waterfront* in New York and we're going to have to use a local cameraman"—they're having trouble finding a cameraman that they like, and this fellow Kaufman applies.

Boris Kaufman working on *On the Waterfront*. Photo courtesy of the Margaret Herrick Library, Academy of Motion Picture Arts and Sciences.

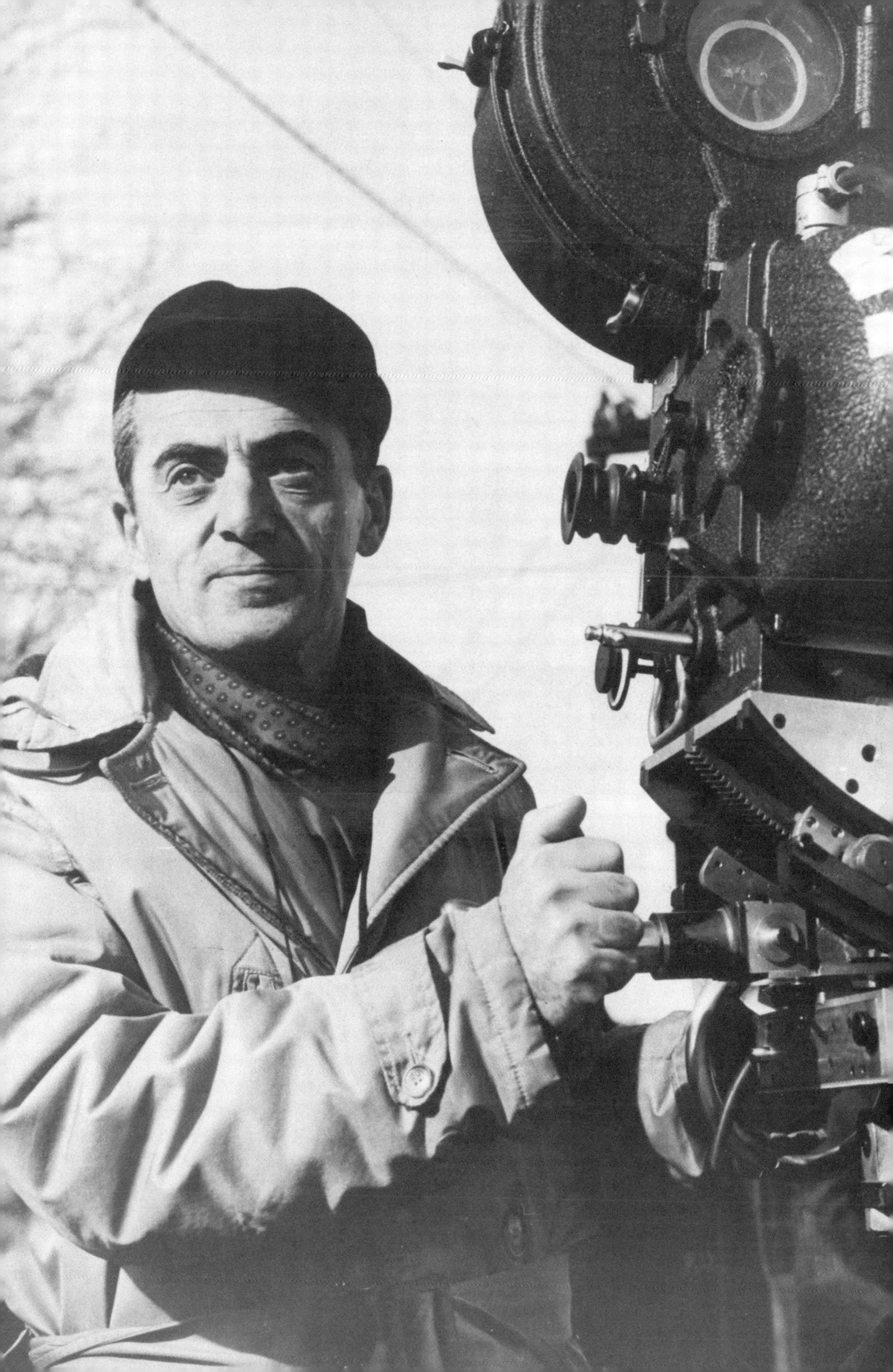

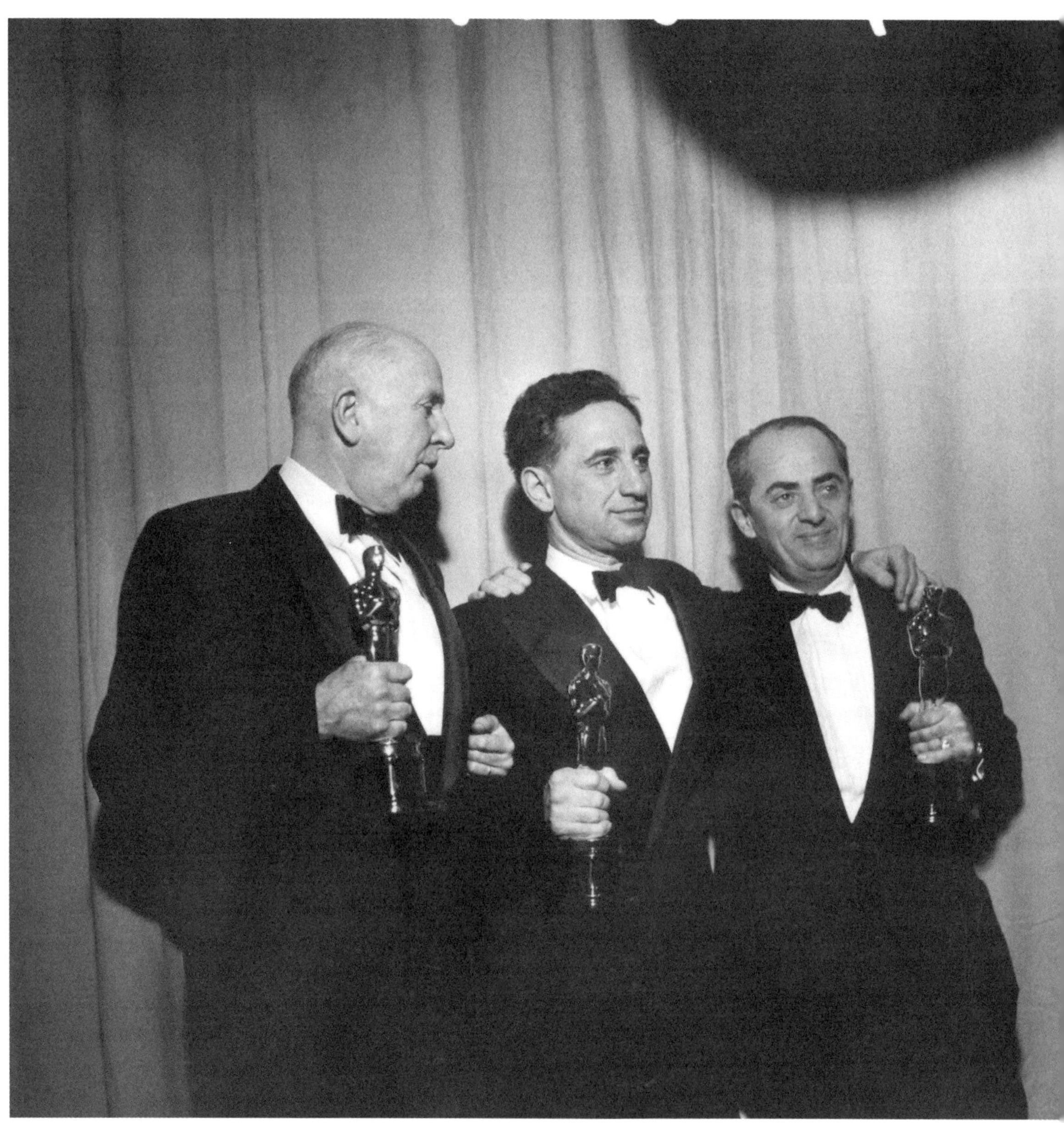

Richard Day, Elia Kazan, and Boris Kaufman at the 1954 Academy Awards.
Photo courtesy of the Margaret Herrick Library, Academy of Motion Picture Arts and Sciences.

Kaufman writes a letter to [director Elia] Kazan and he says, "I hear you're going to do a movie about the waterfront in New York. Well, when I was in Europe, I made a waterfront movie. It was called *L'Atlante* [1934] and directed by Jean Vigo." Kazan says, "Oh, I've heard of Jean Vigo. Maybe we can see that film at the Museum of Modern Art. And we can talk about it."

The point is that Kaufman hadn't been a director of photography on a movie since 1939 and that was in France. He escaped from occupied Europe in 1940. He comes to the United States. He can't get a job in Hollywood and they're not going to hire him in Hollywood. He doesn't have a union card there. He's lucky to get into the country. So he spends the next dozen years working in the East, first for the National Film Board of Canada and shooting documentaries up in Canada. Then he works for the Office of War Information, making documentaries down here in the States. He began shooting two-reel shorts for Paramount Pictures and commercials.

He's working on all kinds of stuff but no feature pictures. Yet you might say, "Well, no feature pictures for thirteen years—obviously he would've left the Business and gone into something where he could make a living, but he could make a living here as a cameraman working in all these other genres." Then when the offer to shoot a feature picture comes he says, "Here I am, and I have this training and guess what—I know how to film outdoors in winter and I can work inexpensively and quickly and I can work under shifting weather conditions"—and all that.

Part of the thing that surprised Hollywood when *On the Waterfront* won eight Oscars was the cinematography, because they thought, "New York cameramen—it all looks like a newsreel. That's what they can do in New York?" They have Local 644 there, but all they know was newsreels. And they had their eyes opened by the photography of *On the Waterfront* and these subsequent films that Kaufman and other people in the East did.

Kaufman won the Academy Award for that. He tried to get a job in Hollywood on the strength of how great *On the Waterfront* is and they made him a member of ASC [the American Society of Cinematographers], but forget about working in Hollywood. They said, "Well, no, we don't care that you've won the Academy Award and [are] a member of the ASC. If you want to work out here, you can come out and we'll start you with the bottom rung in the union. And then you can work your way up for a few years."

RUSSELL ENGELS (GAFFER): At the very beginning, the people my father worked with—back then there was Boris Kaufman, and he was a very tough old cameraman. He demanded a lot. Boris would go on a set, and we would go into a bedroom set and basically, we had a big 10K and a 2K backlight and maybe a fill light—three lights, basic set-up, very basic. He liked that and put cookies and cutters and little things in front and took three or four hours to light one scene, and that was understood. Boris was lighting.

RICHARD KOSZARSKI: Boris Kaufman never shot a film in Hollywood, but he had a pretty good career in the East instead, which was good for the people in the East because he trained crews. He trained his operators and his assistants and his gaffers and they trained other people and so on and so forth. So in a sense, instead of Hollywood simply siphoning off all the good people to work there, they actually prevented the good New York people from coming there.

Already, you see that the classical Hollywood studio system is over—everybody working under contract, all the films pre-sold to the theater chains. Now these films are going to have to basically sell themselves on their own. And the creative packages are going to have to be assembled piece by piece. They're going to have to get a director from here and these actors. It's very different from the way movies were made in the time of *Casablanca* [1942], where Jack Warner would just go through his little Rolodex, see who was under contract, and they'd fill out the cast and crew in an afternoon.

CRAIG DIBONA (DIRECTOR OF PHOTOGRAPHY, CAMERA OPERATOR): Arthur Ornitz was the [camera] operator on *On the Waterfront* for Boris Kaufman. That's where I first met him. My father had to do a [camera] repair. They were doing *On the Waterfront*.

Remember the end of the movie where he walks up through all those longshoremen? I remember I was like six years old, and Boris Kaufman had a brute light, which at that time I had never seen one, so I say, "Well, how interesting—a light with a smokestack," and there was a guy on a ladder feeding the carbon arc. And he's looking through a little glass on the side. I'm like, you know, "This is fantastic," but what amazed me was he shot it down through all those guys playing the longshoreman. And there was so much flagged off that out of that brute light was just this one beam that went down and picked the actor up as he came all the way up. I thought it was just so interesting to watch and that was the first time I'd ever been on a set and actually saw something like that. But I never forgot it. That's sixty-five years ago.

RICHARD KOSZARSKI: It's an interesting example of how changes in technology affect the way films are made. *On the Waterfront,* for example—James Shields was the sound man on that. He's a New York sound man. And that's one of the first films that has a lot of outdoor location work that is recorded with direct, live sound. And they had the equipment—portable film recorders—I mean, they could drag it around; a couple of men could carry it from here to there. They didn't have Nagras yet.

ELEN ORSON: Some of the filmmakers coming out of Europe had different kinds of equipment than we had here. Our television pedestal cameras were very heavy. Our film cameras were very heavy. It took a whole crew to move them around and set them up. And the European cameras were more like the Arriflex, and then the Eclair and the Bolex came out. Nagra tape recorders, UR tape recorders, and Sennheiser microphones.

These are all coming out of Switzerland, Germany, and France. And filmmakers like D. A. Pennebaker and Jonas Mekas and people in that [documentary] genre are all experiencing this new wave as it's happening in France, and all the art films that are coming out of France, and they're using the European cameras that are very portable. You can go on location; you don't have to have sets.

RICHARD KOSZARSKI: One reason they were able to film so much of that picture on location in the actual tenement buildings on Hudson Street in Hoboken was because for several years now they had been using this kind of equipment [smaller European equipment] on documentaries and non-fiction films. Same thing happened with magnetic tape. The first American studio films to record on magnetic audiotape were made in the East. Again, because the people in Hollywood didn't want to use that stuff, they didn't know if it was going to be any good. In the East there were various reasons to take a chance on it.

BILLY WARD: You ever heard that one about the art director on that? My understanding was when they came to New York to do *On the Waterfront* [the unions] said, "Look, you have to have an art director," and they said, "Well, we don't need an art director. It's all on location. Nothing's real." They said, "That's why you have to have an art director,“ so they said, "Well, we have an art director on staff in California—Richard Day," so they said, "Okay. Well, that meets the requirement." Well, anyhow, the movie finished and premiered. It got nominated for best art direction and it won and he came up, he took the award, and said, "Thank you very much." He'd never been to New York. [laughs]

LOCAL 52 NEWS

VOL. III, NO. 4 JULY–AUGUST, 1965

23 NEW CONTRACTS THIS YEAR

LATEST NEWS

WALSH GIVES LOCAL 52 ULTIMATUM: ORGANIZE N.Y. INDUSTRY OR I.A. WILL

I.A. President Richard Walsh laid it on the line at a special Local 52 Executive Board meeting, called to hear the I.A. head give his position on what he expects Local 52 to do in meeting the present situation in New York. Present with Brother Walsh was Assistant International President Walter Diehl.

President Walsh told the Board that either Local 52 goes all out in organizing the New York film industry and all qualified people working in the industry or the I.A. would take whatever action it considered necessary to accomplish this itself.

In a meeting that lasted almost four hours, the Local 52 Board headed by Jim Gartland and Bill Swift, asked Walsh many pertinent questions to clarify exactly what Walsh wanted and how it would affect the interests of the membership. (Gartland interrupted his vacation to be at the meeting.)

Walsh's primary argument, from which nothing could shake him, is that he intends to dry up the source of film labor supply so that non-union shops would be forced to seek I.A. contracts to obtain competent production crews. This, he maintained, would also effectively shut out NABET or any other group that may have any idea of setting up an organization in N.Y.

Walsh intends to ask the I.A. General Executive Board for blanket powers to do whatever he considers essential to keep and make New York an I.A. film town. The I.A.

(continued on next page)

Since January 1965, twenty three new producers have signed basic I.A. contracts with Local 52 and other I.A. unions.

Included among the 23 are five who signed up during the week of August 1 – a period when the NABET situation was boiling over.

With these additions, Local 52 now has union contracts with 151 film companies of various kinds. Everyone of the important commercial producers, all the major theatrical companies operating in New York, the TV newsreel networks and many of the top industrial film makers are signed with Local 52.

However, there remains a sizeable number of companies working non-union in New York *(see Editorial, Page 2)*.

Here are the names of the 23 companies added to our growing network of Local 52 union shops:

Arista Films, Barogroves Prod. Inc., Calfas Prod. Inc., Cavalier Films Ltd., Cadmus Films Inc., Cine-Mix Corp. Recording Studio, Coleman-Meyers Inc., Derutinsky Studio, Directions Inc., Drew Lawrence Prod., Famous Artists Prdo., "The Group", Focus Presentations Inc., Gold Dolphin Ltd., Group Communications, New Directions Film Co., Inc., Pegasus Prod., Jack O'Reilly, Tarot Assoc. Inc., Video Craft International Ltd., Ken Walker Prod., N. Weissman Prod. Inc., Victor Motion Pict., Inc., Production International Corp.

WHAT'S IT ALL ABOUT? WHERE DO WE GO FROM HERE?

To deal with the present situation in the industry, particularly as it affects our Local, we are presenting an Editorial (see page 2), a letter by Joseph Zukoff (see page 6), and a hard-hitting, plain talk examination by Dave Golden (see page 9).

July-August, 1965 Local 52 Newsletter. Courtesy of Jimmy Archer.

The 1960s

RICHARD KOSZARSKI (FILM HISTORIAN): The amount of production in New York would go up and down, up and down. There was production in other places too, and then suddenly there wasn't any production. The Texas coast was going to be the big production center. Plenty of other spots around the country. Money was put into establishing them as a regional production center. But when that light flickered out it tended not to go back on again.

Now in New York City, when the light flickered out, the workers, the electricians, the photographers, the writers, the actors, the carpenters had other related businesses and industries that they could go into. They could go back into theater. They could work in nightclubs. Radio would hire electricians and writers and musicians and performers, and television.

TOM PRIESTLEY, JR. (CAMERA OPERATOR, CINEMATOGRAPHER): My uncle was the camera assistant and a camera operator on a show called *Cinerama*. *Cinerama* was shown on the first 180-degree screen. There was only one theater that was equipped to handle it. And basically it was three cameras—the slight overlap—and they had, like, a panoramic view of everything and, I mean, they went all over the world. They flew in a B25 bomber with this guy, Paul Mantz, who was a famous aerial pilot, used camera platforms, and stuff like that.

RICHARD KOSZARSKI: Even in those years when the production of feature pictures in New York City dropped into the single digits, it's not as if everybody left and they demolished the studios. They did what they could to repurpose those buildings and to redirect their jobs.

TOM PRIESTLEY, JR.: [My father] never wanted to be in the Business: "It's full of drunks. And it's not a steady job." My father was a product of the Depression. In those days, you get married, have a steady job, have a family, and all that stuff. He didn't want to be in the film business because he worked for NBC News. He was a newsreel cameraman. He traveled all over the world. He met famous people. He did all kinds of stuff, and I thought that was very exciting. He was going to Hong Kong and Europe and Africa and all kinds of places.

His brother, my uncle Jack Priestley, was the cinematographer on a very innovative TV show called *Naked City* back in the early sixties. I wanted to visit the set. I was in college. It was 1958, 1959, something like that. I'd never been on a set before, and I just fell in love with it. And I said, "Oh my God, this is for me." I loved the community effort, the camaraderie, and just the fact that you weren't doing the same thing every day. It was appealing, and that's where I started in 1961.

Jack was the director of photography. Andy Laszlo was the camera operator. And he won an Emmy because *Naked City* is basically the first TV show that was actually filmed on location. New York had very few studios back then. It was very, very deficient in studio space and most real estate was valuable and they didn't want to dedicate it to movies. So they had a hard time maintaining those kinds of stages. There were a few, but not very many.

This [*Naked City*] was on Fourth Street on the Lower East Side, between Second and Third Avenue. It was an old bar mitzvah hall that they converted into a stage. It was not very elegant, but since they were outside most of the time they only had one or two standing sets, and one was the police station. And then maybe the captain's office, stuff like that. TV was very popular back then.

RICHARD ADEE (**PROP MASTER**): When I got out of the [military] service, I bounced around for a year or two, and my wife finally said to me, "What are you going to do with your life?"

I said, "I'd like to try and get back into the business my dad and grandfather were in."

So I actually—I shaped the union hall [Local 52] for, like, a full year—eight, nine hours a day. Every day. Then I would come home—I'd drive a cab, and work in a gas station, pumping gas. It was tough. They had a meeting room with a big table where we used to sit, guys that were working on permits at the time, and everybody was gone but me. I'm sitting there all alone. Barney Brady slides his window open—it was like a two-way mirror. He says, "Hey kid, come in here."

So I go into the office. He says, "What's your name?"

I said, "Rich Adee."

He said, "You're Charlie Adee's boy?"

I say, "Yeah."

He says, "What the hell is wrong with you? You're sitting out there all this time. Why don't you tell somebody who you were?"

I said, "Because I wanted to do it on my own."

He says, "Your grandfather was an original green card carrier for this union, and you didn't bother to come in here and tell people?"

I said "No."

So he sent me. I don't remember the movie, but they were building a set, which was Macy's department store on stage. Jack Wright was the property master. I think Jack Flaherty was also there as a prop, and Bobby Ward was a grip. I remember those three guys. And there was a guy, John Olstat. He was a drapery man. They had drapery guys back then in the Business, and I worked on stage dressing a set.

It was a Friday. And the union called over and said, "Knock all the permit men off. They're going to work all night long. We're sending union guys over." That's how they did back then. No permit men allowed to work overtime at any point.

Jack Wright said to the [union] business agents, "I'm keeping this kid."

He says, "You can't keep the kid. I'm sending over union guys."

"I'm telling you right now, if that kid goes, I'll shut the job down."

And it shoots on Monday morning, and I was the only guy at that point that ever worked overtime in the union as a permit man. And that's the only job I ever got out of the union.

GARY MULLER (**ASSISTANT CAMERA OPERATOR**): It was a father-and-son business for years. It was difficult to break in if you didn't have the proper last name.

TOM PRIESTLEY, JR.: There was a lot of nepotism in the business. If you didn't like it, you weren't going to survive.

BILL REYNOLDS (PROP MASTER, SET DECORATOR): For a lot of it you'll almost need some kind of directory to figure out which families are connected with which, because that's the way it happened then.

TOM PRIESTLEY, JR.: I was lucky enough to become the first assistant [camera operator] on a TV show in 1963 called *The Nurses*. The producer of *The Nurses* had two shows going, *The Nurses* and *The Defenders* [1961-1965]. *The Defenders* was a more popular show. E. G. Marshall was the lead in that show. I think when I got into the union they had just finished shooting *West Side Story* [1961] on the Upper West Side, which is now Lincoln Center. It was all those five-story walkups, four-story walkups, with the exterior fire escapes. That was all kind of like empty in there. The city was just getting ready to tear it all down.

GARY MULLER: Tom was probably the best first [camera] assistant in New York by hundreds of yards. Nobody could compete with Tom, and then Tom became probably the best camera operator in the business.

TOM PRIESTLEY, JR.: [On *The Nurses*] everything was gray walls—no pictures on the walls—so you could shoot a closeup against any wall anywhere and just go. The other thing, too, with black and white, is that you never had white. You never had white costumes. Everything was painted either a light blue—the shirts they wore [were] light blue or a light gray because the film couldn't handle the difference between the reflective property of white and the other factors in the scene. So the actor never wore a white shirt.

BENNY RAPPA (SCENIC ARTIST): The first thing my father did was have a grayscale [for paint]. Each studio had their different scales, but he made it common to everyone. Gray #2, which is like a warm gray. Gray #1 was like a pure white, but not so pure. The #5 and #6 were, of course, charcoal gray, and all the way to black. There are about eight different levels. So, if you wanted to paint a surface, you simply said, "Paint half of this #2 and #4 on the bottom." The colors had to be standard. I don't have it anymore, but we actually had the original charts that we used for reference, so we'd never be off on these colors.

He invented that. He made it universal. He is definitely a borderline genius. He has tons of energy dedicated for industry only. He doesn't go off on the bottle or any other substances. He just went right home and went right to his art room and produced artwork at home.

MAGGIE RYAN (SCENIC ARTIST): [Scenic artist] Gene Powell was telling me stories about how, at the 1964 World's Fair, they would get enough wages for a week to buy, say, a Volkswagen, and houses back them were $10,000. They got more money. He said when he went to his accountant, the accountant said, "Are you a lawyer?"

RICHARD ADEE: One of the first movies I was on might have been *The Group* [1966]. They locked the stage doors. Nobody could get out of the studio. We were there for the whole weekend. We couldn't get out. And everybody was gambling and drinking. I mean, it was like one big roaring party.

BILL KANE (PROP MASTER): I think *The Group* was one of the first ones I did as a set dresser.

BILLY WARD (ELECTRICIAN, GAFFER): I've done some things before that. I worked on *The Group*. Sidney Lumet directed it.

RICHARD ADEE: I think The *Group* was one of the first movies that I was working on.

BILLY WARD: 1966. I was about twenty-one. I don't think I was in the union at that point. I think it was a shift getting into the union because you couldn't get into the union until you were twenty-one. *The Group*. That was a big color movie. We went up to Connecticut. We did some up there. It was a big flop. It was a long movie at the time, too.

RICHARD ADEE: It was about Vassar college girls. We were shooting in 1 Fifth Avenue. It was a very fancy restaurant-bar-type place. And these girls are sitting around a round table and they're telling stories.

One girl would be talking. The camera would be here. Everything had to be right on the table. And this one is eating raw clams in the scene. I always have spit buckets at eating scenes so that they don't have to swallow and eat it. When they move the camera, they just spit it in a bucket. So, this broad never spit them out. I had a burlap bag—I swear to God, this high—and we're shooting, like, seven, eight hours, and this broad eats clams after clam—she must have ate twenty dozen clams. I'm not exaggerating.

I go home that night and I said to my wife, I said, "I got a problem." She said "What?"

I said, "I got this goddamn woman on the set. All she does is eat clams all day, and we never finished the scene. We had to go back the next day to pick up where we left off the day before. What the hell can I do to stop her from eating clams?"

She says, "Oh, I'll give you something. You ever hear of ipecac?"

You usually use it for children if they swallow pills, and I sprinkle this stuff on clams. Well, she didn't get down half a dozen clams. She starts throwing up. Diarrhea, throwing up. They shut the whole crew down for the day. Everybody went home.

RUSSELL ENGELS (GAFFER, ELECTRICIAN): We did a black and white one, *The Incident* [1967], which was on the subway.

ALEC HIRSCHFELD (CAMERA OPERATOR): That [*The Incident*] was my first movie in New York and my second movie with my dad. For a year prior to that, I worked for him during the summers as sort of an unofficial camera trainee because I was too young to join a union. But my dad was part of this big studio, MPO. He made a job for me, basically. I was taking advantage of nepotism.

For two summers, I was sort of a slate boy and camera reports keeper while learning the ropes and loading magazines on TV commercials. Then his company [MPO] wanted to break into feature films. They did one. I think it was called *The Spy Who Loved Me* [1977], which was shot in Jamaica. And I'm bringing it up because the camera assistant on that was Michael Chapman, who went on to make a lot of nice movies with Scorsese. I worked with Michael on *Taxi Driver* [1976], and then the second one I did was in Denmark. I just graduated from high school and he [father] took me to Denmark as a camera assistant. We did a movie called *Days in My Father's House* [1968], which was, I believe, never released in the United States. Then the following summer I did *The Incident* with him. And that was really my entree into New York filmmaking. It was a good little film. I came up in the business with my dad, so I understood the union.

RUSSELL ENGELS: That [*The Incident*] was one of the first movies I worked on way, way back. And Ed McMahon was in it, and young. Beau Bridges—he was a kid, probably about eighteen years old or something. That was a subway movie, but they had a subway car built in the Biograph studio. That's the one my grandfather worked in sometimes. And my father did also, of course. It was one of the bigger studios in New York before they burned out that whole area. The owners of the buildings would burn them out just to get rid of the tenants. It became a terrible area for a while. But the studio was there for a long time. That was what they called Fort Apache. It was up there in those days. And the riots and burned out buildings.

TOM PRIESTLEY, JR.: Black and white was slowly phasing out. I think the first color show I worked on was a TV show in New York called *Coronet Blue* [1967]. It didn't last very long, but that's when we started getting more and more color.

BILL KANE: I worked on the first *Out-of-Towners* [1970], with Jack Lemmon, not the second one [remake, 1999]. I was the prop master on *Out-of-Towners*.

RUSSELL ENGELS: I worked on the first *Out-of-Towners*. I worked on the second *Out-of-Towners,* but the first *Out-of-Towners,* Dusty Wallace was a gaffer. That starred Jack Lemmon and Sandy Dennis.

BILL KANE: Oh, geez. Jack was great. Sandy Dennis, she was great. We worked a lot at night at Central Park.

One of the big effects was Jack standing on the manhole cover—when it started rumbling and he jumped off and it exploded, flew up in the air. I had fake manhole covers made up out of wood, and then the impressions, plastic impressions that I put over the wood, and then the only thing that scared the hell out of me was we put the air cannon in the subway underneath the manhole cover and no problem—no problem—no problem until I ignited it and it went so far up in the air. I go, "Oh shit. I hope it doesn't come down and hit him on the head." We were lucky. It just fell off onto his side.

I'm trying to think how we pulled the [flash]pot or whatever, maybe inches below the surface. It was right under the manhole cover, and we set it off, but it was so high. I got real nervous when it went off, but no problem.

RUSSELL ENGELS: It was very hard in the train station when they first arrived in New York, and it was a garbage strike and all that. The train station was a very difficult working day. We had to light with the old 10Ks. It was a hell of a lot of work on that one because of the old lights that we had to use, and the station was still full of black soot from the trains.

Right now, you can see the ceiling, but back then it was black. That famous Stieglitz picture with the shafts of light coming in—that was the train smoke that would hang in that whole building all the time. When we were dragging the cable around, it was in this black soot and mud. We came out of there looking like coal miners every day.

CHRIS SOLDO (FIRST ASSISTANT DIRECTOR): Under the [Mayor John] Lindsey administration, under what was then called the Department of Commerce and Industry—it later became the Department of Cultural Affairs—a film unit was set up under his administration. There were various people that were like the front person—at one point Beth Meyerson, a former Miss America,[1] was head of this department. What they did was set up a one-stop permitting system where they made it a very, very clean process by which you could get through all the city bureaucracy and get your approvals. That system still exists today in the film office.

There was a woman named Mary Imperato who was hired. Mary was the motion picture/TV permit person. She was legally blind. She died a few years ago. She lived well into her nineties. She was like the production manager's best friend. The production

1 Meyerson led an interesting life. According to her *New York Times* obituary, she was the first and only Jewish Miss America (1945). She worked as a city official on behalf of two mayors; for one—Edward I. Koch—she was instrumental in helping get him elected. She also ran for Senate, appeared regularly on three different television game shows, survived cancer, and was tried and acquitted on charges of conspiracy, mail fraud, obstruction of justice, and using interstate facilities to violate state bribery laws, in a case that garnered international headlines and attention for Rudolph W. Giuliani, the United States attorney in Manhattan at the time.

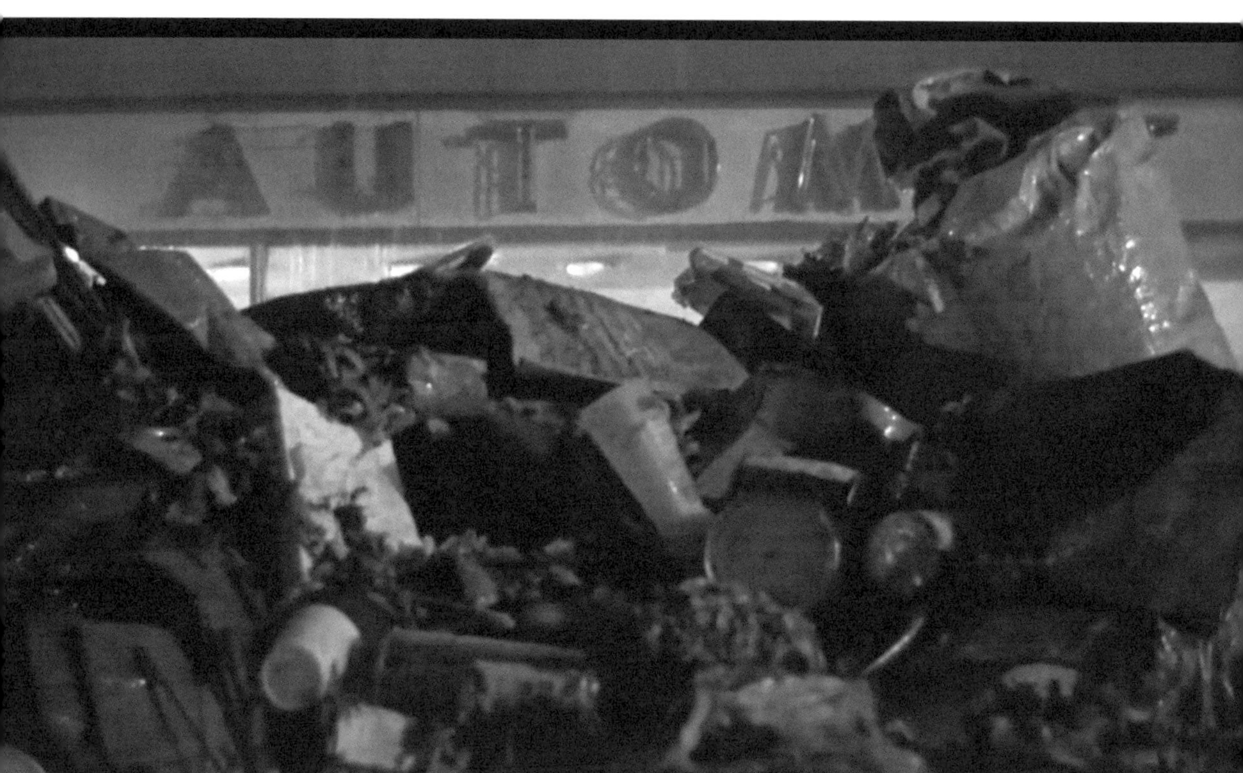

manager would call Mary and say, "Mary, we want to close down the Lincoln Tunnel at night." She would get it done. And she would get it done because the Lindsay administration was basically saying, "Give these filmmakers whatever they want. We want their work here." Now, ironically, it was a time in the City when there were garbage strikes and there was high crime. A lot of the scripts that were getting produced did not particularly paint the City in the most golden light. However, New York became an extremely friendly place to work.

Mary shared the office with one other woman who happened to be my mother. My mother was the parade and block-party permit person. So, in this little office at 455 Madison Avenue, if you wanted to close the street, you'd go and have a meeting with either my mother, if it was a block party or parade, or with Mary if it was a film. You'd start going through the process of getting the closures and permits. Obviously, Mary was very popular with the production managers. I mean, she was just an amazing Italian-American woman, just was like—nothing would stop her and legally blind. She could dial a telephone, but she really couldn't see you.

ALEC HIRSCHFELD: When I went to film school at NYU, I saw it from a whole different angle. I saw directors like Martin Scorsese coming up from being a kid in Little Italy to getting a scholarship at NYU and then becoming a world-class director. It was a whole different pathway [to working in the film industry] than what I had been aware of.

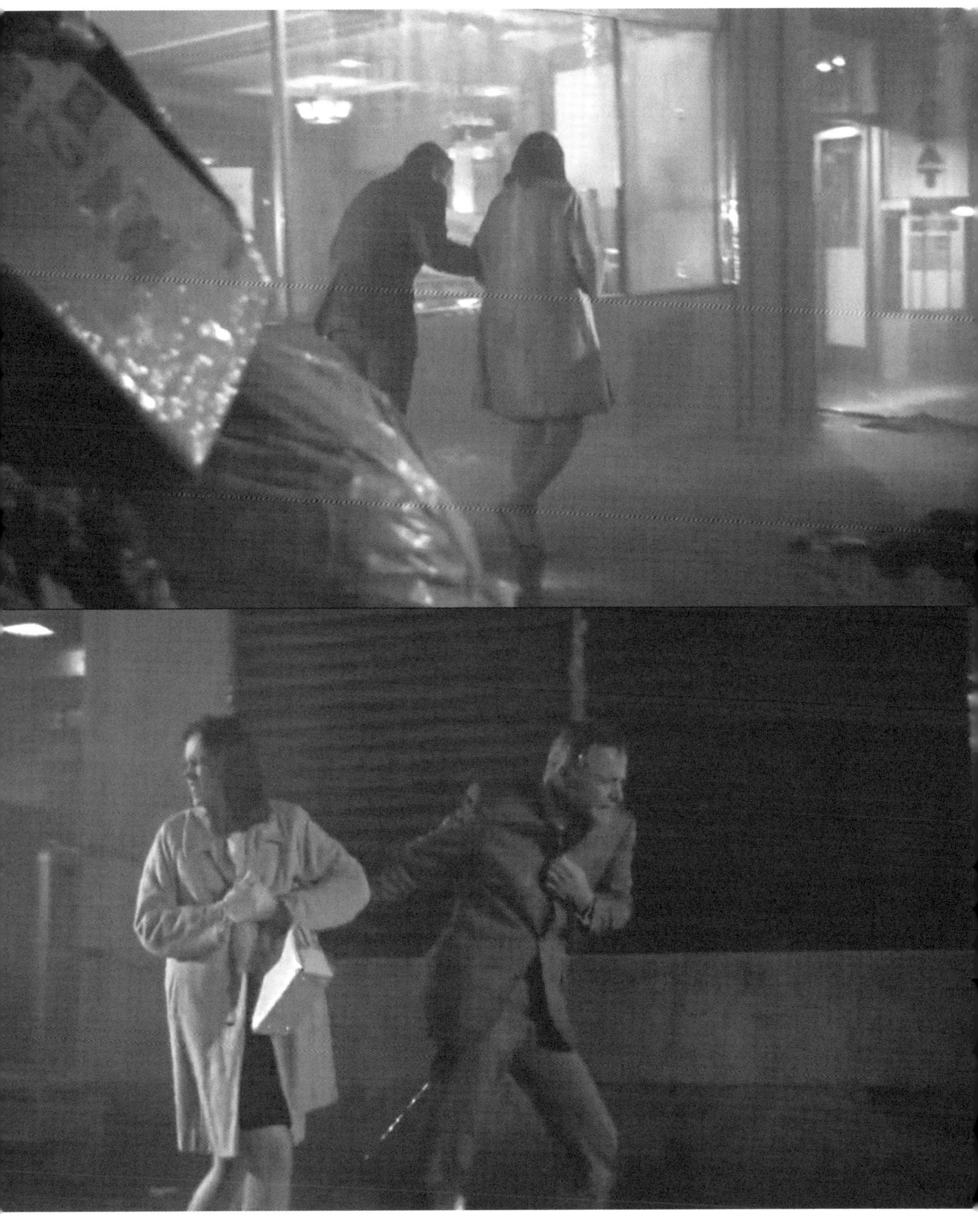

Stills from *The Out-of-Towners*.

Midnight Cowboy

(1969)

TOM PRIESTLEY, JR. (FIRST CAMERA ASSISTANT, *MIDNIGHT COWBOY*): I worked on *Midnight Cowboy*. I thought it was going to be the biggest bomb in the world because we shot it out of context.

RICHARD ADEE (PROP MASTER, SPECIAL EFFECTS, *MIDNIGHT COWBOY*): I tell you, one of the best movies I've ever seen.

TOM PRIESTLEY, JR.: Very interesting film. I mean, it was very avant-garde for its time. Very different. I truly love the director, John Schlesinger. And it was the first time I understood what a director was about and what his role was.

I had to pay more attention to what I was doing. This time, I was more accomplished, and I could observe Schlesinger giving direction to Dustin Hoffman and Jon Voight. I saw what a great influence he was, and he was very good with them, and it stuck in my mind as, "Wow, he really knows what he's doing."

RICHARD ADEE: John Schlesinger was the director, and he was making two versions of it. He was making two films. He was gay, and he was making one for his compadres and one for everybody [else] to see. Because in the movie it was a love friendship between two men. But a straight friendship. They loved each other as friends in the movie. But then he would do a different version.[2]

It is almost 7 P.M. when Schlesinger, famed as the director of "'Darling,'" calls it a day. But before he leaves, he sits down in a yellow canvas chair with his name on it and talks about the film, the first he has attempted in this country. He says it"s about a swaggering young Texan (newcomer Jon Voight) who comes to New York to find fame and fortune through the favors of love-starved wealthy women—and finds loneliness instead. He says it will show how "markedly hostile" New York can be, and how two men (Hoffman and Voight) can love each other without being gay. But he hedges when asked about a rather explicit homosexual scene in a 42nd Street theater balcony. "It's not an unusual scene for the average American movie." And then he goes home.[3]

—*New York Times*, July 14, 1968

2 As of this writing, there is no confirmation of a gay cut, but all of us here want this to be true, so take that as you will.

3 Judy Klemesrud, "Dustin Hoffman: From 'Graduate' to Ratso Rizzo, Super Slob," *New York Times*, July 14, 1968.

TOM PRIESTLEY, JR.: There's a lot of famous shots in that movie too, of Dustin Hoffman and Jon Voight walking down Fifth Avenue, at lunchtime with the crowd. He shot it with a long lens, like a 400-millimeter lens. And they're walking along; he's got the cowboy outfit on. Ratso Rizzo's got the crappy looking outfit he had on. One of the funny stories I remember was when I first saw Dustin Hoffman playing Ratso Rizzo, the first time he came on his set, I was saying to myself, "How could they hire an actor with such bad teeth?" And then I realized that these were prosthetics, that he slipped over his own teeth to make him look more despicable.

RICHARD ADEE: A lot of weird shit went on.

TOM PRIESTLEY, JR.: I never worked with people like that. I never knew these kinds of people. I mean, all these strange people, and I was like, whoa, I just got to step back and just watch and try to do the best job I could. It was like another world for me.

RICHARD ADEE: We were shooting a scene. We were shooting in Filmways. We were doing like a "drug luck" party, all drugs. And Frankie Iannacone was my second man. Frankie knew everything about drugs. He grew up on the Lower East Side, Hell's Kitchen, so he was into all that kind of stuff, and what they did to shoot this party scene was they went down to the East Village and rounded up all these druggies on the streets—brought them to the studio and locked the studio, Didn't let them out and gave them drugs, alcohol, all this shit. This went on for, like, three solid days. They slept in the studio. They ate in the studio. They couldn't get out. All the big doors were locked.

David Moshlak was the sound man. He had this long bushy hair. He fell right in with the hippies. So, they dressed him up like one of the hippies and he had a Nagra [tape recorder] underneath his garb and he would walk around the set. All these people were smoking dope, shooting up—they were doing everything. Everything. We had cameras up on the grids. We had camera guys walking with cameras, with the Steadicam. That's just when the Steadicams developed, and Dave would walk around—that's how he recorded it. I think it was live.

Another thing about Frankie. We were shooting in Filmways, and we were getting ready to do this big party scene. The director or somebody said, "I want to see a couple of what they call a smack."

I said, "What the hell is a smack?"

He says, "It's got to do something with drugs."

"Oh," I said, "I got the man who knows all about that."

I get a hold of Frankie. I said, "Frankie, what's a smack?"

He says, "You don't know what smack is?"

I said, "No."

He says, "I'll bring a couple in tomorrow to show you."

I said, "Okay."

Right up the street from Filmways, like a block or two, there's a police precinct up there. The cab pulls up to the studio, and as Frankie gets out he drops one of these smacks.

There's a cop about thirty feet away: "Hey you! Hold it right there!" Frankie looks at him. He looks at the thing on the ground. Then he opens the door to the studio, and he comes running in. He says, "You got to hide me. You got to hide me!"

I said, "What the hell's going on?"

"Just hide me."

So, I take him. There was two stages there. I take him from one stage to the other. And then there's a trap door on the other stage where the basement is. I said, "Get down in the basement."

The cop comes in. He's searching all over the studio. "Where is this guy? What's his name?"

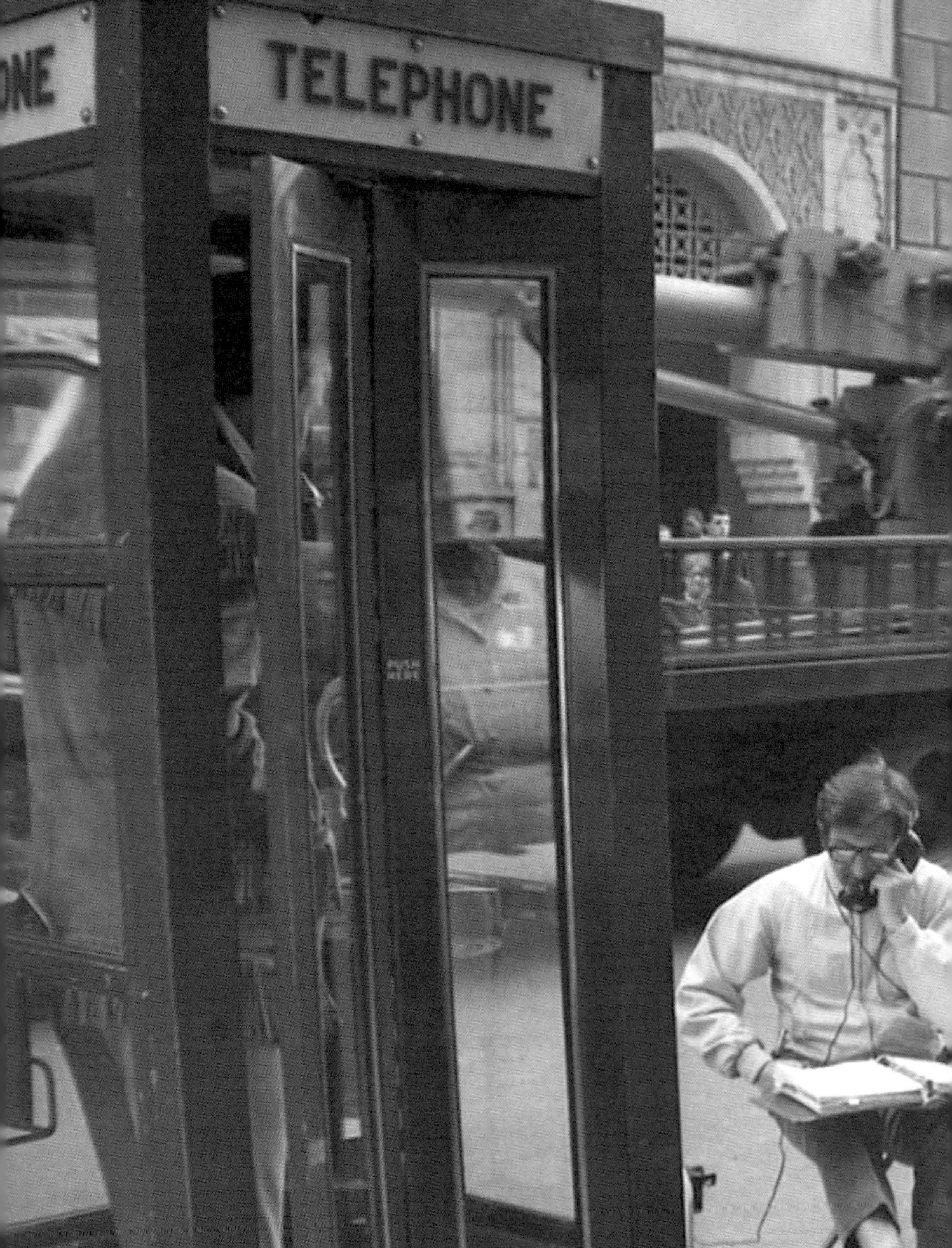
ONE
TELEPHONE
PUSH HERE

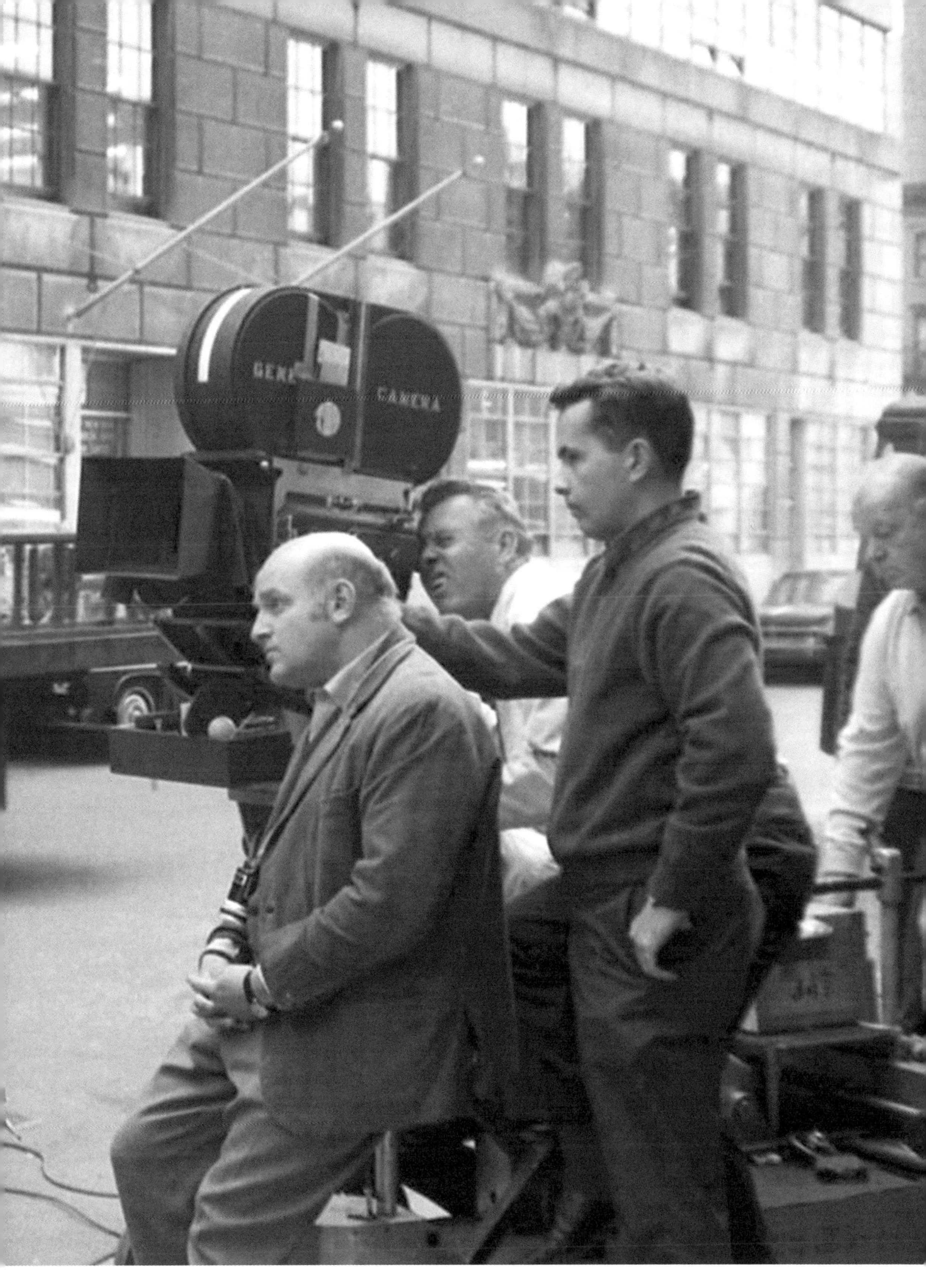

(Left to right) Nicholas Sgarro, John Shlesinger, Dick Kratina, and Tom Priestley, Jr. Photo courtesy of MGM Studios and the Margaret Herrick Library, Academy of Motion Picture Arts and Sciences.

"I don't know what the hell you're talking about. What do you mean? Nobody came in here."

"I know he is here. I'm looking. I'm going to look all over."

Never found him. The cop left. Frankie comes out with the smack bag, the one he kept. A smack is a package—it's got a needle, spoon, and tourniquet, all that kind of shit. They call it a smack. That's the language that the druggers used.

TOM PRIESTLEY, JR.: I'm just a kid from Long Island. What the hell do I know? It was quite an experience.

RICHARD ADEE: On *Midnight Cowboy* we did a great shot. Shot this snow scene down in Little Italy. It was about two city blocks. I had all this snow up on fire escapes. It was in the summertime. People were coming down, looking, and saying, "What the hell? Is this snow?"

You know where Vincent's [restaurant] is? I think it's Mott and Hester. We shot *Godfather* [1972] there. We did a lot of shooting there, and it was, like, the middle of summer. They came to me and said, "Well, we got to do the snow scene." I contacted—I think it was Jay Peak, a New York ski place. They chartered a single-engine plane and flew me up there to go over all this equipment to make snow. I researched it all. It was beautiful stuff.

I signed them up and they're going to come down and do the snow scene, but it was really warm—the highest temperature it could be for the machines to work back then was 32 degrees. Otherwise, you just get water. So that was out.

Then I went to [prop vendor] Modern Artificial and they had this artificial snow, plastic, and we did a whole city block down in Little Italy from—I think it was Mott and Hester. I think we were on Hester Street and what I did, I put crews all up, like the second or third story with these big vacuum machines, big blowers and boxes, and boxes of this plastic snow. Then I filled the street with snow and then I used cotton to drape the window edges and stoops and all that kind of stuff. It really looked beautiful. People were down there because we had all the lights on. It was a night shot. You would never know it was fake. The snow was plastic poly. You could get it in different sizes. Used to get it in crates. And then I had these—they were like reverse vacuum cleaners—they're blowers—and I'd fill up crates on different things and we'd blow it off with fans. And in studios we used tumblers.

I had a guy come in from California. He wanted snow effect, so I set the whole thing up and he says, "What the hell is this?"

He says, "Where's the feathers?"

I said, "Feathers for what?"

He says, "That's what we use in California for snow." I swear to God. That's why you come to New York to shoot a snow scene. Have you ever seen snow that goes up? I says, "You look at any pictures you shoot in California where they use artificial snow—half the fucking snow is going up. Some of it's coming down, but a lot of it's going up. And then they have it on their clothes."

He says, "Well, that's what we use. I want chicken feathers."

I said, "Well, you're not getting fucking chicken feathers. You're in New York. You're getting what I'm going to give you."

And after the scene the guy says, "Holy shit, this stuff is great. What is it?"

I say, "Poly paddles." You could get it in all different sizes—if you wanted it small like a blizzard or you wanted big flakes.

TOM PRIESTLEY, JR.: There's a rape scene in *Midnight Cowboy* and it was done at an old, abandoned farmhouse in Texas. Before we went in there, the snake wrangler went in to make sure there were no rattlesnakes. We were shooting nights. At about four o'clock I went to the production office and the guy was

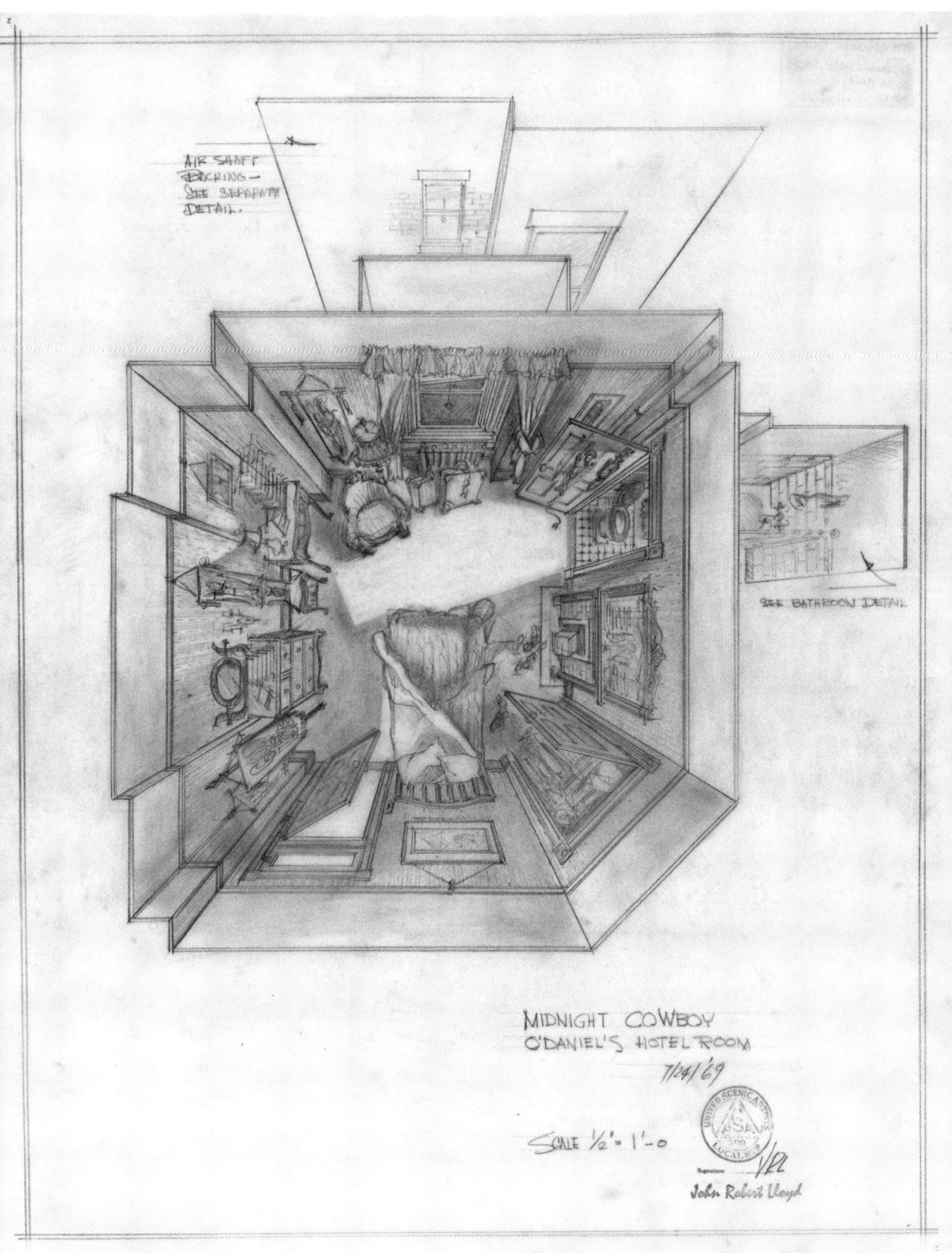

Midnight Cowboy O'Daniel's hotel room production drawing by John Robert Lloyd, 1969. Image courtesy of MGM Studios and the Margaret Herrick Library of the Academy of Motion Picture Arts and Sciences.

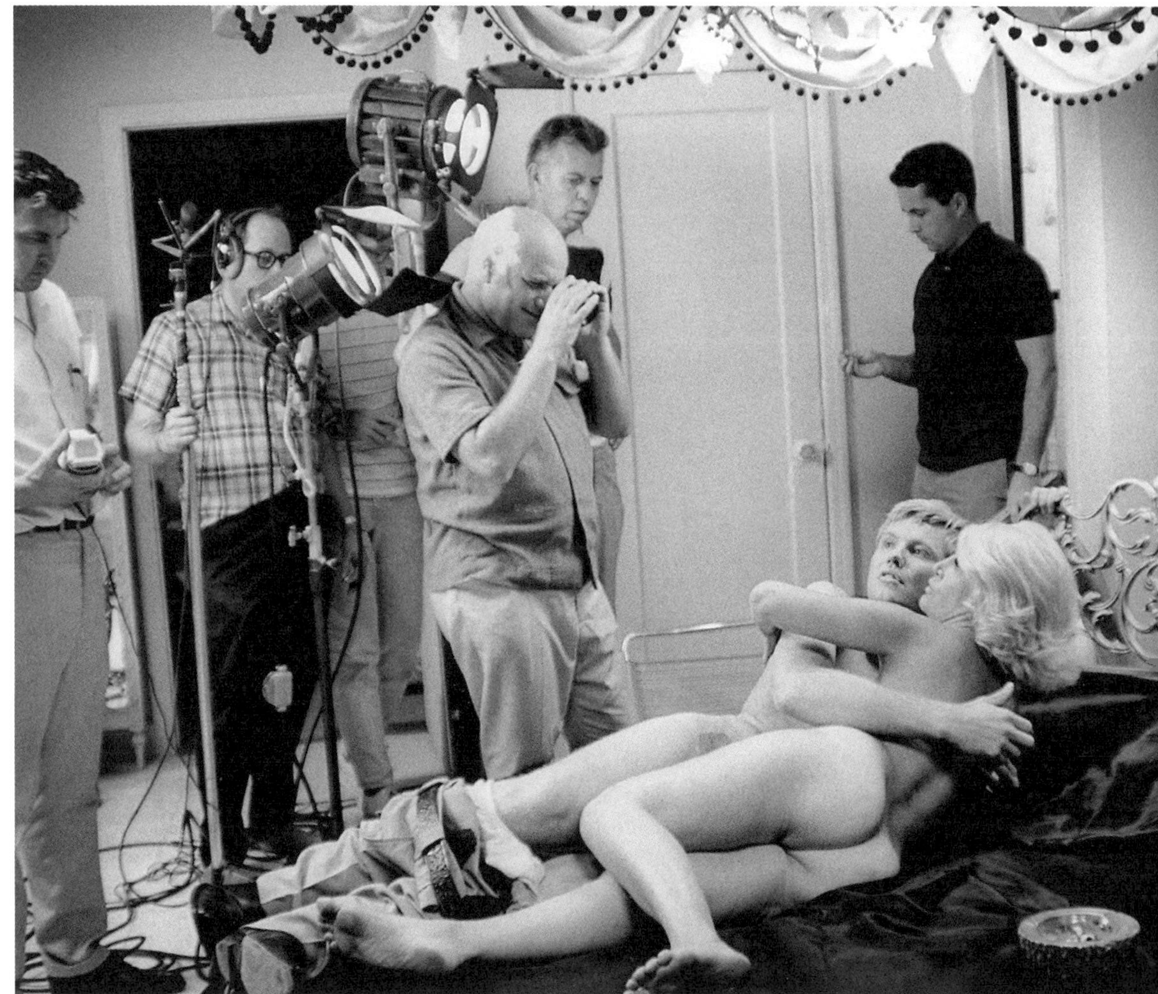

saying, "I got twenty-five rattles. Got them all out of there."

We finished that night's shooting and the next night we had to shoot more. I come back and I see the guy comes out of the house and says, "Yeah, I got about twenty more rattlesnakes."

I said, "Where were those twenty rattlesnakes when we were shooting the first night?" And he started to laugh. Because I didn't know if there were rattlesnakes all over there. It was dark. You couldn't see anything, and everything sounded like a rattlesnake rattle. It was windy and hissing, and I was like, "Oh my God"—it was crazy.

I was walking and I heard a sound. I jumped about three feet in the air and ran. I didn't even look. It may have been nothing, but I wasn't taking a chance at all.

RICHARD ADEE: They went to shoot out in Texas. I couldn't go because either Troy was being born or my daughter was being born. So I had to send my second guy, Frankie Ianacone. He's a New York guy.

He's out there and calls me. He says, "Rich, you're not going to believe what happened."

Shooting *Midnight Cowboy,* 1968. John Voight and Sylvia Miles, with Tom Priestly, Jr. and crew in backgound. Photo courtesy of PictureLux / The Hollywood Archive.

I said, "What?"

He says, "I hear all these noises I never heard before, these weird noises, and I didn't pay any attention. I was cleaning the brush around the house and all this kind of stuff inside the house. The noises were all over."

I said, "What the hell was it?"

He said, "I don't know. I called some people, and they came in. Next thing I know there's a guy in there with these big sticks, and there were rattlesnakes all over the place." He didn't know what a snake was. He grew up in the Lower East Side.

TOM PRIESTLEY, JR.: Another scene we're going to shoot out at this big farm out somewhere in west Texas. So we go out there, and I tell you, it's lush as far as you can see. I mean, miles, it's green. I don't know what the hell they were growing. So in between all of this, you've got these pumps going up and down. I said to the guy, "Wow, look at all these water pumps here, watering the vegetation."

He says, "Them's oil wells, boy."

I thought an oil well was the thing with the derrick shooting all the way up in the air. And they are pumping twenty-four-seven, all the time—oil coming out of the ground, money, money, money. And these people were loaded. I mean, they were loaded. A young kid came out—I guess he was about eighteen. I said, "Where's your parents.?" He said, "They took the family plane down to Peru to go skiing."

I guess they had a few bucks, but my impression of oil wells—I was embarrassed, but what the hell do I know about oil wells? I'm from New York City.

TOM PRIESTLEY, JR.: We stayed in Big Spring, Texas, and there were only two hotels there. I think it was Ramada and a Holiday Inn or something like that. As we finished shooting, everybody goes to take a shower or goes downstairs and have a drink, and there's a guy at the door, the sheriff kind of guy. He says, "Got to check your guns at the door, boys. No guns allowed inside."

And I'm thinking, "Guns? I don't own any guns." These guys are pulling out guns and giving them to the guy. I said, "Holy shit." And there were only two bars in town. And I think the sheriff owned both of them. And that was Big Spring, Texas.

RICHARD ADEE: I get called in. Might have been *Midnight Cowboy*. And the two of them had a big office. One guy had a desk here. The other guy had a desk there. And I go in.

I said to Kenny [Utt, the producer], "One of the PAs said you wanted to see me?"

"Yeah. Hal Schaffel wants to talk to you."

I said, "What's up, Hal?"

He says, "I'm looking at these timecards and there's only twenty-four hours in the day. How could you come up with this kind of money?"

I said, "I don't know. I don't know what timecards are. I don't make them out. Get Frankie in here. He makes the timecards."

And Kenny and Frankie Anacombe were like this [holds two fingers together] for some reason. I don't know. I think maybe Frankie was giving him some pot or something, and Kenny was an old guy—no spring chicken—but I think that's what was going on. I never saw him smoking, but I think that was the thing that they had.

Frankie comes in and the four of us are there, and Hal Schaffel starts questioning Frankie.

And then Kenny says, "Al, listen, if Frankie says there's more than twenty-four hours in a day, then there's more than twenty-four hours in a day, so there shouldn't be any questions."

Al says, "Okay, if that's what you say."

And that was it. We were on triple time, over and over and over and over. Frankie's just writing these numbers down. But I'll tell you, it was good. It was a great scene.

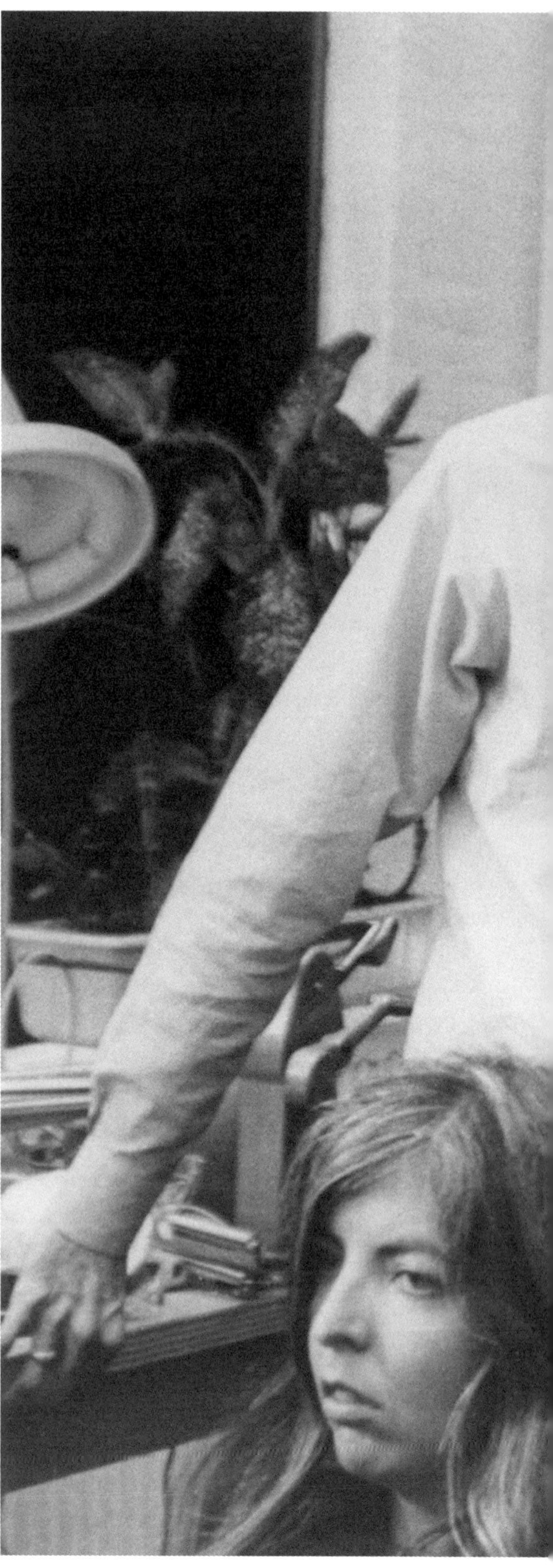

ELEN ORSON (CAMERA ASSISTANT, *WOODSTOCK*): I heard about a job where they were looking for an assistant editor to sync dailies for a documentary for a company called Wadleigh-Maurice Productions. I go uptown and I'm trying to fix my hair. And I hear that they're connected to PBS Channel 13. I'm ready for anything—I don't know what—and I walk in, and there are all these hippies. They're all young, they got long hair—the girls are wearing long skirts and there are a lot of women and there's a lot of people working in this place, and they were making a documentary—they needed an assistant for a show about some outdoor leadership training school in Wyoming, in the Grand Teton Mountains.

They had figured out an ingenious way to sync up these dailies. They showed me how it worked because they didn't have a cameraman hooked up to a soundman, but they were able to read the pilot tone. The sound guy, Larry Johnson, figured out a way to rig a Bic pen on the transfer machine, and when it saw that the sync pulse from the camera was present the pen would move over to the other side of the track and I would know that that was where I was going to find sync.

I'm eyeball-syncing this stuff with no slates and no sync reference at all—it's all eyeball. I'm working on this thing, and the Woodstock festival was coming up, and we had been hearing the radio ads all summer long that this was going to be the biggest concert ever and it was going to be three days of this group and that group, and everybody was going to be there, and why don't y'all come? I was

Woodstock

(1970)

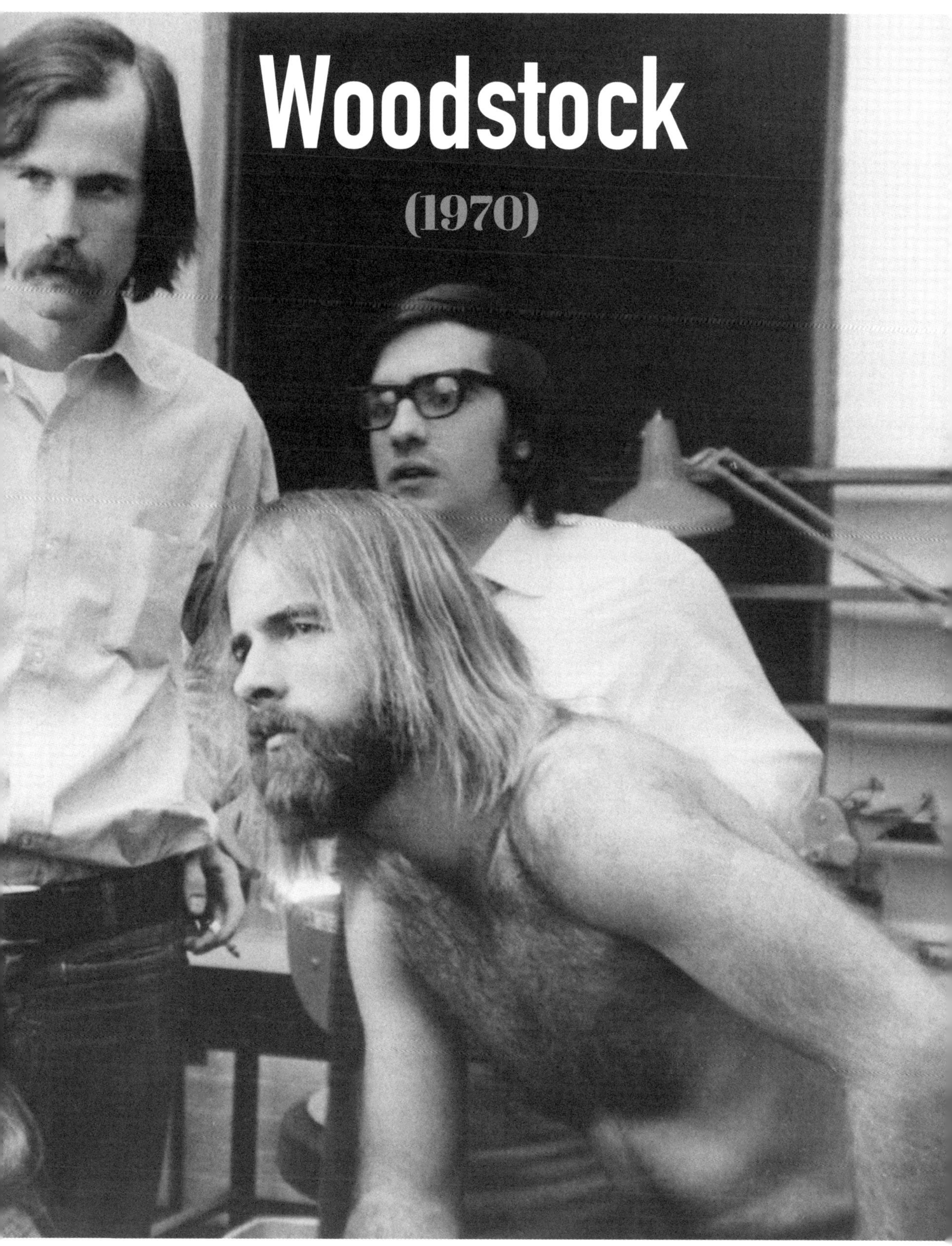

Thelma Schoonmaker, unidentified man, Michael Wadleigh, and Martin Scorsese working on *Woodstock*. Photo courtesy of the Margaret Herrick Library, Academy of Motion Picture Arts and Sciences.

going to try to go to it. I'm now sixteen and my mother's going, "No, you're not going to that," and I think, "Oh, damn, I'm not going to be able to go to that concert because I've got this job. I can't just take off for three days. I can't do it—too bad—oh, man."

All of a sudden, the phone starts ringing a lot and there's a whole lot of hubbub going on in the studio, and the buzz on the telephones was that we were going to try to shoot the *Woodstock* movie. One week before the concert is supposed to begin, we get the green light and they go ahead and they say, "Okay, we're shooting the movie." So they send a scouting team up to the location in New York State.

STEVEN J. JORDAN (PRODUCTION DESIGNER): It was the summer of 1969. I was between junior and senior year at Julliard. I got a job at ABC Camera—that was a camera equipment rental house on 44th and 9th, around the corner from F&B Ceco, which was sort of my first taste of the Business—the interesting thing about that job was the summer of '69, and I remember that weekend in the rental house, the shelves were bare, every piece of equipment—sound equipment, camera equipment, grip equipment—empty. It was quite fascinating. I'm sure everyone was either planning news footage or documentary footage or feature film footage. The equipment just flew off the shelf for that weekend.

ELEN ORSON: I get a call—it's Monday night before the concert—I get a call from [editor] Thelma Schoonmaker and she says, "Elen, we need all hands on deck. Is there any way that you can come up and help?"

And I said, "I'll ask my mother."

I asked my mother, and I told her, "Well, mom, we're going to have hotel rooms and I'll be with working professionals and I don't have to hitchhike. I'll have a ride." And she says, "Okay." She knew that I was making decent money, and it was important to our family at the time because my father was forced into early retirement and we were having a lot of financial trouble. So this was good news because that meant that I was going to be pulling in $350 a week at the age of sixteen. Those days, that was a lot of money.

I went up and met up with the crew the day before they started shooting, and Sonya Polansky, who was the production coordinator, got everybody, all the assistants, all sitting around in a group and said, "Okay, who knows how to load a magazine?"

I put my hand up, and other people put their hands up. "You, you, you. You're on the camera crew. You're going to be loading magazines." And I'm thinking, "Great. This is wonderful." It turns out that they were shooting with Eclairs, and I only knew how to load an Arriflex. I told them, "I don't know how to do this, and I don't think this is the right place for me to learn." It's a pretty important job to put the film in the camera, and if you do it wrong you scratch the whole roll—blow it. I said, "What else can I do?"

They assigned me to Ted Churchill, one of the cameramen, as his assistant. All the cameras were hooked up to the same power source with AC electricity. Part of my job was to make sure that the cameraman, as he was moving around with great fluidity, didn't trip anybody with the AC line and that nobody got hung up in it. I was following him with the cable and watching his magazine footage counter and I'd tap him on the shoulder and say, "Okay, you're about to run out," and I would have a new one in my hand, and he would whip that one off and I would throw that into his hand and slap it on, and maybe the whole operation took six seconds. That's how I spent my weekend working on the stage on the crew, hardly sleeping, not eating. By Sunday, the meat had all gone bad, and I got food poisoning. That took a little wind out of my sails.

The first thing they assigned Ted Churchill to was to get the shot of the opening of the festival where the crowd was getting bigger and bigger and bigger and bigger and bigger, and so my job was to climb up and down the towers, with fresh magazines for him, climb back down with his spent mags, and make my way through the crowd and go back to the loaders under the stage and get two fresh ones and get back up on the tower.

I had the agility to be able to do that, and that was only until sunset that night. Then we didn't have any more camera crew on the platforms up there. It was too dangerous. They had all the big follow-spots up there. So the lighting guys were at the very top of the tower. And our camera platform was maybe one or two rungs down from there. It was just scaffolding really. We thought it was really secure, but after the big rainstorm we found out that some of them had actually slid in the mud, so that's why they kept on saying, "Everybody stay off the towers," because that would've been bad if it had come down. The third day, the cameraman I was working with went home because I think he had a gig on Monday.

He took off on his motorcycle and I was reassigned to one of the cameramen who had been out in the field interviewing the people at the festival, not the performers. Then we were on the back of the stage, and I was about five feet away from Janis Joplin, and she was electric—like somebody had plugged her in. I could have touched her, probably, if I had tried.

I'm in the movie a couple of times just because I got caught in the crossfire. It's like shooting a poker game or a dinner scene where you've got everybody all around the table and it was part of the genius of the editing of that film was actually in maintaining the axis. I'm talking about the axis you have established when somebody is looking to the left of frame, and then what you're never supposed to do is cut to a different angle where they're actually facing the right of frame because of that other angle. You're supposed to know where that line is and not cross over to the other side, unless you're doing it on purpose and directly for an effect.

There was also a lot of desire to do documentaries that defied logic because there was no market for documentaries. You couldn't get a theatrical documentary together. They were rare. *Woodstock* was rare that it went into the theaters, and it was three hours long. And Warner Brothers fought them, saying, "Nobody's going to want to sit for three hours and watch a movie," and we said, "Well, yeah, they are, actually." The popular image of the festival itself is because it was portrayed so realistically and so truthfully in the documentary. When people think of Woodstock, they think of that movie.

The French Connection

(1971)

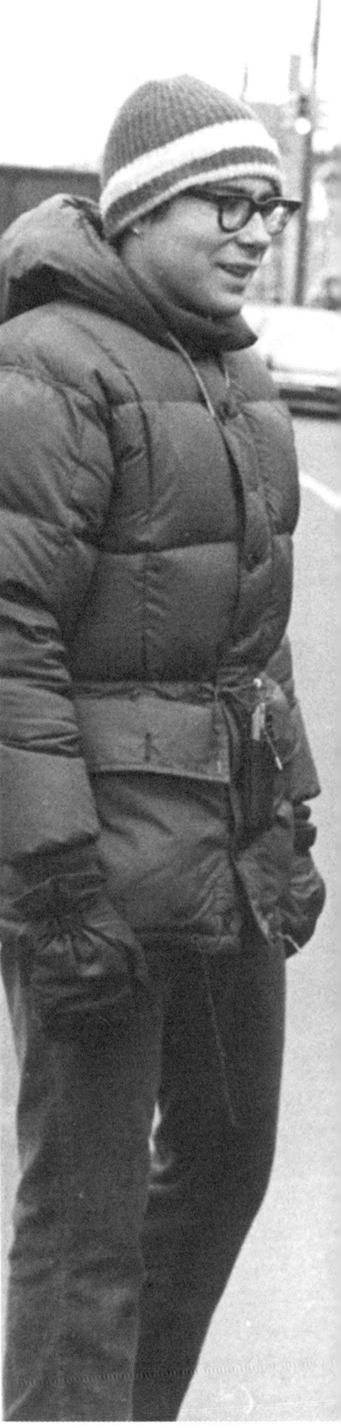

One afternoon Phil [D'Atoni] told me about a book he had optioned by Robin Moore, author of The Green Berets. *The book was nonfiction and told the story of the largest heroin bust in the United States. It was called* The French Connection, *and it focused on the exploits of two colorful New York City detectives: Eddie Egan and Sonny Grosso. I couldn't get through it; it seemed dry and procedural on the page, and it wasn't until I flew to New York with Phil and met Egan and Grosso that I was able to see a movie in their story.*[4] —William Friedkin

GARY MULLER **(SECOND ASSISTANT CAMERA OPERATOR, *THE FRENCH CONNECTION*)**: Billy [Friedkin] was a very unique man. We became friends during *The French Connection*. I was, like, twenty-one years old and here were all these famous New York detectives—Sonny Grosso, Eddie Egan, and Randy Jurgensen. These are real-life detectives, real-life cops, and this is New York.

RANDY JURGENSEN **(NYPD DETECTIVE, TECHNICAL ADVISOR, *THE FRENCH CONNECTION*)**: When I first got the call to come to a location in Manhattan, where they were starting pre-production on *The French Connection,* they hadn't even cast it yet. The screenplay was written. By the way, it was turned down four times—twice by the same studio.

4 William Friedkin, *The Friedkin Connection: A Memoir,* Harper Perennial (New York), 2013, pp. 143-144.

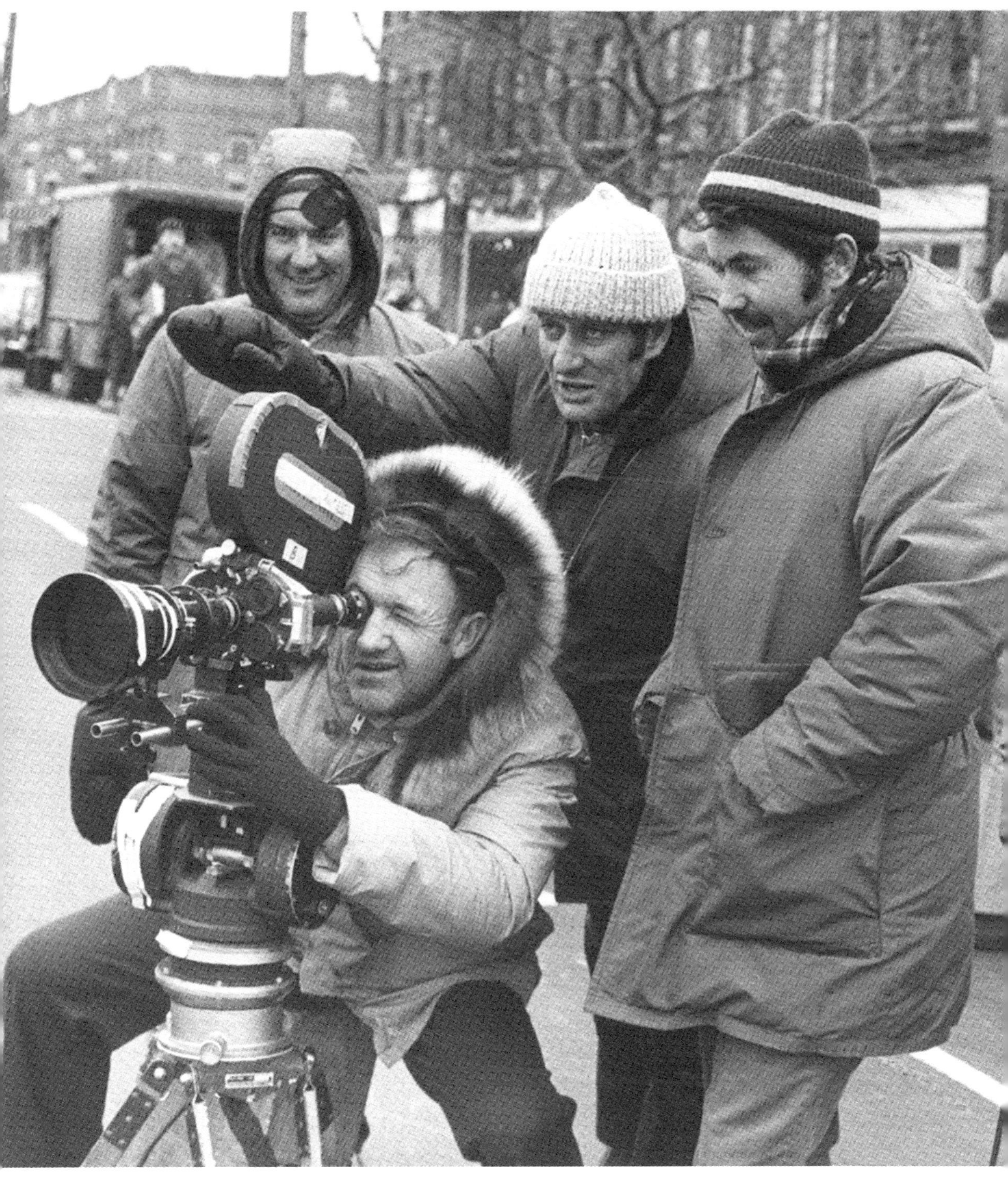

Keeping warm in between scenes on *The French Connection.* Photo courtesy of the Margaret Herrick Library, Academy of Motion Picture Arts and Sciences.

I met thirty-year-old Billy Friedkin. He had done *Boys in the Band* [1970]. When I first got there, they had me tossing people. "How would you toss somebody for drugs or for a gun or something like that?" The person that they had me doing this to was [legendary newspaper columnist] Jimmy Breslin. I couldn't believe that he was going to be the first person to play Eddie Egan in *The French Connection*. However, I was then tasked with—this is the phrase that I like to use—before it was going to go on reel, they had to see what it was like for real. I took Gene Hackman, Roy Scheider, and Billy out on narcotic raids.

These were not staged raids. These were real raids, where my information said, "This is what was happening here." I would take them, and I would be the first one through the door, and they would follow me and, of course, I had a couple of other detectives with me, and we would go in there and it was a shooting gallery. There were needles, and there was heroin and cookers. There was all of that to see. But it didn't end there.

When I took them back into the precinct, there was fingerprinting, there was photo taking, there was marking the needles, and if there was a gun—sometimes there was a gun—it was thrown on the floor. It was easy just to charge everybody with the gun, then charge one person with the gun. These arrests were like numbers. They came to court with me.

By the time that this was over, Billy Friedkin could have been a narcotic detective and certainly Gene and Roy were. They were. I turned them. I learned very early on that actors are sponges. They were absorbing all of that.

Friedkin and crew working on *The French Connection*. Photo courtesy of the Margaret Herrick Library, Academy of Motion Picture Arts and Sciences.

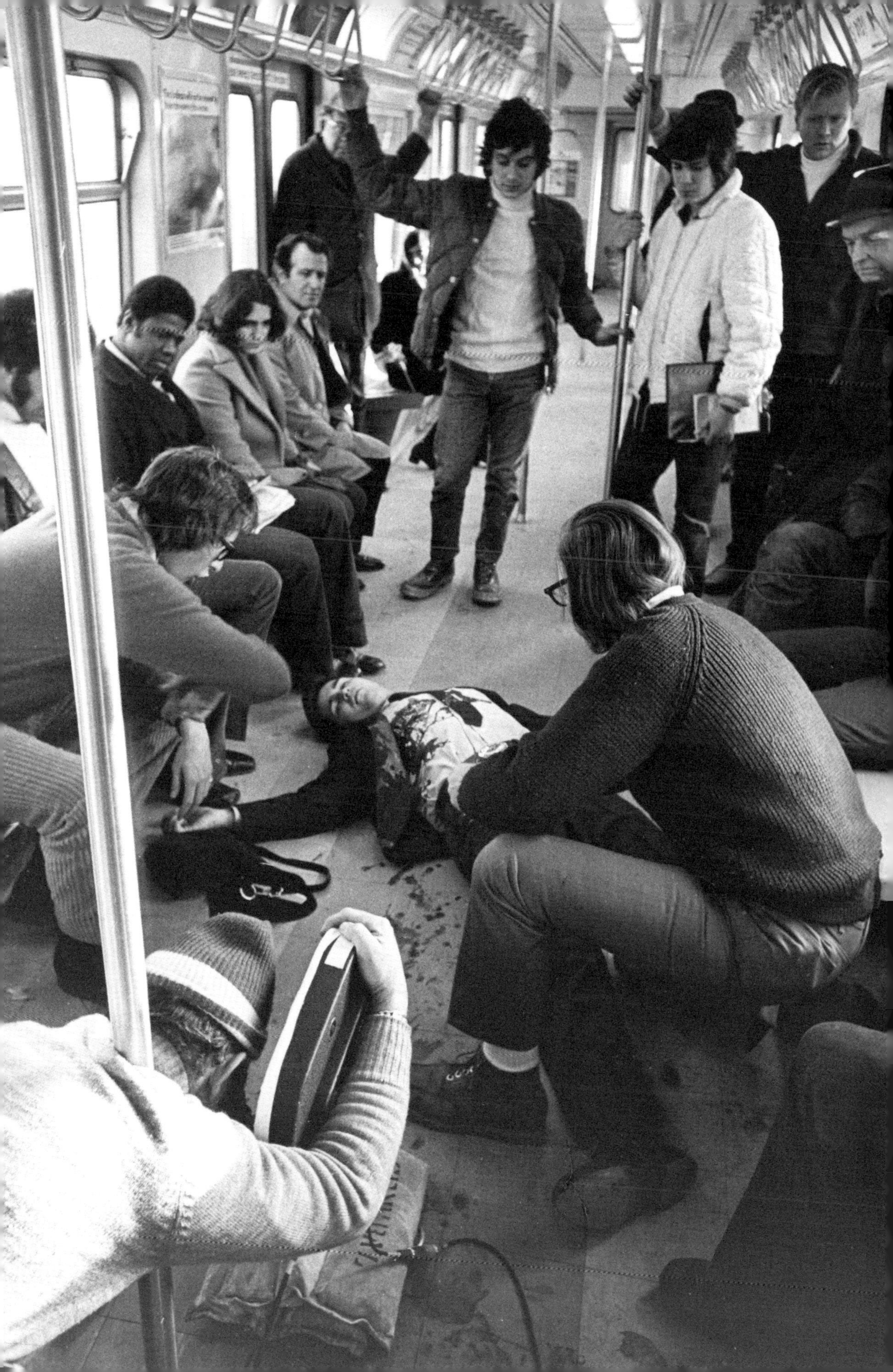

I went on stakeouts and busts until I knew what they said and did in every situation. While on the job, on lunch break, they'd reveal more details of the French Connection case and the personalities of the other players.[5]

—William Friedkin

TOM PRIESTLEY, JR. (FIRST ASSISTANT CAMERA OPERATOR, *THE FRENCH CONNECTION*): He [Billy Friedkin] loved all the guys—Eddie Egan, Sonny Grosso, and Randy Jurgensen. And those guys—I mean, these guys were tough guys. We were doing a scene in a bar down on the Lower East Side by the Pike Slip where the fishing boats come in and stuff, and it's where I think the *Daily News* or one of the newspapers, or the *New York Post*, they print right there. So all the workers for the *Post* are down there. The guys would set the type and all that. They were pretty big drinkers, and Billy had some of the Damon Runyon guys in there, and they started sitting around drinking and talking. We were photographing them. They didn't even know it.

One guy was a famous arsonist. His name was Marvin the Torch, and he started telling [on camera] about all these buildings he was burning down. They finally had to stop. They had to confiscate the film, take it away. The guy could go to jail. Billy loved all that shit. He would go out in the police car with Grosso and those guys. He just loved all that stuff, privy to all these great insights and things, and he would use some of it.

Gary Muller told me a story. I couldn't believe it.

GARY MULLER: Billy says to me one day, "Hey, Gary, why don't you go with these guys tonight and go bust a few people's heads?"

I said, "What do you mean?"

He said, "Go ride in a squad car. They'll let you go."

So I say, "All right, whatever."

Just about when we're about to wrap, Egan comes over and he said, "Kid, get in the car."

I said, "I can't get in the car. I got to go."

"No, you're coming with us."

So, they went down and had a drug bust similar to the raid in the movie and they arrested all these people, and I'm standing there watching them with guns out and all that stuff. I'm saying, "Holy shit." When they came back and reported to Billy that I actually went and did it he said, "You got a pair of balls kid—that's great."

We became friends.

RANDY JURGENSEN: *The French Connection* on purpose was shot looking gritty. I learned what that was. It's not this bright Technicolor like *Bullitt* [1968], which was shot in San Francisco with the blinding sun and the colors so lit. No people on the street whatsoever.

TOM PRIESTLEY, JR.: Gene Hackman was great, and Roy Scheider. Working dawn and dusk night shots—I thought Owen [Roizman, cinematographer] did a great job. I mean, just to capture New York the way he captured it, and just the look of it and the feel of it—the pulse of the city. There's a great sequence when Hackman's trying to follow the Frenchman on Madison Avenue and the guy is ducking in and out of buildings. He's looking at reflections in the mirror, all kinds of stuff. And then they go down into the subway and Hackman follows him. The Frenchman gets on the subway. Hackman jumps on, and the Frenchman jumps off. Hackman jumps off. The Frenchman jumps back in again. And the train takes off.

That was all done with a 35-millimeter handheld Arriflex. It was used in a lot of motion-picture making, but it wasn't a sound camera. It was noisy. So, if there's any dialogue we'd bring the other camera in and

5 Friedkin, *The Friedkin Connection*, p. 148.

shoot the dialogue. But most of the movement, the camera operator was in a wheelchair, and he followed Hackman, moved around, and then even got up and stuff like that.

It was a working subway. I think we had the platform for a certain amount of time but just put the guy handheld in the wheelchair and wheel him around. I mean, it made it smooth enough that you thought it was a regular shot. I mean, if he had a walk with the guy. Today they probably would accept it, but back then it wasn't accepted. It was being a little bouncy, too much movement in it, but that's how we did it. A lot of stuff was shot like that.

BILLY WARD (KEY GRIP, *THE FRENCH CONNECTION*): I don't particularly care for him [Owen Roizman]. I don't think he was a nice guy. He's all about himself. He wasn't a terrible camera person—he actually had some talent—but he wasn't a particularly nice guy.

TOM PRIESTLEY, JR.: The thing was, when we got into the streets, it was kind of like a semi-documentary type of situation. Old slums, run and gun, stuff like that. But one of the biggest factors was that it was freezing.

BILLY WARD: We worked hard. It was cold as hell that winter.

TOM PRIESTLEY, JR.: That winter was colder than hell. I mean, it was *cold*. We were outside working, and I couldn't wear gloves sometimes because some of the things on the camera were so small and delicate. There were times when I told Owen I had to go inside because I can't move my fingers. It was a very difficult shoot.

GARY MULLER: Everybody stands around. I used to have to climb under the trains and put the camera rigs up there, and you're young and you think, "I want to pee in my pants to get warm." It was just outrageous how cold it was touching metal. You can't wear gloves because you're touching metal. My God, my hands hurt now thinking about that.

RANDY JURGENSEN: You look at the *French Connection* chase. It's dark and gritty and crowded. That was New York City and Billy captured it.

GARY MULLER: Don't forget—filmmaking back then in New York—the police catered to it. They would block streets, especially when we did *The French Connection*. There were no laws that you had to wear a helmet or be strapped in. God, I can remember days in *The French Connection*, you do ninety miles an hour, holding on for dear life, chasing a car. There's no safety, which obviously wasn't the best of times, but you didn't know any better.

BILLY WARD: Obviously, in the big scenes, they [Friedkin and the camera operators] just took themselves in natural light, and I remember originally in pre-production we talked about all those scenes. We were never supposed to have a car crash. Everything was near misses. I remember the prop man—"outside prop" we used to call him at the time—he got the cars for us, and he worked on the set. He says, "Holy shit, I rented all these cars."

And they were all smacked up. The first time we started doing the second-unit work with the car scenes, [we crashed the cars] from when the slate went down until everything was crashed all over the place. Billy must have known what he was going to do, but he didn't tell anybody.

TOM PRIESTLEY, JR.: There were four cameras mounted on the car for the famous chase sequence underneath the el—one on the front, one over his shoulder, one on the floor looking up, and one on top of the roof. They ran all four cameras, and you let them go.

BILLY WARD: We were lucky we didn't kill people. It was a little crazy. It got out of hand. Billy got a little taken away with himself. But it worked out.

It seemed hopeless. We thanked him [the Transit Authority rep] and asked if he'd let us shoot the subway cat and mouse between Popeye and Charnier. "That could be arranged," he said. We didn't want to push our luck further, so we got up to leave. As we got to the door, he said, "Just a minute."

We turned back, "I said it would be difficult, not impossible."

"What would it take?" Kenny [Utt, line producer] asked.

Without hesitation the Transit Authority guy said, "If I let you shoot what you described, I'd be in a world of trouble."

"Right," said Phil.

A long pause. Remember, Phil is Sicilian from The Bronx. "What would it take?"

"Forty K and a one-way ticket to Jamaica."

"Why one-way?" Kenny asked.

"Cause when the film comes out, I'll be fired."

And that's what it took.[6]

—William Friedkin

RANDY JURGENSEN: I was a lifetime member of the East Coast Stuntmen's Association. They were rehearsing the end of the car chase when the Frenchman comes off the train, and he lost his gun on the train. He comes out. He's really staggering. He's really hurt. He comes to the top of the stairs and Gene gets to the bottom of the stairs. Whatever Gene hollers out to him—I mean, the Frenchman puts his hands up and he turns to sort of like—he got his hands up. Gene Hackman shoots him right in the back. He falls. This was all done by the stunt people, and I was there on the scene, and I was the backup. We always backed each other up.

Don't forget this is not the beginning of the picture. We're really into the picture now. I had no qualms about going up and speaking to Billy Friedkin. I went up and I said to him, I said, "Billy, you know what? Look, the guy's lost his gun. He's got his hand up. This is murder, shooting him in the back."

Billy says, "No, don't worry about it. This is going to work."

I kept it up. I said, "But Billy, I'm telling you now. This is murder."

Billy Friedkin said to me in no uncertain terms, "I'm the director. That's how we're going to do it."

That was it. That was the end of that. I will fast forward to twelve hundred people in the theater at one of the premieres that we had—well attended by celebrities, so forth and so on. We come to that scene, and I'm standing in the back, and that scene happens. There's that moment of silence. Then twelve hundred people are up screaming, and Billy Friedkin runs up the aisle to me and he says, "It works for them, it works for me, I hope it works for you."

To put the salt in the wound—that's the friggin' poster!

TOM PRIESTLEY, JR.: Finally, we get to the end of the show and it's a wrap and everybody's having a beer or something on a tailgate, and Billy says, "Look, guys, I love you all, but I got two or three more days of B shooting with extra stuff. We'll just put the camera in my car and we'll take a couple of guys and we'll shoot for the next couple days. I got to have this stuff. I mean, it's just important and I need it, and this would be a great way to get it."

Kenny Utt, the production manager, says, "Billy, there's no more money. It's over. No more money."

We never shot another foot of film. He's sure we have got to have this. "I got to have this stuff. I need it." There were some directors who don't want the show to end. And there were some directors that don't want the show to start. And Billy was notorious for that. He starts on a show, and I think he would find

6 Friedkin, *The Friedkin Connection*, pp. 174-175.

an excuse to slow down or stop production or something. He'd do it. He was always famous for firing the cameraman or firing somebody.

GARY MULLER: I've done so many pictures and so many strange things with Billy. I was one of the ones who never really got attacked by Billy.

TOM PRIESTLEY, JR.: Gary Muller told me a story. He was doing a show somewhere out in California when something happened and Billy yelled, "Everybody on the right-hand side of the camera is fired!" And the whole crew ran over to the right-hand side.

GARY MULLER: Down and dirty. Available light. Go shoot the shit in the street. Everybody wanted to emulate *The French Connection*. I didn't do any of them, but how many movies in New York were made with a chase scene after that?

RANDY JURGENSEN: I'll give you just one last story. Sonny and I locked up seven guys for narcotics. It was felony. We're going to court and so you bring them down from upstairs to the court and you put them in what they call a holding cell. The holding cell is the last place that they appear before they come out to the court to be arraigned. Sonny and I are waiting to bring them out when all of a sudden in the back of the court, the screaming and the shouting! It was so loud that the court officers took the judge from where he was, and they took him back in his chambers. That's how loud the screaming was going on. We run into the back and there's our prisoners, along with other prisoners. There were two broken noses. There was a pair of fractured ribs. One guy, his ankle was totally dislocated. They were walloping the shit out of each other. Corrections separated them. *What the hell is going on?*

The one guy that we locked up turned and said, "We told those people over there, they ain't shit. They ain't nothing. We done got locked up by the *French Connection* detectives." That's what started the fight. These guys were proud that they were arrested by the *French Connection* detectives.

You know, when Gene Hackman gets up there [at the Oscars] and he started saying, "Thanks to Eddie and Randy"—within the police department, aside from the jealousy, I mean, we became rockstars. We became rockstars, for chrissakes! It was unbelievable. We went to the Copa one time to see Bobby Darin—we were announced! We were announced at the Copa: "We have the *French Connection* detectives with us, Sonny Grosso and Randy Jurgensen." I was sort of dragged into this thing. It all came about because I was a narcotics guy.

The Godfather

(1972)

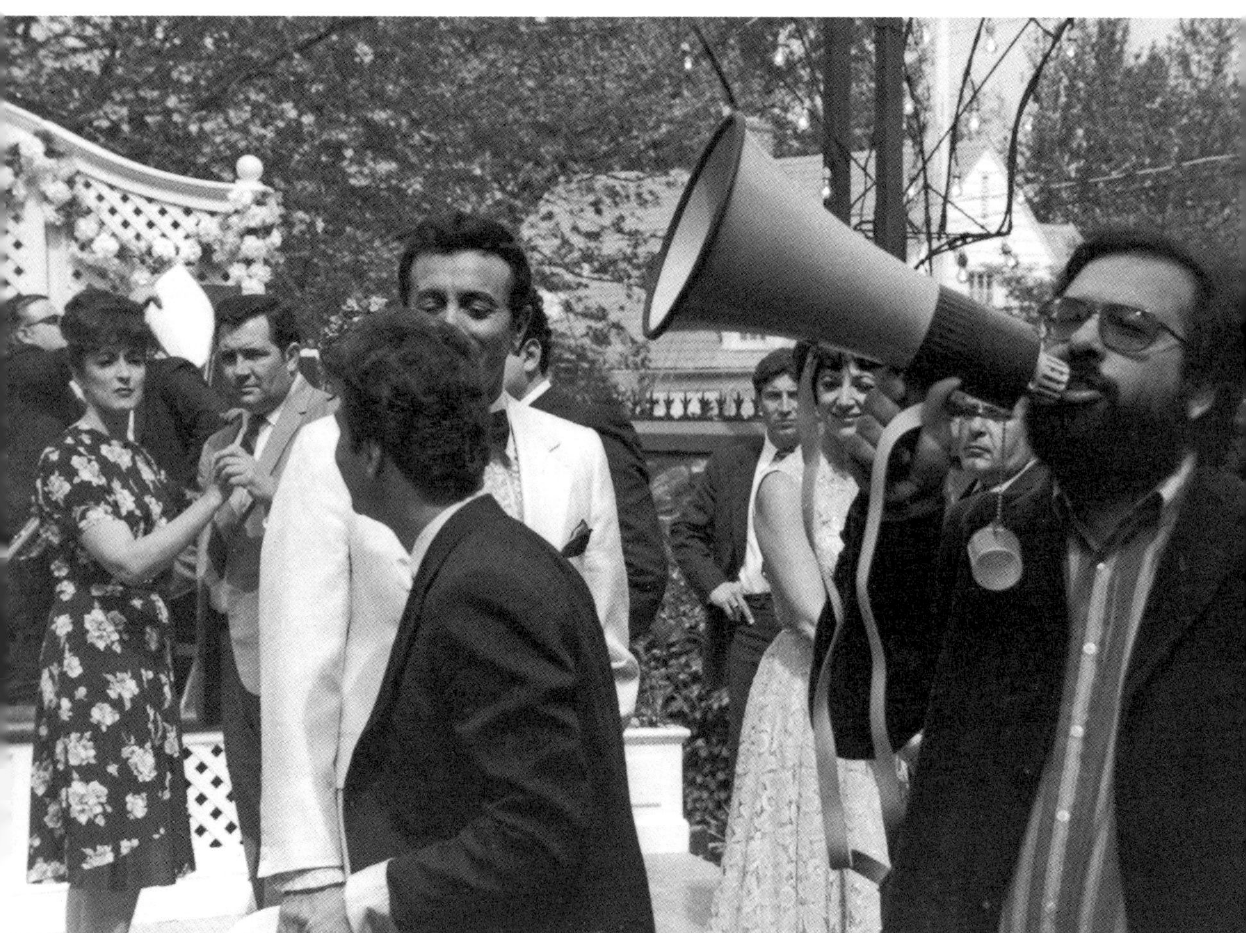

Francis Ford Coppola on set of The Godfather with cast and crew. Photo courtesy of the Margaret Herrick Library, Academy of Motion Picture Arts and Sciences.

RICHARD ADEE (**SET DECORATOR, *THE GODFATHER***): How I got the job on *The Godfather*—actually, I don't think I ever read a book in my life ever, other than in school—and everybody was saying to me, "You got to read this book. You got to read this book." It was *The Godfather* by Mario Puzo. It wasn't a week after I read that book, I get a phone call asking if I'm available to work on that film.

RANDY JURGENSEN (**SECURITY DETAIL, ACTOR, *THE GODFATHER***): Because I never went to school for any of this. I just came in, and I really came in at the top. I mean, the first two movies that you're going to work on are going to be *The French Connection* and *The Godfather*? I was sort of spoiled when I came into the industry.

RICHARD ADEE: Oh God. We had a lot of problems on that thing. When we first started—the Italian Anti-Defamation League—they didn't like that book at all.

We secured this compound. Somewhere. I forget where it was in Long Island. But then we weren't allowed to shoot there. So they kept looking for new places. They found it on Todt Hill in Staten Island, and it was a small compound.

In the very beginning, they wanted to put a wall around this compound. I was in the studio. We were shooting at Filmways 125th Street, and this dump truck pulls up to the stage and dumps all these rocks on the stage. Everybody's going, "What the hell are you going to do with these things?"

The scenic artist came over and said to me, "We're going to make a wall." They built a frame on stage, and they put all these rocks—like, instead of being vertical, it was horizontal. Then they took fiberglass, made a mold, popped the stones out, and then they painted it to look like a stone wall, and it looked like—I mean, it was perfect.

So we're out in Staten Island and we're getting the whole compound ready for shooting. And three of these guys with the funny noses come up to me and says, "We're putting fifteen guys on the payroll."

And I said, "For what?"

He says, "For this wall."

They were the mason guys. And I said, "It's not a real wall."

"Don't give me that shit."

"It's not a real wall"—so I said, "Come on, go over," and I tap on it.

He says, "What the hell is that?"

I says, "Come on around the wall, on the inside." And it's all two-by-fours and battens holding it up. The whole wall was as big as this yard. It was fiberglass. The scenic artist did a fabulous job on that.

We were shooting the wedding scene there.

JOE CIRILLO (**BACKGROUND ACTOR, *THE GODFATHER***): I remember Coppola actually speaking to us, saying, "Don't think of this as a movie. Think you're at a wedding, a real wedding. I want you to enjoy yourselves as if you were really at a wedding, and you can go around eating, do whatever you want, whatever you would do normally at a wedding. That's what I want you to do here." And it really felt like a wedding.

RICHARD ADEE: I had made contact with this restaurant in town, and they made the wedding cake. They had these big casks, big wine barrels, sitting around, and we had, I don't know, a couple hundred extras. Coppola says to me, "I want to put wine in those barrels."

I filled all the wine barrels for the wedding scene with grape juice. Coppola says, "Give me a glass of that. What the hell is this? It's not wine."

I said, "You can't use wine. These extras will be drunk in two hours. You'll never get anything done."

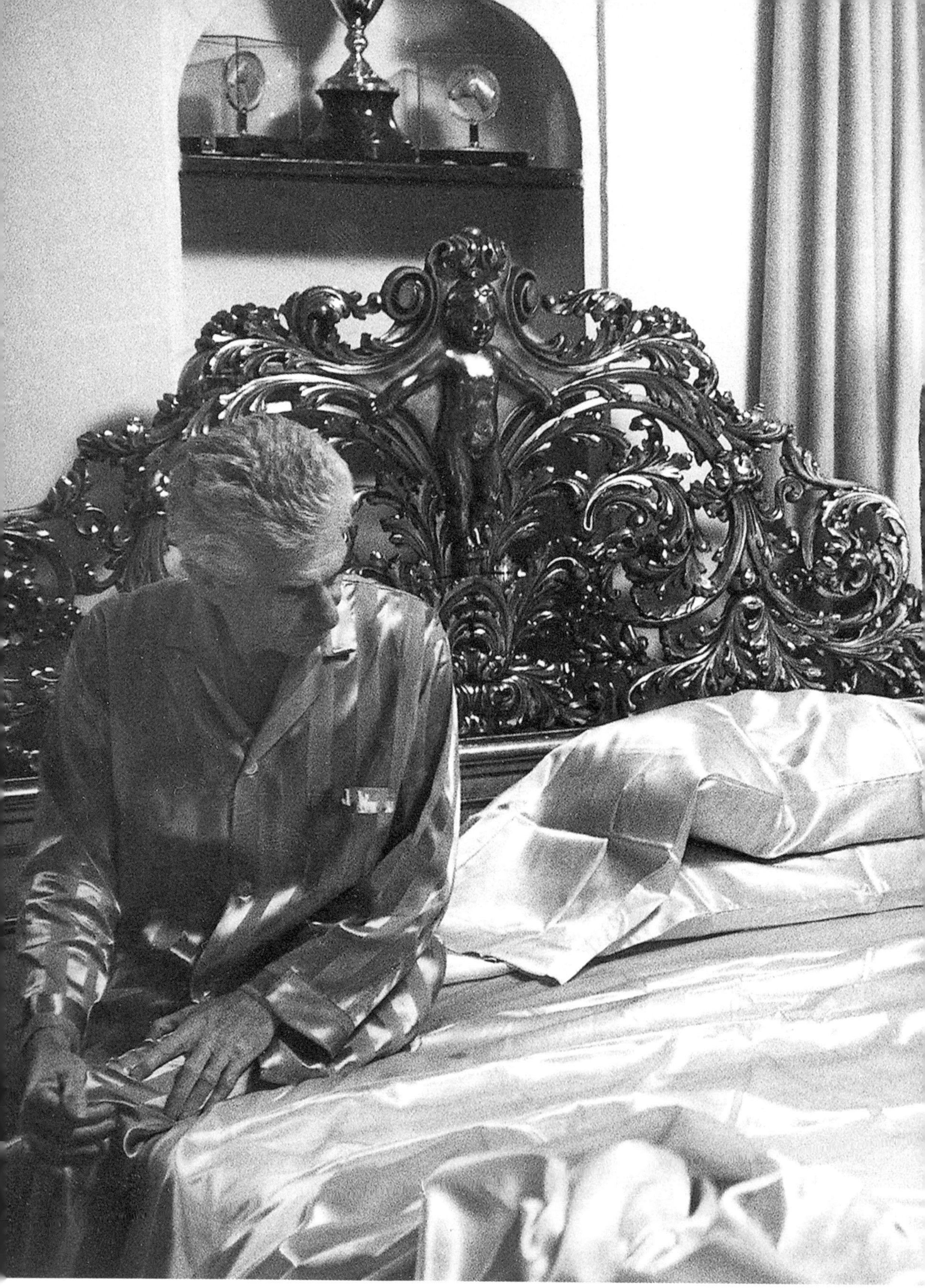

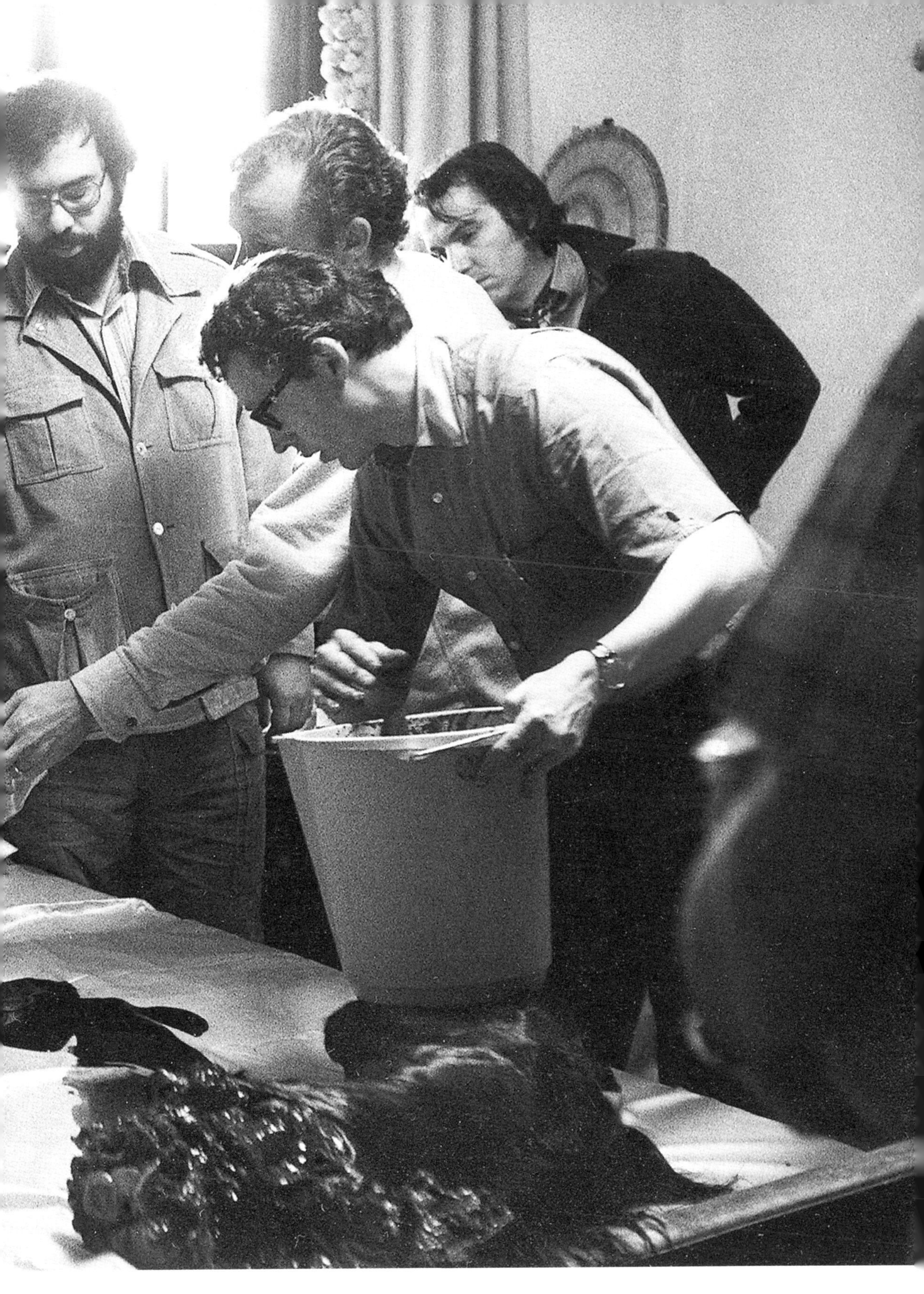

The infamous horse head scene. Photo courtesy of the Margaret Herrick Library, Academy of Motion Picture Arts and Sciences.

You know extras from working on sets. They put the food in their bags. They steal it. They strip everything. He says, "No, I want wine."

Back then the prop guys would make all the contacts for promotions, promoting stuff. I had a tractor trailer come in—just cases and cases—hundreds of cases of wine—and I filled the barrels.

Then we are shooting and everybody's shitfaced. All the extras are getting drunk, and they're slobbering all over. "I told you, Francis, that you're not going to be able to shoot. They're going to all be drunk.

"Yeah. Okay. Put the grape juice back in the thing."

We dumped the wine, and I had hundreds of cases of wine, and I gave it to the whole crew. I used to give it out to everybody.

JOE CIRILLO: They did tell us certain foods we couldn't touch because they were sprayed. But everything else there was real food. I'm Italian background, and I remember that they even had what they call *capuzzelle,* which is a lamb's head that people were actually eating. It was incredible. There wasn't a food that was missing.

RICHARD ADEE: Over where the Meadowlands is now there used to be slaughterhouses—used to be pig farms there—and they would slaughter all these horses. I went over and I told the guy, "I need a horse's head."

He said, "Okay."

I says, "But you gotta euthanize the thing. I want the head chopped off with an axe, and I want all the entrails and everything hanging out of it."

"What the hell? For what?"

I said, "Well, we're doing a movie and I gotta have this."

I had a stuffed taxidermy horse's head, a fake one. It was always on the truck—on the call sheet for, like, the next day shooting—we're going to use the horse's head.

And what I did—I had a box about the size of this table—painted gray and holes in it, like, two-inch holes all over the top, and had a shelf in it, and nobody could understand what this crate was. The only one that knew about it was [key prop] Frankie Anacombe.

TROY ADEE (SET DRESSER): And Bobby Wilson, Sr. [props and special effects].

RICHARD ADEE: And the director. They're the only ones that knew about this. I had two of those boxes made up and the reason the shelf was in there was for dry ice. I put dry ice on the top and holes going down.

TROY ADEE: The cool air would go down and keep the actual horse head fresh.

RICHARD ADEE: I had the horse's head in the basement of Filmways. Had it there for a couple of weeks with dry ice. Kept it frozen all the time. Every day or two put in dry ice. We get out to shoot the scene and we rehearse the scene in the bed. And then Coppola says, "We're going to break for lunch—everybody take a half hour for lunch."

We break for lunch, and he says, "Okay, get the head—bring the head in."

So I put the head in the bed and gallons of blood. I used to make my own blood and poured that in. And then we come back from lunch and nobody knew it. The crew, nobody—just three people knew what was going on. I say to this actor [John Marley], I said, "Get in the bed, I'll help you in the bed. Don't touch anything. Just do what I tell you."

TROY ADEE: It's dark. There's no lights on.

RICHARD ADEE:—and I put him in the bed, and Coppola says, "I want more blood in the bed—more blood, more blood."

I just peel the covers back and put more blood in. So then, when he started rolling the camera and he says, "Action," he [Marley] wakes up, he feels something, and he opens

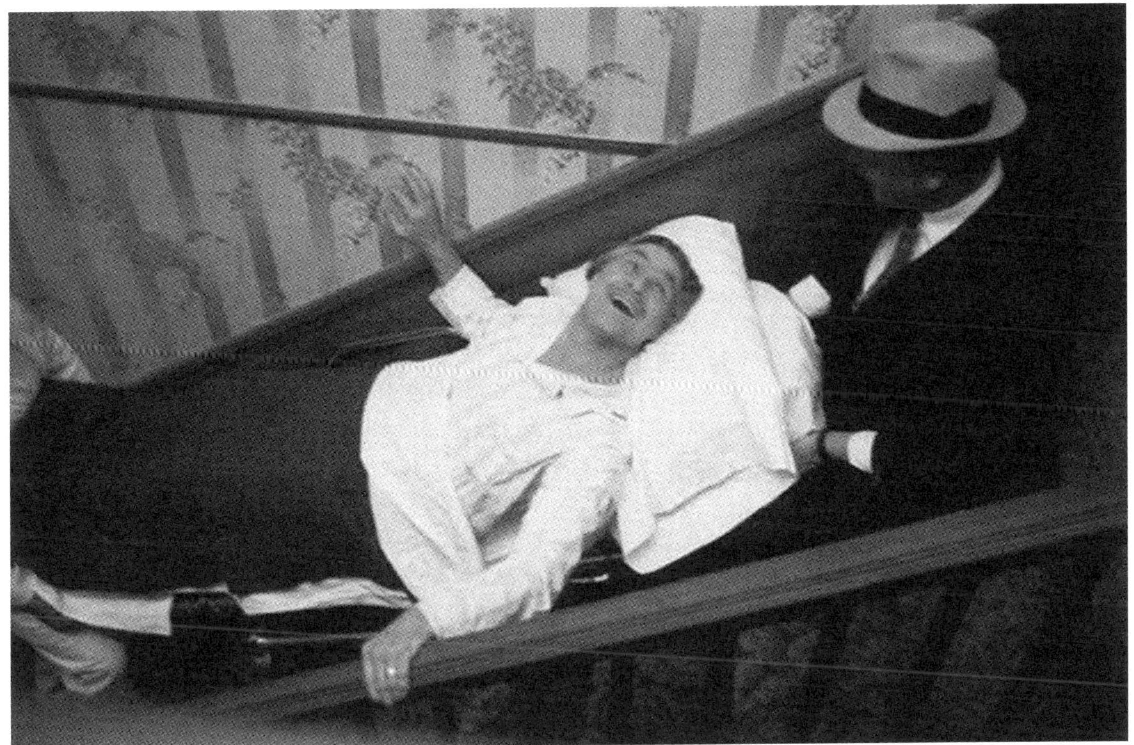

his eyes and he throws the covers back and here's this head with all the guts and shit hanging out.

TROY ADEE: The guy lost his mind.

RICHARD ADEE: That was it. One take.

RUSSELL ENGELS (BEST BOY, RIGGING GAFFER, *THE GODFATHER*): On *The Godfather*—Brando is very serious, of course, and all of that. Well, he had to be carried up the stairs on the gurney. And if you look at that part when he's sick, he said, "I want two strong men. I'm not letting no weak actor or anything like that carry me up these damn stairs."

They dressed up two grips. They're in the movie because they've got to carry him on the gurney up the stairs in his house.

RICHARD ADEE: Rippy and Joe. Rippy was Eddie Cameron. Coppola says, "Let's use him and him."

They were both construction grips. Both animals. I mean, really, they were *animals*.

So they rehearse the scene, [Brando] comes in with the stretcher—take him off and walk him up the staircase—piece of cake.

"All right. Go to wardrobe—get ready."

RUSSELL ENGELS: When they're getting the white suits on and all that stuff, Brando has other people load the bottom of the gurney with a couple hundred pounds of sandbags.

RICHARD ADEE: Coppola says, "All right, give me twenty sandbags—fifteen sandbags—put it down under and then put a sheet over it. Then we're gonna put Brando in there and take him up the stairs."

Everybody knows what's going to happen. Rippy the big guy, he gets one end and he's backing up the stairs and Joe, the short guy, he's on the bottom. They had it all lit and everything.

"Okay, roll camera. All right, action!" They roll the stretcher in. Then they picked him up

Set photo from the gurney prank. Photo by Steve Schapiro. Courtesy of Getty Images.

with, like, the hand stretcher, with the two poles in.

RUSSELL ENGELS: "I only want to do this once. I don't want you guys to give up on me"—and Brando pumped them up as they're carrying him up the stairs. They can hardly move. And they're lifting and grunting. There's no way they're going to back down.

RICHARD ADEE: You could see Joe—he didn't want to admit this fucking thing is heavy. And he's straining. He's really strained, and Rippy is on the other end. Rippy gets up maybe two, three steps and Joe's, like, one step.

BILL KANE (PROPS): And the camera's up the top of the stairs looking down, and the one grip is trying to lift and he is making faces.

RUSSELL ENGELS: And they're grunting and groaning going upstairs, and you see Brando's stomach laughing under the sheet.

RICHARD ADEE: And they drop the stretcher off the staircase and then at that point everybody starts to laugh—the whole crew, and Brando was laughing his ass off, and Rippy and Joe going, "What the fuck is so funny? You know how heavy this goddamn thing is?" The two of them were cursing and they're recording all that shit. They don't cut the camera; they let the camera roll.

BILL KANE: And with that Brando rolls out with the sandbag: "You sons of bitches."

RUSSELL ENGELS: You don't expect that from him, but he had a good sense of humor that way.

RICHARD ADEE: Oh, it was so funny. We had some good times.

RICHARD ADEE: When we did *The Godfather,* special effects here [in New York City] wasn't that good. It was mainly prop guys that did it. It wasn't a real category. A little bit later on it became a category in the union. When we did *The Godfather,* a guy came in from California, a special effects guy—fabulous man. His name was A. D. Flowers. He was an older guy, probably in his late- to mid-sixties—a genius.

We had set up special effects up on the second floor in Filmways, and I go up one day and he had one table laid out, a big aluminum table, eight feet long, six feet wide. He was making candy glass, breakaway windows, bottles, and all that kind of stuff. At the time, we used to send to California for breakaways because nobody here knew how to do it.

We had to do a scene that was like Times Square. It was a billboard of the Camel [cigarettes logo]. Remember the camel? It would blow smoke rings in Times Square. These big white puffs. I said to him, "How the hell are you going to do that?"

"It's a piece of cake."

He came in and he had this big Sonotube. It's about this big 'round, sticking out the window up on the fire escape. And what he did, he took a big sheet of rubber, put it on the end and attached it, and then drilled a hole with a smoke machine—filled it with smoke. And all he did was tap the rubber. And it goes out and makes a perfect ring. I thought that was genius. I'll tell you, the man was unbelievable.

I had a guy working for me called Eddie Drohan. His son is in the Business. Troy is friends with him. I put Eddie Drohan in charge of special. I said, "Whatever A. D. Flowers wants or does, I want you there. If he works twenty hours a day, you're staying with him. I want you to learn everything you can from him. I want you to learn the candy glass, breakaway windows, bottles, and this and that."

Shooting gag on *The Godfather*. If you look closely you can see the effects person holding the wires to the squib. Photo courtesy of the Margaret Herrick Library, Academy of Motion Picture Arts and Sciences.

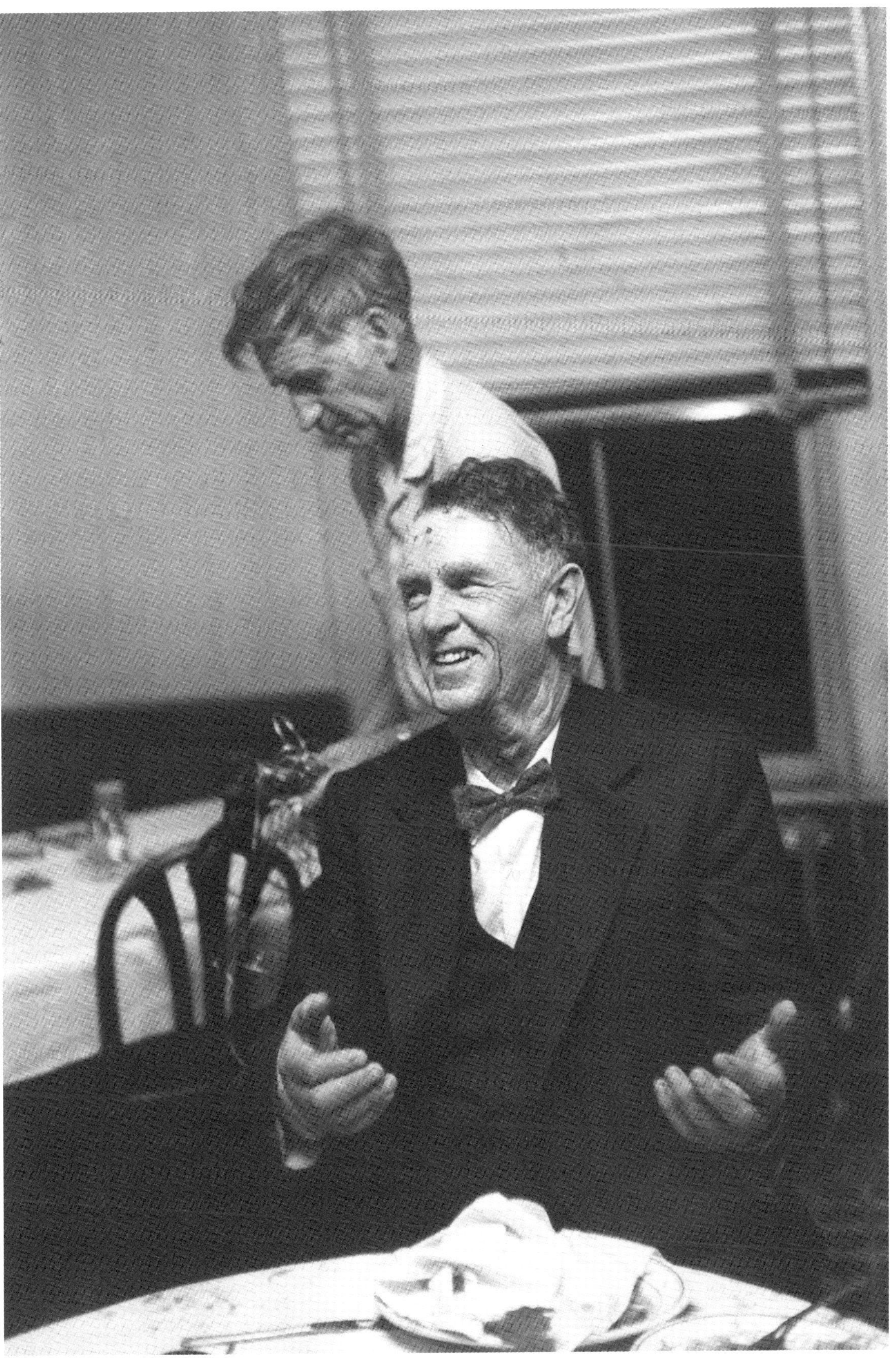

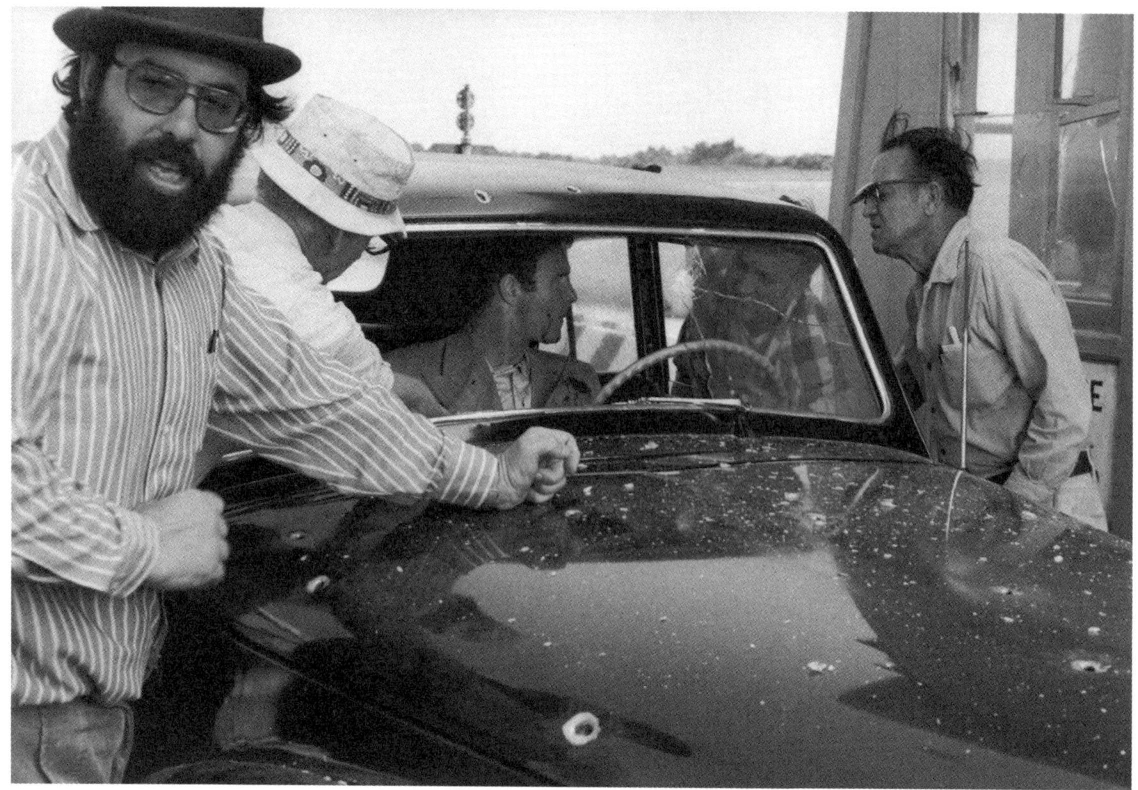

Flowers enhanced "The Godfather" with his own formula for movie blood. In addition to Karo syrup, which gave the substance a blood-like consistency; dish soap, which allowed it to be easily washed out of clothing; and red dye No. 2, Flowers mixed in blue dye No. 1. The last ingredient was crucial to making the fake gore look real by preserving the proper color value on Technicolor film.[7]

—*Los Angeles Times*, 2001

RICHARD ADEE: I did a lot of bullet hits. When they're in the restaurant and Michael shoots the guy in the forehead [and] kills him—well, what we did there was we got a false hairpiece and filled a plastic bag with chopped meat and fake blood and put a leather shield under a toupee and then set that away. But you really didn't see it in the film.

You put a leather thing on their head. It's the same on their clothes. It's a squib, but it's on a leather pouch. It's about a quarter-inch of leather. I mean, you can feel it, but it's not really bad. And then what we used to do is—you get shot, you got a suit jacket or something. We'd have a whole bunch of suit jackets, the same, just in case of takes four or five, but we would take them and then turn them inside out. We set the squib—you put a squib there with a condom, fill the condom full of fake blood, and then you take the suit jacket or pants, jacket, whatever it is, and from the inside you would take sandpaper and really rub it until it just about goes through the material. It won't penetrate.

When we did the tollbooth on *The Godfather*, we shot that—I think it was

7 Elaine Woo, "A. D. Flowers; Won Oscars for Special Effects," *Los Angeles Times*, August 21, 2001.

Above: Tollbooth shooting on *The Godfather*. Opposite page: Gordon Willis on *The Godfather*. Photos courtesy of the Margaret Herrick Library, Academy of Motion Picture Arts and Sciences.

Mitchel Field out in Long Island. It was funny because we had the carpenters build just, like, the island where the toll booth was, and the scenics painted it concrete and all that. We get the whole thing set up. Now we only had two cars, two Lincolns. There were only two of those make and model registered that year in the entire country. They tried every place to find extra cars and they couldn't. We had one that we could rig with squibs for bullet hits. We set the whole thing up and roll camera. He pulls up and all of a sudden the machine guns, they riddle the toll booth—the glass and all that kind of stuff, the car. So Coppola says, "That was great! That was super, but I need one more. I have to have another. I'll be in my camper—call me when you get it ready."

The thing was destroyed. All the bullet hits and everything. We picked the whole unit up, turned it around, and brought the car in from the other end, and we had the other end of the car squibbed, and the only thing we replaced was the glass and a clock in that thing. I said to the PA, "Go get Coppola."

Coppola came. He said, "No way. They didn't fix that! Not even twenty minutes went by."

CRAIG DIBONA (CAMERA OPERATOR): Back in those days, you went to dailies the next night—every night you went to the lab and you watched it, and you started to realize where you could get away with stuff and where you just couldn't.

Now you could take the color away completely and re-colorize it—you can do anything you need electronically. The bad part about it is the studios feeling like, "Hey, the DP [director of photography] doesn't really need to be there for that. We can do all that and make it look the way we want it." So now you're not the author of your image.

There's a downside of it also and when I used to work with Gordy [cinematographer Gordon Willis], I remember one time he said

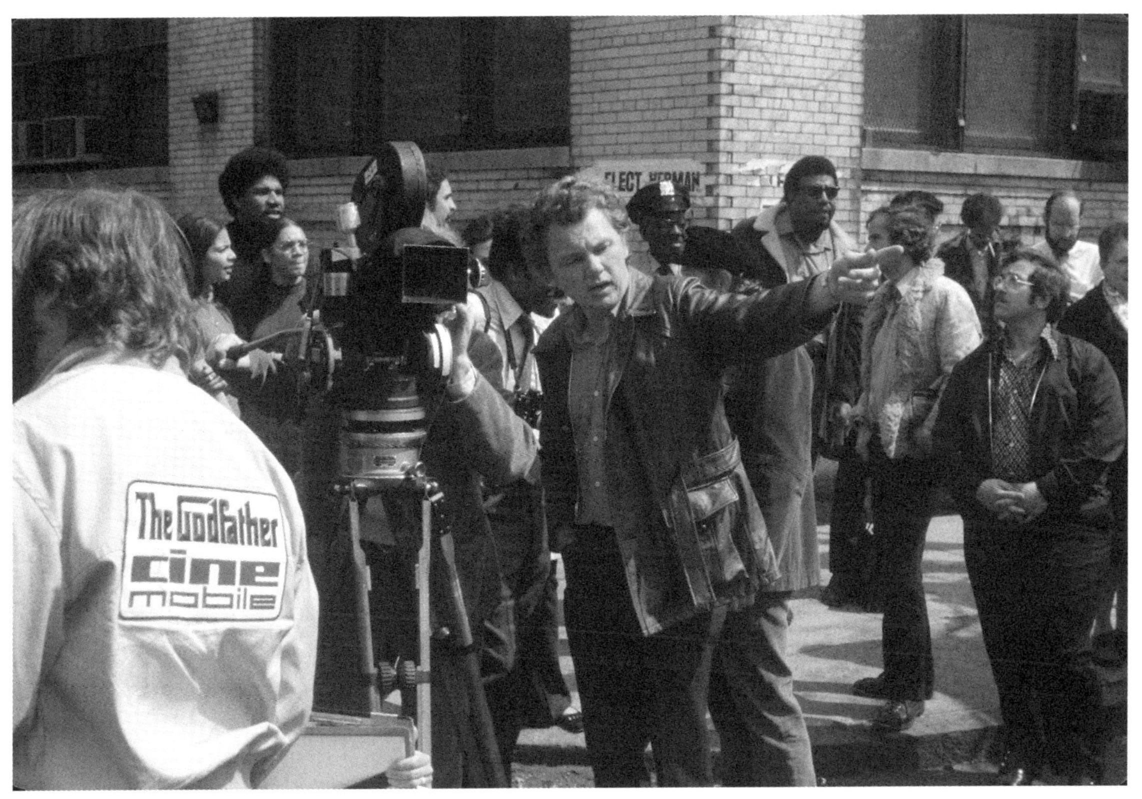

to me, "You know what I hate about Kodak right now is they're taking the D-Max out of all this stuff."

D-Max is where you get your blacks. What happens is you're gaining [film] speed—there were film stocks that were 8 ASA [referring to the American Standards Association exposure-index numbers]—you know, how much light you need? Now you've got stocks that they're going, "Oh, yes, you can push this through," so you can make it 400 ASA and then you can push it and you can go to 800 ASA and what you're giving away is the blacks, and the blacks are just as important to him. What he [Willis] would do is he would give them the negative that they couldn't screw with.

In this particular case, I felt that the film should be brown-and-black in feeling, and that occasionally it should be hanging on the edge from the standpoint of what you see and what you don't see. A lot of cameramen work to increase the quality of an image, but in this specific case I'm working to decrease it. Most cameramen work to make the image as structurally sound and smooth as possible, but it's been my personal feeling that this isn't the best way to handle a contemporary story—and now that I've thought about it, I'm convinced that it's absolutely the wrong way to photograph a period story.[8]

—Gordon Willis, *American Cinematographer*, 2020

CRAIG DIBONA: The original *Godfather*, it wasn't something where you say, Okay, well, print it in the middle. We could always make it darker or lighter. You couldn't make it lighter because what happened was, he [Willis] gave you nothing in the blacks purposely.

RUSSELL ENGELS: Well, it was dark. The lighting on *The Godfather*? Everybody complained that the cameraman was going to lose his job: "He can't do it. They're going to have raccoon eyes."

RICHARD ADEE: If you watch any of his [Willis's] movies, there's never anything in white. Cream, tan—everything is muted. He wouldn't let you on a set in a white shirt. The guy was crazy. He's fucking nuts. We shot a scene in a diner for *The Godfather*. It was called a "mattress," where bad guys hung out after they did a hit or something. And we lit that thing. He lit the whole freaking shot with lanterns. I mean, you couldn't see anything. I hated his photography.

RUSSELL ENGELS: He stuck to his guns and literally made it a famous style of lighting. Everybody after that was building these bay lights which were the black roll-up cloth around. He invented the light on that show *Klute* [1971], and the grips and electrics all put that together and said, "Here, make this portable—hang it up in an apartment building." And that's what happened. That's where it came from.

They had things before that, mostly out in L.A. for big sets. They had these hanging "chicken coops" [in the middle of the set], they called them. They were galvanized steel. And the lights were in that. Basically, the same type of thing, but not very portable, and you couldn't take them into an apartment or any kind of a building on location. But the bay light—you could take that style of lighting on location and move in any way you wanted.

CRAIG DIBONA: Gordy [Willis] changed the film industry, because in *Godfather*, all of a sudden, Paramount's going, "Well, you know we really can't see these people's eyes." He said to me, "That was by design. I want these people to look sinister."

8 Gregg Steele, "On Location with *The Godfather*: A Discussion with Gordon Willis," American Society of Cinematographers (En-US), February 20, 2020, theasc.com/articles/on-loacatiom-with-the-godfather-a-discussion-with-gordon-willis, retrieved July 16, 2023.

He basically would shoot with these bay lights that keep the light off the walls, and you'd see these very sinister-looking people.

But then you look at *All The President's Men* [1976] which is a lot of fluorescents in a newspaper room—totally different look. The idea is you have to look at things and decide what you want it to look like.

RUSSELL ENGELS: I liked him [Willis]. He's tough on some people and if he liked you, if you were a good friend, he'd take care of whatever had to be done. But boy, I'll tell you, he was tough on production. He was a tough man.

We were doing *Godfather*, and Francis Coppola set up a shot and the guy walked on one side of the chair in the house, and Gordon got on the camera, set up the shot, and they re-marked him on the other side of the chair. And it went back and forth three or four times. And Francis came up and said, "I'll shoot my pictures my way!"

And Gordon said, "You're not going to do anything as far as photography goes." Then he got up and he said, "Get yourself another camera man!"

That was three weeks into *The Godfather*. We were all in shock because we had done four or five movies with Gordon before *The Godfather*.

That's the reason we were there as a crew. He went over to pack his bags up in the camera room and Francis got on the dolly and said, "All right, I'll shoot it myself." And everybody walked off. They wouldn't shoot with him. We were all with Gordy. We worked five jobs with Gordy. Who was the new guy? [laughs] We didn't know who the new guy was.

So he went upstairs and kicked his door in his dressing room, and we thought he shot himself with the noise it made. Later that day they [Willis and Coppola] got back together, and they worked for a number of years after that—a lot of shows. I think Gordon stood his ground because he wanted the guy to go on one side for lighting or composition reasons. He wanted it one way and he got his way. He would stick to his guns.

Nowadays, I think most of the cameramen wouldn't dare do that.

CRAIG DIBONA: Nowadays, people just shoot. There are some people who are really talented, but the problem is there's a pushback from networks and studios that want it to look a certain way. He wouldn't let them do that, and I give him a lot of credit for it.

Look at those movies now—people are trying to emulate that style, but just thinking of the nerve he had to actually do that when they were turning around and going, "Wow, we can't make it brighter. We can't do it." Hey, that's what he wanted it to look like, and you look at *Godfather II*—to me, it's probably the most beautiful film ever shot—looks like an oil painting—looks like they went back in time. But it's unfortunate because I don't see that happening too much anymore.

The Exorcist

(1973)

In order to achieve a result on a film like The Exorcist, *I've got to coordinate the efforts of these eighty-five people every morning, and every one of these people comes in with special problems and hangups, and none of them are getting paid as much as I am, and none of them will get as much credit. Yet, all of this is unspoken between us, and we come together because we love the work.*
These are people who contribute to movies, guys whose names you'll never know, they'll come up and say "why don't we do this shot from here?" and by God, they'll be right.

—William Friedkin, director, *The Exorcist*[91]

TOM PRIESTLEY, JR. **(FIRST CAMERA ASSISTANT, *THE EXORCIST*)**: *The Exorcist* was far more complicated than *French Connection*.

STEVEN FELDER **(PRODUCTION ASSISTANT, *THE EXORCIST*)**: I wound up being the office PA on *The Exorcist*. I'd go out and get Bic pens, paper, and lunch. Billy [Friedkin] always wanted Papaya King, which was over on the East Side, so I'd have to go over there, and they let me take a cab that time so I could bring the hot dogs back warm. Then they said, "Listen, why don't you bring Dick Smith [pioneering effects makeup artist]"—who was the head makeup guy—"and Max Von Sydow"—[actor who played] the old priest—"breakfast every day?"

I said, "Okay, all right, what's involved?"

"Well, you're going to have to be there at 4:30 a.m. with whatever they want to eat."

There weren't that many all-night diners or places, but there was one close to the studio, and I would go get them egg sandwiches and coffee and sit with Max Von Sydow until the office opened for three hours.

TOM PRIESTLEY, JR.: They would come in at four o'clock in the morning to start making up people and then sometimes we wouldn't even shoot them that day. I mean, it got to be crazy. I felt so sorry for him [Dick Smith]. And at one point he almost revolted. I think he finally got somebody in to help him, but he was the first one to create and apply the facial

9 William Friedkin, quoted in "William Friedkin's *The Exorcist*: The Most Terrifying Film We Ever Laid Eyes on," Cinephilia Beyond, https://cinephiliabeyond.org/william-friedkins-the-exorcist-the-most-terrifying-film-we-ever-laid-eyes-on/, retrieved October 3, 2025.

Opposite page: William Friedkin, Own Roizman, Enrique Bravo, Dick Smith, and Linda Blair, *The Exorcist*. Image courtesy of the Margaret Herrick Library, Academy of Motion Picture Arts and Sciences.

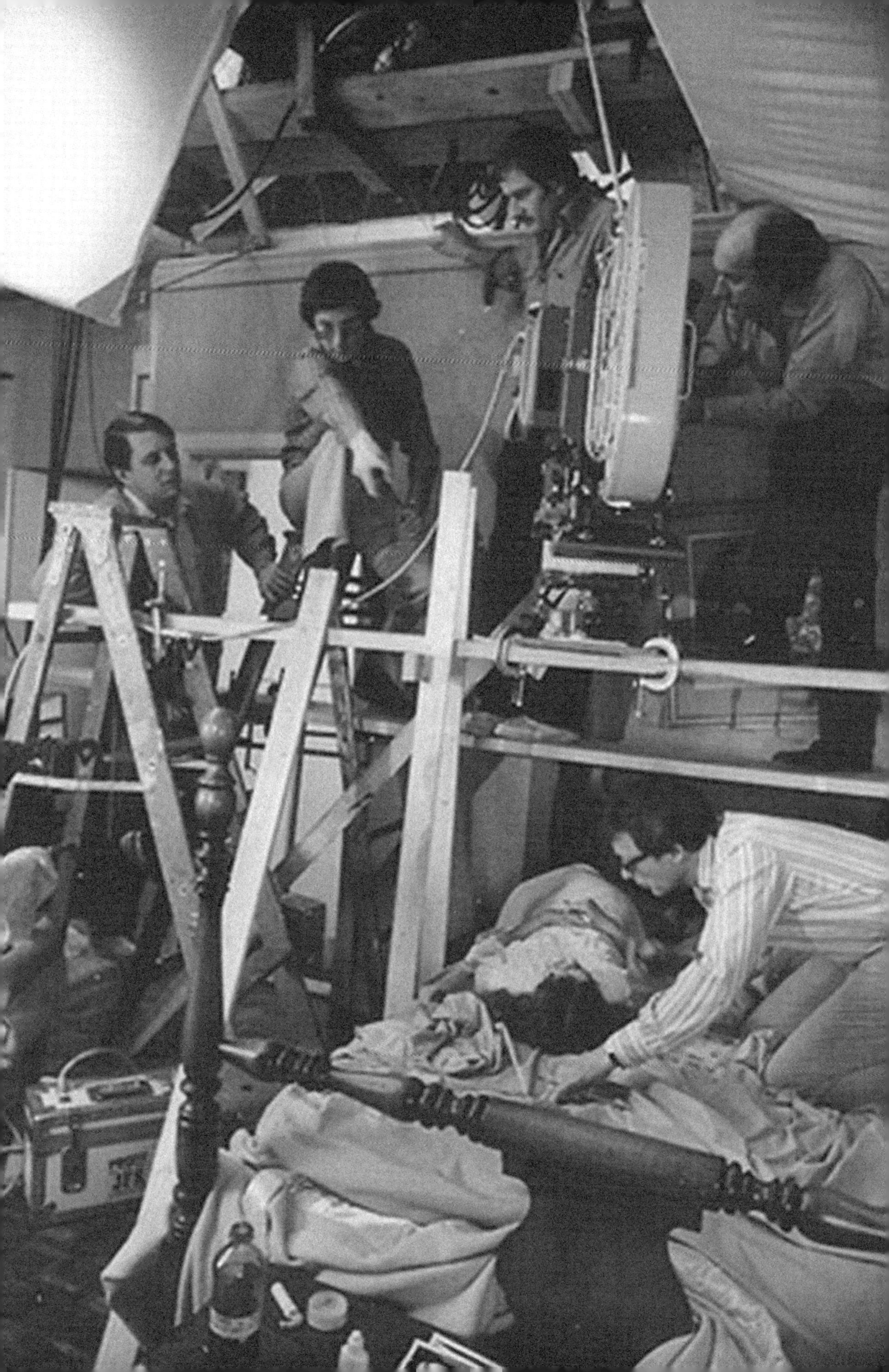

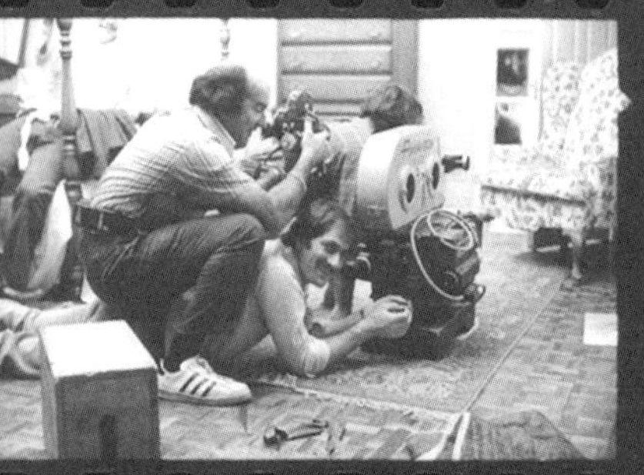

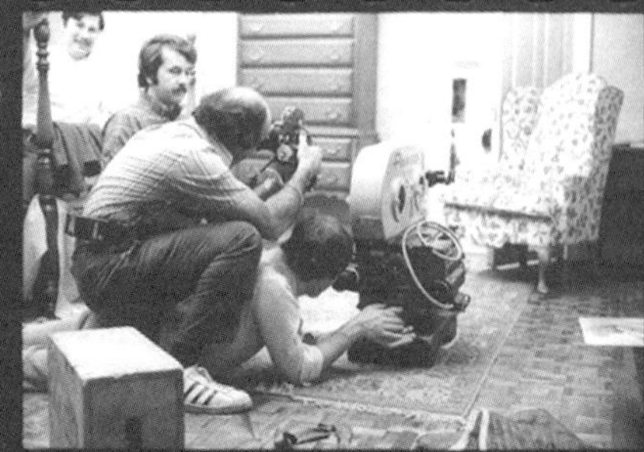

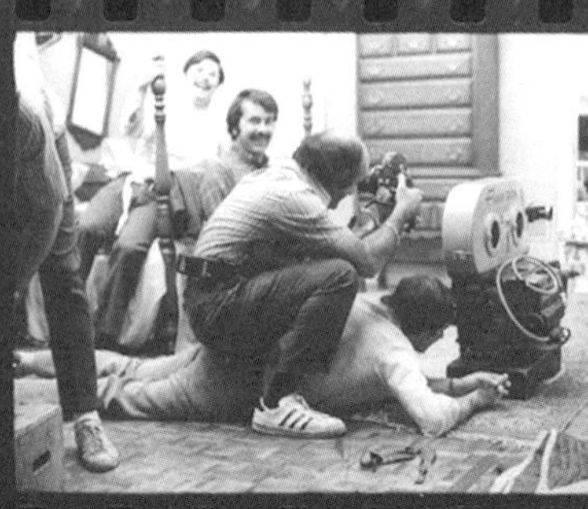
SAFETY FILM
KODAK TRI X
→2
→2A
→3
→3A
→4

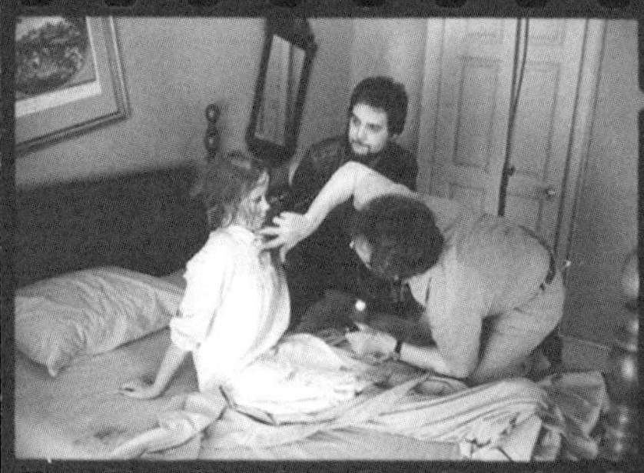

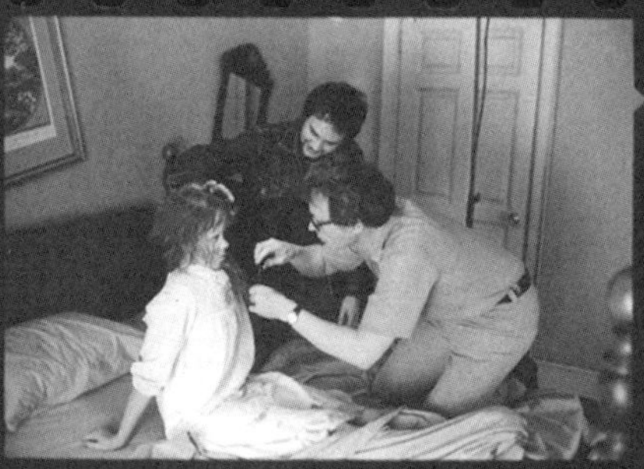

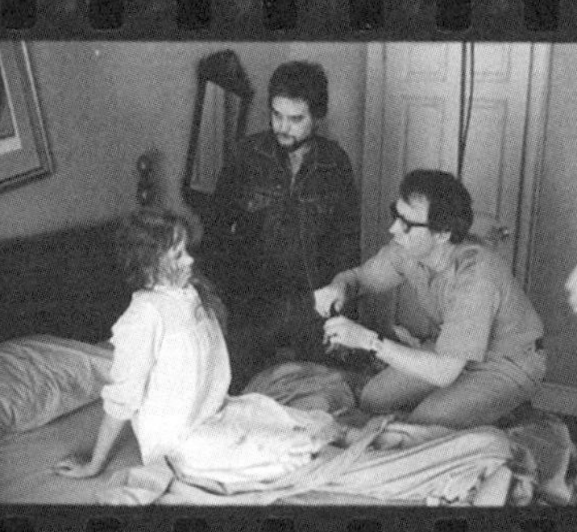
KODAK TRI X PAN FILM
→8
→8A
→9
→9A
→10

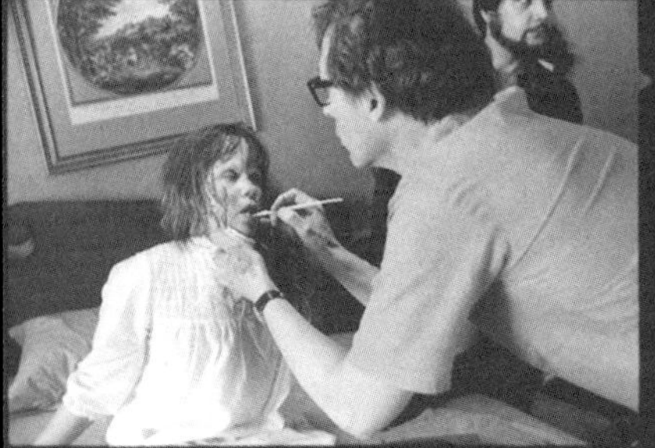

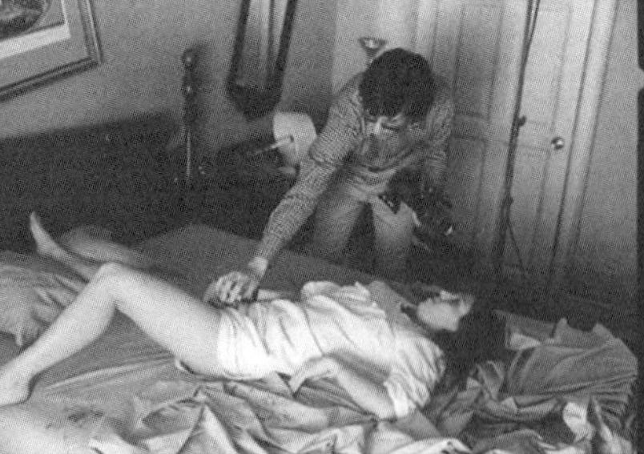

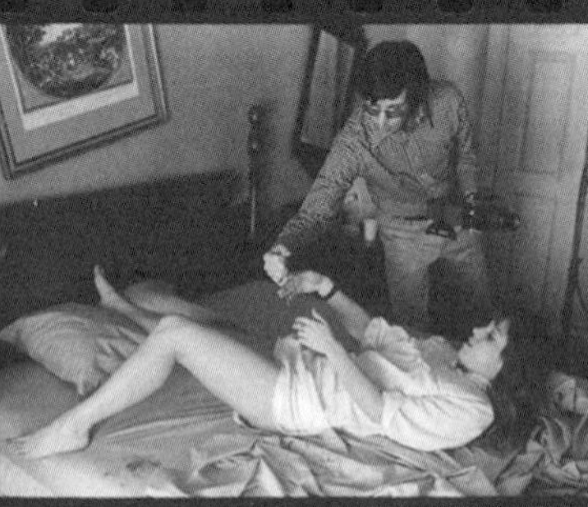
RI X PAN FILM
KODAK SAFETY FILM

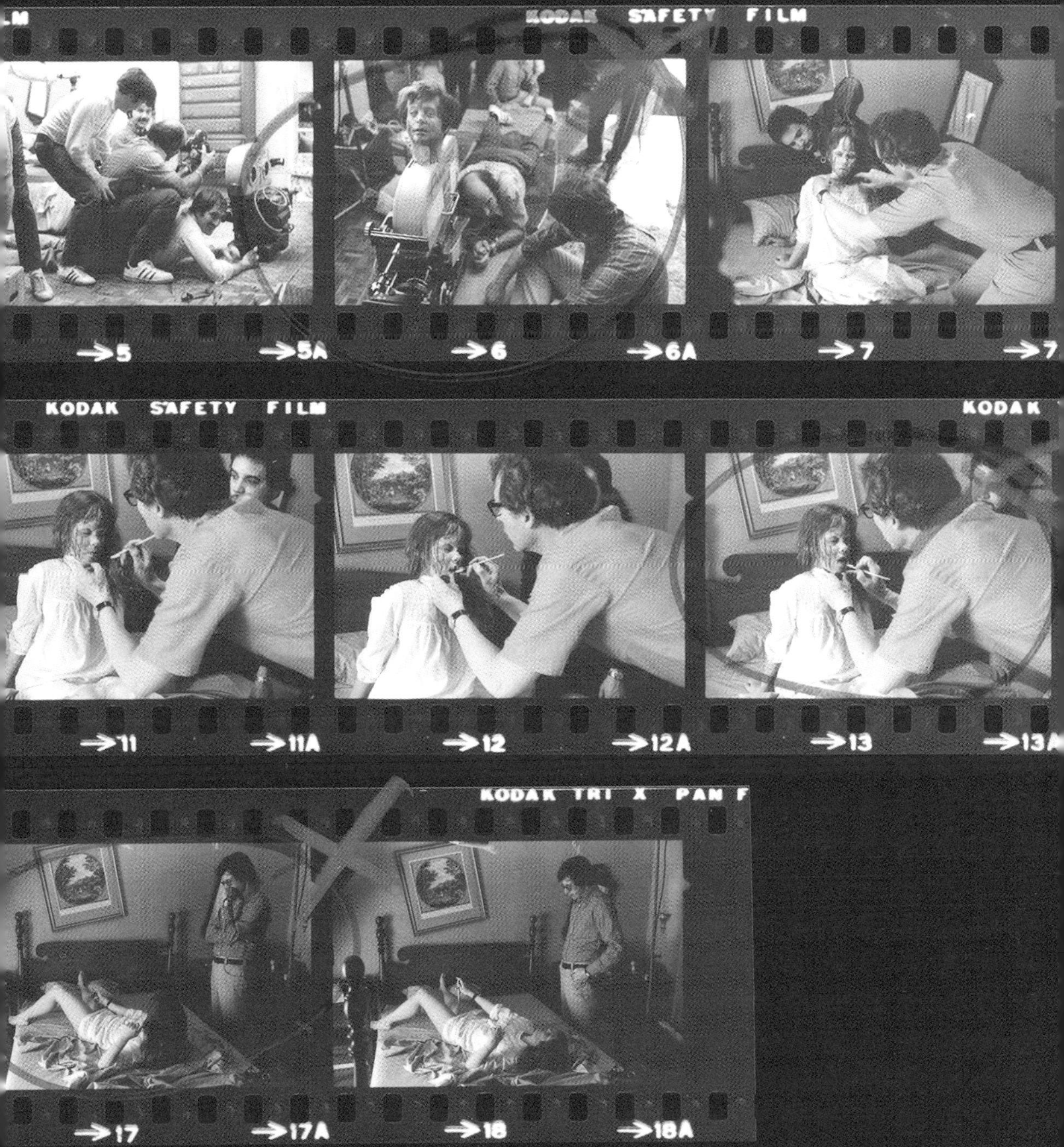

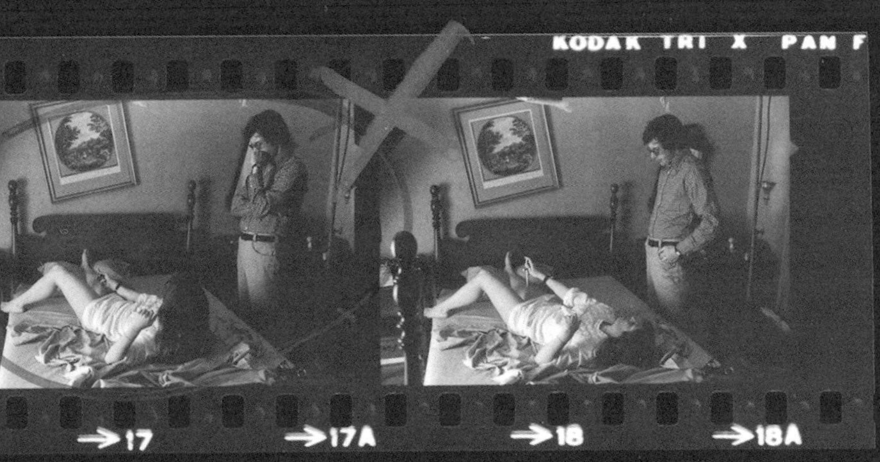

Contact sheet of *The Exorcist* by Josh Weiner. Image courtesy of the Margaret Herrick Library, Academy of Motion Picture Arts and Sciences.

prosthetics that he could alter—it was like a rubber or something.

STEVEN FELDER: He basically invented all the prosthetics for Max Von Sydow—aged him thirty, forty years.

TOM PRIESTLEY, JR.: Max Von Sydow was a young man. It took hours and hours to apply it every day.

GARY MULLER (SECOND CAMERA ASSISTANT, *THE EXORCIST*): I didn't quite understand why the studio was coming down so hard on Billy for taking so long, me being young and naïve—little did I know we were days behind that turned into months.

TOM PRIESTLEY, JR.: We were supposed to be in Georgetown for, like, two weeks. I think we stayed six.

GARY MULLER: I think we overextended our stay in Georgetown by a month.

TOM PRIESTLEY, JR.: We were there so long they had the scenic artist gluing leaves back on the trees because the leaves had fallen off.

GARY MULLER: Because it wasn't supposed to be winter.

TOM PRIESTLEY, JR.: They got Smilax, wrapped that on, and then glued the leaves. These poor bastards were putting leaves on a tree.

GARY MULLER: We had two main sets. One set was *the cold set.*

TOM PRIESTLEY, JR.: [Friedkin] wanted to see the actors' breath. They refrigerated the entire stage.

GARY MULLER: The sets would get refrigerated down to like minus thirty degrees, and then we'd run in, turn the lights on, and shoot, and then when you could see your own breath dissipate we'd go back outside and we'd wait to get it cold again.

TOM PRIESTLEY, JR.: It was so noisy in there. We couldn't stay in there. We had to leave. We would come in in the morning, set up the shot, do the lighting as much as we could, step out, wait for the refrigerator—it might take two hours to refrigerate the set—run back in quickly, get the actors in, and try to make the refinements and shoot. Somehow, we could only do two or three shots a day. Christ, it was impossible! You couldn't speak to anybody. You couldn't hear what they were saying.

STEVEN FELDER: It snowed one day on the refrigerated set—flurries from all the people's vapor just kind of flurried down.

TOM PRIESTLEY, JR.: A lot of shows in California, they would go to an icehouse and build a set in the icehouse and shoot. But here we did it on the stage and it took forever. And it was kind of nerve-wracking too, because you felt the pull of falling behind, getting all the work done. We just couldn't go any faster.

BILLY WARD (ELECTRICIAN, *THE EXORCIST*): Friedkin was a little nutty.

TOM PRIESTLEY, JR.: He used to burn Limburger cheese on the set because he wanted to create a demonic odor for the actors to react. The only people sick were the crew. The actors had perfumed handkerchiefs walking around until they had to act.

BILLY WARD: In order to get a reaction out of the actors, he used to have a gun with blanks, and he would shoot the gun off to get a reaction.

TOM PRIESTLEY, JR.: We were shooting at the Georgetown University chapel, and behind the camera was a desecrated statue of the Virgin Mary. It was covered up. She had a penis and all kinds of weird shit. So this priest is going to come in, walk, and genuflect at the beginning, walk all the way down the row of pews, genuflect again, stand up, and then they would pull the cloth off of the desecrated statue. He

[Friedkin] was trying to get a reaction, and the priest didn't do anything. He just stood there. He was a real priest, I believe.

Billy was frustrated as hell. So they go to do it again. And this time the priest comes down and genuflects. He comes over to the thing, over to the altar. Billy yells at him. He turns. I was right behind him on the side of the camera. Billy comes up right behind me, puts the gun out in front of my face, and fired *bam, bam, bam* at the priest. He must have been hit with a little bit of what they call the wadding from the dummy cartridge. He thought he was shot and fell down on the floor yelling, "Billy, why did you shoot me? Why did you shoot me?"

GARY MULLER: "I've been shot! I've been shot!" I swear to God, he crapped in his pants. We're in a sacred church in Washington, D.C., and Billy shoots the gun off, so you go from one extreme to another.

TOM PRIESTLEY, JR.: I mean, it was pathetic. He could have had a heart attack. It sounds funny now, but it was sad.

STEVEN FELDER: Usually when there's a hot set you say, "There's a hot gun on set"—we make people aware that we're going to fire blanks. The young priest just literally jumped out of the socks, as did most of the crew. The only one he [Friedkin] told was the camera operator. But you watch that film again, you'll see a moment when Jason [Miller] just jumps out of the socks. Billy's very volatile—a fantastic director, but a really volatile person on set.

TOM PRIESTLEY, JR.: He tried the shotguns on the stage too. He wanted to get a reaction from Max Von Sydow. I'm looking at the actors—hand is on the focus knob—and I'm trying to work. All of a sudden, behind me—*boom, boom*. Everybody's supposed to react. But it doesn't have the same effect. You think it's going to have a certain effect. It doesn't have that effect. But that was Billy's way of getting people's attention.

BILLY WARD: The priest, Max Von Sydow—he knew after a while it was coming and he would kind of shriek before the gun would even go off. And so one day Eddie Quinn—he was the grip on it—took a dead chicken and when Friedkin shot the gun off he threw the dead chicken over the top of the set.

TOM PRIESTLEY, JR.: He [Friedkin] went crazy. He stormed off and left.

BILLY WARD: Oh, Jesus. I thought that was funny. And then the assistant director said to his assistant, "Give me a glass of water and two tranquilizers."

TOM PRIESTLEY, JR.: Another night, the scene where Jason Miller goes out the window and goes down the steps—the famous steps in Georgetown that leads down to M street—we took the existing house and built an extension façade on it so that the stunt man could go out the window and land on the steps. The guy came out the window, down the steps, and he winds up on the ground. What they did was they put this high-density foam on the top of the steps so when the stuntman hit it he wouldn't crack his head open.

The body should wind up lying face down. And when he turns it over, you see the real actor.

Billy's screaming, "More blood, more blood, more blood!" Bill Farley [hairstylist] is down there putting blood all over stuff. And he turns around—he's got all this blood on his hand, and he starts to lick it. Someone in the crowd on the side starts throwing up all over the place, thinking it's real blood. He doesn't know it's Karo syrup and red dye or whatever the hell it was.

STEVEN FELDER: They had Mercedes McCambridge—very famous actress—doing voiceovers, and we were running her voice

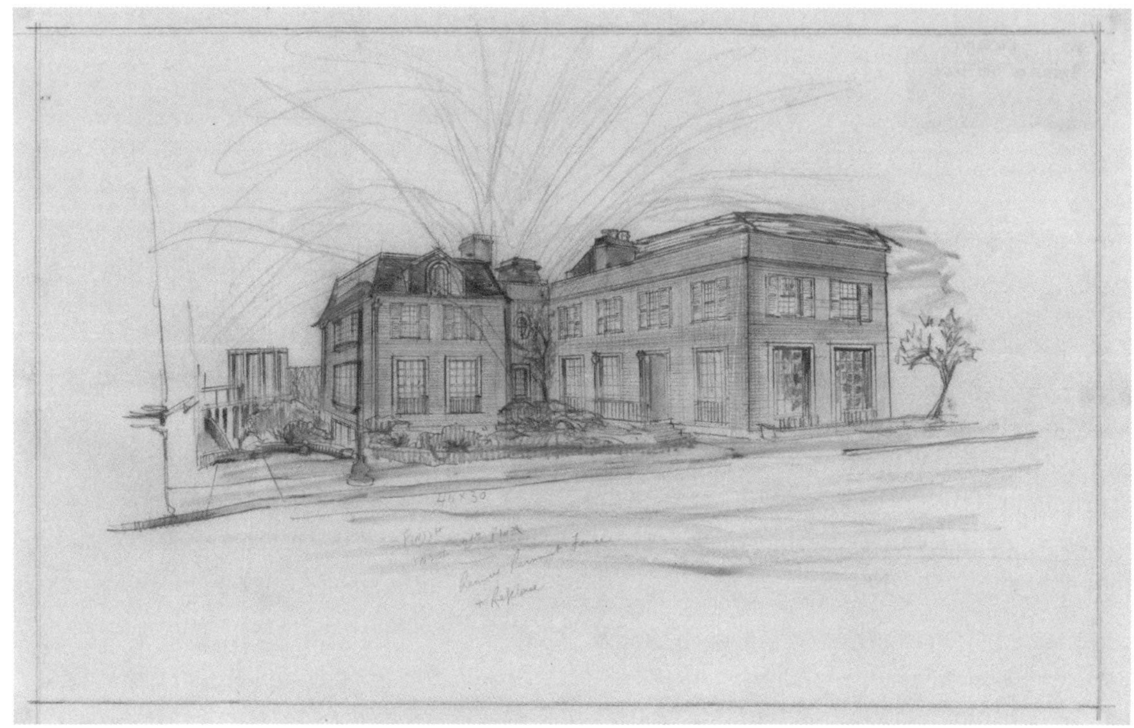

through different instruments and sound distortions, like a saw, an old giant bandsaw, two-handed wood saw that woodsmen use, and all that kind of stuff.

BILLY WARD: [Chris Newman, sound mixer,] was out of hand. We went to Georgetown. He wanted the traffic pattern to be changed so that he could have his good sound. I'd say, "Chris, what are you, crazy? They're not going to change a traffic pattern over Washington for you." And he'd say, "If you don't ask, you never get anything."

We used to use the zoom lens, the 10:1 zoom, which tended to be almost like a bit of a horn, and you could hear the camera a little bit because of it. So he had them cut out a hole out of a brand-new mattress and put the mattress over the camera.

He won the Oscar for that movie.

TOM PRIESTLEY, JR.: We shot about six or eight days before we moved into the studio where the set was built. This was the interior of the house in Georgetown, the kitchen, the foyer, living room, the bedroom upstairs.

We had gone over to Movie Lab at, like, 55th between 10th and 11th to look at the dailies. The stage was on 54th on the corner of 10th Avenue. When we were walking back Billy said, "Let's stop on the stage." We went inside onto the stage itself. And we were looking at the set—beautiful set, two-story, really nice-looking.

I'm standing there. The guys are talking and stuff. I see Owen [Roizman, director of photography] and Billy over on the side looking in through the window in the kitchen and talking. They're trying to lay things out and discuss stuff. Finally, Billy looks up, he walks over, and he says, "Get the production designer and the art director down here immediately." These two guys come down, their chests puffed up. They think they're going to get a big, great "atta boy" from Billy for the job they did.

Production drawing for McNeil house by John Robert Lloyd for *The Exorcist*. Image courtesy of the Margaret Herrick Library, Academy of Motion Picture Arts and Sciences.

He said, "This is the worst piece of shit I've ever seen. Tear this fucking pizza parlor down and build me a set or you both are fired. Call me when it's ready." And he walked out the door—bam. I'm like, "Holy shit." And no one knew why. I never knew why for the longest time, but they tore the whole set down and rebuilt it. I think we were off for a couple of weeks. The crews were working around the clock to finish the damn thing to get it done so we could start shooting.

I talked to Owen. I asked what happened. He told me when he and Billy were looking at the set, they built the set like a real house. You couldn't take the walls out. You couldn't remove anything. And that's all Billy had to see.

This is a great way to get a couple of extra weeks of prepping while they're building a new set. But they *were* wrong. They should have built wild walls, so they could take the walls out to bring the camera and stuff around. I don't know why they did it that way.

GARY MULLER: I enjoyed Billy, but you had to hide from Billy because Billy would fire people if he didn't think you were motivated enough. It was his way or the highway. It took me over the years to figure out why he would fire people—it was because he wasn't ready to start a film or start an important sequence.

TOM PRIESTLEY, JR.: He would tear down sets to buy time—anything to buy time.

GARY MULLER: He fired a special-effects guy on *The Exorcist* because the curtains were blowing too rhythmically. He wanted unrhythmic curtain-blowing.

TOM PRIESTLEY, JR.: We showed up at four o'clock on—I think it was a Friday night—to shoot the arrival of Max Von Sydow with Owen's lighting. Then Friedkin comes up and he says, "No, no, this is not what I want." And he's never told anybody what he wanted. He said, "I want this light to come out of the house and hit him. This beam of light."

Owen said, "There's no place to put the light that won't be in the picture or even mounted anywhere." I don't know who made the suggestion—cut a hole in the damn roof and put the light in there! They had to go over there, get permission from the owners, cut a hole, get everything mounted, get the thing set up. You know what that cost? It's the signature shot of the movie. But it was never discussed [prior to shooting].

He [Friedkin] loves all that shit. Creating controversy. He can go off and have dinner with somebody while everybody's scrambling around trying to fix this shit.

STEVEN FELDER: Somehow my responsibility became bringing the film back [to New York City] from Georgetown: "We want you to fly down to Georgetown every day with negative film from Technicolor, pick up the developed film, bring it back to the lab." Seventy-three round trips on People's Express Airlines.

GARY MULLER: I'd hand him the ten rolls of film, he'd take it to the lab, and he'd bring back the stuff.

STEVEN FELDER: I'd go to LaGuardia every day, fly down there, watch some of the filming, wait until they wrapped and whenever they did their film cut off. I'm flying down there with a hundred thousand feet of negative. At that time the Teamsters needed to be paid cash, and most of the crew had to be paid cash. So, they'd [the studio] give me cash, negative film, and Panavision equipment.

I mean, if I knew then what I know now, I probably would've gone, like, to Brazil and start my own studio or something! In hindsight I found out you can't really service Panavision equipment because they only rented it, so with Arriflex I probably could have pulled it off.

GARY MULLER: I always tell him [Felder] he was one of the best people to fail upwards.

STEVEN FELDER: I remember I got a raise from $125 to $150, and I thought I was making amazing money. David Salven was the production manager—he was a real character, a legendary kind of guy—hard drinker, but good guy and he was Billy's kind of guy.

TOM PRIESTLEY, JR.: Then there was the time Billy said he wanted a black dog, and they brought a white dog. He wanted a white dog when they bought a black dog—whatever dog he had, he started spraying it with spray paint. People said, "You can't do that!" He's spraying. This dog is yelping and screaming. Finally, they said, "No! Stop! Billy, stop!" But this is the kind of shit that went on. He loved it.

STEVEN FELDER: We had these priests from the Bronx. They were all our technical advisors, and everybody was freaked out about this movie. This movie hit a tone with people—not just as a horror movie, but I think it was more about the religious undercurrent of exorcism—scared people to death—the devil, possession, Satanism.

I wasn't on the beginning of the show which is probably one of the best openings of a horror movie ever. It was shot in the deserts of Iraq.

TOM PRIESTLEY, JR.: But at the end of the movie Owen and Billy weren't even talking—they weren't even speaking. They hired a cameraman named Billy Williams from England to shoot the [desert] sequence, which is ironic because I got married in Las Vegas in 1979 and Billy Williams was my best man. But it's one of those things. I think they went for three days. They were there for, like, two weeks and someone told me he [Friedkin] was getting goats and cutting their throats—sacrificing goats to bring the vultures and stuff. I don't know. I wasn't there.

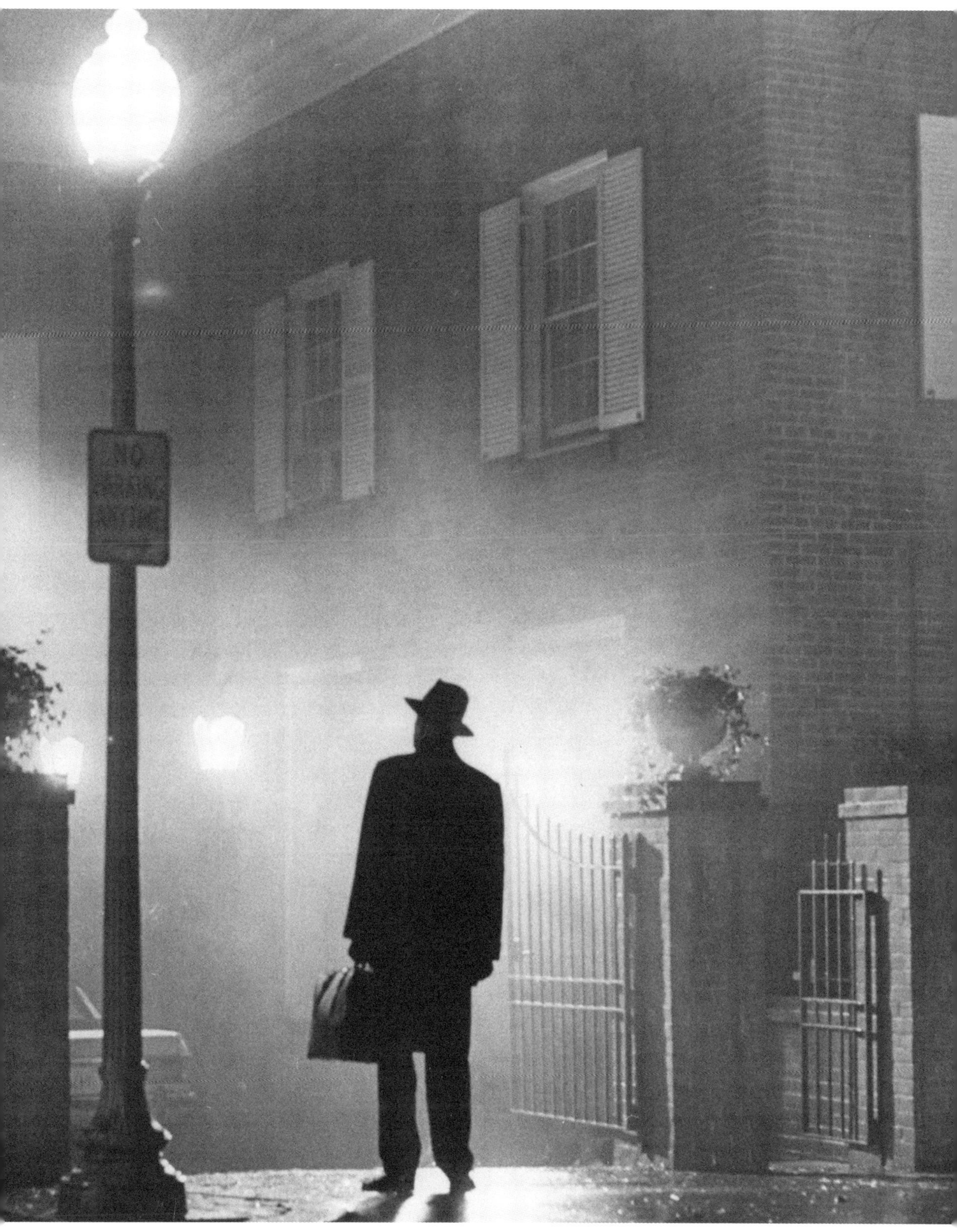

Promotional still from *The Exorcist.* Photo courtesy of the Margaret Herrick Library, Academy of Motion Picture Arts and Sciences.

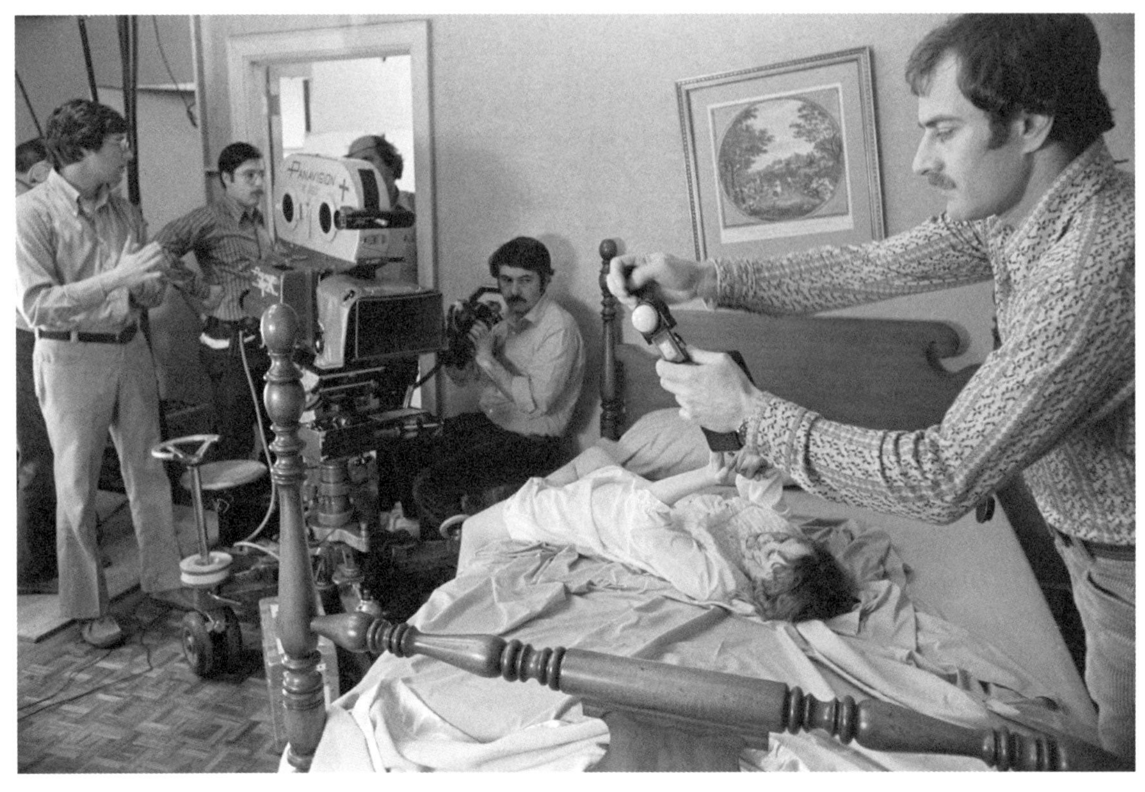

Above: William Friedkin, Gary Muller, Enrique Bravo, Tom Priestley, and Owen Roizman on *The Exorcist*.
Opposite page: Dick Smith, unidentified man, William Friedkin, Owen Roizman, Gary Muller, Enrique Bravo, Tom Priestley, Jr., and stand-in Eileen Dietz on bed.
Photos courtesy of the Margaret Herrick Library, Academy of Motion Picture Arts and Sciences.

STEVEN FELDER: It was a frightening film for a lot of people at the time. First of all, most of the crews were Irish Catholics. This was a little bit close to home for them. One of the Teamsters' teenage daughters had a nervous breakdown. Jason Miller, he and his family were walking on Rockaway Beach and motorcycles came out of nowhere and ran a kid over—just weird stuff like that. One day the set caught on fire.

GARY MULLER: We had a mysterious fire on the cold set over a weekend. All the overhead fire sprinklers were drained so they wouldn't crack when it was in cold mode, so there was no liquid in them to put out the fire.

STEVEN FELDER: You know the guy who played the director [Jack MacGowran], a good character actor, he died of a heart attack the day after he wrapped. The girl Linda Blair—she was a total pro, did everything they wanted her to do, and didn't seem to have any real effect.

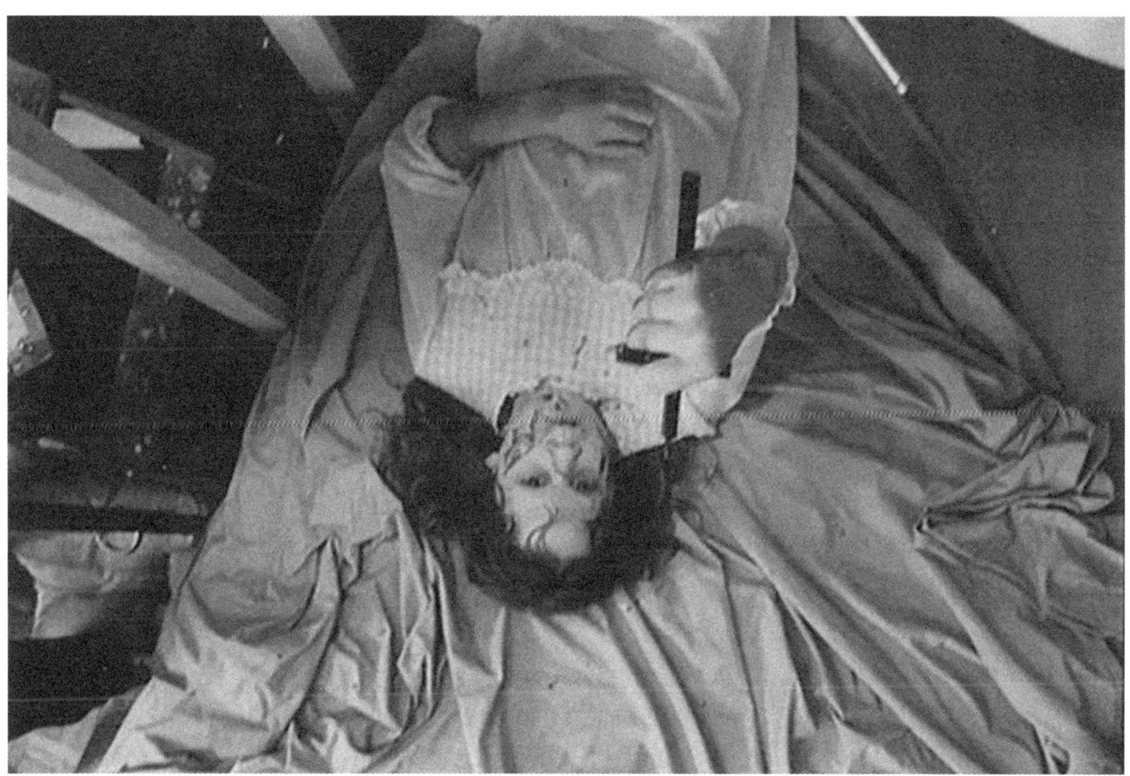

TOM PRIESTLEY, JR.: We had just come back from Georgetown, and we went to dailies one day and we were watching the rest of our stuff. The second unit went down there [Georgetown] to shoot some stuff. The second-unit stuff comes on and Billy stands up in dailies and says, "That's the worst shit I've ever seen in my life! Throw that shit away!" and he takes out his dick and tried to piss all over the counter in the dailies. They finally stopped him.

GARY MULLER: Billy would go look at dailies and come back and say, "We have to do this over again." Billy was extraordinary—he had a vision—but I think he was always trying to bankrupt the studio by reshooting and reshooting until the studio said, "Enough already."

TOM PRIESTLEY, JR.: [Billy] had a big run there for a while, but he abused everything. He pushed everything beyond the limit. It was a shame because I think he had a lot more great movies in him, but he just never—Hollywood, they give you enough rope for you to hang yourself or save yourself.

They're very good at that. And if you make money for them, they give you more money. If you lose money, you don't get as much. If you lose more money, you don't get any—it's one of those deals. It's still a business. We all love it. We love the artistry and everything, but it's still a business.

BILL REYNOLDS (PROPS, *THE GREAT GATSBY*): I got in and my world changed. I graduated that year and I went up to Newport, Rhode Island, on *The Great Gatsby,* which was a fabulous experience. I had the most amount of fun and it was just laughing.

STEVEN FELDER (PRODUCTION ASSISTANT, *THE GREAT GATSBY*): I wound up getting hired on *The Great Gatsby* as the mansion security in Newport—Rose Cliff, where all the mansions were.

BRUNO ROBOTTI (CHARGE SCENIC ARTIST, *THE GREAT GATSBY*): The reason they picked Rose Cliff was because they have the biggest ballroom in Newport.

STEVEN FELDER: *Great Gatsby* was my second job, but I wasn't really an AD at that point. An old set decorator/prop master—a wonderful man named Herb Mulligan[10]—came one day with a book and said, "Hey, can you help me with this?" He said, "We need to find these cars." Because New York prop guys handle picture cars.

I had to find Robert Redford's car, Mia Farrow's car, Bruce Dern's car—all these characters' cars—and fortunately it was New England, so we had all these car clubs up there.

The ADs on that show liked me and I started doing background action and controlling the crowds.[11] But the car search was an amazing adventure.

BILL REYNOLDS: The drinking was certainly in full fever when I started. *Gatsby* was almost exclusively shot at night. We would pray for purple in the sky so they wouldn't be able to keep shooting. You would get to four and five in the morning and you'd get knocked off. That'd be it. We never went home. We went to a bar, and there was pretty much one bar in Newport—probably thirty of us or more.

We'd start at 4:30 a.m., maybe 5:30 or 6 a.m., and this band of Englishmen who were obviously together would show up, and so we got to talking and everything was cool. I think it was actually Rusty Engels who said to them, "What the hell are you guys going to do for the rest of the day? We're going to bed."

They said, "Well, we have a yacht race to run." It was the America's Cup. It was the Australian team, and they won the next circuit.

BRUNO ROBOTTI: It was amazing how much work was done. I mean, those guys—you should have seen them on rainy days. I mean, they lug this lumber that they used to carry so many loads that their feet would sink in the mud. You cannot believe it. The amount of work that was done, it was unbelievable. The drinking did not affect it.

Matter of fact, the director [Jack Clayton] used to consume about a bottle of Hennessy a

10 I sent several carefully worded letters to Herb Mulligan asking for an interview. At the time he was the oldest living member of Local 52. He sent me a note which read, "Sorry—unable to help you—only remember the fooling around and drinking!" He passed away September 25, 2023.

11 ADs (assistant directors) commonly start as production assistants and then move up by doing background (extras) control and then becoming second assistant director who are tasked with coordinating whatever the extras are doing in the background of the scene. It's an important job.

The Great Gatsby

(1974)

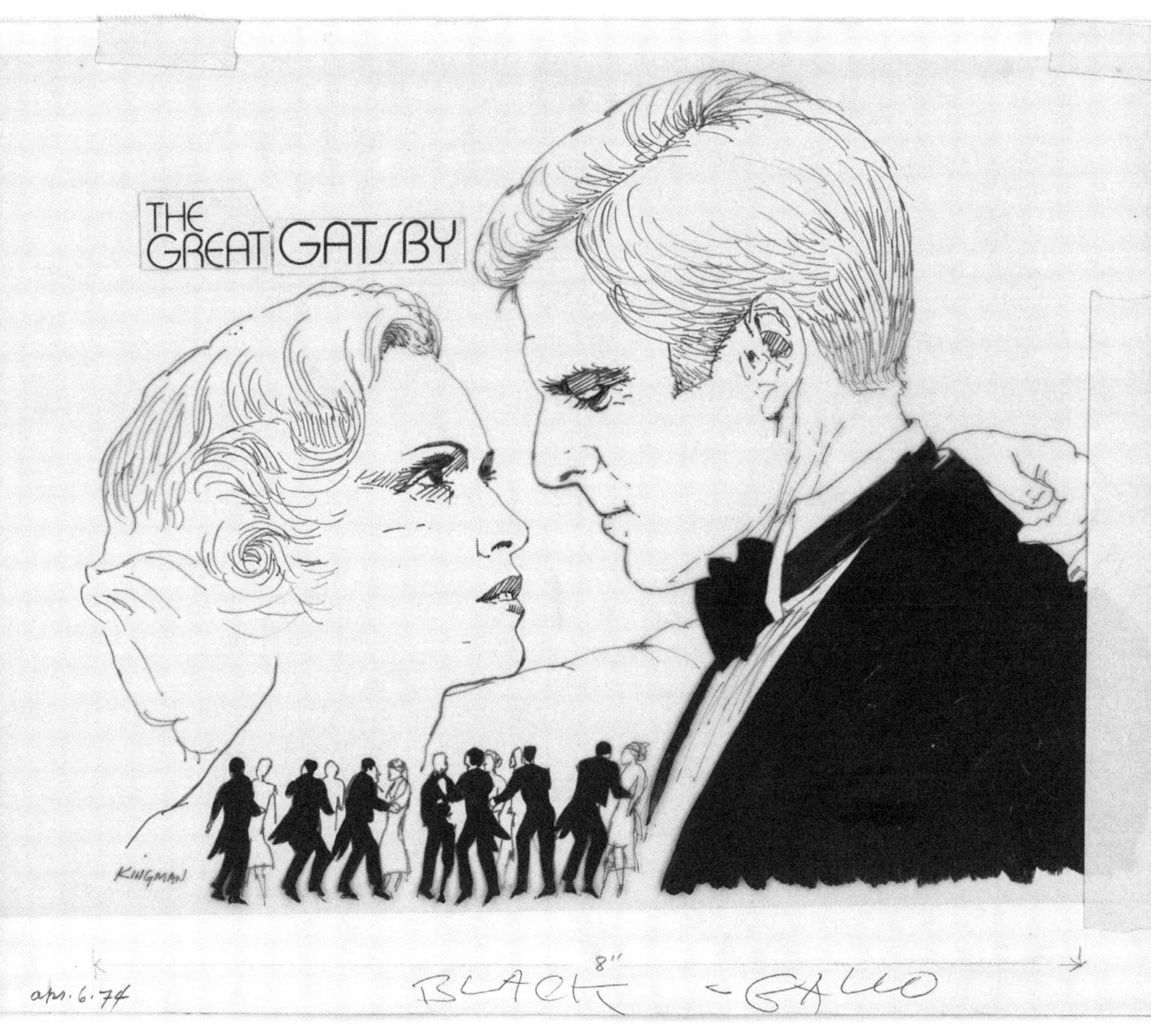

Television advertisement layout for *The Great Gatsby* by Dong Kingman, 1974. Image courtesy of the Margaret Herrick Library, Academy of Motion Picture Arts and Sciences.

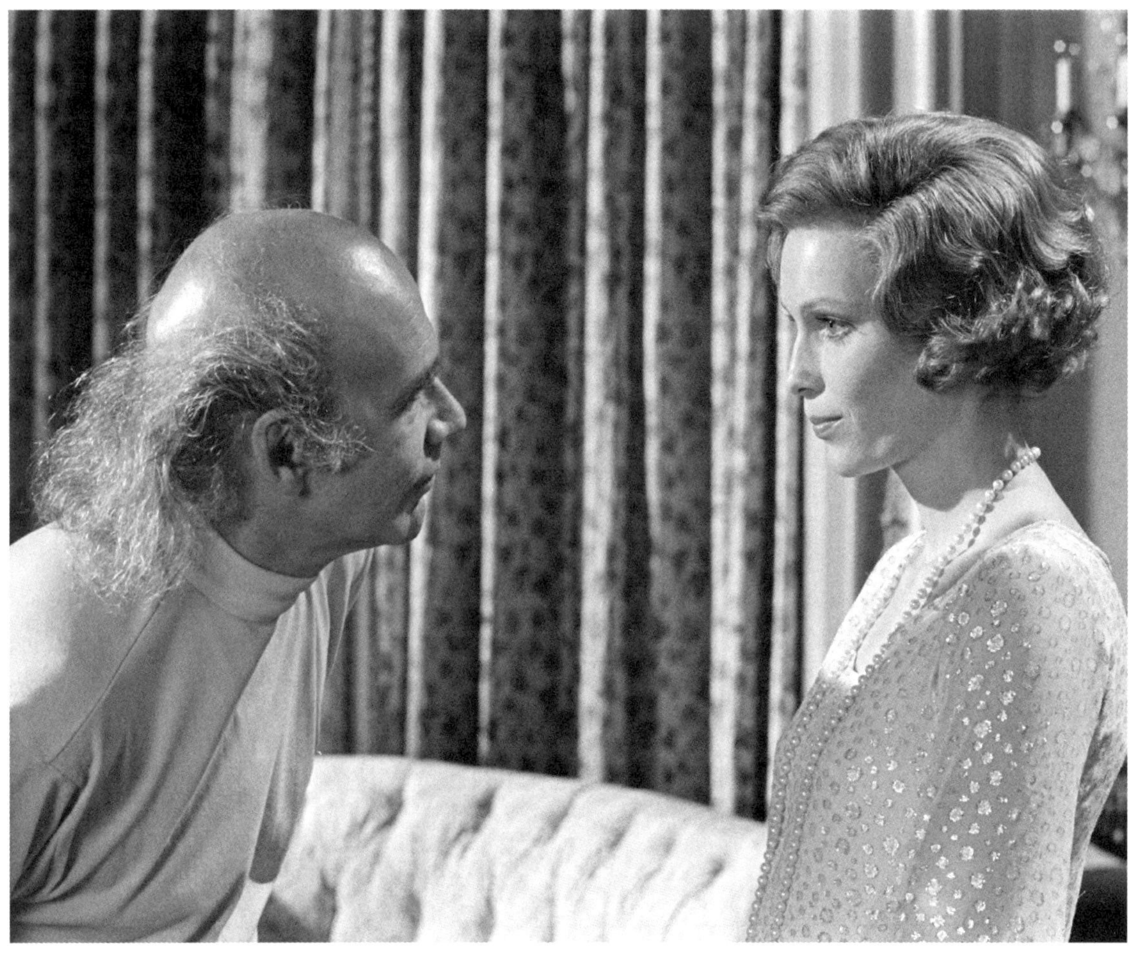

day, and at the end of the show he gave a party on the terrace on Rose Cliff. Beautiful.

RICHARD ADEE (PROP MASTER, *THE GREAT GATSBY*): I was on *The Great Gatsby,* and the director [Jack Clayton], what a fantastic guy. Always carried a knife, a bayonet-type knife, in his boots, and he always wore boots.

We were shooting up there and my truck was on the grounds, and we broke for lunch and my guys, all my crew—and we had a ton of people up there—they'd come, they'd grab their lunch from the caterer and come on my truck, sit on the tailgate. I had lounge chairs, folding lounge chairs, and director's chairs. And they'd all sit around and have their lunch. But one of my toolboxes wasn't a toolbox. It was a bar. It had a quarter keg of beer in it and a spout on the outside. The only thing you saw was the spout. I had a little thing that disguised that. So, we are there and we're all having a beer and lunch, and Clayton comes walking by and he says, "Rich, do you mind if I join you?"

I says, "No, come on."

He sits down and says, "How are you guys drinking beer? Where'd you get the beer?"

I say, "Oh, you want a beer?"

He says, "I'd love a beer." One of the guys jumps up on a truck, gives him a beer.

He says, "Holy Christ, what is that?

So, I say, "Well, that's on my truck all the time."

Director Jack Clayton and Mia Farrow working on *The Great Gatsby*. Photo courtesy of the Margaret Herrick Library, Academy of Motion Picture Arts and Sciences.

He says, "Really? How did you make that?"

I said, "I had the carpenters make it for me."

He says, "Can they make another one? I want to put it in the woods, so anytime anybody wants a beer they can go and have a beer."

I said, "Sure."

We were shooting at one of those big mansions up in Rhode Island and it was a big, wooded area where the equipment was. I had one made up, got the keg and the cooler, the tap. And he [Clayton] was so happy. I never paid for it. The company paid for it. They didn't know it, but they were paying for it.

BRUNO ROBOTTI: Production manager used to send two kegs of beer every day in front of the grip shack for everybody in the morning. The beer was there all day, for everybody in the crew. If you wanted a cold one, you'd go there and take one.

BILL REYNOLDS: One of the people that I really admire and is just a mountain of a man and very knowledgeable is Dusty Wallace, who was the gaffer. Again, it was at the same bar, or that might've been the hotel. He was questioning whether the bartender was being honest with us. There was a pile of money on the table. You put a pile of money on the table, take out what you want, and then we'll figure out what your tip is later. Apparently Dusty or someone caught the bartender [dipping] into the pile a little bit more than they ought to.

So Dusty takes out a buck knife. Now a buck knife extended is probably eight inches long. It's intimidating as it sounds. He whacks it into the middle of the money right in the bar, looks the guy in the eye, and says, "I'll give you money when you need it."

One of the stages, Fox Studios on the West Side, and a number of the smallest studios—there were a lot of studios in Manhattan—they were all DC. They weren't AC. The safety boxes today are different. But he [Wallace] used to have the pigeon boxes for electric. He would literally put his fingers in it to tell what voltage was, whether it was AC or DC, and I would think, "How the hell can you do that?"

CRAIG DIBONA (CAMERA OPERATOR, *PRIZZI'S HONOR*): You know why they call Dusty Wallace "Dr. Wallace," right?

He was a bear. He was an electrician. We used to work with Andrzej [Bartkowiak] all the time, and he worked with Gordy [Gordon Willis] also, and one time he was living in Long Island, and he was a heavy drinker, and this tree goes down and he's cutting the tree with a chainsaw, and he's got a gin and tonic in the other hand, and the chain popped out the saw. It kicked back and it got caught in his ribs and he calls 911. He sends for another drink, and they walk in, they go, "What are you doing?" He goes, "I know they're not giving me one of these where I'm going."

Dr. Wallace. The next day he shows up at work.

CRAIG DIBONA: We're shooting *Prizzi's Honor* [1985]. Dusty and this guy, Freddy, his sidekick, they must've been drinking most of the night and they realized, "You know something? We're never gonna get to work in the morning. Let's just drive to the set, and we'll sleep in the car and we'll just get up there.

BILL KANE (PROPS, *PRIZZI'S HONOR*): They're in a Volkswagen and they park in a Volkswagen and they go to sleep. When the crew comes in, in the morning, they see them sleeping and they get canvas . . .

CRAIG DIBONA: Mouths are open—their heads are back. The other guys took a piece of black duvatyne [heavy black cloth used by grips to hide light] and they put that over the car.

BILL KANE: They slept all day.

CRAIG DIBONA: We're doing the scene where Jack Nicholson comes out after this wedding and the car is right there. They must have kept waking up and seeing it was dark and went back to sleep. Now they look at their watch like, "Holy shit!" and you see the door open up and you see this duvatyne and they're squinting.

And the whole crew stopped and applauded. John Huston goes, "Who are those guys?"

"Oh," I said, "those are electricians."

Then he goes, "Well it seems like they got a good rest."

I am telling you, man—this business. You could never have as much fun in any business, but you want to know something? It's a lot of good work.

BILL REYNOLDS: It was a Friday night toward the end of the movie. And I was at the right place at the right time. We were going into a hotel, and I caught the DP [director of photography] giving Dusty a bottle of Cutty Sark, and, for whatever reason, Dusty notices me looking. There was nothing to it. But he noticed me, and he gives me half a smile. The next morning, he was looking a little ragged, and we're bullshitting around and he said, "Kid, I sunk the ship last night." There is a ship on the front of the Cutty Sark bottle. He was an amazing man, an amazing talent. But if you look at the outside of the box, you will never understand or appreciate the talent that was there.

I used a light meter in my early films, but not on the last 20 or 30. I found that as the schedules were getting tighter and tighter I didn't have time. But I found I could automatically give the set the right amount of light. I then realized I didn't need the meter, so I gave it up.[12] —Douglas Slocumbe

BILL REYNOLDS: I know it's not my domain, but everything about the business interested me and I learned as much as I could about every department and how they did things—but it took a mustache, or a foreign accent, and sometimes both. They were the only ones that did the old hard lighting, meaning a lot of light unrestrained.

RUSSELL ENGELS: Oh yeah. We didn't have HMIs[13] or anything back in those days.

BILL REYNOLDS: There was a furlough of cable which is probably more than an inch, streamed all around the mansion, and that was in DC. It wasn't alternating current; it was direct current. They were mostly using the brutes, the arcs, which only work on DC. So, anywhere they wanted they could pick up power and be able to have these lights because, again, it was Doug Slocombe and it was the old-time lighting of hard Hollywood lights, which means every fucking light.

BILL KANE: We had John Weber. He was in the German army. He was an engineer in the German army and when he came to the United States he went to work for York Avenue Cadillac, and because John worked on submarines he was a terrific, terrific engineer. He built three huge silent generators that were on flatbeds. He had three of them on the set on *The Gatsby* and they were running almost twenty-four hours a day. One of the electricians had to be watching over them, watching the gauges, and it was bleary. We'd be working night and day sometimes.

RUSSELL ENGELS: We worked three major generators just for the house area, and there were thousands of amps each burning all those lights in the ceiling of the place and the windows and it was extremely hot.

12 Bryant Frazier, "Seven Stories about the Late Douglas Slocombe, B.S.C.," Studiodaily.com, February 22, 2016, https://www.studiodaily.com/2016/02/seven-stories-about-the-late-douglas-slocombe-bsc/, retrieved January 24, 2023.

13 Hydrargyrum medium-arc iodine lights, modern low-wattage movie lights that emit very little heat. The current industry standard.

Nick's cottage was one spot. He was funny—when they opened up and they showed Nick [Sam Waterston] and he comes to the door and you see right out the back door out to the ocean—so it [the light meter] was at f45 out there. And everybody's saying, "Well, what do you want to do? Do you want to hang a double net off the back door?" and cameraman Dougie Slocombe is a funny guy—he said, "Oh, no, no, no. We'll light up the inside." So we put three arc lights in this little, tiny cabin inside on low stands, and one big matching group in the ceiling of the place, to backlight him at the door. And it was so hot in there. It had to be over 140 degrees.

The director says, "Let's get going because I want to get this done before you melt my actor."

BILL REYNOLDS: On *The Great Gatsby,* we were in a small room photographing a clock on a mantel and it was old, English DP [director of photography, Doug Slocombe]. We had an arc inside with a 10K kicker—you could have cooked that clock—but that's what they did—that was the old school, the really, really hard lighting, and it was a great look, but it took time, took electricity—it was every available light.

RUSSELL ENGELS: The carbon arc was the best daylight light we had before HMIs and they're huge—225,000 watts. The fumes burn inside the head, but the fumes that come out of the top exhaust pipe and all that—you have to pipe them out of the room and all that or you'd smoke the room right up. But the electricians, we all hit the arcs and literally jumped out the windows to get out of there because it would get so hot so fast.

They weighed about 250 pounds, so it was a heavy carry with two men walking down the street basically, or whatever—then to mount them on the stands and all that. It was a good lift. You'd burn your arm a little bit when you're changing the carbons inside door. You open the door up or pull the head apart and you'd have to change the carbons as they burned down. There were times you got a little flash, and you'd call them sergeant stripes on your arm.

BILL KANE: At one point they're bringing in provisions into the kitchen, into the chateau, and they're coming in and the director says, "I want a lot of lobsters." You could put a false bottom on those barrels, so you only have to put a couple of dozen lobsters on those barrels, thinking that they're full. "But I want you to get the biggest lobster that you can find. And I want a guy coming in with it on the tray."

The outside prop man [finds] there's a lobster house where all the lobster boats come in and unload into these huge tubs of water with flowing water from the bay, just circulating. The guy is looking, looking, looking. He goes, "Here you go."

And then he says, "Wait a minute, wait a minute. Here's one. This is a big one."

And how big was it? Like forty pounds. It was huge. And when we brought it, the actor brings it in and they shoot the scene, then all the guys around, all the crew go, "All right, let's go cook up."

The director [Jack Clayton] turns around, says, "No fucking way."

Newport, Rhode Island, had a sidewalk that goes at the end of the big lawn, and you go down the steps and you have the bay, and he says, "Put that into the bay—I'm going watch," and they go down, and the steps are going into the bay. They placed the big lobster into the bay, and it just walked away back into the bay.

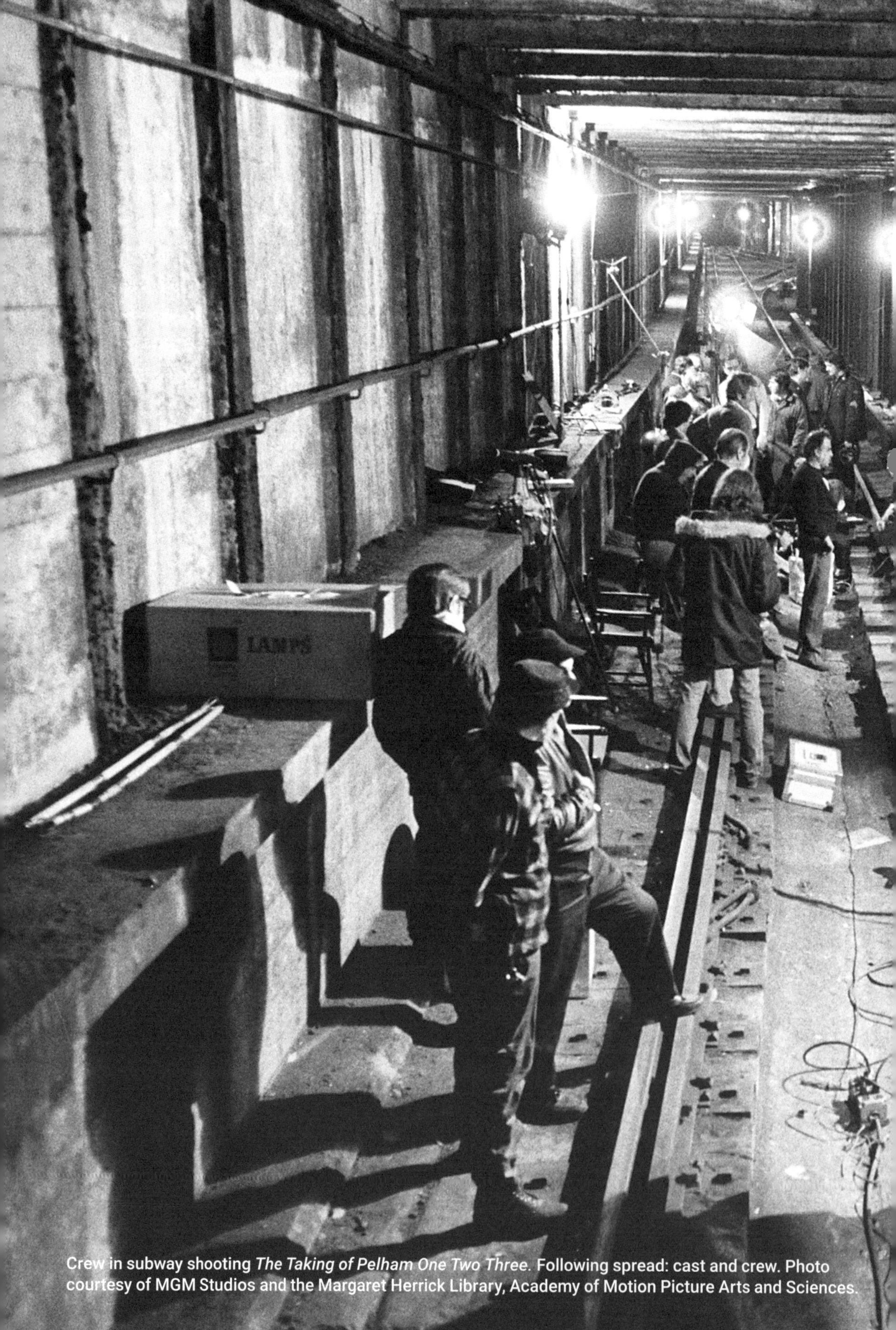

Crew in subway shooting *The Taking of Pelham One Two Three.* Following spread: cast and crew. Photo courtesy of MGM Studios and the Margaret Herrick Library, Academy of Motion Picture Arts and Sciences.

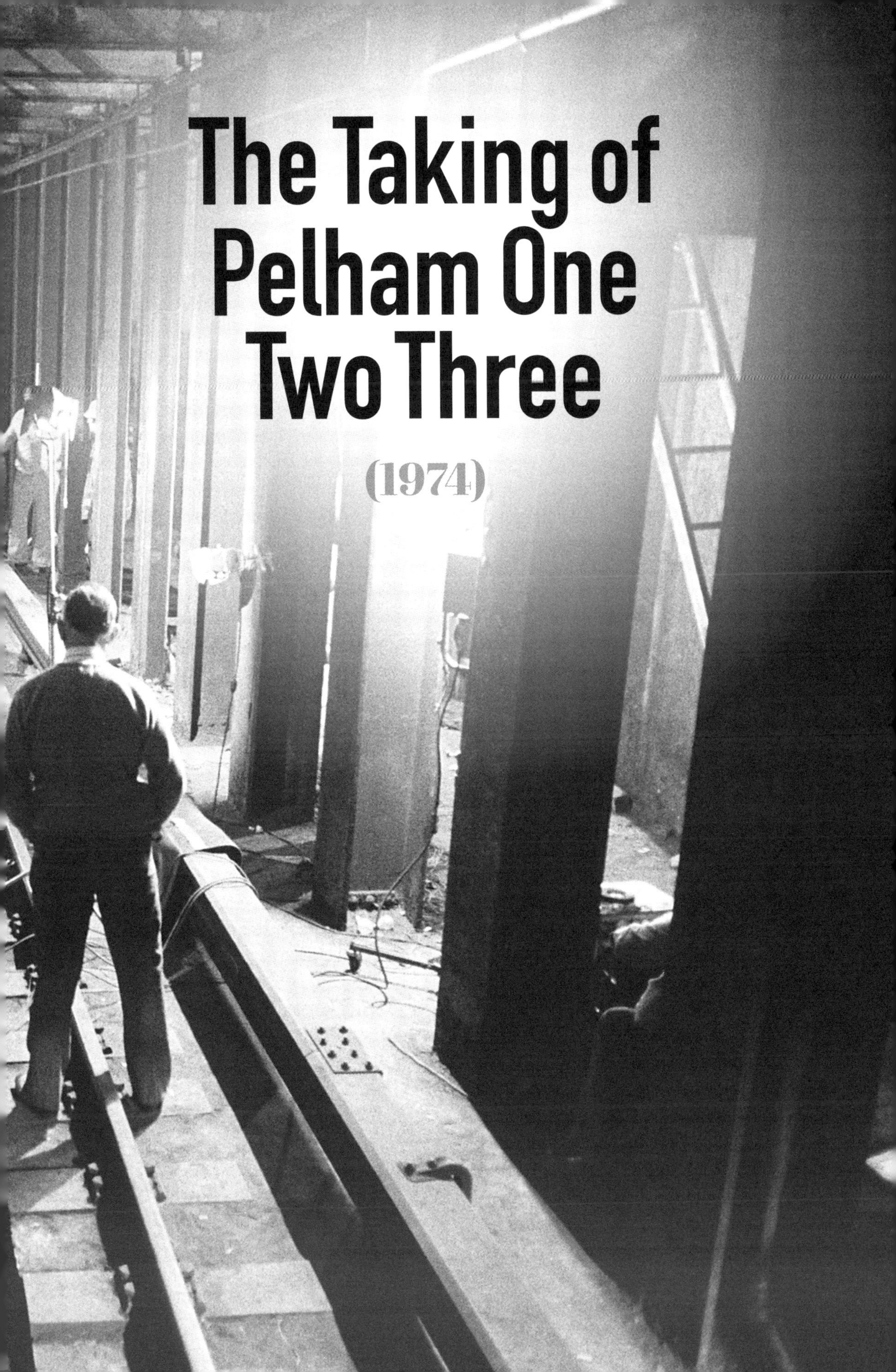

The Taking of Pelham One Two Three

(1974)

GARY MULLER (CAMERA ASSISTANT, *THE TAKING OF PELHAM ONE TWO THREE*): God. *Pelham* was a very difficult movie. Joe Sergeant was the director. It was a long picture. Winter into spring. I think it was probably one of the biggest pictures in New York for a while in the subway system. It was the only game in town. It didn't matter when the picture started because we were underground. The weather didn't matter. We did a lot of scenes outside, but a good portion of it was done underground or done in the studio replica.

TOM PRIESTLEY, JR. (CAMERA ASSISTANT, *THE TAKING OF PELHAM ONE TWO THREE*): Then, most of the subway stations were underneath the City Hall in Brooklyn—I believe Hoyt-Schermerhorn, over around Church Street.

RUSSELL ENGELS (ELECTRICIAN, *THE TAKING OF PELHAM ONE TWO THREE*): It was fairly dangerous at times because you'd have to clear the tracks and let a train go by, and there were only so many places you could get into, like staircase areas or little alcoves, that they would actually let you stay down there.

There was a slight bit of training beforehand, but not like they have today. Now you've got to go through a whole safety course to get anywhere near the subways.

CRAIG DIBONA (ADDITIONAL CAMERA OPERATOR, *THE TAKING OF PELHAM ONE TWO THREE*): I'm going to tell you something that people don't even realize, that I learned only from being down there that night. You had a guy, he had glasses, and he would take us down where we were going to be, and he would show you—"Don't touch this, don't touch that," you know. No problem.

And then you'd see a body, and what would happen is old bums would go down there to stay warm and they'd be drunk and they'd hit the third rail and they'd fry. You never see it on the news. He said, "Oh yeah, we get them every week." We never even knew about it. It was eerie.

GARY MULLER: I remember this famous electrician, Salty Meyerhoff—he was one of the extra electricians on there. He was way in the distance; he was dragging a cable. Somehow it hit the third rail and thank God he let go, but it sparked for what seemed like forever. It was probably a minute to a minute and a half in all. You saw the whole tunnel lit up in silhouette. You're thinking, "Holy shit, this is what happens if you touch the third rail."

The French Connection was dangerous, but we had really good professional stuntmen. Being twenty-one, you don't give a shit about life. But now I'm a little bit older and wouldn't want electricity to kill me. So that was the fear.

TOM PRIESTLEY, JR.: At lunchtime we didn't even leave. We ate lunch down on one of the subway platforms or whatever they had in there. They brought in a couple of ping pong tables so the guys could play ping pong and amuse themselves.

GARY MULLER: Some of the train-car scenes were done on a set. Some of them were done in a dead-end location where they would have to bring power in. Dusty Wallace was the gaffer. They would have to bring in a whole bunch of power because back then film speed was not what it is today. And the cameraman worked at a low light level, but the ASA of the film was slow, so you needed to bring in a lot of lights.

I remember the grips and electricians saying they had a tough time.

RUSSELL ENGELS: You had to change all the bulbs, and you had to change them five at a time because they're all on 660 volts. So if you plug one in the wrong way or something like that, they would blow the others up and you'd change hundreds of these lights, because we're looking down the track one way and then you'd spray[paint] the back of the light or the front of the light toward camera so it wouldn't be blowing out.[14] But the back of the light would go into the station.

Then they go down the other end of the station and shoot backwards. But you had to change all of the bulbs the other way and take these out and they were sprayed on the opposite side. So you had huge containers of bulbs, one for one direction, one for the other direction. It was so archaic in those days, because that's the only way you could do it. Now you can post-process most of that.

TOM PRIESTLEY, JR.: On *Pelham,* I think Owen [Roizman, director of photography] had a vision. The focus is more selective because you're using what they call longer lenses, focus lenses. Where the focus is less, there's less depth of field; basically, you isolate this part of the frame that you want the audience to look at. And the rest of it falls off[15] quickly because, one, you're working with low light levels to have a tunnel in the car, and, two, the focus is very selective. So everything in the background is kind of blurry and soft and it's a very different look, but I think it was the proper way to shoot it.

ANGELO DIGIACOMO (ASSISTANT CAMERA OPERATOR): New York started to get hot when the Panaflex came out because you could move the camera easily, instead of a [Mitchell] BNC, and they did a lot of *Pelham One Two Three* on the tracks and with the small camera, because it would have been impossible to do with the big camera.

GARY MULLER: I was young, and I worked with Friedkin a couple of times by then. I had done *Klute* [1971]. I was more aware of camera movement and even working on *Shaft's Big Score* [1972], how he [director Gordon Parks] would talk about camera position and how important it was. What was the lens going to see? Because he knew. He was a still photographer. So I became more aware of cameras, angles, and screen direction. It's like an evolution.

TOM PRIESTLEY, JR.: It was a challenge. It kind of wore you down. But like anything else, the film people have to get through it, get it done somehow. I don't know how many shooting days were involved in the show. It wasn't physically as difficult as it was mentally difficult to adapt to all the stuff down there.

GARY MULLER: It was a physical movie. We were working someplace in Brooklyn, in some square of the Brooklyn train tracks that weren't used anymore. They were a dead end. And every time he [a train] drove by, I don't know how it didn't kill us—the dust and the iron ore and all that shit—even the masks.

TOM PRIESTLEY, JR.: We used these tunnels that haven't been used in thirty years, maybe forty years, and not well maintained. So you've got everything from rodents to dust to steel filings. God knows what we breathed in down there. We weren't even wearing a mask. This is 1973.

GARY MULLER: We were just breathing this crap in. That was like Friedkin on *The Exorcist*—going back about safety—people were burning fucking rubber tires inside the piers for smoke. Burning rubber tires!

TOM PRIESTLEY, JR.: We should have been wearing masks and hazmat. We wore the jumpsuits—we covered our shoes and everything because it was just—every place you turn it wound up being black soot and all kinds of stuff. Gary and I and the camera guy all bought, like, these utility jumpsuits at Sears Roebuck, and we put them over our clothes because it was filthy down there. It was absolutely filthy and dangerous as shit.

One shot we did, we went down to the length of this platform. It was a service

14 Blowing out: overexposing the film so that everything looks too white.

15 By "falls off" he means the background falls out of focus.

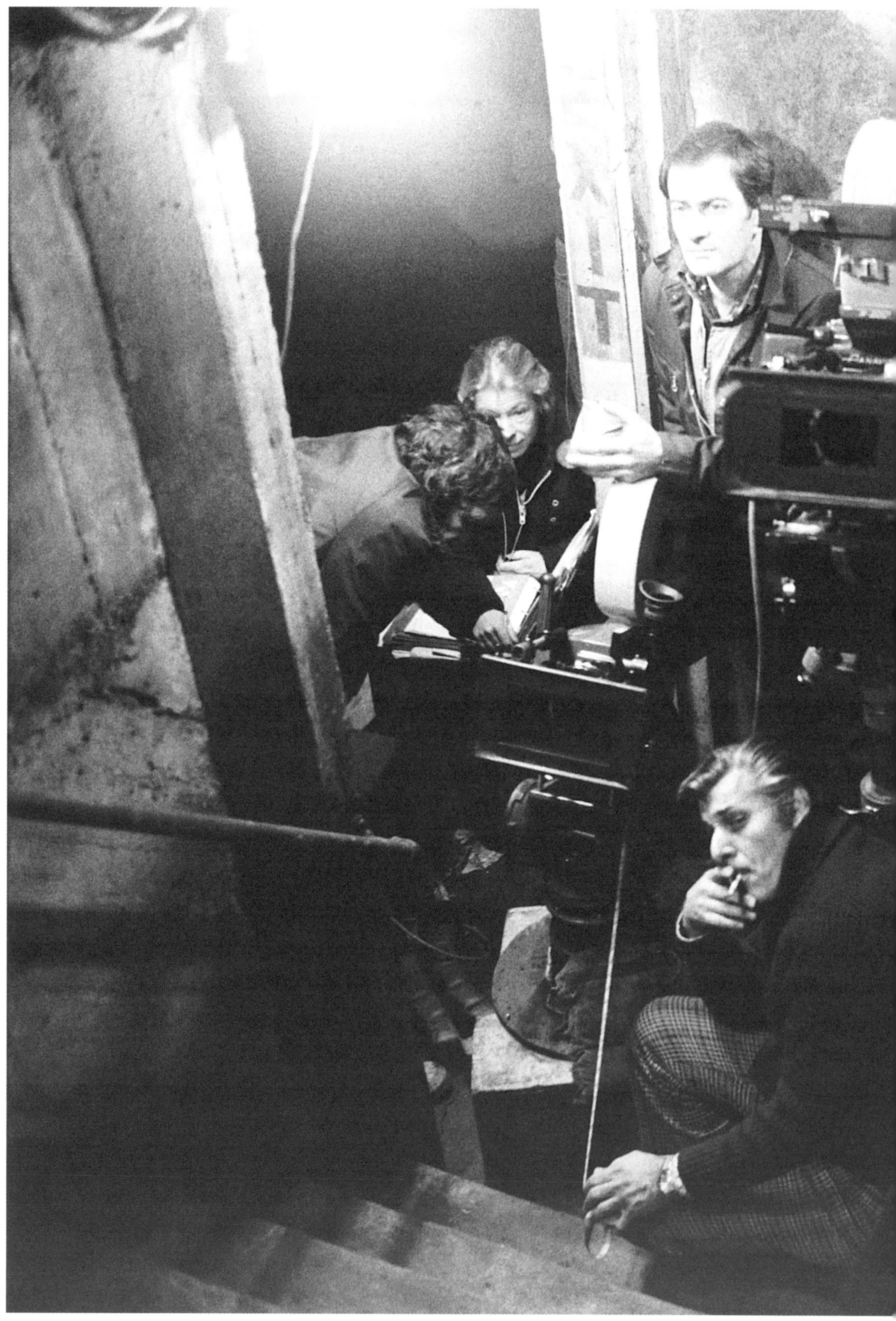

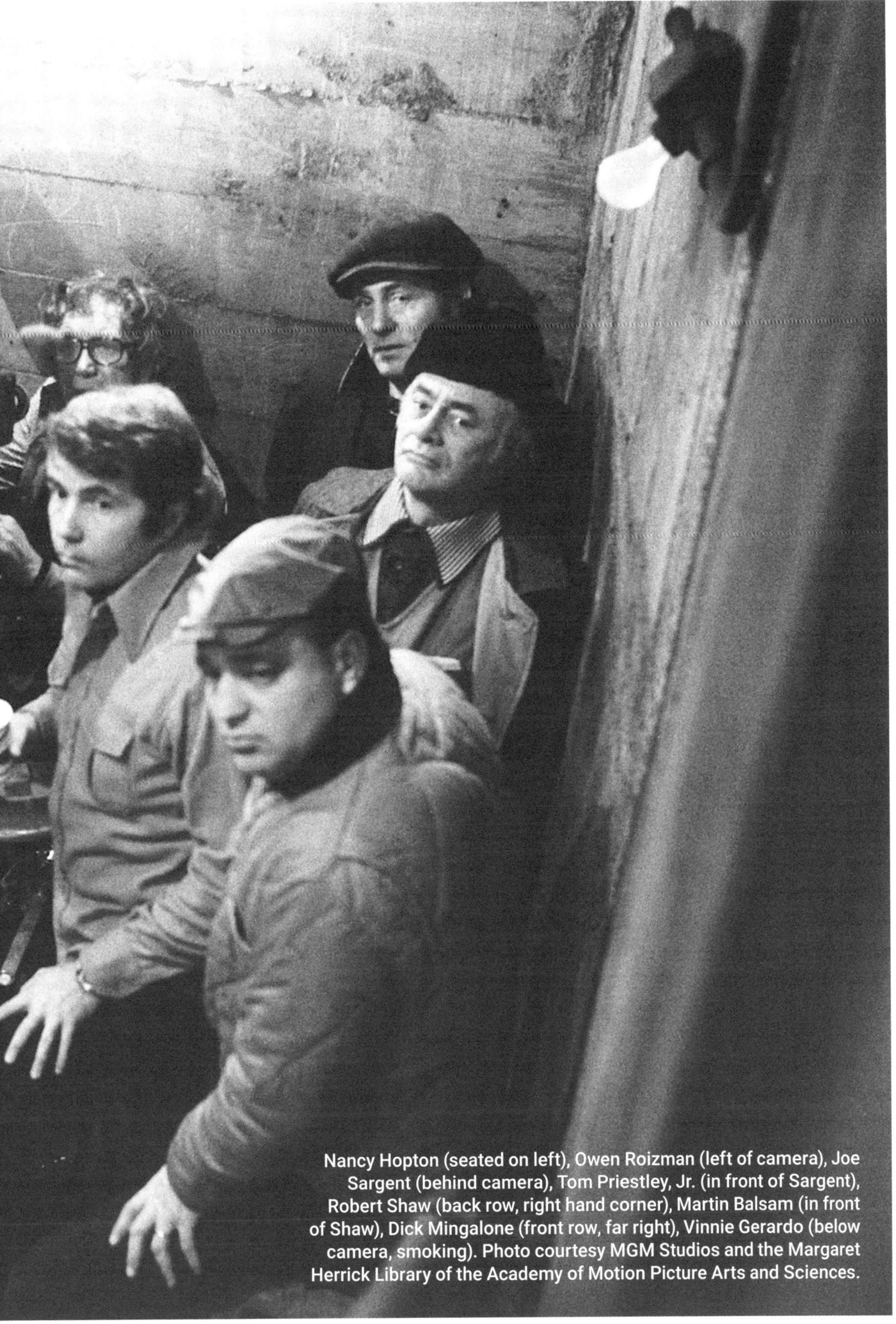

Nancy Hopton (seated on left), Owen Roizman (left of camera), Joe Sargent (behind camera), Tom Priestley, Jr. (in front of Sargent), Robert Shaw (back row, right hand corner), Martin Balsam (in front of Shaw), Dick Mingalone (front row, far right), Vinnie Gerardo (below camera, smoking). Photo courtesy MGM Studios and the Margaret Herrick Library of the Academy of Motion Picture Arts and Sciences.

platform, and we were in an alcove and we were going to shoot the train coming down the tracks at us. We turned the camera on—the train's about, maybe two hundred feet away. By the time the train had got opposite us, we couldn't see the train at all. There was so much dust and crap in the subway system, and it was all turned up by the movement of the train. It was like a fog. The entire train was obliterated—you couldn't see it—and I was, like, four or five feet away from it.

We said, "This is crazy. We're not going to do this again." You ever worked around trains? It's dangerous. In the subways it was really bad. There was no safety—there's no safety switches in there that turn the power on and off at certain areas. The guy who was in charge, the subway liaison person, would call back to the central headquarters where the power comes for these rails and tell them we're working on the tracks so don't apply any power to these tracks. But, as a safety precaution, he took a pipe and wrapped a bunch of chain around the track, the third rail. And if he turned the power on and that thing explodes, get the hell out of the way from the third rail because it's power on the track. That was the safety measure we had there. That was all.

CRAIG DIBONA: In fact, the original *Taking of Pelham One Two Three,* the producer was Stephen Keston, and they wanted all this footage of the trains going through, So they gave us the Hunts Point line. Remember, when they [the characters] steal the trains, they're going seventy miles an hour because that's what the top speed is, and I was going to shoot on a Sunday night through the glass where the driver drives, but it was so scratched, so I stood on the front of the train and he [an assistant] held onto my belt. I handheld those shots.

And they wanted one of the wheels going by, so I got down in, you know, the little alcoves in the subways, in the walls, and I squatted down, and he said, "How much room you got?"

And I go, "Oh, good—I'm a good eighteen inches from the wheel."

He goes "Good."

They back all the way up. The one thing I hadn't calculated was, when this thing got to full speed, it would literally be like a plunger and suck me towards the train. And as hard as the train was coming towards me—as it was going by—I pressed with my left foot and my right foot down hard. You ever drive on the highway to go by a trailer truck and it sucks your car towards it? I got sucked right to it—literally fell by the tracks after the train.

They packed up—they said, "That was a shot." I said, "Just let me get in the train."

I'm telling you, I was so scared, it almost killed me. Keston was an old friend of my father's and he said, "I don't know how I'm going to explain this to your father."

I used to do all these things. They put them in the movie—a hundred bucks for the night, cash. I was happy, but you know something—you're learning. That's what the whole key is. I would have done it for nothing.

TOM PRIESTLEY, JR.: Film tends to sanitize things. You don't see all the dirt and all the crap, especially at night. It all looks kind of, like, nice and safe and pretty, but it really isn't.

GARY MULLER: We had an underground unit and then we had an above-ground unit doing second unit. Just the chase scene—I think Jack [Priestley] shot the chasing scene for Owen, but when they cut it together the studio didn't like parts of it, so we went back and did more of it.

BRUNO ROBOTTI (CHARGE SCENIC ARTIST, *THE TAKING OF PELHAM ONE TWO THREE*): We did a lot of fun stuff. When the car crashes into the balustrades, on the railing there, we made it out of Styrofoam—carved them all out. In those days, everything was done pretty much by hand. There were no machines making this—I mean, to the point we used to even paint all the police cars. We used to do all the [silk]screening and apply them on the cars and all the police signs and all that stuff. Everything was done by hand.

TOM PRIESTLEY, JR.: It was great. I mean, it was a great cast. Joe Sergeant was a really great director.

GARY MULLER: Robert Shaw was quite the actor. He was very standoffish, but not unpolite. The director, Joe Sergeant—I think he was so far over his head. Some directors really know how to take command of a set and tell actors what to do and discuss the scene—blocking with the DP [director of photography], what he's looking for—but Joe had to visually see it before he could work it out with the actors.

TOM PRIESTLEY, JR.: Robert Shaw and Marty Balsam went out to lunch one day. They came back loaded. I mean, they were loaded, the two of them—they must have been drinking martinis or something—and Shaw had this scene to do, so the director propped him up against the wall and he had to shoot each line one at a time so he could get it out. People were holding his legs and keeping him up. It was embarrassing, but they had to get through it.

We shot in the studio up on 127th Street and 2nd Avenue, the old Filmways studio. We shot the interiors—like, the control command center and stuff—with Walter Matthau.

BRUNO ROBOTTI: The nerve center of the subway system with all the lines and all the lights and all dimensions going on was all fake because we weren't allowed to go there and shoot; there would have been too much of a distraction. This is serious business, running the subway system. So we had to replicate all this.

We used an abandoned station. It was Court Street in Brooklyn. It was closed at the time, and we silkscreened miles of tiles and we kept changing. The [tile] grid changed for the different stations that the shots required. The tiles were all silk-screened.

It was on contact tape and, like, blasting tape—what we called blasting tape,[16] anyway—and then just apply it to fake walls and—yeah, I mean, it was miles of it—the Seventh Avenue line at 28th Street and all that and all those numbers with tiles. We replicated all those things.

TOM PRIESTLEY, JR.: A tough movie to make. I don't think the people appreciated how difficult it was to work on that show when they saw the movie.

CRAIG DIBONA: Making movies in the city, man—let me tell you, it's a little bit different than going out in the country.

16 Blasting tape is short for sandblasting tape, which is a stronger kind of masking tape.

Network

(1976)

GARY MULLER (SECOND ASSISTANT CAMERA OPERATOR, *NETWORK*): The next big picture was a [Sidney] Lumet picture.

TOM PRIESTLEY, JR. (FIRST ASSISTANT CAMERA OPERATOR, *NETWORK*): He [director Sidney Lumet] had everything laid out because he grew up [working in] live television—*Playhouse 90* [1956-1961] and all those things where you had to lay out the whole hour and a half. There's no taping. You'd shoot it and that's it. You had to be right on the ball, and so everything he did was laid out to the point where he had all the control. There was no turning back. Go, shoot, go!

He was so precise and mechanical about everything to the point where I wished sometimes he would take a little more time with the scene. "Get the actor—boom, boom, boom." He'd just go.

Sidney is smart. The greatest secret to making great movies is having a great script. If you don't have a great script, you're in trouble. You can hire the greatest actors, the greatest cinematographer, production designer. If it doesn't translate on the page and onto the screen, it's not going to work. He would try to get great writers to do it because he knew it was well-crafted, and that was half the battle.

Paddy Chayefsky was the writer on *Network,* and his deal was you couldn't change one word of the script, not one letter, without his approval.

GARY MULLER: If he [Chayefsky] had "the" in the paragraph, you had to say that word. He and Sidney would always argue about dialogue, and there were a couple of times that Sidney would not be happy because, of course, Paddy would ask for another take because the words weren't correct.

TOM PRIESTLEY, JR.: He had the power then to do that.

GARY MULLER: Bobby Duvall was ranting and raving one day in the office doing a scene. He was having a hard time with his words, the way he wanted them to come out.

TOM PRIESTLEY, JR.: I don't think they changed four lines in the whole movie—three lines—very little. I mean, very few writers ever get to that point in their career where they can do that. In fact, on all the movies I've worked on, he's the only one that I know that had that standing.

GARY MULLER: *Network* was a very unique picture. First of all, knowing Sidney Lumet well and knowing that he's fast—he doesn't want to wait—so hiring a cameraman of Owen Roizman's caliber and who has the tendency to be slow—I know there were conversations between Sidney and Owen about working faster, and he said he'd work faster. He had to prove to the world that he could be a fast cameraman and efficient.

TOM PRIESTLEY, JR.: Everybody should have worked with Sidney Lumet at least once in their life, because he's the most efficient director they're going to work with. He wouldn't even shoot an entire scene. He'd just shoot the beginning and say, "Okay, stop. Let's do the end. I'm not going to use the middle."

And he wouldn't even shoot it. He would do coverage and one take, and if you've made a mistake you'd have to have a good reason why you want to do take two. I don't think I ever did more than two or three takes on anything that he ever did.

GARY MULLER: A few times in my career with Sidney I've asked for another take.

TOM PRIESTLEY, JR.: We shot a lot of *Network* at the MGM building on Sixth Avenue and 55th Street. We all had these black cloth robes around, so they wouldn't see our reflection in the glass. There was glass everywhere.

GARY MULLER: That was in a live building. It was in midtown Manhattan. That made it difficult to bring the equipment up and down. We stayed in that set for weeks. It wasn't a long show.

TOM PRIESTLEY, JR.: *Network* was a long shoot.

GARY MULLER: I don't think that there were more than forty shooting days with Sidney.

TOM PRIESTLEY, JR.: It was like fifty-something days. I mean, the guy was unbelievable. [In some] kind of medical facility or something we did, like, sixteen setups in eight hours.

GARY MULLER: But we ran around like crazy. I swear we did that in under eight weeks, maybe seven.

TOM PRIESTLEY, JR.: I only had one fuck-up and it wasn't a fuck-up, but, again, it was Owen with all the white cards[17] around the camera, and it was on *Network*. There was a scene with Bill Holden and the scene was he was just sitting there talking, and Sidney said, "Well, stand up and sit into it."

When he sat into it, he sat close. I pulled the focus, and I flipped on the magnified. I had the operator looking [at the] magnified to see if it was sharp. He said it looked sharp, but it

17 Tom Priestley, Jr., on *Three Days of the Condor*: "I remember Owen was into this new thing where he put these white cards all around the camera to reflect the ambient light onto the actors, and that was very nice, except I couldn't see anything. I was trying to follow focus on the side of the camera, and I had to look—stick my head way out. It destroyed my whole optical destination. I couldn't decide whether something was three feet, and he wouldn't change. It would be crazy. I would always try to guess before I went out there to see how close I was, to train my eye—to know—to be able to discern the distances as close as possible."

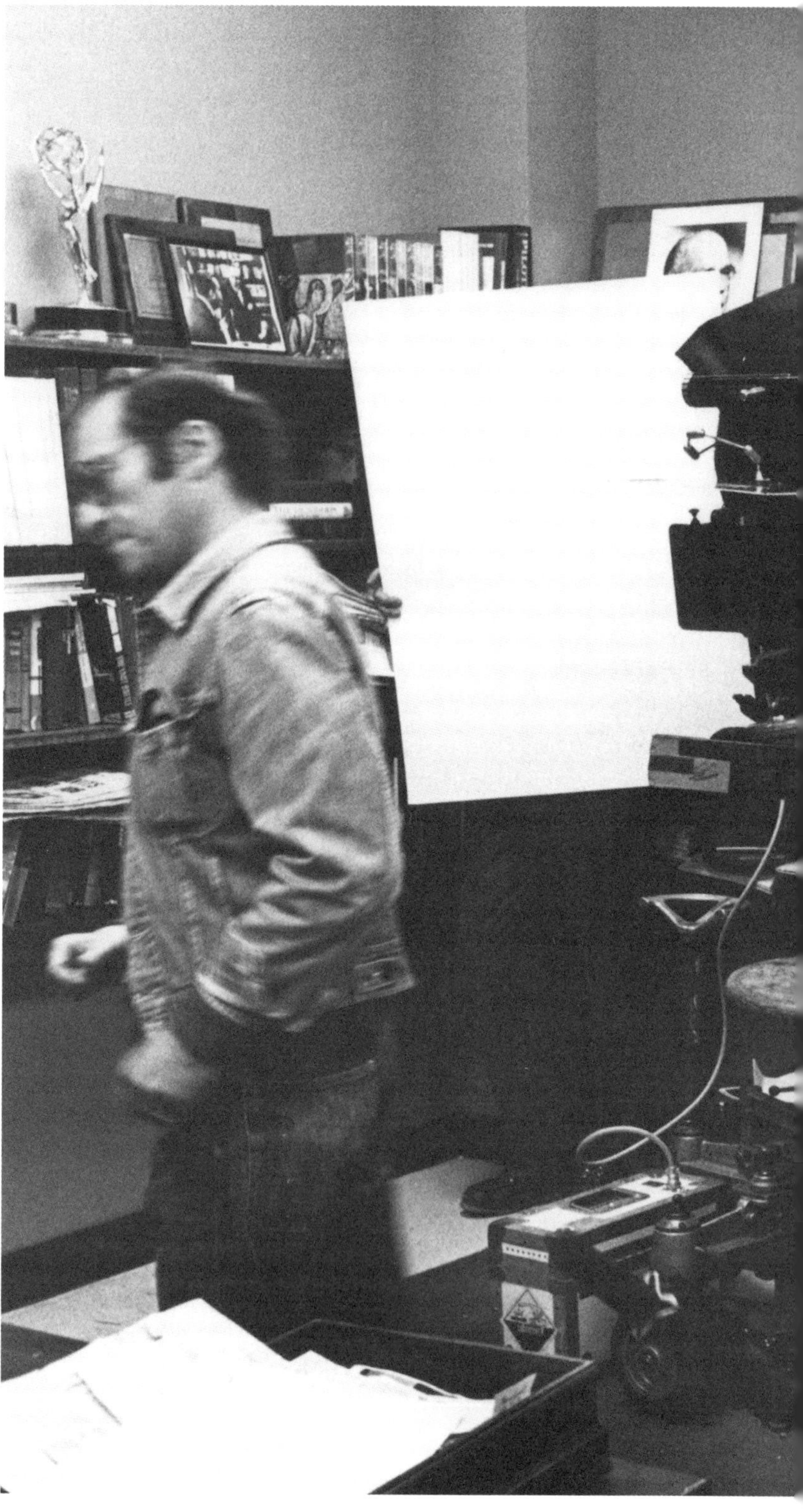

Sidney Lumet, Fred Schuler (looking in camera), Tom Priestley, Jr. (back turned), Owen Roizman, Vito Ilardi (with boom mic), Gary Muller. Photo courtesy of the Margaret Herrick Library, Academy of Motion Picture Arts and Sciences.

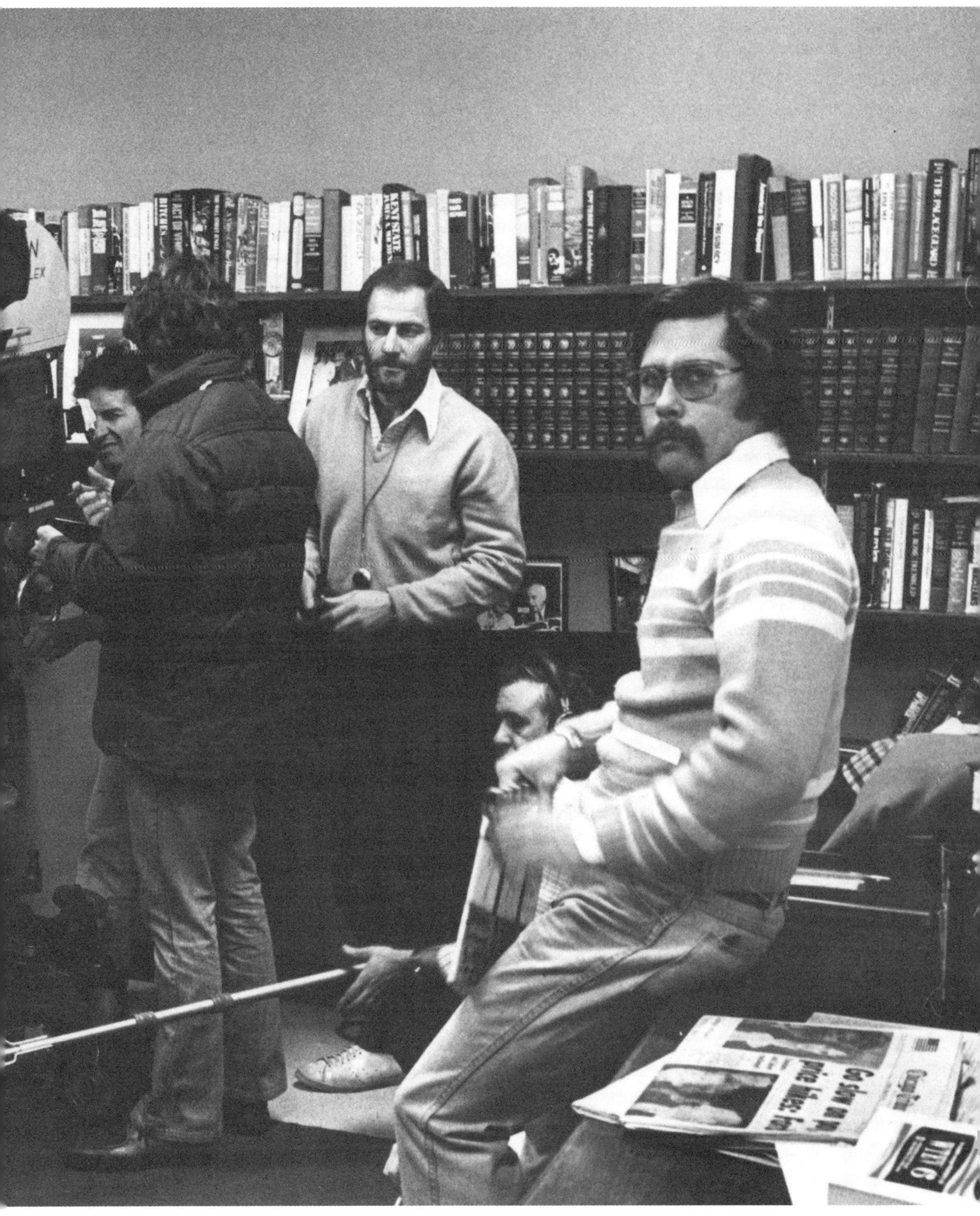

wasn't. When we finished, I asked Bill Holden just to freeze, and I measured. I was off about a couple of inches, maybe two or three inches. I said to Sidney, "Please, we're right here. We could just do it over again?"

And Sidney's, "Oh, no. It's all right. I'll look at it. If it's not any good, we'll redo it."

GARY MULLER: Tommy asked for another take, and Sidney wouldn't give him one. He was pretty adamant about one-takes. Like I said, as a technician, as the focus puller, if you can do a Sidney Lumet picture you can probably work for almost any director, or any cameraman.

TOM PRIESTLEY, JR.: Never redid it. It's in the movie. It pissed me off. It just pissed me off, because I told him it wasn't any good, but he wouldn't reshoot and we were there, three or four more minutes. He wouldn't do it. I don't know why he was always in a hurry. Boom, boom, boom. It's very rare that I ever asked him to do something over because I made a mistake, but you're going to get caught once or twice somewhere, and I got caught there. If you ever see *Network* again, it's one shot of Bill Holden sitting in a chair—I forget what the location was—and it's slightly out of focus.

We had a scene at night—Bill Holden and Peter Finch were out on the street somewhere—and Owen didn't want to use any lighting, so they got these lenses at a very, very wide aperture, like a 1.8, whatever it was. I think he used one light for the whole thing, and I had to follow focus and a depth of nothing.

I said, "These lenses are soft when they're sharp."

They were shitty lenses. They were fast and he [Roizman] wanted to show Sidney he was fast.

GARY MULLER: It was incredible how Sidney would get all these incredible performances out of actors for one take.

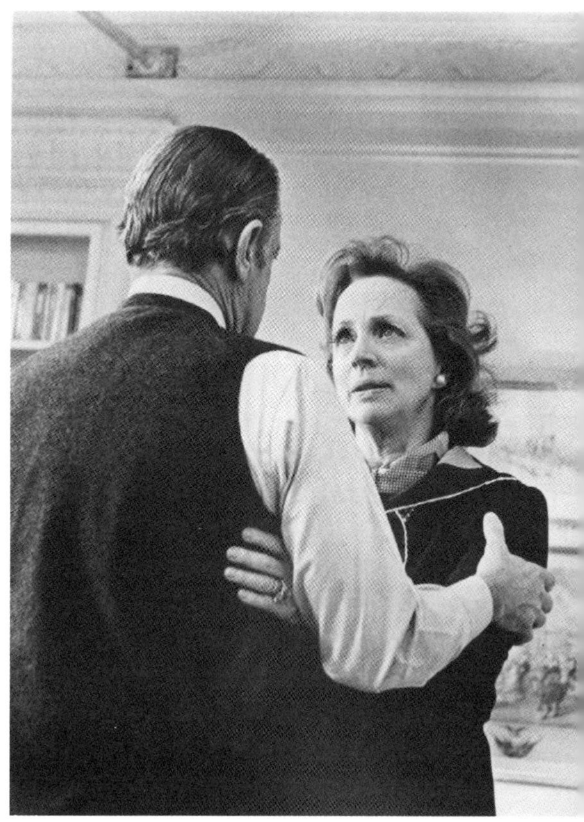

William Holden and Beatrice Straight in *Network*. *Photo courtesy of the Margaret Herrick Library, Academy of Motion Picture Arts and Sciences.*

TOM PRIESTLEY, JR.: You watch *Network* again—you watch Bill Holden and Beatrice Straight, Faye Dunaway—some great performances in that movie—it was brilliant. There are some scenes in *Network*—especially one of the most famous scenes where he confronts his wife in their apartment, in the kitchen, and he's telling her he's going to leave her. Beatrice Straight was the actress. I do believe she won the Academy Award for that scene.

GARY MULLER: Beatrice Straight played Holden's wife. She won the Academy Award for Best [Supporting] Actress for one scene and one take in the apartment.

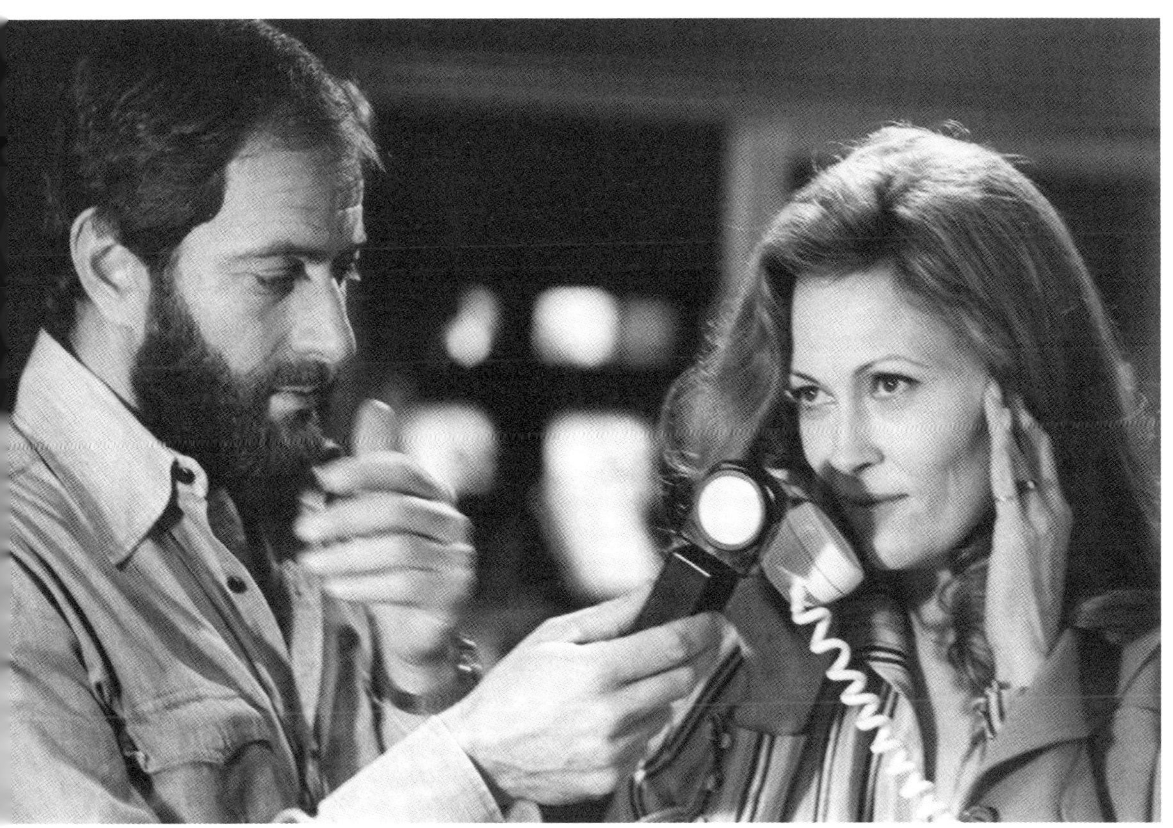

TOM PRIESTLEY, JR.: That's the only scene she had in the movie. No one knew who she was. She was basically a Broadway actress. I don't think she had made very many films, but, I mean, the crew just absolutely applauded both actors when the scene was over. It was such a moving scene, and it was shot in one of those great New York apartments on the Upper West Side.

GARY MULLER: We were on 55th Street, in the MGM building, way up, and Sidney wanted all the windows open to see out.

TOM PRIESTLEY, JR.: I think those floors we shot on in the MGM building were empty. I hear giggling coming out of this room. I can't see anything in there. "What the hell's going on?"

GARY MULLER: Bobby Duvall was really funny. He was ranting and raving one day in the office doing a scene, and he was having a little hard time with his words the way he wanted them to come out. It was a difficult scene for Bobby. So he pulls his pants down and he moons all the secretaries in the adjoining building. It was quite comical. It sort of brought him back to his reality and got him into character.

There was a whole cast of characters there with Duvall. Ned Beatty was in there, and Bill Holden. Holden was a great actor, just to listen to him.

TOM PRIESTLEY, JR.: I always remember Bill Holden. He could read the telephone book, and you'd say, "Bill, that's incredible." His voice was so powerful. Everything about the movie was first class. Of course, the stuff with Faye

Cinematographer Owen Roizman lighting Faye Dunaway. Photo courtesy of the Margaret Herrick Library, Academy of Motion Picture Arts and Sciences.

Dunaway was great. I had worked with her before, on *Three Days of the Condor* [1975]. She didn't know who I was. She knew Owen.

GARY MULLER: Owen took his time lighting the women.

TOM PRIESTLEY, JR.: She loved Owen because Owen would take a lot of time to light her face, and she liked that. Not that she needed a lot of time. There's a great line in the movie. There's a scene out in a motel, out in the Hamptons, and he just had sex with Faye Dunaway's character and they were discussing things. They started talking, arguing about marketing or management, and he [Holden's character] said, "What do you know about life? You only learned life from Bugs Bunny." That was the Paddy Chayefsky line.

GARY MULLER: At the end of the picture, Sidney came to me. He knew my father. My father worked for him in the early days, in live TV. He used to call me bubala—he said, "Bubala, you don't want to be a cameraman for the rest of your life—let me make you a production manager. You're good with numbers. You get the budget right for your department, and my production manager tells me we need some more people in the office."

I said, "I'm not a desk person, Sidney. I need to be out in the streets."

He said "Okay, think about it."

I thought about it, and by the time I thought about it he took two other people, and they turned out to be producers. So that was really my only regret in fifty years.

TOM PRIESTLEY, JR.: We were wrapping a location and I'm standing by the camera, taking the film out the camera, and Sidney is right next to me. He's got a habit of whenever he finished the scene he would fold the page in his script—fold it into quarters—so that when an entire movie was shot, there were no pages to be seen. Everything was folded. Anyway, Paddy Chayefsky runs up to Sidney, says, "Sidney, that was so perspicacious of you to do so-and-so." I'm, like, two feet, three feet away from Sidney, and me, big mouth, I say, "Perspicacious—what a great word. It means having great mental insight and vision."

And Lumet and Chayefsky turned and looked at me like, "How the hell would you know that word?" Because I'm a camera assistant. The backstory is during the show I wanted to improve my vocabulary, so I bought this book on how to improve your vocabulary, and the night before the word was *perspicacious*.

GARY MULLER: That was a classic Lumet movie. Now, was it going to be a blockbuster? It was well-accepted, and I think it was nominated as the Best Picture and for a couple of the other ones. But it was New York. He wasn't going to win. It [the Academy] was anti–New York. New York pictures didn't win.

TOM PRIESTLEY, JR.: The problem—look at all the TV shows. They got nine producers and all. I mean, it's making a film by committee and it gets to be confusing. In the old days, it was one director, one vision. The one thing that most directors could not get was final cut.

COMMERCIAL BREAK #1

RICHARD ADEE (PROP MASTER, SPECIAL EFFECTS, SET DECORATOR): I was doing a commercial one time, and we're upstate New York on a farm. I don't remember what the commercial was about, but they wanted this rooster on a fence post, one of these rail fences.

So I had this guy there—he had half a dozen roosters—and he put them on the fence and they wanted the rooster to cock-a-doodle-doo, flap his wings, scream like the sun was coming up. So we did it, like, ten, fifteen takes—nothing worked, so I said to the director, "Let me go down. Let me set the rooster up. I think I can get him to work."

He said, "Really?"

I said, "Well, I can try it." I said, "This jerk is not doing it. I want to get home today."

He says, "Okay." So I go down—had two other guys with me—go down, take the rooster, put him on the fence post.

And I yell back to the cameramen and the director. I said, "When I tell you to roll camera, this is going to be a one-take, and I'll jump out of frame. But it's just a one-shot deal. I'm not promising anything. Okay, ready?"

"Roll camera. Okay. Jump!"

They're on a long lens. We jump out at a frame, and all of a sudden, the rooster cock-a-doodle-doo—he's going crazy. So I said, "Did you get it?"

And they said, "Yeah, that was great. How'd you do that?"

I said, "Well, I talked to him, told him what I wanted."

"No, come on. How'd you do it?"

I said, "Listen, if I told you how to do it I would be out of job."

I didn't tell anybody, but I had a T-50 staple gun in my pocket. Staple gunned around his toes so he couldn't move. We had needlenose pliers and we just pulled the staples.

Annie Hall

(1977)

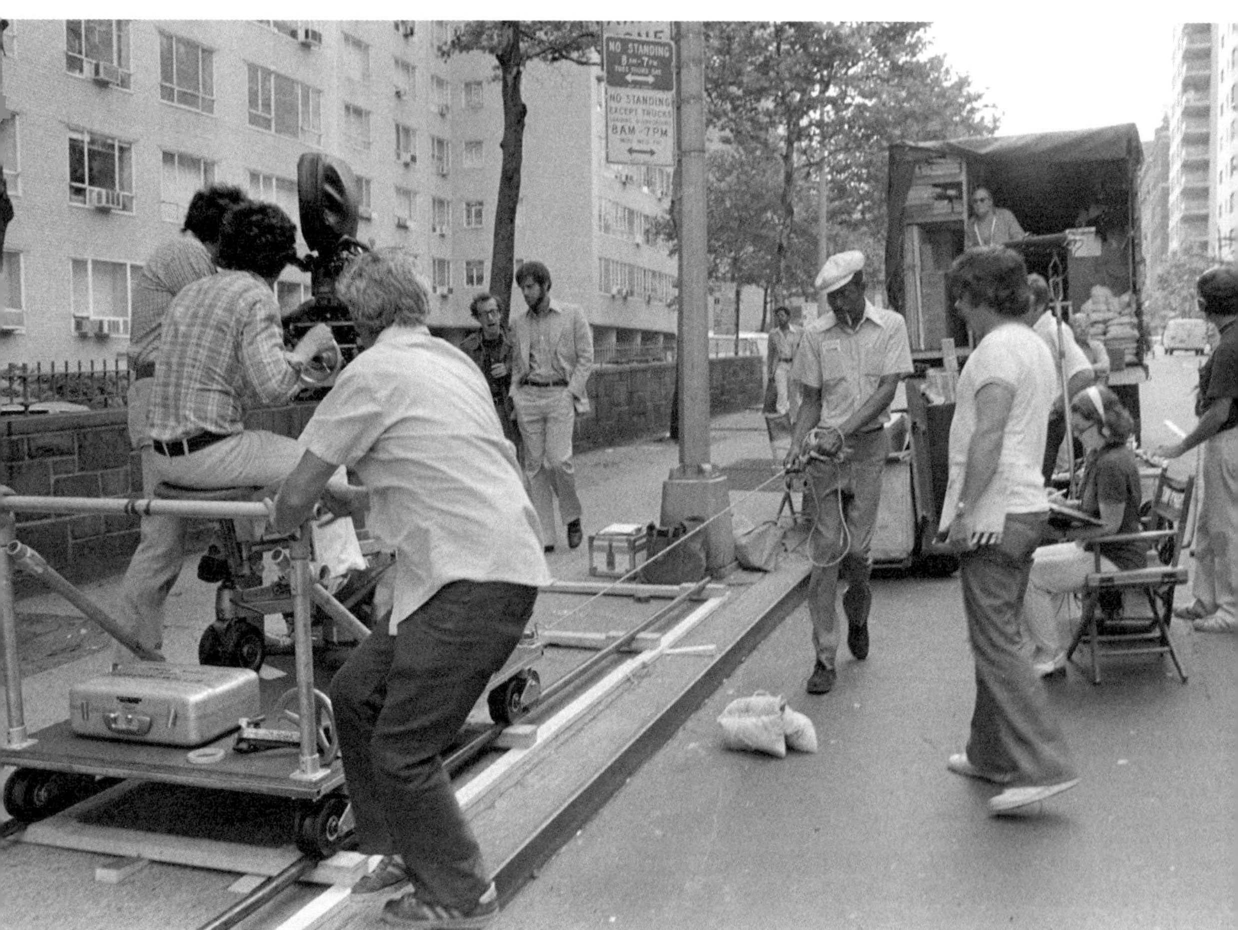

Dolly shot on *Annie Hall.* Photo courtesy of the Margaret Herrick Library, Academy of Motion Picture Arts and Sciences.

The things I enjoy all tend to be a little crooked or a little off. I have a tendency if something doesn't feel that way when I begin to work on it, I'll bend it that way. Just trying to present it in a way that's more interesting on certain levels. Woody was always open to things being a little bit off. It would sort of appeal to both of us at the same time. We'd set up these shots where he and [Diane] Keaton were talking back and forth. I'd say, "Okay, you leave, we let you go. Then we'll leave her on the screen, you're talking off screen, then you come back in and then she leaves. So you're exchanging places." "But you won't see me?" "Yeah, but we'll hear you." That's more entertaining and more eccentric.[18]

—Gordon Willis, director of photography

GARY MULLER: We did *Annie Hall* with Gordon [Willis] and Woody [Allen]—another fortunate period in my life to work on such a great picture. I didn't even know if it was called *Annie Hall* back then. It could have been "Woody Allen's Spring Project 1975."

TOM PRIESTLEY, JR. (FIRST ASSISTANT CAMERA OPERATOR, *ANNIE HALL*): Woody is a really talented guy, sweet guy, but you never called him Woody. You called him Max. That was his name on the set—Max. And he only spoke to, like, two or three people—Gordon, the assistant director Fred Gallo, and maybe the script supervisor once in a while.

GARY MULLER: You had Gordon Willis, who was dictating to Woody when he could shoot because of the sun—"No, we can't shoot in the sun. Everything's got to be overcast."

We'd go inside if the sun came out, or we wouldn't shoot.

18 Mark Feeney, "The Willis Frame," *Cinephilia & Beyond* (originally published in *The Globe*, June 30, 2015), cinephiliabeyond.org/the-willis-frame/, retrieved June 13, 2023.

STEVE SAKLAD (ASSISTANT ART DIRECTOR, *RADIO DAYS* [1987]): Carlo Di Palma, the DP [director of photography] who was Woody Allen's DP for a series of movies at that time, invented a thing called "blue sky cover," which I had never heard of before, and I don't think I've heard it since, but basically Woody Allen abhorred shooting on sunny, blue-sky days. He wanted every single exterior to be gray, overcast, shadowless, and you can feel it in the movies.

TOM PRIESTLEY, JR.: Gordon Willis was different because Gordon set everything. Everything was really very strict. I think he [Allen] was afraid of Gordon in a way, but he respected his talent, and Gordon moved him to a style that became iconic for his movies. The long walk-and-talks, the split screen, shooting people off camera, having dialogue and not shooting him and just listening, one person—all that kind of stuff. That was all Gordon Willis.

I respected Gordon because he could put more information into the frame that was pertinent to the story than anyone I've ever met before.

RICHARD ADEE (PROP MASTER, *ANNIE HALL* RESHOOTS): I knew Gordon pretty well. He lived in the next town. I used to see him shopping and we had a good rapport. So we're doing something in this flower shop, and something dropped into frame. He yells to the prop foreman, "Get that fucking thing fixed!"

I go up on the ladder and he starts hollering at me, cursing. Now my back was to him, and I turned around and I said, "Who the fuck do you think you're talking to?"

And he looked at me and he says, "Richie, what are you doing up there?"

"Who the fuck do you think you're talking to? You're not gonna talk to people like that."

And that's the way he was—nasty as hell, really nasty.

GARY MULLER: Woody and Diane Keaton and the lobsters—that was interesting.

TOM PRIESTLEY, JR.: He's [Allen] got to take the lobster out of the pot. Well, we were setting up with a shot and he was in the next room talking to his analyst for about a half-hour to forty minutes getting up enough courage to pick up the lobster out of the pot. I mean, if he was born two hundred years ago and he had to go out and kill a deer and gut it so he could survive, he'd starve to death. He couldn't do it. He's not that kind of person.

We were out in a house in East Hampton. We were shooting in the woods one day and there were these daddy-long-legs running around, and he asked the grips to get a box to jump on top of the box. He wouldn't get off the box. He thought they were attacking him. He played the whole scene looking down. I think he's playing God—because he's afraid the bugs are going to get him.

We were shooting another scene in an old luncheonette up on the Upper West Side, and it was the only building standing for about three or four blocks. I think they knocked down an old brewery up there, they were going to put up condos and apartment buildings.

We were about a hundred yards from the corner, and a group of people had formed on the corner because they knew the film crew was in the building. I guess by word of mouth they found it was Woody Allen. He said he was worried that other people were seeing [the filming]. The grips put up these big blacks [light blocking fabric] so they couldn't see into the building.

After we finished shooting, he says, "I know: I just figured out what I'm going to do. I'm going to be anonymous," he says. "I'm going to take this paper bag and put it over my head and cut out two eye holes and run out the door and jump in my Rolls-Royce and drive away."

That was his idea of being anonymous. And that's the way he thought. I mean, the guy's a brilliant guy, but, you know, sometimes they walk to a different drummer.

RUSSELL ENGELS (ELECTRICIAN, *ANNIE HALL*): We went out to Coney Island looking at the boardwalk on Coney Island at dawn. They worked out there for three or four days hanging these old signs, and they have all the old signs on the billboards and whatnot. In the background is the parachute jump. The big, tall, iconic-looking tower. We get out there and we do the first rehearsal shot with the dolly, and Woody Allen—who knew that park—he'd say, "All right, I need to see a parachute go down."

And everybody in the production all looked at one another thinking, "Not me. What the hell are you talking about? We never discussed that."

And he said, "Oh, well, it's the parachute thing. I need to see one go down"—and a full crew out there—Coney Island. The guy comes back, and he says, "This thing hasn't worked in forty-five years." He says, "Then we'll shoot something else. Let's get out of here."

And they did. They went over to a ride in the park.

You've got to be kidding me. He of all people should have known that. He was so big with Coney Island growing up, you would think he would have known, but that was the power that he had back then—the whole crew, up and out, moved over. All the set design hanging, all these banners on the big iron work, on top of the buildings and all that. That was all for naught.

TOM PRIESTLEY, JR.: We went to dailies. We watched [a scene] about four or five

From left: Eddie Quinn (head turned), Fred Schuler, Gary Muller, Gordon Willis, Tom Priestley, Fred Gallo on *Annie Hall*. Photo courtesy of the Margaret Herrick Library, Academy of Motion Picture Arts and Sciences.

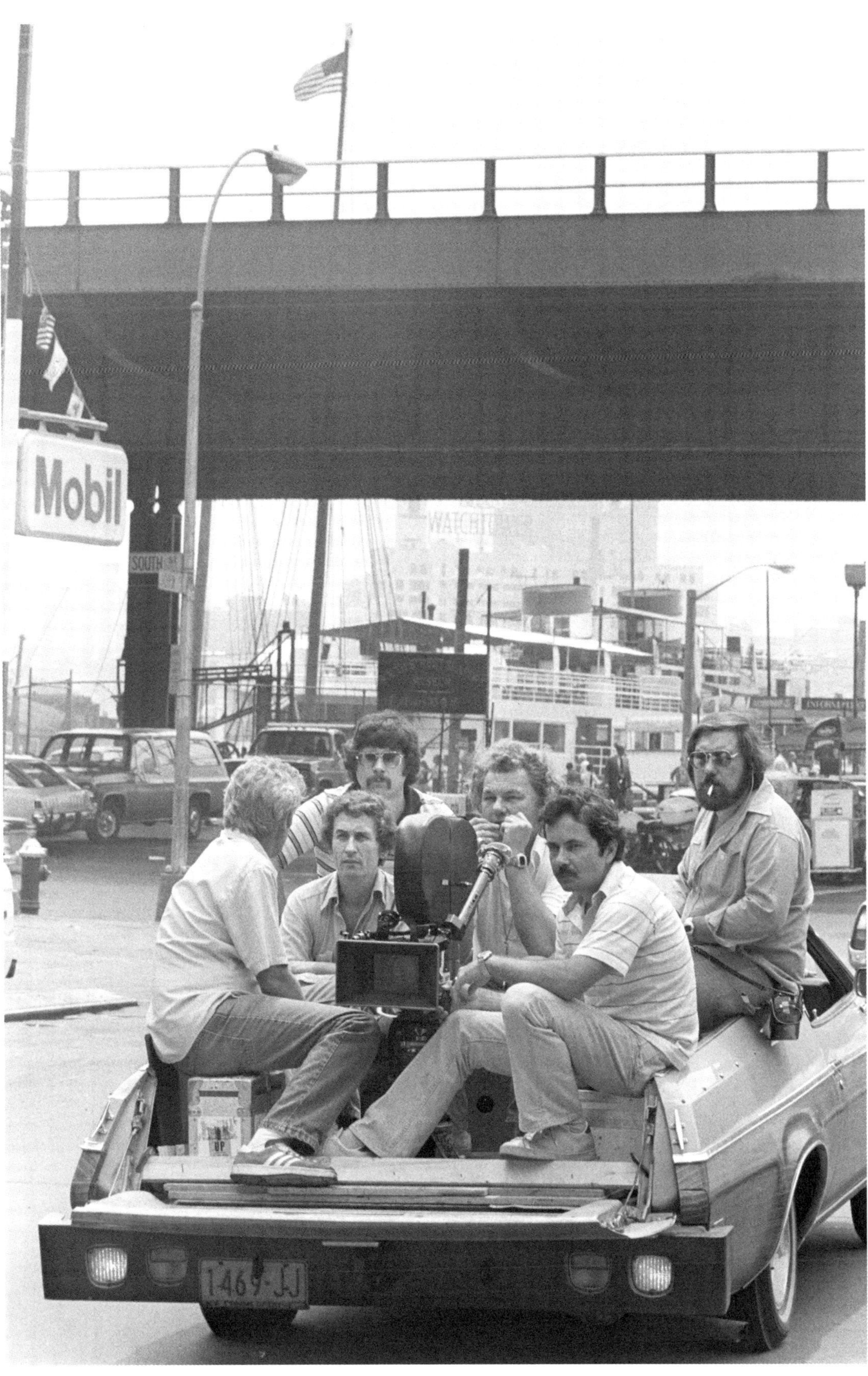
Mobil
SOUTH
1469·JJ

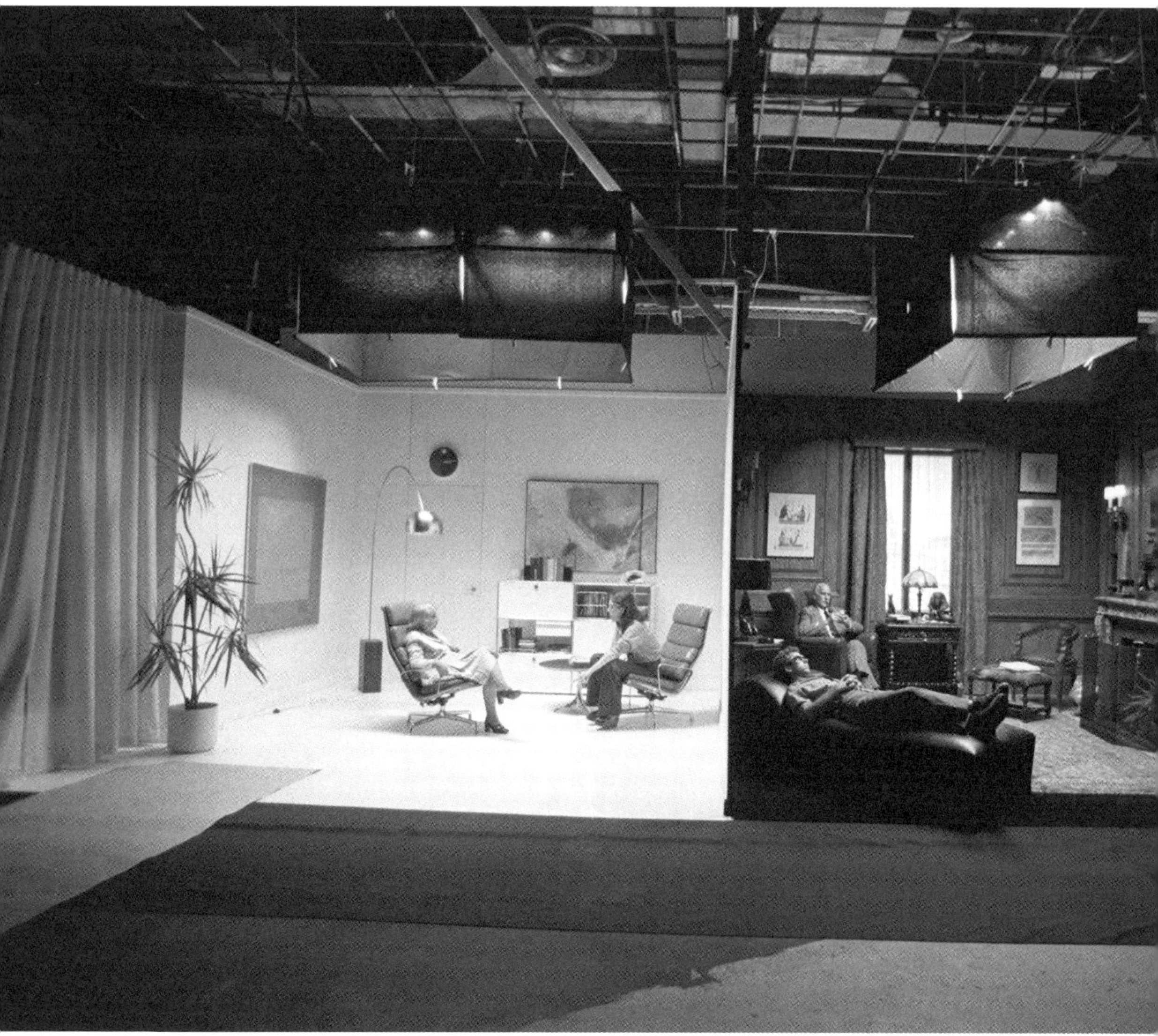

times. Woody kept saying, "Gordon, what do you think?"

Gordon said, "I don't know."

Then finally Woody says. "You see that extra in the back?" It was just there for a second. "See that? I don't like that orange. We better shoot that whole scene over again."

And we did. I mean, he could have cut the thing out. It was terrifying [laughs]—especially when you had really difficult scenes to work on. I just love the fact that you sat in a chair and the lights went down and this image came up and you saw the results of the previous day's work.

How many people get to be part of that in their lives? Most people work on a project and never see the end of it, or it goes off somewhere else. You don't get the satisfaction. This way you get instant gratification for the work you did, or you feel like shit because you screwed up. But most of the time you did well, and it was great. I mean, going to dailies, you see what the result of the work is on the screen at this time.

Set from *Annie Hall*. Photo courtesy of the Margaret Herrick Library, Academy of Motion Picture Arts and Sciences.

You really learned a lot going to dailies.

GARY MULLER: New York, for being such a big city, it was a very small film. *Annie Hall* was obviously a great movie, but it was very . . . how do I say it? I was more of an action assistant. I wanted cars coming at me. I wanted my heart pumping. I wanted the challenge. Not a guy and a girl in a room chatting for ten hours and then the guy screws the girl and the girl leaves. The drama. I think I became aware of that when I did *Annie Hall* because you sit there, and sit there, and wait, and wait, and do a couple of takes, etc. It was mundane. At an early age I was trying to figure out: how am I going to change this? Because, as a camera assistant, you don't pick the movies, the cameraman picks you.

So you can't say no to a cameraman. If you say no, somebody else could be better than you, or you could like somebody better or, "Oh, he doesn't want to work with me. I'll hire this guy again." So, it was sort of coattails. They traveled as a crew, as a unique crew.

TOM PRIESTLEY, JR.: They [production managers] used to schedule in the budget three weeks of reshoots on every one of his films. On *Annie Hall,* we shot for three weeks. They only used two weeks of it. There's a whole week they didn't use. We came back a week or two later and we shot another two weeks, three weeks. But then the one sequence or sequences he didn't like he didn't want to put in the movie. And that was it.

So what do you think a week cost? One hundred and fifty thousand a day—seven hundred and fifty thousand for five days. And most of the guys who worked with Woody had a ten-hour [per day] deal. He never worked ten hours, but that was the deal.

Woody is like a New York aberration. You accept him because New York is full of people like him. These people are slightly different than everybody else, slightly odd, slightly off.

GARY MULLER: I never really talked to Priestley about [*Annie Hall*]. Tommy and I never really spoke much on the set. I have a feeling that Tom felt the same way. Working for Gordon was great, but it was a little boring.

TOM PRIESTLEY, JR.: I mean, it wasn't fun for me to work with him at the time, because you didn't have a lot of creative freedom. Gordon pretty much set everything, set the tone and said everything. Sometimes I'd have to ask permission to speak to him. But he was deep in thought and trying to get stuff and do everything. He was a great artist.

Saturday Night Fever

(1977)

LLOYD KAUFMAN (LOCATION EXECUTIVE, *SATURDAY NIGHT FEVER*): It was a low-budget movie. And, I mean, *Rocky* [1976] the same way. *Rocky,* I think the budget was about a million bucks. I was just on a panel and the accountant, one of the producers, said that *Saturday Night Fever* ended up around eight million bucks. But when I was on it, the budget was well under two million.

TOM PRIESTLEY, JR. (CAMERA OPERATOR, *SATURDAY NIGHT FEVER*): *Saturday Night Fever* was really a low-budget film. I mean, not "low-budget," but lower-budget.

LLOYD KAUFMAN: [Director] John Avildsen had got Norman Wexler back to write the script, the guy who wrote *Joe* [1970]. And Norman Wexler wrote a brilliant script—terrific. And Avildsen is a big location person, so the whole idea was shooting in the neighborhoods that were described in the *New York Magazine* article. It had a different title, but it was about the disco generation and this one kid who loves dancing.

Everybody knew him. When Saturday night came round and he walked into 2001 Odyssey, all the other Faces automatically fell back before him, cleared a space for him to float in, right at the very center of the dance floor. Gracious as a medieval seigneur accepting tributes, Vincent waved and nodded at random. Then his face grew stern, his body turned to the music. Solemn, he danced, and all the Faces followed.

—Nik Cohn, "The Tribal Rights of the New Saturday Night," *New York Magazine,* June 7, 1976

LLOYD KAUFMAN: It's loosely the story of *Saturday Night Fever*—the bridge-and-tunnel crowd versus the Manhattan crowd and how the people over there want to get out of Brooklyn and come to Manhattan. Today Brooklyn is cooler than Manhattan for sure.

TOM PRIESTLEY, JR.: [My] first operating job. The DP [director of photography], Ralph Bode—it was his first union job. He had come from NABET [National Association of Broadcast Employees and Technicians], and he didn't know how anything operated.

BILLY WARD: Ralphie. Nice guy. Good, talented. He had done *Rocky* with Avildsen. That's how he got involved with the project because he had worked in NABET and stuff. He was not in the IA [IATSE, the International Alliance of Theatrical Stage Employees], and this was his introduction to the IA.

GARY MULLER (ASSISTANT CAMERA OPERATOR, *SATURDAY NIGHT FEVER*): So Tom was hired as the [camera] operator, and I was hired as the assistant.

TOM PRIESTLEY, JR.: Gary moved up from being a second to a first and off we went.

GARY MULLER: It was a Robert Stigwood movie because of the music and all that stuff, and he had a concept. He [Avildsen] wanted to do the big Verrazano Bridge scene in the daytime. He wanted to see all of the world and how dangerous it was and this and that. That was his vision, and Stigwood said "No, no. It's got to be done at night."

So, he [Avildsen] got fired, but in the interim—I can't remember who the producer was, the production manager. We went down to an office building, and I brought a camera and I'm waiting to meet my cameraman. I don't know who he is. We're going to do a little screen test between John Travolta and a couple of girls. This guy comes in, opens the electric panel, and starts doing some things. He starts to turn some lights on. Then he comes over and introduces himself to me as Ralph Bode. Well, I didn't know Ralph was just getting to the camera local.

BILLY WARD (GAFFER, *SATURDAY NIGHT FEVER*): Ralph was in the camera department,

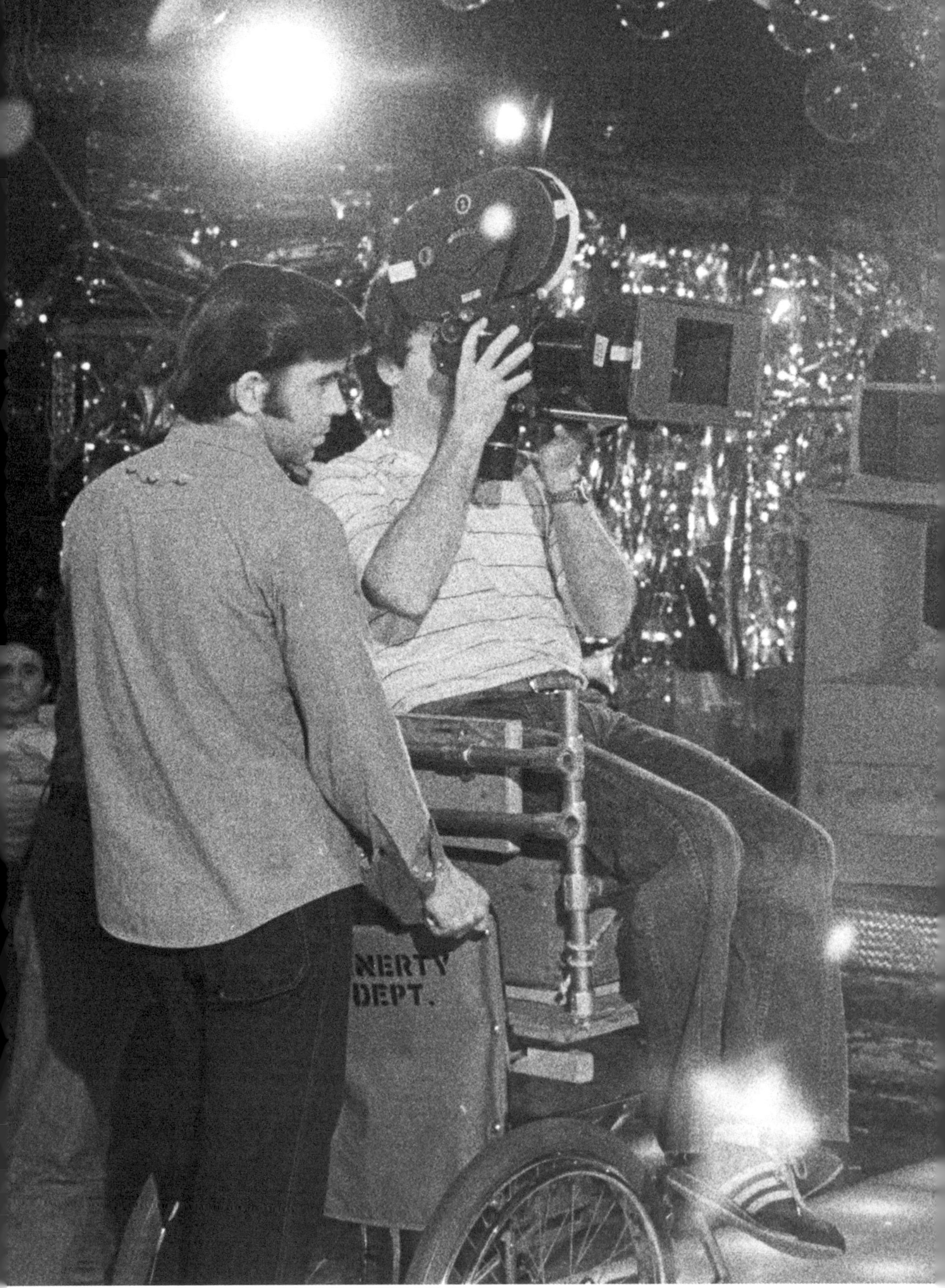
DEPT.

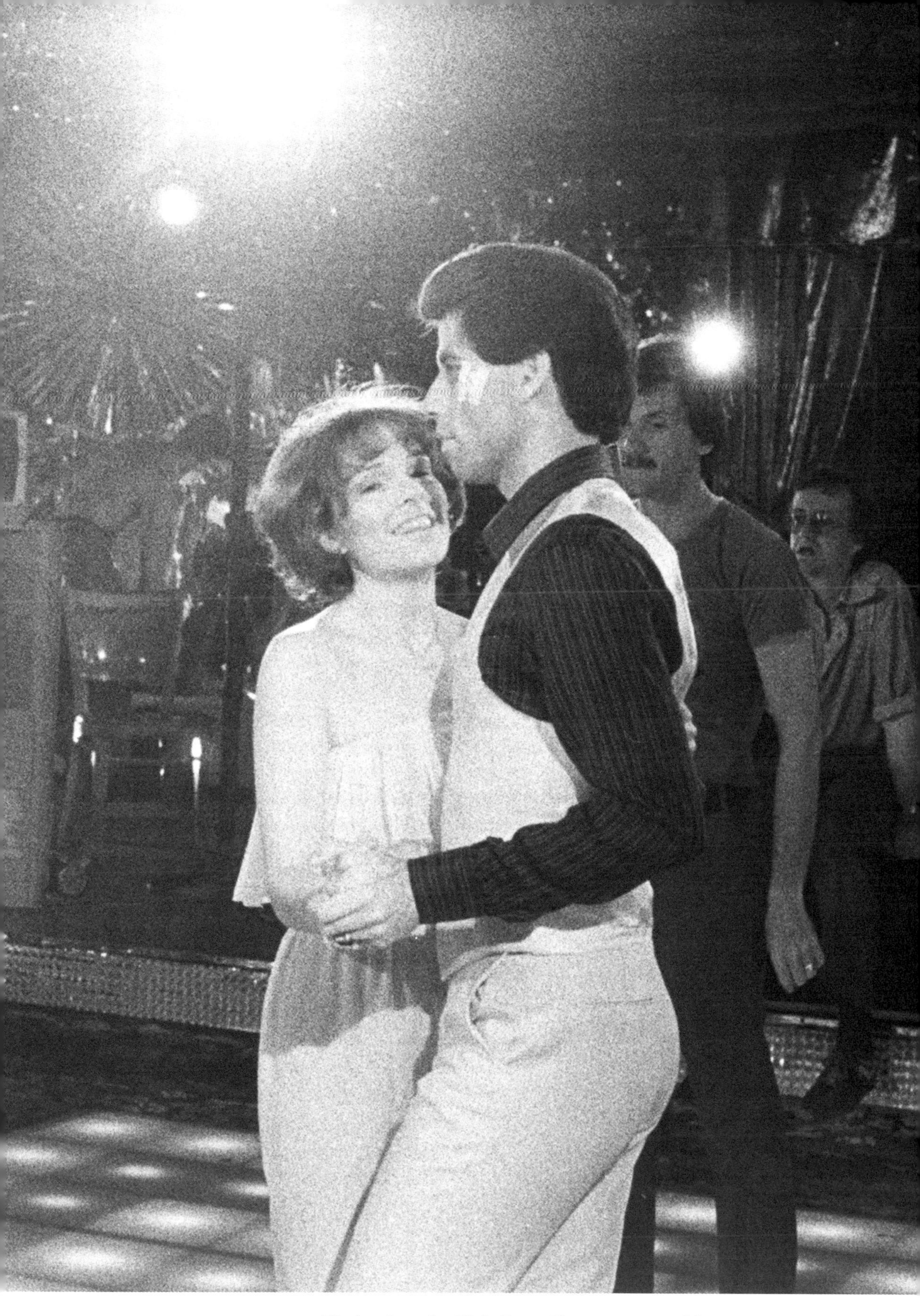

Filming *Saturday Night Fever*. Photo courtesy of the Margaret Herrick Library, Academy of Motion Picture Arts and Sciences.

like a grip, or electrician. I think they [NABET people] had a hard time fitting in. I don't think a lot of people ever accepted them.

GARY MULLER: It was my first and only picture with Ralph. He went in a different direction, and I guess Ralph didn't hire a lot of people he worked with on *Saturday Night Fever,* because I think he felt he didn't . . . how do I say it? He was learning and he wanted to start over with a new crew.

LLOYD KAUFMAN: Avildsen and the producer had me do the production managing on *Cry Uncle!* [1971]. I knew nothing about that, but it's not rocket science. You need the crew. You need a cast. You need equipment. You need locations. I was literally living in the production office, which was up on West End Avenue, 92nd Street, in a flophouse hotel, which is now a magnificent condominium of some sort. It was a little flophouse when they filmed in it too, because they had very little money for locations.

I had to convince people to give us their houses for less than a hundred a day. It was like running for Congress. I hated it. Plus, there was no MapQuest. There was no GPS. It was me and a car in Brooklyn. And I had never set foot in Brooklyn.

Avildsen, who was supposed to direct that movie, brought me on, and I worked for very little in exchange for a big credit, "executive in charge of locations." I was working twenty-hour days at least, and the reason he got fired, according to Avildsen—he says that he was hooking up with a woman named Judy Bowie, who had a cowboy-boot store, and apparently she was the girlfriend of Kevin McCormick, who was the executive producer, who Avildsen told me was hooking up with Robert Stigwood, the top producer who also managed the Bee Gees and had RSO Records and all that stuff. A good guy—all good guys. Everybody was a good guy. But Avildsen says that's why he got fired. There were other issues too, because the staff, in my opinion, didn't give a shit. There was something where he didn't like the Bee Gees.

I had worked with him on *Joe* and *Cry Uncle!,* and we were buddies and I worshipped his talent and he was a great guy. But he's a fighter. He's an artist. And I think it boiled down to he and Stigwood had issues, but he says it was this triangle kind of thing.

I was a glorified production assistant, but I telegrammed Robert Stigwood: "I'd much like to talk to you urgent please meet with me," and most people in the film industry don't return calls or anything, but he actually gave me an appointment, and I went up to his apartment—a beautiful apartment on Central Park West, up somewhere in the seventies—and I told him, "Look, Avildsen is terrific." He had done *Rocky*. "I've known this guy since *Joe,* and you're making a mistake. Take him back."

Stigwood was very polite and just calmly said, "No, it's too late. We've got somebody else coming in."

We discussed who Badham was, then Avildsen suggested that I stay on—as long as I was learning something I ought to stay on—and I'm glad I did because Badham proved to be a terrific director and a good guy also. He's educated—loved movies—a bit older than I, and I got along very well with him.

TOM PRIESTLEY, JR.: [Stigwood] he must have sold a hundred million of the records. All I know is once we heard this track, we knew the movie was going to be good. Up to that point, we didn't know. John Travolta was really unknown. The only thing he had done was *Welcome Back, Kotter* [1975-1979]. This was his big breakout film.

GARY MULLER: A lot of the music for that show wasn't the soundtrack. We had different click tracks. All the words weren't written yet in terms of how they were going to work them into the movie.

TOM PRIESTLEY, JR.: The first eight days, we shot most of the scenes in the house. The slapping scene and "don't touch the hair" and "Attica, Attica!" and then the scenes in the hardware store—that was all done in the beginning because the music wasn't ready.

GARY MULLER: They specifically made this movie to fit these soundtracks, and that's what took some time. I don't know. Maybe that album would be successful, or those songs would be successful, but I don't think they would be as successful if the film didn't exist.

We met Travolta and he was a great guy. Then, as soon as we started to shoot, we had to take time off because his girlfriend at the time [Diana Hyland] was dying of cancer and we didn't even know if the movie was going to go.

TOM PRIESTLEY, JR.: He had to go to California for a couple days for the funeral.

BILLY WARD: Everybody talks about that shot—the feet shot in *Saturday Night Fever*, walking along to the music. I don't know if you remember it, but everybody wanted to know how we did it, and it wound up that John Travolta's girlfriend had been dying. She had cancer. We had nothing to do, so we would be making up shots, and that was one of them—the foot shot that everybody seemed to like.

GARY MULLER: He comes back and he's a little moody, and we start doing these things.

TOM PRIESTLEY, JR.: He [Travolta] came back on a Monday. It was the first day—I caught the famous shot of him walking down the street, swinging the paint can to the music of "Stayin' Alive." It was the first time the crew actually heard the soundtrack of the movie, and everybody said, "This is going to be a fabulous movie," because the soundtrack was brilliant. We did the iconic shot where we start on his feet and we boom up his body and we got to his face and then we see the elevated train behind him and swinging the paint can.

GARY MULLER: We did shots on *Saturday Night Fever* that the grips came up with, wherever they were pulling Tom down a Brooklyn street—he was lying flat on a board, some kind of little western dolly, and then they had rope on both sides of the board and they'd pull up the board and it becomes a shot when he's looking Travolta right in the face.

TOM PRIESTLEY, JR.: You know what a western dolly is? It's a wooden platform—I'd say three by four feet—and has four large balloon tires on it, and it's designed basically to take some of the bumps out of the sidewalk, because all the sidewalks in New York are uneven. They built a rig for me. It took a large piece of wood, like a two-by-twelve, and they anchored it on the base of the dolly with hinges—a cross piece for my feet and a cross piece for my arms—and I lay on this thing and, with the camera in my hand, I was able to get the camera as low as my knuckles touching the ground and looking through the camera.

I lay on this piece of wood. My elbows were tucked in. My feet were on a board across to take my weight. They pulled me down the street. John was walking. My hands are almost rubbing [the ground] sometimes. As we walked to the music, two grips, one grip on each side, had a long board across the wood, and they lifted me—lifted the whole board up with me on it.

GARY MULLER: And then they pulled the board and Tommy up with the handheld Arriflex, so it was eye-level.

TOM PRIESTLEY, JR.: I kind of craned up the body and got to the face, and in doing that I had to adjust my body, move the eye piece down and still hold the camera, which worked out fine, and that was the shot. I mean, it would take some productions a whole day to make that shot with fancy equipment. It took us a couple of hours. An army of twenty-five out there.

But also, remember, New York back in those days was the poor relative. We didn't have all the fancy equipment they had in California. We had to be very innovative with plywood and clamps and rigs. So the guys were innovative and just incredibly talented coming up with solutions to these problems.

GARY MULLER: We did some strange filmmaking for dancing. We patched ropes around Travolta and Tom, and he would hold the Arriflex and spin to get those spinning shots.

TOM PRIESTLEY, JR.: We were tied together, and we both lean back against the rope, And then as he moved to his left I moved to my left. We were counterbalancing each other, and we spin around. I had the camera on him. And that's how the background was so fast.

BILLY WARD: It was just a simple thing. Almost like a hula hoop that the cameraman and the dancer had at the time.

TOM PRIESTLEY, JR.: The nightclub was tough because it was a real location—it wasn't a set—and the ceilings were low—and smoke and everything else, and it was hot in there. Somehow they got a crane in, and they did a couple of crane shots, which was amazing.

BILLY WARD: I think we had to take a wall out of the disco place to get the crane in there at the time. Jimmy Finnerty was the grip.

TOM PRIESTLEY, JR.: Jim Finnerty was the key grip on the show, which was great. Eddie Knot, who was a World War II vet, came into the business and worked on a lot of Lumet movies. He could do more with a couple of wedges and a two-by-four and some clamps than anybody I've seen in my life, and these guys came in with great knowledge and background and it really helped a lot.

BILLY WARD: He [Finnerty] was a clever guy. Of course, he went on to do producing stuff, but we kind of started together. We did the Verrazano bridge.

GARY MULLER: The stunts—hanging over the Verrazano bridge—I remember Finnerty putting a rope on my waist and then hanging over the fucking Verrazano bridge looking down.

TOM PRIESTLEY, JR.: I did a shot on the Verrazano bridge. I had John's shoes on and his pants and I had a handheld camera. I'm out on the beam over the water and I'm trying to simulate John tripping, and Jim Finnerty—the only safety line—I mean, Jim Finnerty holding my belt behind me, and that was it. A long way down.

GARY MULLER: Jim Finnerty was the dolly grip and Jimmy, again, was one of the best grips ever, man. He was good.

TOM PRIESTLEY, JR.: I had faith in Jim Finnerty, and I had faith in my ability, and we did it, but I wouldn't do it now.

GARY MULLER: Well, they wouldn't let you do that now. You have a remote camera that would go over the edge.

TOM PRIESTLEY, JR.: There's one shot I really loved. It was John and the guys coming out of the nightclub onto the street, and the camera pulls back, which is the western dolly again, and I'm doing the handheld only. I'm standing and they come all the way down the street and they come up to the car and [Paul Pape's character] Double J is in the car. He's screwing some girl, and they're banging on the window, and that was all done handheld on a western dolly.

GARY MULLER: Grips were very creative back then. Steel wasn't a big part of the business. Everything was wood and biodegradable with a hinge.

TOM PRIESTLEY, JR.: He [Badham] was okay. He was having an affair with the leading lady and that's why she's in the movie, and everybody wanted a job. She worked, but she can't dance. They had a kind of tiptoe around that. I thought it could have been cast better, but that's me.

GARY MULLER: The only downer for me was Karen Lynn Gorney. That's the girl who the director, John Badham, had the hots for. She wasn't a good-looking girl. She was a nasty girl, and she thought she was it because she was the star. He could have picked a much more attractive, much more vibrant character, but I remember there were words about that. They weren't going to make any more changes because they spent all this money already changing directors.

BILLY WARD: I think we were in Studio 54 for the wrap party. They did a dance contest. My wife was dancing with John Travolta, and she won the prize. They sent us to some island for a week. It was nice.

GARY MULLER: I'll never forget at the end of the picture they had this great wrap party. Back then it was symbolic to get a crew jacket at the end or a gift or something. They gave us these beautiful gold chains with a quarter-ounce of gold. You open your shirt up and show your chest hair type of thing, but it was worth a lot of money, and then when they gave the girls in the crew—the females smaller ones and they gave the guys bigger ones. It was a big wrap party.

Myths and Legends

GORDON KRAUSS (CARPENTER): A carpenter I knew a long time ago said that he called everybody a bunch of carneys. And I think it was true. It felt like everybody was a character of some sort.

CHRIS QUILLES (GRIP): I've got so many aliases, it's not even funny. Growing up, everybody had a name, and once you get it you can't get rid of it. That's your nickname, bro. What are you going to do? You can't fight it. The more you fight it, the worse it is.

JOHN LOWRY(KEY GRIP): Yes, the nicknames were unbelievable, the Flying Squirrel and Fat Sam—when my mother met him, he was like, "Well, I was three hundred pounds when they gave me that name."

BILL KANE (PROP MASTER): Jack Flaherty was very, very well-educated, but funny. He could tell stories. We had guys that could have been actors. That's why we were famous. Local 52 was very famous for one-liners.

RICHARD ADEE (PROP MASTER, SPECIAL EFFECTS, SET DECORATOR): I could give you a list of guys that I gave nicknames to. Bobby Wilson—well, he looked like the Doughboy, so I gave him the nickname Doughboy, and he had a brother—his nickname was Chicken Legs, and Freddy Weiler—he was an outside prop—I nicknamed him Mile-Away because every time you needed him he was a mile away. And then there was Mumbles, Mort Lowry.

CHRIS QUILLES: I got a check on my wedding day that wasn't even in my name. The guy wrote "Chris Lopez" on a check and my ex-wife said, "You invited a guy who doesn't even know your real name?" It was his wife that didn't know my real name. He knew my real name, because he knows my father.

HENRY DUYS (CARPENTER): Since I drove a hearse they started calling me Gravedigger.

CRAIG DIBONA (DIRECTOR OF PHOTOGRAPHY, CAMERA OPERATOR): Oh God, it was Wacko who used to work with Dusty Wallace. One day we're shooting at night and he's up on a fire escape because he would do all the rigging on the fire escapes with the lights, and he said, "Well, I got a lot of time," and he goes into a window, and lays down in some lady's bed and goes to sleep. You can hear her screaming, and Wacko—you had to see what he looked like.

Wacko is like, "What the hell are you screaming at? I'm just sleeping here."

LOCAL 52 Nicknames

John MAZZONI = Johnnyboy = DUKE
Nick Mongelli = Nicky boy
3 John BOIZ = RAGE
4 Joe Finnerty = POCKETS
5 John Finnerty SR = FATHEAD
John Finnerty JR = JUNIOR
7 Chris Lenard = Carbone
8 JACK Finnerty = YONKEL
9 JACK FlareTy = FLAP JACK
10 Bobby Royal = BULLET
11 Bobby Paquette = WILDMAN
12 Billy KERWICK = THE BEARD
13 KEVIN KNOT = Kong = Baby huey
14 Vinny Guarrello = MEATBall
15 James Dolan = PEACHES
16 Jim Dolan = PacKY
17 Dusty Wallace = JOHN
18 HaroLD Sasso = HELEN
19 Tommy PraTe JR = Muffin
20 Bobby PraTe = Rubber HEAD
21 Billy Cassidy = THE WHIP
22 Charlie MERRES = THE LAPPER
23 Bobby Dolan = CHiefy
24 MIKE OATES = CLEM
25 JOE VALLE = BIG GUY
26 PAT TEASTRA = SQUARE WHEEL
27 MAT MILLER = Saloon FACE
28 Charlie NASTagia = Rubber LEGS
29 JACK MarTorello = Mummbes
30 Tommy Lowery = POPCORN

31 Bill Lowery SR = PAPA BEAR
32 Rory WALSH = THE GUPPY
33 MIKE Gerrity = FLOUNDER
34 STEVE Rooney = SMOOTHIE
35 DANNY Vanbloomberg = DENISE
36 JOHN MAZZOLA = BRONCO
37 Greg MAZZOLA = SHadow
38 Frank PRimevera = ROLO
39 CHris PRimevera = PRIM
40 Frank PROSCIA = PRO
41 George ROSEN = TURTLE
42 EDDIE EGAN = Double E
43 LOREN Levy = Baby Jesus
44 ED ABELE = Godzella
45 Paul Haligan = SARGE
46 Tom Gilligan = MOON
47 Kevin Giligan = HAIF MOON
48 MIKE BUCK = HAIF BUCK
49 NORMAN Buck = BUCK
50 Jim MANZIONE = HAMMER
51 Bobby McGAVIN = MAGOO
52 John FORD = WHITEY
53 Bobby Florence = FLOSSIE
54 Jimmy Dillenger = SKinny
55 JACK KENNEDY = Mindy
56 Kenny Goss = PUTTY NOSE
57 STEVE Woods = WOODZE
58 William McGavin = Cardboard CuTouT
59 Bobby ZeTTeberG = BZ
60 Billy Ward = Golden BOY

61 MIKE PROSCIA = BURNOUT = MAGUBA
62 Lou PaTraglia = BAD LOAD
63 JOHN PaTraglia = PANCAKES
64 William Glatt = DUSTY
65 Frankie LaTerra = WACKO
66 Larry OlarKEN = SweeT Pea = LOLA
67 BOBBY VOLPE = Poison TUNG
68 Jim FiTzpaTrick = BOOMER
69 Kevin FiTzPaTrick = BeaMER
70 JOHN BURKE = RED
71 Kevin Burke = RED
72 Jimmy GRAY = THE Rebel
73 Richie FORK = SNEEZIE
74 Buddy McBride = ToasTie
75 MIKE Delaney = ANGEL
76 JAMES Malone = MUGSY
77 Joe VIANO = STUBY
78 EDDie Quinn = WHITIE
79 Phil Purificato = CUTLETS
80 Tom Kudlek = Cuddels
81 Robert Meyerhoff = SALTY
82 Ronnie PaTraglia = Pirhana
83 Jim Pollard = Super GRIP
84 Bobby Brennan = FRED FLINTSTONE
85 Bobby Conners = DINGER
86 FRANK ITRI = THE TANK
87 PAT Johnson = CRACKS
88 MIKE MonTGOMERY = MONTY
89 JIMMY Miller = DON Rickels = Bemmie
90 GEORGE PaTsos = GREEK

91 MIKE FABIANO = BERKOWITZ
92 BOBBY STOCKLIN = STOCKS
93 KENNY FUNDUS = GERBER
94 EDDIE DROHAN = TAZMANIAN DEVEL
95 BOBBY CONNERS = DINGER
96 Dickie FALK = LUCKY
97 JOE FORTUNATO = BLOCK
98 ANTHONY KLEIN = THE DUECE
99 JEFF MAZZOLA = BABY
100 DICK QUINLAN = CRAZE
101 JOHN CorbeTT = THE CRUSHER
102 VicTOR HUEY = THE CHINAMAN
103 Glen PanGione = SNAKE
104 Billy Miller = THE BAD PREIST
105 FRANK DiDio = Frankie Plans
106 TOM RYAN = TUG BOAT
109 ED Kammerer = RiPPie
110 JOHN BOBICK = BURBS
111 MIKE BIRD = THE BIRDMAN
112 TOMMY YOSTPILE = YO
113 MIKE BETZER = PUPPY
114 LEE Sheret = FRANKEN GRIP
117 ARTIE BOYD = PlumBOB
118 JOE Kampher = SQUEAKY
119 CHRIS MARKKUNAS = SNAGEL TOOT
120 John Gabriel = Johnny RoTTE
121 JOE Badalluco = BANGER
122 Chris Quilles = Coco + Lopez

Chart by John Mazzoni photographed by author in the *Law and Order SVU* grip department.

KELLY BRITT (**ELECTRICIAN**): There's legends—a couple grips on a Friday would cash their checks and go to JFK and sit there and look at the board and say, "Where do we want to go?" They'd buy round-trip tickets and go somewhere for the weekend and then fly back, like, late Sunday night.

RICHARD ADEE: Well, there was a story that I heard when I got into business. They'd get Salty [Meyerhoff, props] stewed to the mickey. They'd empty his pockets, take him to the airport, put him on a plane, send him somewhere—down to the islands, South America. He'd wake up—and he wouldn't know where the hell he was!

They did this a number of times. He was just a carefree guy. He didn't give a shit.

RUSSELL ENGELS (**GAFFER**): It got more and more corporate as it went along. Back in those days, a lot of the fun—the production departments would cause it or start it. I remember a story my father had. He was out in Colorado, and he said, "You know what? We're not having any fun. Let's send for Salty Meyerhoff."

Just out of the blue. He was Willie [Meyerhoff]'s brother, a prop. He was well-known. They knew he'd have a few martinis on the way out, and they would all go to the airport to see Salty get off the plane, and this is the production department. They sent a big blonde out there running after him saying "Salty, you came back! You came back, my love!"

She gave him a big hug. Salty said, "Oh, I really like this town."

Then a guy comes out: "You're the son of a bitch that's stealing my wife!" Salty's face went white. And the whole crew was watching from the fence on the side. But can you imagine production managers or producers setting that up today? That's unheard of. You don't do anything to disturb anything, no matter what. That five minutes is going to cost you. It's now $32,000 for five minutes. That little joke cost us.

RICHARD ADEE: But Salty—they were doing a movie in Jackson Hole, Wyoming. Some of the crew set this thing up with the judge, the police station, the sheriff, everything. They get Salty stewed to the mickey. And they lock him up in jail for the night. The next morning, they come and they wake his ass up.

He didn't know where the hell he was: "What's going on? Why am I here? What did I do?"

"You'll find out. You'll find out what you did. Get yourself cleaned up. You're going to court this morning. Take him to court." There's all these people in the courthouse—most of, I guess, the crew or something. Judge says, "How do you plead?"

He says, "I don't know. I don't know what I did."

And this goes on back and forth. "You got a lawyer? You can't tell me you don't know what you did."

"What's the charge, your honor?"

"Murder. First degree." He shit in his pants and it was all a hoax. This is what they did with this poor guy.

Contract on Cherry Street

(1977)

GARY MULLER (**FIRST ASSISTANT CAMERA OPERATOR, *CONTRACT ON CHERRY STREET***): That was a Frank Sinatra movie. I was young, twenty-six years old, and I was responsible, and Frank came to me and said, "Kid, you get one take. I've got to be out of here. One take," and he had his mob with him. He was very pleasant. The acting was terrible, but it was Frank Sinatra.

RANDY JURGENSEN (**SECURITY, *CONTRACT ON CHERRY STREET***): You were never waiting on Sinatra. Sinatra did not blow his lines. Sinatra didn't miss his mark. He would only do it one time. You better get it.

We had a blackout in the city. Sinatra staying at a hotel fourteen floors up. Sinatra walks down fourteen floors. It's five blocks from where we're shooting outside of Studio 54. Now, Studio 54 has air conditioning—they had their own generator. The city is in bedlam—it's a blackout, and everybody's taking advantage of it. They're breaking into store windows.

Sinatra is walking five blocks, and it must be 85 degrees out, humid. The shot means that Sinatra turns the corner—the camera is on him turning the corner, walking over to the car. Sinatra bends down and looks into the car from the passenger side where the two guys are sitting. It will come to me who the two actors are that are sitting there, and he says the line, and then he turns and he walks into Studio 54.

I accompany Sinatra wherever he goes. He goes into Studio 54. Nobody moves from the camera. It's like death quiet. You could hear the riot five blocks away. Somebody says, "You didn't get the shot, right?" Gary or whoever it is doesn't take his eye out of the camera and he says, "No." [Laughs] They say to me, "Randy, you got to go tell Mr. Sinatra that we didn't get the shot."

I said, "Okay,"

I always called him Mr. S. I don't know why. I go in there. I said to him, "Mr. S . . ."

And he looked at me, and he's lighting up one of his unfiltered cigarettes and he says to

Sinatra in his first TV movie!

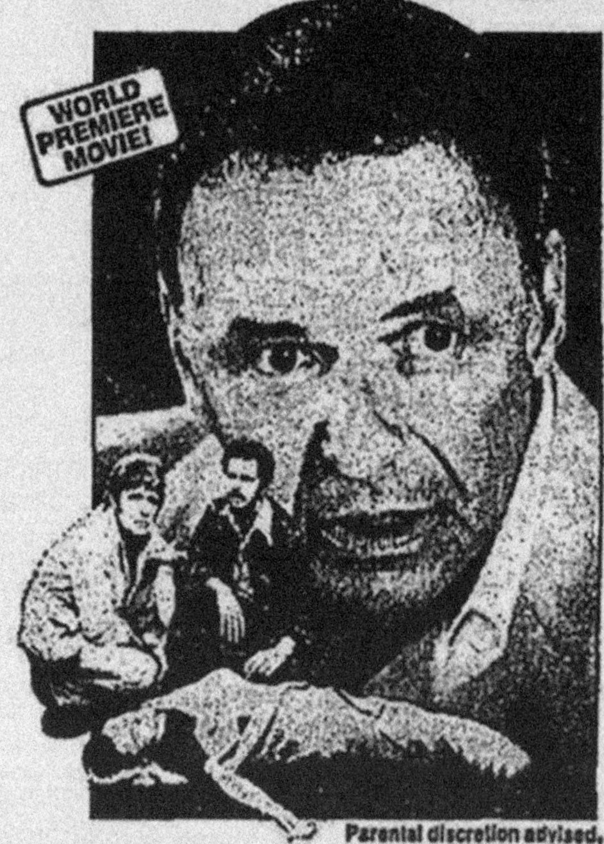

7PM
"CONTRACT ON CHERRY STREET"
Frank Sinatra
Harry Guardino
Martin Balsam
An angry detective devises a scheme to set gangland "families" at each other's throats... putting his own neck on the line, too!

5

Contract on Cherry Street television advertisement.

me—honest to God, quote me—he says to me, "Randy, we're working in here."

I said, "Of course we are."

I walked back outside, and I give a thumbs down: he ain't coming back. He's not doing it again. We're not getting the shot. But movie magic: they got the lines of what he said, they dress somebody that looks exactly like Sinatra, from the waist on down, right? He comes over to the car and they shoot that. They shoot from the waist down. They got Sinatra walking away. They hook it up to Sinatra walking away with the Studio 54 footage. That's how it works. But that's not what the shot was.

GARY MULLER: Jilly Rizzo was still there. Jilly was his bodyguard, and Frank would come up in a black limo and get out and he had a suit on and say, "Here's what we're doing."

It was stressful.

RANDY JURGENSEN: I'm working with Frank Sinatra, and not only did we go to dinner with Sinatra, but he also actually got a limousine for my wife and myself, and we went out to where he was appearing for one night. Thousands of people and we're right up front.

GARY MULLER: He gave us all front-row seats. We had a good time.

RANDY JURGENSEN: Jilly came up to me and said, "Can I see you in the hall?

I said, "Yeah."

I had just come down with Sinatra. We were in the Village. He says, "Here, Frank wants you to have this."

I opened it up. I looked at it. He gave me a solid gold St. Francis medal with a solid gold chain. Jilly put his finger to his lips. He said, "We're going to the restaurant a little later on. Please accompany us."

It was Jilly's [restaurant], and we sat over there. We talked about every goddamn thing that there was. Of course, all he would say is, "How did you lock up so-and-so?"

GARY MULLER: A lot of these New York movies run together. They all become the same because you see the same people. All you do is change the name on the slate. If you do one picture after another, it becomes like a factory. I did three jobs in a row where I didn't have a day off. I finished a show on Wednesday, and they waited to shoot the next show on a Thursday. We drove up with the same fucking camera truck and the same sound department. "Ready? Let's go."

The Wiz

(1978)

The Wiz *would be the first film to shoot in the reopened and renamed Kaufman Astoria Studios in Queens, the very place Sidney's only movie appearance to date in* One Third a Nation *was filmed in 1939. He had been a vital force in getting the studio back up and running, helping to raise money and its profile. Much of the movie would be filmed around the city, the New York State Pavilion at the site of the 1964 World's Fair became Munchkinland, and along the yellow brick road Dorothy would encounter homelessness, labor exploitation, heroin, prostitution, graffiti, garbage and political corruption.*
—Maura Spiegel, *Sidney Lumet: A Life* (2019)

GARY MULLER (FIRST CAMERA ASSISTANT, *THE WIZ*): One of the biggest—one of the worst movies ever made in New York—but one of the biggest was *The Wiz*.

CASSANDRA SAULTER (SCENIC ARTIST, *THE WIZ*): Of course, everybody talks about *The Wiz* because there's no one that didn't work on *The Wiz*.

TONY GAMIELLO (SPECIAL EFFECTS, *THE WIZ*): It was a massive, elaborate job. I mean, probably about three-quarters of the people who worked in the industry in New York at the time were on that job. I remember at one point they cleaned out all the electric houses, rental houses. They had to send to Philadelphia to get more cable and stuff.

DAVE FRANZONI (ELECTRICIAN, SET DRESSER, *THE WIZ*): My dad was one of the few people that did *not* work on *The Wiz* because he was cleaning up on commercials and everything else.

GARY MULLER: Local 52 was scraping them [workers] from the woodwork because I don't think there was any other picture shooting in New York at the time.

DAVE FRANZONI: I jumped on *The Wiz* for four months, pretty much for the rest of that year—as an electric for two weeks and the rest of the job as a set dresser.

JOHN KASARDA (ASSISTANT ART DIRECTOR, *THE WIZ*): Tony [Walton, production designer]

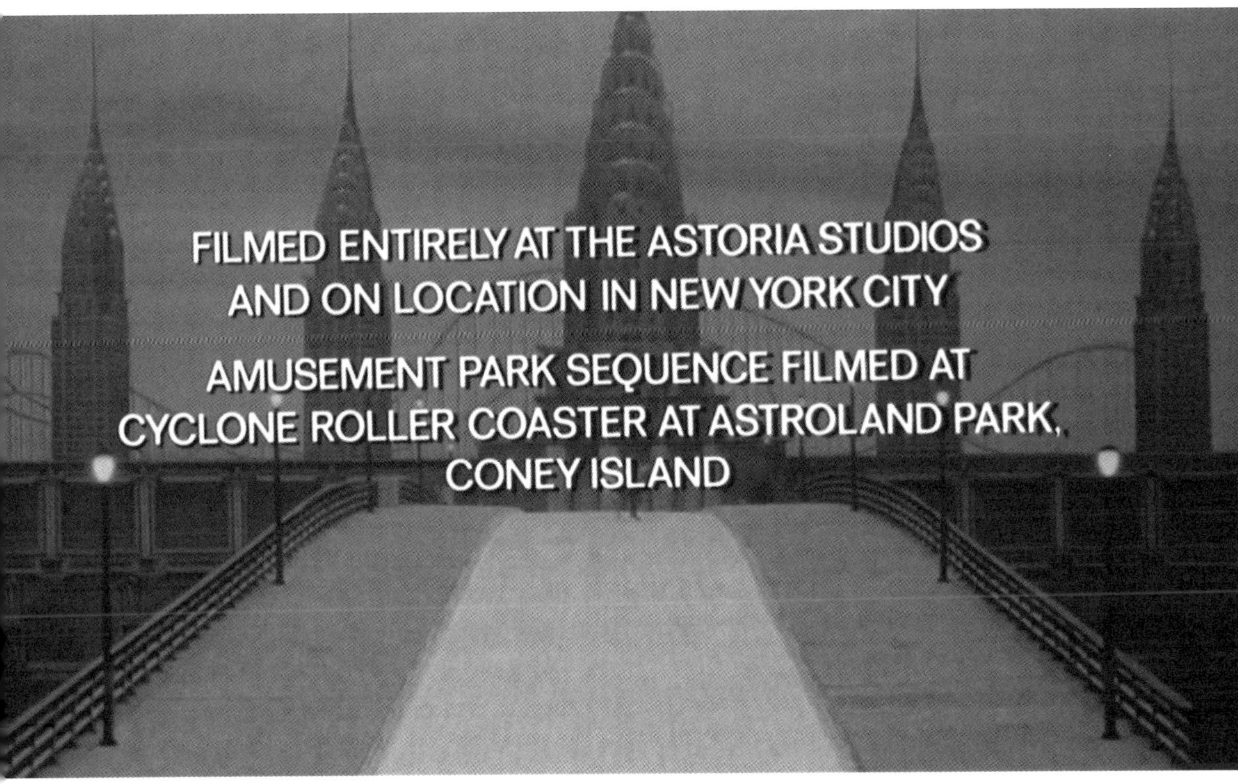

did a wonderful job of designing it. But it was a huge, huge production. In fact they reached beyond the unions to bring in people who were in, like, the Sign Writers Union or the House Banners Union because so much work had to get done so quickly the union couldn't staff everything. I think a lot of people stepped up. The demand was so great that people really advanced in the scenic ranks or the draftsman ranks or all of that.

Yes, I was a lowly draftsman, but I got a chance. It was a real eye-opener. I got a chance to see—kind of get a worm's-eye view of how movies are made and walk around the sets and even some of the locations. It was pretty exciting, actually.

TONY GAMIELLO: *The Wiz* was a musical set in New York; it's supposed to be an urban setting. They were down at the World Trade Center; they were down different bridges and in different places in the city. It would cost a fortune to try and build that stuff in a back lot someplace in Hollywood. So, you do it in New York and you just lay down yellow-brick-road linoleum and you shoot it.

BILL REYNOLDS (PROPS, *THE WIZ*): It was done in the Big House, Kaufman Astoria [Studios].

BRUNO ROBOTTI (SCENIC ARTIST, *THE WIZ*): In 1920 they built the Kaufman Studio, the Big Stage, which is still the biggest and the best studio on the East Coast.

JOHN LOWRY (GRIP, *THE WIZ*): To me, *that's* a stage. You don't see stages like that anymore.

CASSANDRA SAULTER: There are certain jobs like *Scenes from a Mall* [1990] and *The Wiz*—only about two or three movies—where we used the entire height of Kaufman Astoria Studios.

BRUNO ROBOTTI: You can actually build a five-story building in there. It's just amazing.

CASSANDRA SAULTER: It had been used by the Army Pictorial Center when everybody who was working in movies in New York went west. The Army Pictorial Center made those venereal-disease films and marching films, but they didn't really alter it [the building] at all from the movie business, so that stuff stayed.

JOHN LOWRY: It was abandoned for so long. I don't know if the army still owned it at that time or whether they donated it.

MAGGIE RYAN: I used to go into Astoria because it was such a mess back then. It was just a big hole, and it was all concrete and dirty and hadn't been used, really, since the thirties. *The Wiz* was the first movie to come back there. And so I used to go in with Tony and watch them film. I'd wander around.

TONY GAMIELLO: A rumor started years earlier, back in the thirties, that Groucho Marx hid a suitcase full of money behind one of the walls downstairs, so everybody would go along and banging on the walls to see if it was hollow and if there was something back there.

CASSANDRA SAULTER: The bins were full of powdered paints. There was a painted frame that used to move up and down. Kaufman Astoria was designed like a Broadway stage, basically, or a shop. I think the paint frame was still usable when I was working there in the seventies.

TONY GAMIELLO: *The Wiz* really revived the Astoria studios. This is the film that revived those studios and started getting it renovated and getting it back to working so we could bring more work into New York.

JOHN LOWRY: The main stage—they'd pull a floor up and that'd slide open. Then down in the basement, that floor would pop open and then there was the Olympic swimming pool. So that way they could do the big shots of these musicals with the swimming and stuff.

TONY GAMIELLO: One day, we were working in the effects shop downstairs—all of a sudden, we hear a big crash.

JOHN LOWRY: The forklift was coming fast with a whole bunch of masonites.[19] We'd moved the benches away and we felt the floor shaking.

TONY GAMIELLO: This whole floor gave way when the guy went over with a forklift full of plywood and the whole forklift fell in a hole.

JOHN LOWRY: The floor gave way, and what was happening—water from outside was leaking into the pool and the water was sitting there and the moisture rotted the big beams and stuff.

TONY GAMIELLO: When they covered it over, they just put in whatever beams, but they didn't really fill it solid, so you could walk on it, no problem, but it wasn't strong enough to drive a heavy forklift over it. He went right down into the pool. Luckily, there was a cage, and the guy didn't get hurt. The guy driving it climbed out and ran across the street to the Thunderbird Bar to get a few drinks. Scared the hell out of him.

JOHN LOWRY: When he fell in, it was like a deck of cards, all the masonites, and that's what kind of saved him. It stopped him from falling down another forty feet or so.

TONY GAMIELLO: They had to go down there with welders and construct a ramp and then have other forklifts hoist up [the fallen forklift] with chains to get it up the ramp.

19 Very heavy smooth-surfaced wood composite boards.

GARY MULLER: That set—the scenic artists. Every one of them should have won the Academy Award. They were just incredible.

CASSANDRA SAULTER: *The Wiz* employed eighty scenic artists.

BEVERLY MILLER (SCENIC ARTIST, *THE WIZ*): *The Wiz* was the first big movie I worked on with Gene Powell, who was an incredible master and mentor to many scenics [artists]. He was a World War II vet; he had been a prisoner of war. He and Ernie Southern and those guys worked very hard within the union to create what we have now. They fought for us to have welfare and pension and organizing as a more twentieth-century labor union.

Gene was very good at encouraging young artists to join. You have a career that afforded us a middle-class life. Gene lived up here in Valley Cottage. I live in Nyack. We had a lot of scenics move up here and it was all because of Gene Powell.

He hired me and I became one of the sculptors on *The Wiz*. Duke Bouton headed our sculpture unit, and unfortunately we started using a two-part material. After one day I came home and I was saying something is wrong because my skin is burning, even though I was wearing gloves, and of course we were in a very unventilated room and using very toxic material.

We produced all the gargoyles that surrounded the big hall in the Wiz, and I remember Gene Powell asking who wanted to go up in the captain's chair to touch up all the gargoyle heads once they were in place, and I of course volunteered to go up thirty-five feet in the captain's chair, which was a lot of fun.

GARY MULLER: We'd go in and do wide angle and closeups, so you couldn't see the gargoyles on the sets.

BILL KANE (PROPS, *THE WIZ*): Everything we did on a large scale. They put the façade of the New York Public Library in the stage with the lions, with the side lions walking.

TONY GAMIELLO: The library set had a tilted back and angled the set into the center, so it would compensate for the camera lens and didn't look distorted because it was such a wide shot.

DAVE FRANZONI: You don't see a lot of what we made and what we designed on screen. I mean, it was like, are you kidding me? It was crazy. It's pretty amazing.

CASSANDRA SAULTER: You're on this big floor of Kaufman Astoria and they're actually painting the front of the New York Public Library as a drop. They painted a drop to use in the movie. And that was Bruno's gig.

BRUNO ROBOTTI: Gene was amazing. I worked for him on *The Wiz*. As a matter of fact, on *The Wiz* I ended up doing three different jobs. That's how long *The Wiz* lasted.

TONY GAMIELLO: The talent of the carpenters—they made, like, a thirty-foot-long replica of the Duisenberg car, all out of wood.

DAVE FRANZONI: I also met one of my idols—Albert Whitlock. He was a British matte painter. He was in the industry for a long, long time before even *The Wiz*. But he would do matte paintings for special effects. And the guy is considered the tops in the business outside of—another big guy from Disney was Peter Ellenshaw that came out of that generation.

I was pretty much in awe watching this guy work. Some of the plate paintings he did for *The Wiz* were just amazing.

GARY MULLER: Sidney had to go to California and ask Universal for another five or six million to start shooting and finish production. We spent all the fucking money in pre-production. There was no money left—nothing—gone. We spent twenty million. There was nothing left to put film in the camera.

TONY GAMIELLO: They had [a scene] where these sewing machines would melt down.

RICHARD ADEE (PROP MASTER, *THE WIZ*): I think they were from Singer. I did all the rigging—tables and all that stuff. They all melt.

You know how we did that? Took hot plates and we had wax duplicates of all the machines. We just hit the electric and started the hot plates. The things just went down.

TONY GAMIELLO: When I was in the effects department, I just started in the business. I did my first big job, and they had me making this wood framework nineteen feet long so I can mount explosive squibs and smoke bombs, alternating them, and wiring them in series. You had to wire them just right, otherwise it'd be a misfire. I had to make twenty of these, enough for twenty takes. I was there for, like, two weeks working on this—cutting the things out of wood, assembling them, doing the wiring and everything else. They had the big door opened where the evil witch entered, and that's when they had a shortcut in the floor where the things that I made for the smoke bombs and the explosive squibs went off. When she enters, you see all these sparks and smoke—colored smoke, flame, and everything—so it was a big number.

And that was designed by the old master special-effects guy, Tony Parmelee. He designed the flame-thrower for the Wiz's mouth so that he could adjust it and get a big billowy flame or a sharp-focus flame. He had taken chemistry in school so he could change the chemicals in the flame-thrower and make it a blue flame or a yellow flame or an orange flame—a green.

We were testing that flame thrower in a parking lot we were working in. Tony Parmelee had a great sense of humor. Tony says, "Watch this," and he hits the button and flames come out of the flame-thrower and went up the hood of a car one of the guys was moving. You never saw a guy put it in reverse and shoot out of here so fast. Those flames were licking up the hood of the car right up the windshield.

He scared the hell out of the Teamster. Like I said, he had a great sense of humor.

RICHARD ADEE: They wanted fish dancing on a plate for some scene. I drilled holes in the bottom of the plates. They were on a table, and I just put rods up by the heads. I could make the things just move on a plate. I'm down there with these rods, doing this like a puppet.

TONY GAMIELLO: The Wiz's head was made by an outside scenic department called Fantasy Prop headed up by Eoin Sprott—a hell of a nice guy and a master. The artwork on the mechanical men was done by Eoin's people.

MAGGIE RYAN: Eoin used to do a lot of wonderful things. He was just off the main stage in Astoria—he had a shop there—and he did all the breakaway lions and things like that for *The Wiz*.

TONY GAMIELLO: My father would hook up all the mechanisms and solenoids and wires and stuff to make the mechanical men actually move and work. We set them up at Coney Island at the big rollercoaster there, the old one—the Cyclone.

GARY MULLER: The great Ozzie Morris, a cinematographer from Britain—he'd light up forty-nine lighters in one direction of the World Trade Center Plaza. It was fucking huge. It was so bright. It was as if you're shooting daytime, and it was nighttime.

DAVE FRANZONI: The big dance scene at the end—well, there's something that was missed totally in the film. You don't get it at all [i.e., viewers don't notice]. Yeah, I mean, at the Trade Center we did—what was it—47,000 light bulbs under the dance floor, something unbelievable.

BILL REYNOLDS: The lighting was just magnificent colors and dancing and the Yellow Brick Road.

GARY MULLER: The easy part of that picture was shooting. The hardest part was prepping. When you talk to [Bill] Reynolds, ask him how many yards of fucking yellow linoleum they put down across America.

TROY ADEE, SET DRESSER, *THE WIZ*: Rolls would come by—a fucking thousand feet—and the scenics had to paint the Yellow Brick Road on it.

TONY GAMIELLO: There was a crew that all they did was put Yellow Brick Road all over the place. We get to Coney Island at five or six in the morning to set up, and the whole rollercoaster—it's covered with Yellow Brick Road linoleum.

BILL KANE: I did the Yellow Brick Road. There's an area where five roads come together—we covered them all in Yellow Brick Road.

When Sidney comes in, he says, "Wow, Billy, great. Oh, I love it. I love it." Sidney was always gracious.

GARY MULLER: That was the longest prep I ever had in my career. We had to test the yellow linoleum. We had to test skin color versus fabric color. Tony Walton was the greatest designer, and he would want a test of this and a test of that.

DAVE FRANZONI: Tony Walton was great. Really nice guy, too—not temperamental, like, throwing tantrums, as far as I remember. He may have done a little of that, especially working with Lumet.

BILL KANE: We did the bridge over the Long Island Expressway. We also had yellow sawdust to fill in gaps along the edges. We also did the bridge going over the East River. And that was an all-night job, where we did Yellow Brick Road from the sidewalks on the other side of the highway, up the ramp, Yellow Brick Road, over the highway, and then up a ramp, and then up over the East River to the point where you can't see anymore.

TONY GAMIELLO: We were in Brooklyn for the big blizzard scene. They had brought in two huge fans that were propelled by airplane engines from cross country on these big flatbed trailers. They had big trailer trucks full of this polystyrene snow, like a plastic snow, and several of us had to shovel the snow into these big hoses. They would suck it up to the fans [that] would blow it out into the street, and we would just keep feeding it. When they were shooting it, the intensity of these fans with all the snow—there was so much snow. It was, like, blinding—only the cameraman through the lens could see what the hell was going on because it was so blinding. And after we finished with it, all the guys, including me, had this polystyrene snow in your ears, up your nose, in your clothes, everywhere. A separate crew came in after we finished shooting it that night—they came in with bulldozers and dump trucks to pick up all the snow. My car was parked two blocks away and had snow on it.

DAVE FRANZONI: Believe it or not, we closed down 8th Avenue on a Friday night for the scene where the hookers are taunting Dorothy. We laid dolly track across the whole of 8th Avenue. They had these giant billboards for the shot with giant lips creating rings of smoke coming out of them. The only problem was they mounted them on the air intake for one of the theaters and Victor Borge was performing a show there. Sucked in all the smoke into the theater, and they had to evacuate the theater because they thought the theater was on fire.

CHRIS QUILLES (GRIP): I remember my grandfather carrying me on the set of *The Wiz* and I met Michael Jackson and Nipsey Russell. I had no idea who these people were. Michael Jackson was just the Scarecrow. I had no idea who he was.

RICHARD ADEE: Oh yeah, Michael Jackson, he was good—a little weird, but he was great.

TROY ADEE: My father brought my sister and I there one day when we were little kids. I got locked in the fucking elevator with Michael Jackson.

Michael Jackson was the Scarecrow and, instead of being stuffed with hay, it was garbage, and his nose had Reese's Peanut Butter Cups [wrappers].

He wanted to try his fucking acting skills on me, so he is asking me some shit, and I start telling him stuff. He's like, "You're a liar."

I'm like, "What?"

But he made me cry.

He's like, "You're a goddamn liar."

Like, six times, and I'm, like—I'm this little kid—I'm like, "Why is Michael Jackson calling me a liar?" He sees that I'm, like, clearly getting upset, and I start crying, and he's like, "Oh, I was just acting, I was just showing you, like, how acting is."

You can't buy that when you're a little kid. You know what I'm saying? Unless someone says, like, "All right, look, this is a fight scene, and this guy is going to push you, and it's not really a push." My dad's like, "What's going on? "

And I was like, "Nothing." We come home, and my sister's like, "We got stuck in an elevator with Michael Jackson and Troy was crying. He's such a pussy."

GARY MULLER: Oh my God. I remember what Nipsey Russell did to Michael Jackson. It was the weirdest thing. Nipsey put a pornographic picture in his script of a woman's part, and Michael opened it up and he had no idea what it was and he was screaming. He couldn't work the rest of the day. He was in shock. I remember it. I could see it in front of me. I could see the set, and Sidney was so furious. It was frigging outrageous.

Richard Pryor, he was the Wiz. He went fucking nuts a couple of times. I think he had his meltdown right after that. Sidney came in screaming and yelled at him: "Fucker. Hey, you're working for me," etc.

TONY GAMIELLO: There was a guy from *Time* magazine who was photographing. But for some reason there was one scene when we had made this mockup of a subway station where you had the exit gate, the spin-around—they were swords.

Lumet didn't want them [photographers], even though the guy had permission—he didn't want the *Time* magazine guy photographing it—so he had them [assistant directors] confiscate the film. Lumet felt it was revealing a motion-picture secret.

GARY MULLER: Sidney was very careful about running photographers out back then.

TONY GAMIELLO: This is not like a military operation here. I mean, it's a movie. So what if you're revealing something? I mean, it's fantasy. But Lumet took things a little too serious. Some directors are very serious; some are not serious at all.

GARY MULLER: This movie was shot in less than ten weeks.

DAVE FRANZONI: In fact, it was a shame. because the still pictures that we all took looked better than what showed up on the screen.

GARY MULLER: You got to dailies—you don't even see the shit. Tony Walton would get so pissed off. He said, "Sidney, you don't even see the fucking things up there," and Lumet would say, "They [scenery] don't act." He was set in his ways.

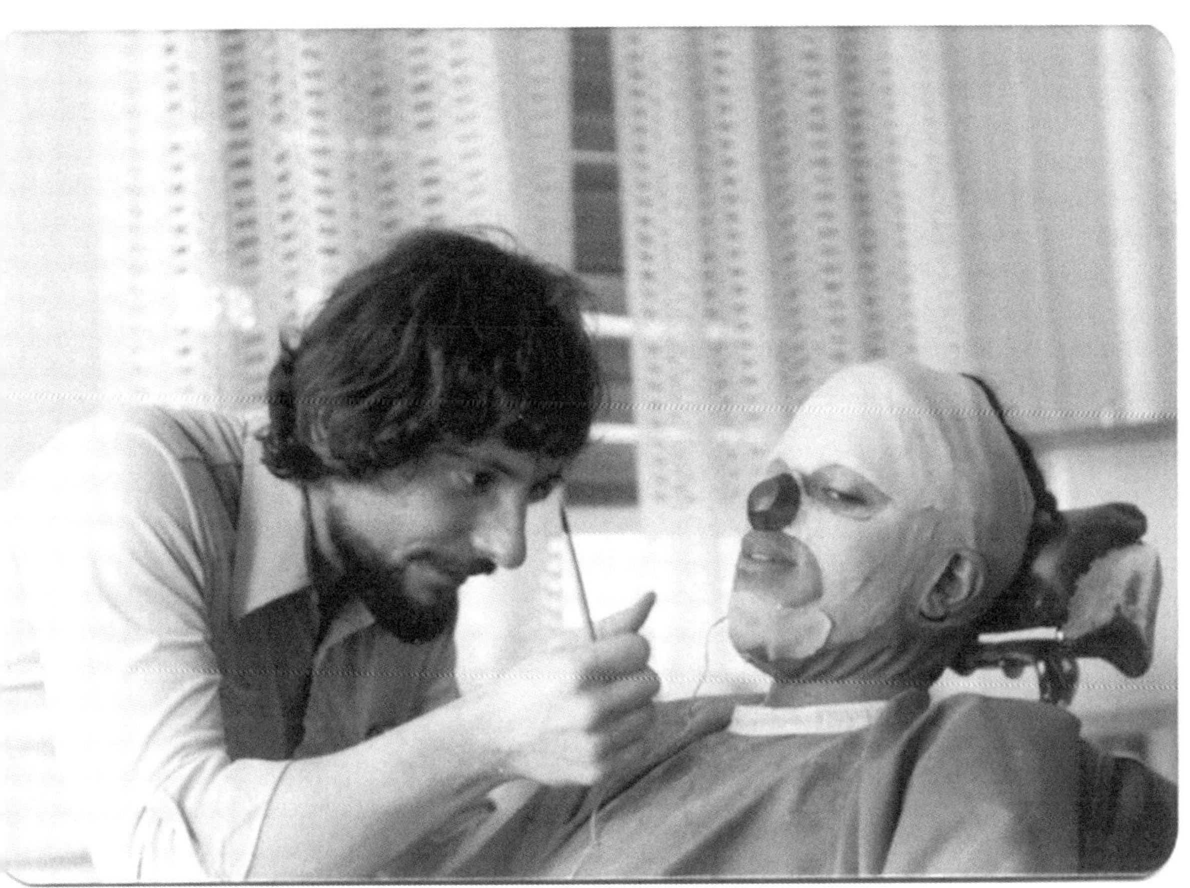

That's another reason why the picture got hurt, because we shot everything wide angle. We didn't do closeups. We didn't have time.

BILL REYNOLDS: The workshop was the biggest waste because they just walked through it, and we did a lot of dance routines in it but it was looking in one direction or the other. There physically wasn't a square inch of that workshop that wasn't magnificent and didn't deserve to be photographed. And it wasn't shot. I think just from a cost standpoint, he could have saved so much money if he said, "This is going to be the shot and everything else doesn't matter."

DAVE FRANZONI: The evil witch's throne is a toilet bowl, and what happens is she gets flushed down the toilet, which you don't get in the movie. You only understand that if you were on the set, because we built it and you watched it, but in the movie you missed that whole joke. And that's when the Winkies rip off their suits and the whole big dance number—it was amazing what went into it.

TROY ADEE: So back to the toilet bowl—they had cut this big hole in the floor to go to the basement. When Dorothy kills her—Diana Ross threw water on the witch, and she melts. Then the Cowardly Lion went up and hit the toilet, flushed it. There was a chair in the toilet

Michael Thomas working on Michael Jackson's makeup on *The Wiz*. Photo courtesy of Christine Domaniecki.

with a track that went down to the basement with her sitting on it. It was amazing. I'm like, "Holy shit."

GARY MULLER: One of the main reasons it wasn't a hit was because Sidney took Diana Ross's character away from her. He made her cut her hair short to look like Dorothy and that woman couldn't sing after that, she was so upset she had short hair. When we started to do closeups, the lip sync was terrible. Diana didn't give a shit, and they couldn't sync the music, so the music and the sync was off.

And we couldn't get close to the actors because they're fucking lip-syncing. The lip-sync guy in charge, you would hear him in the headset: "The music, Sidney," and he would say, "Not now, Bubie. We'll fix it in post." Everything was about fixing it in post. Well, they couldn't fix it in post, so they couldn't use the medium closeups.

I guarantee you—God rest his soul—that Sidney would not want this picture on his résumé. One of the reasons why I went back to working as a second [assistant camera operator] was that my brother was doing a very difficult picture with Sidney, *The Verdict* [1982], and I would drive him to work and all that stuff.

I'm sitting on a crane with Sidney. Sidney always wanted to go up on the crane and see the shot. Sidney always had to visually see the shot. There were no video monitors or anything back then. I took the seat next to Sidney and rode the crane up. We were talking and *The Wiz* came up.

I said, "Didn't we shoot here?"

He said, "Don't remind me, Gary. Yes, I know. But this will work for this shot." It seemed as if I touched a nerve. So Sidney says to me, "Was that fun for you?"

I said, "No, it wasn't fun, Sidney, to be honest with you. It was stressful because you got so stressed out."

He said, "Gary, I'm going to tell you this, and this is true. I would rather do twenty one-million-dollar pictures in my career than that one twenty-million-dollar picture. Wouldn't you rather do twenty pictures with me for one million than that one twenty-million picture?"

I said, "Sidney, I'd go anywhere with you, but yes."

And it was true. If there was any other director on *The Wiz* and that happened, they would have got fired, but Universal knew that only Sidney could finish the picture in eight to ten weeks mostly using one camera.

COMMERCIAL BREAK #2

JOHN MAZZONI (GRIP): The [union] hall called me: "John, we're sending you on location. You got to meet the van downstairs." So I met this Winnebago. "Where are we going?" I forgot who the electrician was. He said, "You're the key grip. Just in case we need anything."

It was like a quick commercial all the way up in Armonk with Terry Bradshaw. Terry Bradshaw just won the Super Bowl. I said, "Oh my God, I'm going to meet Terry Bradshaw." I'm just a kid. I'm twenty years old. I get into the Winnebago and I'm looking out the window. We get to the location—we're there—and I go, "Oh my God, this is going to be unbelievable."

"This is a Red Man Chewing Tobacco commercial, and you just listen to what I say. We've got no lighting here, John. We've just got to put the sticks down, and we're going to put the camera on and everything will be fine."

"All right." I don't know what I'm doing.

"All right, listen, we're going to put Terry Bradshaw on this log fence. Terry sat on the fence and he feels funny on it because it's round. Could you make a little platform for him?"

"Me? You want me to make a platform?" I have to get a piece of wood. I have to figure it out. So I said, "But how big should I make it?" He goes, "I don't know." He says, "Why don't you find out how big his ass is?"

So I go over to the Winnebago. Terry opens his doors: [Southern accent] "Can I help you?"

I said, "Mr. Bradshaw, I'm the grip. They want me to build a little platform so you could sit on the fence, but I don't know how big your ass is." So he turns around and he says, "Measure it, kid."

So, I measured his ass and I got twenty-seven inches. I'll never forget it. I measured twice. I said, "Okay, thank you, sir."

"Okay, kid. I'll see you later." And I built this wooden thing and he sits on it.

He is going to sit on it and sings this song. And we're waiting and waiting. I look and see this camera I've never seen before. It's a big camera. It's a television camera. It was a big, square camera—it was weird. So I look at the camera—I'm looking in it. I was fucking around and I went, "Oh, this is nice," and I point it up at the sky. I'm looking all around. All of a sudden, about ten minutes later: "Somebody's burned the iris of the camera!" You can't point those cameras to the sun. In those days, that was really studio work.

"Come over here." We all got together. "Did anybody point this camera to the sun?"

I'm saying, "Please don't pick me. I hope nobody saw me do that."

So I go, "What? What do you mean?"

"Did anybody point that out to the sun?"

I said, "Oh, it wasn't me. It wasn't me."

The assistant cameraman says, "We can't work. We need a new fucking camera, and we have to call the city to get one up here in Armonk." It must have cost them thousands of dollars to get that camera back. What do we do?

We've got nothing to do. So I'm sitting there. I didn't know what to do. I was so scared. So, I say, "Listen, Terry, why don't you throw me a ball?" Because now we're waiting for the camera. It's going to take three hours. So he throws me a football. I caught it in my chest. I thought he broke my freaking ribs, right? I go on: "I can't wait to go back to Brooklyn and to Bensonhurst and tell all the boys I caught Terry Bradshaw's pass. Nobody's going to believe this. Nobody."

I'm all excited. So I said, "Hey, listen, why don't we choose up a game?" We've got a couple of hours. So Terry says, "I'm in."

I figured I'd get the PAs. They were young, and I was young. "Me and the three PAs against you, the producer, the writer, and another producer." So, it's four against four. So Terry goes, "All right."

We start playing the game in his horse field, right? We're playing. We're in the horse fields. We throw the ball around. We lose five to two. I'll never forget that. We were just kids, but he's drawing passes and we can't stop his passes. It's impossible. He's killing us. So, at the end of the game, he wins. I go, "Terry, would you do me a favor?" I remember. I had my work boots on, these work boots. And I had a little guinea-type cap on, this little newspaper cap—my favorite cap. I still have that cap today. I kept it because of that day. So I say, "Terry, you've got to throw me a pass. You've got to throw me a pass like it's Lynn Swan."

He says, "Yeah, go ahead, Johnny Boy," and I run and everybody's going, "Go, Johnny, run, run!" and I'm running in this horse field, and all of a sudden he stops and he puts the ball down, and they're all laughing, and so I stopped. I go, "This son of a bitch ain't going to throw me a pass." He made me run all the way. All of a sudden, he throws it. I go, "Motherfucker." I start running. "Oh, I've got to catch this fucking ball. I can't miss this ball. This is the best day of my life." I'm running. "Please, God." I stretch out diving straight out—the ball goes into my hands! I catch the ball, I hit the ground, and the ball flies out—incomplete pass—and I slide into this mud which isn't mud—it's horse shit.

I have horse shit all in my clothes, horse shit in my mouth. I'm on the floor—missed a pass—feeling like a real jerk. I get up and they're laughing. I come walking with the football and he goes, "Hey man, you stink."

I go, "It's horse shit." It was in my mouth. He goes, "Well, get that guy out of here. I don't want to smell him anymore." We do the commercial. They have to go out—they have to get me new clothes. I have no clothes to wear. I'm covered in horse shit. They went through like a dollar store in town, and I remember because I came out with the new clothes and he goes, "You smell a little better, Johnny Boy,"

I go, "Thank you."

And he sat on the fence with his guitar and he's singing, "Hey, mister, what you chewing? Chew what all the pros are chewing. Red Man, the king of the pros."

I was a singer at the time. And I said to him, "Why don't you give it a little more—" I'm trying to tell him because he's singing, "King of the *pros*," and I said, "How about 'King of the *pro-ohs*'?" and he did it.

He goes, "Listen, I don't want to talk to you."

I have to get back to the Winnebago. Terry says, "He isn't coming with us." They got me a t-shirt and new pants, and they sent me in a car service from Armonk back to my house. It cost them about $200 then. I'll never forget. He wouldn't take me,

If you want to smell my hat, I'll bring it here next week. It has a little tint of horse shit smell after forty-six years.

The Brink's Job

(1978)

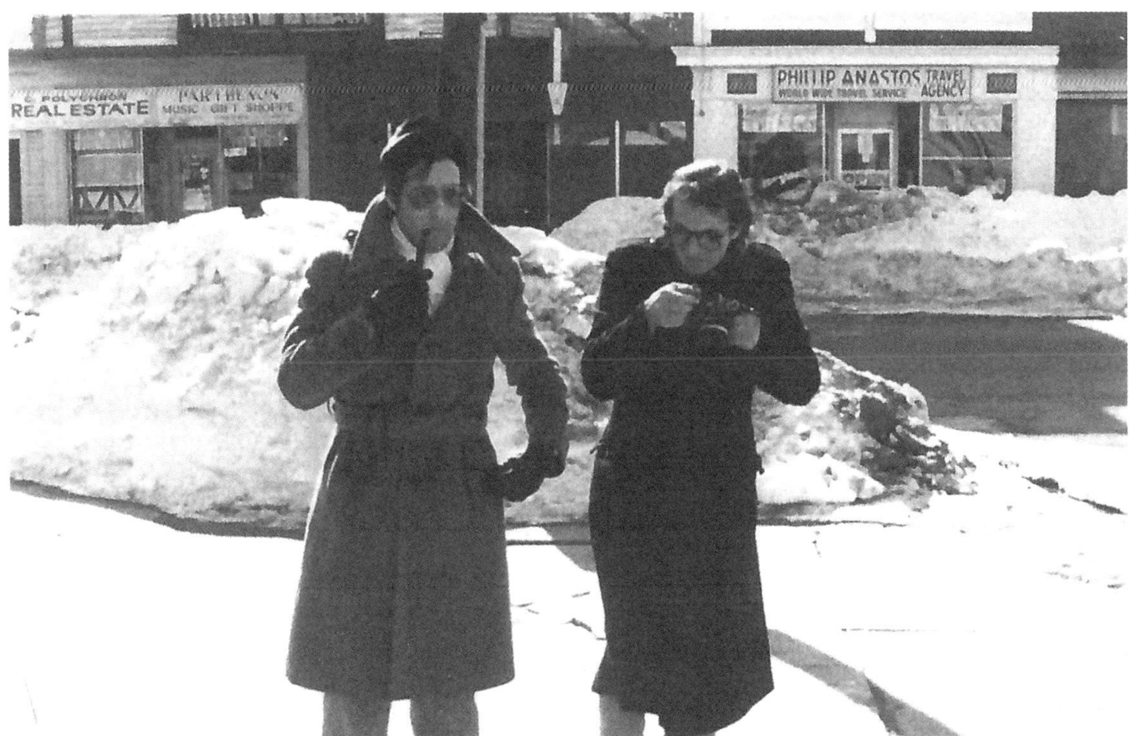

GARY MULLER (**ASSISTANT CAMERA OPERATOR, *THE BRINK'S JOB***): We went to Boston in February to do a screen test of some local talent, real mobsters. That's when the big snowstorm hit. Shut the whole city down for weeks. I was stuck in a Copley Plaza Hotel. Couldn't go anywhere. The hotel ran out of food. To get out of the hotel, you had to climb out the first-floor window and you're literally walking across Copley Plaza, twelve feet up in the air, walking across cars.

We're in pre-production now. Billy [Friedkin, the director] was having problems with the set. They wanted to match the real locations [of the depicted robbery] and details. Dean Tavoularis, famous production designer, built them exact replicas. There was no way to get light in. Billy was like, "This sucks."

RANDY JURGENSEN (**PRODUCTION SERVICES, *THE BRINK'S JOB***): I learned that Billy Friedkin, when he was replicating something—I mean, it had to be right down to the T. We're making movies about the 1940s, the ties that the people are wearing better be from the forties. That's the way that

William Friedkin and Dean Tavoularis in Boston working on *The Brink's Job*. Photo courtesy of the Margaret Herrick Library, Academy of Motion Picture Arts and Sciences.

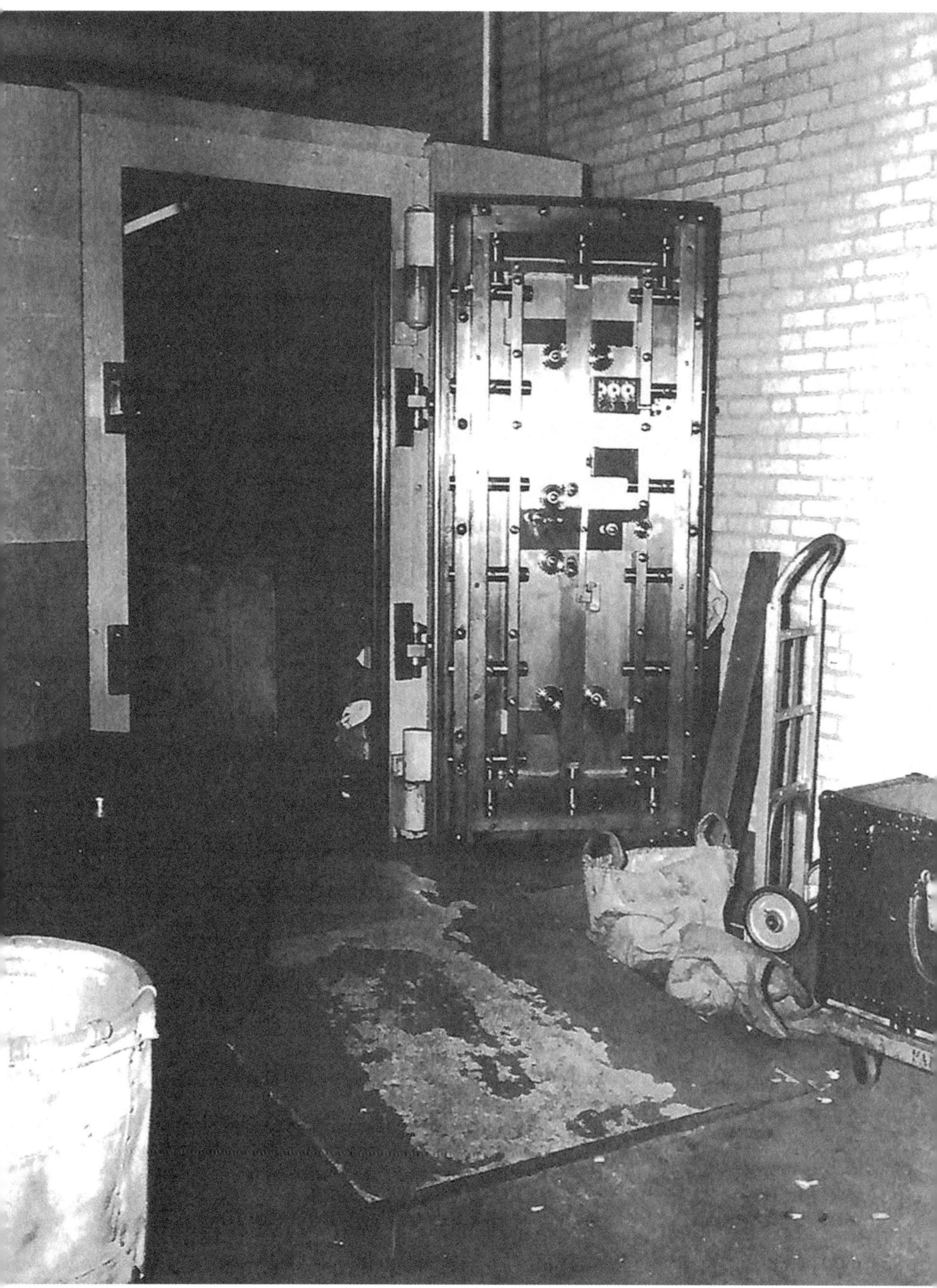

he was, and he paid attention to every one of those details.

True story—the original Brink's doors, they were out in Minnesota. Guess who had to go out to Minnesota to get those doors? They flatbedded the doors in from Minnesota, up to Boston. Just for that scene.

I went to the bank. I signed out on one hundred and eighty thousand real dollars. Not prop dollars. I have pictures of me and Billy and them dancing in the money that they spread out all over the floor.

GARY MULLER: Billy picked Andrej Bartkowiak to shoot *Brink's Job*.

I said to my brother, "Here it comes."

"What do you mean?"

"He's gonna fire Andrej. We're going to the DP [director of photography] store."

I could [tell] he was gonna fire Andrej. He came back from New York one Monday morning. I mean, he was disgusting. He walked around in the same black sweatpants. The guy's making six times as much as everybody else.

We're, like, into week number three of our five-week prep up in Boston. We get going and we're supposed to shoot every Friday night. We go out and do a test. He comes to Billy and says, "Listen, it's my wife's birthday. Can Hank [Muller] shoot the test with you? Because I gotta go back to New York."

"The break of your life, and you want to take off for a fucking birthday party? Just so you can go fuck your wife? You know what, pack your fucking bags. You're fired."

"Billy, Billy, I got to go. I can't do this stuff now."

In front of like six or seven people. He just fired him. Andrej pleaded.

"No, get the fuck out of here."

Called production manager. He was done. So what do we do for a DP? Dino has this great idea. Dino says "Billy, let's bring in some Italian DPs. We'll check them out."

Every Wednesday some Italian DP was flying in. I couldn't even remember their names. Every Friday night we would go to this pier in Boston. It was dark and they had streetlights. He wanted natural lighting. He gave the guy four hours to light and then would shoot it and then we'd get a phone call the next day: "How was it?" "Okay."

Come Monday morning, we'd all go down to the Cheri Theatre in Boston. We're watching the dailies—Billy says, "Send this wop back. This sucks."

I went through nine cameramen in preproduction! Billy wasn't ready to shoot the picture, so he kept on stalling.

TOM PRIESTLEY, JR. (CAMERA OPERATOR, *THE EXORCIST, THE FRENCH CONNECTION*): It was his [Friedkin's] excuse to buy more time, usually. That's usually what he does. He creates a situation. In fact, they asked me to come work on it, but I had enough of Billy.

GARY MULLER: Dino [De Laurentiis] was doing *The Blue Lagoon* [1980]. He was having a lot of problems with that. Billy and Dino weren't getting along. I'll never forget: De Laurentiis flies in from Italy, from Hawaii or whatever resort they had that turkey *The Blue Lagoon* shooting—"Billy, what are you doing to me? You're bankrupting me."

I never could forget what Billy said to him: "Yeah, Dino, I'm trying to fucking bankrupt you, you dumb guinea." Just like that.

Finally, we have to start shooting. He [Friedkin] turns to his gaffer, Norman Leigh, who was a very famous [Local] 52 gaffer: "Let me ask you something—the DP tells the gaffer where to put the lights, right? You know what?

The actual door from the robbery the film was based on.
Photo was found in Dean Tavoularis's research for *The Brink's Job*.

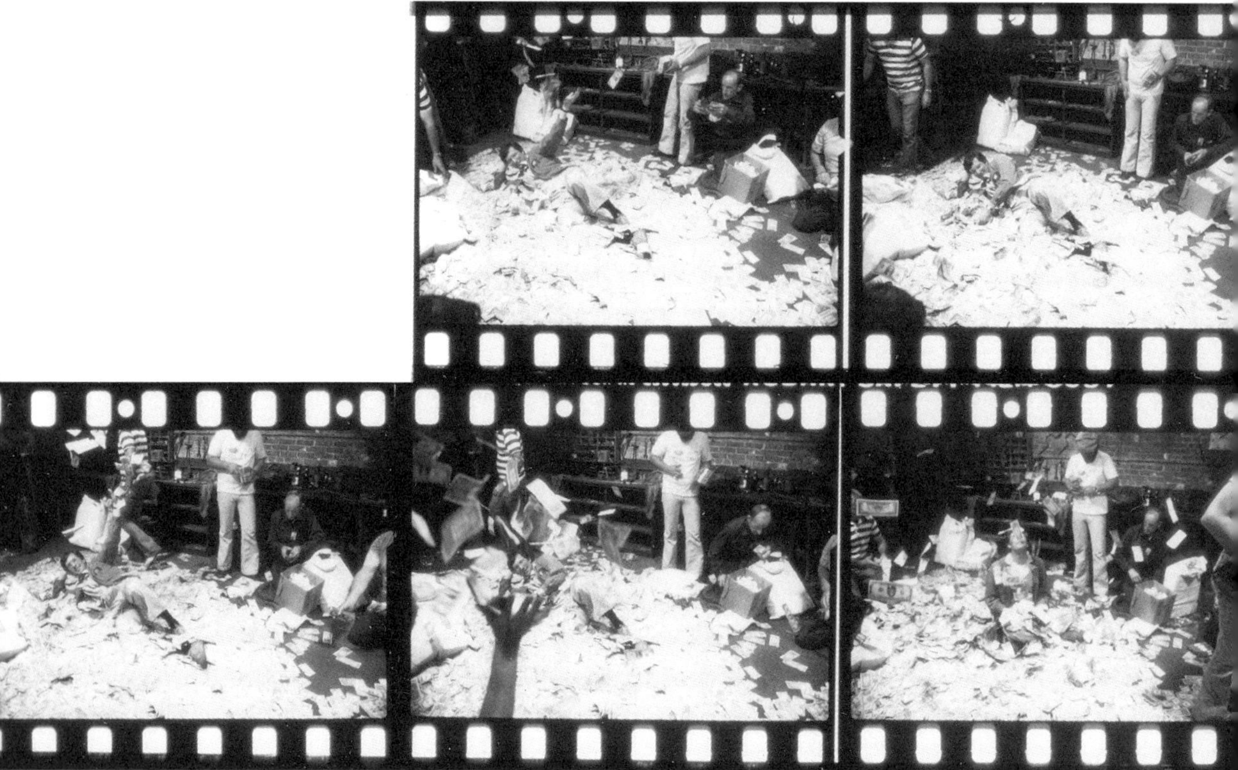

What the fuck do I need a DP for? I got a great camera crew, great operators—Norman, you're my fucking cameraman. We'll start shooting on Monday."

He's making the gaffer a fucking DP. We knew that he would always hire the wrong guy the first time, to stall production for two or three weeks so he could get ready.

Then the union came in—"Norman can't be the cameraman." The unions were strong. Billy says, "Well, put a standby on him," so we had a standby—you know what a standby is, right? A union [Local 644] guy standing by—do nothing, be like a Teamster and jerk off—and then finally, years later, they said that was illegal, you can't do that. Standbys went away.

And then we got a delay another week while we figure out what to do with Norman, and we start shooting. It's okay. It's not the best, and Billy's yelling at the operators. We don't have a leader. We're running a—I don't know—maybe back then it was a ten- or twelve-million-dollar picture. We're running around. It's chaotic. Billy is getting more and more frustrated. I hoped we'd all get fired. I've been in Boston six months already, and I think we've only shot, like, four days.

Friedkin told me many times in private, he tries to do the shit stuff the first two weeks in the movie, because his concept was, later on, you're comfortable with the actors, you're comfortable with the crew, you know what their limits are. You do the crap first. [If] you got enough money left over, you do it over again. At the end of the picture, you throw that shit away. Once he told me that every picture we did, I would say, "Oh, I guess we're not going to use this shit."

"Oh yeah, don't tell anybody," and then, as he became "Billy Friedkin," it became more obvious.

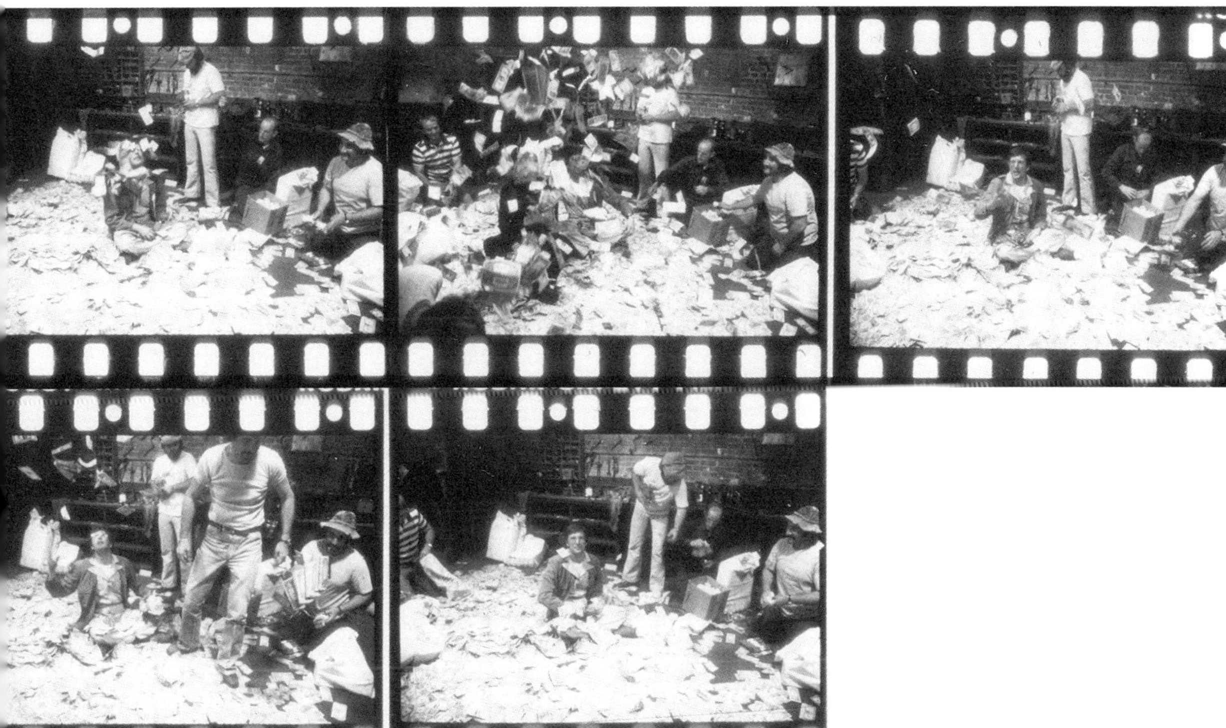

RANDY JURGENSEN: He's tireless. I mean, when we're outdoors and if the sun wasn't exactly right, we waited until the sun was right for Billy to get his shot.

GARY MULLER: The market downtown Boston at Faneuil Hall, which was just reopened back then. It was really beautiful. It was a long walk-and-talk. Peter [Falk] and Allen [Goorwitz/Garfield] were talking about robbing something and we shot the first couple days, and it was totally overcast. Of course, the next day it was sunny. We can't shoot, so we got to do something else.

The producer says, "Let's reshoot."

No, no, no, that was too good. We will be on cloud watch. So, wherever we were, if there was a rumor that the clouds were coming, we'd run downtown to get ready and then of course if the clouds didn't come over we didn't shoot.

RANDY JURGENSEN: In 1968, I got into a shootout with a low-life. When I say "low-life" I don't mean it the way it's used now, but low in their life in the mob. They were soldiers, but they were not made men. A uniformed cop was shot and killed by these guys. I then exchanged shots, got them both. They were headed for the electric chair. There was a fifty-thousand-dollar price put on my head and the district attorney's, and also the judge.

I'm up in *Brink's*. I have a beard, not a big beard. Louis DiGiaimo [casting agent], he also has a beard. We're sitting in a restaurant, and it's got the purple grapes and all that stuff. It's really Italian. I'm sitting with Billy Friedkin, Louis DiGiaimo, and all the guys. Two federal people show up while I'm having dinner. They come over to me, and they don't know me from Louis because of the beards.

"Who's Randy Jurgensen?" I was quick to come back with, "Who are you?"

I don't know who these people are. "We work for the federal government. We are Coast Guard agents. We're here to inform you that one of the prisoners that you arrested has escaped. The mob broke them out of prison."

I had to catch a plane immediately to come home. I then had twenty-four-hour, seven-days-a-week protection for my home. I got kids and a wife. Once I saw that that was secured, I then flew back, to finish *Brink's*.

GARY MULLER: We had all these cars, so every car had a Boston Teamster, and it was crazy. William Bratton, my driver, had a gun strapped to his ankle. They all were carrying. They were all hoodlums.

STEVEN FELDER (PRODUCTION ASSISTANT, *THE BRINK'S JOB*): I got all the cars for *The Brink's Job*. It was pretty straightforward. I mean, I have some tales of, you know, dead Teamsters [on the] payroll in Boston.

GARY MULLER: There were always picture cars for the Boston Teamsters—every driver in each car. They did phantom drivers, and they were paying their wives. They were paying people that were dead. Later the FBI came in and they got Billy Bratton, the driver, on mail fraud, and this and that. He went to prison.

The four are members of Local 25, International Brotherhood of Teamsters, in Boston's Charlestown section. They were charged in a 31-count indictment handed up by a federal grand jury with hiring "no shows," making false statements, racketeering, extortion, and obstruction of a criminal investigation.

Arrested were Joseph F. "Gus" Manning, 74, trustee and general organizer of Local 25, of Somerville; William C. Bratton, 46, of Medford; and Hartley Greenleaf, 51, of North Reading. Indicted was Ernest C. Sheehan Sr., 64, of Braintree.

All four were charged with violating a federal racketeering statute which carries a maximum penalty of a $25,000 fine or 20 years in prison.

During the filming of the Brinks story in Boston's North End in 1978, starring Peter Falk and produced by Dino De Laurentiis, movie spokesmen had complained about the pressure exerted on them by the Teamsters union.

Lawrence Sarhatt, special agent in charge of the FBI Boston office, said the Teamsters "routinely supplied drivers for motor vehicle equipment such as chauffeured limousines, campers, lighting equipment, etc., used by the movie industry when shooting on location throughout most of New England."

Some of the indictments charge the defendants violated mail fraud and interstate transportation laws by issuing paychecks to individuals who performed no work.[20]

—UPI, June 12, 1981

RANDY JURGENSEN: We were all brought before a grand jury. There were no indictments. There was no nothing. It mainly focused on the payoffs, who we were paying off, or who they were paying off and so forth.

STEVEN FELDER: We didn't have a [Teamster] captain for a couple of weeks, until this guy got paroled. [laughs] They stole my Bolex camera system out of one of the trucks. It was a pretty amazing experience, but they wouldn't let me in the Guild. I left for another job to get into the DGA [Directors Guild of America].

RANDY JURGENSEN: A little later on—not connected—a Teamster was shot and killed.

GARY MULLER: And the fucking dailies. Billy would call Joey Violante [technician, DuArt Film Lab] every morning on a daily: "How were the dailies? In focus? Out of focus?" Joey

20 "The FBI Said Today Four Teamsters Have Been Indicted . . . —UPI Archives," United Press International, June 12, 1981, https://www.upi.com/Archives/1981/06/12/The-FBI-said-today-four-teamsters-have-been-indicted/6270361166400/, retrieved October 9, 2023.

and Otto [Paoloni, technician, DuArt] did all the movies of the sixties and seventies, up until he retired. They'd have to tell producers what got fucked up, and then he'd have to tell them, "You have to do this shit over again. It's no good."

You have to picture this: we're in Boston, in a Cineplex. It's a Friday afternoon. There's about twenty of us. Peter Falk decides to invite himself, which is a no-no for Billy. Peter Falk walks in with his wife and Friedkin yells out, "Who's that trashy broad you got there?"—just ranting and raving and bagging on him—"Get the fuck out of here."

It was a very tense day because we were having problems. Billy says, "This looks like shit. What the fuck are we gonna do? This is not representative of this movie."

The light inside [the Brink's vault room] coming in was too ambient, was too bright, and Norman didn't know how to pump up the light inside, so it was underexposed, and it looked like shit; it looked like a homemade movie. Billy couldn't fire the guy. He's, like, on cameraman number twelve.

They go back and forth. Norman is blaming the lab, so Otto Paoloni comes up: "This is what I got to work with. Why don't you hire a fucking cameraman."

After we see this—I mean, it is shit—and Norman and Otto start yelling at one another. It was so bizarre. I'm on my knees. My brother and I are crawling out on our fucking hands and knees to sneak out.

Billy is screaming, "This is the worst shit I've ever seen!" and he whips his cock out and sprays it all over the screen, puts his fly back in his pants, and waltzes out. He stained the fucking screen so they couldn't show anything in the theater that night. The company had to pay the money.

We changed labs. We limped along for I don't know how long. We had editor Bud Smith. Billy didn't like slates. He says the editor sits on his ass in a cold room with air conditioning—let him find the scenes. Fucking Billy was nuts, and got crazier and crazier.

RANDY JURGENSEN: Whitey Bulger was running Boston at the time. There's a scene that takes place on a roof. This takes place in the 1940s. All you see are television antennas.

"Randy. They can't be here."

You have to have a meeting with *the man*. When *the man* says take down the antennas then the antennas come down. I'm double-talking here. You know, there were certain moves we couldn't make without talking to certain people. You had to get permission.

STEVEN FELDER: We had guys who had just gotten out on parole come on our set to be technical advisors for the robbery they committed twenty-five years before. They were on a set all day like celebrities. Friedkin loved that kind of thing.

RANDY JURGENSEN: I met them—Specs O'Keefe and the rest of them portrayed in the movie. One night, we go to dinner. This is a nice restaurant. We're sort of sitting on one side of the room. People [mob guys] are sitting on the other side of the room.

Paul Sorvino is a singer. One of them comes over and said, "Paul, would you sing us a little bit of opera, sing 'The Way It Is'?"

Paul says, "No, no, no, I'm tired. I'm not going to sing."

The guy then came back and mentioned a name; Paul Sorvino got up and was singing an opera.

One afternoon during the shoot I got word that the cutting room had been robbed by two masked men. The assistant editor, Ned Humphreys, was pistol whipped, and the editor, Bud Smith, was told to hand over all the exposed reels to the masked robbers. Later a call came into the production office, demanding a $1 million ransom for the film, and the Boston police were alerted. Press and television crews were all over the story, and *it was national news for three days: the film was stolen for ransom! The negative was safely stored in a lab in California, and could easily be reprinted. What the robbers took, they didn't realize was worthless.*[21]

—William Friedkin, *The Friedkin Connection*, 2013

GARY MULLER: There was this famous lock-picker. I think they got him out of jail to teach the actors how [to pick locks]. He's on parole but he's out there robbing things. Something happened and a guy didn't get paid when he was supposed to get paid.

He gets a whole bunch of his hoodlums and he goes to the editing room and he pistol whips the editor and he takes the dailies, holding them for ransom. We shut down for a day because we were fearful of something else happening. Anything to shut down.

RANDY JURGENSEN: They took it [the film reels] and wanted ransom money. The FBI come in and the FBI got the phones all set up. We knew when the phone call was gonna come. They pick up the phone and Billy says, "Yeah, this is William Friedkin . . . Yes . . . Okay . . . Listen, get a projector and put it up, then go fuck yourself," and he hung up the phone. The FBI dropped their teeth. They couldn't believe it. Billy had another copy. He never told anybody.

RANDY JURGENSEN: I'll tell you how well-calculated it was. The biggest scene in that movie is turning Boston back into the 1940s. We took three days of filming that he wanted to capture everything—the cars, the trucks, the go-carts—every single thing he wanted—Peter Falk walking through the mob.

That's the raw footage that they stuck us up to take—the most expensive shot in *Brink's*.

GARY MULLER: Then the producers finally came down to Billy: "You got two more weeks." He says, "Fine—I'll have a finished picture," because you knew the first two weeks we were going to reshoot and then probably by week nine we really get into the movie.

That job just went on and on and on. Like, I can't remember it ever ending.

STEVEN FELDER: Thirty-five years later, I'm producing *CSI* [2000-2015] and Friedkin comes to do an episode, and so now I'm his—quote unquote—boss because TV directors are subject to the restrictions of the episodic TV. We got along well. It was good.

He would just lay into the writers about the script. Saying, "I'm not doing this crap." I mean, he was a handful, but everybody knew his vision. He was responsive to me as a producer—not necessarily me personally, but to my role. We drove around all these really horrible neighborhoods in East L.A. to find what he was looking for and that was a great kind of bookend to that [*Brink's Job* experience].

GARY MULLER: Steven was a PA [production assistant.] He used to hand me a bagel and a cup of coffee every morning. I mean, I've known Steven close to fifty years, almost my whole career.

We were having an argument one day on *CSI*. It was the first and only argument we had. It was about something a video guy was playing with the GoPros, and it got screwed up. Then the executive producer tried to blame it on me. Steven comes in; I said, "Hey, dude, come on. What are you talking about? You're the best guy that I know that failed upwards from the bottom to the top. What are you breaking my balls for?"

"Yeah, you're right. You didn't fuck up. I can't blame you. I got to blame the other guy."

He says to the guy, "You're fired. Get out of my sight."[22]

21 William Friedkin, *The Friedkin Connection*, pp. 357–358.

22 Steven Felder passed away February 19, 2023, from cancer, a little over a year after I interviewed him.

6 L

Four Gunmen Steal Reels of Film About $2 Million Brink's Robbery

Special to The New York Times

BOSTON, July 28 — Three armed men handcuffed four film editors in the offices of the Brink's Productions Film Company here today, the police said, and escaped with 13 reels of valuable footage of a movie about the famous 1950 robbery of the Brink's Security Company.

The authorities dismissed speculation that the robbery might be a publicity stunt. "We are investigating this as a serious crime," said Police Superintendent John Doyle. The police suggested that the motive might be extortion.

William Friedkin, director of the $12.5 million movie, said it would be several days before the value of the stolen footage is determined. Friedkin also said he was not certain if there were copies of the film. "It may be irreplaceable," he said. There were reports that parts of the original negative were taken.

Asked for Scenes With Extras

The robbers entered the unguarded editing room on the seventh floor of the production company's Stuart Street headquarters shortly before noon and ordered the film editors to turn over specific footage, said Mr. Friedkin. "They knew exactly what had been shot and they asked for the scenes involving a lot of extras," he said. "In other words, the scenes that would be most difficult to reshoot." The sets for those scenes alone reportedly cost $1 million.

Mr. Friedkin said the movie, for which filming was scheduled to be completed next week, could be "damaged" if the footage is not returned, "but it is not our intention to reshoot the scenes." He added, however, "This is definitely not the end of the picture."

The robbers entered and left the Brink's offices by using a public elevator, said police. They gained entry to the editing room by saying they were sent by a Brink's production executive, then held the four film editors at gunpoint, handcuffed them and threatened to kill them if they did not hand over the film. The police are withholding the names of the victims, two of whom were assaulted but not seriously injured.

Superintendent Doyle said the film editors provided the authorities with only sketchy descriptions of the assailants. "They were so scared they could hardly talk," he said.

F.B.I. Has Been Consulted

The Federal Bureau of Investigation has been consulted, Superintendent Doyle said, and will enter the case if an extortion attempt is made.

Mr. Friedkin said he would not speculate on the motive for the robbery. "This is certainly not the first time film has been stolen. It usually turns out to be some disgruntled person or persons. Sometimes it is for ransom," he said. "The most important thing is that no one was badly hurt."

Police officers have now been posted in the Brink's editing room, Mr. Friedkin said, and armed guards will remain on the premises as long as the film company is in Boston.

Local Police Provided Security

Before the robbery, security on the film set was provided by local police. Peter Falk, the film's star, had a private bodyguard.

When asked for his impressions of the crime, Mr. Falk, best known as the television detective Colombo, asked with mock gravity, "How many of them were there?" A production aide then told Mr. Falk he should not discuss it with the press.

A production assistant, asked if she thought the theft was a hoax, replied angrily, "Sure, and we thought it would be a real gag to beat up a few editors and throw this place into complete turmoil, just as we're all ready to go home. You've got to be kidding."

The movie, titled "The Brink's Job" has been filmed entirely on location in Boston during the past three months. It has been financed by Dino de Laurentiis, and is due for release in December.

The film deals with the Jan. 17, 1950 holdup of the Brink's counting room at the North Terminal Garage here. Seven men wearing Halloween masks stole a record amount, first reported at $1,219,000, then later at $2,700,000. Eleven days before the statute of limitations ran out on the crime, in 1956, one of the men confessed and betrayed his fellow robbers.

$37 Billion Military Bill Agreed on by Conferees

WASHINGTON, July 28 (UPI) — House-Senate conferees agreed today on a $36.9 billion military procurement bill that includes $210 million for cruise missiles and $1.9 billion for a nuclear carrier that President Carter opposes as too costly.

Senator John C. Stennis, Democrat of Mississippi, the leader of the Senate conferees, said the bill was $1.5 billion more than Mr. Carter asked, $946 million below the House version, and $854 million above the Senate proposal.

The bill authorizes $30 million for sea-launched cruise missiles, $160 million for air-launched missiles and $20 million for ground-launched missiles.

Cruise missiles are small pilotless aircraft that carry nuclear warheads and, along with bombers and other land-based and sea-based missiles, form the United States' strategic defense against a Soviet nuclear attack.

The conferees also approved the procurement of 36 F-14 fighters at a cost of $689 million. The Administration had asked originally for only 24, but both houses added a dozen.

p n s c k p o d a a C i i b p S D e S w i s n t c

New York Times, July 29, 1978.

The Warriors

(1978)

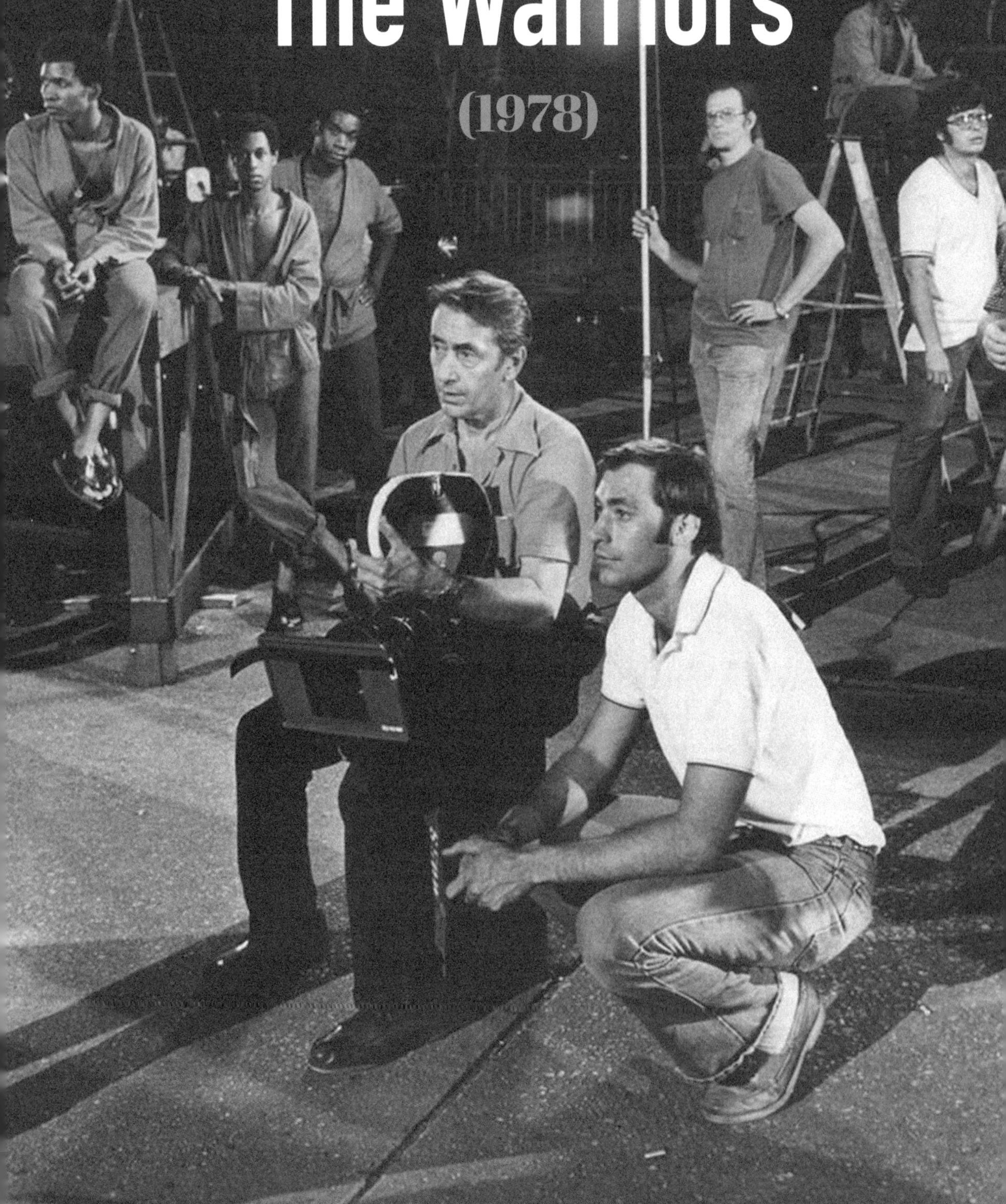

JOHN LOWRY (GRIP, *THE WARRIORS*): I'd go in when the hall was up at 57th Street, and you'd take a one-man elevator up, and you'd sit in the hall and the sliding window would open up and they'd give you a paper—go show up over there. In 1976, I went and took the test, got voted in. Then I started to get established. My father said, "Look, I opened up the door—you're in. Now, good, bad, or indifferent, you're not going to live off of my shirttail. You go out and you make your own reputation."

I enjoyed the business. I grew up in it—building car rigs out of wood in the driveway with my father and stuff. Then the first movie that I worked from beginning to end was *The Warriors*.

MICHAEL F. BURKE (ELECTRICIAN, *THE WARRIORS*): *The Warriors* was a crazy job and there was a lot of shit going on because of the subways. They were talking about how this movie was going to create violence in New York. It was a very controversial movie when it was being done.

RUSSELL ENGELS (GAFFER, *THE WARRIORS*): I think seventy-two nights of shooting.

MICHAEL F. BURKE: A lot of nights. It was crazy. It was an unbelievable time, and it was an unbelievable job.

JOHN LOWRY: It was supposed to be an eleven-week job, and four weeks was going to be nights. It ended up going over and was eleven weeks of nights. That was back when it was double time.

MICHAEL F. BURKE: I don't know if the pay scale was still triple time or it was six [hours' pay] for eight [hour guarantee]. That was the pay rate and then you got paid in cash if you wanted it on Thursday nights. We would play with the exemptions. You could go exempt or ninety-nine dependents and not have any taxes taken out. So, you would get an envelope with $4,000 on a Thursday night and then people would buy a house from one job.

JOHN LOWRY: If I had known—that's just when we bought our first home—I could have ended up paying for the whole home, really. I should have done that.

MICHAEL F. BURKE: This was 1978. You're making four grand a week. The president of the United States, I think, only made $200,000 a year back then, and we were doing $120,000 cash.

RUSSELL ENGELS: Andy Laszlo was the cameraman. He's a real gentleman—nice man. We worked for him a number of times.

TOM PRIESTLEY, JR. (CAMERA OPERATOR): I think Andy started actually in Korea. He was a combat cameraman in Korea, I believe, and then got into the union and then came on that show. Fantastic guy. He's a class act. His family was very wealthy in Hungary, but they had to leave because of the Communists.

MICHAEL F. BURKE: *The Dain Curse* [1978] was the first job we worked with Andy, and he liked us. We did *The Warriors*. We did *Somebody Killed Her Husband* [1978] with Farrah Fawcett and Jeff Bridges. We did, like, a string of movies with Andy. He tolerated me putting my costumes on and stuff like that.

RUSSELL ENGELS: Mike [Burke] was on it and Mike's father, Red. He was a character.

MICHAEL F. BURKE: Billy Kane was a prop, and he knew all the restaurants. Rusty liked to eat

The "lost summer" filming *The Warriors*, 1978. Photo courtesy of the Margaret Herrick Library, Academy of Motion Picture Arts and Sciences.

too. So we always made a point of knowing where the [good] restaurants were, wherever we were shooting. One of our favorite restaurants was an Italian place on the east side of maybe 61st Street between 1st and 2nd.

There was Ernie, who was the manager. There was a Little Mario and Big Mario, the waiters. We knew these guys, and they knew we were in the film business. So somebody would go over and pre-order, and [then] we would go. I would bring Andy back a piece of cheesecake. Andy was always watching his weight, but he loved cheesecake. I would come in and hand him the cheesecake at one o'clock and he would give me that look, like, "Ugh, thank you." It was always worthwhile endearing yourself to the accounting department, and to the DP [director of photography]. These are the key people.

MICHAEL F. BURKE: It was just the very beginning of having walkie-talkie systems. Companies didn't provide walkie-talkies for the set. You bought one of those cheap little plastic walkie-talkie systems for your department so you could try to communicate because, otherwise, someone would have to run down there and yell at somebody to put a net in.

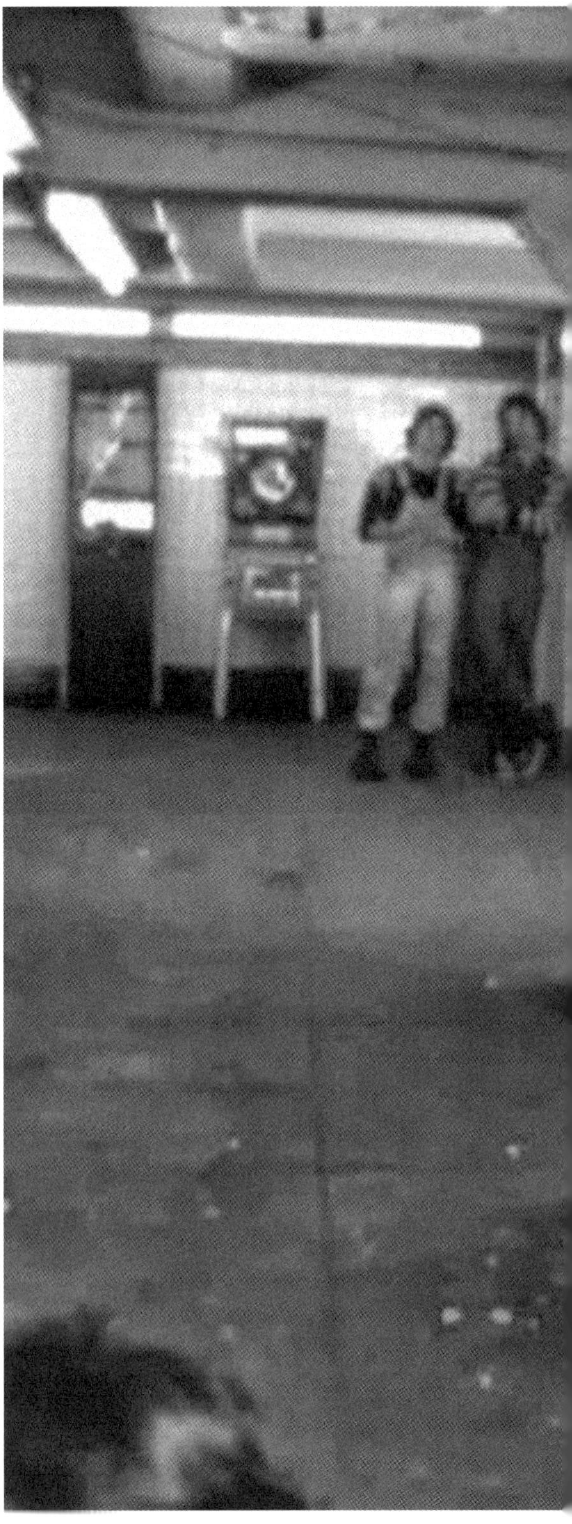

BILL KANE (PROP MASTER, *THE WARRIORS*): In the *Warriors* script, nobody was killed after the shooting in the park. But we had one actor [Thomas G. Waites], of the group of Warriors who was breaking the director's [Walter Hill] balls. When we were in the subway, it got so bad. It was not scripted, but he [Hill] says, "All right, he gets thrown off," and then the train comes in and that was it.

I feel very bad about the whole thing. We weren't getting along very well. I'm perfectly prepared to think that some of it was my fault. He did have issues—he had

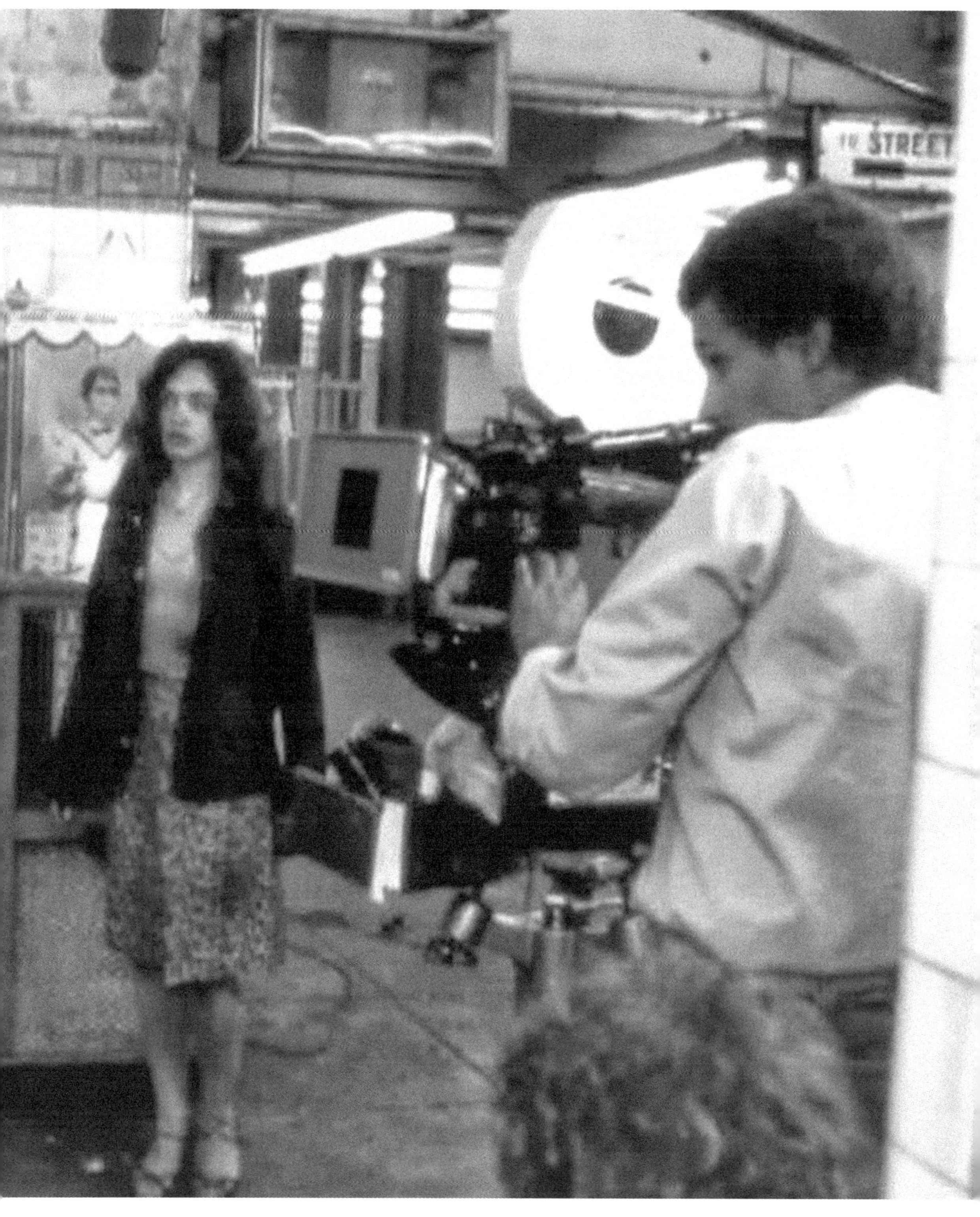

Deborah Van Valkenburgh and crew, *The Warriors*, 1978. Photo courtesy of the Margaret Herrick Library, Academy of Motion Picture Arts and Sciences.

some problems in his life and it just wasn't working. So I took him out of the movie and did a quick rewrite and gave a lot of his material to the Michael Beck character. I'm not proud of this at all. I think had I been a better director, I might have gotten through to him better. But he was, we felt, beginning to be a disruptive force. He's since apologized. He's written me a couple letters.[23]

—Walter Hill, interview with *Screen Rant*, October 19, 2022

MICHAEL F. BURKE: I was in charge of the timecards and stuff like that. There was a person on the job, a girl who was following the production. She wasn't paid, but she was just following and had an interest in the film world. Maybe she was a director's assistant or an intern. We became buddies.

I think she worked during the daytime. So I would say, "You mean you've got a regular job and you're doing this and you're not getting paid? That's crazy."

I said, "You know what? Let's have some fun. I'm going to make a timecard out and put it with your name with your hours, and I'll submit it as a joke with the electric department." This was in November. We make out the timecard and I submitted it for sixty hours: forty hours regular and twenty hours overtime and submitted it. The following week, the paycheck shows up for her and I thought, "I can't believe they paid this." So, I give it to her.

She says, "What am I going to do with this?"

I said, "I don't know. I put it in, and they paid it. This is crazy."

We then broke for Thanksgiving. She had Thanksgiving dinner with three brothers who are all lawyers. They said, "You can't cash that check. If you cash that check, it's fraud, and if you don't give it back it's going to be on the books, but it won't be balanced."

She hands the check back and says, "My brother said we've got to get the check back." So, we go up to Frank Marshall, who's the producer. I was friendly with Frank too, because I used to bring him Irish coffee from our truck.

Celeste and I go up to Frank and say, "We need to talk to you for a second."

He said, "Why? What's up?"

And I explained the whole situation. I said, "We did not do this with the intent of taking any money from anybody, and we don't know what to do with the check, so we figured if we give it to you as the producer, you would be understanding." He says, "Fine, I'll take care of it. No problem."

Larry Gordon is the executive producer. There was a bad day in the office and the producer has had it up to here, and he calls John Stark [unit production manager] into the office about shit that's going on on the job, like locations they've lost or whatever it is.

He's yelling at John and says, "And besides that, there's people on the fucking payroll that are not even working on this job."

John Stark looks at him as if to say, "What are you talking about?"

"People are being paid here that are not even working on this movie."

"I don't know what you're talking about."

Larry Gordon now has the paycheck, and he hands the paycheck to John Stark, and he's now a puddle of pee on the floor. He's completely caught off guard and is now being crucified and has no answer for anything. "How many other people are not on this fucking job and being paid?"

You can imagine the venom that was flowing out of him at that point. He was saying to me, "You motherfucker. You fucking ruined my career. I'm going to fucking kill you."

And now I'm on my knees in the phone booth, cowering in the corner of a phone

23 Warren Elliott, "The Warriors Director Regrets One Main Character's Death," Screen Rant, October 19, 2022, https://screenrant.com/warriors-movie-fox-death-walter-hill-response/, retrieved June 4, 2024.

booth. The phone doesn't even reach the ground and I'm lying on the ground with the phone while he's cursing at me: "This is the last day you are ever going to work in the film business again. I am going to fucking kill you."

I'm thinking, "Oh, my God."

The additional complication is that they send the check back to California because there's an accountant in New York but there's also a California film accountant, so they have to send the check back to California to be canceled and they want to know why it was canceled. The accountant in California now finds out what it's about and now he's furious that he issued a check to somebody who wasn't on the job and wants to know who does the timecards and who is in charge of this department, and it's me. This guy now wants my scalp. It comes back that Michael Burke cannot be on the job. He's not to get a paycheck because if this guy Dan Bernstein [the California accountant] finds Michael Burke, he's going to kill him.

I told Rusty [Russell Engels] what had happened. He was aghast. I said, "Russ, I took the check. It was not meant on purpose or anything, and we gave it back to Frank Marshall, the producer," and he said, "Okay,"

RUSSELL ENGELS: He got in trouble for that. He finally had just turned it in and admitted that mistake, and they weren't too happy with that—that they had to get rid of that evidence, I guess.

MICHAEL F. BURKE: So, after work, there's a meeting that goes on with John Stark, Rusty, and Andy Laszlo the DP. [Russ Engels] said, "The issue is that you [Stark] did not check the timecards. So, because you failed at your end, you want him [Burke] to go and—and if he goes off this job, I'm leaving this job as well." Andy Laszlo, the DP, says "Rusty's not leaving this job. I'll tell you that right now." So I got to stay on the job. But I am now going to work as my sister. I did the last month of the job as Glynnis Burke. I would still do the timecards and everything, but I had another electrician sign everything and would go hide when California would come to deposit the money.

Walter Hill was the director, and Frank Marshall would say, "Hey, Glynnis, how are you?" They knew about it and laughed. I tell you, it had a happy ending, but it was a lesson learned to think twice before you decide that something is funny.

RUSSELL ENGELS: Mike was a lot of fun. I guess he pushed it a little too far with the payroll [laughs].

MICHAEL F. BURKE: On *The Warriors*, we had three or four cases of beer delivered to our tailgate every night. It was a long hard job, and there were other substances that were readily available. But that was not unique to our job.

One time we were shooting over in Riverside Park at 96th Street, and there was a deluge, and they couldn't shoot anymore. So we wrapped early, about one o'clock in the morning. Billy Hines was driving the John Weber generator truck. It was a big generator truck. Normally at one o'clock in the morning, I go home and get a good night's sleep. But no—we were like, "It's one o'clock in the morning. We just had lunch. We could go out now. So let's go to the after-hours bar, over on 81st Street and First Avenue."

We double-parked the tractor trailer at two o'clock in the morning on First Avenue and we'd go into this after-hours club. Everybody's doing blow. You go there until five or six o'clock in the morning. You come out, put the sunglasses on, and then go home or go back to work. It was a crazy time. This was 1978. The drug world was quite expansive in the film industry and all of society back then.

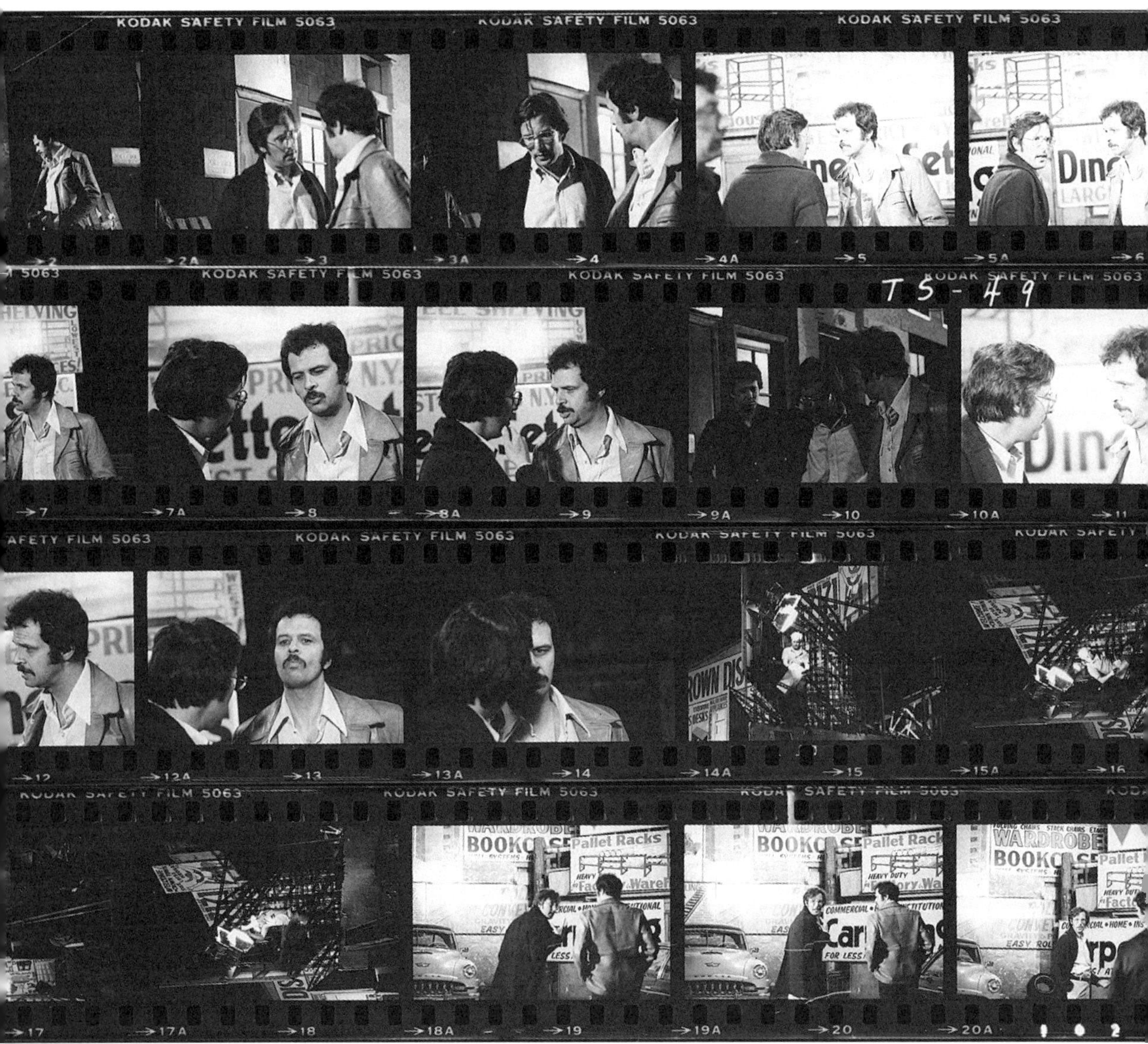

Randy Jergensen and William Friedkin on set. Image courtesy of the Margaret Herrick Library, Academy of Motion Picture Arts and Sciences.

Cruising

(1980)

GARY MULLER (ASSISTANT CAMERA OPERATOR, *CRUISING*): My girlfriend was the producer–production manager. Basically Billy [Friedkin, director] tried to put together a strong crew because of the subject material. He didn't want a whole bunch of new people on the crew. He wanted people who knew each other because we knew we had to swallow a lot. No pun intended. We would be very committed.

RANDY JURGENSEN (SECURITY AND THE REAL-LIFE SUBJECT OF *CRUISING*): We went to Texas, he [Friedkin] was trying to buy a book called, I believe, *Honor and Money*. But it didn't work out. We were on our way back from Texas. He said to me, "Randy, you did a stint working on [the murder of] gays in the City and so forth and so on."

I said, "Yeah, I did. I got a gold shield outta that. I broke that case. Why?"

He said, "I'm buying a book—it's written by Gerald Walker—called *Cruising*, and I'm buying it for the title only." He said to me, "Randy, I don't want you to read the book."

I said, "Okay."

To this day, I've never read the book.

He said, "You're going to tell me all the things that you did while you were there. That's the story we're going to do."

I said, "Okay."

And sure enough, I got a call and it was Billy and he said, "Randy, I'm stuck."

I said "Where?"

He said, "No, no, I'm here in my apartment. But I'm stuck. I'm stuck on the story. I have to get the cop into the guy's apartment, but I can't go get a search. I can't do this. Nobody has to know this. How do you do it?"

I said, "Well, Billy, if I was the cop, this is what I would do." I said, "We now know that the cop knows the perpetrator's route. We know his schedule. He gets up. He runs. He gets on a bus. He goes someplace, blah, blah, blah, and the apartment is empty."

Billy is listening. I said, "Billy, I'm going up the fire escape—shimmy up the ladder—have a newspaper—stick it in the fan that's in the window—the fan will stop—and go into the apartment. I don't know what you wanted to go in there for."

He said, "Holy shit."

I said, "If somebody is going to say to me, 'What are you doing outside the fire escape?' I'm going to show them my shield. I'm going to tell them—like I did one time in a basement when we had a wiretap going on, and the super came down—I told him we're tapping for Communists."

"Communists?!?"

"Yeah. And if the cops ever showed up in uniform, I would show them my badge and wave them off and say, 'Go, go. No, I don't need any help.'"

What was gonna happen? Nothing's gonna happen to me.

GARY MULLER: Randy Jurgensen was famous for [investigating and breaking] the Harlem mosque case.[24] The shootout up there. These guys are fucking badass cops. That was the fine line—were they cops, or were they criminals? These detectives like Eddie Egan were guys you didn't want to fuck with, and obviously you didn't have a phone like you do now, but you had their phone numbers, and the people who they liked, if they got in trouble—"Here's my number—I'll get back to you."

RANDY JURGENSEN: I never fingerprinted anybody. I did place people under arrest, but they never saw me in court because I was undercover. My face was painted. I had a nickname in the Village called Sparkle. I told this to Billy. I was on 14th Street walking with them, "cruising" as they call it, and I saw the police car go by. I was scared.

The clubs would have theme nights where patrons had to dress like cops, wear only jockstraps, or even go completely nude. [Interviewer] Kermode asks if he ever visited the clubs on those nights, and Friedkin replies, "Yes, and I was the ugliest guy in the room. Nobody ever hit on me."[25]

—William Friedkin, commentary on *Cruising* DVD

RANDY JURGENSEN: Then, of course, I was able to get Billy Friedkin into the club. It was police night. Billy says, "Let's dance."

I said, "What?

He said, "Come on, Randy. Let's get up and dance!"

There I am, a New York City detective, a pretty well-decorated detective, and I'm up there dancing. So is Billy, and he's rapping. I said, "Billy, if this ever gets out . . ." He couldn't wait to tell people!

GARY MULLER: That was a movie that Billy decided he picked his favorite operator, Jim Contner, who was my partner and my brother's partner. He said to Jimmy, "You're gonna be my cameraman."

Jimmy said, "Nah, I just wanna be your operator."

"No, you're gonna be the cameraman. I don't have the money to fire you. This won't be like *The Brink's Job*. We're going to get through this together. We're going to do this together. We're gonna make it work. I promise you."

My brother and I said to Billy, "Listen, Billy, we love you, but if you do let Jimmy go, we're also gonna leave."

He said, "All right, we'll work through this."

In pre-production, Billy invites the three of us up to his apartment right off of Fifth Avenue. Had a great view—I mean, gorgeous. Of course, there's a doorman and you go out and you open the door in the foyer. I said, "This looks like the set of *The Exorcist*."

Basically, the construction crew on *The Exorcist* finished his foyer. They used the wood to make it a foyer. This was in today's market a twenty-five-million-dollar apartment. He just divorced Jean Moreau. He said, "Moe, look at this." (He used to call me Moe.) He opens a window, and I see an alley straight down the ten floors.

24 The 1972 Harlem mosque attack occurred on April 14, 1972, when a New York police officer was shot and fatally wounded at the Nation of Islam Mosque No. 7 in Harlem. The officer responded to a fake emergency call and was shot and died from his wounds six days later. The incident sparked political and public outcry about mishandling of the incident by the NYPD and the administration of Mayor John V. Lindsay. Randy was the lead detective and wrote a book about it called *Circle of Six: The True Story of New York's Most Notorious Cop-Killer and the Cop Who Risked Everything to Catch Him.*

25 Rob Hunter, "31 Things We Learned from William Friedkin's *Cruising* Commentary," Film School Rejects, September 3, 2019, https://filmschoolrejects.com/william-friedkin-cruising-commentary/, retrieved May 12, 2023.

I said, "What's that?

He said, "The other night I took out some china and bounced it off the buildings like flying saucers."

"What do you mean china?"

"Yeah, dishes—the 1800s or something—I didn't want them in the house anymore."

That's how fucked up he was. We're in there and we're talking about the mood, which is a dimly lit room. This dimly lit room is very dramatic. Billy is saying, "Okay, I want this." He whips out five or six of the most pornographic male pictures. I'm not a prude or anything, but these things are like—guys have, like, eighteen-inch private parts.

It was just crazy, and he said, "You see the shade on this? You see the light on this?" I'm not saying not to photograph these things, but this went on for, like, two hours, and then the butler—whoever was there—brought us coffee. Like I really wanted to eat cookies.

Then he said, "Now you guys go out and get a camera and just go around."

Don't forget the West Side Highway still had the overpass. It wasn't torn down yet. But when you come off the West Side Highway it used to be elevated all the way down to Lower Manhattan, where gay bars are and all that.

We'd have to go at night. We go and take the camera in the car and shoot this stuff and really looked at—okay, this is very interesting because the last time he [Friedkin] did that with a cameraman on *The French Connection* he fired him and Owen Roizman took over.

I said to Billy, "Isn't this a repeat of *The French Connection*?"

"No, no, no, no, Gary. I just need to get a feel."

"Okay, we're on board." I felt at that point in my career and my relationship with Billy I could be a little more man to man. I wasn't a kid anymore. You know, it's more like, "Hey, we want to do the best for you." He picked the look, and I thought it looked pretty well for a New York picture and in those circumstances. But the movie basically was a simple movie to shoot.

RANDY JURGENSEN: Al Pacino was chasing a killer. I chased two killers. One guy was Black, one guy was white—they were called the salt-and-pepper team.

GARY MULLER: If I remember correctly, there was only one murder, but the way the script was written it was seven, but Billy got frustrated it was taking so long, so he cut out six murderers.

RANDY JURGENSEN: I got them. I was promoted twenty-four hours later to detective for breaking that case. It took me six months. I had an apartment down there.

GARY MULLER: Now him [Friedkin] and Pacino were really on the same page and then one day he [Friedkin] says, "I don't understand this fucker. He just doesn't listen." I thought he was listening to him.

We go up to 125th Street, to the famous bridge with the humongous arch looking back at New Jersey. It's the elevated West Side Highway.

Billy says, "Okay, put the camera here, down low, 20-millimeter." Now this is Pacino's scene and it's in the movie—he's contemplating something. We got the 20-millimeter on a high hat shooting up. It was a small figure—beautifully composed, no moving—just Al Pacino sitting on the back of this bench looking up at this thing.

Billy and Al are sitting on the bench probably for thirty-five, forty minutes while we're waiting to shoot and Jimmy's [Jimmy Contner, director of photography] saying, "The light."

Billy says, "Fuck the light."

We started shooting midday. We shot all the stuff in the morning. We're shooting and shooting and reloading and reloading, shooting and shooting. Billy goes to Pacino,

"Al, you're not giving me what the fuck I want. What's the matter with you?"

Al says, "Billy, fuck you." Turns around and—think it was Burtt Harris, who was the first AD [assistant director]—he says, "Burtt, grab the fucking company. I want to take a late call tomorrow. The only fucking thing I want to do tomorrow is this scene. So, let's take twelve-o'clock call." Billy said he wanted the camera [call time for] two o'clock. He still made you come in at six o'clock in the morning.

Billy always wanted to be on set with the actors at, let's say, nine o'clock, so if we had to light, [it would be a] fucking five-o'clock-in-the-morning crew call. We'd be there at five o'clock, doing nothin', playing cards waiting and be ready by nine. Then we'd have to eat lunch at twelve[26] and he's like, "What do you mean, you motherfuckers are going to lunch? I just got here. Fuck you!" We'd have thousands of meal penalties because we couldn't go to fucking eat.

We did ninety-nine fucking takes of Al mumbling to himself over two days. That was it. Ninety-nine fucking takes. I asked Billy about it years later: "Just forget it. That guinea couldn't give me what I wanted." From that point on, Pacino—I don't remember how far into the movie it was, but the Pacino–Friedkin love turned.

Al was angry—and Billy trying to fuck him over—and his whole nuance of the character changed. I think Pacino was having some problems with the sexuality and his part with Karen Allen.

RANDY JURGENSEN: I knew Al Pacino from *The Godfather*. I said, "Al, I don't want to really overdo this—but this assignment, Al—I mean, honest to God, this assignment took a lot out of me. Six months, you know—it wasn't every night that I slept down in that apartment and stuff. I went off, and I went and got laid."

GARY MULLER: I would wrap—I'd go back and pick up my girlfriend [Jennifer Ogden]. I don't think we were married at the time, but we were living together and sitting in the production office for an hour or two and heard her side of the tragedy of the day. That made my days very long. We'd go to bed together. We get up together. We'd eat together. Unfortunately, in this Business, it was the norm.

RANDY JURGENSEN: There was a point where—I don't want to say I got sick, but there was a point where I couldn't do this anymore. I could not do it. I told the captain and that's where you see Paul [Sorvino] saying to Al Pacino, "Look, you're our last hope—you got to continue to do this. You got to do this." These are the things I told Billy.

It's on the screen. It's hard to explain, but you can see Pacino losing himself throughout the movie and especially looking in the mirror and the music playing and stuff like that. You can really see it.

TONY GAMIELLO (SET DRESSER, *CRUISING*): We were shooting what they call social clubs. They were in the basements of these old buildings. Some of them you go into, and you can see the mist in the air [because it] was so humid in these places. And after the electricians ran that cable for the lights, it looked like they came out of a coal mine. Really grungy places.

BRUNO ROBOTTI (CHARGE SCENIC ARTIST, *CRUISING*): There were some locations that were pretty disgusting, so I'm not sure that I want to . . . We actually shot in a basement where they used to have all these sex—they had shut it down because two people had died in there.

[They] opened the place, and it smelled of urine. We went downstairs. I said, "Look, let's

26 Union rules state that we have to break for a meal after six hours. If we go longer, the producers have to pay out meal penalties to all the crew members, and it can get pretty expensive, so producers generally try to avoid that.

get this freaking thing done and get the hell outta here. This is disgusting."

TONY GAMIELLO: We had to build these racks with chains that would equal like a swing seat you'd use for fisting.

GARY MULLER: The walls were paper-thin. One day, like, seven o'clock in the morning, we got the camera in there—we're all set to go, roll sound, be quiet—and we hear *chhhh-ch, chhhh-ch* . . . the guy in the next room was getting whipped. You hear a guy going, "Harder! Harder!" Billy's like, "Roll that soundtrack."

It happened again in another place. We're in the middle of the scene and the guy comes busting through the fucking door and he's got his leather mask on, and his thing is hanging out, and screaming, "You guys are interrupting my sex! It's costing me $500 from this guy!"

It was fucking bizarre, and then you gotta pay the guy off. Billy's bodyguards take the guy and calm him down. The sideshow behind the scenes of *Cruising* was better than the movie, probably.

The morgue scene at 13:00 was the first time a feature film was given permission to shoot in an actual morgue. The city's Chief Medical Examiner, Michael Baden, was fired for that decision, but he went on to a lucrative career as an expert forensic witness.[27]

RANDY JURGENSEN: There never ever had been a film set in the morgue with real body parts. That's how *Cruising* opens up. I knew Michael Baden very, very well. In fact, that's the opening scene of *Cruising,* and that's me in the morgue.

Some of the parts were found in body bags belonging to NYU's Medical Center Neuro-Psychological Division which is where he filmed a scene for The Exorcist *[1973]. An extra in that scene, a radiographer named Paul Bateson, was later charged with being the serial killer responsible for those body parts and was convicted of murder. Friedkin went and spoke to him while in custody, and Bateson admitted committing the first murder but having no recollection of the rest.*[28]

GARY MULLER: The gay community [was] in arms about it.

RANDY JURGENSEN: I did the security in *Cruising*. I'd be down there with a radio—long-distance shots at night and stuff like that. I'd be on the radio on a separate band, and I would be talking in general to the camera man: "We're good. He's good."

GARY MULLER: But we were driving around doing shots, and hundreds of protesters downtown screaming because I think word got out that Billy altered the script and how it was a gay killer killing gay people. I don't remember who the *Village Voice* reporter was that wrote the story [Arthur Bell].

The blowup began when the film was shooting on location in Greenwich Village last summer. Arthur Bell, a gay activist who writes for The Village Voice, spearheaded protests against the production, even urging harassment and sabotage to shut the company down.

Bell was quoted as saying, "I feel like the Godfather of the gay movement. I put out a contract on Friedkin's movie, and I feel confident that it can be stopped. If it gets released, we'll hit the distributors . . . The script has no social value; everyone comes out looking bad—cops, gays, even the city."[29]

—*Washington Post*, February 18, 1980

27 Hunter, "31 Things We Learned from William Friedkin's *Cruising* Commentary."

28 Hunter, "31 Things We Learned from William Friedkin's *Cruising* Commentary."

29 Gary Arnold, "'Cruising' Off Course," *Washington Post,* February 18, 1980, https://www.washingtonpost.com/archive/lifestyle/1980/02/18/cruising-off-course/67800f4b-23cf-4a7e-b055-3b4f643fdbc3/, retrieved May 16, 2023.

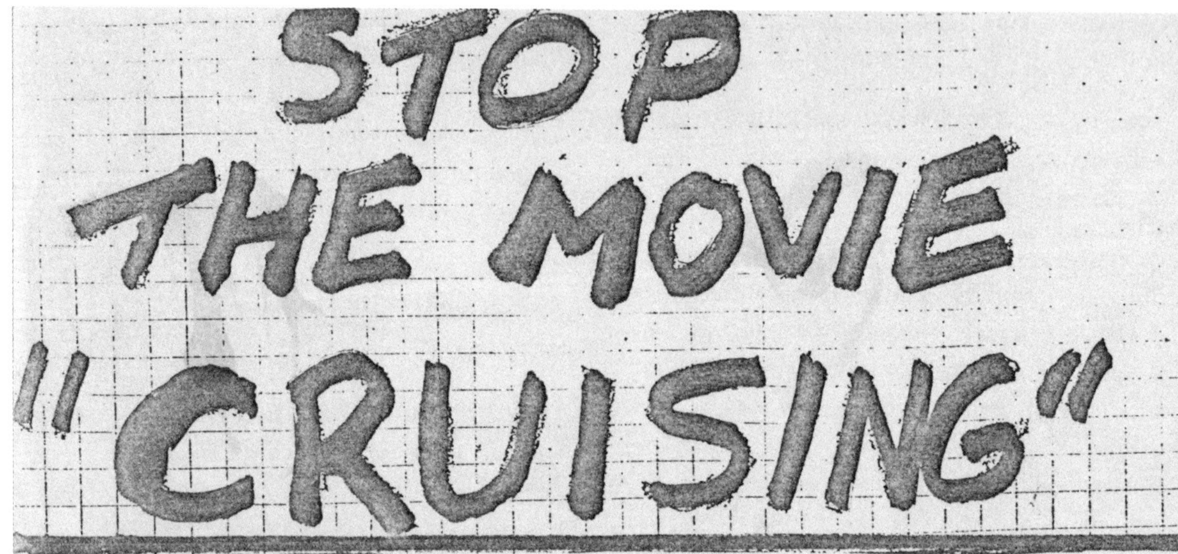

STOP THE MOVIE "CRUISING"

IS THIS FREE SPEECH?

OUR right to free speech and the right to redress grievances were trampled to dust last summer during the demonstrations. We were attacked by the police time and time again for merely assembling.

THE City not only supported, but financially backed, the filming against the protests of the majority of Lesbians, Gay males and many liberal and revolutionary organizations. Three Gay bars were raided only a day after they had cancelled their contracts with the film.

NUMEROUS attempts to meet with the filmmakers met with zero results.

THE City government decided that only Big Business had the right to "free speech" and funded it with OUR tax dollars to boot!

WHY WE'RE AGAINST THE FILM

MURDERERS of Lesbians, Gay males and Transpeople often get only misdemeanor charges. Isn't that encouragement enough for anti-Gay bigots without a film depicting us as the meek seducers of murder? Isn't anti-Gay hysteria widespread enough without a film showing Gays murdering Gays?

IT'S still too difficult for the vast majority to come out without a film depicting our streets as alleys of death.

GAY SEX IS NOT A PROBLEM

WE'RE not objecting to sexual content or to S & M and Leather subjects. Now, however, it has become a question of defending this segment of the community -- and the community as a whole -- from attack. Lesbians, Gay males and Transpeople across the continent must know that we can organize for the right to live our lives as we choose to live them. Hollywood flab and the city government cannot dictate our rights on whim and profit.

for further information phone:

GAY ACTIVISTS ALLIANCE

674-4198

"Stop the Movie 'Cruising'" New York Public Library.

TONY GAMIELLO: They were recruiting gays from the community for extras, so select pages of script would be released. They knew what was in the script, and they would know where they were shooting, and a lot of times there would be protesters to greet us.

GARY MULLER: They were always protesting, "Hey, ho, hey, ho, movie crews gotta go!" Trying to run us out of the area. We had police protection, and we would have to park our cars, like, fifteen miles away, and then they'd bring us to the location.

Bell had also called upon gay men the production had hired as extras and background color to "be aware of the consequences" of the picture; about twenty of those men quit, and some who remained served as spies for the community, leaking valuable, confidential information about the company's movements, which allowed activists to better disrupt location shoots.[30]

GARY MULLER: Somebody had loose lips. I don't know if somebody left sides somewhere—somebody left a script somewhere that was stolen or given. I don't know. I know there was subterfuge, and we never got call sheets.

RANDY JURGENSEN: Call sheets or not, I mean, they just knew. They just knew where we were, especially at night.

GARY MULLER: We were told where to report, and somehow leaks were still coming out. The office staff was all a mess and very tight-lipped, and there were very few people who had access to where we were going—what we were doing and one-liners.[31]

30 Jason Bailey, "Making Sense of 'Cruising,'" March 21, 2018, https://www.villagevoice.com/2018/03/21/making-sense-of-cruising/, retrieved May 16, 2023.

31 Advance schedules with essential information. They are called "one-liners" because of their brevity.

TONY GAMIELLO: If we were shooting outside some nights, you had people blowing whistles to screw up our sound. You had people on fire escapes with mirrors to reflect light to screw up our lighting. Everybody felt a lot of tension because there were protesters everywhere. You're allowed to peacefully protest and as long as you don't do any violence, but it was screwing up the shoot. It made it much more difficult when everybody was on edge.

GARY MULLER: There is a headline in the *New York Post*. There's a picture of my assistant, the late Scotty Rathner, holding a slate up—a whole fucking headshot of him doing the slate—and now everybody knows who this guy is. I mean this is, like, fucking nuts. They were out to get us.

RANDY JURGENSEN: In no time flat, when we were out in the street, you had fifty to a hundred people screaming. We couldn't get the lines out a lot of times.

GARY MULLER: Somebody found out that we were gonna do night running shots, and we rigged the vehicle twenty blocks away and had police follow cars behind it.

We had four Panaflexes on, which, at that point—usually you'd only put two cameras on the back. That was unheard of then. We'd added extra cameras to get the scene as fast as possible. The film [magazine] lasts eleven minutes and we would just roll and roll and roll until he would cut the shit out. We rehearsed it. We go down the West Side Highway. We go and make a U-turn in front of the gay place, and we come up the street. But now the driver gets confused. When we make the U-turn, we're supposed to come in front of the police barriers, not behind the police barriers.

The driver makes a big U-turn, and he winds up behind the crowd, not in front of the crowd, so the crowd now turns. Now, all of a sudden, eggs and bricks and bottles, with the six or seven of us trapped in this fucking camera car—they're pelting us with bottles. Now it becomes fearful.

We had two of Billy's detectives with us. One pretty big guy jumped on the back of the fucking camera car, started swinging at Billy and one of Friedkin's bodyguards—I mean, fuckin' cold-clocked this guy. He hit him so fucking hard he went flying out of the camera car, and then Burtt's yelling, "Drive, drive, drive!"

Lucky it didn't kill anybody. Cameras got hit. People got whacked. We'd go back to home base and everybody's spent. That's it. We're fucking done for the night. We have fucking eggs on us—the back of the camera car—broken bottles. They realized: okay, we can't do this this way.

RANDY JURGENSEN: Somebody threw a Coke bottle. It hit [producer] Jerry Weintraub. My brother took him to the emergency room. He got three or four stitches. Al Pacino is out in the street. I couldn't get any closer to him to make sure that he was going to be A-okay.

GARY MULLER: Billy Miller. God rest his soul. He passed away. He was a key grip, and he was in the back there defending us. This is like hand-to-hand combat. I mean, towards the end it got very, very dicey: "Oh, am I gonna get killed today?"

RANDY JURGENSEN: What's never told, what's never addressed, is—and I don't want to exaggerate, but on the other side of the street there were people hollering just as loud in support of the picture.

The marchers, who chanted "'Cruising' must go," gathered at dusk yesterday and went first to Pier 40, where the film company has its headquarters, the police said, then proceeded along a number of streets toward the Village, disrupting traffic. At about midnight, the police said, many of the demonstrators sat down in the street at the Avenue of the Americas and Fourth Street, blocking traffic in the Sheridan Square for up to 30 minutes. They were dispersed by about 100 police officers from different precincts. "There were a lot of them," said Deputy Police Inspector Vito Valle.[32]

—*New York Times*, July, 27, 1979

GARY MULLER: They stormed the production office a few times. It was very intense.

TONY GAMIELLO: We had a shop at Pier 40 where we would have a lot of set-dressing stuff and costuming. One day we were doing some preliminary stuff for that night shoot. There were but a few of us there as most of everybody else was at the location. We see all these guys coming up the ramp and we figured that these guys found out we had a shop and were probably protesters.

One of our guys says, "Get ready to call 911," and people are getting hammers and grip stands—they're getting ready for a fight. Well, when they get off the top of the ramp, we're ready for what the longshoreman used to call a "Pier 6 brawl" at Pier 40, but anyway we were ready for this fight, and then all of a sudden one of the production guys says, "There is the wardrobe [person]."

They were bringing these guys up and cast them as extras to come up to be fitted for wardrobe and everything! And we thought they were protesters. We're ready to beat the daylights out of them, and then it winds up, luckily, that a production guy there already recognized them.

GARY MULLER: Every day there was confrontation. The streets were blocked off and the media and protesters—it was very stressful and very intense.

32 Les Ledbetter, "1,000 in Village Renew Protest Against Movie on Homosexuals," *New York Times*, July 27, 1979, https://www.nytimes.com/1979/07/27/archives/1000-in-village-renew-protest-against-movie-on-homosexuals-cruising.html, retrieved May 11, 2023.

TONY GAMIELLO: If the police had stepped in it would have escalated. Then there would have been a riot. They tolerated certain things as long as nobody got hurt, because it's like—there's a fine line. But there again, these guys have the right to protest peacefully, but not violently. They don't have a right to do bodily harm to people.

GARY MULLER: Obviously, some of the scenes went a little bit further and more X-rated, and we did some pretty gruesome stuff that couldn't be on the film, and I always thought of that as Billy's perversion to watch at home—people putting lightbulbs where they don't belong and getting rushed to the hospital. We were in a location, and we put our lens cases in the closet and later we went in the closet to get a lens change and there's two guys in there doing their thing.

RANDY JURGENSEN: I remember we had a private screening for the protestors. At the end of the screening, Billy Friedkin walks all the way down and he's going to take questions, and the questions are getting out of hand; they're pointing fingers and people are standing up and they're shouting. Billy Friedkin can handle himself. He's a tough kid from the streets of Chicago. I ran down to the bottom of the screen to where Billy was, and I took over and I said, "What you're seeing up on the screen there—Billy Friedkin saw it in person. Because I did it. I was the cop that was there."

There was a hush that came over. But that lasted maybe about a minute. Then back they came again to attack. But I tried to take the weight. For whatever it was.

GARY MULLER: Cut to a year later—maybe two years later—I get a call—a few other people get this call: "I represent somebody who represents Billy—just deny everything."

"Okay. What are we denying?"

"Deny everything."

A couple weeks go by—get a phone call like, "Hi, I represent Joe Blow."

"Who's Joe Blow?"

"Joe Blow got the shit kicked out of him two years ago in the back of the camera car. He's suing the production company, suing Billy Friedkin, suing blah blah blah for multimillion dollars. Lost his use of his left hand."

A couple of days after this call, I got this other phone call from somebody representing Randy Jurgensen.

Then we get a phone call from both lawyers. Basically, I remember what I said: "How do I know what happened? I was fighting for my life. There were eggs and I had bottles thrown at me. I was in the corner holding a camera case up in front of my face. I said, 'Shit I'd love to get out of here alive.'"

Well, everybody said the same thing. That went on for a couple of months. I don't know if they settled out of court. I never brought it up with Billy again. It was something you didn't want to relive.

RANDY JURGENSEN: If you really look at it, It's about the cop. It's about the cop losing himself, basically losing his identity.

TONY GAMIELLO: One of the toughest jobs we had ever worked on and one of the few jobs we got a bonus at the end because of stuff we had to deal with.

GARY MULLER: Billy put me in a lot of compromising positions and always thanked me for it. Somebody had to do it.

The Coldest Day in the Business

(1978)

DAVE FRANZONI **(GAFFER)**: Have you talked to Mazzoni? Well, he could tell you—him and I and our fathers were on a movie years ago—and you just ask him what the coldest day in the business was and it would be this day back years ago. It was some movie. I don't know the name of it either. It was shot under one thing and it was released under something else.

JOHN MAZZONI **(GRIP)**: It was called *The Rip-Off,* but there was another name for the movie: *The Squeeze.* It had two names. They were mad at us in New Jersey. The Jersey Teamsters were mad. They made a bad sharp turn by our craft service table and crashed [into] Dennis Maitland [sound mixer], Tommy Saccio [prop master], and a couple other guys. They went to the hospital. It was a big thing. We had a big fight with them.

DAVE FRANZONI: The local Teamsters in New Jersey try to run us over and hit a couple of us. It was horrible. The wardrobe lady punched the Italian DP [director of photography] because he grabbed her on the ass. Mike Saccio's dad was the head prop guy on it—Tom Saccio. He punched the director [Antonio Margheriti] out one night.

JOHN MAZZONI: Everything went according to plan for the day. We shot. Those guys were in the hospital. Maitland hurt his groin. Tommy broke his left arm. It was about nine, ten degrees out—crazy. We shot the whole day, but a car had to blow up. Tommy Saccio was supposed to blow the car up, but he's in a hospital bed. The Italian director is asking, [accent] "Where is Tommy, where is Tommy, where Tommy? We have to blow this car up. I told him, I told him!" So Tommy comes back from the hospital. It's nighttime now.

Everything's forgotten. We know those guys are okay. We heard they're not dead. And it's nine degrees and a truck pulls up making us steak sandwiches. I will never forget. So, me and Johnny Mazzola—we're the grips—they give us the steak sandwiches. It was so hot—it was smoking. When we bit into it, it was actually almost cold again. So, I bit into the sandwich and I see the director Antonio by the car going, "I can't believe. This car was supposed to be rigged. Where is Tommy? Where is Tommy?" And we're like, "What the fuck?" It was only me and him. It's freezing. Tommy comes walking over: "What's the matter? What happened? Do you realize that I was in the fucking hospital all fucking day? Who the fuck are you talking to? Who are you yelling at? Don't talk to me like that. I'll fucking knock you out."

[accent] "You don't ah-knock, ah-no! You don't ah-knock, ah-no!"

"Don't talk to me like that." He said, "I didn't know what happened. There was nothing I could do."

"Fuck-ah-you. Fuck-ah-you." I remember holding my sandwich. I was looking at him. He came from the bottom—uppercut. He hit Antonio in the bottom of the chin, uppercut, and knocked him right on out cold. Boom. The guy hits the ground, but we hear his head hitting the concrete. I'm still trying to bite my cold sandwich. Tommy says while pointing at him, "Fuck you. Never fucking talk to me like that again."

And he walked out and he goes, "I quit."

Johnny looks at me. He goes, "What do we do?"

I said, "Maybe we better quit too."

And we both ran away.

Wolfen

(1981)

BILL REYNOLDS (PROPS, ***WOLFEN***): *Wolfen* was a clusterfuck.

GARY MULLER (CAMERA ASSISTANT, ***WOLFEN***): *Wolfen*. That was fucking cold. Holy shit.

MICHAEL F. BURKE (ELECTRICIAN, ***WOLFEN***): It was a really hard job. It was a lot of night work. It was really cold. We were up in the Bronx during the *Fort Apache* time. The Bronx was burning. It was just rubble up there.

MICHAEL ZANSKY (SCENIC ARTIST, ***WOLFEN***): The first movie job I did was a job called *Wolfen,* where we built a church in the East Bronx, just a few blocks from where I grew up. It was a burned-out war zone at that point.

TROY ADEE (SET DRESSER): You'd get off the avenue and you would drive, and it would be miles, and it looked like something out of a movie. It looked like Beirut. Miles and miles of all the buildings were just totally decimated. I'm like, "Wow, you guys did a lot of work here." I'm a ten-year-old.

My dad's like, "No, this is not the set." This is the burned-out buildings—cars everywhere, fucking dogs.

KIM MAITLAND (SOUND RECORDIST, ***WOLFEN***): That was 1979—first job, and I had just been dropped off in the City for the first time in my life to live, and now I'm, like, shooting in South Bronx. I also never made more money than I did on that particular job. It was nights and weekends, and we had double time on weekends and double time after 2 p.m., which we no longer have. So the contracts have changed a lot over the years, but it was a crazy job.

TROY ADEE: There's a kid up on this hill and it's like just rubble and burned-out shit. Everything there was, like, fucking sketchy. So this kid is up on this mound far away, and he comes down to see us and the cop's like, "What the fuck do you want?"

The kid's like, "There's a house on fire over here."

So he goes, "Go call the fucking fire department." Back then there were phone booths, but none there. They were all knocked over.

Up on that hill, I guess there was a phone booth, like, one of the freestanding ones. He calls the fire department, and he comes down and the cops said, like, "Get the fuck outta here." I'm this little kid and I'm like, "Wow, those guys are mean." The fire department comes and they fucking hook up to the hydrant and everything, and they roll the hoses out, and the kid's standing there. They fucking open up, like, a two-inch line right at the kid. I was like, "What the fuck is going on?"

He's like, "This fucking kid called a fake fire in."

I'm like, "Really? Did he really? Why would he go through all that trouble? Maybe there's a fire over there."

My dad's like, "Troy, don't." They blasted him. I mean, that's not a joke. That's not like a garden hose—fucking knocked the kid right out. Who the fuck knows?

But I was like, "I want to go home."

My father was like, "Don't you leave my side," because it was fucking really bad.

MICHAEL F. BURKE: They got somebody walking off with one of the portable generators. A guy was stealing one and pushing it down the street in the Bronx, a quarter of a mile away from the set. The cops are driving by. They see some guy pushing this little Honda generator down the street. The electric truck caught on fire. It was something.

MICHAEL ZANSKY: We're in campers. They're putting up a church, which is, like, a five-story church that's all burned-out and wrecked and everything else. I get there and I don't know—I don't know anything about this. This is a movie job. I have no background whatsoever in it.

They said, "Well, look, we're going to build this. Go into the trailer." Everybody was set up in trailers. We're going to build this church. I look at these plans and I'm, like, saying, "How long have we got to do this?"

And they said, "Well, it's gotta be done in four weeks." and I'm, like, looking at this thing and I'm thinking to myself, "Four fucking weeks on this." This is a fucking gigantic construction. What are all the bricks? Oh, we got to paint all the bricks, blah, blah, blah. The steel structure and everything is five stories high.

So in the first couple of days of the job I don't know anybody. I go in the camper first thing in the morning and there's this sheet of glass with lines of coke. The grips are there, the carpenters are there, the scenics are there. I'm thinking to myself, "Oh, this is an interesting meeting we got here." I mean, this is insane. It's a mountain. We're talking about a snow-capped mountain on this sheet of glass.

MICHAEL F. BURKE: There was a lot of cocaine use. I'll even go one further—I had a full-size tank of nitrous oxide, and I brought it to the job one time and we lashed it to the truck and we would go to the truck and do balloons of nitrous.

MICHAEL ZANSKY: I leave the camper, and I'm working with this guy that I never saw again. He was a very neurotic fellow—scenic artist—we're working together. It's probably within the first week or so of being on this job. We're up on a scaffolding and lifts and we're talking. He turns to me, and he looks at me, and this is my intro.

He says to me, "Who do I fuck to get off this job?" And I just burst out laughing.

I said, "How long you been doing this for?"

And he says, "I'm not even sure."

He says, "I'm not sure how I got here."

I'm thinking to myself, "What the fuck is going on?"

TROY ADEE: We go back to the Big House and that's where we had the command-center set. I'm sitting there and, like I said, I'm ten. I'm sitting in the control center and the grid—you know the grid at the Big House—it's, like, seventy feet [high]. I'm sitting there in this control center and it's like, all the high-tech shit from back then—it's, like, twenty television screens.

I'm sitting there and all of a sudden a fucking crowbar comes out of the grid and fucking sticks right into the fucking floor—like, fucking one foot away from me! My father walks in—my father's like, "What the hell was that?" It fell out of the grid. So my father freaks out. The only way up to

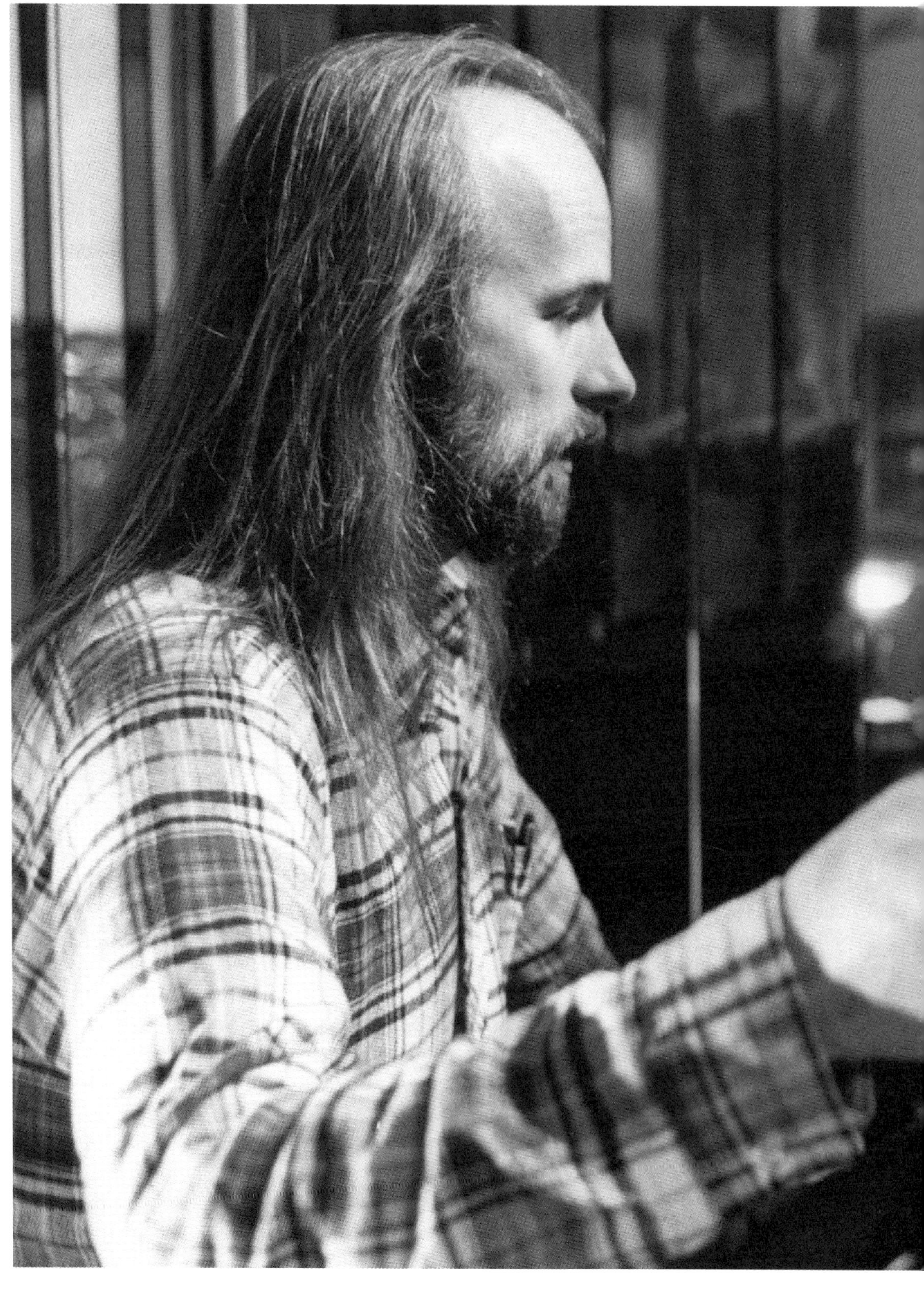

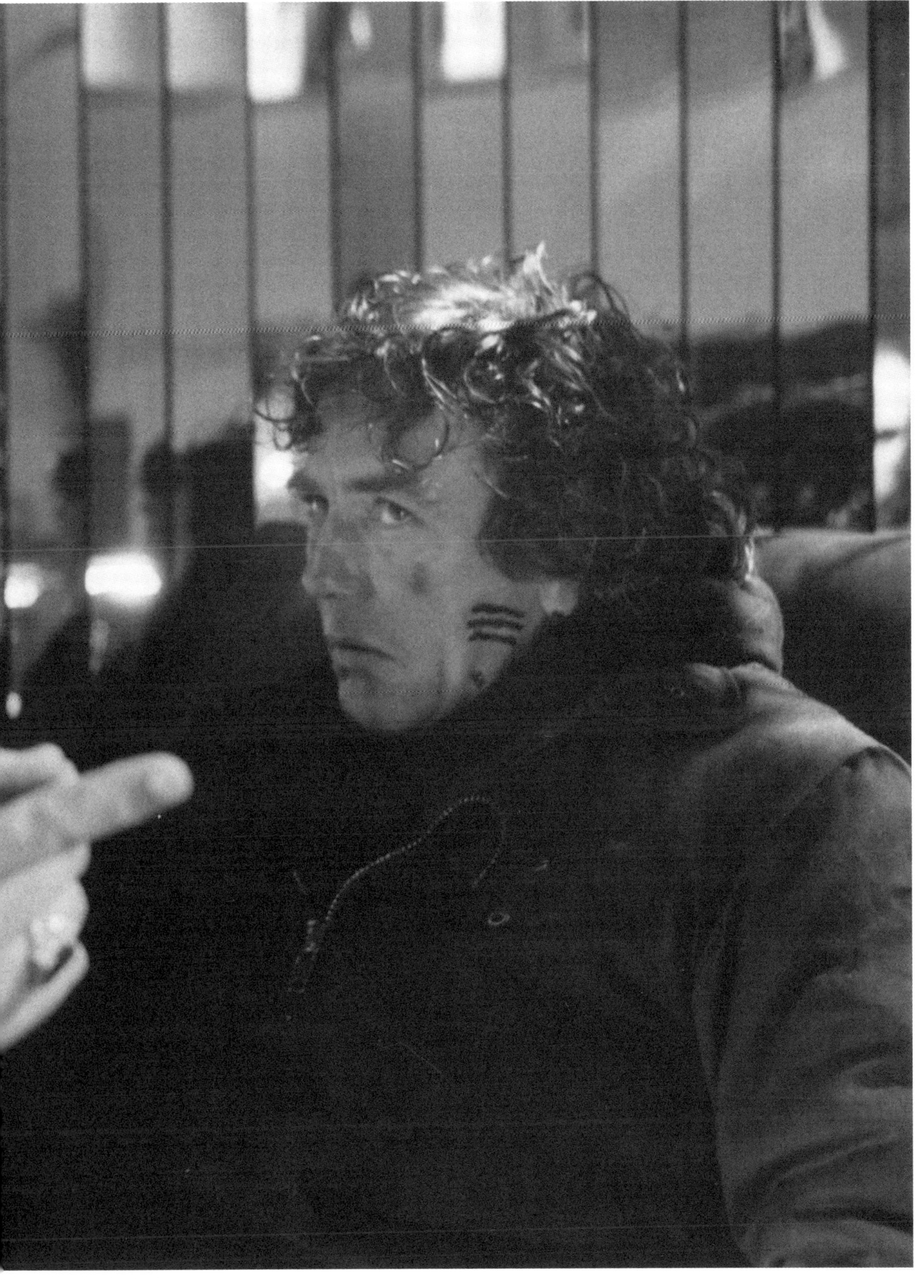

Michael Wadleigh and Albert Finney, *Wolfen*. Photo courtesy of the Margaret Herrick Library, Academy of Motion Picture Arts and Sciences.

the grid is that staircase all the way up to the thing. My father was, "Who the fuck is up there?" —and back then you heard the stories of *Wolfen*—cocaine and drinking. My father goes up there, there it's fucking [name redacted]. He's up there. He can't even walk straight. And when I got home, my mom's like, "How was work?"

STEVEN FELDER (FIRST ASSISTANT DIRECTOR, *WOLFEN*): Gary Muller and I were shooting some second-unit stuff in the Bronx—Dresden, we called it. I think it was Jerome Avenue in the 220s or something. In the church—there was half a church there that they built as a set where the wolves kind of hung out and a lot of scenes were in that building.

We were shooting some general stuff down there, and bullets were bouncing off the top of the building. We had to stop for a while and the cops came and figured out what was going on—people taking pot shots at us, because we were in a gang neighborhood, obviously.

TROY ADEE: We pull up—it's an old fucking burned-out church. These two cops pull up from Fort Apache and they say to my dad: "What the hell are you doing here?"

My dad goes, "I'm with the movie."

The guy is like, "What movie are you going to? What are you looking for?"

My dad's like, "We're shooting a movie *here*. That old burned-down church right there is our set."

And the guy in the patrol car gets out and he's like, "That church?"

"Yeah, we just finished. We built it."

The guy goes, "That church has been here since all these motherfuckers burned all this shit down."

My dad goes, "We just built that church."

And then the guy is like, "You don't know

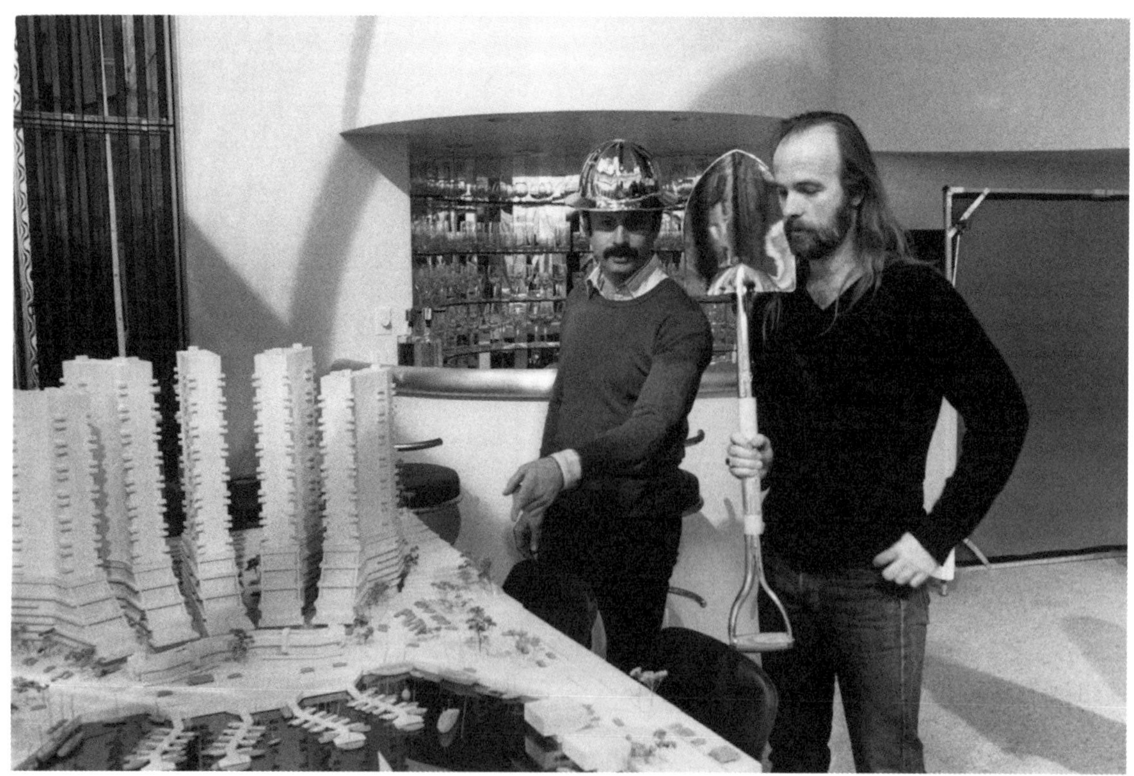

Rupert Hitzig and Michael Wadleigh. Photo courtesy of the Margaret Herrick Library, Academy of Motion Picture Arts and Sciences.

what you're talking about." He's like, "Let me see some ID," to my father.

My father's like, "What?"

He goes, "Let me see your license." My father's like . . . you know how my father is.

Again—I'm, like, ten. "Oh, god, dad." There we go again.

The guy says, "Step out of the car." My dad steps outta the car. He is like, "Listen to me. We're shooting this movie, *Wolfen*. We just finished building that church."

The guy's, like, talking to his partner—calls into the patrol, "Do you know anything about a movie going on here?"

And the captain goes, "Yeah, they're building something down there."

And the cop is like, "I got some guy down here telling me that this burned-down old church that they just built."

And he's like, "I don't know what they're building down there, but I know that they're doing something."

I'm standing out there now. My dad goes, "Come with me." So he walks up to the church and there's rubble everywhere. I mean, it just looks fucking awesome. My dad goes up to the side of it, kicks the side of it—like, the cornerstone—and he puts his foot through.

He's like, "This thing has been here for a hundred years?"

The guy starts touching it, and the inside is all burned out and the stained glass is hanging. The guy's like, "You got to be kidding me. This is incredible."

MICHAEL ZANSKY: Now the church is standing and there's scaffolding wrapping this building. You know, it's gotta be several hundred feet long and, you know, I'm on the ground and I'm spackling and doing the bricks. We have to paint the bricks and—blah, blah, blah, whatever. It's burned out, and I'm on the ground there. All of a sudden—I mean, I'm knocked to my knees. I get hit in the back of my head by what I think is a rock, it's so heavy. I think, "Oh shit, I'm going to die here! A few blocks from where I grew up." I feel the back of my head. I say, "Oh, fuck, it's my brain." What I pick up is wet—it's moist and it's spongy. I'm on my knees. I'm like, "What the fuck?" and I pulled my hand around thinking I'm going to see blood. It's a huge clump of spackle, and I'm thinking to myself, "What the fuck?"

I look up and it's just another scenic artist—this guy, Paul, that I had met at this job, four or five stories up with a big grin on his face, smiling at me. I think to myself, "That's the son of a bitch I'm going to kill. All right, I'm going to just fucking kill him." I say, "Okay, fine. You motherfucker. I'll get even with you."

Well, about a week has passed. It's now—I'm on the scaffold way above five stories in the air, whatever, with a spray gun and with a raw umber black spray, to spray-age the whole thing down. I see he's on the ground now, and he's moving around on the ground, and wherever he goes on the ground I'm there with the spray. By the end of the day, you can't see his face, all you see is the whites of his eyes. He's covered in dots. That's the beginning of my saga working on films.

KIM MAITLAND: The director was kind of kooky—Michael Wadleigh—and my father told me that, during the interview to get the job, Michael Wadleigh had an orange on his lap, and he broke it open with his hands and said, "Do you see this? I want to hear this. This is what I want to hear. I want to hear this sound of this orange." He wanted it to be like a "smell vision" of the wolf when they were, like, looking through the woods and through the park for the wolves. He wanted to be able to hear it.

STEVEN FELDER: Michael Wadleigh—very eccentric hippie who had done *Woodstock*—he was a long-haired hippie guy—drove around with a hippie chick in a VW van. He wouldn't allow the Teamster to drive him to work, which made them nuts. Very anti-establishment type of character, but a nice person—you know, not stoned, not crazed, just eccentric. He and I tried to get the show organized.

ANGELO DIGIACOMO (CAMERA TRAINEE, *WOLFEN*): Michael Wadleigh got the movie because he was supposed to do *Woodstock* ten-year anniversary and it never happened, so they owed him a movie, and he had read Whitley Strieber's book *Wolfen*, [but] he wasn't a real movie director. He was kind of overwhelmed by the whole thing.

MICHAEL F. BURKE: I think *Wolfen* was a King-Hitzig production—Alan King and Rupert Hitzig. So Alan King comes to the set in his Rolls-Royce. It was in an accident and has a dented front end to it. I made up a sign posted, like the charities where they have a thermometer, and you want to raise the goal: "It's wrong that Alan's Rolls-Royce is damaged. So, please can you all get together and help fund the repair of his Rolls-Royce," with a thermometer. We started it at seventy-five cents, and it had, like, a dollar twenty-five, and our goal was, like, two hundred thousand dollars. We had that up in the back of the truck. Whatever shit we could do to help.

BILL REYNOLDS: Bill Garrity was a gaffer and did very well. I never knew him as that. He became a unit production manager, and I only knew him as a unit production manager. But he was formerly [Local] 52 and broke that glass ceiling. The funniest story I can remember about him was on the show *Wolfen*.

We're on Delancey Street or somewhere downtown, and it was a typical *Wolfen* day. It was a total screw-up, and the screw-up was coming from the top. So Bill was a little guy. He was probably five-foot-seven in heels. He was a short man, but he was clever and well-spoken. Rupert Hitzig was the producer. Bill Garrity was the unit manager, and the director [Michael Wadleigh] was very tall. He was probably six-foot-five.

Bill was old-school, and Bill did drink, and it was probably the middle of the afternoon and something really stupid happened. I can't remember what it was. But he walks up between these guys. Now, Hitzig was taller than Bill, but everybody was. Hitzig was probably six foot, something like that, but he's almost half a head above Garrity. And the director is a full head and a half above Garrity. He gets in between them. He looks up at Hitzig and says, "You? I wouldn't trust you to produce pencils."

He spins around to the director and says, "And you, I wouldn't let you direct traffic on a play street."

I almost rolled over on the ground. This is in front of everybody and, with this, he storms off.

STEVEN FELDER: I was hired as a key second [assistant director] on that job, and my first responsibility was to deal with the wolves as actors. So we had all these wolves with their names—they were on the call sheet. It was about six of them, and I worked with the wolf-trainers, and their progression [into bigger wolves]. These wolves came out of Montana. George Toth was the animal-trainer. We found a place—Spaceland Zoo or something, in New Jersey—for them to stay, and we had meetings with the ASPCA and New York Police Department and Traffic and Security on how we were going to run these schools around Wall Street, which was some of the things the script called for, and they decided that we need eight-foot cyclone fence with a three-foot top of cyclone and barbed wire, because the wolves could jump over that fence.

TROY ADEE: And not, like, an eight-foot fence cage, because these fucking wolves would fucking jump—like, a fifteen-foot fence all around that church—like, three city blocks. Those wolves were like horses.

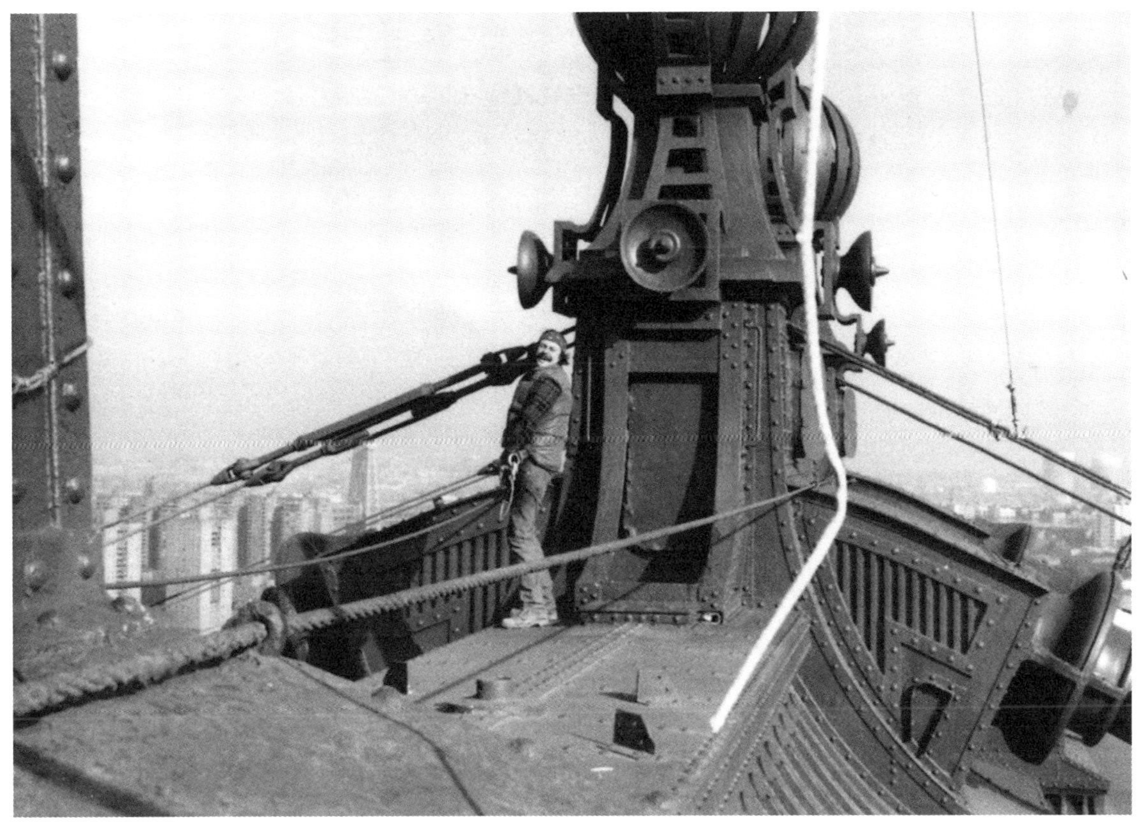

TOM PRIESTLEY, JR. (CAMERA OPERATOR, *WOLFEN*): I just think it was the Humane Society making sure that they wouldn't get out roaming around.

STEVEN FELDER: We pretty much walled in Wall Street around the New York Stock Exchange for a couple of blocks—had to put it up at night, take it down in the morning, so that Wall Street could open. We shot a couple weekends.

TOM PRIESTLEY, JR.: We were down on Wall Street. They looked like big German shepherds—that's what I thought they were—and the trainer kept saying, "Don't look at the wolves' eyes." "Come on, get out of here, man." There's no such thing as a tame wild animal as far as I'm concerned

STEVEN FELDER: My responsibility was to bring wolves to the set and then talk with the trainers about which wolves are ready that day or not. There was a growling wolf that had a puppy that had gotten his paw caught under one of the fences, and the trainer that released that puppy—when it [the puppy] grew up, [it] always associated that trainer with the pain [it] had felt under the fence, so as soon as that puppy saw that trainer it would go into full snarling, drooling wolf mode. That's the one we put in the back seat of the police car with this actor. I think his name's Richard O'Neill. He was a good character actor. He was the police chief. So he's sitting in that car doing surveillance and this wolf pops up right over his shoulder. She [the trainer] was outside the window; that wolf didn't even know he was sitting there. That wolf was so focused on her, growling and drooling, literally a foot away from his head; it was an amazing performance right there, but that was like one of our days.

Grip Harold Halligan peeing off the top of the bridge.

I got to know these wolves. I went out to the pen with them, and I'd always liked dogs, big dogs, and they're kind of like—you gotta picture a shepherd that at any moment could bite your hand in half. Their jaws are superpowerful. They're really intelligent. They are big dogs, just smarter and stronger than we are. So I'd go out to the pen, and two or three of them and, you know, kind of play with them—roughhouse them a little bit on the jowls and pet them, and they're all happy and they're circling and everything. The next thing I know is one of them that's nipping at my Achilles tendon—there's another one nipping at my kidneys on the other side, and the other one's kind of keeping me focused and that's how they play.

That's how they're going to take down the prey—the moose, the deer, whatever they're hunting—they sever their Achilles tendons or a hamstring or something, then it's down and that's it—you are done. It was an interesting experience, but that went really well. They were playing, but that's how they play, but I was totally comfortable with it—until it got a little bit over the top, you know. They're like babies.

TOM PRIESTLEY, JR.: I never saw any instance where they were actually aggressive. They tried to do closeups to where they bare their teeth and all that stuff. That takes a long time.

MAGGIE RYAN (SCENIC ARTIST, *WOLFEN*): I did the mechanical wolves with Eoin Sprott, and I was in charge of taking all the gristle out and tenderizing the skin—they'd get the skins from Canada—and it was against the law because they were protected animals. It was against the law to even have them sent into New York state, let alone work on them. I probably could have been arrested or prosecuted.

STEVEN FELDER: So, you know, I'm sitting around one day and the location manager—I think was Peter Macintosh—called me in. He said, "Hey, listen, we're going to go scout the bridge today."

"Okay, all right—what time?"

"Four o'clock be down by the Manhattan Bridge on the Manhattan side."

We go out there and then we meet the bridge people, and they say, "Okay, put this on," and it's a harness, like a climbing harness, and I step into it and it wraps around your waist and you got two hooks, two clamps on either side, and said, "We're going up."

"We're going up where?"

"We're going up to the top where we're going to shoot."

So myself, Wadleigh, the production manager, and these technicians from the bridge go from the runway, climb up on the lowest fat cable that runs up the center. It has all these down cables, every four or five feet. We step onto the main cable, and we start to shush our way up, and so you go to the next upright cable, support cable, you unhook one side, you hook your head, you unhook the other side, you hook your head, you shush up like you're kind of—almost, like, cross-country skiing kind of motion—until you get all the way up—up to the top.

At the top, you're leaning a little bit back because there's a door that is in the superstructure of the top of the bridge. At that point you unhook and you lean as fast as you can into that opening to a four- or five-foot ladder that takes you up to right on top of the bridge.

Okay, so that was that afternoon of scouting—I did it once—my knees were pumping like a slalom athlete—but I'm very athletic. I've done some risky physical things. I wasn't unconfident, but it was like, "Well, this is crazy." Then, coming down, we stood up there. It was windy, and if you're not afraid of heights then you're okay. Coming

Michael F. Burke working on *Wolfen*.

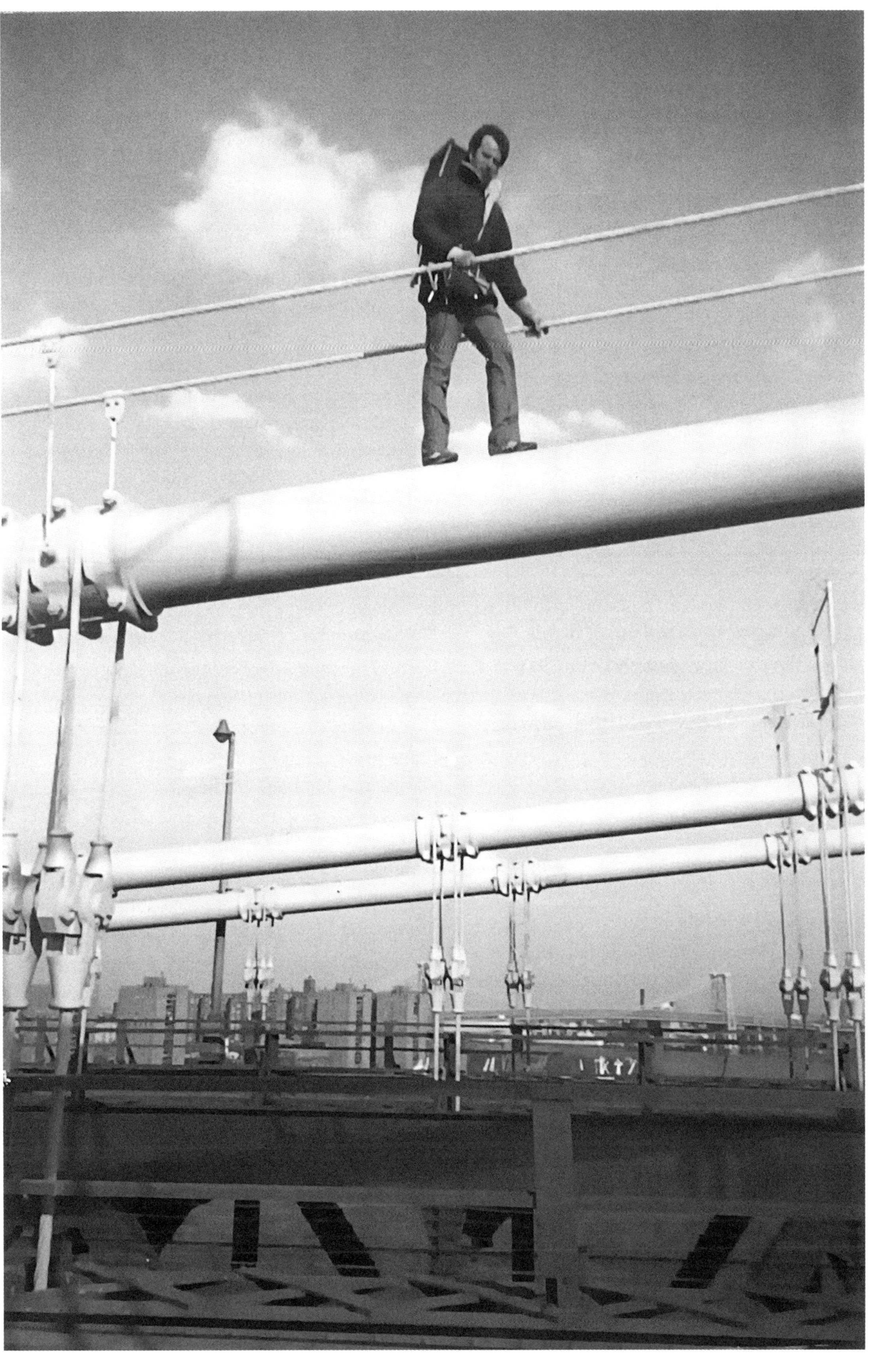

down, it's the opposite—you shush, you unclip, clip, clip, clip, clip. So I asked the guy, "What happens if I slip?"

He said, "If you slip and you hook in with two, you're probably okay. If you slip and you hook in with one, you might dislocate your hip."

I said, "Lord, so I'm dangling here with one clip and a dislocated hip—what happens?"

"Then we're gonna have a big problem with you—we're going to have a hard time getting you down. That hasn't really happened."

We became kind of confident. It's weird how your body reacts to these things. Well, that was the first scouting trip. Then we had to do another one [scout] with the other technical people. We had to decide how many people [we] are going to have up there, how we're going to bring the equipment up, and everything else.

BILL REYNOLDS: We had an antenna that we made, and we put it up on top of one of the balls on the east side of the Williamsburg Bridge on the Brooklyn side, the north tower.

We created this thing. Now to get up there—and I think I might've been the only prop, but I was with a bunch of legendary grips. They went up there and put that up, because technically it is a prop. We carried this thing up those wires. Everybody was represented.

STEVEN FELDER: By the second time going up, I was confident. It's funny—if I tell you I paint a line on the ground ten feet long—I said, "Hey, just walk one foot in front of the other on that ten-foot line"—no problem. I raise that thing two feet—I walk across that thing—four feet in the air—you're like, "I better really concentrate," right?

Five feet, six feet, eight feet, ten feet—in you go—"I don't know how to walk anymore—I forgot how to walk." The mental thing was: it's just one foot in front of the other. Just walk. It doesn't matter if you're a hundred feet off the ground or one foot off the ground,—it's the same walk, which was interesting, you know.

We had all the macho Irish grips coming on one of these scouts—construction guys, they literally pissed their pants before they even got off the roadway. This was something they were not going to fucking do. The first AC [assistant camera operator]—feisty little fucker—he eventually went up there bitching and moaning all the way.

BILL REYNOLDS: It was great. It was fabulous. People have been up higher. I know there's been some guys that were up on top of the world—Verazzano. But I think there's an elevator that goes up to the top of that. I don't think you have to climb up. That's stuff you can't do anymore.

STEVEN FELDER: I don't remember exactly who went up on the bridge other than myself, the camera operator Tom Priestley, Jr., the director, and Albert Finney.

TOM PRIESTLEY, JR.: There were some really good performances there, and Albert Finney's in the foreground. I'm standing there with the camera up on top, high up on the structure of the bridge. Eddie Olmos is on the left and the director, Michael Wadleigh.

We were up there for seven hours. The platform was about seven feet wide and about fifteen feet long. That's all the people that stayed up there, and it got so late in the day. The sun was setting behind us. We're getting camera shadow. I had to lay down on the ground and hold the camera—shoot up so I wouldn't have the camera shadow all over the actors. They finished the last part of the scene. I mean, it's unbelievable.

STEVEN FELDER: So we set this up on a Friday night on the Manhattan Bridge and, of course, the incoming traffic is on the north side of the bridge and the outbound traffic is on the south side of the bridge from Manhattan but doesn't look good. So we wanted the traffic reverse, so it looks like the limo's coming out of Manhattan rather than into Manhattan.

If you're on the Brooklyn side of the bridge, you're looking right at Manhattan with cars coming at you, which is not how it is because it is on the other side of the bridge.

All right, so we had to stop traffic. They had to control all the traffic on the East River Drive, so we can get a limo streaking across the bridge where they want. So, working with the TPS [Transit Police Service] at the time, there's a couple of guys I've worked with over the years—I think his name is George—he was one of the head guys.

We got this thing locked up—I can look all the way down the East River, literally from the Manhattan Bridge to the Midtown Tunnel, and traffic is bumper-to-bumper locked up, on a Saturday night. I'm getting ready to cue the limo to come and, while Eddie is walking up the bridge, because they're following this limo guy and they're kind of being wolves and they're kind of alter-ego things—all of a sudden, from behind the camera the officer starts walking into the shot. He just starts walking like a freaking zombie, and he had his hand on his gun and his holster, and I had known the guy for years. "Hey, George, where you going? We're rolling, George. Where you going, man?"

He starts walking like a zombie down the fucking empty roadway—pointed, blaring, and it's totally New York City chaos, and he starts to walk to the edge of the bridge, to the rail. At this point, I radio to my second. I said, "Get the other TPS guy. There's something wrong here. Get them right away." He's got his hand on his gun, he's looking over the bridge, he's ready to jump, and, luckily, the other TPS guys showed up and they stopped him. He had some mental problems and just flipped.

Anyway, we got the shot and moved on to another day.

BILL REYNOLDS: [*Wolfen*] was coming from the culture of the American Indians. The American Indians worked on high steel.

STEVEN FELDER: I had to go down to this Lower East Side sort of tribal club they had and talk some of them into being extras. They're all steel workers. Mohawks traditionally did all the high-end work. "Well, you have to be on the bridge—not on the top, but you have to be kind of climbing and doing some stuff. "

MICHAEL F. BURKE: I remember hearing Rupert Hitzig on the telephone one night at Battery Park City yelling at somebody, saying, "We cannot go into April." He was screaming because they took away all his points. It was just a nightmare. It went on forever.

BILL REYNOLDS: I always remember *Wolfen* above all for it being the coldest frigging winter I can remember. They built windmills because it was supposed to be Dutch at the end of Manhattan on the battery. And we had a lot of night shooting with that.

Oh my God, that wind coming off the lower harbor—it was just hideous.

MICHAEL F. BURKE: There was a scene where the girl is found dead at the Battery Park on this sculptural, whirligig—it had some sails, it was a small merry-go-round with sails that would be interacting with the weather—and this girl is found mangled, mauled on this thing at nighttime, and the next morning Gregory Hines—he's a cop—and he comes down to the scene of the crime, but they didn't get to shoot it when they were supposed to shoot it. So they came back to reshoot it in January, and thirty-mile-an-hour winds were coming off the Hudson, and it was fifteen below zero at two in the afternoon.

So Gregory Hines has to dress this part for that other scene, which is in a short-sleeve Hawaiian shirt, and he's doing the walk-and-talk in Battery Park while the other detective is explaining to him what just happened the night before. So Gregory Hines—they're feeding him ice cubes so that the frost doesn't come out of his mouth when he's speaking.

And they're trying to do a take and Gregory's shoulders—you know, when you're cold, how your shoulders are up above your ears? So they're doing the walk-and-talk and they're saying, "Gregory, you've got to relax your shoulders."

He says, "Do you realize where my people came from? My people don't bring their shoulders down in this kind of fucking weather." So they had to wrap. They couldn't do the shot. He could not get his fucking shoulders down long enough.

STEVEN FELDER: Eddie Olmos was amazing. He ran into the ocean. I had to stay with him one night and cue him to strip his clothes and run into the ocean at Coney Island in the middle of winter. Part of this transition [to wolf in the script]. It was pretty dangerous, actually.

Albert Finney was just amazing—what a trooper. When we were shooting the opening in Battery Park it was probably minus twenty, and him and the former Miss Finland were out there, and in between takes he would say, "Come into my trailer. Let's talk about what we're going to do the rest of the day and night— stuff like that. So I go into his trailer, and he'd break out a little brandy flask and we share a couple shots of brandy, until it was ready to go and then he'd get back there and do his thing.

MAGGIE RYAN: With *Wolfen,* we used to have the thing where the grips like to sell [playing] cards on Fridays and you would put twenty dollars on a card and there were fifty-two cards.

STEVEN FELDER: The Teamsters always had their Super Bowl pool, and it was, like, a hundred dollars a box—a hundred boxes—and so one day Finney comes up to me, says, "Hey man, you got ten bucks I can borrow? I only got ninety bucks. I want to get in on this."

"Ten bucks—never going to see that ten bucks again," is what I'm thinking. Give him ten bucks. Super Bowl Monday comes in, he goes, "Hey, Steve, here—here's your ten bucks, and here's the rest of the ninety." He won ten thousand dollars; he gave me a thousand. Yes, he was a regular person.

MAGGIE RYAN: And of course the person who won the ten grand was Albert Finney and he was already on penalty making ten thousand dollars a day because the movie was running longer than it should.

STEVEN FELDER: The other kind of interesting aspect, I think, of that film was the "wolf vision," which they experimented a lot with. Somebody in the show had contacted the Israeli military, because they had just started to use infrared vision on the border with Palestine, and so they had this night-scope headgear and cameras. So they found this guy and he smuggled the stuff out of Israel into JFK and, funny enough, one of Billy Friedkin's ex-con bodyguards brought this guy in. This guy, Jerry Murphy, was like an ex-con kind of tech advisor for all these kinds of illegal things that happened.

So we smuggle this guy out to the set one day to do these tests on a pier in New York and how they have this thermograph type of looking thing now, but it shows heat lost from a house for instance. It'll go green or red and it'll show you where the leaks are.

We're out on the pier somewhere with the gizmo that attaches to the bottom of the Panavision camera and then the film runs through it. It kind of exposes it in whatever way it worked to show heat loss. It's the middle of winter. We stick [Wadleigh's] totally braless hippie girlfriend out on this frozen pier and literally you could see through her dress. We started out with a coat—take the coat off, take the sweater off—okay, just be in your regular coat—and you could see the heat loss in her body, going from warm red and it starts going green until she's frozen; then we stopped and then something happened with the camera. Something malfunctioned—I don't know what happened exactly—so that thing didn't work. It was an interesting experiment, so now we have to smuggle the guy back to Israel.

RUSSELL ENGELS (**GAFFER,** ***WOLFEN***)**:** Michael Wadleigh, the director, wanted it done that way. They didn't have the technology yet. So we had a guy named Kent Remington and he promised him that the computers were going to be able to make you do this the way it's written in the pages, and he hired this guy, a good friend of his, and we all thought, "Well, he's getting 1800 bucks a week. Holy crap! And he does nothing."

But he promised Michael that the computer age was on the way, and he said that you could get 256 colors and change them anytime you want—you can make a red into a green, like you can do nowadays in film of course, but it was before its time. They had it written on paper and all that kind of stuff, but nobody had invented the equipment yet or the computer part. So they banked a lot of that movie on that belief that they would get that colorization for the wolf-vision, but it never happened in that time.

STEVEN FELDER: So then Garrett Brown, who had just started to invent Steadicam—it was cumbersome—it took a long time to go from low mode to high mode. It was a very heavy camera. Garrett Brown is a pretty big guy. I think he was, like, six-five. Strong guy could handle it—not too many other guys would do it at a time because he was inventing it.

We wanted to have this wolf-vision where they're going to look for their victims through the rooms in Dresden, through Central Park. So we rigged a golf cart with the Steadicam with the [animal] trainers. We were a little bit isolated, but the trainers would go down to an end point, and one trainer would stay at the beginning point and release the wolf running through the paths of Central Park during the day.

So we would just follow the wolf with Steadicams. What they did was also in this story. They could follow the thermal print of a person who had just been there so, if you're walking, when you leave a thermal impression for a certain period of time from your body heat in the snow or on the grass or whatever. Anyway, they went through all these mechanizations to figure out what to do with wolf-vision and how they see things and all that stuff, and then I think in the end they just wound up reversing the negative. If you watch the film, you'll see—they just reverse the negative. All the blacks are white, and all the whites are black, and then I think they colorized them a little bit, so the simple technique wound up working.

RUSSELL ENGELS: Michael Wadleigh took the picture to his Colorado mountain camp, or house, or whatever. It took six months, I think, before he came back with a cut that was over four hours, and then the producers—the first time they sued a director and won. They got power over the picture. They took it away from him and cut it down to two hours or whatever it was and brought it out that way.

Mr. Wadleigh says quietly: "I'm not angry at King-Hitzig or Orion. I blame myself. I keep asking myself how I failed to handle the people. Now the Directors Guild of America has gotten new language protecting directors in postproduction creative rights. I hope the new language will give directors who want to do more than entertain—who have a point of view artistically, politically or socially—courage to stick by what they believe in the face of producers who oppose them until they can get their version to a public audience."

—Aljean Harmetz, "Wolfen: A Case of Director's Rights," *New York Times*, August 4, 1981

The World According to Garp

(1982)

TOM PRIESTLEY, JR. **(CAMERA OPERATOR, *THE WORLD ACCORDING TO GARP*)**: George Roy Hill—great director—great man, just a lovely man—another one of those directors, you never hear him utter a harsh word. He did *Waldo Pepper* [1975]. He did *The Sting* [1973]. I think he did *Butch Cassidy and the Sundance Kid* [1969]. You never hear him yell or nothing. Robin Williams was great.

Robin was incredibly sensitive to the crew, to the people who don't always get the recognition they deserve for the various jobs they do during a shoot. Robin knew everyone's name and could always get a laugh—not a laugh aimed at himself, but a laugh that recognized others. He gave various favorite crew members special nicknames. Our camera operator had famously combed-back, black hair that had considerable amounts of product in it, keeping every hair in place in all kinds of weather. Robin dubbed him "Teflon Man" and would do hilarious riffs as an archeologist in the distant future finding "Teflon Man" with his hair still perfect.[34]

—Glenn Close, 2014

34 Roger Friedman,"Glenn Close on Friend and Colleague: 'Robin Williams Was a World Treasure,'" *Showbiz411*, August 13, 2014, www.showbiz411.com/2014/08/13/glenn-close-on-friend-and-colleague-robin-williams-was-a-world-treasure, retrieved August 16, 2023.

TOM PRIESTLEY, JR.: He was never off. He was on all the time, telling jokes, fooling around—never stopped. I don't know how he did it. It was unbelievable. Always had some shtick going thing—boom, boom, boom, boom, boom—all the time, he never stopped.

TONY GAMIELLO **(SET DRESSER, *THE WORLD ACCORDING TO GARP*)**: Believe it or not, while we were there shooting, James Cagney lived up in that area. He came to visit our set because he knew the DP [director of photography]. It was just something to see him on set. He was probably in his eighties.

PHIL KENNEDY **(SCENIC INDUSTRIAL, *THE WORLD ACCORDING TO GARP*)**: The first movie that I ever worked on was something called *The World According to Garp*. Bruno [Robotti] was the scenic charge. And it was done at the Big House—[Kaufman] Astoria Motion Picture Studio.

TOM PRIESTLEY, JR.: We shot a lot of it on Fisher Island off the coast of Connecticut.

TONY GAMIELLO: We were staying in Connecticut. We'd get in the van. They drove us down to the ferry. We'd take a forty-minute ride on the ferry every morning out to the island. At this mansion we had to create a beach where there was none. We had to put I don't know how many truckloads of sand. We

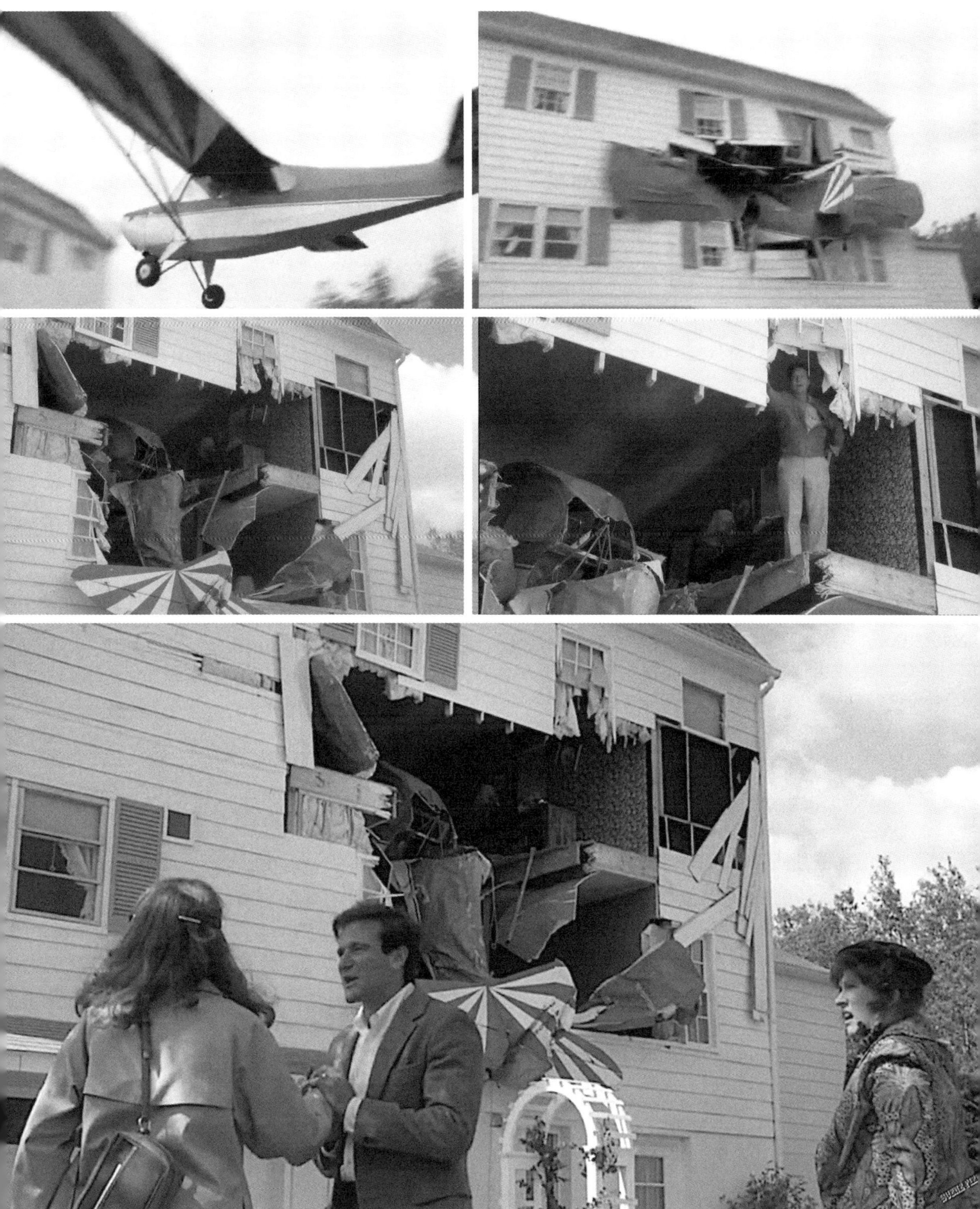

created a small cemetery where there wasn't one. We had to put kinds of tombstones and stuff. And then the inside—we had to revamp it for three different eras or periods in time. It was a big, big set.

BRUNO ROBOTTI (CHARGE SCENIC ARTIST, *THE WORLD ACCORDING TO GARP*): We built the funeral up in Fisher Island, and we made that stone out of a piece out of wood—make it look like different colors of granite.

TONY GAMIELLO: He [Robotti] had another great old-time scenic, Sante Fiori—that guy, I mean, he can make a piece of wood look like marble, and in fact I saw a guy mistake pieces of wood for marble: "Hey, give me a hand with this piece of marble," and they pick it up—"Oh, it's light. It's a piece of wood."

These guys were very talented.

BRUNO ROBOTTI: Sante, when he reached sixty-five, he said, "I'm not running movies anymore. I can't do this." He didn't like the responsibilities anyway. I got the job through him and then [he] went to [be] my second anyway.

TONY GAMIELLO: My father and I are out at Lincoln Park, New Jersey, airport for about a month. We had to reduplicate the back end of a house that we shot in Eastchester and a plane was supposed to crash into it. They had the sides held up with telephone posts, and in the middle was, like, balsa wood where the plane was going to hit with a big net behind it.

BRUNO ROBOTTI: We set up all these fake houses, all set up for the camera, and that's where the crash took place.

TONY GAMIELLO: The plane only had, I think, enough gas to go one loop around. He had a cage around him so he wouldn't get injured inside.

TOM PRIESTLEY, JR.: They dug a foxhole for me on the ground. I was standing in the foxhole with the camera and getting ready to shoot. And the plane starts to fly. I start to roll the camera, and the plug comes out from the battery. I shout, "Get the plug!"

He [assistant cameraman] put the plug in backwards. "No, no. Turn around. Reverse it."

And all this time I'm trying to follow a plane because I got to get this shot. I'm the one to get the main shot, him flying into the house. Luckily, we got it back and got it working. I panned the plane right into the house and it worked, but he [assistant cameraman] almost blew the whole shot. They should have taped the end of the plug into the motor of the camera so it wouldn't come loose. We almost blew it. There's no take two on that.

TONY GAMIELLO: After that they [everyone involved] have a big conference because it didn't go exactly the angle they wanted. So, when you see the movie, it's cut and what they did is they came back a couple of weeks later and we had to go into the second floor of this mockup, and we had to put an actual room in there.

BRUNO ROBOTTI: When you see the crash, you see the wallpaper and all of that stuff in the back. We had to do all that. It was all set up.

TONY GAMIELLO: We had to go in there and dress it up with the staple curtains and the plane went into it, and knocked them out—all the furniture, lamps, and everything. We had to reset it all up, and then they placed parts of the plane inside this bedroom set that they made and then continued the scene where the pilot gets out of the plane. In this case, it was the director, George Roy Hill.

TOM PRIESTLEY, JR.: George was a pilot. He loved to fly planes.

TONY GAMIELLO: Then Robin Williams says, "We'll take the house, because the odds of this happening again . . ."

BRUNO ROBOTTI: The set decorator and I got a Warner Brothers helicopter to go out to the location because we each had a crew working there. So the two of us got picked up at 59th Street Bridge where there used to be a helicopter pad and they brought us to Fisher Island.

TOM PRIESTLEY, JR.: I shot some additional photography on it. I had to pick some shots up in a private boys' school up in Poughkeepsie, New York. We flew up on the Warner Brothers helicopter with George. We shot a day or two up there. It was nice.

AL CERULLO (HELICOPTER PILOT, *THE WORLD ACCORDING TO GARP*): I had Robin Williams in the back of the Dauphin. We had a stretcher, a litter in there when he—I forgot what happened to him, but then we flew him somewhere. I don't think there was a stunt. That was just taking him somewhere to a hospital.

TOM PRIESTLEY, JR.: George liked to drink—not when we're shooting but liked to drink afterwards, and we finished shooting up at this boys' school, and soon as they said wrap this Mercedes pulls up. His driver gets out, opens up the trunk, and there's a full bar in there.

The driver gets the glass, takes a bottle of gin, puts about eight ounces of gin in the glass, gives it to George, and George takes it, and he drinks it down all in one gulp. I looked at him. I had chills. I have never seen anybody drink gin like that—whoop—right down in one drink, like it was nothing, and on the show he had his buddy Henry Bumstead that was a famous production designer, and they used to hang out every night drinking. Oh, boy.

BRUNO ROBOTTI: What was interesting for me—the car shots that they did, it was all done in the studio—those nice shots when they're driving. Bumstead came to me and says, "Okay, here's how we're going to do this. We're going to shoot this in the studio. I'm going to give you a sketch. We're going to take eight-foot [height] canvas. You're going to run it so many feet [width]"—I forgot how many feet—"and you're going to paint houses and trees on it."

In the meantime, the carpenters built a drum. Now you remember as a kid watching cartoons, right? You watch how it's the same scenery coming back around? This was the same thing. If you pay attention to it, you're going to see the same buildings going by.

We painted the canvas; we mounted it on this drum. It was sixteen feet. The drum was huge, and it was pivoted so you could turn it. It was in a pivot and [grip] Tommy Gilligan was in the back [turning it] and they [camera operator and director] would say, "Okay, slow it down a little bit, a little bit faster. Okay. That looks good. Keep it at that speed." [laughs]

The camera was all set up with [diffusion] screens. and you know how they diffuse [light] and it's nighttime, and it worked. I mean, not unless you really concentrate on the background that you're looking at. I mean, the scene is so intense that you're not really paying attention.

That was new for me. A matter of fact, there was a set decorator—I forgot his name, he was a little bit cocky whoever it was, I never liked him anyway [laughs]—I shouldn't even mention—but anyway he thought it was asinine to do this. He was making comments about it, and I was totally taken by it, and it worked. But anyway, great, great movie.

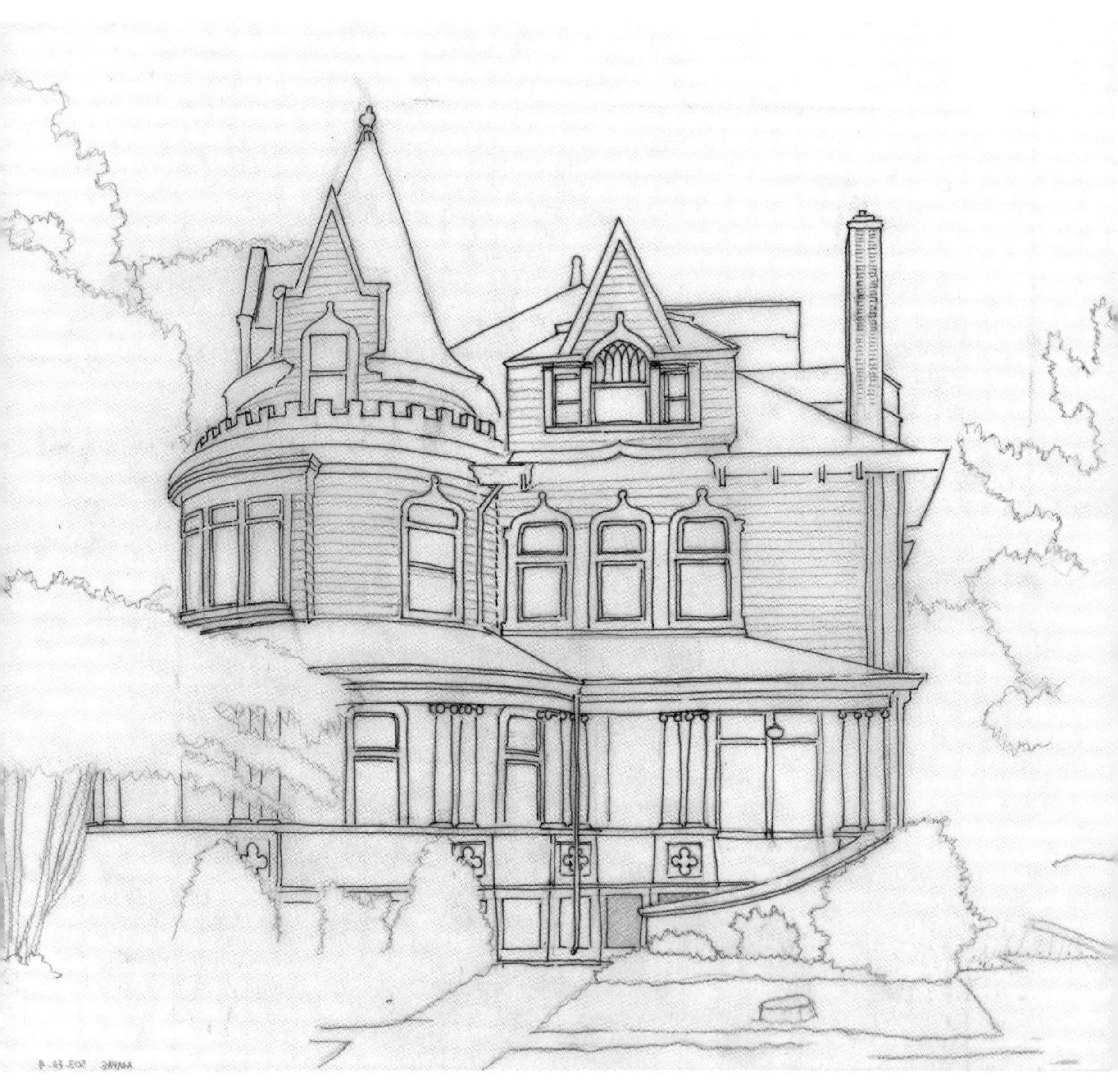

Exterior set design drawing for *Sophie's Choice*. Photo courtesy of the Margaret Herrick Library, Academy of Motion Picture Arts and Sciences.

Sophie's Choice

(1982)

TOM PRIESTLEY, JR. **(CAMERA OPERATOR, *SOPHIE'S CHOICE*)**: When I worked on *Sophie's Choice*, I think the average day was 8:30 a.m. to 7 p.m., with an hour for lunch. We'd come in at eight-thirty. They'd chase everybody up to set, Meryl [Streep] and [director] Alan Pakula, and whoever was on it would go and rehearse the scene we're about to shoot, and then, after maybe twenty minutes or whatever it was, they'd call the heads of the department in, they'd look at the scene, they discuss where the first shot would be, the camera, then they'd go off and get makeup and we'd do all the lighting and all this stuff, and then Alan would go off and do his thing and come back. We might get the master shot, and maybe one or two pieces of coverage, and we go to lunch at one o'clock.

Come back at two, we shoot the rest of the coverage of the scene and then maybe get a heads-up for the scene the next day, and we leave six-thirty, seven o'clock at night. We only shot three and a half pages, most. It was a very relaxed, I mean, beautiful way to do movies, but, as it's been shown, they just keep pushing and pushing. Now, I guess with someone like Meryl, you can't push too much, but she was always there. She was always on the set. I mean, she was a real professional and a joy to watch.

Alan was a very nice man. He was like an absent-minded professor. Doing *Sophie's Choice*, Alan wants to talk to Meryl and stuff, and he's sitting in his chair with the headphones on and he gets up, and he forgets he's got the headphones on, and he's got his book in the chair. So he is walking toward Meryl with the headphones around his neck and he is dragging the chair along beside him. He's trying to talk to Meryl about the scene. It was unbelievable, but that's the way he was.

He and [director of photography] Nestor Almendros were made for each other. I mean, Nestor Almendros—they used to send a PA [production assistant] with him when he went to the men's room because he couldn't find his way back to the set. We used to call him Mr. Magoo—he'd wear these very thick glasses, and the glasses made his eyes look very, very small and beady. If there was a crack on the sidewalk he'd trip over. I'm surprised he lived so long. He was always walking into things, tripping over things. Yet he made this great movie with Terrence Malick, *Days of Heaven* [1978]. Nester was a very sweet man.

All Nestor's career he's basically worked on live locations. He did very little stage shooting and was not used to the luxury of having to take walls out and lift things and fly things away and all that kind of stuff. I had to do a shot on *Sophie's Choice*—Meryl and everybody were coming down the flight of stairs and going to the front door. So in that particular shot I had to take the wall out on the left-hand side of the hallway so I could pull the camera back and follow the actors.

I asked Nestor, "I'd like to take this wall out," and he looked at me like he was frightened to take the wall out because he couldn't handle the empty space that was there. He's used to working in live locations where basically your photography is dictated by the confines of the space where you're in. What they did was, after I set up the shot, he found out how far the camera went back. He brought the wall right up to our backs to reduce the amount of empty space, to make him feel better.

TONY GAMIELLO (SET DRESSER, *SOPHIE'S CHOICE*): *Sophie's Choice*. We did it at the old Camera Mart stage on 54th Street and 10th Avenue. We set up a whole building—like, it was two floors—and the second floor was suspended from the grids with chains because all the floorboards were wild, so they could pull out any section of the floor and put a camera up through it, or a light, or whatever. Then of course we had locations of the exterior of that house in Brooklyn with the old-fashioned curved windows.

TOM PRIESTLEY, JR.: We're scouting the locations. They were going to pick this location that was, like, an abandoned chicken farm which they're going to make into the concentration camp. It was a whole bunch of us out there scouting. It's a big old muddy field. Tommy Prate [key grip] and I are sitting there, and we're watching—we hear Alan Pakula saying, "Nestor, Nestor, where are you?"

Then we hear Nestor saying, "Alan, Alan, where are you?"

And we're saying, "These are two grown men—they can't find each other?" Then we see them; they're backing up towards each other, and we're saying, "This is like the O.K. Corral gunfight in reverse"—these guys are backing towards each other, and eventually Nestor bumps into Alan, and he's so shocked. He jumps out of his boots and lands in the mud in his stocking feet, and Alan turns around—they look at each other.

MICHAEL ZANSKY (SCENIC ARTIST, *SOPHIE'S CHOICE*): I met Dean [Taucher] early on. He had moved to New York from Chicago. I met him at Nolan's Paint Shop in Bed-Stuy [Bedford-Stuyvesant neighborhood of Brooklyn]. I had started to do film work. I couldn't stand [back]drop painting. I couldn't stand scenic shops.

Then we both started working for Gene [Powell, scenic charge] on *Sophie's Choice*.

DEAN TAUCHER (SCENIC ARTIST, *SOPHIE'S CHOICE*): The production manager or the accountant or both had a $60,000 cash-flow for petty cash, because so much was paid for in cash back then. It was a loose account. If you had a receipt, it was fine. The job got done. But at the start of construction in the first week they turned the $60,000 into cocaine to sell to the crew.

[Name redacted] was selling to the construction crew, the whole crew, and he didn't have to put any money up front. He and the [redacted] were splitting the profits, but they put the money back into the till in a week—$60,000 worth of cocaine sales profit in one week.

MICHAEL ZANSKY: [Name redacted]—loudmouth motherfucker, stoned out of his mind on coke along with the other guys that were doing steel work on the building itself—and I'm thinking this motherfucker is really a piece of work. I'm joking around with this son of a bitch. He turns away from me and falls to the ground, just falls to the ground, passes right to the ground. Bang!

DEAN TAUCHER: He ends up having a heart attack and dying on the set in the middle of shooting.

TONY GAMIELLO: We came back from lunch one day—my father, Hans Swanson, and I—and [he's] there on the floor in the lobby with the paramedics working on him, then they took him away. That was it. I saw a lot of guys go way before their time. My contemporaries and the older guys would either drink or drug themselves out, and I knew a lot of guys like that.

DEAN TAUCHER: And they didn't call it a day. They had him carried off the set. Maybe it was an hour break or a long lunch and then they went back to shooting. It seemed pretty cold-hearted.

TONY GAMIELLO: We're working and it's Christmas Eve. Everybody else left after lunch and we were still working at one point and we just said, "Hey, we ready to leave soon? We got families waiting at home." We pulled a mutiny because these people are unbelievable, some of them, and now every production closes down for two weeks so people can be with their families.

TOM PRIESTLEY, JR.: The last two days of shooting [in Zagreb, Yugoslavia], and Meryl comes to the crew and asked the crew if we could combine two days' work into one—she wanted to get home and see her kids. One of the most important scenes in the movie. She's in the commandant's office. She had to make the choice, and she's begging for her child's life, and I think she does it either in German or Polish. I'm on the set with her, with the camera assistant and the AD [assistant director] and the two actors and everybody else is behind the set, watching the video.

It's, like, three o'clock in the morning—crew's tired, everybody's tired, and so we roll the camera. We do the slate. Meryl and a German actor [Gunther Maria Halmer] do the scene. It was great. Everything Meryl does is great. And there's silence, and Meryl's looking around—I'm looking around. So finally, I yell, "Cut!" I run around behind the set where the video village, and here is Academy Award winner[35] director Alan Pakula, Academy Award winner Nestor Almendros with their heads together, sound asleep.

I wake up Alan: "Alan, you got to look at the video." Alan says, "Oh, that's great." Meryl's on the other side of the set—she hears, "Great," and she says, "Good night, folks, that's a wrap. I'm out of here."

And she's gone. Boom, no take two. One take—gone.

TOM PRIESTLEY, JR.: We went to Zagreb to shoot the exterior scenes that were supposed to be Auschwitz. The guy who was the production manager, a Yugoslavian guy, was a survivor of Auschwitz. He also was in Spielberg's movie *Schindler's List* [1993]. He played the maître d' in the beginning who talks to Schindler and gets all the stuff and arranges the people to meet and everything like that. His name is Branko Lustig, and he went on to work in a lot of pictures with Spielberg, but he was the production manager on that job and he controlled everything. He learned a lot from the Gestapo. He was very influential in helping us. They had some other people there, but it was brutal.

It was a very powerful movie because of the sentiment. Meryl was great. Peter McNichol was great. It was a hard movie because of the remembrance of the survivors of Auschwitz, but it was done with great compassion. The scene when Meryl—the first scene, where she gets off the train, and the officer makes her choose between her son and her daughter, was a very emotional scene, and that was shot out in the countryside somewhere in Yugoslavia under Russian control. It was just a depressing place—like, even in the city they had all these

35 He was actually nominated three times, but he didn't win.

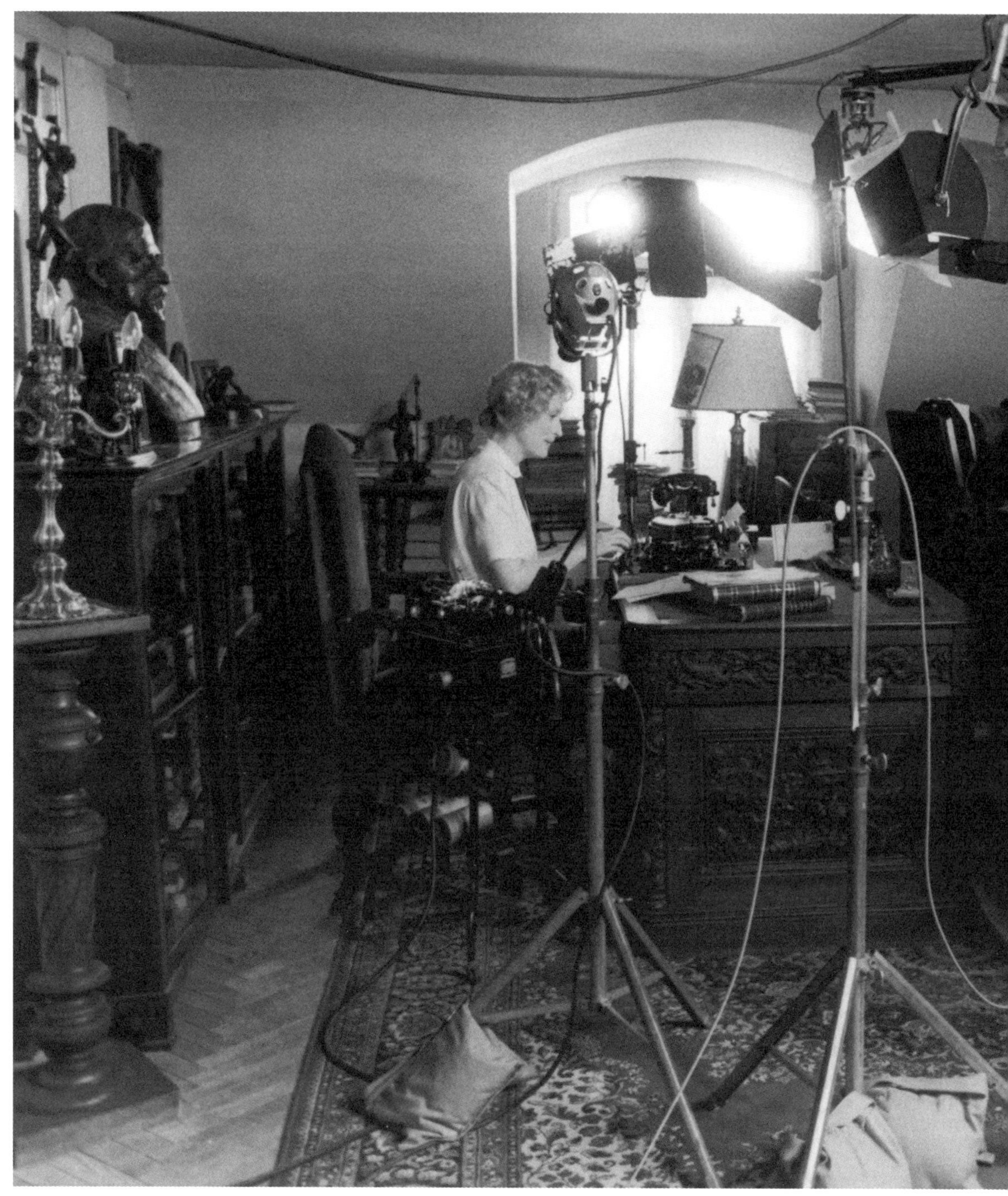

Meryl Streep and Alan Pakula working on *Sophie's Choice*. Photo courtesy of the Margaret Herrick Library, Academy of Motion Picture Arts and Sciences.

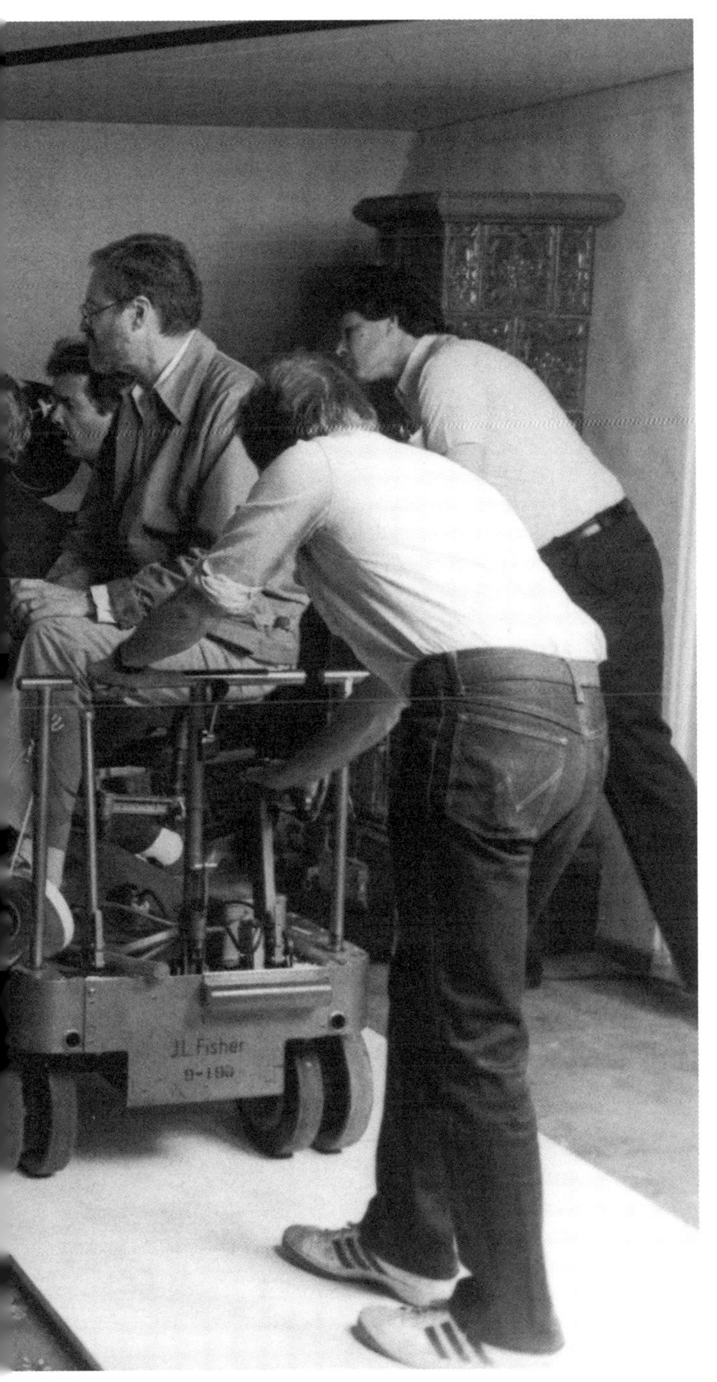

apartment buildings. It looked like Russian prisons. They all had those ugly concrete buildings with just the windows and no balconies and no architectural detail—just awful.

And then the sky was like a yellow haze. They were burning this cheap high-sulfur coal, and it was like a haze of smog—brutal. We also had some people who were survivors, and they talked about it—they had one spigot that trickled water out to like eighty people, and people lived in filth and squalor, and it was just—just the sense of any humanity was gone. They were treated like animals.

One woman—she was a friend of Richard Attenborough—his family sponsored some of the survivors from Auschwitz at one point—she came to visit, and she was talking about how they were treated and they had no food. One woman was working in an infirmary and her daughter got ill, and the Germans would come around and they'd pick out certain people and they'd make you run around the barracks and if you couldn't make the trip around the barracks you went off to the gas chamber, and this one woman's daughter was ill, so she took the daughter and put her underneath a dead body in the bed and covered the dead body up to hide her so the Germans wouldn't find her. Awful.

And this guy Branko Lustig, he was like twelve or thirteen when he was taken to the camps and he wanted to go with his mother and the mother said, "No, you go with your father," because the mother must have known that they were going to get killed, and she told him he could pass off being somebody who could work. He went with his father, and he survived.

Trading Places

(1983)

GARY MULLER: It was epic. That's the movie that started in New York, then we went to Philadelphia for quite a bit. It was John Landis, who was a total scumbag, and it was right after *The Twilight Zone* [1983]. It [*Trading Places*] was such a tense set because the director and the producer and the editor were all from *Twilight Zone*.

That was produced by George Folsey, and one of his nephews, Michael Tadross, who became the famous Michael Tadross—I'm sure somebody's mentioned his name—he was at Paramount for a while. He was a big New York producer.

MICHAEL TADROSS (ASSISTANT DIRECTOR, *TRADING PLACES*): *Trading Places*. John Landis was at his best. I'm sure I did, as far as I remember, four or five movies of John Landis's, and the man was an absolute pleasure and the smartest director I've ever met in my life. After *Twilight Zone,* it was the toughest time ever for those two guys [George Folsey, Jr., and John Landis].

GARY MULLER (SECOND ASSISTANT CAMERA OPERATOR, *TRADING PLACES*): The editor's name was Malcolm [Campbell]. I got friendly with the editor because we were looking at tests. He says, "Hey, do you want to see some stuff?" The fucking guy shows me the *Twilight Zone* decapitation footage—shows me all his shit while they were still cutting *Twilight Zone*. I couldn't believe it.

The filmmaker and his team made a series of reckless decisions that were almost unbelievable. First, they hired two child actors, Myca Dinh Le and Renee Shin-Yi Chen, who were seven and six years old respectively. This was in direct violation of California law, which explicitly forbade the employment of children at night. Additionally, hiring minors always required a special permit, which they didn't bother to obtain. Everything was resolved with a hasty agreement involving Peter Wei-Te Chen, Renee's uncle. He acted as a representative of the families and accepted a cash payment on their behalf, without any formal contract or insurance.

The deal was closed quickly by associate producer George Folsey Jr. without informing the casting crew or the on-set firefighters. Landis was eager to cut through the red tape and quickly shoot the scene. After all, the children would only appear briefly on screen.[36] —*El País*, August 29, 2023

GARY MULLER: Landis wanted to fire everybody—didn't think this guy was good, that guy was good. Everybody was walking

36 Miquel Echarri, "'Keep Rolling': The Decision That Resulted in the Tragic Deaths of Two Children and a Hollywood Actor," *El País English,* August 29, 2023, https://english.elpais.com/culture/2023-08-29/keep-rolling-the-decision-that-resulted-in-the-tragic-deaths-of-two-children-and-a-hollywood-actor.html, retrieved November 26, 2023.

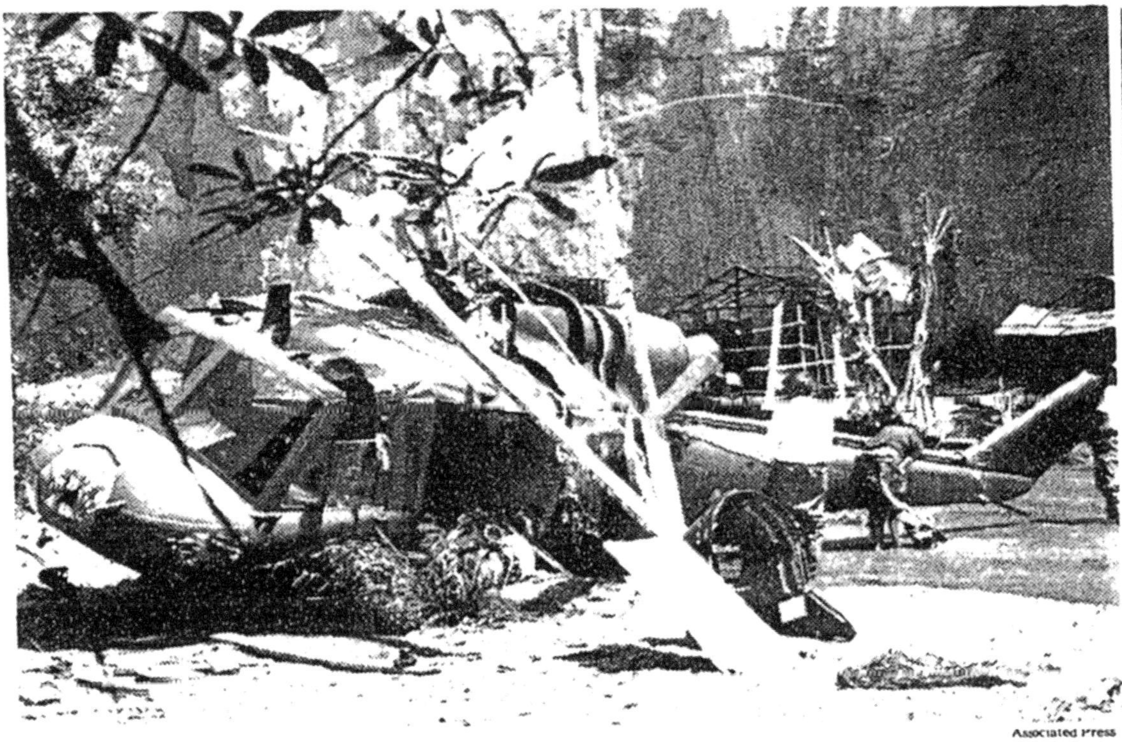

Associated Press

Wreckage of helicopter after crash yesterday during filming on set of a segment of the film "The Twilight Zone."

Copter Falls, Killing Actor and 2 Children on Set

Special to The New York Times

LOS ANGELES, July 23 — Vic Morrow and two Vietnamese children the actor was holding in his arms were killed early today when a helicopter crashed while they were making a movie northwest of Los Angeles.

The tail rotor of the helicopter, carrying a camera crew, had been hit by debris from explosives detonated in a Vietnam war scene.

Mr. Morrow and the children were struck and killed by the main rotor of the helicopter as it pitched into a river on the set, DeWitt Morgan, the Los Angeles County fire inspector, said. The child actors were identified as Renee Shinn Chen, 6, of Pasadena, and My-ca Dinh Lee, 7, of Cerritos, a sheriff's deputy, John Radeleff, said.

The three persons were killed as they were running through a set that resembled a Vietnamese village. More than 100 movie extras and production assistants witnessed the accident, which occurred during the filming of a scene for a film based on "The Twilight Zone" television series.

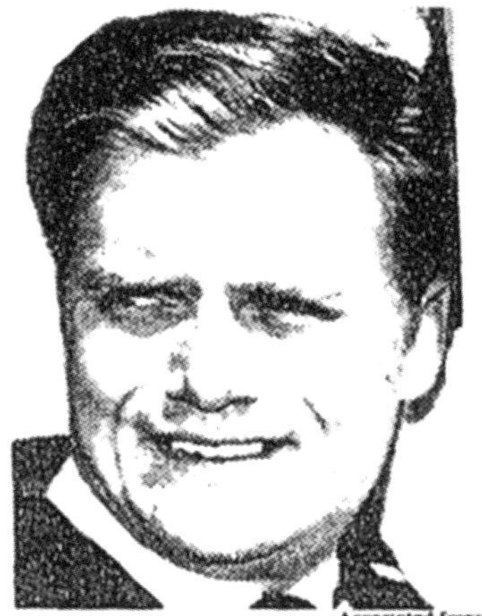

Associated Press

Vic Morrow

The accident occurred at about 2:30 A.M. at the private Indian Dunes Park, 40 miles from here. It was the last session of shooting directed by John Landis for Warner Bros. Mr. Landis, director of "National Lampoon's Animal House," was in charge of one segment of "The Twilight Zone," a four-segment anthology. The other directors were Joe Dante, George Miller and Steven Spielberg.

"There was a village along a bluff being involved in war," Mr. Morgan said. "They were going to have a helicopter doing rockets and bombs, explosions and fireballs. The debris from one explosion hit the tail rotor, and the helicopter landed in the river."

Also injured were the pilot, Darcy Wingo, who was listed in fair condition with a cut hand and injured neck; the camera operator, Roger Smith, in fair condition with leg and neck injuries, and the production manager, Danny Alingham, and Randal Robinson, both in good condition with minor injuries.

Career Spanned 27 Years

Mr. Morrow, whose entertainment career spanned 27 years, created the role of Sgt. Chip Saunders in "Combat," which ran from 1962 to 1966. He began his career directing Off Broadway productions, including "Death Watch," "The Maids" and "The Firstborn." He also had a role in an Off Broadway production of "A Streetcar Named Desire."

Mr. Morrow, who was 51 years old, made his film debut in 1955 in "The Blackboard Jungle." His other films included "Tribute to a Bad Man" in 1956, "Men in War" in 1957, "Portrait of a Mobster" in 1961 and "The Bad News Bears" in 1976, in which he played the coach whose team battled Walter Matthau's ragtag Bears.

Mr. Morrow married Barbara Turner, the actress, in 1957, and they were divorced in 1965. They had two daughters, Carrie, 24, and Jennifer, 20.

New York Times, July 24, 1982.

around him on pins and needles. I was working for an English cameraman, Bob Paynter, who was a great guy. He would laugh, and all he wanted to do was drink beer.

We're out in the streets of Philadelphia, and Jack Volpe, a famous dolly grip who is a nice guy and sort of off the wall—we're doing a dolly shot and it was cold—he had his Eddie Bauer hoodie up with the fur, and he's pushing the dolly back and forth, and out of nowhere he blurts out, "Oh, guess we're not going to kill anybody tonight." And Landis was standing right next to him. Had him fired on the spot. Well, that became a big brouhaha. Jack went home and got paid hour by hour for the whole job. Every hour we worked he got paid.

Even Eddie Murphy was cracking jokes [about *The Twilight Zone*], and Landis is just getting really uptight. Eddie is trying to keep everyone cool.

So now we have to go to an island to shoot this sequence. We're at this island and we're shooting and shooting. We had a helicopter scene to shoot. This is the opening sequence where they cut back and forth with Dan Aykroyd on the boat.

We had just found out—not many people knew—that Landis was not allowed to be within twenty-five miles of the helicopter scene. I think it was Paramount Pictures who wanted him off the island. They didn't want him anywhere near a helicopter. They said, "That helicopter cannot take off if he is anywhere near. He can tell the AD what he wants and then he has to leave."

So we're having a dinner and there's, like, thirty people at this table, and the helicopter pilot is there. Now the next day we're going to start this two-day sequence with the helicopter and the pilot. It was a great time. I mean, Eddie was funny, [Dan] Aykroyd was funny, everybody was funny, and the pilot was drinking, and drinking, and drinking. I mean, *drinking*. His forehead was about to touch the top of the table. And I believe Sosna said to him, "Don't you think you had enough to drink? We have to fly tomorrow."

He's got his head in the plate of pineapple, and he picks his head up, and, like, throws his shoulders back, and he stares right at Landis and he says, "Nobody has to fucking worry. As drunk as I am today, tomorrow morning I'll be sober as the judge, and I won't cut anybody's fucking head off." And he got up and walked away. Well, needless to say, that was the end of dinner. True story.

I mean, towards the end, I would say stuff to Landis—you know, he'd be looking at me and I'd say, "John, what's your problem? Come on. Let's go."

DON NACE (SCENIC ARTIST, *TRADING PLACES*): I think my first movie was *Trading Places,* and it had Dave Lowry and Gene Powell and Bruno Robotti and all these scenic artists, the old guard, and I couldn't believe how much fun they were having. I worked in commercials before I decided to become a shop man.[37] I was doing okay. I was doing ad concepts and stuff, but my agency kind of fell apart. In ad agencies, everybody's at everybody's throat all day long: "This isn't good enough," "This has got to be better," "We don't have time to do this," "I want this on my desk now." So here I'm working, and these guys sit around and they make jokes all day long. I was just dumbfounded at how much fun they were having.

BRUNO ROBOTTI (SCENIC CHARGE, *TRADING PLACES*): They put us up in this beautiful hotel in Philadelphia, and it ended up being the hotel where they had the Legionnaires' disease. They didn't tell us. Once I found out, I also found out you couldn't open windows in that place. I went to my friend, the grip, and said, "You must have a crowbar, right? Can I borrow it for the night?" He said, "Sure. Don't kill anybody."

37 "Shop man" is an old term for scenic industrial, a position in the scenic artist department that does the cleaning, orders the supplies, etc.

I said, "No, don't worry about it." It was wintertime, but I didn't care. I'd rather freeze. I opened that window just enough to get air in. The crazy stuff that you do on location.

TONY GAMIELLO (SET DRESSER, *TRADING PLACES*): We spent quite a few weeks in Philadelphia shooting and it was strange. There was an old historic building there that was a bank. We turned a good part of it into the Stock Exchange, because they couldn't get permission to shoot in the Stock Exchange in New York and we were shooting in Philly for other things, so we fabricated this whole Stock Exchange thing, and we had to run cables out windows and into other windows and stuff, because back then they had all these computers that were from the eighties, and so they had to make them work. We worked all day and all night.

We had a big, huge sign that they had to rig some cable and hang it off the balcony, and then you can see it down below that it said "Stock Exchange" to hide the bank sign, and we can only do it later in the evening, after nine o'clock, because they wouldn't let you tie up the sidewalk during the day when pedestrians are walking.

But anyway, to hide the cable we had a couple of scenic artists—harnesses and ropes tied around them secured so they could angle up the ledge of the building with long handle brushes, on poles, long handle rollers and brushes to paint the cables so they blend in with the building. You didn't see the cables holding the sign because it was a historic building—they wouldn't let us screw in a bolt into the building and they wouldn't let us damage the building.

In fact, they had a production office across the street from the hotel, and you could see the light was on, and, like, every once in a while, you see them come to the window. They were monitoring what we were doing.

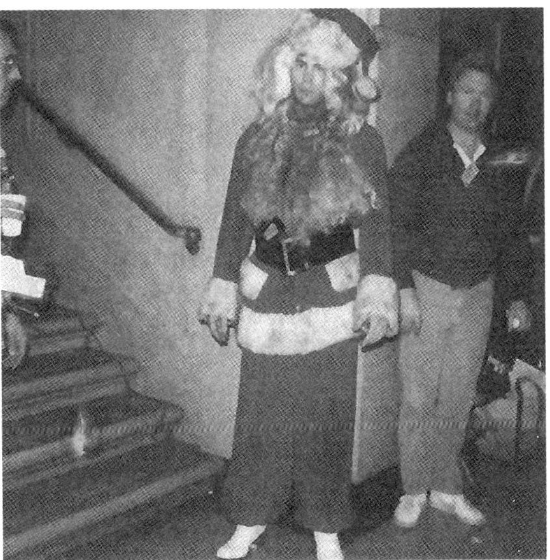

We were working so many hours that, when we were finishing up in Philly, Dan Aykroyd sent out a memo inviting the whole crew to one of the penthouses for a party that week. The invitation says, "To inaugurate the fifty-six-hour work day, we're having a party at the penthouse. All are invited."

GARY MULLER: I was amazed at how good the movie turned out, how funny it was.

We were up in the Bronx, in some godforsaken old apartment that we had to walk up three flights. Dan Aykroyd was in a scene with the salmon under the Christmas Santa Claus outfit. He's laying there and he's got a big piece of salmon under his suit thing, and he's having a hard time with the dialogue—it was simple dialogue—and went on and on, and I was like, "Oh God, I've never seen Dan like this before."

Aykroyd sits up with the salmon in this smelly Santa Claus outfit and says, "John, we have to wrap." He said, "This is the first time in probably five years, I'm not stoned, and you know why. I can't work anymore."

He got out of bed and left. It was the anniversary of Belushi's death. That was a weird situation.

Wardrobe test polaroids of Dan Aykroyd on *Trading Places*.

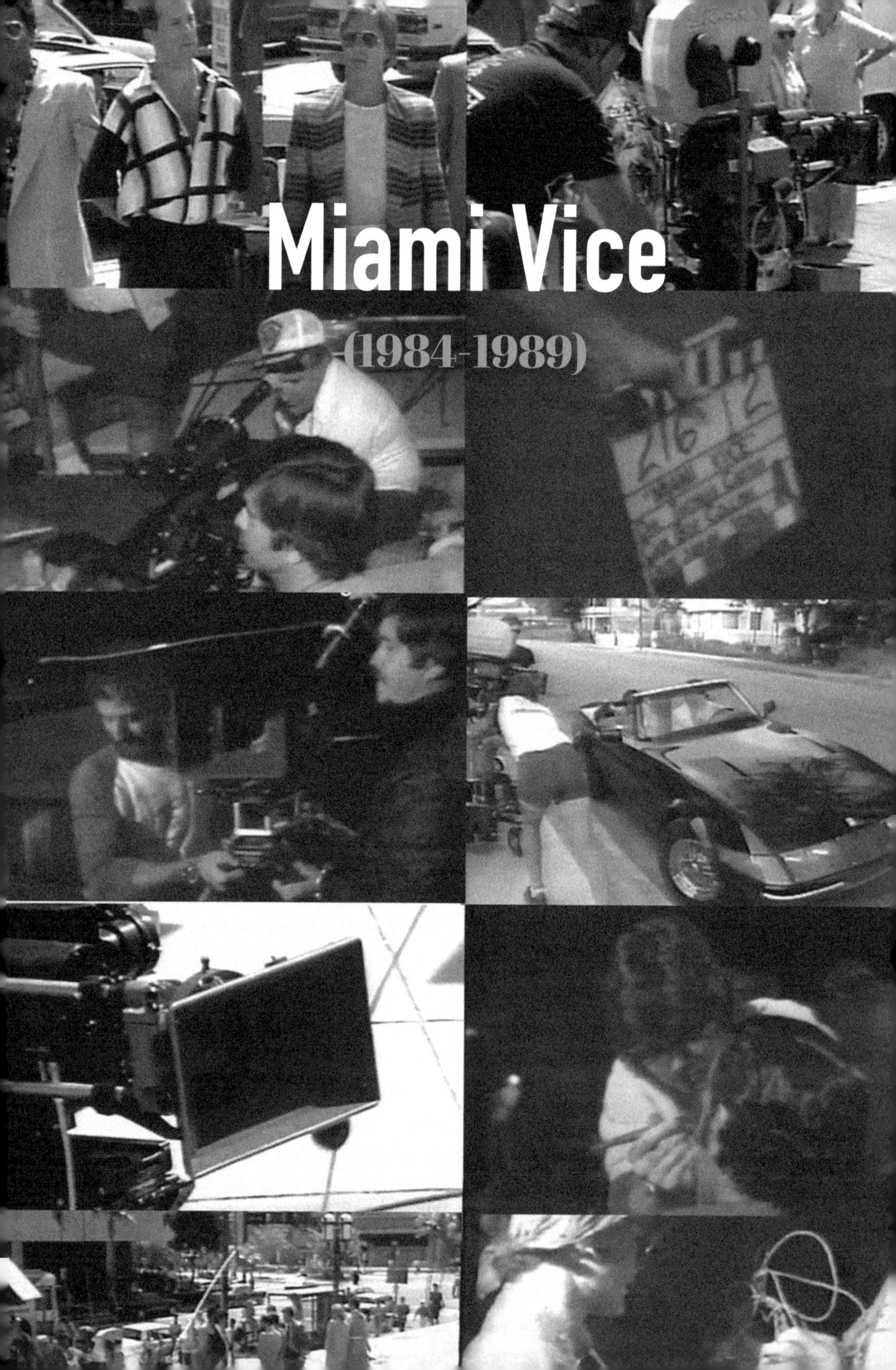
Miami Vice
(1984-1989)

STEVEN FELDER (FIRST ASSISTANT DIRECTOR, *MIAMI VICE*, SEASON 3): I just did season three. I think the first-season pilot part was in New York. I got called down to do second half of season two. They had a lot of problem with ADs—I got called to come down and replace somebody—I don't even know who I replaced—and I remember they said, "Listen, Don Johnson is a handful. He's a nightmare. We don't know how long you'll last."

I said, "I don't care. I'm in Miami. What's the big deal?" So they had their hotel set up on Collins Avenue—the office is in the hotel—and when I went into production office there were these boxes of white hats and black hats that said "Miami Vice" on them, and they said, "Okay, well, here's your white hat, because it's hot down here."

"So what's all the black hats for?" "That's when you get fired. That's your going-away gift." So I go down there and kind of figure it out, and there's a fair amount of New Yorkers down there—ex-New-Yorkers—Enrique Bravo was the camera operator—Tom Priestley, Jr., was one of the DPs [directors of photography]—Jimmy Contner was one of the DPs.

TOM PRIESTLEY, JR. (DIRECTOR OF PHOTOGRAPHY, *MIAMI VICE*, SEASONS 2 & 3): Television is a great place to learn. I mean, you can do a television show, you can do anything. I did *Miami Vice*. We did it [an episode] in, like, seven days. I think back then, '85, we didn't have co-DPs. I was able to go out and scout the location. I'd show up and then I have to shoot it, whatever it was. If they had a real difficult location, they would drag me out there at nine o'clock at night to show me it so they could say they showed it to me, but by going there, I couldn't initiate anything, because it was nine o'clock at night. I'm going to be back there at seven o'clock in the morning.

They just did it to satisfy their so-called requirements and then say, "Well, we showed him the location." I mean, it was run and gun.

STEVEN FELDER: A lot of guys who were feature guys—it was a lot of snobbism between being a TV guy and a film guy, and even as I have my résumé built up with film, people would go, "You, you're a film guy—you don't know how to do TV." Now, I started doing a lot of TV—they said, "You're doing TV. You don't do film." There was a feature crew and a TV crew. TV was popular, but most of it was done in studios in L.A.—*Mannix* and these horrible shows—but location TV work was pretty new.

DEAN TAUCHER (PRODUCTION DESIGNER, *MIAMI VICE*, SEASON 3): I got asked to take over *Miami Vice* as the designer. Our union was not part of the IA [IATSE, the International Alliance of Theatrical Stage Employees], and they wouldn't give me an art direction credit because I was not part of the Art Directors Guild, which was an IA local, and the only credit I could get—which they didn't want to give me that either—I was the "visual consultant," I was the production designer.

STEVEN FELDER: When I first went down there we had this big setup—there was a crime scene and [characters] Crockett and Tubbs show up early in the morning on Ocean Drive in front of all of the Art Deco hotels, a dead body, and a car crashed into a palm tree.

And so I've been warned about Don [Johnson]. We did a big rehearsal with camera, we shot some background extras, we did all this stuff to give him a later call, and so he comes out. He always changed shit. He's always late. He's always wired up, and I went up to him and said, "Hi, Don, I'm number thirteen"—I was the thirteenth AD in, I think, two and a half years—I said, "We're ready to go."

He said, "We were ready to go? I didn't rehearse anything."

I said, "All you got to do is come out to the car and walk up to the spot and then we'll get the coverage."

"Okay, great. I like that." And that's how we started off. Really good.

Don was just coming out of a couple of things—he wasn't a big star. They wanted to do, like, an *I Spy* combo of black and white actors with the other guy, Tubbs, Philip Michael Thomas. So they started off even—like, even screen time, even dialogue, even involvement, even everything, and then Don eventually realized—and so did the audience—that he's, like, a super TV star, super-good-looking, knew how to work the camera, knew the character, very thorough, very prepared, but difficult, really demanding, and so I got along with him pretty well, most of the time.

We did a lot of big stuff. We rigged, like, four Panavision cameras on the Ferrari and set them off to do seven pages of dialogue with a couple of police escorts, and they would just drive till we finished. We would close part of the freeways to get on these off-ramps and stuff, even during the day—do these high-speed chases and these montages that [the show] was famous for. It was an exciting show. "What are we gonna do today?"

"Today we're going to take a boat down the Inland Waterway by Indian River, and we're going to have it launch itself out of the water across Lincoln Drive onto a flatbed."

That was a lot of fun on that show. Crazy fun.

DEAN TAUCHER: It was the case where you used to know special-effects guys because they were always missing a digit. They were the crazy guys from World War II or the Korean War who just loved blowing shit up, and they found a way to keep doing it after they got out of the service.

On *Miami Vice,* I made a warehouse. They put plastic explosives every place that two pieces of wood bent and wired the whole thing up. They had seven cameras on it to see the explosion. The explosion was so big, the exposure burned out on every camera to white instantly, so they got nothing out of seven cameras. They broke 250 windows in the neighborhood, and the aftermath was an empty parking lot because the entire set disappeared.

It was just rubble on the ground.

STEVEN FELDER: We were on these cigarette boats that Don had gotten involved in, eventually racing cigarette boats with a sponsor. Turns out on Netflix there's a thing called *Cocaine Cowboys* about these two cousins that began smuggling cocaine in speedboats from Bahamas. Those were our technical advisors and the guys that we had been involved with. We didn't know they were smuggling at the time, to get us into the speed cigarette boat world. There was this whole underworld of stuff going on.

We'd have production meetings and we talked about, "Okay, the bad guys do this, and these are dealers." We'd have our tech advisors: Miami tactical police come in with duffel bags and plastic suitcases, open them up, and say, "Look, we just confiscated all these guns at Miami International—which ones you want to use? These are plastic Glocks that go through X-ray—these are this thing—this is an AK-47—this is this—this is that. You guys can get first crack at using these things if you want it."

So there was a lot of that, plus it was so much cocaine floating around in mid-eighties it was crazy. I had a guy so high one night, he fell out of a forty-foot Condor [a boom lift]. He had an anxiety attack—fell out of a Condor.

The Cotton Club

(1984)

KEVIN LADSON (**PROP MASTER**): When I came in, it was the early eighties and I honestly wanted to get in the Business because my mother was going around shooting home movies and I said, "Boy, that looks like a lot of fun. I want to do that for a living." I started to inquire at my high school, and they basically gave no information, but I lived in Astoria. Astoria Studios was there, and so basically I said, "Let me see what's going on here." I heard they shot *The Wiz* there. I heard they shot *Wolfen* there.

At the time they were shooting in there with *The Cotton Club*. Let me see if I can get into *The Cotton Club*. See what it's like. I was always held back by security, could never get in, and then I got on line with the extras, who were all Black. I snuck in with the extras and got on set. I had my camera, because I didn't know any better. I walk away from the extras and I start taking pictures of the *Cotton Club* set. Francis Ford Coppola sees me and curses me out: "Who the fuck is this guy with a camera taking pictures?"

I'm like, "I want to be in the movie!"

But he didn't want to hear that, none of that shit. So this older Black guy with a sailor's cap says, "No, no, no. He's with me. He's all right."

He asks, "What are you doing here?"

"I want to be in the movie business. I want to see what it looks like."

He says, "Listen, come with me."

At that point, they broke for lunch and had a big commissary. I didn't even know what a commissary was, and he says, "You want lunch?"

I said, "Yeah. Okay, thanks."

I went and had my salad, and things that were familiar to me. I asked him, "Well, what do you do?"

He was actually Gregory Hines's father [Maurice Hines, Sr.] and was one of the advisors. Because he was part of the jazz era, they had Hines, Hines, and Dad. That was their first group. He showed me around and said, "You got to get into the union."

I said, "Well, how do I get into the union?"

He says, "You got to work on the film."

It was Catch-22. Still, I decided that's what I wanted to do.

BRUNO ROBOTTI, CHARGE SCENIC ARTIST, *THE COTTON CLUB*: Robert Evans was supposed to direct the movie. We were already in production. We were already building sets when they brought in Francis Ford Coppola. I don't know what happened. It was money from Las Vegas.

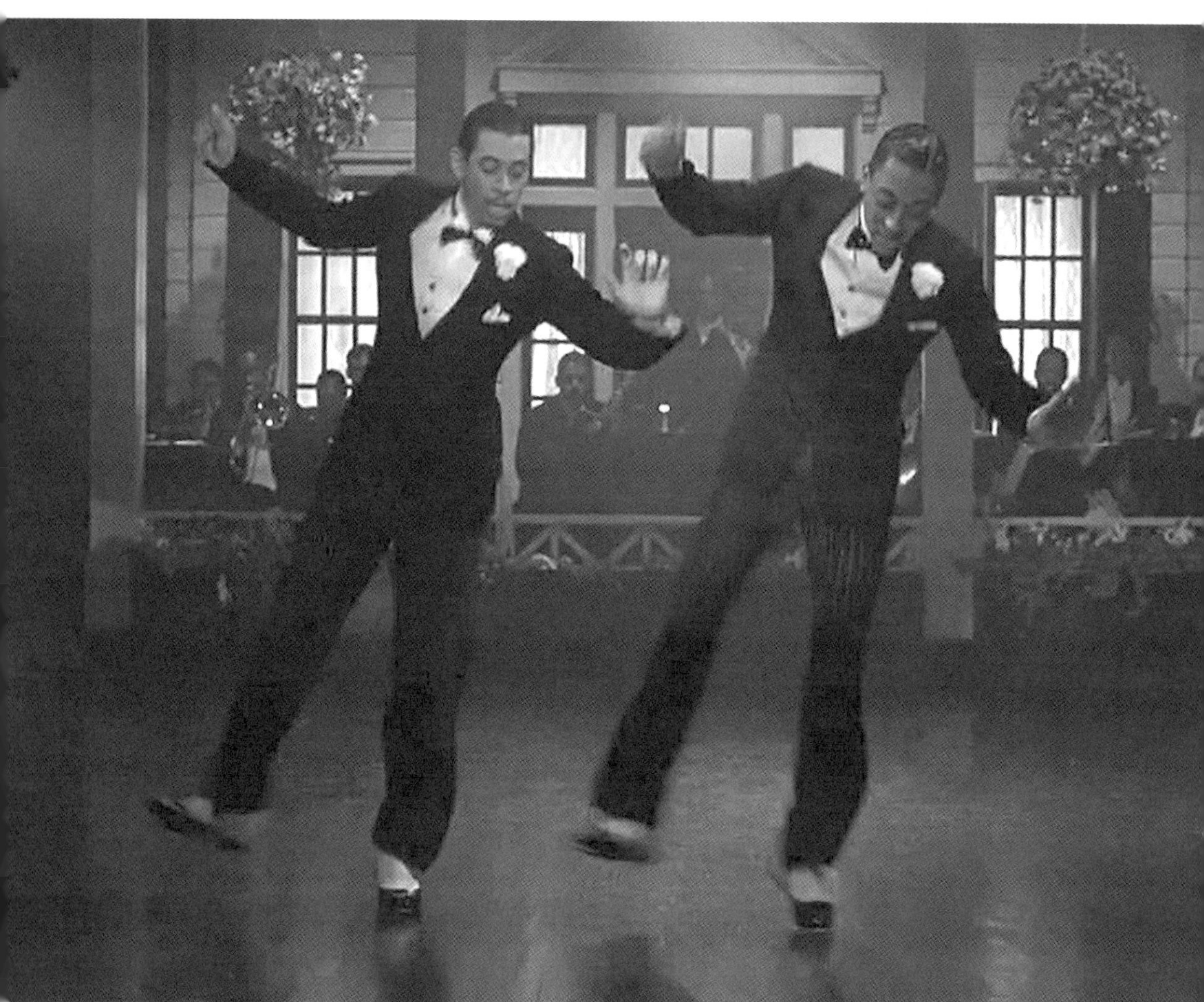

Maurice and Gregory Hines tap dancing in The Cotton Club, 1983. Photo courtesy of the Margaret Herrick Library, Academy of Motion Picture Arts and Sciences.

ANGELO DIGIACOMO (SECOND ASSISTANT CAMERA OPERATOR, *THE COTTON CLUB*): Francis, his company was going bankrupt, but again, because he was producing this, he brought in a Las Vegas guy, Cusumano, who, as part of the—well, the whole thing started with Adnan Khashoggi, an arms dealer, putting money up.

The girl who got it started, one of the associate producers [a former Miss California, Melissa Prophet], did absolutely nothing except introduce these two people. And she caused a riot on the set one day because she came to the Harlem set in a T-shirt that had no sides, no bra.

"Francis may have the one financial situation worse than mine." Evans says. "But I'm not sure."

Some of the supporting players in this drama include a Union Carbide executive, a pair of Las Vegas casino operators, Arab arms dealer, a murdered vaudeville promoter named Roy Radin, and Pulitzer Prize-winning novelist William Kennedy. Those who managed the finances speak of a skyrocketing budget and squandered millions and intrigues aided by pretty young women. What Evans originally presented as a $20-million "sure thing" became a $47-million gamble, and the backers often did not know if they would have the money for the next week's shooting.[38]

—*New York Magazine*, May 7, 1984

ANGELO DIGIACOMO: They got the money from Vegas, but one of the Cusumano brothers had a girlfriend who was an exotic dancer—her costume was a python—he wanted her to have a part in the movie, and so they gave her the part of the cigarette girl, and she could not hit her mark. I had to show her how to back up, like, three steps because she had the tray and the cigarettes in front and she goes, "I can't see with this thing in front of me."

BRUNO ROBOTTI: One of the provisions was that the girlfriend was the cigarette girl. They put her in the movie.

ANGELO DIGIACOMO: Had you gone to central casting, she would have been there for this part. She was perfect.

MAGGIE RYAN (SCENIC ARTIST, *THE COTTON CLUB*): There was a lot of wastage in that movie. But he [Coppola] decided he was not going to have a lunch break. He was going to do it California-style. We had large tables at one end of the stage, just full of food all day long. They had roasted pigs in there. They had everything you could think of just laid out, and everyone could just come and have food and carry on shooting.[39] He didn't want to stop for any break. That didn't last very long because all the employees of Kaufman came down to eat too, and it ended up costing him too much money.

. . . even law clerks connected with the picture were flying first-class, riding in limousines, and staying at top hotels. Travel and living expenses were budgeted at $1 million. Other amounts included $1,644,404 for wardrobe, $460,000 for makeup and hairstyling, $256,000 for security, and $247,000 for catering. Coppola had discarded the "French hours" as impractical, and drivers were pocketing more than $1,200 for a 60-hour week. The carpenters were making upward of $900. All told, the shooting was costing Doumani and his brother at least $1.3 million a week.[40]

—*New York Magazine*, May 7, 1984

ANGELO DIGIACOMO: The costume designer, Milena [Canonero], wanted to spend hundreds

38 Michael Daly, "The Making of *The Cotton Club*: A True Hollywood Tale." *New York Magazine*, May 7, 1984.

39 This is also called French hours. No formal lunch break, but catering rolled out all day so you can just eat whenever you want.

40 Daly, "The Making of *The Cotton Club*."

of thousands of dollars on period underwear, and they said, "What the fuck are you talking about? Nobody's going to see the underwear!"

MAGGIE RYAN: I think there was a lot of drug money coming in.

ANGELO DIGIACOMO: There were times when there were no prints[41] on the roll—I didn't send it in to be processed. I'm saving money, right? Why do you have to process something that you're not going to look at? But that's Francis's thing. And in fact, I just read that he went back to *Apocalypse Now* [1979] to get old footage. Francis found out because he said, "Go look through blah, blah, blah," and they said, "Well, we don't have that," and he called me in and he says, "Why aren't you sending this?"

He liked me—I guess because my name was Italian or whatever—but he says, "You have to do these. I'm sorry, you have to send this all." It was, like, 30,000 feet to send in with no prints, but he wanted it processed.

MAGGIE RYAN: We were into production and suddenly the checks bounced.

BRUNO ROBOTTI: Friday came and there was no money, no checks. They had to regroup.

MAGGIE RYAN: So everyone got together—grips, electricians—they all said, "The checks are bouncing, so we're not working."

And we all stopped work. We would come in and sit. Coppola had one of those silver bullets [mobile homes] on the stage as his office and he would come out of that and start talking about how "We're a family. Your money will be fine, but we're a family. We have to continue working."

Everyone said, "Nope."

Coppola returned to New York. He arrived at the studio on Wednesday morning only to find that Evans and [investor Edward] Doumani had failed to deliver the payroll. On union orders, the cast and crew refused to work. "Francis was in the middle of the stage, telling the entire cast that he was going to pay them," [producer assistant] Jane Bartelme says. "I thought his lawyer was going to drop dead on the spot." By 11 A.M., Doumani had dispatched the money to the studio in an armored car.

Wages in hand, the cast and crew went back to making The Cotton Club. *The unions required Evans and Doumani to post bonds. And most of the people on the picture began cashing their checks on the spot. An assistant director named Henry Bronchtein says, "I'd take my check and deposit it that night at Citibank, but I'd make sure I deposited it that night."*[42]

—*New York Magazine*, May 7, 1984

BRUNO ROBOTTI: We stopped working for a few days and when the money showed up we went back to work.

MAGGIE RYAN: In the end, they had to do cash, so every Friday the guys would come with suitcases full of cash. They took over a room with six or seven four-by-eight tables, all lined around the walls with people behind them. There'd just be stacks of hundreds, tens, and twenty-dollar bills.

You'd come in with your name, and they'd be counting out your money and giving it to you. They had a couple of guys with them with guns and rifles to protect it, because it was, like, a quarter-of-a-million-dollar payroll, and at that time we didn't pay any tax because you were allowed to do ninety-nine deductions. Everyone got a lot of money.

ANGELO DIGIACOMO: Francis wanted to record on video what was happening, which wasn't always something done on a movie at the time. Francis wanted the kid—who has since become a DP [director of photography],

41 When working in film it was common to only print the negatives of what the production thought they might actually use, to save money on printing costs.

42 Daly, "The Making of *The Cotton Club*."

Mitch Admundsen, who drove his Silverfish across the country with his girlfriend. Francis was used to him doing the video, but when they got to New York the union said, "No, you got to have [Local] 52 guys doing it, and not just one guy—you got to have two guys." So that's a real 52 thing.

And of course they have three sound people too—that was the other interesting thing and I have never seen anywhere else, but it was Francis's guy—Nat Boxer was head of the department. I had read an article in some film magazine where he talked about his theory of sound recording, and he felt like the most important thing was the placement of the microphone. He says, "Any moron can push a button, but you've got to put the mic where it belongs." This guy was serious about it—an artist.

Boxer taught me to wear the same clothes every day. He would wear the same uniform every day. He had the darkest blue scrubs, but they weren't scrubs—there were pants and a shirt in the darkest blue. He didn't like black, but it was the darkest blue, almost black, with no reflection, so he could get in just like the assistant; he got in there and he didn't want to reflect. He said, "I have a closet full of the same uniform."

Then I became known as the Man in Black, because I only wore black, and they would make fun of me because I would wear sweatpants. After all, getting black jeans is not always easy.

. . . the "Silverfish," an Airstream RV that provided audio support sets as well as an environment for both creating and editing film. Fully equipped with video viewing and recording machinery, the Silverfish served as an electronic hub for all of the sounds and images. With wires attached to each of five stages at the old Hollywood General Studios, the Silverfish captured the sound and image from each stage. As Thomas Brown, who supervised the design of the Silverfish said, "Francis envisioned an environment where image, sound and data flowed like hot and cold water."

—Zoetrope.com, Coppola's company website

ANGELO DIGIACOMO: They parked the Silverfish on the stage in Astoria.

MAGGIE RYAN: One of the older scenics got quite drunk [laughing] and he went banging on the door demanding that Coppola come out: "Come on out of here, you bum!"

ANGELO DIGIACOMO: When he needed time to write—again, this was with [writer] William Kennedy there—he came out of the Silverfish and he looked at the set and said, "You know what, this lighting is all wrong. Let's change direction."

All because he wanted more time to write, he made the DP do everything 180 degrees different. It bought him time so he could polish what he was working on. He would come out of the Silverfish with clouds of pot smoke.

BRUNO ROBOTTI: I got a call from Dick Sylbert who had recommended me to his brother Paul. I already had done two movies for him, and he asked me about it. Geez, I was elated. Dick was a big name too. He was a production designer. He had already won two Academy Awards at that time. I think I started that a month later.

Organizing a movie is very important, and on *The Cotton Club* one of the things that I think made it successful was that I had three crews, three teams. Gene Powell was doing all the murals, I had Jack Hughes doing the locations up in Harlem, and Bill Drake, Jr., was doing all the backgrounds.

DON NACE: *Cotton Club* was one of the first really big movies they decided they'd do in Kaufman Astoria. So Kaufman Astoria, inside stage 5, looked exactly as it does now, but all the rooms around it were totally wrecked. All the doorframes had been taken off. There was lumber piled in the hallways—the window frames rotted off—there was trash everywhere. So there was really nothing except the stage itself. They had to clean out rooms and they didn't even deal with the outside part of it. The lobby wasn't even there. It was a total wreck. And then the basement was full of water.

So, to avoid going down the steps to get to the lower parts of rooms where they could use the stages, they just chopped a hole right in the floor and put down a ladder. So you would be on the main stage at Kaufman and then somewhere between one of the sets is a big hole in the floor, and you climbed down the ladder and there's another hole in another wall and then you climbed on that ladder and there was a bigger room where they were doing the *Cotton Club* [back]drops.

BRUNO ROBOTTI: It was amazing. The average staff I had was about thirty-five and it went up to close to fifty during different times.

DON NACE: It was phenomenal. They filled about sixty or seventy scenics on it. It was a big change in the union.

BRUNO ROBOTTI: Dick Sylbert was an amazing production designer. At the beginning of the movie, he brought me into his office. He said, "I want you to think about this movie with this palette in mind. It's going to be white, silver, and tobacco color. Everything is going to have this kind of a palette in the movie."

So he kind of prepared me. He started describing all the different sites and so on, and his last words were, "I'm here every day. Anytime you need me, just come knock on the door and come in."

ANGELO DIGIACOMO: There were two brothers, the Sylberts—one was the boss, and one was the second—and they built the set, and they made the doors too narrow for the dolly to fit through. [Director of photography Steven] Goldblatt says, "What the fuck are you doing?"

And he goes, "Well, that's how wide the doors were."

"This isn't a fucking museum. We're making a movie here."

BENNY RAPPA (SCENIC ARTIST): There was no digital stuff. The backgrounds had to be painted. There was no photograph background. The signs had to be painted. So you had a whole six people in charge of just signage. They had to be very good at it.

I worked in a bad area back then, Harlem, 125th Street. Our job was to paint a marquee. It was the actual Cotton Club on 125th Street and we had about ten other scenics for approximately a month and a half. But we had to have an armed guard watch our cars, and to watch us. It was a tough job, because we were scraping this lead paint off this building. It was tedious, and it was cold, but at least we had fun.

Then, after about two months of that on 125th Street, we went back to the Big House. It was just amazing. The whole stage A was just loaded with scenery. It was almost like you were inside of the marquee that I was doing, which was the Cotton Club. They had to use a tar type of paint. Now it's illegal to use that stuff. They used it to get the look of old-fashioned smoky walls. It's like a diluted tar, and we just smeared it around and rub it off. It had to be padded just right.

The fancy artists painted beautiful murals. We were all green and new to the business. Bruno Robotti was like a sergeant, a general. You made sure you didn't even question him. The name Bruno alone just intimidated you. [laughs]

BRUNO ROBOTTI: No, I try to create a relaxing atmosphere. I would always do the initial samples for the production designer and then go from there. We have so much talent in the union that I would let them go, let them create.

If you take creativity away from anyone, they get bored and they start creating nothing. They just follow orders. I saw many guys running jobs where they would impose themselves on everything and then you lose interest, and that's one thing I didn't want. I didn't want people to lose interest in what they were doing.

BENNY RAPPA: Maggie Ryan was in charge of the pigeon shit. In *The Cotton Club,* they had a roof, and she had to go to different parts of Brooklyn and actually get a pallet and match pigeon shit. She did such a wonderful job, you'd swear it was pigeon shit because you can't have actors go into a big pigeon cage on a rooftop shot with real pigeon shit. She made it look exactly like pigeon shit.

MAGGIE RYAN: On *Cotton Club,* they were doing all sorts of things that no one would ever see, and it was all toxic. Everything was toxic. Everything was oil or resin.

Bruno had his nieces employed—Leslie, and Cassandra, and Rosanna—and he was running for union officer, so he had to employ a few more women—I was one, Pam [Lenau], and Polly [Wood-Holland]. Then, three of us got pregnant and he was suddenly having three pregnant women on the crew.

CATHY NASCH (SCENIC ARTIST): Bruno had Maggie in this room painting enamel because they used to use a lot of toxic materials. That was part of the culture too, to man up and use them. Well, he had a bunch of, like, older—I'll put it this way—primadonna scenic artists. One of the scenic artists [Paul Tappenden] marched in and told Bruno, "This woman is pregnant. You need to go and put her in a job that's not quite so toxic."

BENNY RAPPA: Maggie's daughter became a lawyer.

BILL KANE: I worked mostly doing some special effects, smoking up the place.

ANGELO DIGIACOMO: There was a lot of smoke. The special-effects guy was Billy, and Steven [Goldblatt] would go, "More smoke, Billy, more smoke!"

And at the time that was pretty toxic shit.

BILL KANE: We used at the time what they call the Igeba, which is almost like a cannon. You put juice into this little box and then it emits the smoke.

ANGELO DIGIACOMO: One of the [Sylbert] brothers' girlfriends was a set dresser. Anyway, the girlfriend walks out and there's three hundred extras for a nightclub scene and she has a respirator mask on. It was a riot, and the fucking AD [assistant director], Bob Girolami, has a fit: "Get the fuck out of here. Don't you ever come back. What the fuck are you trying to do?"

We were doing another scene in a nightclub and there was a scripted fight, and a glass broke and cut somebody. [Camera operator] Mike Stone cut the camera and Francis freaked out: "You can't! My directing teacher told me that I'm the only one who yells 'cut'"

We never knew if he was kidding, but he didn't like anybody else but him to yell "cut."

BRUNO ROBOTTI: I swear to God, they shot two movies there. It was said that there were so many dance sequences, they could've produced another film with just the dancing on the period.

ANGELO DIGIACOMO: We spent four days shooting "Stormy Weather," and it's not even in the movie—it's just a cut in the transition—it's just a brief clip.

BRUNO ROBOTTI: And Gregory Hines—my God. When they were shooting, I used to lose the crew. [laughs] When they were doing dance sequences and the singing, everything stopped to watch Hines. And do you know what? I didn't care. I let them do it. I was taken by it. So was everybody else. And I said, "Ah, fuck it, let it go."

Death Wish 3

(1985)

MICHAEL TADROSS (ASSISTANT PRODUCTION MANAGER, *DEATH WISH 3*): I worked on two movies with a guy named Michael Winner—British director. I did a movie called *Scream for Help* [1984] and *Death Wish 3*. He was the wildest human being the Lord ever created. May he rest in peace. Michael Winner was absolutely crazy, but I enjoyed his craziness. There's a guy that ninety percent of crew members hated.

STEVEN KIRSHOFF (SPECIAL EFFECTS, *DEATH WISH 3*): *Death Wish 3*, that was my first real big effects movie I ran. That was crazy. We had an English director who hated all of us.

TOM PRIESTLEY, JR. (ASSISTANT CAMERA OPERATOR, *DEATH WISH 3*): I actually worked the last three days of *Death Wish* [1974], the first one. I came in as a second camera, and it was so bizarre. Michael Winner wasn't talking to the actors, the cameramen weren't talking to Michael Winner, and the actors weren't talking to anybody. The gaffer was directing the film with instructions from Michael Winner. This is how crazy this shit is. I couldn't believe it.

MITCHELL LILLIAN (KEY GRIP, *DEATH WISH 3*): We shot in East New York, a really unfortunate neighborhood. There'd be lunch set up for the crew and then Michael Winner would have his table and it would be fenced in and he'd have china and crystal and real silverware and stuff like that.

MICHAEL TADROSS: He wouldn't have lunch with the crew. We're all using plastic forks and paper cups, and he's got fine crystal, fine china brought in from England. It's strictly wine at lunch for him, and I had to get him Cuban cigars, which were illegal.

TOM PRIESTLEY, JR.: He used to have a guy who would follow him with his director's chair, and if he would try to squat to sit down the guy had to slide the chair underneath him.

Cast and crew filming *Death Wish 3*. Photos courtesy of the Margaret Herrick Library, Academy of Motion Picture Arts and Sciences.

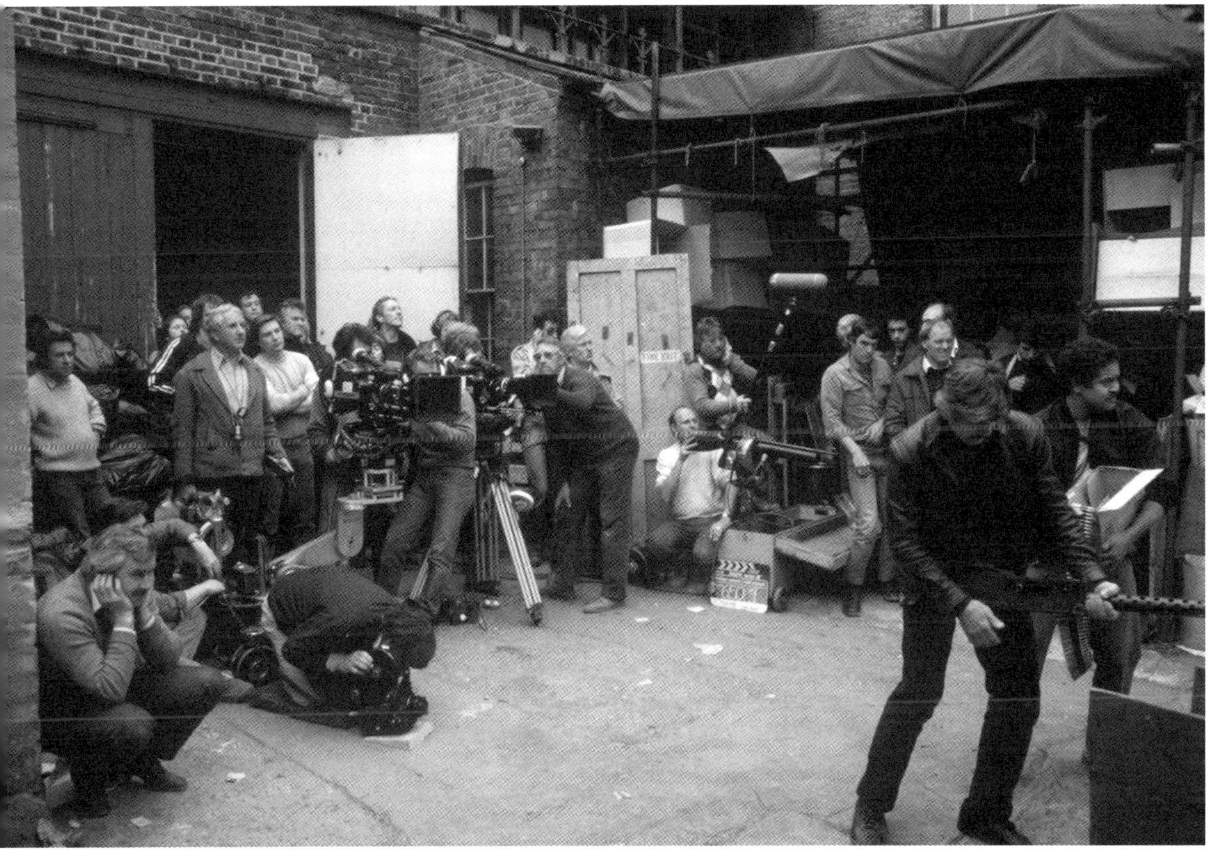

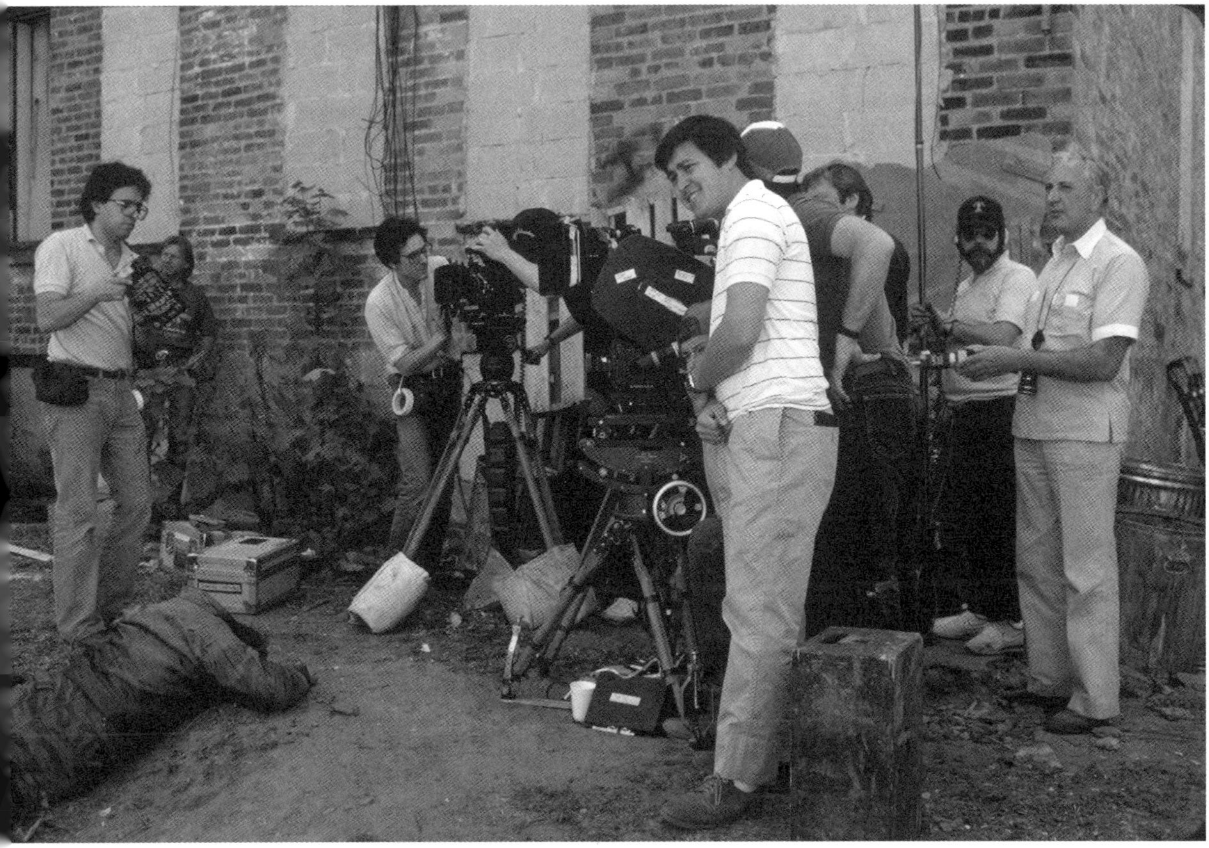

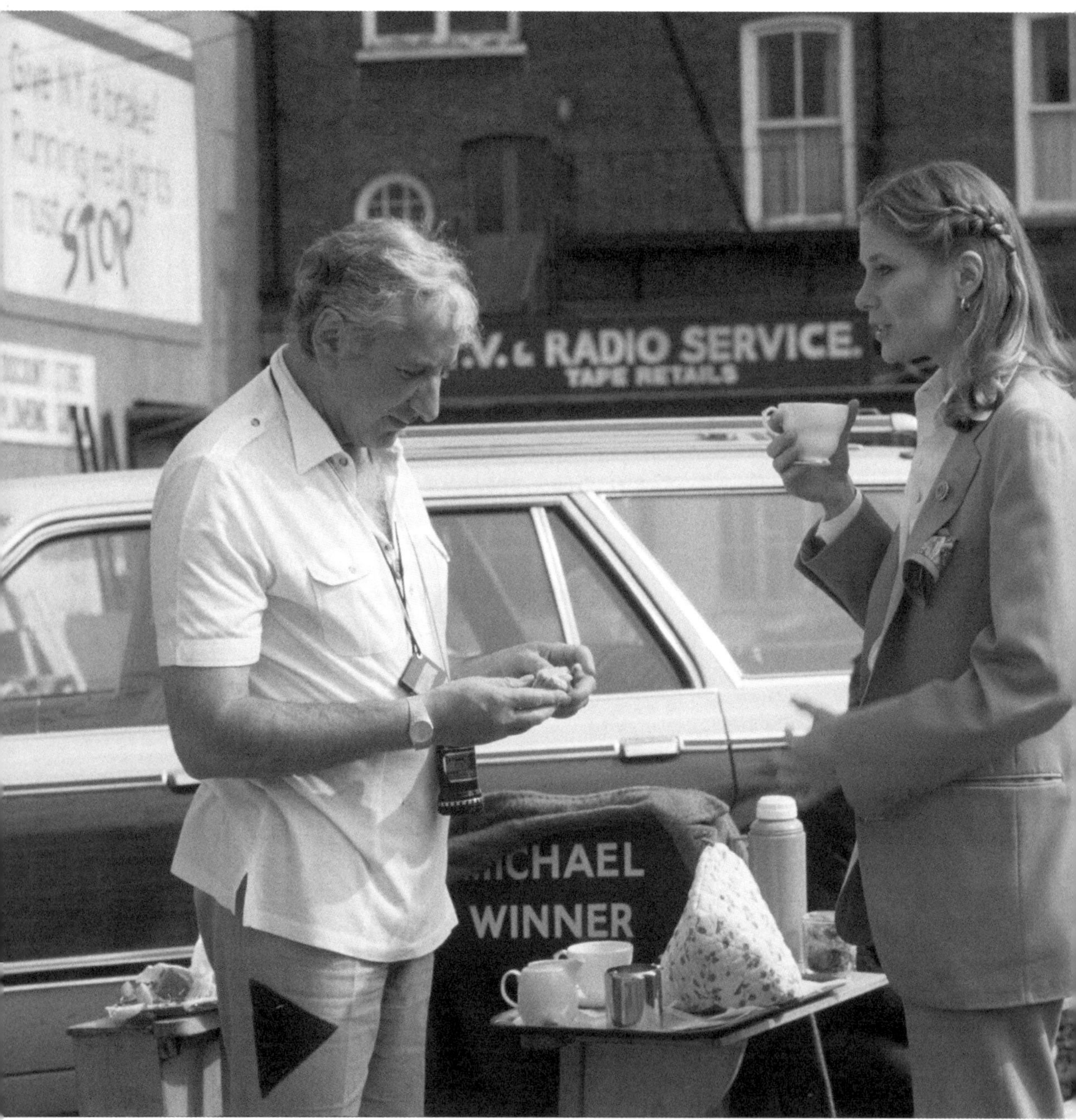

Deborah Raffin, Michael Winner, and his chair *Death Wish 3*. Photo courtesy of the Margaret Herrick Library, Academy of Motion Picture Arts and Sciences.

MICHAEL TADROSS: Mike Winner had a custom-made director's chair made in London. It had these big flaps on the side, made out of wood. One side had three different plates in it—china and knives and forks—and the other side held wine glasses and crystal. It was higher than everybody else's, because he talked down to everybody. He would say, "Why do I come to the set and my chair is not

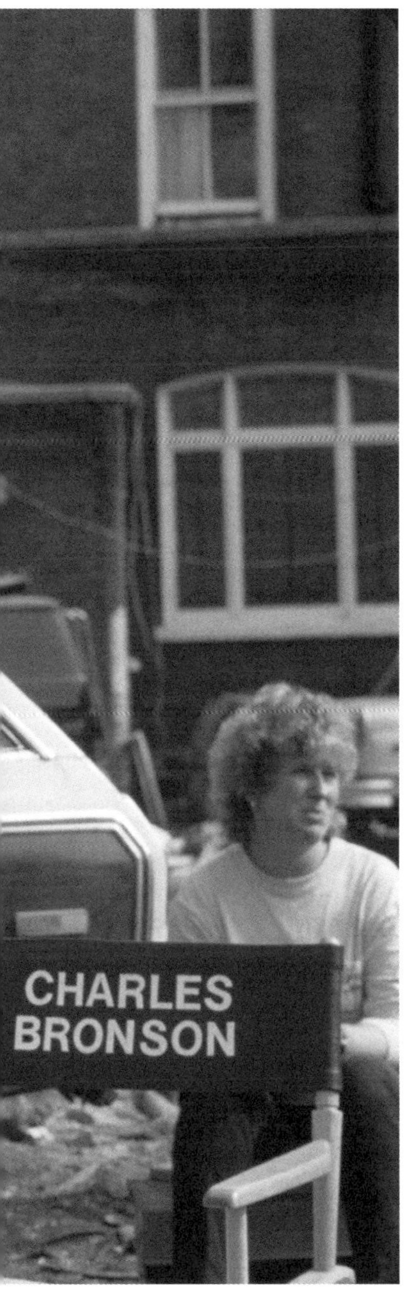

on the set?" I said, "Michael, I don't know. I'm not the prop man here." They would do it purposely, just to annoy him.

They had this whole thing planned—on set on North Avenue, outside New Rochelle High School. Winner asks, "Where is my chair?" and all of a sudden the prop guy said, "Oh, sorry, Mr. Winner," runs across the street to the prop truck, gets the chair. He's crossing North Avenue and the car is coming. The props guy said, "Oh my god," put the chair down, and he runs away, and the car comes in—a million pieces all over North Avenue. They worked it out with the stunt guys.

Winner spits out his cigar. He's holding his chest: "My God, my God." As he's falling backwards, the other prop guy fixes his chair under his ass. Dicky Allen and the carpenters made a fake one out of balsa wood. "Fucking Miguel, did you do this?" He's screaming at me. I knew nothing about it, but I never laughed so hard in my life.

STEVEN KIRSHOFF: Michael Winner was horrible, and he would do things to me—like, you're in the middle of putting out a fire and he would go, "Next," to another location, and he says, "Okay, where's the bullet?"

Like, I'm still putting out the fire. He goes, "Okay, Mr. Kirshoff, another amateurish performance—one that I'm getting used to seeing on a daily basis." That's how the guy would talk to everybody—not just to me—but I was so freaked out, man. Plus, Charles Bronson was kind of a dick also, so it was . . . I earned my money on that, let me tell you, man.

MITCHELL LILLIAN: We did some crazy stuff. That was a lot of fun. Those were like wild days. You'd never do that stuff today—massive shootouts and cars blowing up on city streets. You'd never get permission to do that.

Also, people [New Yorkers] weren't sick of the film business like they are now. People were intrigued. You didn't have people getting upset with you. Occasionally you'd be keeping somebody up at night, maybe get upset with you, but not like it is now.

Izzy and Moe

(1985)

STEVEN FELDER (FIRST ASSISTANT DIRECTOR, *IZZY AND MOE*): *Izzy and Moe*—Jackie Gleason and Art Carney recreating the true story about the two hustlers from the Depression era who decided the only way they could get by is to portray other people and pull these scams off, so they would get into these characters, being salesman or being this or that.

STEVEN KIRSHOFF (SPECIAL EFFECTS, *IZZY AND MOE*): That was kind of an honor—Jackie Gleason and Art Carney.

OCTAVIO MOLINA (SET DRESSER, *IZZY AND MOE*): *Izzy and Moe*—it was a NABET [National Association of Broadcasting Employees and Technicians] TV [movie].

STEVEN KIRSHOFF: Any movie that was any decent, you grabbed up all the NABET people that you know.

OCTAVIO MOLINA: Basically. Gleason was very abusive. He had this guy who was a "do-for." We used to call him do-for, the personal assistant, and he always had to stand by with a box of menthol cigarettes, ready to give him a cigarette, and then he would just throw out the cigarettes everywhere, because he never finished them. We were shooting in these stages on the river. They were tinderboxes, basically. There were not enough stages in those days. It was basically a pier. We're going nuts.

JONATHAN HERRON (FIRST ASSISTANT CAMERA OPERATOR, *IZZY AND MOE*): He had an assistant whose apparent responsibilities were to bring Jackie tissues and cigarettes.

He'd go, "Mel, cigarette!" "Mel, Kleenex!" and Mel would come running over with a cigarette, give Jackie a tissue. And Mel was probably Jackie's age. He'd clearly been with him for a long time. And Mel made far more than anybody on the set. I mean, rumor had it that Mel was making $20,000 a week, in 1986.

And they were exactly what you'd expect. Jackie would come in and do a take, go back to his trailer. Art Carney was kind of laid back and would occasionally sort of hang out on set and tell stories.

OCTAVIO MOLINA: Art Carney of course, was the opposite—he was a really very nice person, very quiet, kept to himself—but Gleason was a real dick.

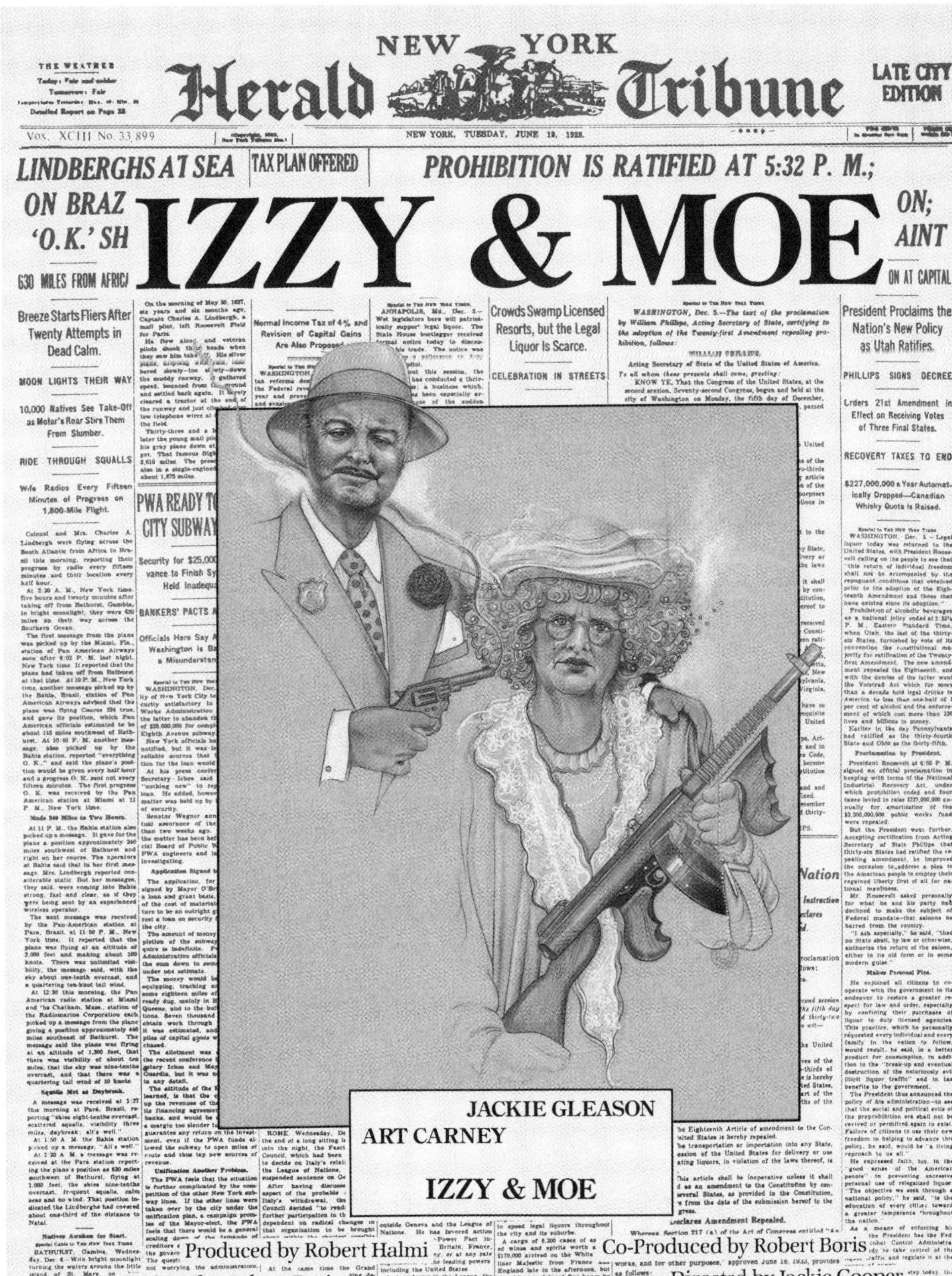

Izzy & Moe poster art. Image courtesy of the Margaret Herrick Library, Academy of Motion Picture Arts and Sciences.

STEVEN FELDER: I think this was the first reuniting after *The Honeymooners* [1955-1956]. So Carney had done good films, a really good film with Walter Matthau. Gleason had not done that. He did *The Hustler* [1961], and I don't know what else he had done after *The Honeymooners*. But he was difficult. He was a star, and he didn't like being there, being on set doing anything.

In 1985, a year after Carney starred with James Cagney in Cagney's last film, a TV movie called "Terrible Joe Moran," Carney agreed to reunite with Gleason for another TV movie, "Izzy and Moe." According to Michael Seth Starr in "Art Carney: A Biography," negotiations over contracts dragged on for months because Gleason insisted on being paid more than Carney, and Carney, who'd won a cartful of Emmys as well as that Oscar, no longer wanted to be relegated to the status of second banana.

Producers settled the squabble by agreeing to pay Gleason something extra for "composing" the musical score for the film, even though Gleason didn't know a note of music and, throughout his composing career, merely hummed tunes that others would transcribe.

On the set, Starr reports, Gleason was "surly, drunk and belligerent." Carney dealt with his difficult co-star by avoiding him as much as possible. When reporters showed up on the set, Gleason would make a great display of his affection for Carney, yet he barely acknowledged him the rest of the time.

But Art Carney, who'd endured many years of working with difficult co-stars—Gleason probably being the titleholder as most difficult—dealt with it calmly and uncomplainingly.[43]

—*Washington Post*, November 12, 2003

43 Tom Shales, "Honeymooner's Best Man," *Washington Post*, November 12, 2003, https://www.washingtonpost.com/archive/lifestyle/2003/11/12/honeymooners-best-man/4f39e026-7dd1-498e-a9be-6774637e72e7/, retrieved October 12, 2025.

STEVEN FELDER: Gleason had hated the paparazzi. There was this one guy, Steve Sands, who was always on the streets of New York taking candid shots. We had to chase him.

When I knew what was going on in the streets, I'd hire two or three big extras to be in the crowd. I said, "Your job's to stay in front of this guy all day long." So, he became one of Gleason's targets. He hated the motherfucker, and so Gleason wouldn't come out of his trailer if there was paparazzi on the street. We had a lot of scenes like that.

JONATHAN HERRON: Steve [Sands] got arrested on that job. He got taken away in a police car, which was gratifying. I don't think Steve was in the union at that point.

STEVEN KIRSHOFF: Jackie Cooper was the director. He [Steven Felder] was the first AD, or the production manager. I can't remember.

STEVEN FELDER: They hired Jackie Cooper to direct, who was a childhood actor in *The Little Rascals* who was pretty much a full-fledged jerk.

OCTAVIO MOLINA: Jackie Cooper was a nice man on set. Look, he didn't have to be nice to me. It was a pleasant experience.

JONATHAN HERRON: Jackie Cooper was completely old school. I remember the first day he gathered everybody around, and I had been told some of this in prep. He said, "Okay, these are very seasoned actors. They know their lines. They don't really need rehearsals. They might do one rehearsal, but that's it. They're going to do one take, maybe two. So everybody needs to be ready when we bring the actors. If you need extra time with stand-ins, that's fine. I don't want to do relighting, focus, marks, or anything with first team. When first team shows up, we'll be ready to shoot. So take all your time you need with second team. So we're going to get through our days. I know all of you like to get home for dinner with your family, so we are going to do our best to make sure we have reasonable days, and I'll let you know. If it looks like we have a day that's scheduled long I'll let you know when we get started so everybody can make arrangements."

So that was actually true, and then Jackie and Art would come on set and you do one take. And I would say 95% of the time we got it in one take and we'd move on. But Jackie Cooper was quintessential Hollywood. He had some of these little quips that he'd use all the time that were very funny, like the cameraman would say something like, "Oh my God, Jackie, we have to go again. There was a little flare on that car in the distance," and Jackie would say, "Oh Peter, don't worry about it. They won awards for that in Italy. We're moving on." I think you had to have somebody with that sort of Hollywood street cred to tell Jackie Gleason what to do.

STEVEN FELDER: I had two major confrontations with Cooper, and I'm not a very confrontational AD. One was on the steps of the federal building where they're going to court, so it was period lockup. We had the streets from, like, 7 a.m. to noon—period cars, period extras, the whole thing—and they're supposed to get out of a car and walk up the steps and I think they had a conversation at the top of the steps.

So Cooper—I think he was drinking, so he was never prepared, and he was arrogant, aggressive, and all that stuff—so we ran out of time—we got the shots he wanted to do, another big master. I said, "We're out. The DP says we're out. We're done. We got to get off the streets."

So we're, like, in the middle of the steps—I'm telling him this—so he starts walking up two steps to be above me, just yelling at me, so I walk up a step above to get on his level. He walks up two steps to be above me to yell, and then I walk up two steps to be even. By the time we finished it, we got up the top. Everybody was wrapped anyway, because I'd already called a wrap.

So then we got to the big finale, and we staged this thing where I guess they made a bet, and I forget—one had to kiss the other one's ass in Macy's window: "I'll kiss your ass in Macy's window on Christmas Day," or something. So we had this whole set-up in Macy's on Herald Square in one of the window displays with all the actors from the show. We got, like, a whole Norman Rockwell kind of home set.

We had, like, a block and a half, and to shut down New York, even though we had the TPS [Transit Police Service], it was really difficult because people didn't care. They weren't gawking at it. It wasn't fascinating. They just wanted to go do what they wanted to do. So this was during Christmastime, so everything was all jingle bells, and decorations everywhere and all that stuff. So we had some traffic passing by, and Cooper had decided that he wanted the cars on the sidewalk, from the window.

When we'd had all our meetings, they [TPS] said, "Okay, you can do all this, but we have to keep it open for pedestrians between cuts and you cannot have any vehicles on the sidewalk." He [Cooper] starts ranting and raving at me: "Where are the cars that I asked for on the sidewalk?"

"Jackie, we talked about this in the meeting. We're not having any cars on the sidewalk."

"I want cars on the fucking sidewalk! I want them right fucking now!" He starts screaming at me in Herald Square like a lunatic. I'm just standing stone-faced. And then my TPS cop friend comes over to see what's going on. I said, "The director would like some cops or some cars on the sidewalk."

"Let me talk to him."

They go over and talk to him: "Mr. Cooper, we had our meeting. There'll be no cars on the sidewalk, and if you persist we're going to arrest you."

So they drag him off. They kind of strong-arm him, but they never arrest him. They just say, "Listen, you only have the street till eleven" or whatever time it was; if you want this shot, we'll help you get it, but there are no cars on the sidewalk."

They walked him off. [Producer Robert] Halmi finds out about this the next day—Cooper must have called him or something—says, "What happened? You—you got Cooper arrested?"

I said, "I didn't get him arrested for anything. He violated what our permit said. The cops were very cooperative. We got the shot as planned. He's just out of control."

JONATHAN HERRON: They had to do a scene–they had to be under a car. We were in a studio with this old, this antique car, and we had to get Jackie Gleason under this car. So we put him on a creeper dolly, and wheeled him underneath the car. And he was like a turtle on his back. He couldn't move once he was under there, he was stuck under there until we pulled him out. And it was sort of revenge on him for being this sort of primadonna the whole time that here we had Jackie stuck under this car and he was going to stay there as long as we needed him to. [laughs]

An Impostor

ALEC HIRSCHFELD (**CAMERA OPERATOR, *THE EQUALIZER***): We had a different director for almost every episode. So the other director shoots and then they stand by for the editing and then they go off to another show, and so we once had a director come in that no one knew. He was just hired based on credits out of the directors' membership book.

The first morning we were just shooting from a fire escape—people coming in and out of buildings—so not really much directing to do there. In the afternoon, we go inside to an interior set and we have a family, parents, and one child who had just lost their home, and then they're in a single room at the hotel, and that's a very dramatic scene with the parents arguing and the child listening. So they read the sides. There's no mystery as to what the scene's about. It's time to put it on its feet, and the actors ask, "What should we do?"

And the director says, "Whatever you want."

Geoffrey [Erb, first assistant director]'s eyes start to roll. "Oh, this could be trouble."

So, he [director] said, "So you could sit down in the bed or you can walk around," so naturally the actors say, "Oh, we'll walk around."

And so they're thinking: is there any idea of where they should go?

And the director just kind of looks up in the air and says, "Show me what you want to do," and so Geoffrey asks, "Could we just kind of keep them to one side of the room, so we have a place to put the camera?" and Geoffrey helps him to the blocking and sets some marks and sent the actors away [to hair, makeup, and wardrobe].

And he [Geoffrey] asks, "Well, how do you want to shoot it? Is it going to be a moving master, closeups, over the shoulders? What do you want?"

The director takes out a cigar, cuts the end off, lights the cigar, takes a big puff, blows a steady stream of smoke into the air and says, "I see many, many possibilities," and he walked off the set without telling anyone.

Turns out the guy was an impostor. He and an agent had contrived to steal the name of a director who had just died or was in the hospital or something like that, and he had the same name, and they sent this guy in to direct the episode. So Geoffrey and I wound up directing the first three days, and then they got rid of the guy, and the show's film editor quickly got a director's card and directed the rest of the episode.

An impostor! To me, this is only going to happen in New York.

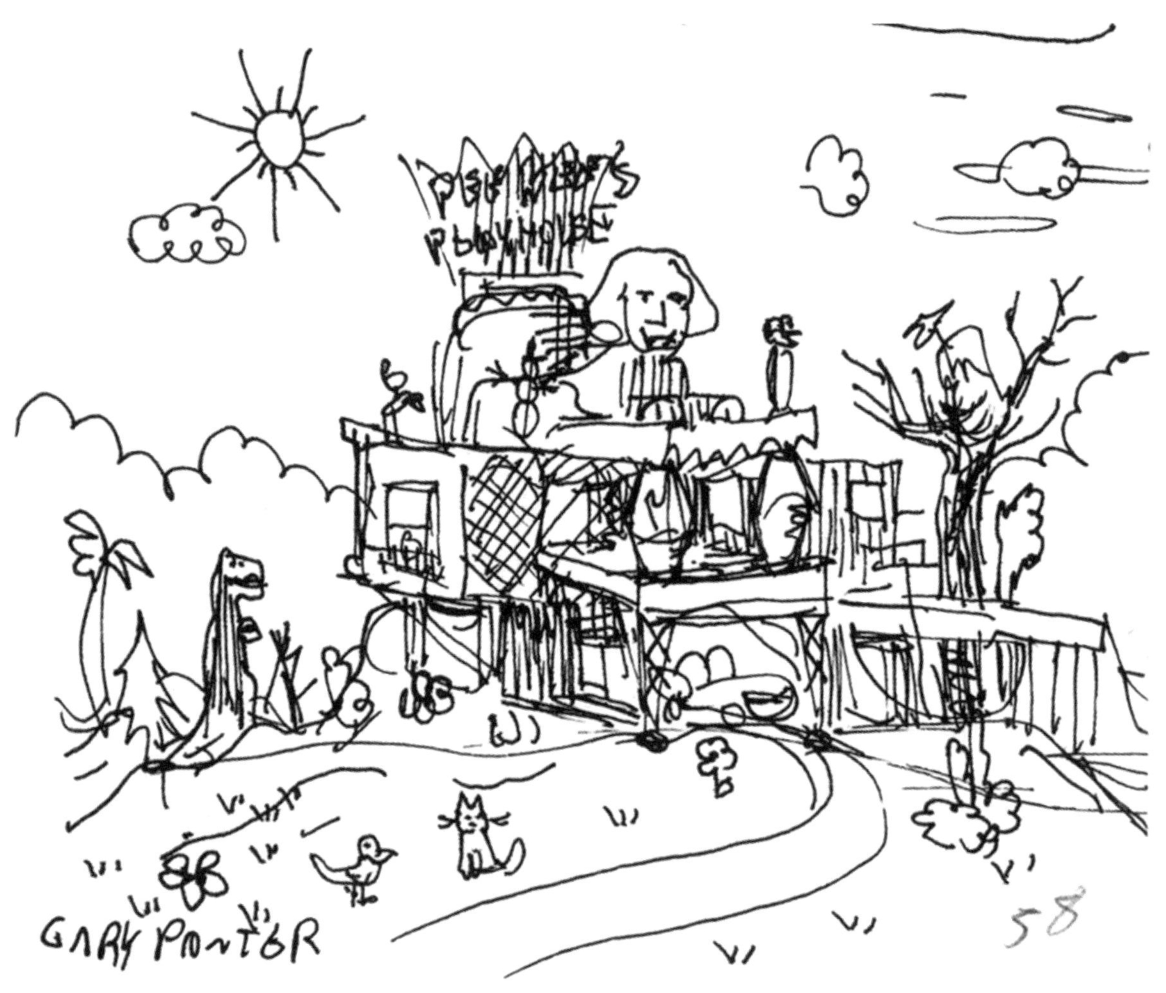

Early sketch of Pee-wee's Playhouse by the artist and production designer Gary Panter. Image courtesy of Gary Panter and the Margaret Herrick Library, Academy of Motion Picture Arts and Sciences.

Pee-wee's Playhouse, Season 1

(1986-1987)

KEVIN LADSON: I was nineteen. After *The Cotton Club*, the best way to get in is probably to work for free. I would look in the Yellow Pages for film companies, and the only one I saw in the Queens phonebook was Eoin Sprott. He was located right in Astoria Studios. I think I worked with him maybe for one day, volunteering on something. But ultimately my big break came from *Pee-wee's Playhouse*.

This is when we were prepping the first season. They needed people to work in a warehouse to remove these heavy cast-iron sewing machines, because it was a sweatshop—they wanted to clear that out and make it a shooting studio for a puppet show. They said, "Yeah, the Muppets are going to be shooting here." No one said anything about Pee-wee or *Pee-wee's Playhouse*.

As we're getting these sewing machines out, all of a sudden someone says, "This isn't a Jim Henson production. This is a Pee-wee Herman production."

We're coming back from lunch and we're on the elevator, and I said, "Pee-wee Herman? I saw him on the David Letterman show. He sucks!"

We get off the elevator and a guy says, "Oh, okay. You screwed up now, man. You see that guy with the long beard and the long hair? That's Paul Reubens. You just said he sucked in the elevator! You just said that!"

Now, he didn't look like the Pee-wee I saw on David Letterman. He was covered in a beard and long mustache and everything. I said, "Oh my God, I'm a goner."

We had one week before they were to start building the set. I'm like, "I'd appreciate it if I could work on the set," and I didn't think I would because word would get around that I said he sucked, but I did. I ended up working, and then we built the set. Then, the second day of shooting, Paul Reubens comes up to me. He says, "What don't you like about my act?"

He remembered! [laughing]

I said, "No, I didn't mean to say that." I was just fumbling for words, but I didn't get fired, and they actually started paying me after that.

SHARON ILSON-BURKE: I knew the production manager, Daniel Lupi, who was a friend of mine. I had worked on other films with him. He brought me into the project and I thought, "Oh, this looks like a lot of fun." We designed all the makeup for that first season. I loved Paul Reubens. He was the nicest, nicest man. He was great to work with. That was definitely one of my favorite jobs to work on.

KEVIN LADSON: We never went outside. We always shot at 480 Broadway. We were always inside, so we never came onto the street.

SHARON ILSON-BURKE: It was on the second floor in a loft building. It was, like, right by where Canal Jeans used to be in SoHo. We didn't have enough power in the building, so we had a generator on Crosby Street and, you know, they used to throw the cables out the window.

KEVIN LADSON: They were smart enough to hire a Teamster, who ran the generator, so they avoided some of the union entanglements with the Teamsters, but it was a low enough budget that the IA [IATSE, the International Alliance of Theatrical Stage Employees] didn't want anything to do with it.

SHARON ILSON-BURKE: The Teamster who drove the genny truck was so bored that he came up and helped run the light board.

KEVIN LADSON: *Pee-wee* was non-union. That's how I got in.

SHARON ILSON-BURKE: The set was really amazing. It was like nothing you had seen before, and it was so perfectly of that time.

KEVIN LADSON: Gary Panter [artist and production designer] is an amazing artist. Then the guy who did the soundtrack, Mark Mothersbaugh—and Cyndi Lauper was the voice of the opening song.

Working in New York at that time, I mean, it was great because New York was just at that time where all the stores were still mom-and-pop. Canal Plastics and Canal Rubber and Pearl Paint—you had to go to very specialized stores to get these things. It was very hands-on.

You had to go out and hit the streets for these kinds of things, and particularly for *Pee-wee's Playhouse*, there were all these artisans, and people who I'm sure are legends and not even knowing it.

I had an advantage that I could draw, so I was able to pre-visualize things. I could visualize what I would see and then I could build it if I needed to, so props was a better fit, and then if it was a wacky enough show, like *Pee-wee's Playhouse*, where we needed to have fake ice cream or a [giant] foil ball or things like that, I could be creative to figure it out, and then with Gary Panter and all the creative art people that were there, they would say, "No, Kevin, do it this way," or, "We cut foam this way." I learned a lot in that one season. Some techniques I still use right to this day.

SHARON ILSON-BURKE: [Paul Reubens] would take naps, like, on that bed, on the set, because he had no place to lie down in his dressing room. He said, "Sharon, don't worry, I sleep like Dracula," and he would lay there with his hands crossed on his chest to keep his makeup perfect. He's dark—he's a Sephardic Jew—so that makeup is like this pale, milky sort of milkmaid's complexion. Pee-wee was supposed to be a preadolescent boy.

I did Paul and Jambi the Genie. Those were my two characters I was doing from scratch, because they were a lot. Karen [Reuter Fabbo, co-key makeup artist] was doing a lot of the other ones who had smaller roles and were in and out, but Jambi was a big job and Paul was a big job.

KEVIN LADSON: [Art director] Sydney Bartholomew was the one I worked for [on] *Pee-wee's Playhouse*. He was really—I would say my mentor, and then he would go around saying that he discovered me on the street corner, selling fried chicken. I said, "Man, I'm going to punch you in your nose."

We joked around back and forth, but he really was showing me how to do things, how to build things, how to be creative, step up and just create it—if you see it build it, and that's from the Gary Panter school. We're building puppets. We had to make the fish and the fish tank realistic, and these guys are puppeteering and I'm the one blowing the bubbles from the fish. But when you see it put all together, that was creativity in the day—where today they may say, "Don't worry about it—we'll do it in post," but when we had to figure it out, man . . . We spent hours at that fish tank trying to figure out how we were going to have water in it, how we were going to puppeteer the fish and blow bubbles through. It looks simple, but it was really pretty amazing.

SHARON ILSON-BURKE: [Sally Hershberger] was a hairdresser, but she was also Sandra Bernhard's girlfriend, and back in that time, it was interesting, because you knew people were gay but you didn't talk about it. Like, I worked with Jodie Foster and I knew she was gay but, you know, you just didn't talk about it. You just accepted people for what they were. We knew Paul was gay, but there was no need to make a thing about it.

KEVIN LADSON: And once we started shooting, I see Larry Fishburne and I remember him from *Cornbread, Earl and Me* [1975] and *Apocalypse Now* [1979], and I was so excited to see him and he's dressed up as a cowboy and I'm like, "Does he really know what he's doing?" I thought they were exploiting him. I didn't get his comedy.

Then, S. Epatha Merkerson, an established actress, is coming in and playing Reba the Mail Lady. I'm like, "Hey, how y'all doing? Yeah, I'm here too!" [laughs]

It was amazing to see, and then it catapulted from there because S. Epatha Merkerson introduced me to Spike [Lee], and that's how I ended up working with Spike for about ten years, because she had just finished doing *She's Gotta Have It* [1986]. The handshaking was across the board. It was very unique at that time because, particularly then, there was so few Black people that it was celebratory when we would see each other on set.

SHARON ILSON-BURKE: It was kind of insane. It was just so funny. Like all the innuendos and silliness. It's like, Miss Yvonne and all the puppets at one time—she went by the puppets and one of them said, "Gee, Miss Yvonne, we don't mean to stare, but you've got the biggest [pause] hair"—things that you're like, "Wow, they did that!" And I remember it was so funny. Like, there was one episode where he Scotch-taped his face. I had to leave the set because I was just laughing too hard.

KEVIN LADSON: At that time you could get your check in cash. So the union guys were teaching me. They said, "Listen, when you get married you want to keep your kit [fee] separate from your check. Keep your kit and give the other money to your wife." They would always have stories, but you could get money in cash.

And that's the thing. People would blow that money, man. Blow—that was the thing that was around in the eighties when I came in. There was a lot of jobs, and when I worked with Paul Reubens on *30 Rock* [2007] we talked about how much drugs was on *Pee-wee*.

There were a lot of drugs on *Pee-wee*. One of the construction guys was like, "Kevin, you want a bump?"

I didn't know what he was talking about. I was naïve. I said, "Man, I haven't done that dance in years." [laughing] I didn't know what a bump was! Even on *Do The Right Thing* [1989], there was a technician—I think it was an electrician—who had a heart attack because they were blowing at lunch.

SHARON ILSON-BURKE: That was a great job. It was really a great job, and me and my friend, Karen, who's since passed away—she was my key and we won an Emmy for it.

Manhunter

(1986)

SHARON ILSON-BURKE **(ASSISTANT MAKEUP ARTIST, *MANHUNTER*)**: It was bananas. That movie was nuts. People were getting cocaine FedEx-ed from New York. *Manhunter*—it's a classic eighties movie. The costumes are amazing.

That was a wild job. I mean, we worked so many crazy hours. We went to different cities because it was a travel movie. It was the precursor to *The Silence of the Lambs* [1991].

JONATHAN HERRON **(ASSISTANT CAMERA OPERATOR, *MANHUNTER*)**: Well, I was a focus puller at the time and I got a call saying, "We're in trouble. We're over budget. We're over schedule. Can you come down? We're adding a camera. We think that's going to speed things up down there." And I don't think this is an exaggeration. It said something on the call sheet like "Day 110 of 61." They were massively over schedule.

It was mostly night work and I was booked for three days. I wound up staying for two weeks. The first thing, they get to set, and there's this giant house that they've built as one of the sets, and there's this big line of people coming out of the door of the set as everybody's having dinner and getting settled in and arriving on set in vans.

And it turns out everyone is getting vitamin B12 shots in their ass from the medic, or it was like a nurse at the time. They were all so exhausted and also coked out of their brains that they just needed whatever sort of chemicals they could get to just keep going and keep shooting.

DEAN TAUCHER **(ASSISTANT ART DIRECTOR, *MANHUNTER*)**: I got a field promotion. They were short-staffed. The crew heads were from New York, the set work was in North Carolina, and then other scenes shot in different cities—Washington, D.C., Chicago, Atlanta—and at some point I get a call: "We need you up here in Washington. You're going to be an assistant art director. You need to be in charge of . . ."

So it's this weird split. I was running the sets in North Carolina, then I flew to D.C. Somebody gave me a sketch of a panel van, a bread truck that was supposed to look like it was some fish company, and out of it the whole SWAT team was going to come out it.

Michael Mann micromanaging the scenic department applying stage blood behind actor Tom Noonan on *Manhunter*. Photo by Gusmano Cesaretti. Courtesy of De Laurentiis Entertainment Group and StudioCanal.

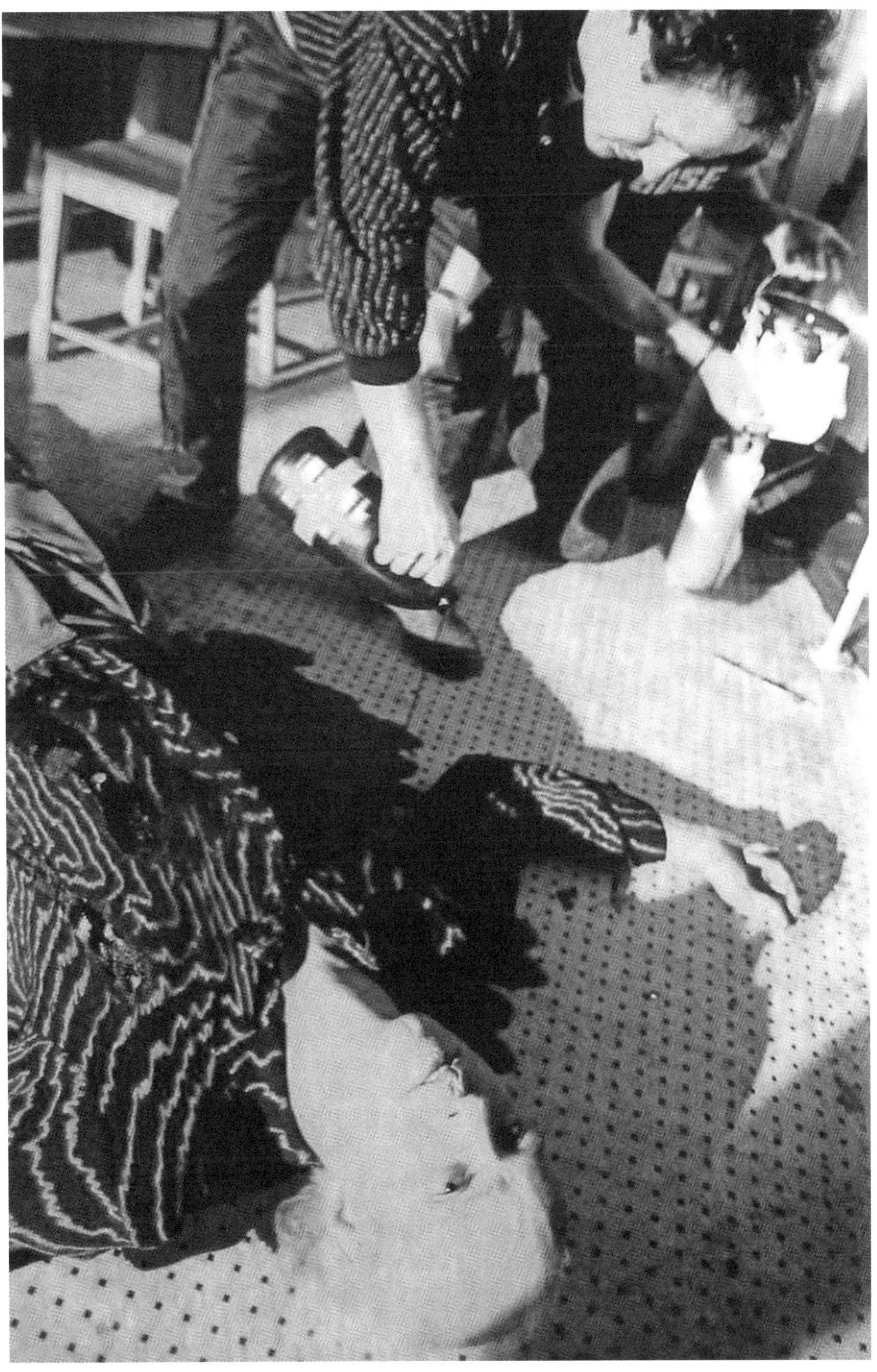

It was shooting the next day, and someone I'd never met before—she was a decorator from New York—comes to me and she says, "Okay, what are we supposed to do inside the van?" I say, "Okay, we're going to paint the inside a medium gray. All the tools need to be black. We need ropes. We need this. We need that," etc.—totally fucking on the fly, and then it was up to me—"the assistant art director." They wanted me to paint the signage, and these fish on clouds with lettering, on both sides of this van. It was shooting the next morning at eight in the morning, and I think I ended up meeting this crew at about two-thirty in the afternoon in D.C., and they hand me the sketch and I say, "I have no equipment."

They say, "We'll get you a warehouse. The truck will be in the warehouse." I said, "Are there lights? Is [there] water? Is there anything?" And I literally got in a cab: "Where's to an art supply store?" I bought whatever I thought I needed, and then I spent the rest of the night with Krylon and some sticky back. I made some rainbow trout and painted clouds on the thing with Krylon and did lettering, and typically the next morning it was all done and the director, Michael Mann, who was a fucking prick, sees it.

He says, "That's great. That's great. Why are there only four fish on each side and not five?" I said, "Because at two-thirty in the morning when I realized I didn't have enough material, I decided that four was going to have to do, because at two-thirty in the morning I couldn't do anything else." I talked back to this fucking prick. Then he goes back where the lettering is and changes the name, just to fuck with me. He knew I had only fifteen minutes before they were going to shoot the fucking thing, so that I had to scramble again and redo the back of the fucking van. He did that just because he could.

Then, because I pulled that off, I was told, "Well, maybe you should go with Mel [Bourne, production designer] to a few other cities," because literally they were sending Mel to each city on his own. There's no production office. There's nothing, and he was going there to prep things without a crew. Then he took me. I took notes, and then he'd go to another city. He left me in Chicago. There was no production office. I had no petty cash. I had nothing. But I grew up in Chicago and I used some connections I had and put a crew together. I said, "You got to trust me. They're going to pay you. It's a big movie." They got paid, but it was because of my guarantee.

SHARON ILSON-BURKE: On that movie, Dino De Laurentiis had this scam where he would bring an Italian crew in from Italy on tourist visas. They would work and not pay income tax, and he wouldn't have to pay tax on them either, because they were getting paid under the table. It's how he kept his costs down.

I was actually giving evidence to someone who was making a case against De Laurentiis at the time. I was drawing cartoons, and I would draw, like, satirical cartoons about things that would happen on the set, and some of my cartoons were used in a lawsuit that came against the company. I was really shocked. I stopped doing it after that because I never thought that something I was doing just for fun would be used like that.

DEAN TAUCHER: They built the set in a swamp right along the river.

SHARON ILSON-BURKE: The killer's house was out in a marsh, and there were speakers. They would blast "In-A-Gadda-Da-Vida" in the middle of the night because no one could hear us. We were so remote. It was, like, the creepiest thing.

DEAN TAUCHER: The scene near the end—the cop played by Billy Peterson finds this house and knows there's the killer inside with another woman, and he is going through this plate glass window to confront this guy.

It was probably six-by-six plate glass, tempered glass with a squib on it, and Michael Mann wanted to see some compression on the glass before it shattered. He wanted to see the glass move a little before it shattered as the guy is going through. Well, I don't know how you fucking do that, but he's having a fit with the special-effects guys because there's only one plate of glass left and the squibs would happen too soon.

So gun-nut Michael Mann had his own armorer with him—the guy says, "I can take care of this." The actor's jumping through the window and the guy uses a handgun and shoots a live round, next to an actor, to break the glass, to get the shot the way Michael Mann wanted it. And God, this set—that looks like it's a stucco building, is actually just plywood—doesn't stop the bullet? It went through the glass—it went through the plywood to the other side of the building and into the special-effects truck. Now, we're in fucking hillbilly North Carolina and they're thrilled that they have a film business. The special-effects guys from L.A. see this and they're totally pissed off at this asshole anyway. They just get in their truck and leave. But nothing happens to anybody.

I wish I remembered the actor's name. But they're trying to do these intense scenes and there's a songbird on the roof that was interrupting the scenes. You could hear the fucking songbird. They kept going, "Cut. Get that fucking bird out of here." Somebody went to throw a rock at it. Boom. It would come back and start singing again. Finally, I don't know if it was the armorer or one of these rednecks with a rifle in his pickup, but somebody went out and shot and killed the bird off the roof of this tin barn shooting right into the flight path of airlines. But they got the scene.

Being on a movie like that with a pushy director, it's like being a member of a cult. You're in it or you're not.

JONATHAN HERRON: And Michael Mann was a little bit of a madman.

SHARON ILSON-BURKE: Michael Mann was kind of wild, and in fact I was the only person allowed to be on set from my department. Sometimes hair and sometimes wardrobe could be there, depending on what kind of mood he was in. He yelled at the hairdresser once and she burst into tears. I went into the room and I said, "What do you want?" and he said, "Well, you know, his hair is lying across his face."

I was like, "All right," and I put my hands in the guy's hair and I pushed it back, and I said, "Well, do you like this?"

And he said, "Yeah, that's better. Stay over here."

I wasn't intimidated, you know?

You're at a job, you can't get emotional about things. It's like, the excitement and the satisfaction comes—especially with people who are considered difficult—the satisfaction is in pleasing them and making them relax. You know what I mean? Because I can see them getting tense, annoyed, and aggravated, and if you're the person that can make them calm and focus in on something else, that's a great feeling of accomplishment. Strangely.

Your job is to kind of interpret something that other people have been masticating for months, or however long they've had a character—the actor, the director, the producers—and you have to figure out what they're trying to say they want the character to look like, you know what I mean? And then you have to kind of let it go. It's like, they could say, "Well, I want her to be very sexy," and you have to figure out, what do they mean by sexy? Because everybody's interpretation of that is different. It's a whole thing. And you have to kind of feel your way around people.

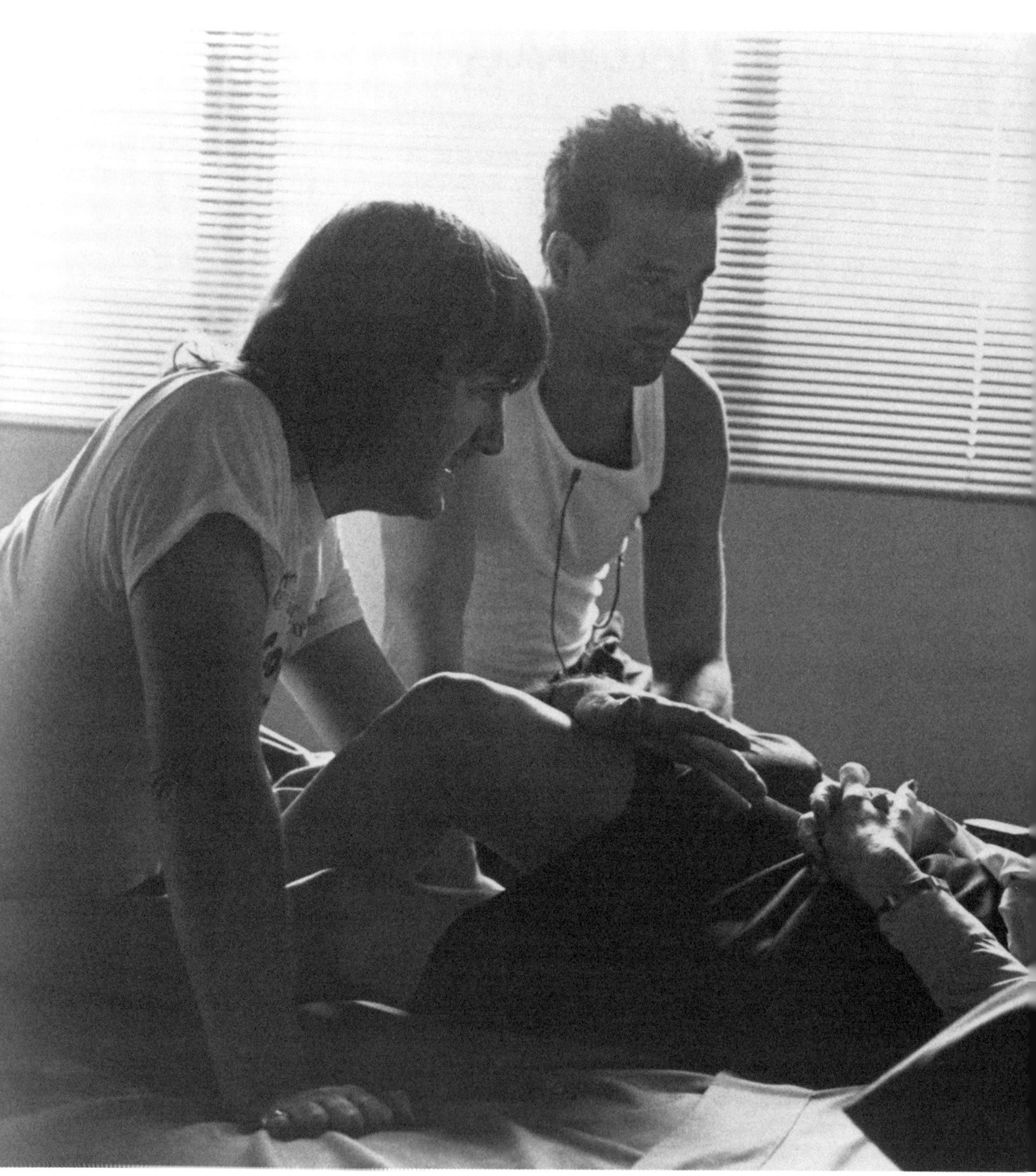

Director Adrian Lyn, Mickey Rourke, and Kim Basinger working on *9½ Weeks*. Photo courtesy of the Margaret Herrick Library, Academy of Motion Picture Arts and Sciences.

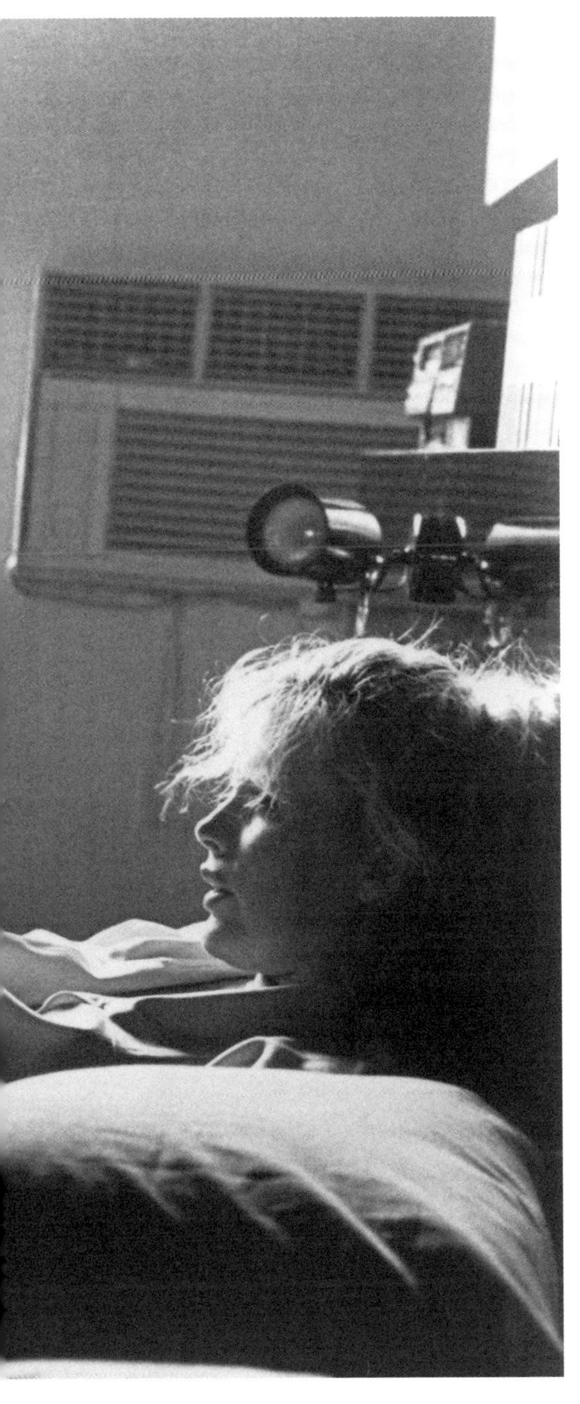

9½ Weeks

(1986)

MITCHELL LILLIAN (**KEY GRIP, *9½ WEEKS***): That was a crazy movie. Oh geez. It was—it was crazy.

BARRY WETCHER (**STILL PHOTOGRAPHER, *9½ WEEKS***): It was a lot of S&M or bondage. Columbia Pictures was going to make the movie and two weeks before we were going to begin they pulled the plug and the rumor was that the president of Coca-Cola, which owned Columbia Pictures at the time, read the script and said, "There's no way we can make this movie. It's just too risqué."

MITCHELL LILLIAN: First of all, we lost our financing in pre-production. Adrian Lyne was the director, and he went out and found three producers and they formed the company. I think that company later became Tri-Star[44] and we had maybe a month of downtime where we stayed on the clock, just the department heads. They kept us busy; we scouted locations and stuff like that.

44 Tri-Star and Columbia Pictures were sister companies both owned by Coca-Cola at the time. They were later merged into Columbia/Tri-Star and then shortened to Columbia Pictures when they were acquired by the Sony Corporation of Japan. To make it even more complicated, Sony resurrected the Tri-Star name in 2015.

BARRY WETCHER: They found other investors.

MITCHELL LILLIAN: Adrian found these guys [Producers Sales Organization] to finance the movie.

BARRY WETCHER: *9½ Weeks* was a very sexual thriller, which Adrian Lyne was so good at. That's his forte is those kinds of movies—the *Fatal Attraction* [1987], *Indecent Proposal* [1993], *Jacob's Ladder* [1990], and *Flashdance* [1983], that's his thing. Later on, I worked on *Unfaithful* [2002] that he directed, the same thing—a sexual thriller.

SUSAN KAUFMAN (SET DECORATOR, *9½ WEEKS*): That was probably the first really big NABET [National Association of Broadcast Employees and Technicians] film, I think one of the first to be here—a feature that NABET got, as opposed to Local 52. This is more NABET than [Local] 52 world, but the art world and the film world weren't far away from each other in the eighties. That film featured Donald Judd and Sarah Charlesworth. I can't remember who else we used. I tried to get Robert Longo.

BARRY WETCHER: Oh God, we shot in a place called Show World. Do you know what Show World is? We're talking 1985, when Times Square was Times Square. On 8th Avenue. I think it was between 42nd or 43rd, or 43rd and 44th, but it was this huge place, man. It was peep shows and live sex shows, all sorts of crazy shit.

The scene in that place is Kim Basinger runs in there through the place and into a theater where there is a live sex show going and as she runs in there there are supposed to be all these topless girls or whatever and they couldn't get enough or find enough actresses for backgrounds to do that.

So, Jimmy Breslin's son, Kevin Breslin, was the PA [production assistant] or location manager, but they sent him out to find actresses. In those days, over there near the Javits Center, there were tons of prostitutes. There'd be hundreds of prostitutes. It's probably six o'clock in the morning and there's Kevin coming down the street and behind him is a couple of hookers that he wrangled. I don't know how much they paid them to be in the movie but that's how they got enough people to be topless in the movie—real hookers.

As I said, Kim runs into the theater where there's a live sex show and they hired a real porno couple to be the couple fucking during this scene, and I mean—I'll never forget, we couldn't buy that place out because they make too much money. You couldn't shut down the entire place. It was a huge place, it was like two or three stories, but we were able to rent one of the theaters in the complex and get in to set up the scene, and then in the afternoon we were shooting.

So here's the film crew locked in one theater while shooting the scene, and meanwhile there are hundreds of guys watching peep shows and the other live sex shows in the others.

I'll never forget this. I walked out of the theater where we are shooting and walked into the next theater where paying customers were watching a live sex show. You had hundreds of men, whatever they were doing—masturbating, whatever they're doing—while we're filming a movie, man—it was really, really crazy. It was a crazy two days.

MITCHELL LILLIAN: Lyne would dwell on a scene too long. He was very set in his ways and if he wanted something that was gray and it was blue, you would wait until they got a gray one or they painted it gray. It didn't matter. There were very few concessions made, and he had an interesting way of working. He really played a mind game with Kim Basinger and Mickey Rourke and got them to have this love/hate relationship in real life. I mean, they would do a scene where they had to be in bed together, but they wouldn't ride up the elevator together to get to the set.

It was insane. There was a lot of tension. He would do crazy things to build an insane tension. He wanted them to be angry, and he got them angry. It was fucked up, and that wouldn't happen today because you have studio supervision now you got stockholders, you got all these bean counters that would get wind of that.

BARRY WETCHER: I'm not going to say anybody was doing it, but that's when cocaine was huge and I'm not accusing anyone of getting stoned while we were filming, but let's just say those were the days of bad drugs.

ANONYMOUS: You're not allowed to use my name on this, but the rumor is that there were receipts being put in for one-hundred-fifty, two-hundred-dollar butter melons for people to get some coke. There were so many drugs. That movie was outrageous.

MITCHELL LILLIAN: When a director finds the financing for a movie, he becomes very powerful, and Adrian was just running with the ball until the bond company came in and put an end to that near the end. There's nobody to tell them "no" when the producer works for the director. Ought to be the opposite.

BARRY WETCHER: We went forever. The completion-bond people took over that film. They took over the movie, so now they're basically—lightly using the word—*producing* the movie. They're controlling every penny that's spent and whatever they say has to go.

Now again, I don't know if this is true, because the reality is that movie went so far over that I left because I had *After Hours* [1985]. The rumor is that when the last roll of film was exposed, that was it. That's how the movie ended. Otherwise, it would have kept going. If they'd given Adrian more film, he would have kept on forever.

SUSAN KAUFMAN: I would say it was one of the most unpleasant experiences of my career and probably couldn't happen today.

COMMERCIAL BREAK #3

JOHN MAZZONI: We did a commercial in NASCAR with Jeff Burton and Rusty Wallace, down in Charlotte, North Carolina. It was a closed NASCAR course. It was 135° on the tarmac and he's doing his thing. We're filming it. [whooshing sound] They're going by me.

So there was a break. We couldn't get to the hotel, and I was dying. I had a Windstar. Windstars were the first minivans—the first minivans with a sliding door. That was the car that the company gave me and Sal Martorano. So I go, "I want to drive around this track. I'm going to use the Windstar that we rented." So I get in the Windstar and Sal gets in with me and I go, "Sal, I'm going to floor this car around this thing." Don't forget the track. It's like this [gestures to indicate a sloped track]. You've got to go fast.

So I'm doing seventy with the Windstar—seventy, eighty miles an hour. Sal goes, "Take it easy." I say, "This is fucking great!" We pull over in the minivan, right? Sal turned white.

We pull over and Jeff Burton goes, "What are you, crazy?" He says, "What are you doing with the Windstar?"

I said, "I wanted to drive it."

He said, "You know, you've got to be careful with it. You want to come with me? I'll show you how to drive around."

I said, "Yeah, you'll take me?" He says, "Yeah, I'll take you." He gives me a suit. I put the suit on. I guess it's a fire suit. God forbid something happens. He put me in a fire suit. He put the thing on with the helmet. He looks at me. He goes, "Don't pee in my suit."

I go, "I'm a tough enough guy. I'm from Brooklyn. I ain't got to pee in nobody's fucking suit."

He says, "I'm telling you don't pee in my suit." I say, "I'm not going to pee in your suit. Let's just go, let's just go." We go.

Oh god! It's 160, 170 miles an hour. I'm thinking, "Wow. What the fuck!" It was just incredible. We went around four times, and we stopped and he looked at me, he goes, "You peed in my suit, right?"

I said, "I did."

I felt so bad. I was crying.

He goes, "That's okay. You're not the first, and that ain't my suit."

And I remember that story because in 1959 my father went to Lake Placid for a commercial. My father was rigging a bobsled—rigging the camera on the bobsled. My father strapped it and tied it. So he did the whole commercial and one of the guys says, "Hey, John, you want to go? Come on. It's a four-man bobsled. I get in the front. You and Vinnie get in the middle, and the other guy will push and we'll do the four-man bobsled. You want to go?"

"I don't know. All right, I'll try it. I'll try it."

He was so scared. "John, I got in that bobsled. I've been in World War II. I've been captured. And I peed my pants." So, he peed his pants in the 1960s in a bobsled, and in the 1980s I peed my pants in a car. I hope my son pees his pants one day for me and my father to keep the legacy going.

Ishtar

(1987)

BRUNO ROBOTTI (CHARGE SCENIC ARTIST, *ISHTAR*): God almighty. We did so much work.

STEVEN J. JORDAN (SET DECORATOR, *ISHTAR*): That was brutal. That was absolutely brutal. There was a rehearsal period in August—I think they were going to start shooting around September, October in Morocco, but it was a music rehearsal period in New York in July and August. I was put on for that initially to get [songwriter] Paul Williams set up with whatever instruments he needed for rehearsals and for Dustin [Hoffman] and Warren [Beatty] to play.[45] My initial meeting with Paul Williams was at the Sherry Netherland [hotel], and I got there around eleven o'clock one morning and I had woken him up and he shows up at the door: "Come on in, man."

You could see, I missed quite a party the night before. We got all these instruments set up, and I was buying gym equipment to ship to Morocco. Number one and number two on the call sheet [Hoffman and Beatty] had to have a certain amount of exercise equipment in their trailers.

RICHARD ADEE (PROP MASTER, *ISHTAR*): Dustin Hoffman. And what the hell is the other guy? They never got along. That was funny.

They were into bodybuilding and weightlifting exercises. They said to me, "Rich, can you get me some kind of equipment? I want this, I want that." So I had the guys make this equipment up for Dustin and he wanted it portable because he wanted it on location. I had to do the same thing for Warren Beatty.

STEVEN J. JORDAN: The rehearsal period goes, then we pack them up, ship them to Morocco. And then I was laid off until they got back to shoot again in January.

RICHARD ADEE: Beatty wanted his own plane to fly over there. He didn't want to get on a commercial flight. And then Dustin says, "Well, fuck that. If he's getting his own plane, I want my own plane." The whole shooting was all about their personalities.

45 In *Ishtar* Warren Beatty and Dustin Hoffman play two terrible songwriters who can't catch a break.

Office.
212-603-0605
1619 BROADWAY RM. 404.
PROP HOUSE - 713-0760

PROP RM. 706-5868

UNTITLED COMEDY
-ISHTAR-

K2 E

Script from *Ishtar*, 1987. Courtesy of James Archer.

STEVEN J. JORDAN: I got a call from [unit production manager] Mac Brown, who called and said, "Look, they've been shooting in the desert for quite a few weeks, and they've not gotten one Moroccan interior."

So we're going to come back to Kaufman [Astoria Studios] and build these giant sets. I was a decorator on that. Bill Groom was the art director, and Bill designed these beautiful sets—beautiful details. I think Bruno Robotti was the [scenic] charge on that. The paint work alone, he did a spectacular job.

BRUNO ROBOTTI: They were supposed to do the palace in Morocco. But the story goes that the movie company ran over a kid crossing the street and killed him. I was told that it ended up that he was the son of a bigwig in the area, and they actually had to leave town really quick. That's how they made it back to New York sooner than they wanted to, and they decided to build this palace, which was huge. A lot of work.

I had a staff of eight people just casting pieces for a couple of months. The stuff was so heavy, it was just above the ten-foot line. The grips had to put in steel plates to put this weight on top of it. It was monumental even for the construction. Paul Sylbert bought me these two books on Moroccan architecture, which were phenomenal to use as research.

STEVEN J. JORDAN: I came in and I met with Sylbert. I said to Paul, "There's no way I can do these sets. I can't do it on Atlantic Avenue in Brooklyn."

I went to Marrakesh and shopped for about two weeks, very much against production. The British producers wanted no part of sending me over there to shop but I went over and shopped for two weeks.

I had a driver and also an interpreter, and we would walk into a store and I'd say, "I'd like to buy five rugs. How much?"

Then my interpreter would grab me by the arm and take me outside and say, "You can't do it like that. You gotta bargain for each rug."

And I'm like, "All right, you do it."

So, we go back in. I'd pick the rug, these two guys, they talk Arabic, and next thing I know it's lunchtime and I've bought five rugs. It was so slow. They'd argue, he'd take me out of the store: "We're not buying them."

And then we'd go back in, and then finally they would come to an agreement. I would get my five rugs. We'd have to drink a glass of mint tea to celebrate the deal. It was frustrating, because in New York you'd say, "I'll take this, this, this, this, and this." Okay, fine. Out there, every time you bought a plate, there was a mint tea ceremony afterwards. It was crazy.

BRUNO ROBOTTI: One day, Paul Sylbert comes to me and says, "You've seen the movie *Casablanca*?"

I say, "Yes. Years ago. Such an old movie, I don't remember."

He says, "Okay, good. Go upstairs in the executive boardroom—there's a TV. Go watch the movie."

After a while he says, "All right. Now you saw the *Casablanca* set, right?"

I said, "Yes."

"We're going to turn the palace into the *Casablanca* set."

We ended up just covering it. It was a sin. When they drag away a set that you've been putting so much energy into at work—it was really beautiful.

BERNADETTE WISE-TUTEUR (CARPENTER, *ISHTAR*): It was enormous. We were up on scaffolding, cutting in the cove molding up above and getting down on the floor to fill in these little gaps. "You're going to see this?" I guess so.

And the scenics had all this plaster stuff

that they did that we had to attach to the wall, which—"Be careful, you'll crack it"—and then it can all come tumbling down and then they have to make another one. The plaster stuff doesn't glue together very well.

STEVEN J. JORDAN: I had a very difficult time with Paul [Sylbert], to be brutally candid and honest. I would see him every couple of days, and we would sit down and talk and he would say, "Okay, everything is blue."

So I'd go out and shop for everything blue, and then I'd see him two or three days later. I was thinking, "I think it's all red now."

And then come in and do things like, "I think these curtains are upside down."

"Paul, they're not."

He said, "Well, they look upside down, let's change it."

All the money I spent and everything else was thrown out and then I'd have to try to justify it with the UPMs [unit production managers] because we were going wildly over budget. Ultimately, I was fired the night before the shooting of that scene. That was the only time in my career, which is well over forty years, I've ever been fired. I took that pretty hot. That was really the catalyst to making the move to design.

STEVEN J. JORDAN: And it was a very tough show and from what I could tell it wasn't a very happy set.

BRUNO ROBOTTI: It was a flop, but it was something else.

ISHTAR

R-1 CONTINUITY FEB. 23, 1987

1 Ext. Song Mart

2 Int. Song Mart - 3 acts, Chuck and Lyle "Nam" (*)

3 Intermission - Marty and boys

4 (*) Int. Club #2 - Blind Lyle (Marty - "spritzer, please")

7 Ext. 8th Avenue - Honduras or Morocco

Ext. 8th Avenue - Chuck "I want to be alone"

9 Int. Bar - "One more for the road" to flashback

10 Ext. Street - Lyle and Good Humour - Hot Fudge Love

11 Int. Lyle and Willa's Apt. - Lyle plays "Hot Fudge Love"

13 PT. Int. Greek Restaurant - "Love in my will"

Continuity notes from *Ishtar*, 1987. Courtesy of James Archer.

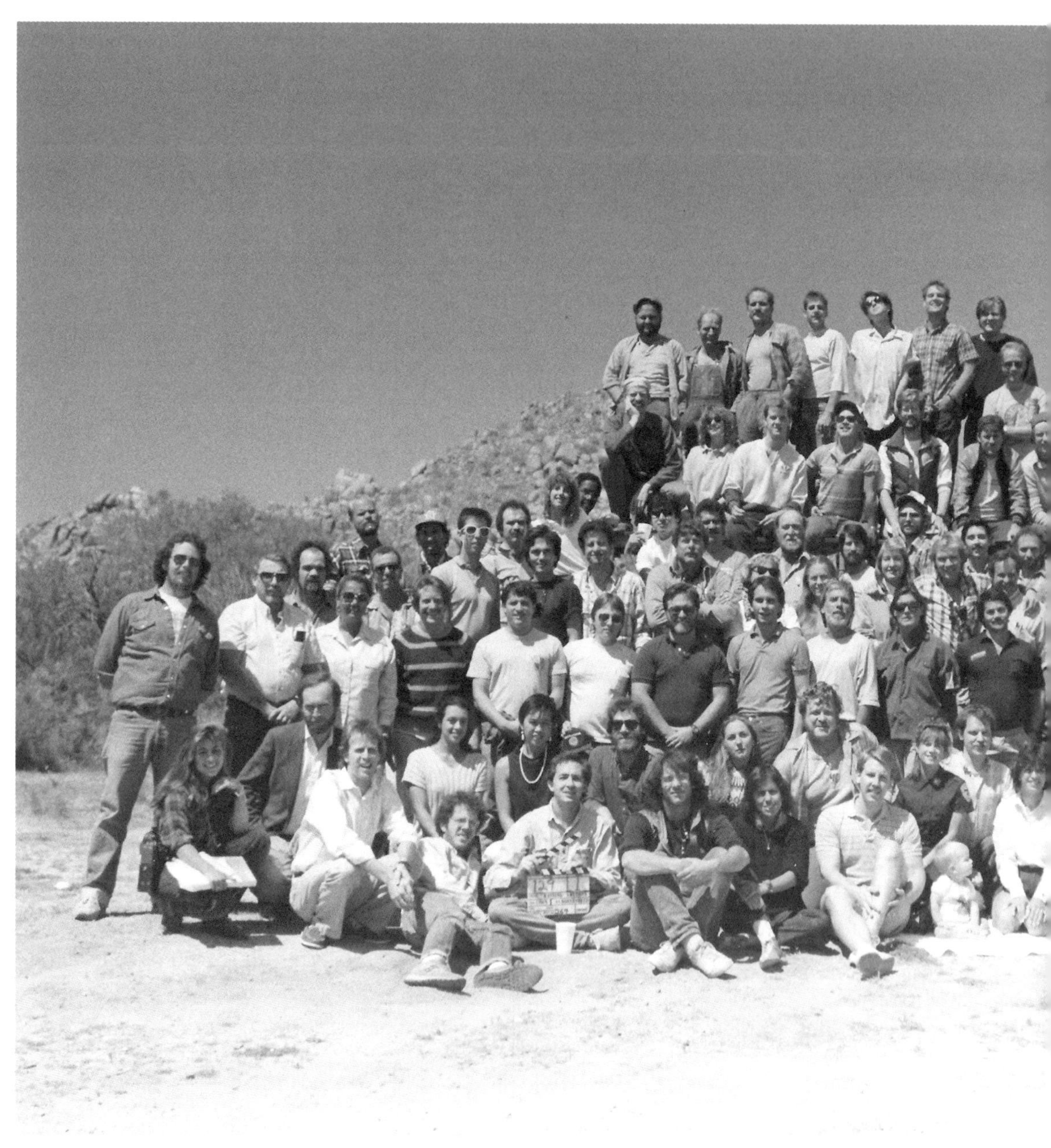

Cast and crew, *Raising Arizona,* 1986, by Melinda Sue Gordon.

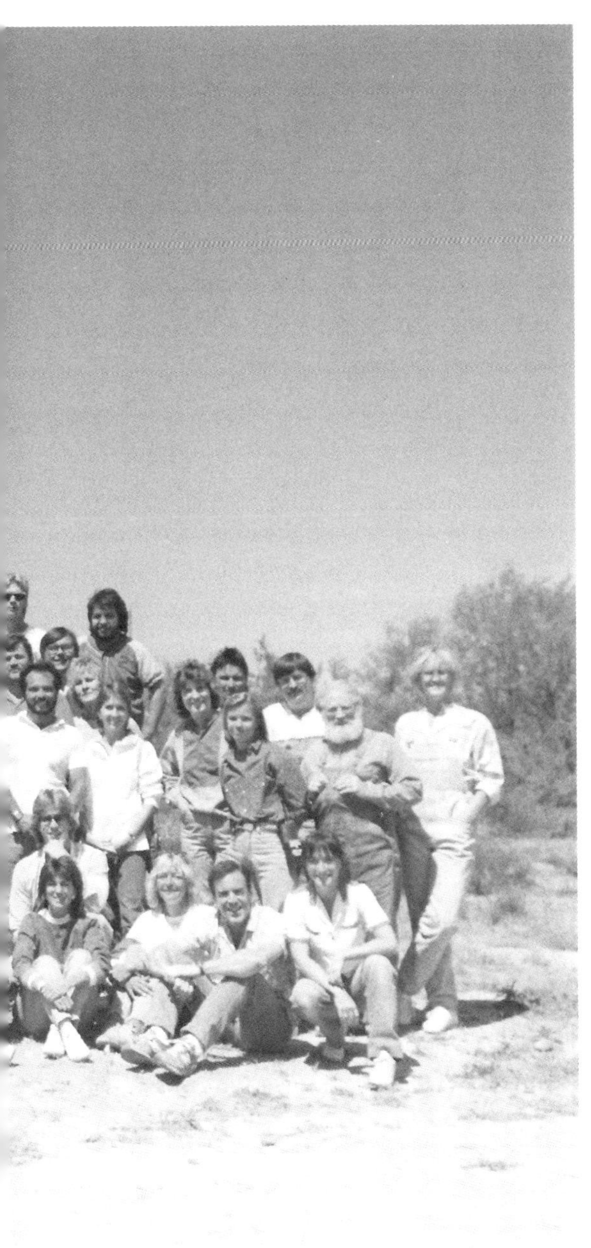

Raising Arizona

(1987)

MICHAEL F. BURKE (ELECTRICIAN, *RAISING ARIZONA*): Barry [Sonnenfeld, cinematographer] had done *Blood Simple* [1984] in Texas [with the Coen brothers]. There was another job in between that we did with Barry in New York, and it was the first time Barry worked with an IA [IATSE, the International Alliance of Theatrical Stage Employees] crew, and he loved us.

So when the Coen brothers got *Raising Arizona*, Barry said, "Look, this is a big job, and we need to shoot it in 35-millimeter, and we need to bring Dennis and Rusty from New York. We need the New York crew. Whatever the cost is, they will make the movie better for us."

Dennis Gamiello, John Lowry, and Brian Fitzsimmons from the grip department and me, Rusty [Engels], and Kenny [Connors] from the electric department. Then Allan Byer was the sound man. I think the prop department came from California. They filled in the rest of the stuff with local folks.

"It was an interesting scenario because there were the New York guys on the film, and we're local Arizona guys who were also working in L.A.," [electrician Bob] Field says. "It was also a mix of union and non-union crews because Arizona's a right-to-work state.[46]

—*Phoenix New Times*, March 17, 2022

MICHAEL F. BURKE: Barry got into NABET, and he did one job that kind of was a big NABET job called *Compromising Positions* [1985]. He then got an IA job. I forget how Rusty [Engels] got the job.

RUSSELL ENGELS (GAFFER, *RAISING ARIZONA*): I think that was their [Coen brothers'] first union movie, and they were a little skeptical about working with the union crew, as opposed to when they did their other pictures. I remember the stories about them being worried about this, that, and the other thing. Then we had such a good time, so much fun, that they said, "I don't know where those stories came from, [that] it's going to be problems. You know, the union guys are going to do this and that. Local 52 people are so tough, or whatever." It wasn't that way at all, of course, but they were, I think, grateful that it worked out as well as it did.

I mean, those stories came from what it was like in my father's days in the sixties and seventies. There were some really tough crews, and a lot of alcoholism, drinking—tough, nasty guys on set.

MICHAEL F. BURKE: They were New Yorkers.

RUSSELL ENGELS: We lived out there for about three months, so it wasn't a commutable thing. My wife and two kids came out. We had a condo and worked from the Scottsdale/Phoenix area. Dick Van Dyke had good-sized buildings built out in the desert, basically out in nowhere, because it was cheaper back then, and did his TV show out there for years, so we used his backlot.

JOHN LOWRY (GRIP, *RAISING ARIZONA*): Rusty Engels brought his family. Then Dennis Gamiello brought his family, and Mike Burke did too. They stayed in the same condo complex. They [Coen brothers] had the refrigerator stocked the first time, they had the school set up, so it was like we just walked out of our home and walked into another home—all the kids starting school. The Coens took care of it all.

RUSSELL ENGELS: It was for such a long time, and it was a good time. The kids got right into their grade level and all the kids were in school together—kindergarten and second grade, for our kids. They still remember a lot about that.

JOHN LOWRY: Two years later we did *Miller's Crossing*—they [Coen brothers] said, "Hey, John, how's Cathy, how's Meghan, how's Kevin, Patrick?" They knew Dennis's kids, Rusty's kids, their wives' names. I was just blown away by that.

RUSSELL ENGELS: Everybody talking about "Is that good for the kids?" I think they had a great time. They made new friends and learned to get along right away. I think they did very well.

MICHAEL F. BURKE: The night before shooting they had a party, and Joel and Ethan [Coen] were there. Joel got up and spoke to everybody and said, "Thank you all for coming here. This is a big movie for us. They say that the risky things about doing movies is stunts, animals, and babies, so we figured we put all three of those in. So we're going to see what happens.

The first day of shooting, we went out into the desert. It's a scene where the lead actor,

46 Benjamin Leatherman, "Coen Heads: How Phoenix Played a Starring Role in *Raising Arizona*," *Phoenix New Times*, March 17, 2022, https://www.phoenixnewtimes.com/arts/coen-heads-how-phoenix-played-a-starring-role-in-raising-arizona-13229220, retrieved April 7, 2023.

Nicolas Cage, was supposed to be running towards this cactus, and he runs into it and then falls down. They described the shot, and they say that's the first shot. So, as soon as they finish talking, everybody takes off. Dennis goes to get the dolly track. The camera department goes to get that. Rusty is like, "Okay, get a cable out here. Get a couple of lights," blah blah blah.

Then the only three people that are still standing in the middle of the desert are Joel, Ethan, and Barry. They are looking at each other like, "Well, I guess they know what they were supposed to do." That was the start of the job.

RUSSELL ENGELS: It was pretty hot, 105° sometimes out in the Western town that we shot in.

MICHAEL F. BURKE: So we had so much fun on that job. We were doing it out in the desert, and the local people were like "Well, you should see when the desert blooms." I would be bitching about being in the desert, like, "It's fucking beige!"

I said, "The person who would make a killing out here in Arizona is somebody who opened a paint store. Is there another color other than beige out here?"

Ultimately, when the desert blooms, the saguaro cactus would have a red pimple on top of it. I'm like, "Oh, this is blooming?" I just had a blast busting the balls of the locals about their desert.

DAVE FRANZONI (ELECTRICIAN): Mike's a great storyteller. Some of the stories are just amazing.

MICHAEL F. BURKE: We set up our camp behind the set that we built on this ranch. We had the beige room. We had the bar set up, we had the grill. We put both speakers in the tree. I took a pickup truck and put a blue tarp in the back of the pickup truck and filled it with water, so we had a pool. We had so much fun on that thing.

I would go into town to the supermarket. It seemed like Scottsdale was a testing ground for brands. If you wanted to test a business model, you'd set it up in Scottsdale and then see how it did. So, they had a supermarket that was called PJ's or JP [probably AJ's Fine Foods]. They would have stuffed pork chops or stuffed quail and all of these really great prepared things for like a dollar ninety-nine a pound—"Oh my god"—so I'd buy all this stuff. We told them we weren't going to have the catered food, so we got our meal money for our lunch, then we cooked our own meals. As they would be filming in the morning, I would be starting up the grill in the back of the building so all of the aroma of grilled pork chops and stuff would be wafting through over the building onto set. We had the production manager and one of the accountants and we had kind of lounge chairs for the two ladies—Alma the production manager and for the payroll girl; I forget her name.

They would come around and sit in the reclining beach chairs. We would make them piña coladas and margaritas and they would sit in the back and listen to music. I had a video camera and had maybe about nine hours of video footage that I filmed behind the scenes of *Raising Arizona*.

DAVE FRANZONI: Mike was taking home movies of *Raising Arizona*. When he showed it to us—I mean, your sides are hurting from laughing so much. If they ever make a documentary . . .

MICHAEL F. BURKE: Barry was with his girlfriend at the time, Susan, who is now his wife, and she was great. I would have fun playing with Susan. We would do little skits because Barry had kidney stones and he had to get taken away in the ambulance once or twice. I did a little skit with her. I would spot Susan walking around the back and I'm like, "Susan, Susan, what are you doing?"

She said, "Well, Michael. I just came from the hospital, and we did a test and Barry passed his stones, and look . . ." You'd see these big rocks in the Gatorade.

After the operation I woke up in a private room with a catheter inside me. This was an interesting twist [. . .]

Four hours later, a knock at the door woke me up.

It was a stripper in a pink gorilla suit, holding a boom box.

"Hi," I said, wondering where we are going with this.

"Hi, do you know where I can plug this in?" said the pink gorilla, pointing to a boom box.

"So, who are you and why are you here by the way?"

"Oh. Sorry." She opened up a card and read:

"Mike, Rusty, Dennis, Earl, Brian and Dave want Sheila—me—to cheer you up with a little striptease. Do you know where I can plug this in? It's the music."

"Sheila. Please don't take off your clothes. Okay? You see the reason Mike, Rusty, Kenny, Dennis, Earl, Brian and Dave have hired you to take your clothes off in front of me is, well, I have a catheter in my penis."

"Catheter?"

"Like a long skinny needle."

"Uh-huh."

"And if you take your gorilla suit off in front of me I might, you know . . . you know . . ."

—Barry Sonnenfeld, *Barry Sonnenfeld, Call Your Mother: Memoirs of a Neurotic Filmmaker*, 2020

RUSSELL ENGELS: Barry's got the tube up there. My God, she takes the clothes off and he says, "I'm going to get an erection and I'm going to break the glass tube in my dick. Whatever those bastards pay you, I'll pay you twice that. Keep your clothes on!"

All the doctors, they followed this person into the room, and they were laughing their asses off. We had a stripper come to the set three or four times for Barry's birthday. You hear that little whistle go up and you go, "Oh, no."

MICHAEL F. BURKE: Tex Cobb was one of the stars of the show. He fought and went fifteen rounds with Mike Tyson. He was a kickboxing or martial-arts champion. He was a rough character, but he's one of the stars of the show. He's a biker and he would come by when he found out about the beige room and the fact we had a cooler full of beer. He would come back, and he was drinking all our beer. Everybody was afraid of him, because he was crazy, so I had to go to the production manager and I said, "Look, I got a problem here." I said, "Tex is drinking all of our beer. Now, we got two things we could do. You could tell him that he can't have any of our beer, or you could pay for our beer and just let him drink our beer." The production paid for our beer.

We were doing a scene, and Tex doesn't know how to ride a motorcycle, of course. They always had a stunt guy doing it. But there was a scene where Tex drives over like a crest of a hill, and then we wrap. He said, "I could do that."

They were doing the second unit, this running shot with Tex. Of course, Tex drops the machine, falls off, and lands on his shoulder and dislocates his shoulder. So, him being an extremely tough person, continues to work with a dislocated shoulder while getting medication for the pain. He winds up, like, putting his left thumb in his belt loop to hold his arm up. Also, he has to go away for three or four weeks for another job in North Carolina.

He came back, but he had to shave his beard and his head for whatever job he was doing at the time. Now he's addicted to pain meds, and he's lost a lot of weight. I don't know if he had his shoulder fixed at that point, but he was getting crazier. He wouldn't come out of his camper. He wanted some dope. It was just getting crazy. I think the day when he was finished with the job, he was threatening that he was going to come back and kill someone, or he'd be suing or wanted more money because you ruined his career. They had to put on security because they were afraid that he was actually going to come back. There was a whole escapade going on with Tex Cobb.

Barry would be going on about Rusty, telling him, "You are, like, the perfect man." He says, "Joel and Ethan, isn't Rusty a man? We're just New York City Jews. But you look at Rusty. He's a man. He's got muscles. He's tough. He has facial hair and a beard."

Rusty would just be like, "Oh god, please stop."

"You are the epitome of what a man is."

Rusty would just laugh and walk away.

RUSSELL ENGELS: We were out one time in the two vans. I think Barry was in the front van with the directors, Jane [Musky, production designer], and everybody else. They hit a wild pig as we were crossing through the desert on the highway. It went tumbling off on the side of the road. They killed it, basically. It's lying there and they're all crying, whimpering about the pig. And then the back van, our van, we're saying, "Get the knife. We'll take that out. We'll gut that and bring it back in and have some ham and bacon." Kidding of course.

Barry was like, "Oh damn, I wanted to be in the manly van. I didn't want to be in the wimpy van."

MICHAEL F. BURKE: This was just Barry. Barry would say, "Would you rather have sex with my mother or Tex Cobb? Because my mother is so ugly."

Barry would present these situations and scenarios and absurdities. He lived in an absurd world. So we had a lot of fun with that. Barry would get letters from Susan. So Barry is sitting on the set, and he's got a letter in his back pocket. I was able to pull the letter out of his back pocket without him knowing, and it was from Susan. Now, I was not going to read the letter because, like I told you, I learned my lesson from *The Warriors*: when you think something's too funny, it's not. So I said, "I'm not going to read the letter that's in there, but I'm going to write another letter, and I'll put it in there." I wrote another letter to Barry, and it says:

Dear Honey,

I miss you so much. You know I just can't wait till we are together again. In the meantime, I took a photograph of you and I had it blown up to a poster size and I put it over the bed so that when I go to bed every night, the last thing I see is your face. I worry so much about you. I was worried for a while about you being out there in Arizona. It's so different than New York, and I hope that you're safe. But then I realize that you are with Rusty, and the electricians who are so good to you, and they take care of you and protect you so I can rest at ease. It would be really good if you could take the electricians out as a sign of appreciation and do some guy stuff with them.

Now I just saw in the paper in New York that Kitten Natividad, who is one of Russ Meyer's vixens, is going to be performing in Scottsdale on St. Patty's Day. It would be really fun if you took the boys out to a strip club and treated them and go to see her. They're so good to you and you're really lucky to have them.

I miss you with all my heart. I can't wait to be with you again.

Love, Sweetie.

So I write the letter. I put the letter back in the envelope, I put it back in his pocket, and he doesn't know. Maybe like a couple of weeks later, on Monday morning, I get to the set, and I hear, "Burke, you're fired!"

I said, "What?"

Barry said, "Sweetie and I were in the car, and we were driving over the weekend, and I said something to her and she said, "What are you talking about?'"

"'Well, it was in the letter you wrote.' She says, 'I don't know what you're talking about.'"

He says, "We drove in the car for another half hour, and nobody said a word and as soon as we got back to the apartment, I went into the bedroom and I got the letter. I pulled the letter out, and I said, "See here, the letter that you wrote."'

"She said, 'I didn't write this letter.'"

It was hysterical, absolutely fucking hysterical. I said to him, "I can't believe you actually believed it. The handwriting is different and it's two letters in one envelope."

Absolutely hysterical.

RUSSELL ENGELS: Mike didn't go too far very often. He did a lot of things that were kind of over the top. He could have caused a whole lot of trouble with that one.

Barry knew exactly what he wanted and how to get it, and we got along well. I know I could do anything for him—that's why I was there—and he trusted me to get his vision. That's the key thing for me. One guy asked me in an interview once, "How come you get a job like that on a regular basis?"

I said, "Well, I go in and talk to the cameraman. I have to learn what you [the director of photography and camera operator] want in a week and forget what I did for the last few years."

I gotta learn his style right away and get it going. I think that helped me a lot, just the fact that I didn't say, "Well, we use 10Ks for this on a regular basis" or whatever, and I knew some people like that, that would say, "Nah, we won't use that light. We'll use this light." I think that's wrong to tell the cameraman what to do.

JOHN LOWRY: They [Coen brothers] are unbelievable people. I had gotten hurt when I was thirteen, but we were going out to do *Raising Arizona* and I said to Dennis, "I don't know if I'm going to make it. Dennis, my back is really bad."

"Just come out."

We were out there at the production meeting, and they said, "Unfortunately we're going to have to bring a process trailer out of California, not to be on the whole job because we'll need it one day, but the cost of the Teamster to bring it back and forth, and the Teamster that stays with it the whole time."

So I said, "I got a Navy welder. I can build you anything." So we built them a process trailer that telescoped in and out. We wanted to do it hydraulically—press a button—but I couldn't get the motors in time.

I had a bad back going out there, but after we built the process trailer—I got it under budget and done on time—I looked back and was standing on the back of the trailer, thinking, "I can't believe that we did it."

Then the Teamster just started the truck without warning, and it was in gear, and I fell backwards and made the ruptured discs worse. I went to them [Coen brothers]—I said, "Look, the doctor says I can be up and walking again soon and my rental stuff I'll put towards the condo." Because I thought, "I'm in a hospital. Why should they be paying this mess? It's not something that really happened on the job."

I had to have this operation for ruptured discs. My bride calls and says, "Dennis just came with an envelope of cash."

I said, "No, Cat, give it back." They made a collection for me. I said, "I'm making more money than the local guys. I can't take it. "When I got hurt, they [Coen brothers] kept me on the payroll. They said to Dennis, "When you have to hire a local guy, you just deduct what the local guy costs and John gets the difference. Just put the hours in and the accountant will work it all out."

They paid me right through.

Mississippi Burning
(1988)

The last month of preparation and the usual frenzy of last minute preparation and the thousand questions a director has to field. Each special effect to go through from fire to rain—each period car and truck to be chosen; each costume, shirt and pair of boots to be checked; each prop—from a dog house to a broken picture frame to be looked at; each pistol and shot gun to be approved; each wallpaper sample and shop front to be selected; each three legged dog; arthritic cow and fetid pig to be considered; each stunt to be choreographed—and the shooting crew and actors hadn't even arrived yet. For a director, undoubtedly the more answers you get right at this point the better the film will be. I don't think there's a director working who doesn't realize that it's a percentage game.[47]

—Alan Parker, "Mississippi Burning: The Making of the Film," 1988

47 Alan Parker, "*Mississippi Burning*: The Making of the Film," 1988, alanparker.com, http://alanparker.com/film/mississippi-burning/making/, retrieved November 7, 2022.

INGRID PRICE (WARDROBE SUPERVISOR, *MISSISSIPPI BURNING*): *Mississippi Burning*. Boy, if I was ever going to write a book about industry, it would be about this project and what it was like to work on this film. God rest his soul, Alan Parker—we just lost him this year [2020].

He was a British director who decided to tell the story of [Andrew] Goodman, [Michael] Schwerner, and [James] Chaney, the three civil-rights workers who were murdered in Mississippi during the Civil Rights Movement. Their bodies were hidden, and the FBI found them. It has also been done on television in movie form, but this one starred Gene Hackman and Willem Dafoe, Fran McDormand, Brad Dourif—some really fine actors.

DANNY MICHAEL (SOUND MIXER, *MISSISSIPPI BURNING*): I'd never worked with Gene Hackman or Willem Dafoe before. That was a really great experience. My takeaway from Gene Hackman is that he could make the worst dialogue golden. There was a lot of dialogue in *Mississippi Burning* that was not that well written, a little bit cringeworthy, but I would actually just sit there thinking, "Okay, how is Gene going to make this believable?" and, sure enough, somehow with his sense of timing and phrasing, and pauses, where you might not have expected it, he'd always make a scene turn out great. I just loved listening to it.

TONY STARBUCK (BOOM OPERATOR, *MISSISSIPPI BURNING*): I mean, my favorite memories of that job are Gene Hackman detesting Alan Parker and basically telling him every day, "Fuck off. Do not give me any direction."

INGRID PRICE: It was a terrific cast, but the shooting conditions were kind of unbelievable. It was just mind-blowingly difficult to shoot because a lot of the film takes place at night, meaning that they scheduled to shoot during the winter months so that the night hours would be longer. Obviously, that makes sense. But what most people didn't realize was that Mississippi gets quite cold at night in the winter—ice on the ground, below-freezing cold. The story took place during the summer. That meant that a lot of times the actors would have to be outside in a tank top and bare feet and there would be ice on the ground. You could see people's breath. It was very tough for them.

The hours were rather long because we were taking advantage of the nighttime when it would get close to dawn. The DP [director of photography] would be yelling, "We're losing the night!" They usually say, "We're losing daylight!" I guess the work is grueling when you're just in the trenches for long hours and the conditions are tough and everybody was dealing with it—the actors, the crew, and everybody.

JOE BURNS (PRODUCTION ASSISTANT, *MISSISSIPPI BURNING*): We were working in and outside Jackson, Mississippi, and then we worked in Lafayette, Alabama.

DANNY MICHAEL: We spent the first—I'm going to say—four weeks shooting at night, for the most part—burning down churches.

JOE BURNS: We're on a scout before the shoot and we're scouting the motel, where all the FBI guys are arriving for the end of the movie. Across the street was a park and there was this odd part of the grass. It was like this big grass street with this odd sort of square in it.

I say to the only owner of the motel, "What is that over there?"

He says, "Well, that used to be a swimming pool. Then when that integration came in those *Blacks* were in there like a bunch of ducks. So, we filled it full of dirt."

He's telling me as a white guy, and somehow he thinks that I'll understand what he is saying. I thought, "Oh, my goodness gracious. That's amazing that you're proud of it."

TONY STARBUCK: In one small town we're in there was an extra, probably in his forties, and we start talking.

He goes, "You're from the north, aren't you?"

I'm like, "Yeah, actually a lot of the people are from the north."

And he is like, "Well, I love the whole civil rights movement because I like nothing more than bashing the heads in of fucking niggers." I just looked at him. I'm like, "Well, we have a difference of opinion about how we feel about things."

DANNY MICHAEL: Although we brought down crew from New York, we still had to hire a local crew, like extra electricians and stuff. And we had some old-timer who was working with the electric department who said something like, "We used to do this for free in the old days, but now you guys are paying me to burn down churches." He was serious. He wasn't kidding.

TONY STARBUCK: Eamonn O'Keefe was the assistant cameraman. Mike Roberts was the [camera] operator. We're shooting the scene

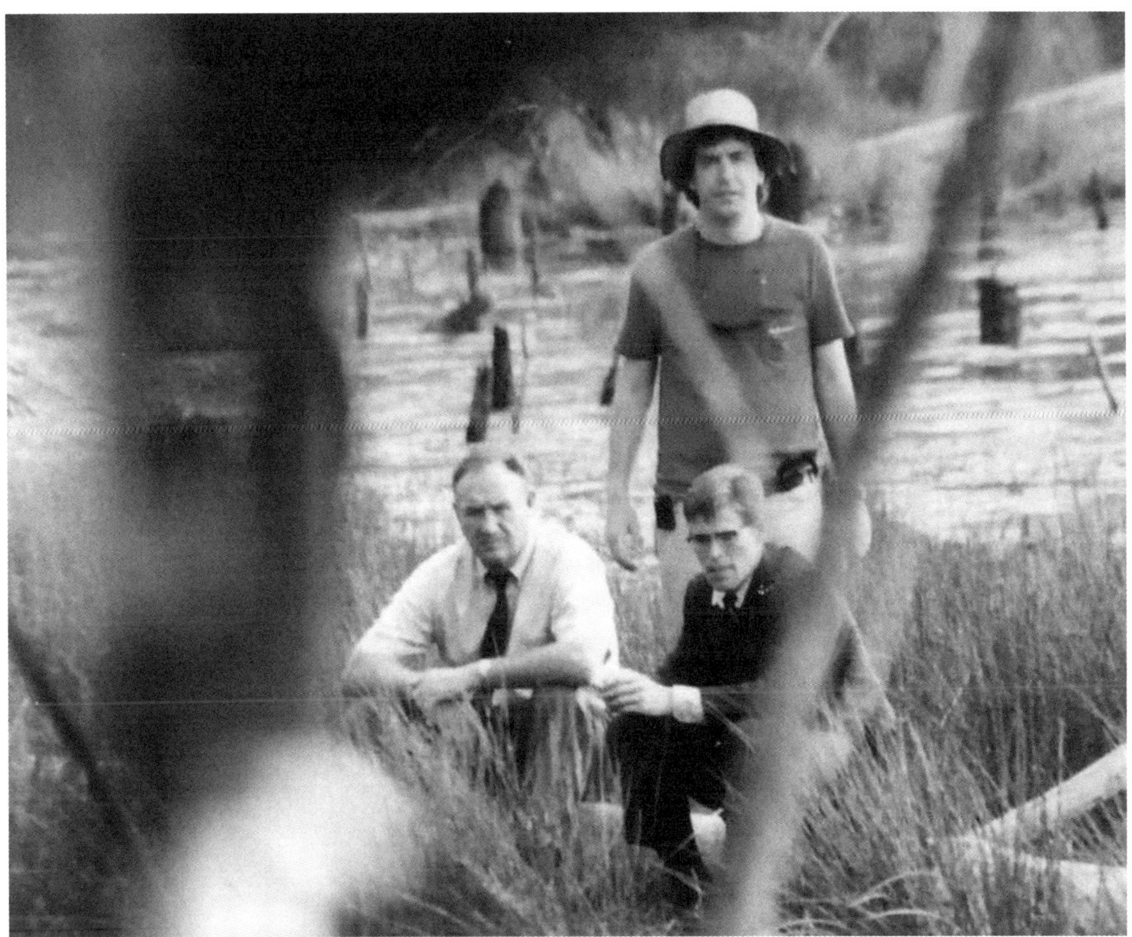

where they dig up Schwerner, Chaney, and Goodman's bodies.

We have this crane on the site, and it's got a big claw that goes down and starts digging. Eamonn is setting the camera. It's all locals. There are no prop guys operating this crane. They bring in whatever local construction company to operate the machinery during the scene.

This is a NABET [National Association of Broadcast Employees and Technicians] film bordering on basically being a non-union film. Eamonn O'Keefe sets the camera, and he walks under the suspended claw and the claw plummets to the ground, misses him by one foot. Everybody looks over at the [crane] operator and he just looks at us. I swear to God he was trying to kill him. There was a lot of hostility about the making of the film from the white people down there, people who participated in the anti-civil-rights thing.

JOE BURNS: We were shooting at this pig farm, way in the country. We're outside of a little town that's outside of Jackson and there's this one cop who is the entire police force. He's the sheriff. He's kind of a heavy-set guy and I'm standing with him. We are going to hold up traffic. It was a period piece and you don't want a modern car driving through.

I'm standing there with him and I have to

Assistant director Joe Burns standing, Gene Hackman and Willem Defoe seated, *Mississippi Burning*. Photo courtesy of Joe Burns.

have a conversation with him. He's chewing tobacco, spitting his tobacco and all that, and he says, "I don't know why you guys have to come down here and stir all this shit up."

He spits.

I said, "Oh, really?"

He said, "Yeah you got more problems with niggers up north than we do down here. We don't have a problem with the niggers down here."

I was thinking, "Wow, there's nobody to help me to get out of this conversation."

For the most part people were very nice, but some of these people I met were right out of the script and they didn't know it.

TONY STARBUCK: [Alan Parker] was a fucking racist—like when we did this crowd scene. They hired all these local Black people for no money or very little money. They're out in the sun and then we're doing one of the funeral processions, and they have these people going by.

And after the first take, the AD [assistant director] goes, "Hey everybody, listen, I know you're new to this. You really can't look at the camera. So let's do it again. Nobody look at the camera." And so we shoot the second take and Parker's looking at the monitor or whatever, and all of a sudden he goes, "Cut! Could we find any more *stupid* Black people?!?"—sort of under his breath, but loud enough.

JOE BURNS: I'm in AA. I've been sober for thirty-seven years. I first stopped drinking down there. I found this AA clubhouse down there called You Are Not Alone. I was in charge of the extras. I ended up having all these people from AA sign up to be extras on it.

Here I felt like I was really meeting people, meeting real people at the AA group, and interestingly enough they always wanted to talk about the Civil War. There's monuments all over the place. They had battles there. The North came down and burned these places down. These people have stories from their families that came from the Civil War era, and this was back thirty-five years ago. Everybody thinks of the Civil War as so long ago, but it's not really that long ago. My father died when he was eighty. He was born in 1921. If you go back just one other person and you're in the Civil War. Anyway, they wanted to talk about the Civil War all the time. I mentioned to them—to be honest with you, nobody's talking about the Civil War where I come from. It was still so close to people.

INGRID PRICE: One of the weirdest things I ever experienced on set was shooting the aftermath of when the Klan had burned somebody's barn down and killed all his animals. Our guys, Gene Hackman and Willem Defoe, were coming to investigate and there was a scene where they were walking around among the rubble of the burned-up barn and talking to each other about it, and so the art department had gone to a local agricultural college and gotten hold of some animal corpses because there's nothing like reality, right?

JOE BURNS: As a matter of fact, they sent me over to see how they [the art department] were doing. We were going to shoot it in two days or something. Aldric Porter was the first AD and said, "Joe, can you go over there and see how they're doing on that set?"

I drive over and the special-effects guy is there with a cow on the ground, and I'm thinking it must be a fake cow, and I said, "That looks real."

He says, "It is real."

They brought the cow there and killed the cow on the spot, on that place, and then they started burning it. He had something he would cut metal with, but it's actual fire and he's burning the cow, burning the cow's ears and everything. It's a real fucking cow. I think it was a dead horse there too.

INGRID PRICE: They had singed them so that they looked like they'd been in the fire and scattered these dead animals around the set.

DANNY MICHAEL: We should clarify. They were real animals that were ill. They were, like, horses and cows that were going to be put to death. So they were euthanized and they were just used in that scene.

INGRID PRICE: We knew they were real—obviously, everybody had been apprised of that—but what we didn't realize was that as the day went on and the temperature got warmer and warmer—these bodies, these animal bodies were starting to bloat and decompose.

DANNY MICHAEL: We did the barn-burning and then the next day we were filming a scene between Gene and Willem, where they were having this big argument in the yard, the burned-out yard. It was hot and the horse body started to heat up and started to literally spew crap.

INGRID PRICE: I remember going out and tiptoeing around these animal corpses in order to make a wardrobe or a mic adjustment or something on the guys, and then we were mincing our way back trying to avoid these corpses. These dead pigs and stuff are starting to ooze and bubble and swell.

Finally, we got the scene, they called wrap. We all disappeared and went to the next location, and what we heard was that shortly after we wrapped and left, those corpses started exploding.

TONY STARBUCK: There were just all these bloated, charred animals lying on the field, and you know what's so funny is that at the time—I don't know—my head was still new to movies—I'm like, "Okay, this is what they do." It didn't occur to me, like, "Oh God, this is, like, the worst transgression and horrible treatment of animals ever." I mean, this is years before PETA—"oh, okay. I guess this is how we do things."

INGRID PRICE: That was so far above and beyond the call of normal film-set duty. But the whole film was kind of like that.

DANNY MICHAEL: Something worth noting about Alan Parker: Alan does not allow anyone to be in his film, any extra, unless he's seen them and approved them.

At the Jackson Armory we had arranged an "open call" advertising on the radio and in local newspapers for anyone, who wanted to be in a movie. Nearly two thousand turned up and were dutifully photographed and ushered through the filtering process allowing me to read with as many people as possible. As always you hope to find someone special for a speaking part, (the "interviewees" in the film were all found this way), but mostly it enables the background extras to be sifted through, so that no-one appears in the film who I haven't seen or approved—the theory being that there's no such thing as a "crowd" scene because at the end of a long lens, in close-up, any individual becomes a principal. The "open call" process consequently enabled us to build up the most characterful and believable background for the film.[48]

—Alan Parker, "Mississippi Burning: The Making of the Film," 1988

DANNY MICHAEL: He wants to know what they look like and pick them out. And he's right, because it means that his guys can pan their cameras across the crowd and they will always look like who he wants them to be.

INGRID PRICE: There was mud all the time—everywhere we went. A fact of life was the mud, and I remember we were so accustomed

48 Parker, "*Mississippi Burning*: The Making of the Film."

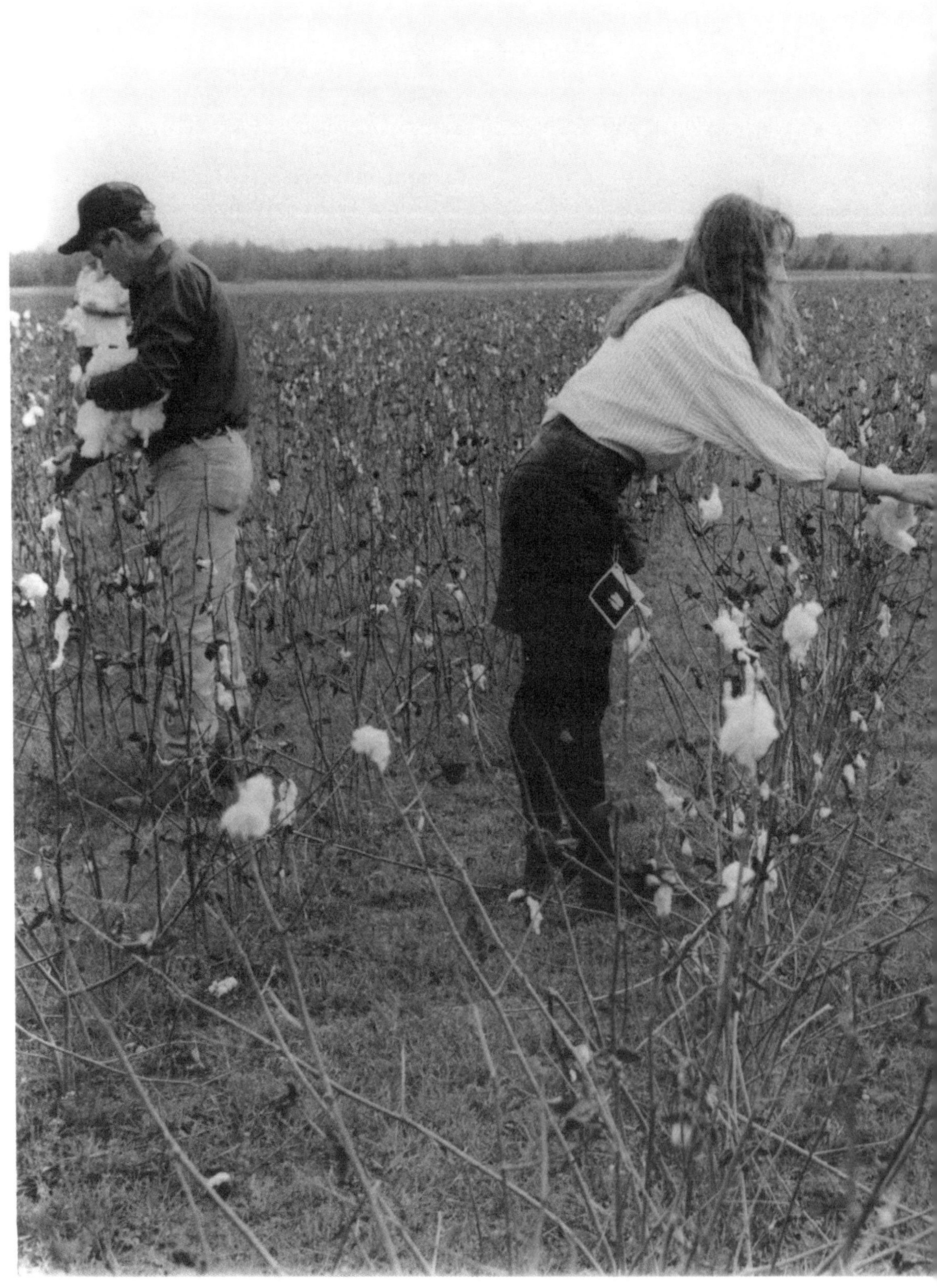

Left unknown, Ingrid Price, and Alan Parker. Photo courtesy of Ingrid Price.

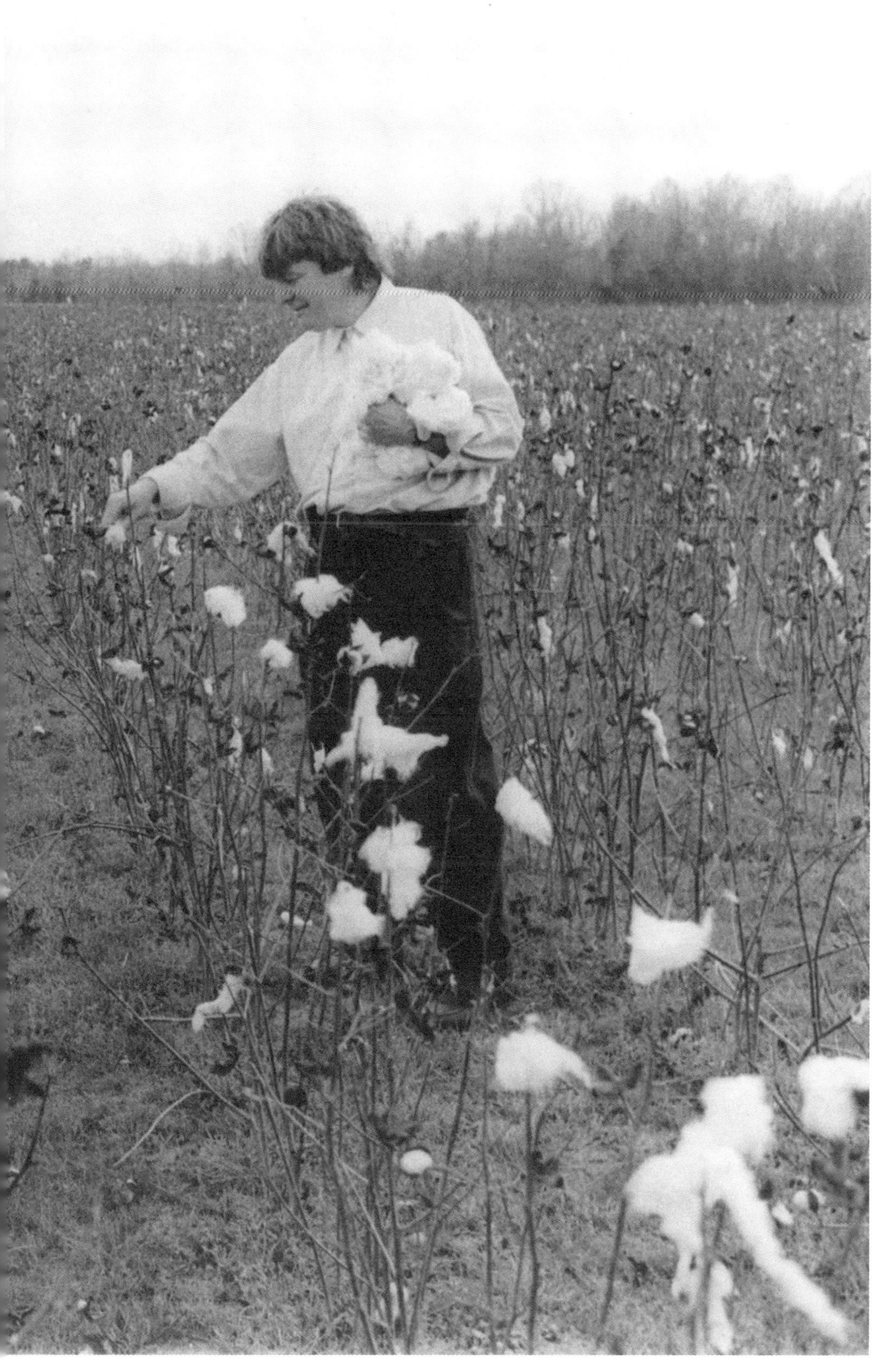

to it. We were shooting out on some farm location at one point, and they broke us for lunch. We all slogged through the mud to the catering tent, and it's muddy in there too. We sit down in our chairs and we're eating our food. We notice gradually that the table is getting closer and closer to our chins. Suddenly we're at the table eating and we think, "Why is this happening? Why am I so close to my food?" I looked down and of course the folding chairs were sinking.

By the time the meal was over, I think the chairs were six inches into this mud and the table was up under our chins. It was just a funny moment where we thought, "Oh gosh. You just can't escape it."

JOE BURNS: That [scene on the] farm where the KKK are dragging—I got to say that everybody felt—I mean, it was such a traumatic scene that the actors are constantly apologizing to the guys. You can sense that everybody feels awful about what we're doing. I can't really explain it, and it rained—it ended up being a rain scene—and it ended raining like a son of a gun, and we didn't go to cover.

We just decided, "Hey, is it going to continue to rain? Okay. It's a rain scene." And it came out absolutely beautiful and dragging them through the mud and all that stuff.

INGRID PRICE: We were doing this shot in the dead of night, and Alan, the director, wanted six FBI guys to go running off into a field. They were going to start at the camera and they were going to run away from the camera out into this field as if they were pursuing somebody.

That's all great, and we've got everybody dressed in attire circa 1964. The FBI people are in their suits, and they've got their little dress shoes on and everything. Then Alan really wanted the field to be quite muddy. Alan loved mud. The more mud, the better. We got the water truck in and soaked the field and made it nice and soupy and muddy and we got the shot. The guys went racing off into the darkness because it was the night. And then the assistant director yelled "cut" on the megaphone when the scene is over. The guys slowly started wandering back—these six actors and not one of them was wearing a pair of shoes.

The guys showed up and I said, "What happened to your shoes? Where are your shoes?"

They said "We don't know, man. They're out in that mud somewhere."

Every one of them had lost their shoes in the mud. Cheryl Kempton and I went out there with flashlights and tried our best to locate the shoes. They were gone. I said to Alan, "I hope you don't need another take because these guys don't have any shoes." Fortunately, we got it on the first one.

DANNY MICHAEL: On my end, what was an amazing thing is Alan Parker—the Brits are tough on sound people, because they're all into their whole visual thing, but he really did not like looping any sound, and a film like that you're very likely to do looping because there's a lot of stuff going on in the image, and we accomplished something that people have no idea we did. There's actually no looped dialogue in all of *Mississippi Burning*. It's all live.

INGRID PRICE: We had a rare daytime shoot. What Alan wanted was to pan across a field of cotton. Unfortunately, we were there in the wintertime and the cotton had already been harvested. The plants were still out in the field kind of dried up, but there was not one cotton ball in sight. There just wasn't any cotton.

It wasn't the ideal time of year to show the cotton in full bloom and the cotton was "dressed," plant by plant, by the entire crew who volunteered to help out the pressed art department to undertake the mammoth task. The ironic reversal of history—seeing so many white guys putting cotton back into a cotton field—was not lost on the crew.[49]

—Alan Parker "*Mississippi Burning*: The Making of the Film," 1988

INGRID PRICE: So the art department got a whole bunch of cotton balls and every single available human body on that set—and I mean everyone from craft service to the executive producer—grabbed a bag of cotton, went out in that field, and stuck cotton balls on those plants until we had filled it with cotton.

It was an amazing moment. I'm walking up the row—I've got Alan Parker on one side of me. I have a great photograph of the two of us sticking cotton on these plants. And I looked to my left and there's Brad Dourif, one of the actors, sticking cotton. I look to the right, there's the executive producer, and right next to him is the craft service guy, all putting cotton. It took everybody and we just did it. You can see Polaroid photos safety-pinned to my fanny-pack. Those were costume continuity photos I had of the actors who were about to appear in the cotton-field scene, as soon as we got the cotton on the plants!

TONY STARBUCK: Alan Parker was a very, very, very effective director—really effective with the crew. If you're in his little circle, it's great, but he was a guy with a temper and vindictive.

A story to me that I thought was just ridiculous was that we had a prop guy—his name was David [Howell]—he was screwing this local wardrobe girl—young, attractive blonde girl—I don't remember her name. Well, it turns out that Alan Parker is also having a thing with her on the side. After, like, a couple weeks, she decides, "I'm going to fuck the prop guy, David"—a sexier, younger, trimmer version—and then basically Parker spent the rest of the film trying to get David fired off the film, which [Robert] Colesberry and [Fred] Zollo [producers] refused to do, probably because of the implications of a lawsuit and also because Colesberry is a cool guy. He liked crew people. He's not going to let a maniac like Parker do it.

This all unfolded with maybe, like, three weeks left of shooting. It was just really funny to be on set and just watch Alan and watch David. David was so cool about it. He's like, "I don't give a fuck if he's the director."

DANNY MICHAEL: Alan was also very superstitious. Like, at dailies, everyone had to sit in the same seat. Literally the same seat you sat in every other time for dailies. If he rode in a van with his DP, and his camera operator, his first AD, and his gaffer, all had to sit in the same seat in the van.

TONY STARBUCK: The other weird thing about Alan Parker is if anybody wore red to set they were sent home immediately—not fired, but you could not wear the color red. Another thing Parker did that was part of his superstition was that he had a shirt made of swatches of the shirts he had worn on every other film he had made stitched into it. He would basically wear one shirt, and he'd have it laundered every day.

DANNY MICHAEL: He was also one of the few directors in the day that had final cut. The studio could not change the cut of his film.

INGRID PRICE: It's just so funny to me. People who think, "Oh, you were a costume designer? Oh, my goodness. It must have been so much fun." Because they're imagining Cinderella dresses, and I'm thinking, "Oh, yeah, it was crouching in a ditch in the middle of Arkansas in the middle of the night. Yes, that was great fun."

What a weird industry to be in, and the potential for strange moments at work is high.

49 Parker, "*Mississippi Burning*: The Making of the Film."

Sidney Lumet in the '80s

BILL REYNOLDS (PROP MASTER, SET DECORATOR): I think a lot of directors were intimidated by New York and had difficulty in New York, whereas if you got a guy like Sidney Lumet or Woody Allen, they understood New York, and they could get what they wanted.

GARY MULLER (ASSISTANT CAMERA OPERATOR): I would say Sidney was probably the most influential person in the film industry. He taught me the most about screen direction, how to block a shot. He was very conscious, technically. On *The Wiz* Sidney would cut the camera if the actors missed their mark, and he'd say, "Bubala, you got to hit your marks."

LARRY HOFF (SOUND MIXER): Sidney came out of directing live TV, and for your half-hour show it took a half an hour to shoot. That was it. Hitchcock shot all these films, and then once he had a TV show he would take his TV crews to shoot his movies. The film crews are too slow. Let's get TV guys in here, because they know how to do it.

BILL REYNOLDS: But without question, he was the most together director. You can have the artistic end of it, and you can have the more mechanical end, and Sidney had enough of the art, but he certainly was mechanical. He knew how to get it done, and shooting on schedule was as important to him as getting the performances.

TOM PRIESTLEY, JR. (DIRECTOR OF PHOTOGRAPHY, CAMERA OPERATOR): A lot of moviemaking is problem solving. You do a major scene and then you try to figure out, well, how can I make it better? What can I fix? How can I make it flow better? How are things going to edit? Things of that nature. It's a constant ever-evolving situation. It's not very cut and dry, except if you work for Sidney Lumet.

BILL REYNOLDS: The schedule was very important to him, and I think that that came from his time in television at the beginning, when it was critical for money and everything else. Of course you can't now, but I would never invest in a movie unless Sidney was directing, because Sidney will come in on schedule, or in front of schedule. He will never be late, and he'll never be more expensive.

Martha Pinson and Sidney Lumet working on *Power* [1986]. Photo by Kerry Hayes.

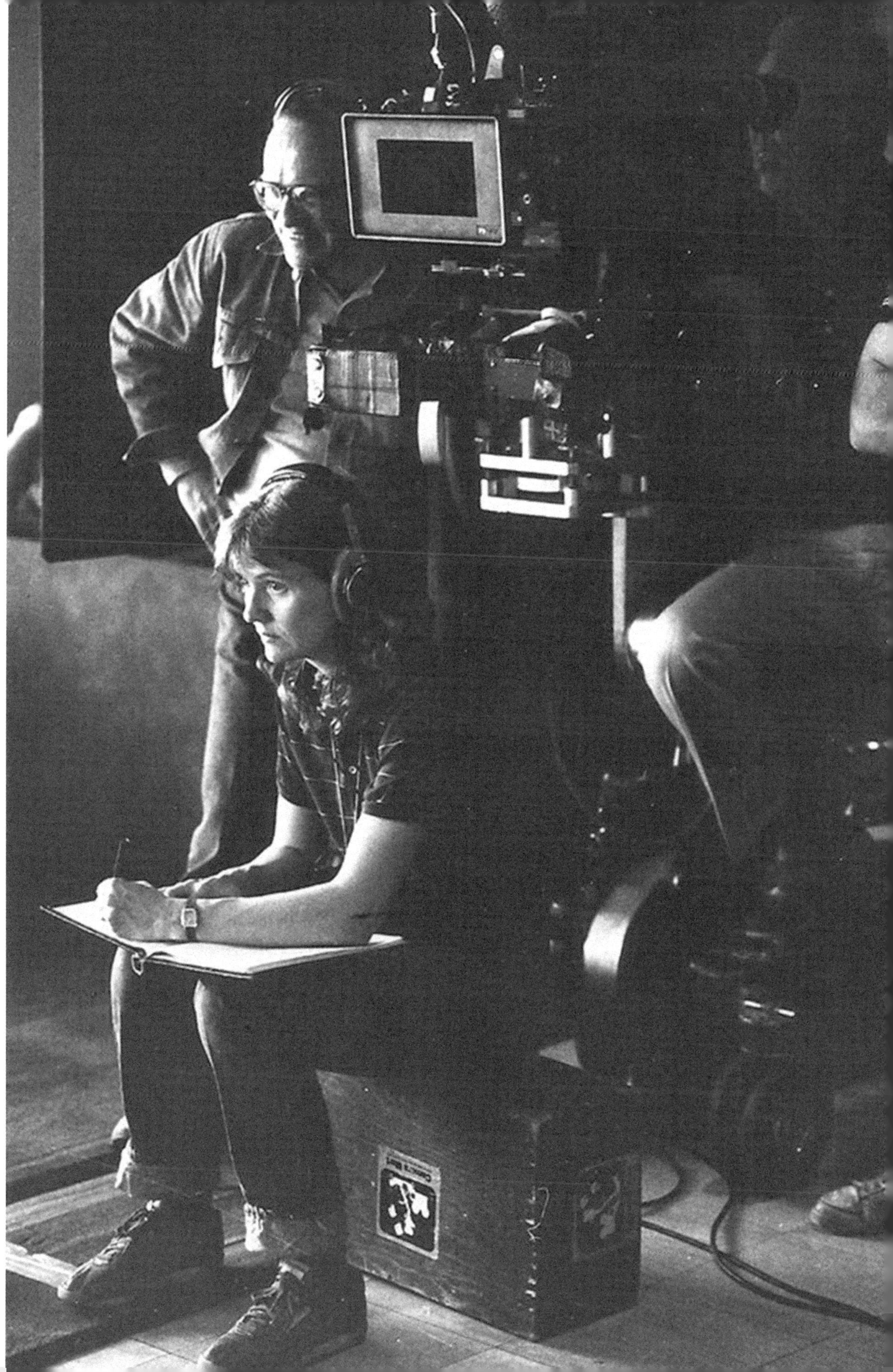

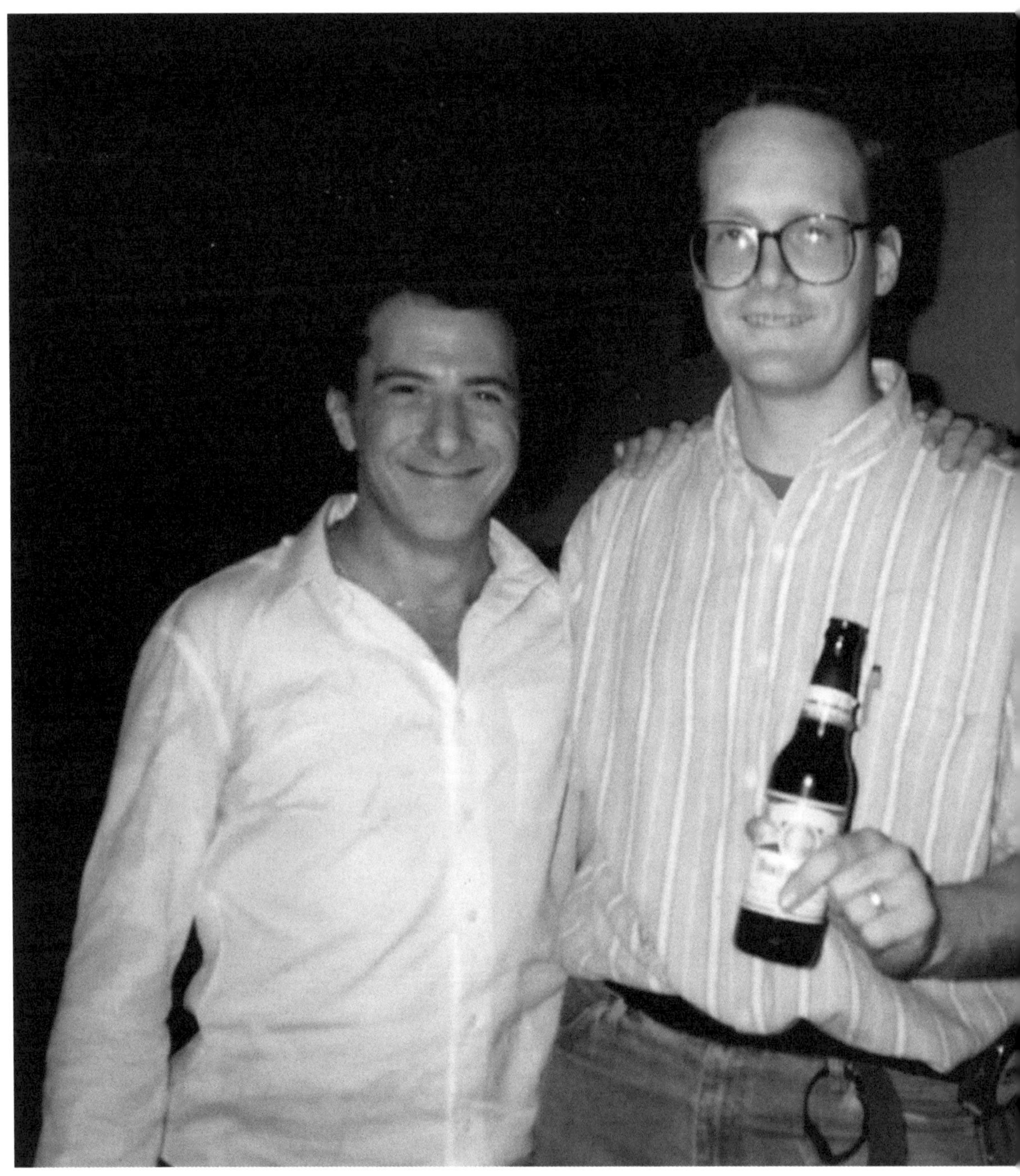

Prop Jimmy Archer with Dustin Hoffman and Matthew Broadrick on *Family Business* [1989]. Courtesy of Jimmy Archer.

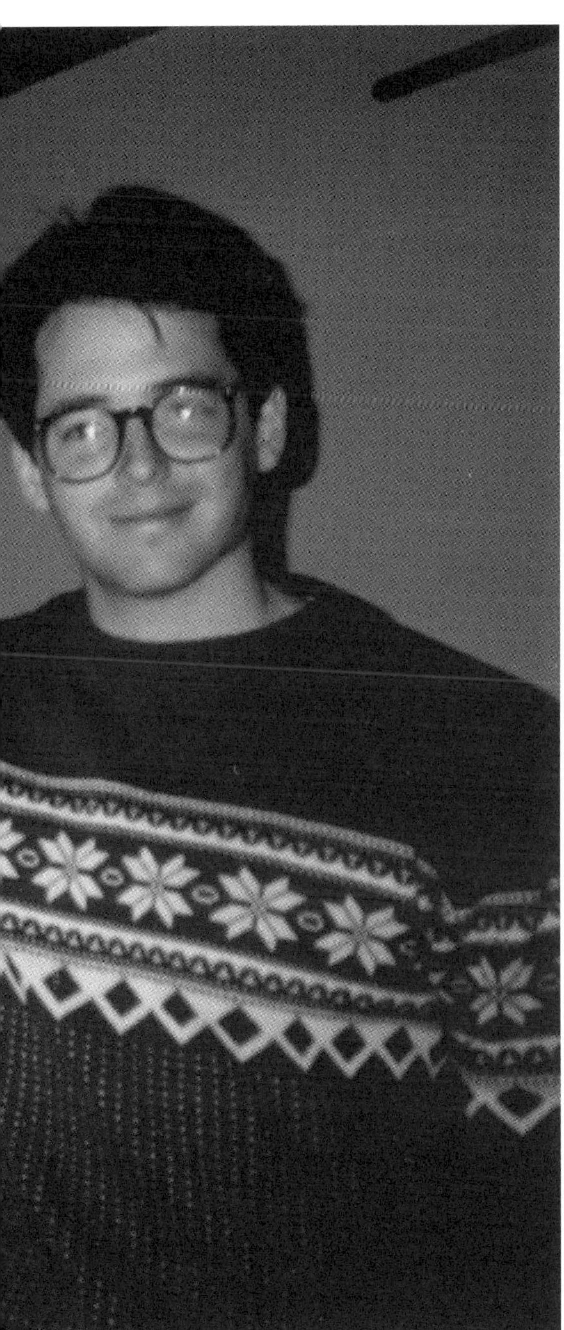

TOM PRIESTLEY, JR.: Everybody should work with a Sidney Lumet once in their life, just to see the other end of the spectrum. I've never met a director like that. I mean, no one's ever come that close to Sidney with the organization and the dedication and the speed.

RICHARD ADEE (PROP MASTER, SPECIAL EFFECTS, SET DECORATOR): I did about three movies with Sidney. He was fabulous. You go on a scout with Sidney Lumet and you'd scout all the locations and he'd say, "All right, camera's here. I want a 50 [millimeter lens] on it, and we'll make one dolly move."

That was it. I mean, that's how thorough that man was. You knew exactly what he wanted.

BILL REYNOLDS: He'd have very elaborate scouts, and he'd say, "Okay, the camera's going to be here." And if it was a period job especially, he said, "It's going to be 24 millimeters here. The left frame is going to be the edge of that building over there. The right frame will be this. You have a 35 [millimeter lens], so don't worry. Anything above the third floor, don't worry about."

And you could say to him, "Well, what about that telephone booth over there? Is that going to be a problem? It's not really in the period."

He'd say, "You know what? It won't be. It's not going to be a problem."

And they [the sound crew] would wire Sidney. He would be on a microphone and a transmitter, and the lemmings behind him, which could amount to thirty people, would all have speakers set up to be able to hear what he was saying. Any question you had about what was going to be required or where he would be looking—this was particularly helpful for the DP [director of photography] pre-planning and that, but the detail he would do, and he wouldn't vary from it.

I remember doing a movie with him on the Upper East Side, and they were having some trouble lighting. I think it was that they didn't account for where the sun was going to be.

It was looking out at the building across the street. It was all black buildings. So there was a big rush to get some lights on that, so you could have some depth, and it didn't look like a black hole behind them. And the DP [director of photography] said to him, "It's going to be a little bit of a while," and I remember Sidney looking at his watch, looking back at the DP, right in the eyes, and saying, "We will be shooting at 11 a.m." And they were.

TOM PRIESTLEY, JR.: He could tell you, "Next Thursday at four o'clock, we're going to be on the corner over there with a 35-millimeter lens on the camera," and, by God, we were there. I mean, that's how precise he was.

BILLY WARD, GAFFER: Sidney used to scout the location, and he would tell you exactly, "The master from here, over the shoulder here, over the shoulder there," and when we came back we shot it exactly as he said, which was nice in some respects, because you knew what you were into. But sometimes something's come out of a rehearsal you feel that could change something.

GARY MULLER: In pre-production, he would rent this Polish Hall out in Lower Manhattan, and every actor had to be on payroll from beginning to end—you couldn't start and leave and come back. You had to be there if you worked, or if you didn't work. You got paid for the entire six or seven weeks.

BILL REYNOLDS: We had taped out the floor to signify the walls, the outside walls, in various colors, so whether it was an apartment or was an office, they could stand in basically in the position. We taped that furniture on the floor so they could relate to it.

MARTHA PINSON (SCRIPT SUPERVISOR): In a big empty room with the set taped out on the floor, and we would just do it. It started with a table-read and then a discussion, and he would show pictures and things, historical or whatever, the location issues, so that the cast would all be educated as to the setting and lots of other factors.

BILL REYNOLDS: I was on *Family Business* [1989]. The talent was Matthew Broderick, Sean Connery, and Dustin Hoffman.

So, this was the first read-through, and they sat down at a conference table. Sidney was at the head, and he gets up and he says, "Gentlemen, I can't believe how lucky I am to have the talents that I have here in front of me. But let me be very frank and very clear right off the bat: there is one final voice. It is mine. You may have heard I only do one or two takes. That is very true, and I stick with that. If you have an extremely good reason, I will occasionally let you have a third take, but I can almost tell you there will never be more than that."

GARY MULLER: Sidney said, "Sean, listen, if I think I got it, that's it. Dustin, no two takes. If you're in frame and in focus, and I like the acting, don't ask."

BILL REYNOLDS: I think Hoffman was a little aghast, but they finished two weeks early.

MARTHA PINSON: I would have my [script] breakdown there, and then he would take it to read certain sections, reading this and that, and then we would do a rehearsal—staging of every scene in the film, in the two or three weeks that was allotted for the rehearsal.

GARY MULLER: The first week he'd do script reading. The second week, there was a PA [production assistant] at the door. When the actor came in the door, he took the script. The actor had to have the whole script memorized. Then the first couple of days they would just block it and then towards Thursday or Friday of the last week of prep the actors would go through it, and then the DP.

Sidney used this famous Mitchell finder, from the old days, and the DP would go down there, and they blocked the shots out.

MARTHA PINSON: Then the DP and a couple of other crew people would come in for a full run-through on the last day. The DP would know what the staging was going to be in each set, each scene. You would know if there was a car or something that they would just sit and pretend they were in a car. We'd use chairs. But we did have the actual size and shape of the rooms with a few basic props, a chair, or something so that they could use it, and so the actor might say, "I want to try this one, like, being insanely angry," and Sidney goes, "Okay, do it," and then he might tell the actor, "You know what, on the day, I think that the anger is good, but sit on it a little bit—just make it a little more subtle." The actors would be prepared as to various things that they would need to do in terms of pace, performance, and character. Everything was discussed.

BILL REYNOLDS: It wasn't as if he didn't want the actors' input. He didn't want input that was going to upset his schedule.

MARTHA PINSON: I think they had those discussions, but it was more private.

TOM PRIESTLEY, JR.: Every actor knew their motivation, what was expected of them—do it, *boom,* gone—and actors love that because they'd come in at eight and go home at five. It was great. I mean, shooting the movie was almost anti-climactic because he had the movie in his head. He was like Alfred Hitchcock. Hitchcock had the whole movie down on storyboards.

MARTHA PINSON: It was well-planned, and they would be thinking about how to transition from scene to scene as it were, or from series of scenes, segments of the film, to, like, another segment that might be a flashback or years later or something.

I worked with Miloš Forman on *Ragtime* [1981] and it's been so long I don't remember whether I had it on paper, something of a shot list, or with sketches. Martin Scorsese annotates his script by taking the physical script and jotting down, both in words and sometimes in images, three quick sketches of how he wants to see something and then we shoot that; we shoot what he plans.

GARY MULLER: Sidney, most of the time—for a camera assistant—he's very difficult because he only wanted to do one take. There's so many shots in Paul Newman's sequence [*The Verdict,* 1982] that are one shot, one take through a couple of rehearsals.

Most camera assistants like to work on the operator's side, the left-hand side of the camera. Very few back then like to work on the other side, the right-hand side of the camera. Sidney, when it was time for a closeup, would come up to the matte box and say, "Bubbie, other side."

He wanted his nose right next to the matte box. What the lens was seeing he wanted to see in an actor's eyes—even if it was a difficult dolly shot, he wanted that—and that's how I learned how to be a really good assistant working from the dumb side of the camera. Sidney always wanted to be near the matte box for closeups.

BILLY WARD: We did a lot of movies with Lumet. At that point, of course, I was a kid. I knew Sidney pretty well at that point. In fact, in those days Boris Kaufman was the cameraman. It was so different back then. We would come in at eight-thirty. We would light until one-thirty, go to lunch, and then come back and start to shoot. In the later years Sidney, he ripped through the script—boom, boom, boom. Once you lit for the master, a couple of corrections—boom, we shoot.

MARTHA PINSON: There would always be a rehearsal when you come to set in the morning. You got to block the scene. And then they go to wardrobe, hair, makeup, and the camera guys, and everybody does their work to light the set, set up the props and everything. It would be six hours a day that we would be there.

LARRY HOFF: I worked a couple of days for Sidney Lumet in Central Park. We have a nine-o'clock call. I think we were done in four hours, and we came in—boom, boom, boom, boom, boom—"This is okay. Let's go home." He shows up at ten. I think we were wrapped at two, something like that.

It's called block shooting. We do it now—where we'll shoot three scenes looking at the judge first or at the witness first. Sidney invented it.

RUSSELL ENGELS (GAFFER): It's very hard on actors too when you break it up like that, because you're doing it just in one direction. There was no over the shoulder, back and forth conversation-wise, so it could be tough on them. The actor would be into the scene and go about two sentences or so and he would say, "All right, cut."

And the actors would say, "What the hell? What are you cutting for?" and he would say, "I'll be over here on this guy when you're doing that." He knew exactly where he was going to use that guy, or that line, or that sentence. Then he was going to be on somebody else or whatever, and he would cut right there in the middle of the scene: "All right, we're done. I got that. I'll move over here." Because it's a lot less days on the job. The general cost would go way down when he could do that.

BILLY WARD: It was almost like he didn't like the process of making the movie—we shot so fast—which was nice because you knew you weren't doing overtime. You could make an appointment that night because you weren't going to be late.

TOM PRIESTLEY, JR.: It's one of those strange dichotomies: you want to work with a guy because he's brilliant, but you don't want to work with the guy because he's brilliant. On one location, on *Family Business* [1989], I think we shot, like, sixty setups in a day.

GARY MULLER: We went into this building, which they let us in on New Year's Eve because they had off. It was, like, this perfect location, and Sidney says, "Guys, I have fifty shots. We'll be done by lunchtime. I promise." Fifty shots.

TOM PRIESTLEY, JR.: In a room—out of the room—"Put the camera here, put it there."

GARY MULLER: He said, "Gary, don't tell me there's a hair in the gate. Don't even look in the gate. I'm taking that responsibility. We'll blow it out. We'll figure it out. Two lenses—film, handheld camera, that's it. I want it lit; I want to go."

Well, in about three and a half hours, we did forty-something shots, and I said, "Sidney, we got three more shots."

He said, "I forgot those shots. We don't need those shots." But in between [script supervisor] Mary Kelly's saying, "Sidney, you gotta do another one. Sidney, [the] screen direction's wrong."

And he's saying, "Mary, what are you taking notes for? I don't need notes. All I can do is cut the slates out and I got my sequence. Please. I don't even know why you came today. You could've stayed home. Just give Gary this slate number. That's all. Please."

It's so funny, though. He was, like, telling us, "Don't take notes." We were laughing our balls off behind him. He was like, "Everybody's getting in my way. I only want four people. I want the actors, I want Tom, I want Gary, and Andrzej [Bartkowiak, director of photography]. You go away, too."

TOM PRIESTLEY, JR.: Andrzej Bartkowiak had to place pre-rigged [lights]. So there were mostly the hallways, which you just point the camera and shoot—maybe he had one light for fill somewhere or something, but basically just pointing the camera and shoot, and that's what we did, and most of the equipment stayed on the truck—just the camera and maybe one or two lights. It's also about getting coverage. The more coverage you have, the better editorial rhythm you can achieve.

GARY MULLER: Man, we worked our balls off. He didn't even have a shot list. He had it all in his brain.

BILLY WARD: There was a time we were working and a couple of days prior the prop man, his father had died, and so Sidney walks on the stage and he says, "Ah, Harold, terribly sorry to hear about your father."

So, Harold starts to say, "Well, he was sick . . ."

And Sidney cuts him right off and says, "Okay. Just grab that couch and pull it over there. Let's go."

He didn't want to hear anything. He just did it for the formality. He was a piece of work, Sidney. But it was fine because, like I said, I knew I was coming home that night and you set the clock because you were going to finish at five-thirty.

JIMMY ARCHER (SET DRESSER, PROPS): One movie, they started in New York, did a shot in Kennedy Airport, went down to Washington, D.C., did a shot there, came back to New York, all in an eight-hour a day.

GARY MULLER: Seven hours, he's done. Get to a point where, Jesus Christ, you couldn't even take a piss. Sidney wanted to work French hours. Why do we have to go to lunch? Sidney's like, "I can take a nap at home."

You could be home. Okay, Sidney, you're making two million bucks; I'm making thirty dollars an hour.

BILLY WARD: I remember Dustin Hoffman working with him, and I guess they explained to Dustin before, "This is how it works," and they had a conversation, but Dustin didn't like that. Dustin always wanted another take. "No, no, no, it's fine. Bubbie, it's great. Let's move on."

GARY MULLER: Dustin was pretty damn good. So then Dustin started—a couple times on his dialogue—he said, "Sidney, I'd like another one. Gary, you need another one, don't you?"

I'm like, "Please don't say that," because he was commenting, "I'm going to fuck up on purpose, because I want another take." He would get under Sidney's skin. I think I've asked Sidney for another take maybe once in my career, and I think the same thing for Tommy [Tom Priestley].

BILLY WARD: I remember one time we were on top of a roof. After the take, the operator said, "No, that's no good. I clipped off his head."

He says, "Oh, it makes for tension. It's beautiful, bubbie. Let's go. Let's go." [laughs]

GARY MULLER: Sidney was a control freak, from beginning to end. Once my brother pulled focus with Sidney, he would say, "I try to say five things to Sidney a day. If he takes one of them, I'd go home and have another glass of beer."

TOM PRIESTLEY, JR.: With Sidney, dailies were at five-thirty p.m. It wasn't like other shows that were nine o'clock at night. The Teamster would have the car waiting for him on the last shot. They'd say wrap, he'd be out the door in the car, down to dailies. By the time we wrapped out and we go get our cars and get down there, he's coming out of dailies saying, "Oh, everything was great. I told the projectionist to hold it for you," and he's gone. We go up and watch it by ourselves. But that was Sidney.

GARY MULLER: The joke in the cutting room was that he didn't have to cut anything. All he had to do was cut the fucking slates off and put the film together and the film was done.

BILL REYNOLDS: Sidney wanted to be on a helicopter on Friday afternoon going to his place in the Hamptons and you knew you were going to get a short day on Fridays if you were on the shooting crew.

In fact, most times, shooting crews are the ones that make the money, with the hours. In a Lumet job, it was the dressers and construction, because you'd think that a set might be coming up two weeks from now and suddenly we've been burning through this, so we're going to get to it a week early. Set dressers always get it last—it gets built, it gets painted, and then the dressing comes in.

There was many a time when you'd be finishing up that morning when you thought you had plenty of time, and the shooters would be coming in to do a pre-light in the evening, where you thought you had the whole day. So the stress really went on construction, and scenics, and dressing. The carpenters are the most old-school blockheads. They're incredibly talented, but they don't like their schedules upset. If you set a schedule, if you said, "You might need a Saturday or you might have to go to twelve [hours]."

GARY MULLER: *Daniel* [1983]—see, that's when that got a little dicey working with Sidney, because we always had a twelve-hour guarantee. We work eight hours and nine hours, but a lot of the crew had a twelve-hour guarantee—sixty hours a week from the prep to finish—and with Sidney, if it was a ten-week schedule, you knew it was done in eight weeks because he would shoot so fast. So you were losing money working for Sidney after a while. And *Daniel* was very close to his heart because it was about the Rosenbergs, and it was part of his political makeup.

He didn't have enough money to make that movie. So he reached out to Burtt Harris, producer, his best guy—reached out to everybody—and said, "Listen, I don't have a lot of money, so can we just work for eight hours?" and we do forty-hour weeks, and working for Sidney for eight hours is like working for fourteen from anybody else. I mean, put a broom up your butt and you could clean the streets in New York. You don't sit down; you don't do anything. I think everybody agreed to work for normal rates and bend the rules a little bit.

I mean, the Teamsters got their money, and everybody else and producers got their money, but sure, okay, we'll do one for Sidney. But he was very tense, very tense. Sidney knew he had to hurry. I think the movie was, like, so politically motivated that nobody understood it. Nobody really cared about it, and then when we went to do *Garbo Talks* [1984]—it was sort of the same—like, "Oh, okay." Everybody anticipated that we would get reimbursed for our previous movie, but no, they said they didn't have enough money, and that was an okay movie. Then we went and did *Power* in, I think, 1986.

TOM WHELAN (UNIT PRODUCTION MANAGER, LOCATION MANAGER): After about six years of working in theater and television, I went back to film school and went to Columbia University. Miloš Forman was the chairman of the department. I didn't see him that much, but he was there. I studied screenwriting and directing. I had seminars with Frank Perry, Sidney Lumet, and Ralph Rosenblum.

The seminar with Sidney Lumet was the most memorable to me. He was also an extremely well-read person. He knew everything about the theater. He knew everything about theater history, European films. He was just amazing. And so the seminar was basically sitting around a table listening to him talk and us talking back and forth.

At the time he was finishing the movie *Running on Empty* [1988], and he took us to the ADR [automated dialogue replacement] sessions. He took us to the editing room. We would go to the editing room with him, and he still had a standup Movieola that he would look at his cuts on, and he would say, "Come over here and look what I'm doing at the Movieola." There'd just be a couple of us there because he would do, like, a very small group. We'd stand five feet behind him. He'd say, "No, get your nose into this screen here and see what I'm doing. You have to see this." And it was an unbelievable experience to watch him work and to be there when he was doing his stuff. None of us had ever been to an ADR session before. And here we have Judd Hirsch in front of us doing his work. It was quite amazing. I never got to work on a production with him. But for me that was a formative experience.

TOM PRIESTLEY, JR.: He made great movies, and he made average movies, but he never really made a bad movie. Made forty or fifty movies, starting, I guess, with *Twelve Angry Men* [1957], which is incredible. *The Verdict* was another great one. The great movies transcend time, you know? You can watch *Twelve Angry Men,* made in 1955, today and it's got carrying power. The same with *The Verdict*. The same with *Network* [1976].

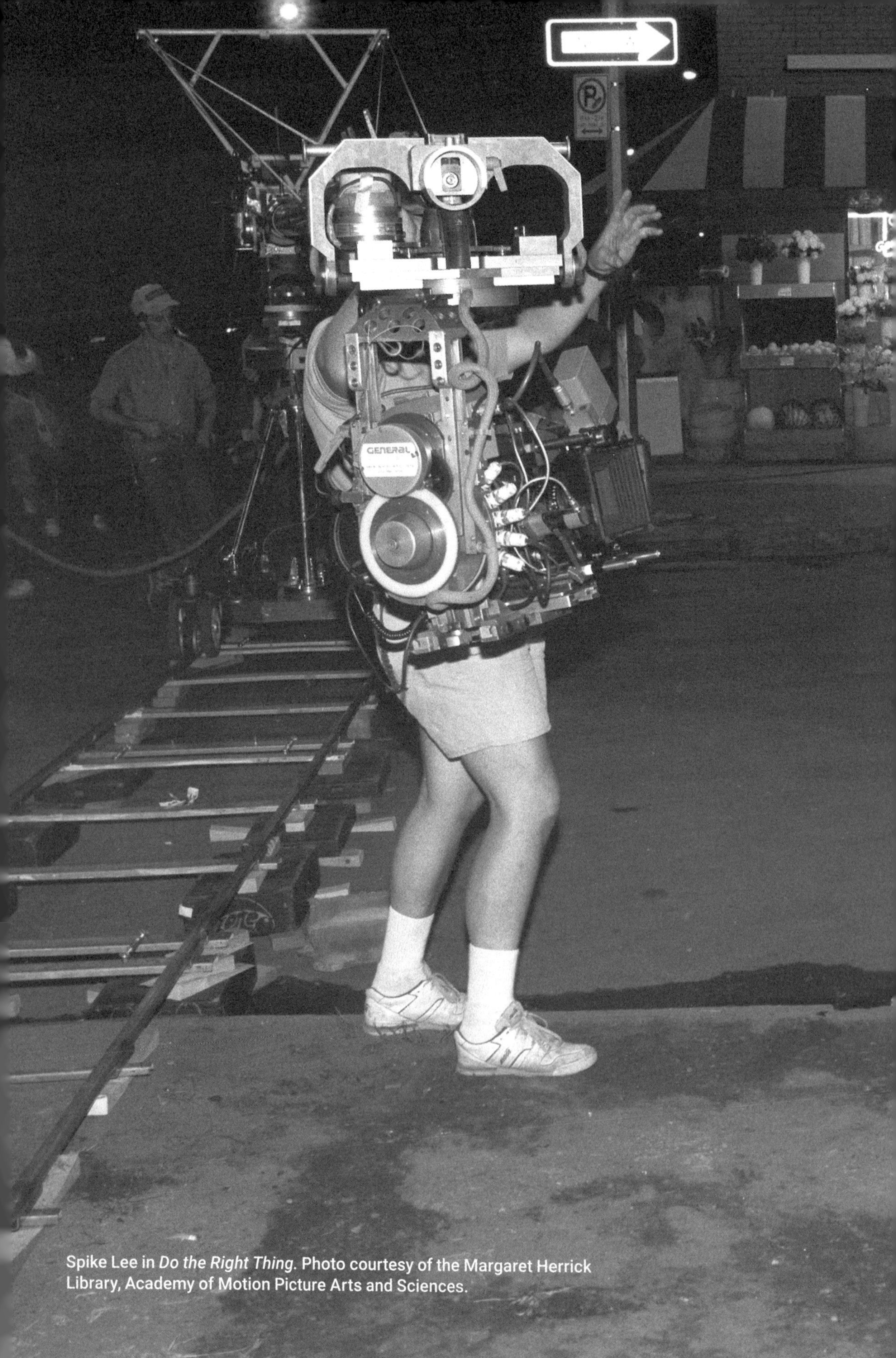

Spike Lee in *Do the Right Thing*. Photo courtesy of the Margaret Herrick Library, Academy of Motion Picture Arts and Sciences.

Do The Right Thing

(1989)

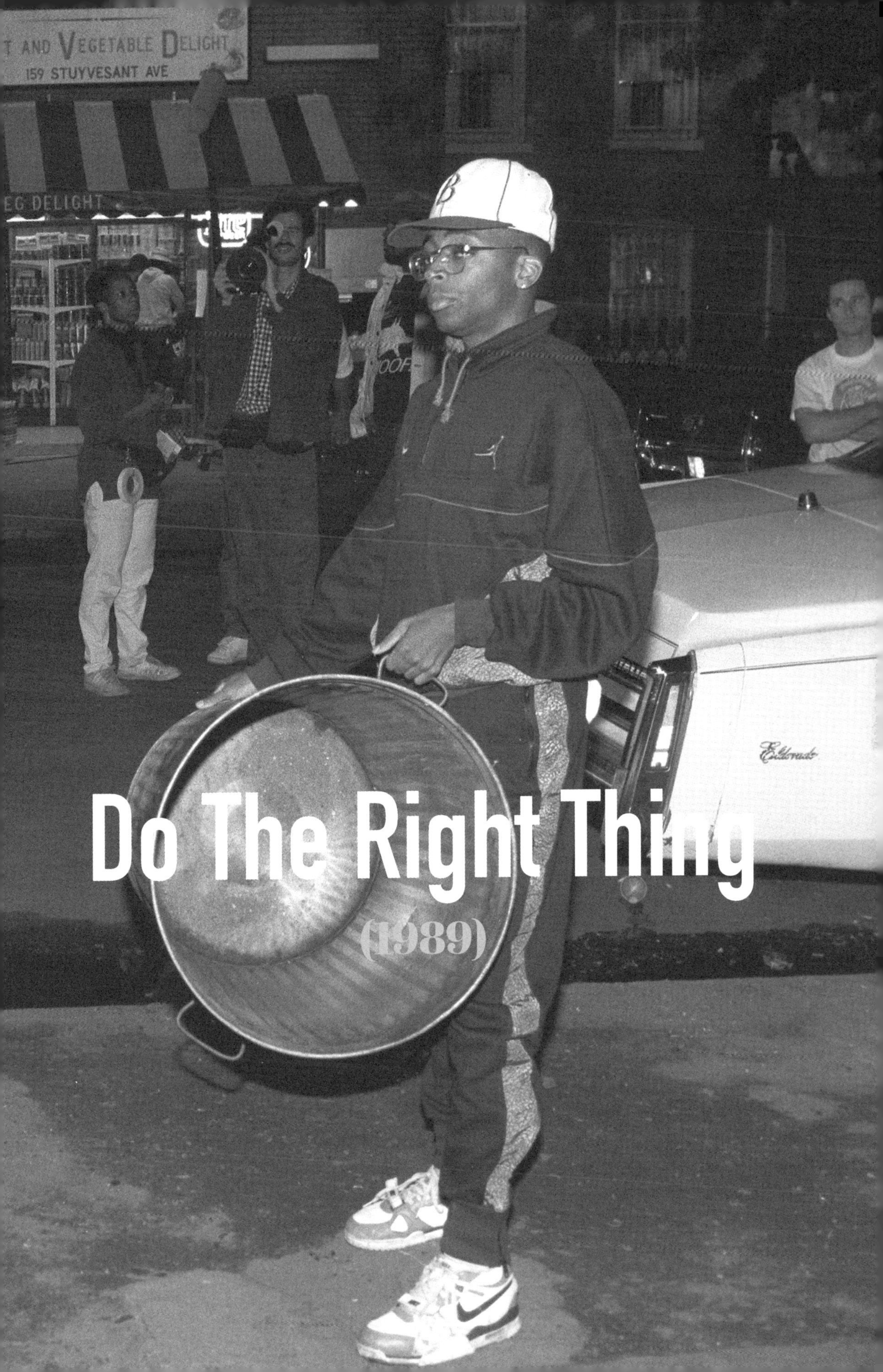

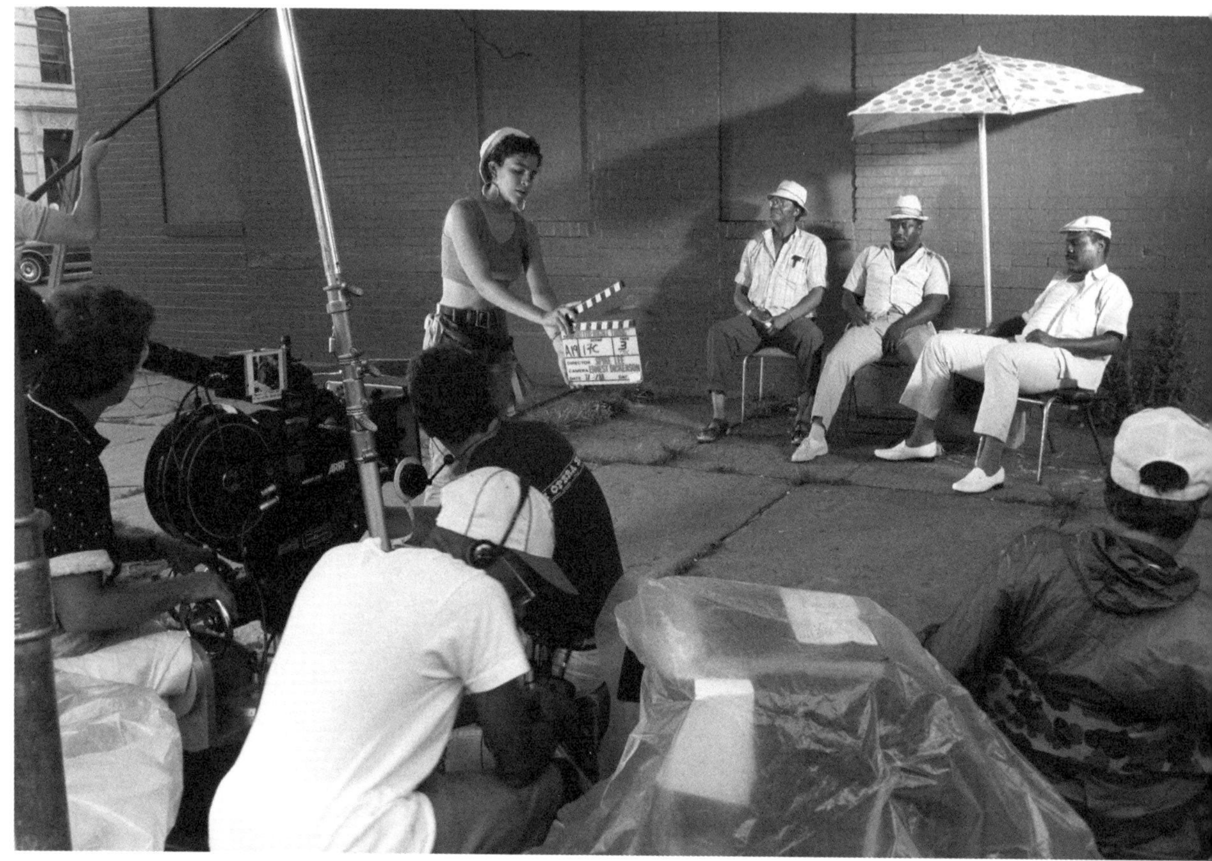

FRANK STETTNER (SOUND MIXER, *DO THE RIGHT THING*): It laid out a view of a neighborhood. I thought that was really, really vibrant to see the different characters, and Spike did bring them to life.

JONATHAN BURKHART (FIRST ASSISTANT CAMERA OPERATOR, *DO THE RIGHT THING*): So I'm living on 46th Street. It's 1987, and I remember I'm walking down 9th Avenue and who comes up on her bike but it's this woman named Tami Reiker. Tami rides by on her bike. We start chitchatting. This conversation changed my life and career. She goes, "Hey these guys are trying to make a movie. They're looking into hiring a camera department. I just interviewed there. Maybe you should go try this one."

I said, "Where?"

"You're going to go to 1842 Broadway. Go up to the sixth floor, knock on door B."

Mind you, there's no internet—no cell phones or anything. I was like, "Okay, I'll give it a try."

And Tami goes off on her bike and I go to this address and I knock on the door and I meet Ernest Dickerson, who shot all of Spike Lee's movies. Today Ernest is a huge television director in Hollywood—super, super amazing guy.

From there he hires me to be the camera assistant on *Death by Temptation*. It came out in 1990, but we shot it in 1987, and on that movie Ernest Dickerson was the cinematographer and the director was a guy named James Bond III. It was an all-Black

Two angles of Paul Benjamin, Robin Harris, and Frankie Faison in *Do the Right Thing*
Photos courtesy of the Margaret Herrick Library, Academy of Motion Picture Arts and Sciences.

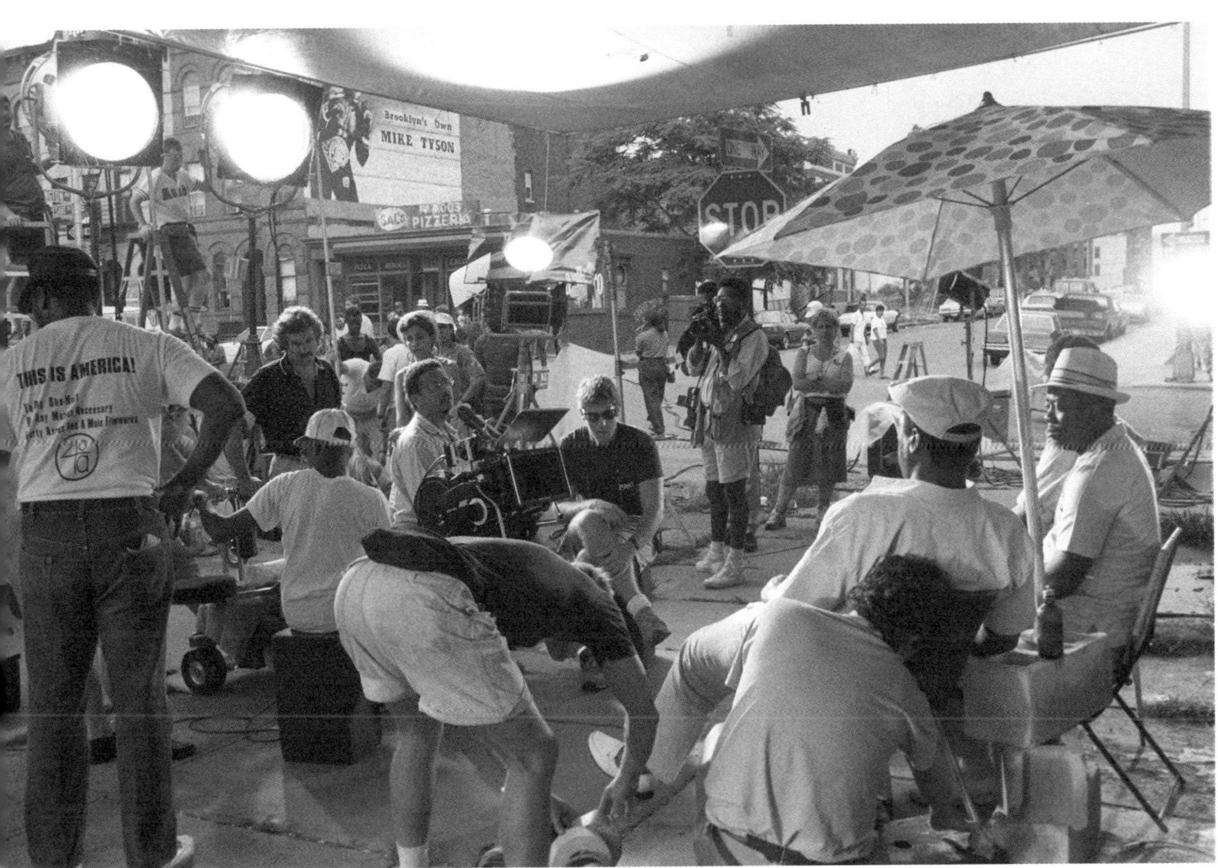

cast, mostly a Black crew, but Ernest hired me as his camera assistant and we got along great.

As we were coming towards the end of the schedule, he said, "I also shoot for Spike Lee. In a week or so he's got a UB40 music video. Will you work on that with me?" I said, "Sure."

I prepped a camera, and I'm on the first day of shooting on this UB40 music video with Ernest and Spike. Ernest introduced me to Spike. He looks at me. We chatted for a little bit. We do a couple of days of shooting. Then there was a Tracy Chapman music video. And from then on I was Ernest Dickerson's camera assistant. Like, he hired me for everything. This was a giant career changer in the hugest way because Spike Lee worked all the time. We were doing all the Nike spots with Michael Jordan and Charles Barkley.

We shot them, like, all the time, and if it wasn't those it was a music video, and now we're rolling into winter, spring of 1988 and I get a phone call from Spike's company, 40 Acres and a Mule. Spike wants to meet me in Brooklyn, and I go, and he says, "I'm making a movie called *Do the Right Thing* this summer. Ernest Dickerson wants you to work on it with him. And I want to talk to you about it."

What I am about to tell you is very important. It changed my career, and still to this day it affects me. So I'm at 40 Acres and a Mule. Spike looks at me and he goes, "Here's the deal. You're a white cameraman." He said, "My goal is to bring as many Black men and women into this industry as possible. This is what's going to happen. You are going to train yourself out of a job. You're going to work on all the films I do—commercials, music videos—and one day I'm not going to call you anymore because I have the department that I need."

And he did that with all departments—grip, electric, set dressing, props, so on and so forth, and he stayed true to his word. He made it clear to me directly to my face: "This industry got to change—there was too many white people doing it—and I'm going to make the change."

I said, "Sure."

KEVIN LADSON (PROP MASTER, *DO THE RIGHT THING*): That's the kind of person Jonathan Burkhart is. I give him a lot of credit because he never shunned the idea of that. That is a known, absolute true story. He is as big a part of that revolution as anybody, because there was no hatred coming in. Jonathan was part of the learning process of people coming in, particularly in the camera department. Spike was very clear—there was no beating around the bush with him, because he was very clear on his mission from the start.

JONATHAN BURKHART: And we had a really great relationship. I lasted, I think, four years, but it wasn't like he didn't call me anymore. I just moved on. After *Mo' Better Blues* [1990], I did most of his movies either, like, day-playing B camera, C camera, or second unit, because my career was actually doing something else at the time.

KEVIN LADSON: My first day was *Do the Right Thing*. I wanted to faint because I saw so many Black people. It was certainly something I had never seen before on a job from 1984 to 1988, when we did *Do The Right Thing*. Prior to that, I was maybe one of five, six, seven Black folks on the job, which was a lot, but then when Spike came in I saw a sea of Black people.

FRANK STETTNER: It was a really good crew, a lot of serious, younger Black people that were in the lower positions on the scale, or on the crew, seconds and thirds to learn the crafts. Top notch people today began on that movie.

JEFF GLAVE (CHARGE SCENIC ARTIST, *DO THE RIGHT THING*): It came through Wynn [Thomas, production designer], but Spike was interested in why are there no Black scenic artists? Why are there no Black crew people? Why are there no Black designers in general?

OCTAVIO MOLINA (PROP MASTER, *DO THE RIGHT THING*): I mean, everybody there who was a minority—myself included—we were not lower class. Everybody had gone to college, well-educated, myself included.

KEVIN LADSON: The hand-shaking was across the board. It was very unique at that time, because, particularly then, there was so few Black people that it was celebratory when we would see each other on set. Ossie Davis tried. He tried with Third World Production, which trained script supervisor Renoir Darrett. She ended up working on *Claudine* [1974]. She ended up working on these films where they did assign people, but it was only ten [Black] people per production. Preston Holmes is one of them, but when Spike came in there were forty, fifty Black people coming into the business.

OCTAVIO MOLINA: My first real key credit was on *Do the Right Thing*. And that was probably one of the best movies I ever worked on besides the porno [*Debbie Does Dallas*, 1978]. [laughs] I didn't realize it was going to be like that at the time, but it was a singular experience.

It was set up very unusually, because there were no trucks. It was always the same location. Everybody had a derelict building basement to set up their stuff. The grips had some kind [of] garage because they needed to build cranes, but we had a garden apartment on the derelict property. The art-department office was on Washington Street. Spike still lived in the neighborhood down by Fort Greene. He had a firehouse.

FRANK STETTNER: I like the idea of it being everything in one day,[50] on one block in the neighborhood, with nothing out. That was an interesting focus for me, and I had a good crew and we all worked together.

[If] Spike said, "No, I want to do it this way," we'd have to figure out, "That's not the classic way to do it, but let's see—how can we do this?" and then we would solve the problem, give him what he needed. It made me think outside the box a little, which is good. That's how you grow things.

JEFF GLAVE: I remember trying to pull the crew together because it was so early in my being in the union that I didn't have lots of people that I could call upon to join me for that kind of job. It was absolutely wonderful and terrible, because I really ended up liking Spike Lee, but he asked to do things that we didn't want to do. I have one specific instance. It was during the Tawana Brawley episode in history with Al Sharpton and everybody, and he wanted us to write on graffiti on one wall, "Tawana Told the Truth!"

And at the time it was pretty clear that Tawana hadn't told the truth, but it was just before it came out that she made the whole thing up, and I remember not being able to ask anybody else to do this because I didn't believe you could ask people to do things they didn't believe in, but I knew I had to do it. I ended up doing that bit of graffiti and I was choking mad when I had to write it because it was so divisive and it's like: yeah, she didn't tell the truth.

The film was a trenchant exploration of the racial politics of New York City at the time, from incendiary trash-talking to police violence and an ensuing riot—even extending to the graffiti on the wall reading "TAWANA TOLD THE TRUTH." (Tawana Brawley became a political flashpoint in 1987 when, as a teenager, she was found in a trash bag smeared with feces and with racial slurs written on her body; she said six white men had raped her, although a special state grand jury the following year declared that she had fabricated the story.)[51]

—*Rolling Stone*, June 20, 2014

JEFF GLAVE: I remember it being the hottest summer ever because we had more than a month of over-95 temperatures and we were working outside on scaffolding every day.

OCTAVIO MOLINA: It was hot as hell, and it was a really interesting experience to be on the same place, like a backlot and the two locations that feature prominently are the Korean deli and the Sal's Pizzeria. They were directly opposite each other. They're still vacant lots because these buildings were just built from scratch. They were literally sets that you could walk into, but they were sets and I don't think the oven worked. I had a guy delivering me all the product [pizzas] early in the morning.

KEVIN LADSON: I got there the first day of shooting, I didn't know that half that stuff was built. The pizzeria was built. The radio station was built. The Korean deli was built. When Wynn told me that, I said, "These are the types of designs that will never win Academy Awards because it looks too real." It was flawless, and the Korean deli was so real that people would actually go and try and shop there.

JEFF GLAVE: Wynn Thomas was brilliant. We made a whole lot out of a little, because we took a row of abandoned brownstones and put windows in them, and we did fake repairs to the masonry and built foam masonry to make stuff look upstanding instead of down and out, and we made it into a cute little neighborhood block, and it was a lot of fun.

50 The plot of the film takes place over one day.

51 Gavin Edwards, "Fight the Power: Spike Lee on 'Do the Right Thing,'" *Rolling Stone*, June 20, 2014.

KEVIN LADSON: Now there's a guy, Bruce Roberts, who worked as a PA [production assistant], and I would see him stealing boxes of cereal [from the Korean deli set]. I said, "Bruce, you don't need to steal a cereal. Just leave the boxes, take the cereal. We need the boxes for the set. Take the cereal, because the rats would get into them anyway." And the pizzeria—Octavio Molina was the prop master on that.

OCTAVIO MOLINA: "Bed-Stuy Do or Die" was kind of spooky so early in the morning or staying up late at night coming home. Like, if we were in scenes where I had police vehicles and I had to reset the vehicle, I would have to go around the corner and drive around. I thought to myself, "I hope nobody thinks I'm a real cop," but nothing like that happened.

JEFF GLAVE: We had the Fruit of Islam as our protectors in the very dangerous section of Bed-Stuy we were in. We had to walk to catering. It was a low enough budget that they actually counted paper plates so that they wouldn't be having people bringing food to anybody else, but we would pass these empty brownstones that had mange-covered dogs living in them and we would slip our paper plates full of food to the dogs so they would have something to eat because we felt so sorry for these walking skeletons.

KEVIN LADSON: I mean, the camaraderie—we became a family at the end of that job, because it seemed all fun, very light and airy, very New York, culturally diverse—until they killed Radio Raheem. Then you could see the emotions of the crew start to shift. That just affected everybody.

OCTAVIO MOLINA: And of course, when they had the scene in the pizzeria where all hell broke loose it was actually more real than I care to remember, which is why I think a lot of people were a little bit in shock. I don't think it was really as rehearsed as I would've thought it might have been, but nothing happened. Nobody got hurt. But there were no fake glasses. There was none of that. And I think it kind of went a little bit out of control.

JEFF GLAVE: Sal's Pizzeria was a lot of fun to build, fun to watch it burn.

STEVEN KIRSHOFF (SPECIAL EFFECTS, *DO THE RIGHT THING*): You do the interior shots where they set the fire on the inside of the place. It was built with double sheetrock, so it wasn't going to burn down for real. The interior stuff was minor. Then the exterior, basically you build sheet-metal hoods that kind of box in the window facing from the inside. Then you run your fire pipes under the eaves. So anything that has fire on it is protected by sheet metal. I use an asbestos replacement; you wrap it into casings.

That one was different because it was like a big storefront, but basically you run propane lines—the slotted pipes you run it to a big manifold, which was either a truck with a manifold or a series of hundred-pound bottles of either propane or map gas or a combination, and, you know, light it up.

OCTAVIO MOLINA: Everybody was lovely. A lovely, lovely crew. A lot of us bonded after that job. I wish I could say the same about our leader, but a lot of people have different opinions of him. He was not an easy person to get along with—for me anyway. I certainly feel like I had a great time doing the movie. It was a very, very great experience.

Coming from an old leftist circle, I thought the movie was a little bit too much like one of those liberal dramas from the fifties. So what is the response? So you start a riot and then what? These people are not going to be able to live in the building or something like that? There's no path to create a greater working-class consciousness. It doesn't offer any solutions.

The other thing that really bothered me about the project was the fact that he was heavily into promotion and we're promoting Nikes and things like that. I guess that's smart, but he was definitely not a purist in any of these politics, so I didn't appreciate that. I don't understand why he had to do it. To pay for the film? Maybe that's why he thought he had to do it?

I can say that the reason I had drawn a jaundiced view was because of certain commercial aspects and the lack of clarity in solutions for the working class. I thought it was kind of commercialized, but of course I sympathized with it. I mean, I consider myself a minority and I identify strongly in that way.

KEVIN LADSON: We would go to dailies, and we would have little cookouts and barbecues after work and everything, and then when John Turturro started doing the lines, "You black moolinyan spear-chucking African Negro," the lady who did craft services went up to him and cursed him out. She couldn't break the reality of him being an actor. She actually went up to him and cursed him out! It's like, wait a minute. We're making a movie. He's really reading lines. [laughs]

You couldn't tell her that Spike was the one who wrote those words. You know, she was so angry. It was so realistic. I thought, "Oh my God." I said, "Either this is a problem or the acting is just that great," and the acting was just that great, because Spike pulled it out of everybody.

KEVIN LADSON: After Radio Raheem was killed, that just affected everybody. I was talking with Jonathan Burkhart just reflecting about that, man. It's still so personal being on set while we had shot that scene, because there were a lot of people going off behind the set and crying, because what we shot was just that powerful.

Jonathan and I, we were crying on the phone after George Floyd got killed, man, and we were talking about being on the set when we killed Radio Raheem and it was the same emotion. We're talking about all these years later. It was interesting to get his perspective, and John Newby, who was another one of the cameramen I spoke to, we were talking about how, when we were shooting that scene, it was so pivotal, so iconic, to what was going on in 2020, and that film always stands out, man. That's a film of the eighties I'll never forget. Never.

JEFF GLAVE: It was really a great job, and I did enjoy that whole group of people from Spike's world and Wynn's world. We worked together for, geez—another dozen jobs easily.

KEVIN LADSON: A lot of people went from *Do The Right Thing* right into *Mo' Better Blues*. Again, it was that family camaraderie and a lot of the actors were in it—John Turturro, Bill Nunn, Sam Jackson continued to be in a lot of his movies after that. It really started to feel like the family, the more movies we started to do with Spike.

JEFF GLAVE: I'm getting emotional thinking about it now, all these years later. We made something good, and we all knew it.

When Harry Met Sally

(1989)

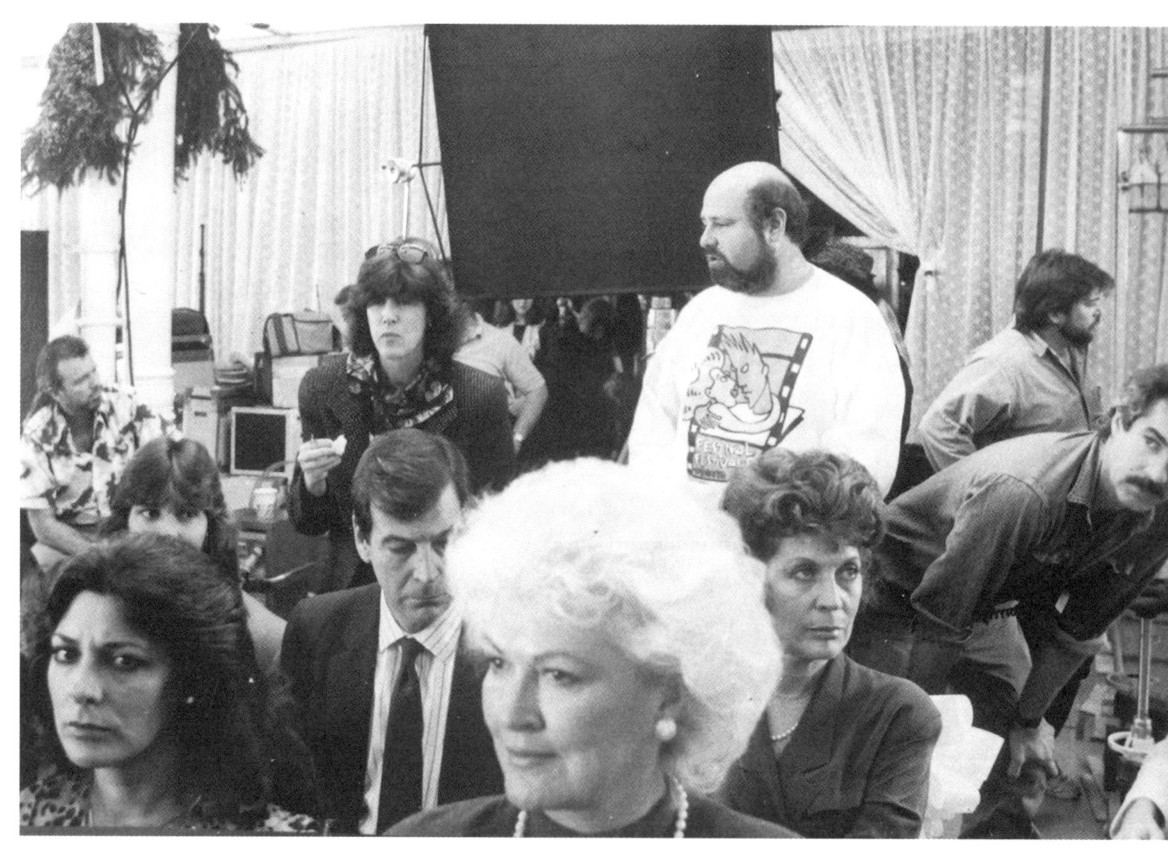

Left to right: Michael F. Burke, Nora Ephron, Rob Reiner, Eddie Lowry, Brian Fitzsimmons. Courtesy of Michael F. Burke.

JANE MUSKY (PRODUCTION DESIGNER, *WHEN HARRY MET SALLY*): When I first came on the picture, Rob [Reiner] lived in Los Angeles, and they were going to shoot the whole picture in L.A. That was a time when everything that was scripted for New York, the studios would try to pull to L.A. because they could save money.

First of all, because of the [cheaper] crew rates, but also the studios had to support these big lots at that point. They're not as big anymore. So they wanted the pictures to be on their stages so that they could pay for the facilities, basically. You had to use their scenic artists, you had to use their whatever, just so they could make their overhead. When I took the job, everyone said, "You have to come to L.A. 'cause we're going to shoot it here."

This had happened to me before. This wasn't the first film where they're yanking me out of New York to go to L.A. When I got there, I told Rob, "Well, I'll start scouting with people and we'll see what happens." I spent about three or four weeks with some scouts, just going all over L.A. to look for the New York stuff, believe it or not.

I just kept saying to Rob every day, "I got to tell you, this is a New York story, like, a romantic comedy. What I'm finding is not what you're going to want." So I took him out scouting a few weeks after I'd been there. The whole day we're all in this van driving around. Steve Nicolaides, who is a line producer, is a good friend of Rob's. I looked at Steve, I said, "Isn't there any way to at least shoot a few weeks in New York for the exteriors in Central Park etc.?"

At that point they had committed to L.A. I'd already started building Carrie Fisher and Bruno [Kirby]'s townhouse. That whole first floor was a set in L.A. They were gung-ho—the whole picture is going to be in L.A. So that set plus one other—I can't remember which other—but I started two big soundstages already with the beginnings of these set pieces.

Rob and Steve finally got the studio to acquiesce, and I think a lot of it was Nora [Ephron], who was a pretty big screenwriter at that point too. I think she had a lot of weight to pull in that decision too, and they pulled the whole picture back to New York with the understanding that the sets I had already started had to be finished out in L.A. So we shot in L.A. I think for two weeks and then moved the whole picture back to New York. Barry [Sonnenfeld, director of photography] started a whole New York crew, and I did also.

MICHAEL F. BURKE (ELECTRICIAN, *WHEN HARRY MET SALLY*): When we started working with Barry, anytime he had a job we were with him until he started going into directing.

JANE MUSKY: Mike was glued to Barry at that point.

During the filming of "Big" I discovered how Depends adult diapers worked. I rarely leave the set, and I don't think any crew member should either. It would drive me crazy when I needed an additional light or wanted to add a piece of track to a dolly move, I'd ask "Where's Rusty? Where's Dennis?" And some crew member would say, "In the bathroom, sir."

"Sir" is crew code for asshole, by the way.

—Barry Sonnenfeld, *Barry Sonnenfeld, Call Your Mother*, 2020

MICHAEL F. BURKE: He had Dennis [Gamiello] and Rusty [Engels] with him in the crew. So it was John Lowry and Brian Fitzsimmons, his grips, and stuff like that.

ANGELO DIGIACOMO (ASSISTANT CAMERA OPERATOR, *WHEN HARRY MET SALLY*): Rob Reiner is truly a gem. He's a guy that comes to work having done his homework, so we never worked more than ten hours a day, which was unheard of. And I saw him lose his temper once: he threw a water bottle because something didn't work out or whatever, and even apologized, but truly a gentleman. Nice guy, very bright. He knew what he wanted, and he worked very well with Barry, because Barry at the time was a hot DP [director of photography], but he had very good gaffers working with him. You can be an adequate DP and look great if you have a good gaffer.

MICHAEL F. BURKE: So Barry and Rob became buddies. Barry set up Rob Reiner with a date who ultimately became Rob's wife.

RUSSELL ENGELS (GAFFER, *WHEN HARRY MET SALLY*): Barry and Rob Reiner together—that was a fun part too—the two of them. I don't know how they knew each other, but it was possibly through Barry or possibly they saw [each] other's work, whatever, and Jane, maybe she had something to say about who can do this or who can do that, but it all fell together, and it was almost the same crew [as *Raising Arizona*].

JANE MUSKY: Barry and I did so much work with each other back then.

ANGELO DIGIACOMO: Barry does therapy on set. He talks and has no filter whatsoever. He hated his mother and would talk about it. Barry's parents were older and Jewish. His mother was, I think, in her forties when she had him, and she was a schoolteacher, and she would take him to the same school where she taught. Barry was a real nerd—glasses, big teeth, skinny, very awkward socially—and the kids in the school couldn't beat him up because he'd say, "I'm Mrs. Sonnenfeld's son—you can't beat me up," so they would beat his friends up and they'd tell his friends, "We're beating you up because we can't beat him up," and that's what used to happen. Barry is a very weird guy.

So anyway, we're eating lunch in the cafeteria in the basement of the [Metropolitan] Museum—we were doing the Temple of Dendur, and I'm sitting with my back to the wall, farthest away from the entrance, and Barry is telling a story at lunch and he's very animated. His mother walks in and I go, "Barry, your mother's here." He went from being animated, talking, telling a story, to a little boy; he visibly shrunk.

RUSSELL ENGELS: Barry could do everything without a [camera] operator. That was unheard of, but in some of the pictures his operator was Mike [Todd Henry].

A number of jokes went on there. Mike was on the camera for [his] first union picture and a little leery about the dolly and who's in charge and operating and all that stuff. How good is everybody? Are they going to take care of him, because he came from a non-union background? All that kind of thing, and we'd put printer's ink on the handles of his wheels and maybe put printer's ink on the rubber eye protector on the camera lens, and you would come out with the big black eye. That broke the ice with that union thing. So that was good.

JANE MUSKY: You know, who could ask for a better job than *When Harry Met Sally*? I mean, first of all, you get Rob and Billy [Crystal] scouting in a van together and laughing for twelve hours straight and stopping every few hours to get a pastrami sandwich. We all had the best time. I mean, there was not a moment on that film I can remember where things felt stressed. Maybe Rob felt it, but we didn't. He was very protective of making this experience wonderful. Nora Ephron was very involved. She always had a great way about her. Things sort of slowed down when Nora came around because she was very mannered in the way

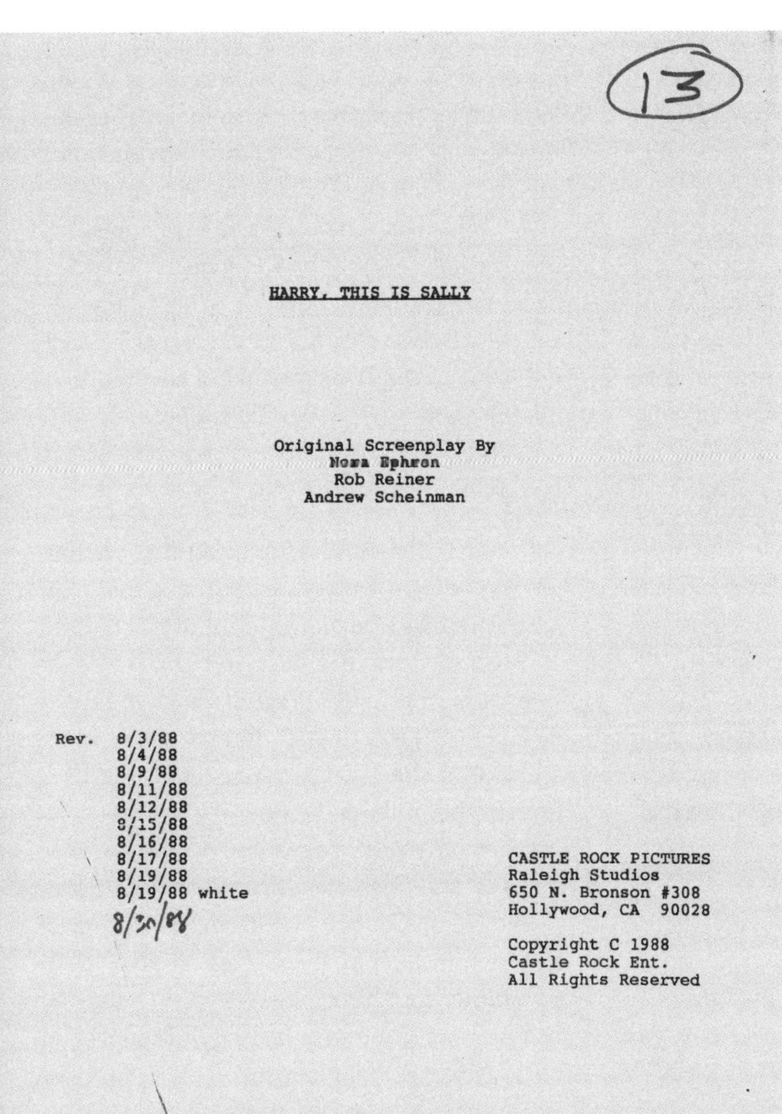

13

HARRY, THIS IS SALLY

Original Screenplay By
Nora Ephron
Rob Reiner
Andrew Scheinman

Rev. 8/3/88
8/4/88
8/9/88
8/11/88
8/12/88
8/15/88
8/16/88
8/17/88
8/19/88
8/19/88 white
8/30/88

CASTLE ROCK PICTURES
Raleigh Studios
650 N. Bronson #308
Hollywood, CA 90028

Copyright C 1988
Castle Rock Ent.
All Rights Reserved

Harry, This is Sally script.

she explained things. It was really a good combination between Rob and Nora, because not only were they great friends but they listened to each other, and we listened to them.

The most stressful thing I can think of was a scene with Meg [Ryan]—we shot her apartment at the Apthorp. The bedroom was the set. We had a small apartment at the Apthorp and Nora lived in the Apthorp—the apartment building—it's on 79th and Broadway and is a famous building with the big courtyard. Meg's apartment was in that building and—'cause back then they were extremely film-friendly.

These were gigantic apartments. They were good to shoot in because you had a lot of room to move around. Meg came to the set that day—and she's the best; I've done three films with Meg, I think—she showed up on the set and it was Christmastime in the story. She and Rob were starting to figure out what they were going to do during the scene. Rob says something like, "Well, why don't we make cookies?"

Meg said, "That's a great idea. I could be making gingerbread cookies." So I'm standing there listening to the rehearsals going, "Oh, hell, we don't have any cookie stuff!" It was like one of those moments where the prop person's looking at me like, "What the hell are we doing?"

It's like seven in the morning, you know? I'm standing there and all of a sudden I think, "Nora's home." We call up Nora. Nora always was known to be this phenomenal cook and very family-centric—making big meals and whatever. I called her up and she was awake, thank God, at 7 a.m. I said, "We have a problem upstairs. She wants to make gingerbread cookies."

Nora was so funny. She goes, "Gingerbread cookies. I have, like, ten different gingerbread cookie cutters." She saved the day. We went down and she literally put a kit together to make gingerbread cookies. I think Meg thought we were just the most amazing art department [she'd come] across at that point.

MICHAEL F. BURKE: You know how everybody comes to the back of the truck and the first thing they ask, "Hey, what are you shooting? Can I be in it?" And I was hanging out on the truck in the back one day, and there are all these people asking me all these stupid questions. So I got a piece of board from the grips and I posted a sign on the back of the truck.

It said: "The name of the movie is *When Harry Met Sally*. There's nobody famous in it and no, you can't be in it." I had maybe entered five questions and answers. Some guy sees me sitting on the back of the truck and he takes a picture of the thing. I don't know if it still exists, but I think it was *Premiere* magazine.[52] And Billy Crystal says, "There's nobody famous in it."

JIMMY ARCHER (SET DRESSER, *WHEN HARRY MET SALLY*): So the scene in Katz's Deli—we had a California property master, and it was me and Dickie Tice doing props in New York and, instead of giving Katz's a flat fee like he wanted, they said, "We're not going to eat that much food. We're going to pay per sandwich and per plate."

I say, "Okay, but it's going to be a lot of money."

Well, we got everything else in the background. What I got to take care of is going to be cheap stuff. Okay, no problem. They do this scene. They break for lunch. No one told the guy behind the counter that the crew—and, I mean, all the [Local] 52 guys, including scenics and Teamsters—weren't supposed to order and just put it on a tab. Well, when it came to time to pay, it was, like, six thousand dollars, and the guy says, "What are you talking about? We were only supposed to pay for sandwiches." Another guy says, "Yeah, but you didn't tell the crew that." True story.

MICHAEL F. BURKE: The funniest thing on that job was when they were doing the famous "I'll have what she's having" routine at Katz's Deli.

I had the idea to make up a bunch of signs. You know how in the Olympics back in the day, before it was digital, they used to hold up scorecards—like, 5.8, 5.7, 4.6, 6.0? I was lining up everybody along the side so when she was finished having her orgasm we would put the signs up and raise them and rate her orgasm.

As I've mentioned previously, a few times from my past experiences when maybe something you think is really funny, it may not be funny.[53] I went up to him [Rob Reiner] and I said, "Hey, Rob, I made up all these signs and we've got all the people over here and when she's finished giving her orgasm we're going to put the signs up and rate her orgasm, and I've got some signs for you."

And he said, "Oh, no, no. Please, don't do that. I was on the phone with her all night long. She does not want to do this. She's so nervous about doing this, and I told her it would be fine— 'just try to relax.' Please don't do this."

I said, "Okay."

And then as I turned away, he says, "You know, that's really funny."

RUSSELL ENGELS: Reiner probably begged him not to do it again and again.

52 We looked extensively for this article until we ran out of time. If you happen to find it please contact us to put in future editions of this book.

53 See chapters on *The Warriors* and *Raising Arizona*.

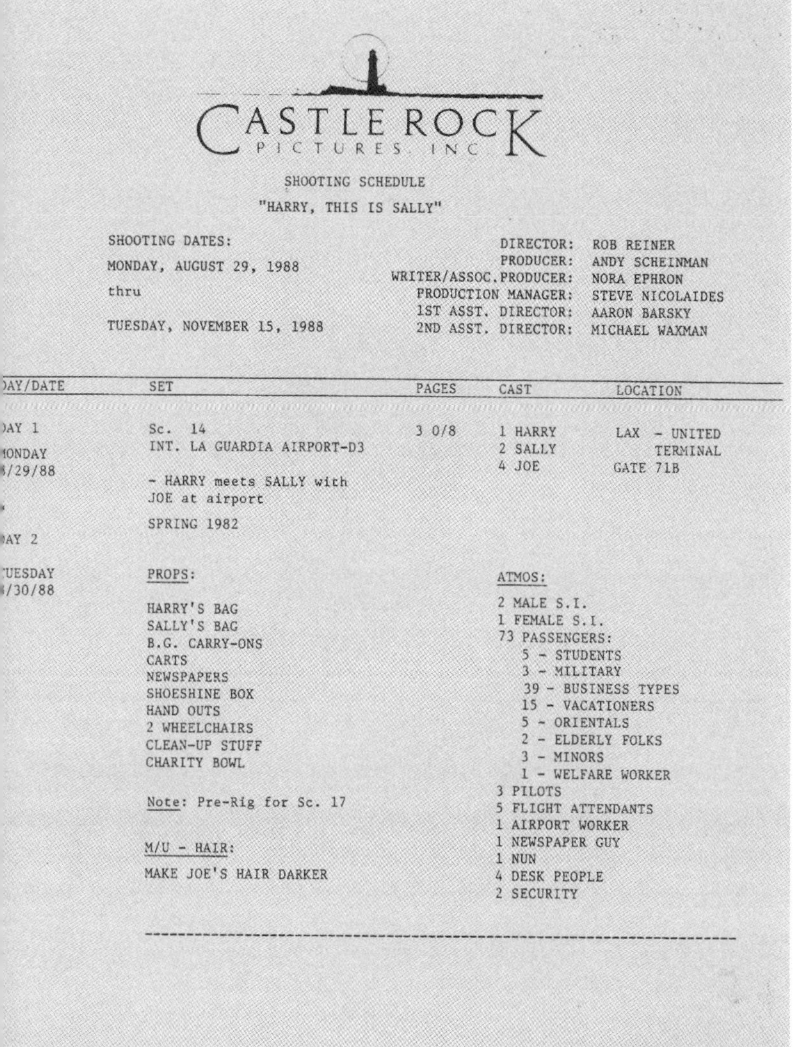

CASTLE ROCK PICTURES, INC.

SHOOTING SCHEDULE

"HARRY, THIS IS SALLY"

SHOOTING DATES:
MONDAY, AUGUST 29, 1988
thru
TUESDAY, NOVEMBER 15, 1988

DIRECTOR: ROB REINER
PRODUCER: ANDY SCHEINMAN
WRITER/ASSOC. PRODUCER: NORA EPHRON
PRODUCTION MANAGER: STEVE NICOLAIDES
1ST ASST. DIRECTOR: AARON BARSKY
2ND ASST. DIRECTOR: MICHAEL WAXMAN

DAY/DATE	SET	PAGES	CAST	LOCATION
DAY 1 MONDAY 8/29/88	Sc. 14 INT. LA GUARDIA AIRPORT-D3 - HARRY meets SALLY with JOE at airport SPRING 1982	3 0/8	1 HARRY 2 SALLY 4 JOE	LAX - UNITED TERMINAL GATE 71B
DAY 2 TUESDAY 8/30/88				

PROPS:
HARRY'S BAG
SALLY'S BAG
B.G. CARRY-ONS
CARTS
NEWSPAPERS
SHOESHINE BOX
HAND OUTS
2 WHEELCHAIRS
CLEAN-UP STUFF
CHARITY BOWL

Note: Pre-Rig for Sc. 17

M/U - HAIR:
MAKE JOE'S HAIR DARKER

ATMOS:
2 MALE S.I.
1 FEMALE S.I.
73 PASSENGERS:
5 - STUDENTS
3 - MILITARY
39 - BUSINESS TYPES
15 - VACATIONERS
5 - ORIENTALS
2 - ELDERLY FOLKS
3 - MINORS
1 - WELFARE WORKER
3 PILOTS
5 FLIGHT ATTENDANTS
1 AIRPORT WORKER
1 NEWSPAPER GUY
1 NUN
4 DESK PEOPLE
2 SECURITY

Harry, This is Sally shooting schedule.

MICHAEL F. BURKE: That was one thing that did not happen.

RUSSELL ENGELS: Jokes like that, they just wouldn't be appreciated nowadays.

ANGELO DIGIACOMO: We were shooting in Silvercup, and we're doing this scene where they make love, and now it's Billy lying awake with his eyes wide open and she's contentedly sleeping—his arm is under her head.

It's an overhead shot. He's lying there, eyes wide open—deer-in-the-headlights "I got to get out of here" look—and his arm is under her head and she's lying cuddled against him, contentedly sleeping with a smile on her face, and he wants to leave and she realizes what has happened and that he doesn't love her and she starts to cry.

And my wife and kids had come to the set and my sons were four or five, and after the scene is over, my older son is standing next to me at the camera and he goes over to Meg and he says, "It's okay. Stop crying. It's okay. Everything will be okay," and the whole room explodes in laughter.

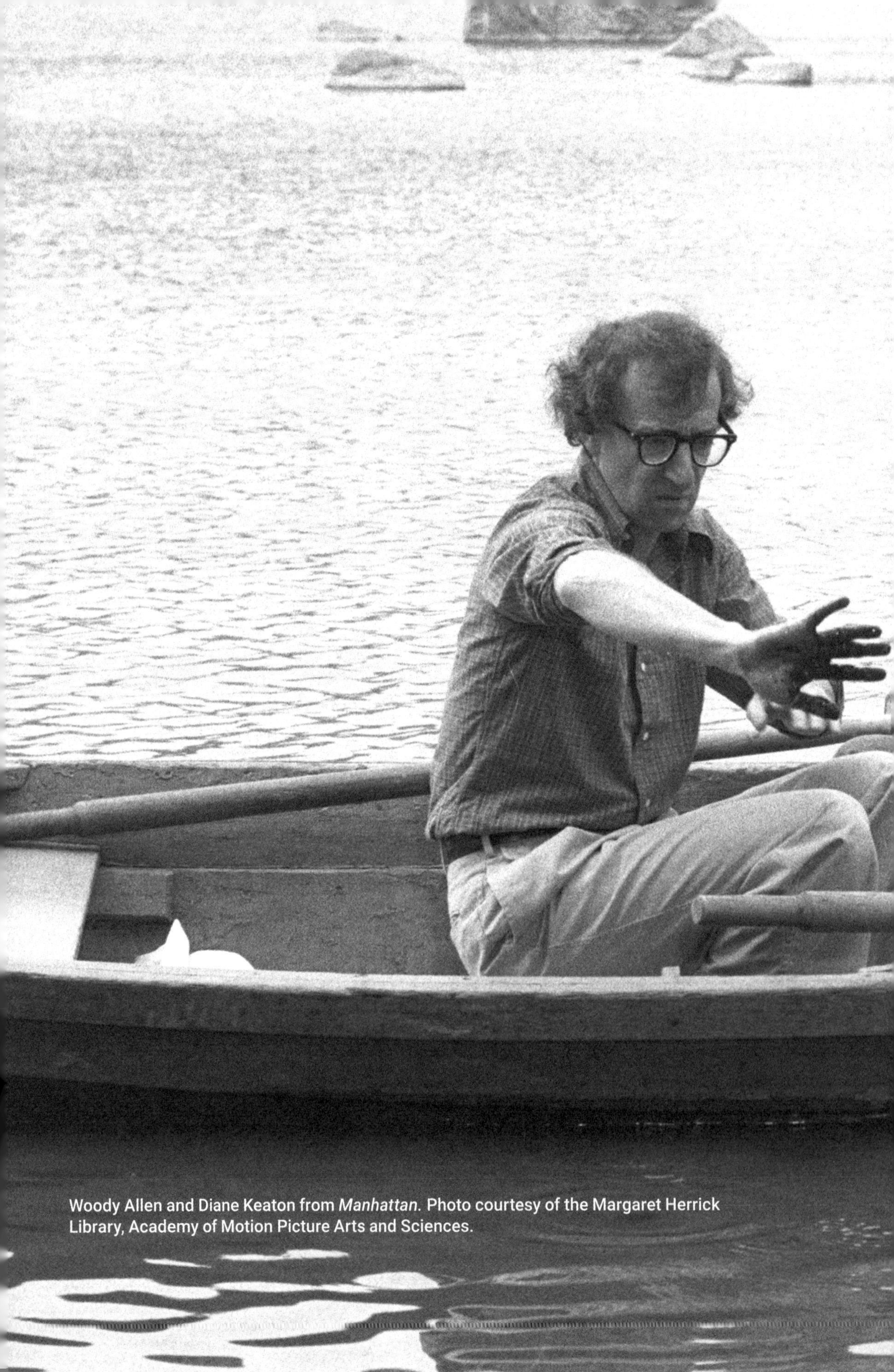

Woody Allen and Diane Keaton from *Manhattan*. Photo courtesy of the Margaret Herrick Library, Academy of Motion Picture Arts and Sciences.

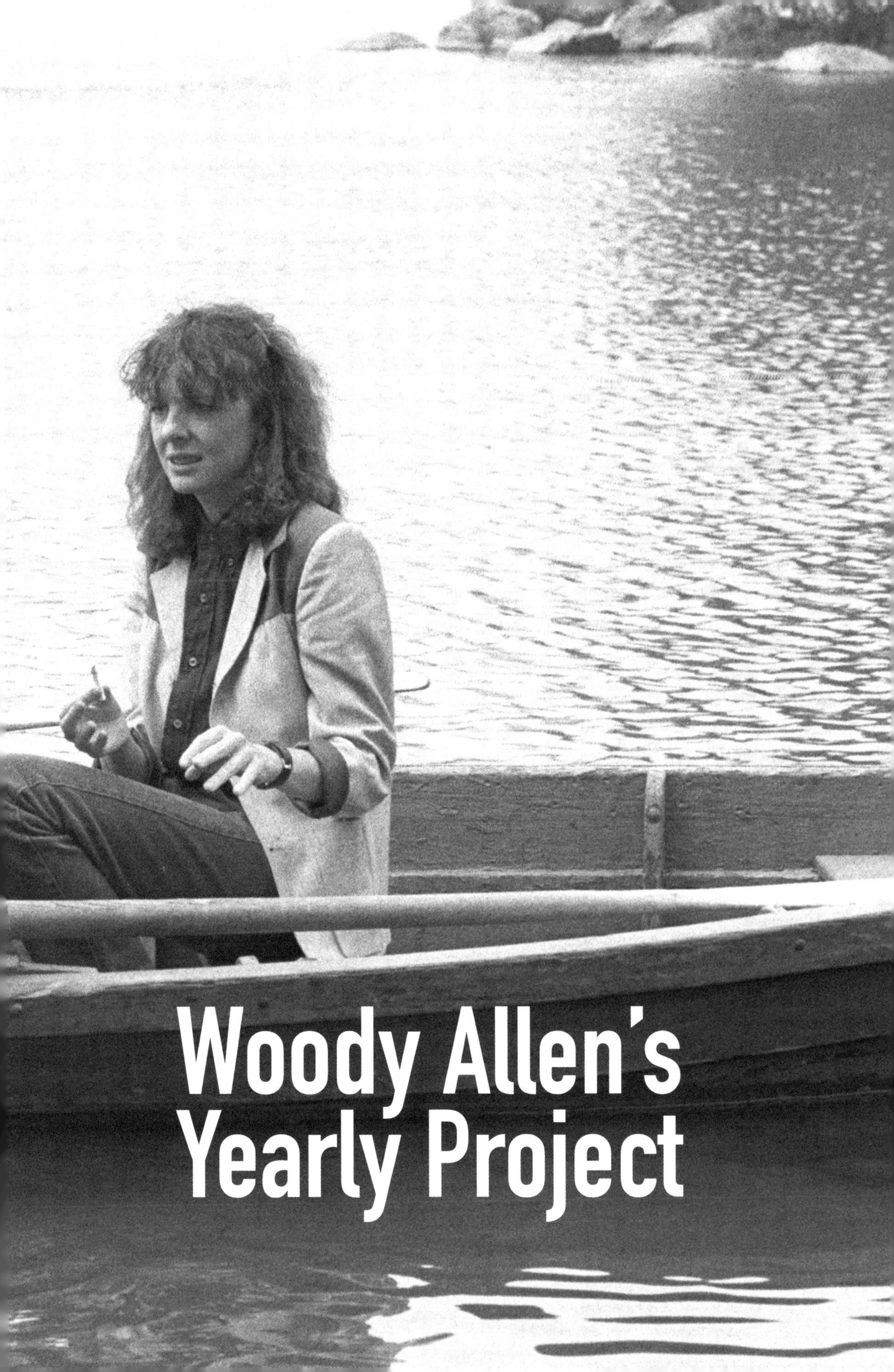

Woody Allen's Yearly Project

STEVE SAKLAD (ASSISTANT ART DIRECTOR, *RADIO DAYS* [1987]): The Woody Allen thing was sort of every single year.

DANIEL GROSSO (LEADMAN, SET DRESSER, MANY WOODY ALLEN FILMS): He never titled his movies. Our paycheck said, "Woody Allen Spring Project '81," "Woody Allen Fall Project '81." So, we did two every year until he couldn't do two every year, and we did one every year, so it kept us busy.

STEVEN GAMIELLO (SPECIAL EFFECTS, *MANHATTAN* [1979]): Originally my dad and Ronnie Ottesen started Effects Specialists, and they had a shop in the basement of what is now Kaufman Studios. They're doing effects on Woody Allen's *Manhattan*. If you remember the movie, the radio-controlled boat in Central Park—the guy gets pissed at Woody Allen and he has a radio-controlled submarine and he puts a torpedo in it and he blows up Woody Allen's boat. I was assisting my dad. I was just handing him this, handing him that, and we blew that up.

Another thing—Woody Allen and Diane Keaton are sitting in a rowboat in Central Park, and they're talking. I'm on one side in waders and my dad's on the other side in waders, holding the boat steady with a rope so it's not leaving frame. You don't hear what they're saying, but Woody's hands are going, and he sticks his hand in the water and comes out with all this black muck on it. We had attached a bucket of water-soluble tar underneath, and he stuck his hand in the tar.

One of the cool things that we did—there was supposed to be a scene—it got cut from the movie—he's supposed to be driving through Englewood, New Jersey. There's a big town square, like a park in the middle, and he sees a Nazi rally on the other end, and he goes driving through the park getting all angry, and he goes scattering the Nazis. He drives up this alley and you hear all these crashing booms, and it's the same car all banged up driving out

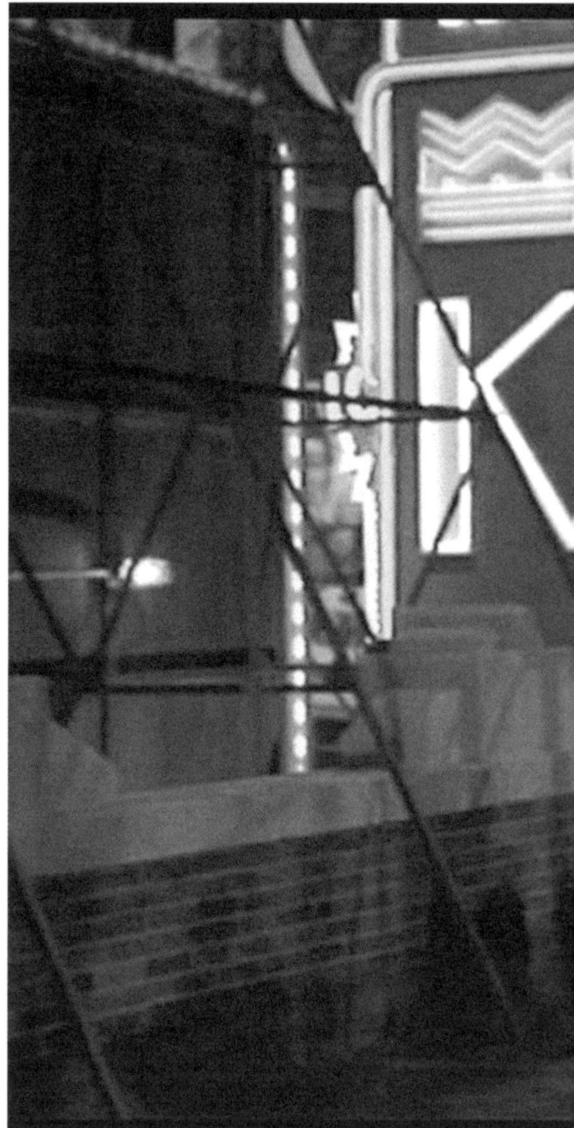

of the alley, and, as it turns, the trunk opens up and this manuscript that he had blows all over the place.

We took out the back seat, we put in these beds, and we had a nitrogen tank in there and we had a release on the hood, and it was set up for two people to lay in the back of this stunt car. We had it all rigged up and my dad and I were going to be the ones [in the car]. He would pull the handle to open it, and I had to turn on the air and then he would blow all the things out. I was just laying there as soon as he pulled the trunk, I turned on the air and he did the rest.

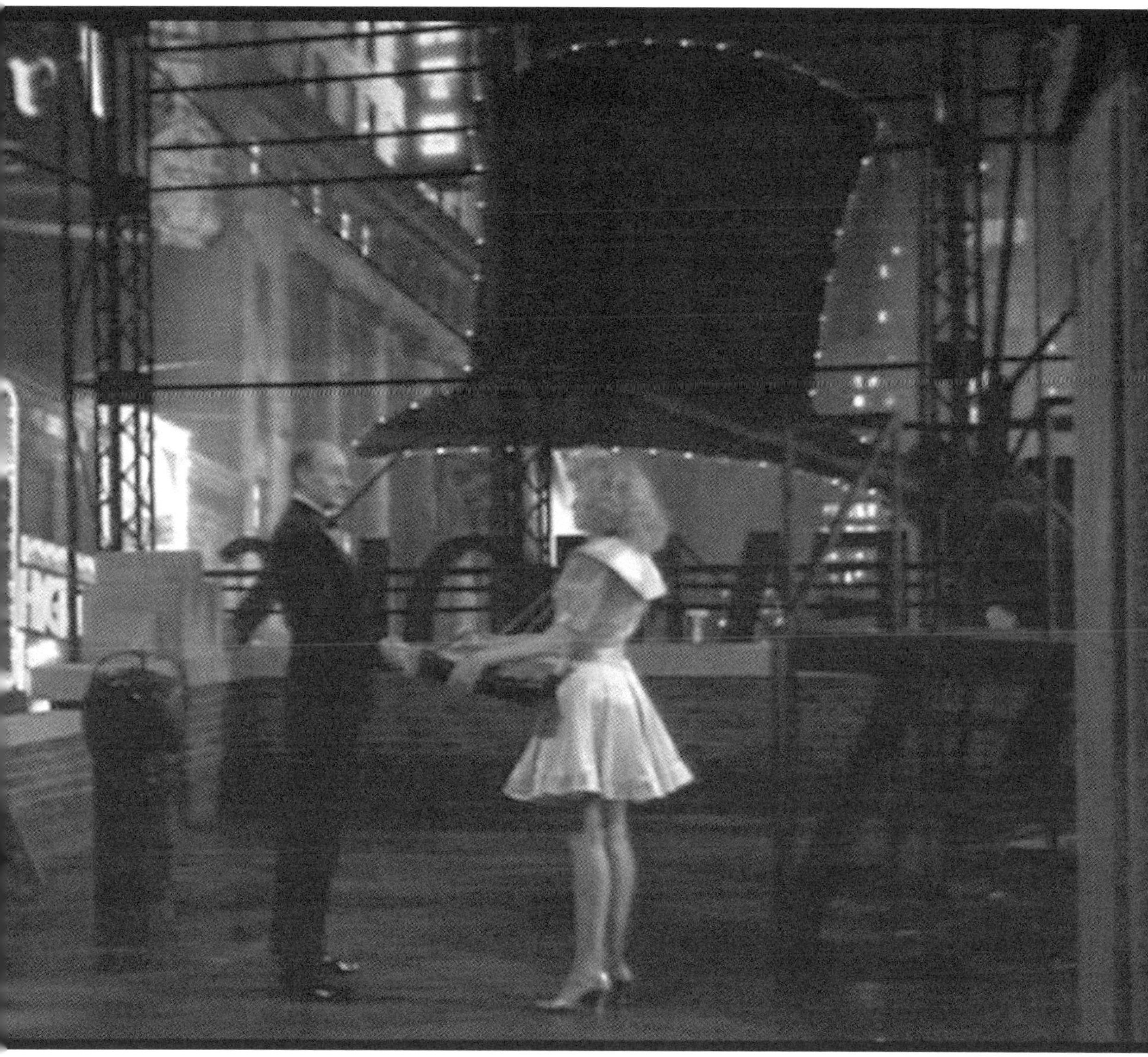

But we had to make this car look all crashed up. First, we got some sledgehammers. It's a 1973 Dodge Dart—it's built like a tank. Before you know it, they get the Sawzall out, they start cutting it—they're lifting it with the forklift—they're bringing the forks down on it and making it dented, banging it all up. The whole thing is all set. We get it out of the basement of Astoria Studios, get it onto a flatbed, and take it out to Englewood. The AD [assistant director] comes over: "Woody wants to know if you could do a spiderweb crack on the windshield."

Normally, we'd get a scenic to just fake it. But my dad got a forklift, he got up on top of

Times Square rooftop set from *Radio Days* [1985-1986]. Photo courtesy of MGM Studios and the Margaret Herrick Library, Academy of Motion Picture Arts and Sciences.

the car, and he just lightly cracked it, and it made a perfect spider web with spider web crack, a circular one. We do the job. They want to do it again, and Woody wants to know if we could make the hubcap roll off when it comes out.

So my dad takes off the hubcap, he gets the pliers, and he crimps all the things that hold it in with pressure and he took Flexowax, which is basically paraffin wax and Vaseline—it's mortician's wax—and he put a little wax of that on it, and we did it again. Bingo, as soon as he came out and hit the curb and made the turn, the hubcap kept going straight as the car turns to the left. "Oh, we love it, we love it, everything's great!"

Bingo. Successful day. They cut it from the movie. [laughs]

DANIEL GROSSO: When I did the Woody Allen movies, all twelve of them, I never got a budget once, not once. We just did the job, and if I needed an extra truck I'd go to the production manager, say, "Helen [Robin, unit production manager], I need a truck for a week," and she said, "All right, get a truck. I'll talk to Pete, and we'll get another truck."

STEVE SAKLAD: The Woody Allen thing was constant employment for [production designer] Santo Loquasto and his team of art directors. That was a sure thing. It did change over the course of the eighties. I would say that the stages of Kaufman Astoria were filled to overflowing, and you had to sort of wait for the availability of the stage to actually get a show there after the mid-eighties or so. *The Cosby Show* [1984-1992] was sort of in residence in one stage, and there were three other TV shows in residence, and then you negotiate to sort of get spaces on the other stages. Silvercup [Studios] was a player, but Kaufman Astoria was the big time. Stage E was the big stage. That was the goal, to get on Stage E at Kaufman Astoria. That was where the giant shows put their acts. For instance, my second show drafting for movies was *Radio Days* [1987].

I love my theater drafting, but it doesn't prepare you for this sort of skill and technical proficiency of the movie draftsman—and to sort of see what the other tables were looking like—see the other drawings, see what those apartment buildings and those interiors look like on the drafting tables of these really top-notch guys. It was mind-blowing and it sort of made me want to be much better at what I did than I knew.

In December of 1985, I worked for two months on *Radio Days* for Santo and Steve Graham, art director. Speed Hopkins was the other art director. I worked on the *New York Times* set—that fantastic rooftop set with the top hat that goes up and down. I was elevating that, but most of my time has been elevating all the façades of the Camel billboard and the built façades of the Astor Hotel and the *Times* building, so, for all the buildings that ringed Times Square in 1930. It was my first time learning about a photo backing. I think it was Pacific Studios who was doing them then, and they had prepared this photograph from the period—a photograph that they had hand-tinted and sent off to the West Coast—all lit beautifully—and all of our built backings were built in perspective to sort of blend into that photo backing at the end of the set, and it was from edge to edge, from fire lane to fire lane, on Stage E at Kaufman Astoria. There was no CG. There was no set extension of any kind. Every single thing was in camera, including the smoke coming out of the Camel billboard—smoker's mouth.

It's such a great set, and you don't know when you're drafting on it how significant or insignificant it will be in the movie, and then to sort of find it being the best signature of that whole beautiful movie. And the movie ends—there's credit crawls and you're seeing the snow falling on this Times Square set and that's sort of the end of the movie.

STEPHEN GEIGER (BACKGROUND ACTOR, *HANNAH AND HER SISTERS* [1986]): I had done extra work on some Woody Allen movies. I was in *Hannah and Her Sisters*. I was in *Broadway Danny Rose* [1984]. But it was nothing. I mean, it was just extra work, and that—at least they called us "extras" then and not now, where you're just called "background," which is, to me, even more demeaning than extras.

One set was in a loft on lower downtown New York, far downtown, like Broadway. This was on *Hannah and Her Sisters*. It was a big loft with these beautiful mahogany windows, and the grips nailed up these big pieces of Masonite to the windows because there was too much light coming in. And Carlo Di Palma, who was the director of photography, came in and threw a hissy fit—ripped down the Masonite and knocked over a giant antique silver samovar that just went flying everywhere. It was at least three and a half, four feet tall. I mean, he was in a rage, and all of us extras, it was a party scene—we just sat there like, "Wow, he is pissed off."

And then Woody came in, and Woody was just, like, very calm. He just talked. You could never hear what Woody was saying. He would go over to Di Palma and say a few things and then finally order was restored and they got the shot and, to this day, even with all the years that I've spent since on movies and TV, I've never seen a fit like that.

STEVEN J. JORDAN (SET DECORATOR, *STARDUST MEMORIES* [1980]): We shot [*Stardust Memories*] in Ocean Grove, New Jersey. There was some religious tabernacle that we turned into our hotel. We were down there for weeks and weeks, and then we built all the stage sets up at Filmways and it was crazy. Filmways—the neighborhood was such that you'd park your car and come out—your battery would be gone. You'd go across the street to this flat-fix place and buy your battery back.

Gordon Willis was shooting it, and we would have these gorgeous bluebird days at the beach and Gordon said, "It's too sunny. I'm not going to shoot today." It was shot in black and white, and the story has it that Gordon was having issues choosing a lab to process the black-and-white film stock, and apparently after a few weeks of shooting we still had all this exposed film in a closet up in Rollins-Joffe production office, and one day it was like, "Well, we really should pick a lab and start processing some of this film."

STEVEN GAMIELLO: Did you ever hear of a guy named Mel Bourne?

STEVEN J. JORDAN: He was an absolute character. We did three or four movies together, and as a matter of fact his son Tim is the executive producer on the show I'm doing down here. I did a number of commercials with Mel, and one day I got a phone call and Mel was getting ready to start a Woody movie. He said, "I'd like you to decorate it," and that was my first feature film.

STEVEN GAMIELLO: When I first got into business, every studio bathroom wall said, "Will Rogers never met Mel Bourne." Will Rogers' famous line was, "I never met a man I didn't like." [laughs] You'd see "Will Rogers never met Mel Bourne" in every bathroom.

MICHAEL ZANSKY (CHARGE SCENIC ARTIST): When I was working on that job in the Bronx, on *Wolfen*, they had port-a-potties where you take a leak or whatever. I go to a port-a-potty and I go and take a leak. In it, in magic marker, "Will Rogers never met Mel Bourne."

I know who Will Rogers is; I don't know who Mel Bourne is. Then over the course of a week every one of the port-a-potties had the same thing with different handwriting: "Will Rogers never met Mel Bourne."

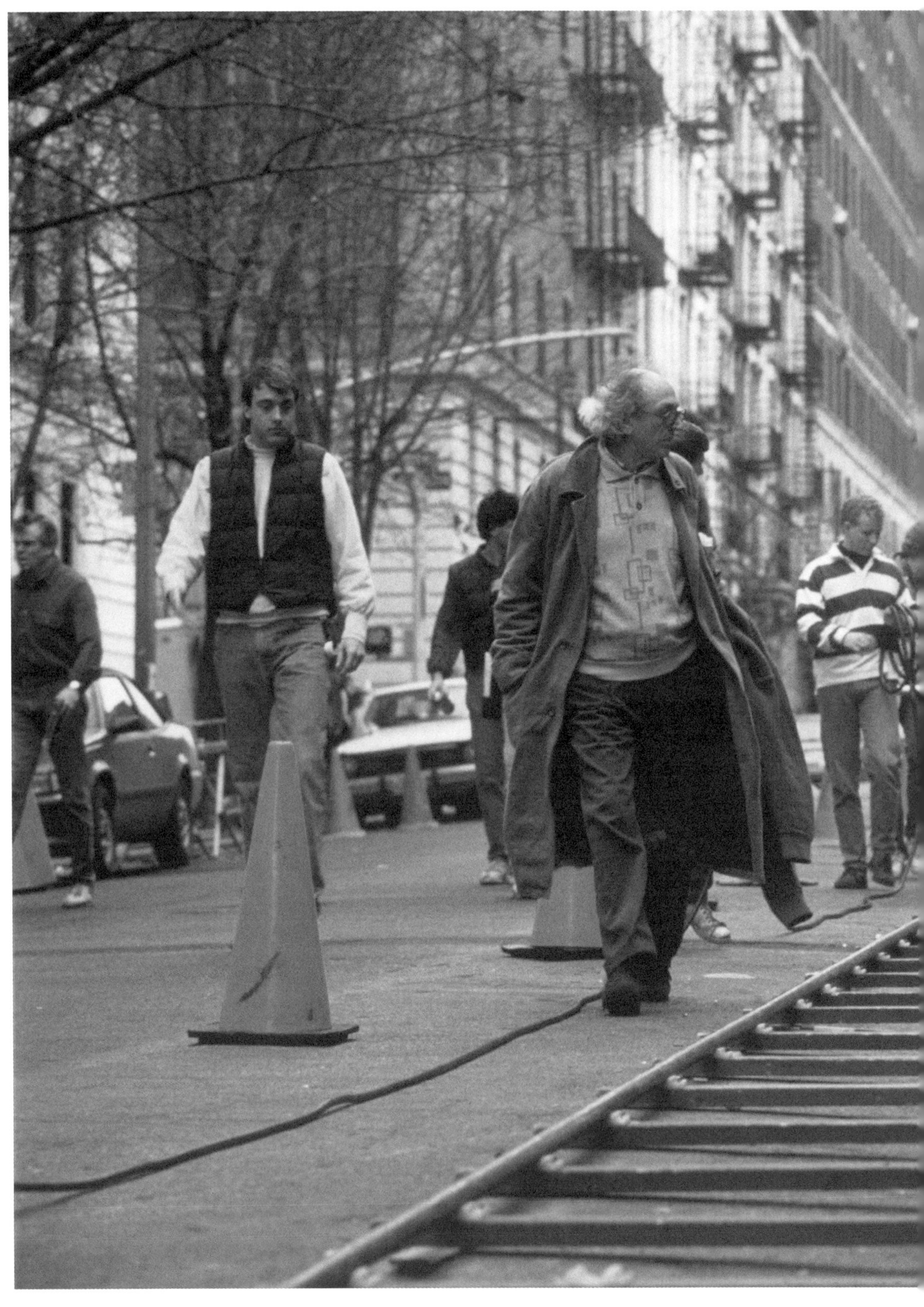

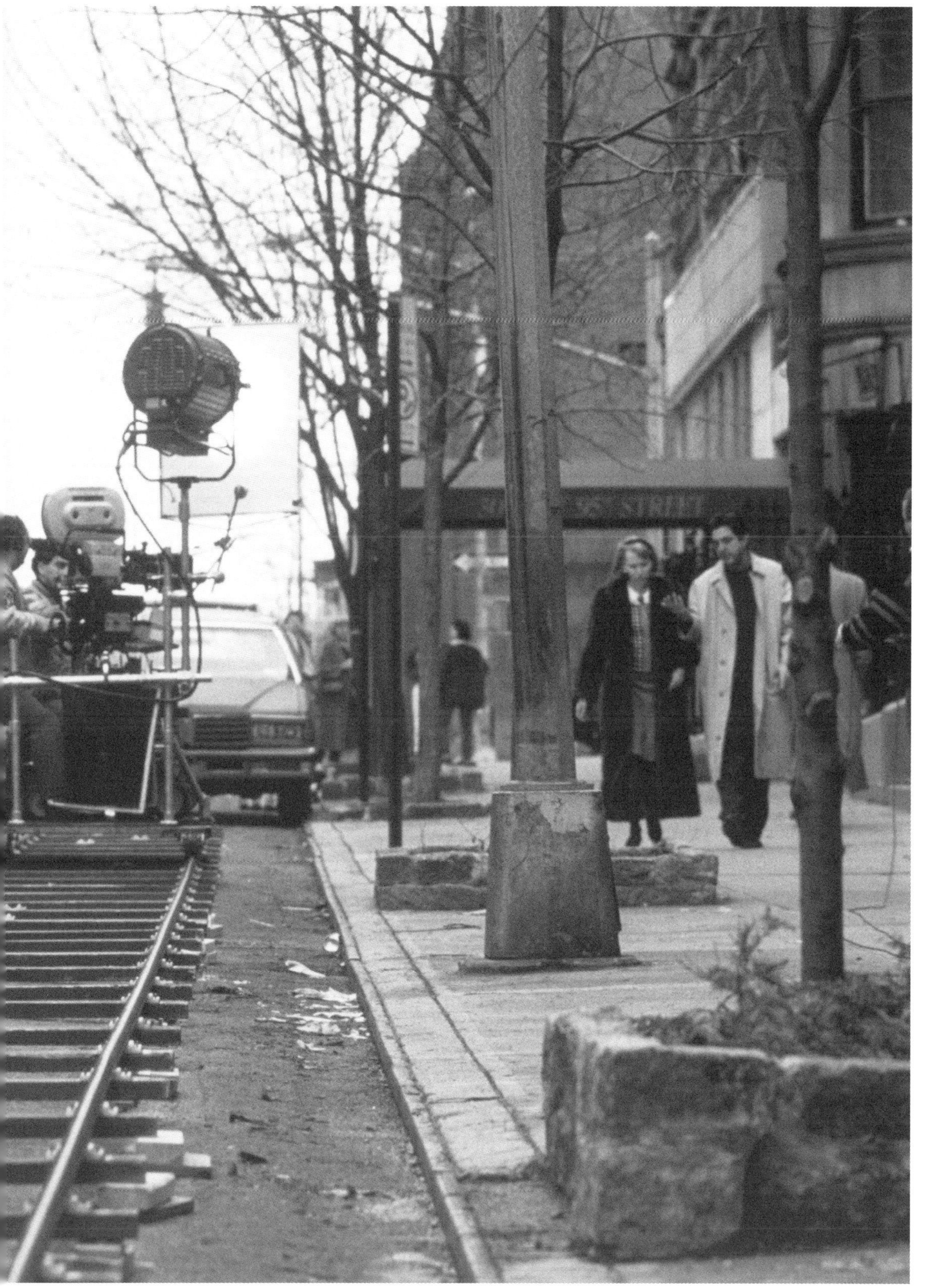

Carlo Di Palma filming *Alice* (1990). Photo courtesy of the Margaret Herrick Library, Academy of Motion Picture Arts and Sciences.

STEVEN GAMIELLO: I was the assistant decorator on *Presumed Innocent* [1990] with Harrison Ford, and Carol Joffe was the decorator on that. Carol was a sweet, older woman. She didn't know shit about hardware. So all of the set dressers hated working with her, but she was a very talented decorator and she was a very nice woman. She hired me to come in to deal with the hardware and deal with all the shit. She told me this story about one of the Woody Allen movies.

Being that she was married to Woody Allen's producer, Charles Joffe—[they] had gotten divorced by then, but she was decorating Woody's movies, so she knew Woody on a personal level, not just the business level.

They had a set made to be the inside of a boat and whatever's on the inside of the boat, including portholes with the little doors that opened, and they were blacked out. Woody comes to see the set, like, a day or two before the shooting and Carol was there and he walks right past Mel Bourne and goes over to Carol and starts to talk to Carol. Mel Bourne had a huge ego, and he was like, "Oh, you should be talking to me, the designer."

So Mel's trying to get Woody's attention: "Woody, look over here. We've got this over here, we got that," and then he goes by the port holes—he goes, "Look, Woody, the portholes even open up," and he opens up one of the portholes and is written behind it, it says, "Mel Bourne sucks." Woody just put his head down and looked away.

DEAN TAUCHER (PRODUCTION DESIGNER): Mel was crazy. There was no separation in Mel's mind from work to anything else, so in the midst of his talking about the job he might say, "Oh, I got to take my laundry. Where's my laundry receipt? Oh, my God. Look at the tits on her." It was his stream of consciousness.

We're at this location, and these two women are painting and he's totally out of line by talking about what they look like or hitting on them or something. They were both sort of tough lesbians and gave him something back. The next thing he comes to me and asks, "How much are they getting paid per hour?"

I told him what they're getting paid.

He says, "They're not worth that. Fire them."

And I said, "What if I can get the rate reduced?"

He goes, "You could do that?"

I said, "I think it would be better for everybody if we get them to take less money and they finish the job."

They were being paid through a scene shop where I knew the owner and I called him up. I said, "This is going to sound crazy, but you need to do this. When you put in the bill, put in the bill so that they get ten dollars an hour and make up the difference in additional paint charges." He goes, "What are you talking about?" I said, "It's either this or I have to fire these women."

How do you deal with a crazy person? It must be what it's like working for Donald Trump.

STEVEN J. JORDAN: He was a tough cookie—very confrontational. I think he loved it. It was a part of his persona. I know grips couldn't stand Mel. They would go for their hammers when he would come on set. He would stir up shit and he'd leave a wake of angry people.

DANIEL GROSSO: Woody was very simple in the sense that he would take a master shot and then he'd go in to do his closeups. It wasn't necessarily about the scenery and the costumes. Although Santo did a brilliant job—he got nominated several times with production design—but he was also aware that Woody Allen movies were about characters and the conversations. In character films, you didn't see the floors that much, you didn't see the ceilings that much—you saw the artwork on the walls, you saw the lighting. He was always big on providing lighting.

They were great jobs to work on because we worked relatively normal hours. They weren't big on overtime, but a lot of it had to do with Santo's ability to manage their job.

GARY MULLER (FIRST ASSISTANT CAMERA OPERATOR, MANY WOODY ALLEN FILMS): Every movie I worked with Woody was short days.

DANIEL GROSSO: Jimmy [Mazzola] asked me if I wanted to come work with him on the set, and he said, "You get more money, work more hours" and stuff like that, but it didn't interest me. At first, I didn't want to work the hours because I had young kids, and I prefer doing projects, on-set dressing, and the same thing with scenic work—you could do nothing all day sometimes, and I just couldn't do that. Some of these guys work twelve, fourteen hours a day and then they go into Saturdays or "Fraturdays," as they call it, and they get one day on the weekend, and I just don't see how you do it. You go home, you take a shower, you eat, and you go to bed, you get up and go to work, and you don't have a life.

We were fortunate that Dave [Weinman], Chris, Ricky, and I, and all the guys I worked with were all the same age. We all had young kids. We all coached baseball, softball, or basketball. Dave made sure that we got the work done, but we worked normal hours, and he didn't travel much. Dave was the number-one leadman in the business. Any job that came in Dave got a call to do, so we always worked, but he turned down a lot of movies that we would've traveled to do. We wanted to stay in town because we had kids, and we don't regret it at all.

GARY MULLER: Woody Allen movies aren't technically challenging. Even as simple as Lumet movies were, they were very technically challenging because it was only one take. Woody did good movies also, but it got monotonous. All he did was change the name on the slate and it's the same dialogue, basically, but Woody is really a great filmmaker.

DANIEL GROSSO: He was very much like Sidney Lumet in that he planned everything he needed to do, and he worked normal hours. He ran the camera for eight hours, ten hours—that was it. When Woody was going through the stuff with Mia Farrow, he had to go to court, like, three times a week, so they would work till one o'clock and the guys—if they were working at the stage—the guys on the crew would set up the next shot today and they'd be gone by two or three o'clock. So it was, and you got paid the normal hours, so it was a good way to live.

MICHAEL F. BURKE (GAFFER): I think because they were smaller-budget movies, relatively speaking, they had to work within those budgets. By not working longer hours, you kept your budget down because the overtime was less. Additionally, because you wrote the script, you had it really as fine-tuned as you could get it, so you knew what was important from the beginning. They were Jewish New Yorkers and were like, "I'm not going to beat this. I live here, I work here, and this is my life," and, of course, Woody Allen would play music every Monday night.

DANIEL GROSSO: He played the clarinet at Michael's Pub and went to the Knick games, so he didn't want to work those nights either. Then the contract changed in 1991. We had just started working on *Shadows and Fog* [1991] in Astoria. They couldn't come to an agreement, but we were fortunate that we already started the Woody Allen job and worked under the old contract. Everybody was out of work, except for us for the next four or five months.

Goodfellas

(1990)

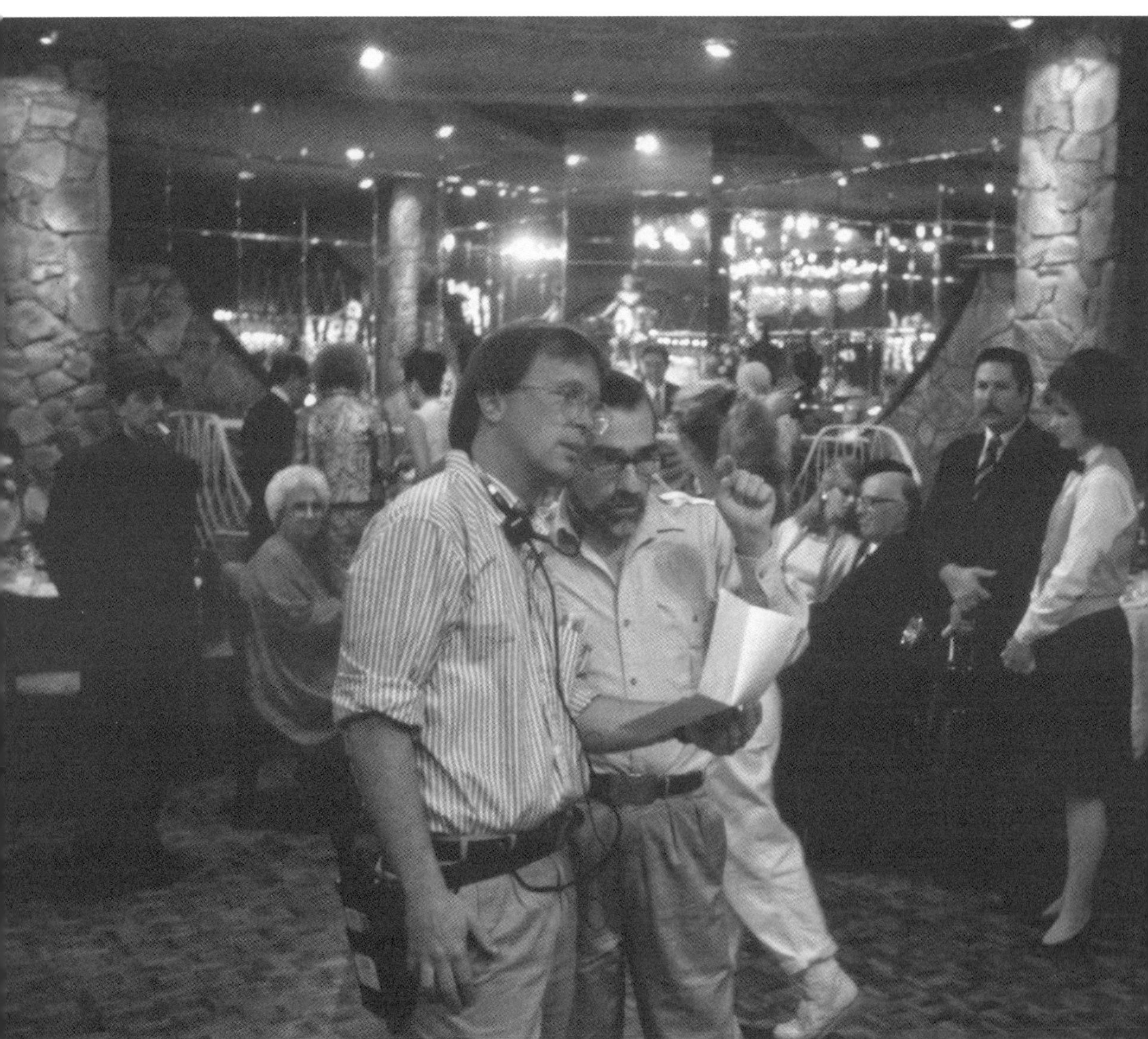

Martin Scorsese and first assistant director Joe Reidy. Photo courtesy of the Margaret Herrick Library, Academy of Motion Picture Arts and Sciences.

JOE REIDY (FIRST ASSISTANT DIRECTOR, *GOODFELLAS*): We had a lot of guys that were not really professional actors. Marty [Scorsese] started working with Ellen Lewis, casting director, and with Nick Pileggi the author. The three of them would go to Rao's. They'd meet people, and she'd take notes on some of these people, and they thought about people for different roles. When I came on, they just had grouped all this, but they didn't have assignments for some of them.

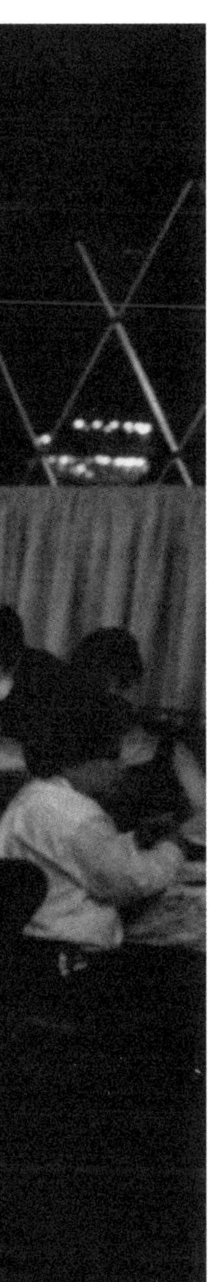

The big, speaking parts—Paul Sorvino, obviously, and some of these other characters were definitely gonna be actors or people on a certain level, but all these gangsters needed a crew behind them. Pauly, the character Paul Sorvino played, needed a crew, Henry needed a crew, and these crews changed at different eras. I made it plain to the production manager, line producer, Barbara [De Fina], that we had to control these people even if they hadn't budgeted this, that, like, the third, fourth, fifth guys that may or may not have had scripted lines, we needed to control them. We needed to make them principals.

So we created these parts. I really pushed Ellen. I said, "Ellen, you know we want to put them in, but we can't just hire them as extras. We have to hire them in a way that we can do all their wardrobe and the continuity and being able to get a hold of them and all that, and I'd rather not leave it to extras casting. It should be our area." So she did a chart that I helped create. I sat with her and Marty, and he made the creative decisions to assign people to different crews. And this was different from some of the other things he'd done. It certainly was a model for what I did on other mob-related movies, that these faces, these people, if they're special, they're often not really actors. They're often the real thing—or, when I say "the real thing," they're not made men; they're connected guys. So we had people who were actors [and] people who were not trained.

Now, when we had them on set, this was like play to them. Many of them had real jobs. One was a former cop. One was this guy used to be a butcher or used to sell furniture or something like that. But they always had a side business in their life. That's why they were connected. And so, when they're now playing versions of themselves in the life, at a social club and all that. Getting their attention, getting them focused, getting them to do that sort of fell upon me. Now, Marty loved talking to them, and they all paid attention to him. They'd all be quiet for him, and they'd kid around with him, and he'd laugh and it was a great tone for the set, but when I needed to get them in control—and other films it got a little worse—I felt like I was dealing with children. Even though I had to respect them. Italian-Americans, respect is a big deal.

But winning them over and feeling that they're part of this—they're important—and to pay attention and focus and all that without punishing them, not disciplining them, not making them feel bad—make them feel they belonged, that they're important and we're gonna miss you if you're not here—that's a job.

Vebe [Borge, second assistant director] was very good at it. I had to be good at it on set to get them to pay attention and often to direct them, because Marty would leave if he had important characters to deal with, and he would let me do the background action. He wouldn't direct the extras. If he didn't like something or if it didn't look right to him, he'd tell me. But I was free to do that. And when we were in small rooms and the social clubs, I did the background and small things. I would set them.

The bigger things Vebe would do, for sure. But that's how that worked. And we always had to be honest with everything to make it feel truthful, and these actors, who are not really actors, would help define that: "No, I wouldn't do that. No, no, no. A guy like me, I wouldn't talk when this guy comes in the room because he's a made guy and I'm not, and I would have to stand up and I have to show my hands"—or whatever. They would say these things, and I would learn from them.

BARRY WETCHER (STILL PHOTOGRAPHER, *GOODFELLAS*): I get a call saying, "We need you to come up to the production office." This is before we start shooting. We need to take a photograph of one of the guys, we need to submit it to SAG [Screen Actors Guild] or some shit like that. I go up to the office. It was in the Brill Building.

I get introduced to this guy. His name is Johnny Manca. He was going to be the consultant for the movie, and the story as I remember it was that he worked for the New York City Organized Crime Task Force.

But he went over to the other side, and he actually ended up working for the Mafia while he was a law-enforcement officer. He got busted for it. And part of his deal for either probation or parole was his job being a consultant on a movie.

So I got to take this photograph of him. We're in Midtown, we walk outside, and now I'm a little worried. I'm like, "Fuck, what if somebody wants to take this fucking guy out? Like, here I am on the street with him." His eyes are darting all over the place, and I'm thinking, "Fuck, maybe there's a hit out on this guy."

That was my introduction to *Goodfellas*. I had worked with Marty before on *After Hours* [1985]. It wasn't an easy movie. There were a lot of long hours, a lot of nights, and working with a lot of real wiseguys.

When we did the Copacabana scene, there were a lot of real wiseguys as extras in that scene. A guy named Tony Darrow. He just recently went to jail, but he actually turned out to be a really good guy, and the guy wanted to make sure that I took lots of photographs of him. He used to pat me on the face, "Hey kid, did you get that? You get photos of me?" Johnny Manca once went over to him and said, "Fucking stop that with that guy," and he never did it again. Johnny Manca turned out to be a good guy to me. He was like an actor, a fake actor. He's like a lot of these low-level mob guys who were put in movies, and then they think they're actors.

A lot of it is improvised. When they were doing their scene where they are playing cards and where Joe Pesci shoots Spider [Michael Imperioli]. There's a line where he goes, "Winky from *whosimwhat*." Irwin Winkler was the producer. Joe was just making shit up, so it was fun.

Ray Liotta worked for about a month before DeNiro worked, so Ray was able to get comfortable, but once Bob came in it was a whole different ballgame because he was the main man. DeNiro—that was at the height of DeNiro's thing—and we were all kind of—I'm not going to say afraid of DeNiro, but there was this mystique about him, about his eyeline. We had to hide from him, but he was actually a good guy.

JOE REIDY: I was a little scared of Bob a little bit. I remember getting in trouble with him because we were running out of light in this one location. Another time, we were in Red Hook, which was not gentrified in those days, and he was dealing with a makeup issue and it was important but not for the day, not for now. I needed him to come out of the trailer. I couldn't rush him. And he took me apart. He lectured me.

He said, "I know that what you're saying is important, but this is important, too." And he's pointing at his hair, getting it right. And he was right. He's correct. And having him angry at me taught me a lesson, as I've learned.

But this is an important note that I got from Marty: "Whatever you can do, I just want the actors happy. Whatever they need, whatever you need to do, I just want them to be happy. I don't want them to have anything else on their mind that gets in the way of the work. If we're gonna get this done, if we're gonna move along on the schedule and all that, the actors have to be right. They have to be in the right frame of mind, and nothing is more important than that." Now, that could be something that has nothing to do with the assistant directors, could be something to do with their deal, with their production manager, or their hotel room, with the people that work for them, the stuff that's in their trailer, and all that, and it's important to him that it's all right because if the actors are happy then they perform better. So I learned that lesson in a big way and, you know, Bob De Niro and I have worked on other movies together, and I was his assistant director later on.

When Henry Hill and Karen are fighting and Marty wanted Henry—that's Ray Liotta—to throw a lamp, we only had one, and before this happened they said, "Well, we gotta get another. Do we have another lamp? Another five lamps?"

So I say, "We have another lamp. We have one other lamp. We don't have another five or six. Marty, how many takes do you think we're gonna do?"

"I don't know. I can't tell you."

And he's right. He couldn't. No one would know. So now we're waiting. We're in Brooklyn. We sent someone out to, you know, Flatbush or someplace, to a lighting store, to get something that's the right period lamp, you know, that would be in their Italian-American household—you know the style. You could find it in Brooklyn somewhere, but to get enough—that it would break. I mean, these are real lamps. These are not breakaways. He's gonna break the real lamp. We waited. We got it. It worked well. We didn't use ten. We used whatever number it was. It was fine. That's what Marty wanted. That's what we gave him. That's what was important.

JOE BURNS (ASSISTANT DIRECTOR, *GOODFELLAS*): I was an additional AD [assistant director]. I had lunch with [director of photography Michael Ballhaus] and Joe Reidy, the first AD. I was lucky enough that Joe invited me. I'm sitting there with him and when you're a PA [production assistant], the director of photography is like a God. He did *The Color of Money* [1986]. He says, "It wasn't my best work. My best work was *Goodfellas*." And we talked about his collaboration with Scorsese, picking the shots and all that. He says, "If you want to see how Scorsese sees the movie, turn the movie on and turn the sound off and just watch it. And that's Scorsese."

And, with that in mind, that's where you really see where the grips and electrics, the camera operator, and the DP, of course, come into being a character in Scorsese movies. They're the ones that are really carrying out his imagination. I've done this now so many times with different directors, and I understand they tell you this in film school, but I had never heard it before.

Have you heard of the "Copa shot"[54]? That was one of the first Steadicam shots that told this story with the camera. I mean, it was a famous shot because it was so brilliant.

JOE REIDY: Early on, Marty had talked about it. He put it in his notes. We knew the limitations of the Steadicam with the 300-foot magazine, you know, in terms of what the weight would be and the length, and

54 Put this book down. Open your browser and type in "Goodfellas Copa shot." Spend the three minutes and four seconds to watch (or rewatch) it and then read the rest of this chapter.

that's what we had to use. We couldn't use the thousand-footer. We had to use the other one. And that would give us three minutes. So we knew we had that limitation.

Well, we scouted the place. He knew the Copa had gone through some changes, different businesses. There was still seating inside. They had the kitchen underneath just like in the movie, and the stage area. But we had to dress it more for the period. So everything had to be more period-accurate, and Kristi Zea our [production] designer, who did lots of great sets in that movie, and all those wonderful places that we had—she did some things.

Marty talked about the [camera's] path and how we could make it longer and have it go through the kitchen, and there was a way of doing it because there was only one door into the kitchen. It looks like two doors, so we would go in the door and then circle around the inside of the room and come out the same door, but it would look different in the time that we came around because there was a scenery change while we were inside, and it was minor, but enough that people had to work and move flats and things like that to do that, and part of it is that when you went through the door to the kitchen it went almost immediately into the Copa main room. There was a little transition, but that thing had to be hidden when we first went into that space.

Then there were a few technical challenges. Michael [Ballhaus, DP] had to do lighting and possible lighting changes. There were certainly lighting changes on the stage—theatrical lighting changes. We had the exterior-to-interior part but that was night exterior. You know, there were things to worry about along the way.

And then there was communication. There was communication from me to the staff that was gonna be inside because our walkies didn't reach all the way in. There would be a relay system. And then the video tape, at the time—you couldn't broadcast far. This was gonna be so far away from Marty's monitor. He was out on the street where it began, to talk to the actors, to direct Karen [Lorraine Bracco] and Ray [Liotta] to give 'em the last bit of encouragement, and then they were off. Then he could listen in his headphones until he lost communication, and he lost video eventually, and so we'd have to go back to number one [starting point]. We knew this in advance. We'd have to go back to number one and play back from the camera for Marty to see the whole thing.

And then with my team, we broke it down in the following way: we had a limit on the number of extras we could have. It was less than three hundred, but they were meant to cover outside, the kitchen, and the club itself, including the band. And so Vebe was in charge of setting the background and the kitchen, which was the most difficult background to set with people who were kitchen workers. They didn't speak English, many of them—they trained all kinds of people—they weren't SAG actors, necessarily. Joe Burns, who came on, who was my key second [assistant director] later on in my career, he did the outside picture cars, people lining up, the doormen, etc., and then Deborah [Lupard] did part of the interior, especially people seated who were being reused from the outside.

JOE BURNS: Scorsese didn't know this, and I don't know if he knows it now, but we did not have enough extras to do the outside and fill the place completely up on the inside. We had miscalculated how many extras we needed. So everybody that you see lined up outside to go into the Copa—as soon as the camera goes past us and starts down the stairs—all those extras go in the other door, down the stairs, take off their coats, and now as we're doing that the camera's going through the hallway and into the kitchen, and then we get everybody and they're in the deep background.

They're obviously not in any foreground shot, because we just had to fill it up to the max. When the camera then pops out and goes into the club, the people that were outside are also inside, and it's all in one shot. We're just doing that on our own. We didn't involve Scorsese in doing that. He wanted people outside, he wanted people inside, and we figured out how we would do it.

JOE REIDY: While we were in the kitchen, the scenery in the hallway was changed. The extras from the outside all came inside and sat down in the club. We had a different group that was already there near the stage and at the front, and then I dealt with the cues and directing the specific extras in the hallway, all of the waiters that set up the table and the lights. I dealt with them. I cued the drumroll, and Henny Youngman—and there was a guy named Mr. Anthony. We pan over to Mr. Anthony. That was a thought that Marty had on the day. He didn't plan that. We had to find somebody in the crowd to be Mr. Anthony. He was never seen again in the movie.

So working out those cues and working out the transitions, we worked all day on the shot and did many rehearsals and, like, fifteen takes at least.

JOE BURNS: We rehearsed it all morning, then broke for lunch before we started to shoot, and I understand from the first AD Joe Reidy that at lunch the producers were trying to talk him [Scorcese] into doing some coverage, like coverage maybe down in the hallway, where he meets the guy, or somewhere in the kitchen—just a little piece of coverage, a cutaway of some sort. He refused to do it. He wasn't going to go along with that. He said, "This is the shot, and this is what we're doing."

JOE REIDY: Larry McConkey was the Steadicam operator. He could make suggestions and things like that with the extras, as needed, and to work certain things, but he was there really to make sure our actors were in frame and we captured it, and had to make sure that the end of the shot was as good as the beginning of the shot when he was rested, because that was really hard for anybody to operate Steadicam and do a long take like that, and I worked with him many times after that.

So we did it. Now, Marty was very happy that this thing that he imagined that was part of his life worked out on the first take. We could do better, obviously—*All these things went wrong in it*—but he saw how this could be better, and he had instructions, like the couple in the corridor and the doorman—we gave him a sandwich at the front—the guy who was in the door down below—things like that sort of develop a little bit along the way.

It took the collaboration and all the help of all these seconds assistant directors: "Joe, can we have these cars come a little earlier. Can we just near-miss on this one? Slow it down so we go right by the tail of that second car? The line shouldn't look like it's opening to allow the camera in. Just have it a little tighter there, so Henry and Karen have to break away, and when they go through we'll have enough time for those people to just get away from the camera, so it's a little closer."

It's those little things I could help with. I can't take credit for it, but I can take part of the credit for it with all the people that helped on it. I'm very proud of how that worked out. I guess, you know, that summarizes how special *Goodfellas* is. It's a classic now.

BARRY WETCHER: Scorsese used to say, "This movie's about ties, beautiful ties."

Miller's Crossing

(1990)

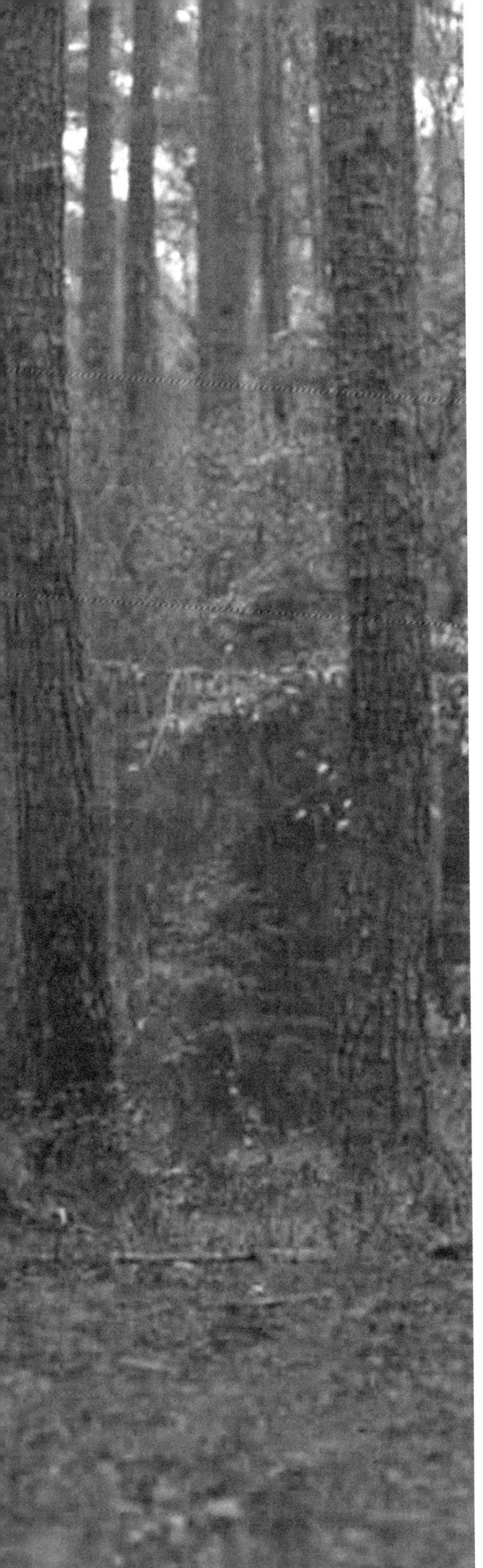

MICHAEL F. BURKE (RIGGING GAFFER, *MILLER'S CROSSING*): *Miller's Crossing* was an epic film that we made in New Orleans. That was Barry [Sonnenfeld] with the Coen brothers and Albert Finney again.

We came down at the beginning of January and the original lead actor was this guy Trey Wilson, and he was doing the Jerry Lee Lewis movie [*Great Balls of Fire!*] in Memphis or Nashville, and then he was coming from there to New Orleans but died from a stroke before we started, so we found ourselves here without a lead actor. They went on a hiatus for a week, and they got Albert Finney to take Trey's place. We had just had so much fun coming down to New Orleans.

ANGELO DIGIACOMO (FIRST ASSISTANT CAMERA OPERATOR, *MILLER'S CROSSING*): It was a low budget. They [directors Coen brothers] were very good. It's very interesting to see how they work; I think they still work the same way now. They're very, very bright and it's amazing that they are so like-minded, but they're not clones. They definitely enhance each other.

RUSSELL ENGELS (GAFFER, *MILLER'S CROSSING*): It's set in the era of the gangster in the 1930s. They wanted to shoot black and white, but the studios or whoever wouldn't have it, but if you look at it close, it's pretty much contrast in the backgrounds, curtains, and walls and colors and all that stuff, and they kept it as close to black and white as possible. The lighting was dark. The design of the show used deep, rich colors and all that stuff.

ANGELO DIGIACOMO: This was when New Orleans was a wide-open town. The Coen brothers didn't want to burn their people out,

Still from *Miller's Crossing*.

so they would give everybody every other weekend off. You work five days, and they paid you for the sixth day when you didn't work.

It's one of the highlights of my career. I loved being down there. They did a very good job in making you feel like part of their family. They got me a one-bedroom apartment so my family could come down.

RUSSELL ENGELS: Away for quite a while, but it was one of those things. My father traveled for months and months when I was growing up—*A Face in The Crowd* [1967] and pictures like that. I was used to it. So it's just a matter of getting your family used to it. When the kids get a little older, they can't travel like that; you can't pull them out of eighth grade as easy as you can pull them out of first.

ANGELO DIGIACOMO: J. E. Freeman, he was the mean guy, the enforcer for John Polito, and we were doing a scene. Freeman's character carried a revolver, like, an American Eagle or something like a .44- or .50-caliber pistol, but it's a revolver.

At the time, crews didn't carry remote focuses as a matter of course. If you needed a remote focus, you order it because it was an expensive specialty item, so I didn't order one; plus, we're in New Orleans. They had to do a shot where he had the big pistol and pointed on both sides of the camera and so I had to stand on one side or the other and I could back away, but I still had to be physically anchored to the camera,[55] so I said, "You're going to shoot on this side, and you're going to shoot on this side and this side—it's just going to be a click—so I'm going to stand on the side where it's just going to be a click and so you won't shoot me."

And of course he fucked it up and wound up shooting my arm. I had one hundred fifty little bleeding things—because it's gun powder and it was a big load—because it's a big gun. He was so embarrassed and so apologetic after that happened. Not that he wasn't already nice, but he was, you know, like, "I'm so sorry." He felt bad for weeks.

MICHAEL F. BURKE: The music, the architecture, the culture—New Orleans really was like New York. The accent isn't that far off from New York. It's like New York City forty years ago. The cost of living was about a third of New York.

ANGELO DIGIACOMO: New Orleans was a very welcoming place for the crew. You could go and hear music, fantastic music in little holes in the wall. I mean, literally, sometimes the entrance was a sledgehammered hole in a cinder-block wall and that's how you got in, and there was—whatever, a very funky band, but the music was almost always excellent. This was New Orleans in its heyday, and I think we went to fifty, sixty Mardi Gras parades because they don't have a parade just for Mardi Gras. They start at the beginning of January, which is when we were there.

MICHAEL F. BURKE: I did three films with Albert [Finney] and became buddies with him.

ANGELO DIGIACOMO: If it was Mike and Albert, there was no such thing as *not* over the top.

MICHAEL F. BURKE: Albert had fifteen days of shooting on the movie, but those fifteen days were like one day a week, so Albert was loose in the city. He was having mint juleps with all the hoi polloi.

He's a horse man, and a friend of mine used to call the races at the racetrack.

RUSSELL ENGELS: Albert, a few years before this, said he was an obsessed gambler. He would wake up at three in the morning and bet on a camel race in Dubai. He was addicted,

55 At this time the assistant camera operator/focus-puller had to get the shot in focus by actually touching the camera. Today the technology has advanced to where it's done remotely with the assistant generally a few feet away from the operator with a small monitor.

and he said he had to stop that. It was just getting way, way out of hand. We went to the horse track that one time, had a nice day at the track—gambling and whatnot—then had dinner afterwards.

MICHAEL F. BURKE: We had one night where we went to a friend's house, a gathering with some waitresses from the hotel where Albert was at. My friend was cooking dinner. Then Albert says, "Let's go out to this restaurant later on for drinks." It's late. Albert calls up and asks if we could come out to the restaurant if they would take us. So the company people say, "Oh, yeah, sure. Come on out here." So we get out there at about ten minutes to 10 p.m. and the restaurant closes at ten o'clock. There are about twelve of us, and we started ordering drinks and food, and we were there until one o'clock in the morning. They're probably ready to kill us in the kitchen.

RUSSELL ENGELS: Did Mike tell you about the car ride?

MICHAEL F. BURKE: I had a 1963 Oldsmobile 98 convertible two-door, sleeps six. This thing was like a boat. Myself, some girl, and Rusty are in the front seat, and Albert and two other girls are in the back seat and we're driving. We make the turn and we're driving down the middle of Canal Street at one-thirty in the morning. Albert is half in the bag. He decides to get up and stand up in the back of the car and start thanking the people of New Orleans for their hospitality and graciousness, so Rusty opens up the passenger side door—it's a really big door—of the car while I'm driving and then hangs on the door. He's car-surfing by scraping his feet along the highway with the door open, hanging on to the door.

RUSSELL ENGELS: We used to call it skiing—you open the door and put your feet down on the ground, but you're hanging onto the door, scraping your shoes along the ground.

MICHAEL F. BURKE: Now I have an eightball of cocaine in my pocket, and I'm smashed to begin with.

RUSSELL ENGELS: He's thinking, "Here I am—got the star in the back of the car standing up and orating, and I got the gaffer hanging out the side door, skiing down the highway."

MICHAEL F. BURKE: And I'm driving down Canal Street at one-thirty in the morning and I'm thinking, "If I hit my brakes, the lead actor of the movie is going to go over my windshield and I'm going to run him over and the gaffer was going to go forward and rip off the door off my car." So I took my foot off the gas and I prayed that the lights did not turn red and I just coasted, and the lights all stayed green. I coasted to a stop. And there were no cops—nobody saw us—and the girls finally pull Albert back down in the back seat, and then I pulled Rusty back into the car. I'm thinking, "The gods are with us."

RUSSELL ENGELS: Mike said, "Oh, boy, we're lucky we didn't get pulled over."

ANGELO DIGIACOMO: One day Joel [Coen] got sick, so we just went out and shot shit. Then the next day Mike and I cruised in his convertible.

After, like, a month down there, Mike could have run for city council. He has a knack for making friends in remote places.

DAVE FRANZONI (ELECTRICIAN): *Miller's Crossing* was the start of Mike's real-estate empire in New Orleans.

ANGELO DIGIACOMO: Mike is still down there now. New Orleans was a place that was not created for him, but he meshed with it perfectly.

MICHAEL F. BURKE: By the end of the job, the locals were asking *me* what's going on at night, what's happening here. And that's why I'm still here, because of *Miller's Crossing*.

Mo' Better Blues

(1990)

VAN HAYDEN (PRODUCTION ASSISTANT, *MO' BETTER BLUES*): I was at a journalism event in July 1986. It was the National Association of Black Journalists convention. They were going to be screening this unknown filmmaker's first feature film that was due to be released in the fall. It was myself and my friend Michelle Norris who went on to work for NPR, ABC News, the *Washington Post*. We're there watching this movie, and that movie happened to be *She's Gotta Have It,* directed by a filmmaker named Spike Lee, and at the end of the movie I was just so blown away by not only the storytelling and the style but the kind of fresh perspective.

I was really impressed by—here's a young African American filmmaker who's telling this story, which I really believe to be a real feminist story about examining the double standard in society with relationships to women dating multiple partners and men dating multiple partners. It totally opened up a window to what my future career could be like. I didn't know there was access into the Business.

I was in Minneapolis. I had a day job working at a hotel, driving the limo for this small luxury hotel, and at night I was also working as a copy editor at my college paper—it was a side hustle—and so I'm doing these two jobs, and a friend of mine from New York told me, she said, "You know, Van, why don't you just write Spike a letter and just say you want to come out and work on his next film he is going to do."

And I did. I remember it really distinctly. It was a Friday afternoon. I wrote the letter, and I was so itchy that I wanted to get that thing off. I drove the letter to the airport post office, so it would be postmarked that day, that Friday afternoon, and the following Tuesday I get a call from a production assistant named Eric Knight, and Eric said something to the effect: "Hey, Van, this is Eric Knight. I'm calling from 40 Acres and a Mule Filmworks, Spike Lee's production company. I've got your letter here and there was just something about the letter that really kind of struck me. I wanted to reach out to you. We got the letter. I am sorry to tell you that we filled all of the production-assistant slots for our upcoming movie, and unfortunately we can't offer you a paid position on the film."

I said, "Oh, gee, I'd be so excited to do this," and Eric could tell that I was sincere and he could tell that I was really highly motivated, and he said, "Well, let me ask you this. If we could get you on as an unpaid intern doing the exact same jobs as that production assistant would have, would that be something that you could do, do you think? We can't pay you. We can't pay to bring you out here. We can't put you up. But you'd have the same opportunities and the same job and the same expectations as our set PAs. I said, "Yeah, that'd be fantastic."

Thank goodness I had some money set aside, and my sister Connie and her husband Stanley in Brooklyn, who I stayed with. That was my first call as soon as I got off the phone with Eric: "You're not going to believe this. I have this offer to come back to New York and to work on the Spike Lee film."

JEFF GLAVE (CHARGE SCENIC ARTIST, *MO' BETTER BLUES*): It was originally titled *Love Supreme*. They couldn't use the title because Coltrane's widow wouldn't release that to Spike.

VAN HAYDEN: She said he could use the music because they had gotten the rights to the music before they'd started, but she was concerned about some of the racy language in the film, so she didn't feel comfortable using it as the title, and I remember driving Spike to the meeting with Alice Coltrane when that decision came down.

JONATHAN BURKHART (FIRST ASSISTANT CAMERA OPERATOR, *MO' BETTER BLUES*): I got a story to tell you about *Mo' Better Blues*. One of the greatest experiences in my life. Nothing will come close to this. When Spike was in prep for *Mo' Better Blues,* he had let the crew know that somewhere within the first couple weeks of shooting we would be filming a birth—actual birth—and he had to make sure we were okay with it.

His sister Joie Lee is the female lead in it with Denzel Washington, and there's a scene at the end of the movie—the character is pregnant in the movie, and then she delivers a baby. Spike had stated clearly, "I want to film the birth. Like, I want to see the baby come out of the vagina."

Now, prior to this, I actually had seen birth before, because when I wasn't making commercials, movies, or music videos, I worked on some docs. What Spike had done was about a year earlier he had posted up at the Harlem Hospital that he was shooting a movie, that he was looking for volunteers giving birth on the days that we were shooting at the hospital—you would agree to let him film the birth, that he would pay the medical costs and put together, like, ten or twenty thousand dollars into a college fund for the babies. So we started shooting the movie and about a week or two into filming, we go to Harlem Hospital and we go to the birthing center.

It's day one, and we load the cameras in, and in the delivery room can only be me, [cinematographer] Ernest Dickerson, Spike, Denzel, the boom operator, and the sound mixer. The birthing center at Harlem Hospital is rather big, and we would wait until the woman got to ten centimeters [dilation].

The agreement was—and the scene was supposed to be—is that the doctor is in the room with the two nurses, like, the real, actual doctors and nurses. When the baby comes out and the doctor's holding the baby with the umbilical cord, the agreement is that Denzel Washington is the first one to hold the baby, kisses it, and then puts it on the mom's abdomen. The camera can't shoot the face of the woman who just delivered because then in the editing room we would cut to Joie and that would be the shot, but it has to come out of the vagina. The doctor holds the baby, hands it to Denzel, kisses it, puts it on the mother's abdomen—that's the shot.

Finally, this woman is dilated. She's signed the releases and whatnot. The mom gets to eight centimeters, nine centimeters, ten centimeters, and everybody's in the room and she's pushing and we're all there. The husband's in there and all this excitement, and all of a sudden the woman who's delivering, who's having contractions starts to cry and she rolls on her side, and I'm like, "What the fuck is going on here?" and you have to understand, me and Ernest are so close we're actually touching the doctor's back. We're, like, twelve, eighteen inches from this woman's vagina, and this whole weird event takes place and she's crying so hard.

We all step back, and I take the camera and we're leaning, standing against the wall now, like, six, seven feet away, and the doctor is trying to talk to this woman and she's a fucking mess. She's just destroyed, crying so hard her body is quaking, but the nurses freaked me out because she's dilated and the baby has to come out and they're checking her pulse and whatnot, and all of a sudden she says, "I need you to leave," and she points to her husband and tells her husband to leave the room and then she asked everybody else to leave, but I can't because I'm holding the camera. It was me and the boom operator who stayed in the room. Everybody else stepped out.

She asked everybody to leave except for Denzel Washington. She's crying but she regains her composure and she leans in and she whispers in his ear. He stands up with this look in his face like he had just seen a ghost and he walks out, and then they wheeled her away. Somehow the baby got delivered in some other room. What she told Denzel was that it wasn't the father's baby. Like, this kid's about to come out of her and the man in the room, her husband, wasn't the actual father.

There's more—the next one. So maybe twenty minutes go by, and we get a call—there's another woman in labor, and she's pushing, she's pushing, she's crowning. The baby gets stuck, and then the baby's heartbeat stops, and right there was a crash C-section. When mom and baby are about to die, they take the tray with the scalpel and they just start cutting her. There's no anesthesia. There's nothing. They cut her right open—like, fucking deep—pull this baby out, get the baby to breathe, take care of the mom. Just fucking blood everywhere. That was fucked up.

The third one. The last one we shot that day was the complete opposite. We broke for

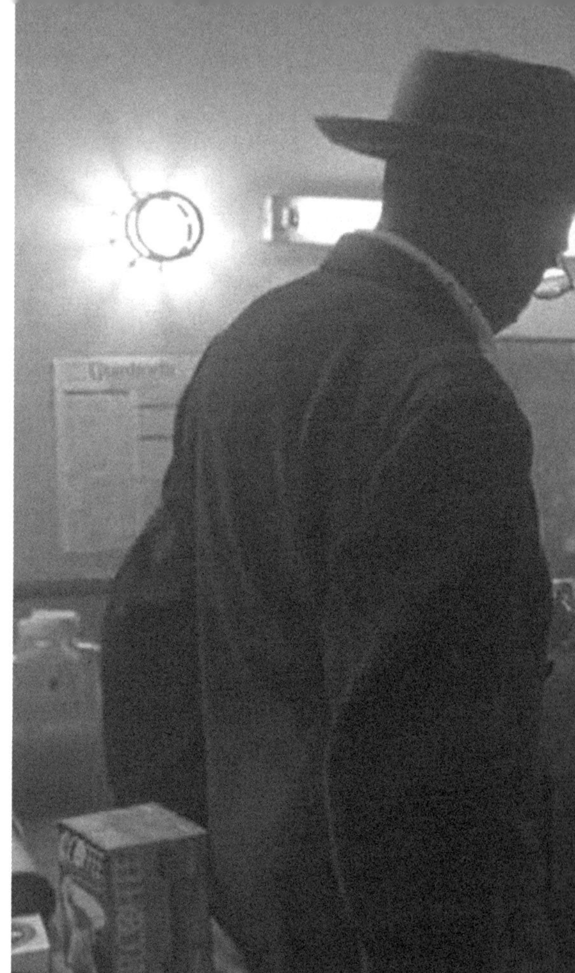

lunch, then right away there's a woman, she's ten centimeters, she's about to deliver. We go to this other room and set up the camera. She gets wheeled in. She's crowning. She's laughing hysterically. She's got her husband and three other kids and all of her friends. We settled in, we're rolling camera, and the baby fucking flew out of her so fast that my left hand went down to help catch it with the doctor. I am not joking.

Balloons, party streamers—it was the absolute opposite. It was the happiest, most beautiful delivery. When I got home, I was a fucking mess. That night I lost my shit.

What a wild day that was. But again, to end it with this woman, a perfect delivery—great happiness, love, affection. That's the way you end the day.

VAN HAYDEN: As an unpaid intern, we weren't being paid anything. At that time, we weren't

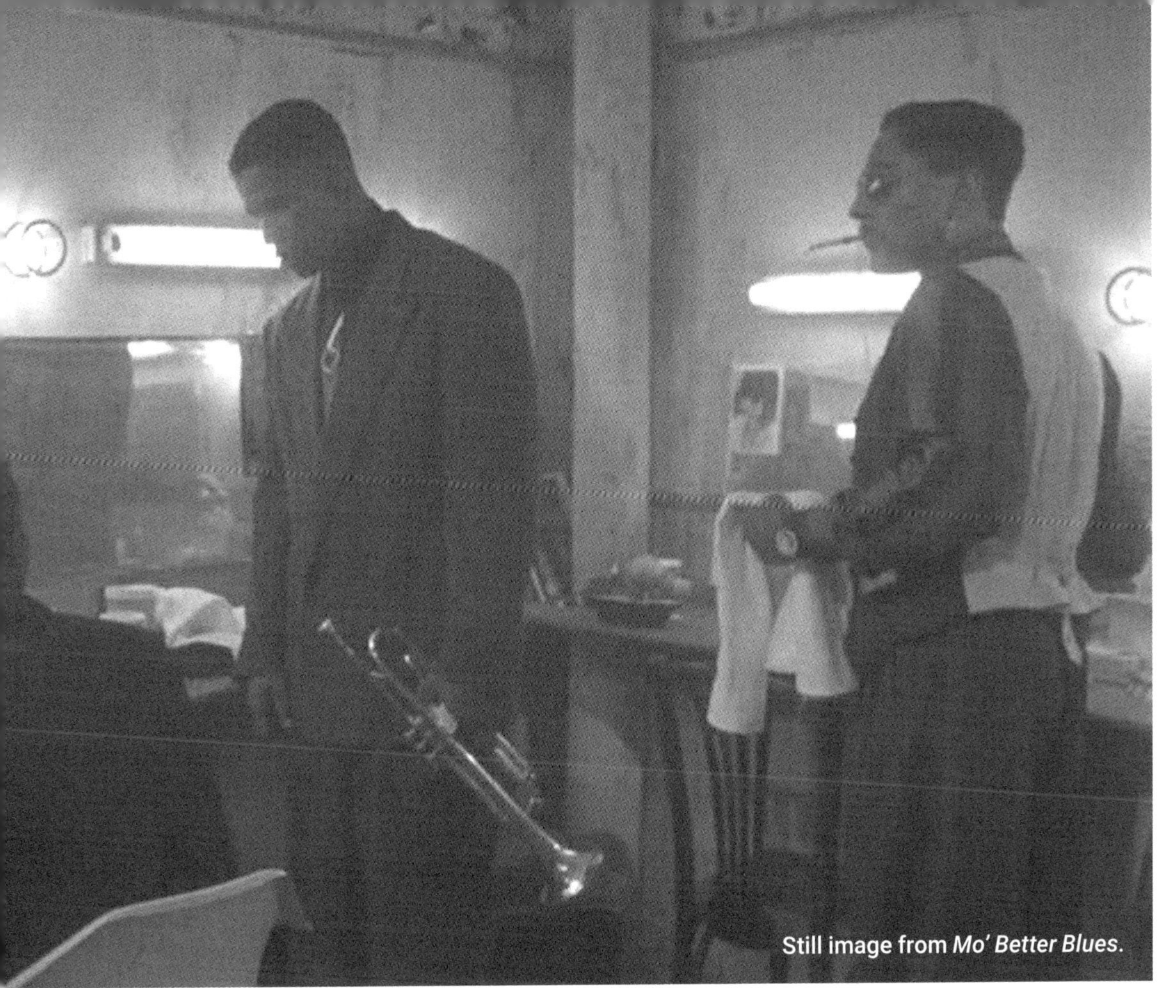
Still image from *Mo' Better Blues*.

being given subway fare to get back and forth to work. You had to get there on your own, your own token, literally. My sister and her husband had relocated from a small apartment in Brooklyn to this big, three-story house in Staten Island that they had purchased. The deal my sister and Stanley set up for me was, "Okay, we'll let you stay here, but on the weekends, in exchange for your room and board, you have to agree to clean all the bathrooms, do all the vacuuming and the dusting.

I took the ferry each morning to Lower Manhattan. Then I got a subway map to figure out how to get to locations. I'll get to Brooklyn Heights on the train and find the connection to the route. At that time Spike always had these early calls at the beginning of the week, so on Monday we'd have a 6-a.m. call, which meant the PAs, the production assistants, and the production intern, we had to be on set at 5:30 a.m.

We always had to be there half an hour before to make sure things were set up and everything. That meant I had to be out the door at about 3:30 a.m.

After doing that for three or four weeks, Spike came up to me and he gave me a little handshake, a little dap, and in doing so he slipped me some cash. I opened up my hand to reveal a hundred-dollar bill there, and he looked around, kind of checking to make sure the coast was clear with him, both ways, left and right. "Don't tell everybody, because everybody ain't getting it."

I just thought, "Wow, that was really thoughtful." And then also it made me realize that even when no one says anything, people recognize if you're there—you're working hard, you're doing the right thing, and Spike was incredibly observant. I think that's what made him a great filmmaker.

The 1990 Producer Lockout

With the expiration last night of a contract between the major Hollywood film and television producers and a production crafts union, New York City is facing a slowdown in an industry that is a source not only of prestige but of badly needed jobs and revenue as well.

At stake is the continued employment of nearly 3,500 workers who toil on more than 100 New York film productions yearly, as well as the future of the city's third largest industry, behind tourism and fashion. Film and television production pumps more than $2.7 billion into the city's economy each year, according to the Mayor's Office for Film, Theater and Broadcasting.[56]

—*New York Times*, November 1, 1990

56 Glenn Collins, "Filming in New York May Be Disrupted by Labor Dispute," *New York Times*, November 1, 1990.

BARRY WETCHER (STILL PHOTOGRAPHER, LOCAL 600): What I remember most about [*Lean on Me* (1990)], besides having to travel to Patterson, New Jersey, was that in those days we had a great contract. You were on the clock once you crossed over the George Washington Bridge. There was no "thirty-mile rule."[57] In those days, even if you worked in Brooklyn, once you crossed anywhere into Manhattan you were on the clock, and the same thing coming back. I used to drive [boom operator] Kim Maitland and we'd be driving home from Patterson, and it'd be, like, a fucking traffic jam at the bridge and we'd be sitting and waiting to go over the bridge in triple time.

In those days we didn't have time and a half. There was no time and a half in those days. After eight [hours], you went right into double time—and then two and a half, that's fourteen [hour day].

57 The 30-mile rule defines a radius around a central production zone (e.g., Manhattan or Hollywood) where standard pay and no per diem apply. Work outside this zone typically triggers extra compensation like per diem, mileage, or housing.

Filming *Misery* in 1990. Photo courtesy of the Margaret Herrick Library, Academy of Motion Picture Arts and Sciences.

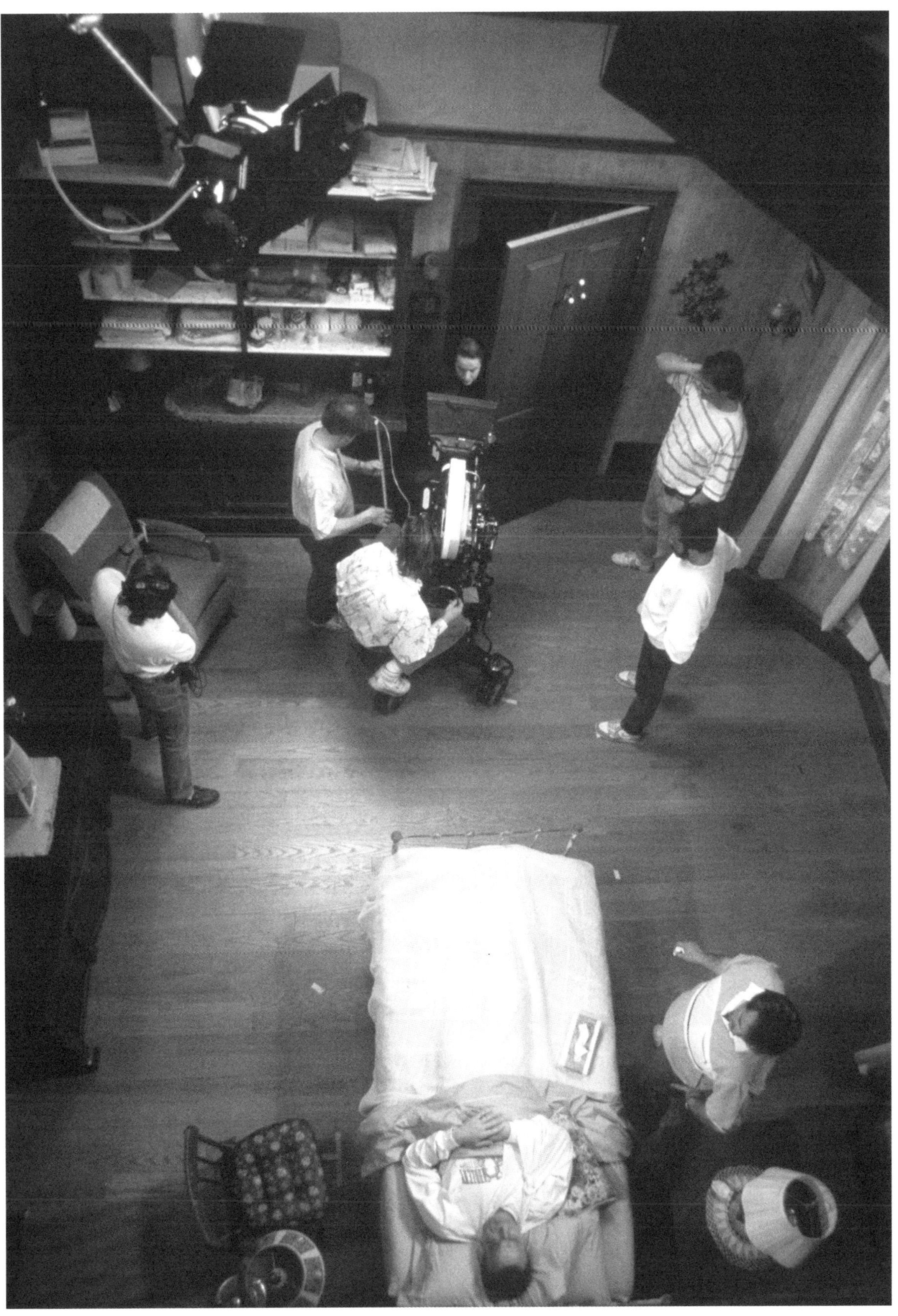

TONY GAMIELLO (SET DRESSER AND PROPS, LOCAL 52): We would get double time and triple time, and we weren't wanting that to get rich, we were doing that so we wouldn't have to work twenty hours a day, like my grandfather did—sleep on the stage. We would do it so we can have a life.

BARRY WETCHER: Once we [Camera Local 644] merged with L.A., in New York we became part of the Hollywood Basic agreement. The Hollywood Basic agreement is an agreement between—I think it's thirteen Hollywood locals and the producers. Those locals include camera, hair, makeup, studio teachers, publicists, [and others]. The Hollywood Basic agreement covers work in the thirteen western states. It's different than Local 52. Local 52 only has jurisdiction in New York and New Jersey and that's it. So my local, when we were three separate camera locals, was 644, then we [and Local 666] merged into Local 600.

TONY GAMIELLO: NABET merged into Local 52. They ended the NABET 15 charter. They expanded our jurisdiction to all New York State, Connecticut, New Jersey, and all of Pennsylvania except Pittsburgh, who already had a local, and Delaware.

BARRY WETCHER: The way that the Hollywood Basic contract is ratified is via the electoral-college system, so you have thirteen locals voting on one contract.[58] For instance, in the late nineties, camera used to have a provision that a camera operator was mandatory: producers had to hire a camera operator.

When the contract was being voted on, my local voted it down by a ninety-percent majority, and the only other local that voted it down was the prop local in L.A., but the other eleven Locals voted for it. It passed because it's an electoral-college system, which allocates votes by how many members you have. Therein lies a big disadvantage of that contract, because you have studio teachers voting on whether there should be a camera operator. They don't give a shit. They don't care.

In my eyes, it's a very flawed contract because you're voting on things that don't really apply to you. So maybe that year the grips got something or didn't lose something, and they were happy to vote "yes."

The Hollywood Basic—their contracts were never as good as the New York contracts, but it was okay. They used to let a lot of non-union work go on there. Then the producers basically pressured them [Local 52] to sign this contract and got a sweetheart contract. That's when they lost nights and weekends and sixth day,[59] and any five days.

After that happened in Hollywood, this is what the producers wanted when it came time for the New York local to negotiate. You heard about the boycott of New York, right? The walkout and then the boycott. My local, the camera local, agreed to the contract. Local 52 obviously did not, and that's when the Hollywood producers boycotted New York.

TONY GAMIELLO: Local 52 was the renegade local.

The producers have promised to steer films away from New York City until an agreement is reached with the union, Local 52 of the International Alliance of Theater Stage Employees and Moving Picture Machine Operators. It provides the sound people, electricians, shop craftsmen, prop people, camera grips, gaffers and set dressers for the city's film and television productions.[60]

—*New York Times*, November 1, 1990

58 Today Hollywood Basic contract includes eighteen film and TV locals.

59 Saturdays were always called "sixth day," which meant you started the day at time and a half or double your normal rate, even if you hadn't worked the previous five days.

60 Collins, "Filming in New York May Be Disrupted by Labor Dispute."

CHRIS MARKUNAS (CARPENTER): Local 52 dug their heels in and they said, "We're not ratifying the contract. We don't give a shit what you do. The old rules apply here. You come to New York because New York is 'the holy city.' We get to negotiate our own deals." So the producers boycotted the northeast corridor.

DON NACE (SCENIC ARTIST, LOCAL 829): I thought the boycott was extremely frustrating because we all knew what was happening. New York had a lot of work, and the reason New York had a lot of work was because the producers were boycotting in L.A. during that contract negotiation. Because their contract was on a different timeframe than the New York contract, we knew what was coming, but we had all this work and we were just working away and working away, and then they settled in California, finally, after about a year.

TONY GAMIELLO: Then they put the pressure on us. They locked us out. It was very little work for about a year, for about two years.

CHRIS MARKUNAS: No work. Scene shops went out. The Slate, one of my favorite restaurants, went out of business, and they finally brought Local 52 around because guys were losing their houses. It was brutal in 1990 through 1992.

BARRY WETCHER: I think it was 1990. The boycott was right after the NABET merger with New York. Basically, nothing was shot there. The 52 guys going, "Hey, they've got to shoot here." Meanwhile, they made the Babe Ruth film in Chicago. Turns out they didn't have to shoot here.

I've gone through about three writer strikes in my career. This was serious. Some people call it the boycott. Some people call it the lockout.

DON NACE: California signed their contract, and within a couple of weeks there was no work in New York. Everything went to California, and we knew it was going to happen. They just picked us off one at a time, like a sniper, and then there was no work. I had *Malcolm X* [1992]. It was the drop painters and the lucky few on *Malcolm X* had jobs. People lost their houses. It was economically devastating.

DEAN TAUCHER (PRODUCTION DESIGNER, LOCAL 829): [In the 1950s], when Reagan was in SAG, and they orchestrated this whole thing where they locked out forty percent of the workers for over a year, and federal law states that if you don't work in an industry for more than a year you're ineligible to vote on union representation. That's what they were trying to do in New York with this strike vote. They were trying to orchestrate a strike. Then the studios were going to do a lockout of us, and they were going to replace us with other workers, and if you did that for over a year then the NLRB [National Labor Relations Board] would hold an election and the new workers would vote for the IA [IATSE, the International Alliance of Theatrical Stage Employees], and 829 would have just been a stump of what it was.

TONY GAMIELLO: Some of us were collecting unemployment and trying to get other work. A lot of guys lost their homes. Some marriages broke up. Because when you haven't worked for two years, it's not good.

BILL REYNOLDS (PROP MASTER, LOCAL 52): They really came for us. We talked about it at that time after the fact, maybe a year or two after the fact—you'd think of the names: "What the hell happened to him?"

And then somebody would say, "Yeah, they got out of Business. They're doing whatever they're doing now. They're plumbers now. They're an outside carpenter now." It drove people away from the Business. And really it was just New York. All of the California locals pretty much were in unison, but we were not connected with them. We had autonomy.

TONY GAMIELLO: People thought we were on strike, and we weren't. They locked us out. Our union president at the time, Frank Schultz, wanted to buy a half-page ad for ten thousand dollars in the *New York Times* to state our side of the story, that we're being locked out, we're not striking or anything like that, and the *New York Times* refused to run it. So much for freedom of speech, so much for the first amendment, so much for unionism. They were anti-union, and they didn't want to piss off the movie companies who were advertising in the *New York Times*. If I saw somebody with the *New York Times,* I said, "Get that rag outta here! They're anti-union scumbags. I want nothing to do with them."

I go to this film festival at Westchester Community College, because I had went there, and at the end they had all these different movie people talking and one of them was Alan Arkin. At the end, somebody gets up and says, "Mr. Arkin, when are they going to end this strike in New York?" Well, I had to raise my hand, and I got up and say, "Mr. Arkin, there's no strike in New York. We're ready to go back to work now. They're locking us out to get into a contract."

And he goes, "I didn't know that." And here's a guy, an actor who's worked in the Business, and he didn't even know they were locking us out. The point was—is they were trying to silence us and then censor everything and not let us get our point of view out, because they didn't want to piss off the movie companies. In the meantime, they put the squeeze on us.

They could do that because movies could be made anywhere. TV shows can be made anywhere. They couldn't do that with Local 1 because, when Local 1 had a problem, then the International would go to them and say, "How could we work this out?" because you can't take Broadway on the road. People come from all over the world to go to Broadway to see plays. Local 1 was a bit more flat, whereas 52 and the rest of the IA locals—you have to give in because they can shoot movies anywhere. Look, they shot *Rumble in the Bronx* [1995] in Toronto. I didn't see any long peak mountains in the Bronx.

So they pit jurisdictions against each other and everything else.

BARRY WETCHER: Local 52 eventually capitulated. I mean—and the story as I heard it—I don't know if it's true because I'm not a member of Local 52—at the time I think Wally Stocklin was the president of Local 52—he was a prop guy who became a Teamster after he retired—the story as I heard it was Local 52 went out to L.A. to negotiate and told the producers, "Okay, we are going to recommend that our members vote for this bullshit contract."

And again, this is secondhand what I'm telling you—I don't know if it's fact—they told the producers they would recommend it, but actually they told the members not to vote for it [laughs], so the members rejected the contract, and the producers went fucking nuts and locked us out. So again, I don't know, because I wasn't there, [I was] never in Local 52, but it all sounds right to me. [laughs]

TONY GAMIELLO: As I remember—and I confirmed with my brother—the way we remembered things is back during the lockout Wally Stocklin [Local 52 president] and Ray Fortune [business agent, Local 52] went out to California to negotiate. When they went out there, they foolishly went without an attorney. All of the seven major motion-picture company producers had representatives there with their attorneys and basically got steamrolled because they just weren't prepared. They came back to New York and they did recommend to sign the contract because it had some good benefits in it.

The producers contended that the local that rejected the contract proposal, Local 52 of the International Alliance of Theatrical Stage Employees and Moving Picture Machine Operators, had reneged on a promise to recommend the deal to the local's rank and file.

The producers, through the Alliance of Motion Picture and Television Producers in Sherman Oaks, Calif., said that they had made concessions in the negotiations based on assurances that Local 52 would recommend ratification.

Yesterday the alliance issued a statement denouncing Local 52's failure to urge ratification as "outrageous and unprecedented."

"Local 52's leadership has no interest in reaching an agreement with the producers," the statement from the alliance said.

Ray Fortune, the business manager of Local 52, denied the allegation. "Wally and I did not have the power to make any kinds of deals," he said, referring to the president of Local 52, Walter Stocklin.[61]

—*New York Times,* April 17, 1991

TONY GAMIELLO: They forced the contract down our throat. They appeased us on some things, like going from time and a half to double time, but what hurt us is the "any eight hours and any five days." In other words, if the production wanted to work Wednesday through Sunday, you wouldn't get overtime on Saturday and Sunday until your ninth hour.

BILL REYNOLDS: If you come in on a Thursday and you're going to work Thursday, Friday, and Saturday, that Saturday everybody else in the crew is going to be getting a time and a half and you're going to be working straight time because that's only your third day.

61 James Barron, "Settlement Defeat Speeds Film Exodus from New York," *New York Times,* April 17, 1991.

TONY GAMIELLO: Years ago, if you come in after three o'clock it was a night call and you get time and a half immediately. Well, they changed that, so the eight hours starts at call. If you're working those nights all week, that's fine, but, if you're on the job for two days, now you couldn't take a job in the daytime because you're working that night, or you couldn't take a job the next day because you're sleeping because you worked all night. It hurt some guys who didn't have a steady with that same production all week.

DON NACE: We [Local 829] went from a seven-hour day to an eight-hour day and from double time to time and a half and other concessions.

BARRY WETCHER: It was only a good move in terms of our pension and health plan. I'm not going to say ours was in trouble, but becoming part of the Hollywood Basic now put us into the motion-picture plan, which was a very viable plan.

That was the one big advantage. But the disadvantage was now we had a shittier contract.

CHRIS MARKUNAS: The International caved on the Hollywood [Basic] Agreement. They caved and we lost triple time, golden time. We lost so much.

TONY GAMIELLO: It's a little different now. That was ancient history, but a lot of the youngsters don't know about that. That's the problem—they get lured into a false sense of security. It wasn't always like this years ago. You didn't have all this TV. Some TV shows would come here for a couple of weeks to get the experience, and they shoot everything on the West Coast in the studio. *NYPD Blue* [1993-2005] used to do that.

JONATHAN HERRON (CAMERA OPERATOR, LOCAL 600): I had a lot of friends who bailed on New York when the boycott happened in 1991 or whatever that was and subsequently they found themselves chasing work. They moved to L.A. because it was busy. Then they moved to Vancouver. It was busy. And then some of them even moved to New Orleans when it was busy. And I just sort of thought it goes from city to city to city. Eventually stuff's going to come back to New York. Isn't it better to have a really strong foothold and reputation in one place rather than dabbling in four or five places where you never really find your feet? And I just stayed and sort of built a credit list, and people liked having me work on their movies. It paid off.

BARRY WETCHER: I mean, we were a real union. Today it's like a club. We were proud, and we were strong, and the producers were afraid of us. That's not true anymore. It hasn't been true for many years. When I started, the guys that were in charge of the studios were filmmakers. Today they're MBAs, so when you go negotiate a contract the guy that's sitting across from you is a lawyer who studied labor relations at school—never been on a film set, ever. He has no clue what it's like to work fourteen hours in the rain in twenty-degree weather, no clue. Doesn't understand what it's like if you don't eat for ten hours.

I think in the past, the producers' job was to negotiate the best contract for everyone. They understood that. I'm not saying they were compassionate, but at least they understood it. Today they negotiate with people who have no clue.

Law and Order franchise

(1990-present)

BARRY WETCHER (STILL PHOTOGRAPHER): There was no TV work in New York, or very little TV work. Dick Wolf is the guy who brought TV back to New York.

BILL REYNOLDS (PROP MASTER, *LAW AND ORDER*): There're so many people that came out of that *Law and Order* school.

JONATHAN BURKHART (FIRST ASSISTANT CAMERA OPERATOR, *LAW AND ORDER*): That show launched a million careers. I've never seen so many key grips become cinematographers, and brilliant ones. *Law and Order* is a machine that has created some of the greatest filmmakers we have.

INGRID PRICE (WARDROBE SUPERVISOR, *CRIMINAL INTENT*): I don't know if it's unique to the [creator] Dick Wolf universe or episodic TV in general, but so many of my friends who actually became producers started as PAs [production assistants], and then they went through the DGA [Directors Guild of America] training program or became production managers. They came up through the ranks.

GARY MULLER (FIRST ASSISTANT CAMERA OPERATOR): I turn on the TV and every day there was a different Dick Wolf thing, and *SVU* was on. I started watching a couple of episodes from the different genres. To see the evolution of the show and how the characters changed—the show has gotten very different and a lot better. It's amazing to see.

BILL REYNOLDS: For a large part, *Law and Order* was replacing the *Movie of the Week* [1969-1975].

ALEC HIRSCHFELD (CAMERA OPERATOR, *LAW AND ORDER*): And then while we were just at the tail end of one of *The Equalizer* [1985-1989], Geoffrey [Erb] got the job to shoot the pilot for *Law and Order* the original. Dick Wolf actually says he "never does pilots." He just does "episode ones," because his shows always get picked up.

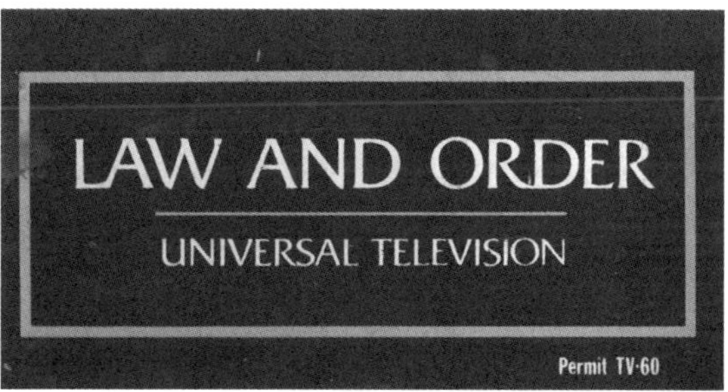

Parking pass for *Law and Order.*

So we did episode one of *Law and Order* for CBS. Some executive at CBS decided not to go ahead with production. Two years later, they got an okay from NBC, and they went to work with a NABET contract. Season two, I think the unions merged, and so it became an IA [IATSE, the International Alliance of Theatrical Stage Employees] show.

DEAN TAUCHER (PRODUCTION DESIGNER, *LAW AND ORDER: SPECIAL VICTIMS UNIT*): It was a real competition between NABET and IA because, with NABET, rates were cheaper and their rules were easier, and at one point the studios had a lockout against the IA of all filming in New York, so the only things that worked like the original *Law and Order* show had a NABET contract.

D. W. PAONE (ASSISTANT CAMERA OPERATOR, *LAW AND ORDER*): Now, that producer lockout was right at the time I was on *Law and Order*. There were two jobs shooting in New York: there was a Woody Allen movie and *Law and Order* and that was about it, and then the Woody Allen movie wrapped and pretty much *Law and Order* was the only game in town.

I would go to union meetings on a weekend and camera operators who I didn't know would come up to me and ask me, "Who operates B camera when you have B camera on?" They were coming to me looking for work. So I was very lucky. But when my time at *Law and Order* was finished, the producer lockout was still in effect, and that's one of the reasons why I started accumulating credit-card debt in the late nineties.

MARLENE ARVAN (SECOND ASSISTANT DIRECTOR, *LAW AND ORDER*): *Special Victims Unit* [1999-present] hadn't come in yet, and *Criminal Intent* [2001-2011] hadn't come in yet. It was a tough show.

D. W. PAONE: In December of 1990, I started on the original *Law and Order,* and it was the second half of the first season, so it was the original cast and, I have to tell you, there were days I felt like the luckiest guy in the world. I was learning how to make movies. I mean, I'm fond of saying everything I know about filmmaking I learned in twenty-two episodes of *Law and Order*. We had top episodic directors come in every episode. Gus [Makris] was a top cinematographer. Eventually, for *Law and Order* he was nominated for four Emmys and won all four of them for cinematography.

This is like film school—like, you couldn't believe because it was a real thing. I was getting paid a hundred dollars a day, and I was getting pension and welfare payments, which means I was getting health benefits. It was pretty damn good.

Other times I didn't feel so lucky because, being the lowest guy in the camera department, it was like having five older brothers again and I got picked on mercilessly. But you know what? It was a small price to pay. So I only thought I was going to be the trainee for that second half of the first season, but I was happy to say they asked me back for the first half of the second season. So, all in all, I did twenty-two episodes, so I was very happy with that.

A friend of mine from General Camera who was a little bit older—and he had a previous career as an assistant director at *CBS News*—he always gave me good advice, and he was a little bit older, a little more experienced, and he said to me, "It's not how good you are. It's if they can stand looking at your face for twelve hours a day," and even [camera operator] Dave Tuttman said to me on the first day of *Law and Order,* Paone, I'm going to see you more than I see my wife. You know what that does to me?"

So it's true. It's really not what you know. It's just how well you get along with these people.

On the Catwalk **by David Paone, 1991.**

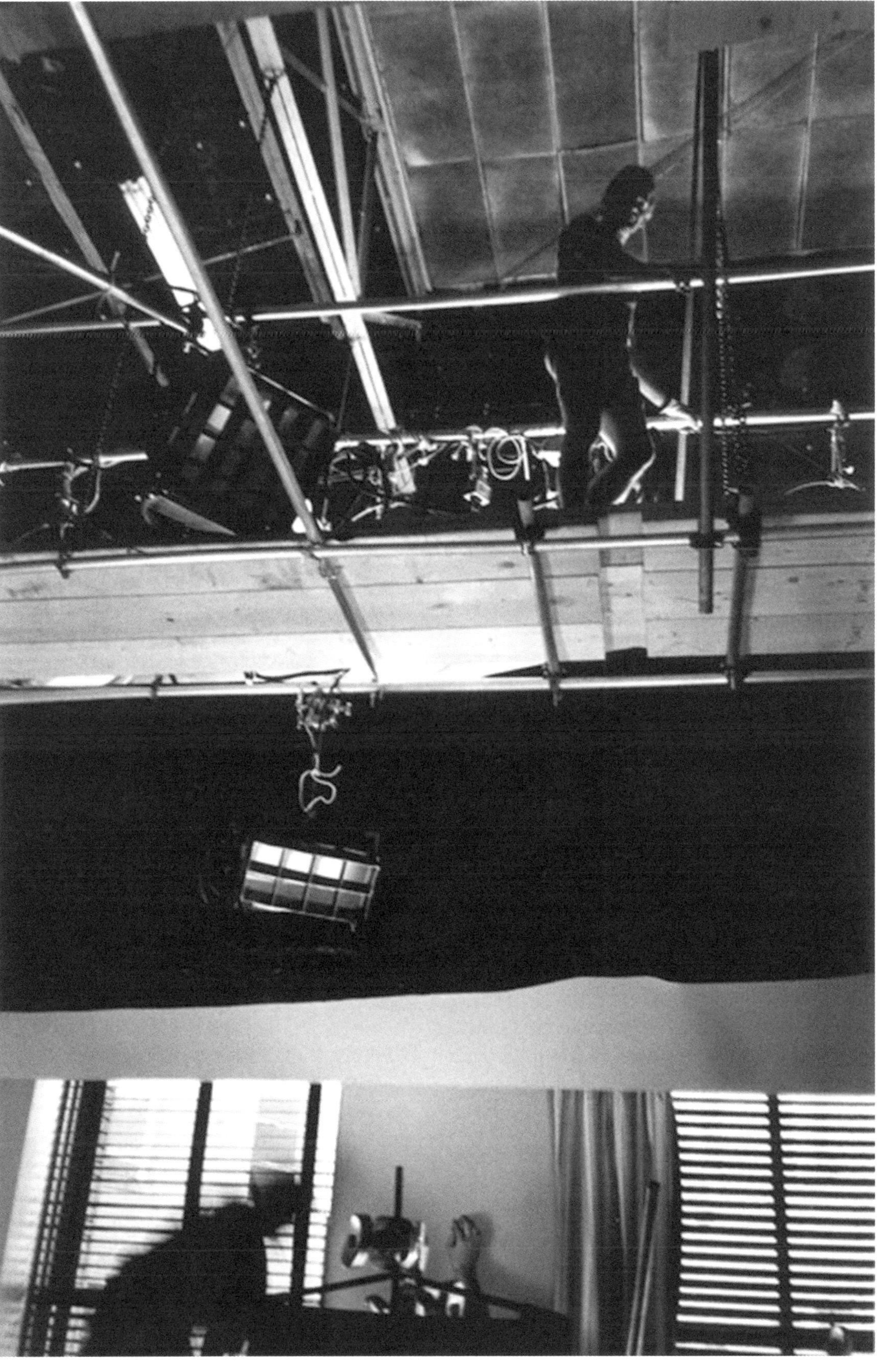

STEVEN GAMIELLO (KEY PROP, *LAW AND ORDER: SPECIAL VICTIMS UNIT*): The two years that we had both Sam Waterston and Jill Hennessy—'94, '95, '96? I remember it was seasons four or five, but Sam Waterston first came on. His office had the window, and in the back was a backdrop of Lower Manhattan, but in reality the Hudson River was behind that window, behind the backdrop outside. So he had a little sailboat in his window. So me and the other on-set dresser—if we were doing a scene before lunch, we would have the front of the boat facing to the right going upriver and [if] it was after lunch we'd turn it and have the boat facing downriver.

We did that for two years. Nobody knew about it. So if I go back and I look at some of those episodes in those years, I could tell if I saw the boat if it was before lunch or after lunch.

FRANK STETTNER (SOUND MIXER, *LAW AND ORDER: SPECIAL VICTIMS UNIT*): It took a while until they built a courtroom. The courtroom was shot downtown in the old Tweed Courthouse up on the third floor. Then eventually they built that courtroom.

DAVE FRANZONI (BEST BOY, GAFFER, *CRIMINAL INTENT, SPECIAL VICTIMS UNIT*): I remember we started the second season of *Criminal Intent* downstairs at the [Chelsea] Pier, and it was loaded with all the first-aid stuff from the 9/11 towers, and of course they never used it because there weren't that many injured people, unfortunately—they were either dead or everyone kind of walked away—but it was loaded with all kinds of first-aid equipment. It was right after we started up right after, I guess, to January 2002, a couple months after 9/11. And then we'd been downstairs [Chelsea Piers] for nine years, and then we came upstairs [to *SVU*] for ten years.

JANE MUSKY (PRODUCTION DESIGNER): There were shows at the Pier back then. I don't think the government owned the space, but the government probably had the lease on the space, and the guy that originally owned the pier that turned it into Chelsea Piers, he was very film-friendly because it was sitting there derelict, and he had the lease on it before *Law and Order*. I can't remember what job it was. There was no heat. So they used to put those big cannonball blasters before the unions ruled them out.

I used to come into work at, like, seven and, you know, go say hi to Fred [Merusi, construction coordinator] and have some coffee with him. Fred would say, "There's this crazy guy—I come here at five in the morning and he's running all around the pier, drawing these things." He said, "You gotta come see this stuff."

So he drags me out into the middle of the pier. The pier then was derelict, you know, and filled with rats. It was really unbelievable. He dragged me out into this section of the Pier and there's all these figures. He said, "The guy's name is Keith something—Hair—Keith Hair." It was Keith Haring coming at night to draw on all these blank walls all over the place. For years—I don't know if you ever saw it—but before the Pier was redone there were Keith Haring figures across the whole front of the pier of this running man he did. I don't know if anyone saved them.

STEVEN GAMIELLO: Now in the early days there was no such thing as on-set [set] dressers. So you had your prop crew, your three-man prop crew—they did everything. They were the on-set dressers. They did the props, they did the cars, they did the guns, food, you name it. So when I first got in, and quite a few years—I would say up until the mid 2000s—that's kind of the way it was when I started on *Special Victims Unit*—it was me and one person on set, and occasionally I'd ask to get a third person. So we did everything between the directors' chairs—the worst is coffee—Chris [Meloni]'s coffee, [Richard] Belzer's green tea—and I had something for everybody.

Then dealing with the guns, dealing with the cars, putting the license plates on it, and all that. So we did everything, and on-scene there are, like, five or six on-set props on the TV show, and half the time they stand around doing nothing because most of them don't know what to do. One just moves the directors' chairs and just talks a lot.

JOHN S. PAUL (**SCENIC ARTIST, *LAW AND ORDER***): We were, like, in New Jersey, in the swampland. Was it near Secaucus? They did about three company moves a day, and the phrase was "go hard or go home." The grips and the construction people and all the team—it was a slog, it was tough, and it was pretty much copacetic. I mean, people got along with each other. There wasn't friction. That was just endurance. That's all it was.

STEVEN GAMIELLO: I remember the hours, especially on, like, the *Special Victims Unit*—it was horrible. I remember having, like, I think it was a 2-p.m. call or 3-p.m. call on a Friday afternoon, and we were shooting up the *Law and Order* stages all night, and then we moved over to the hospital set that they had, and it was almost seven o'clock in the morning and they wanted to add a scene, and I had a big argument with the producer. It's like, "Enough of this shit. Come on, it's seven o'clock in the fucking morning. How long are you going to kill us?"

I had a big argument with him and the crew actually didn't back me up and did the scene. We didn't get out till about eight-thirty in the morning. That's kind of fucked up, and that doesn't do a lot for your marriage. I've had my wife come down with the kids to sets where we're shooting late at night, just so she knew we were shooting late at night and I wasn't out fucking around.

It's very hard. My wife and I were having some problems, and we were separated for a while, and at one point it was, like, actually my last day shooting or my last day of work on *Special Victims Unit*. This is 2001, just before we broke for the summer and we were going to do the *Law and Order* mini-series. I just remember that night I was really down and whatnot, and Chris [Christopher Meloni] and Mariska [Hargitay], they treated me so well, and I'll never forget them for that. They just made me feel so good. They were just really great to me.

But what made me feel really great was Matt [Steve's son] was there a couple of years ago and Mariska mentioned me to somebody, not knowing that he was there, and whoever it was said, "That's his son over there," and then she went over and said hi to him. But for her to remember me it really makes me feel special. She was great.

TONY GAMIELLO (**SET DRESSER, *SPECIAL VICTIMS UNIT***): One day on the set they had as a guest Jerry Lewis. Jerry Lewis is playing—I don't know what—a homeless man, or whatever he was playing. Today, they were lighting, and they're putting makeup on him. He's there doing his old schtick from the fifties, but the guys—they didn't find it funny. They're just standing there stone-faced. Working twelve, fourteen hour days, they're tired. He's there doing all these cornball jokes, and just then I'm walking by the set and he says, "Tough room." He couldn't get a laugh out of them. Not even a smile.

MICHAEL F. BURKE (**GAFFER, *CRIMINAL INTENT, SPECIAL VICTIMS UNIT***): I think Paul Gallo was the key grip, and I think that was his first job as a key grip. He came from maybe *Law and Order* or *New York Undercover*. He came as the key grip, but Paul's got a very gruff voice, and he sounds like he's been in too many boxing matches: "I'm looking to get a crew." So I give him some names of folks to inquire. I call him back and he says, "I got some people. I got

Johnny Mazzoni. He's going to be my best boy grip." At this point, Johnny Mazzoni only really did commercials. He was not really a TV-series guy, and I knew Johnny over the years, so I thought, "Okay."

Francis [Kenny, director of photography] would test people. In the first episode, he was testing me and Paul, to see if we knew what we were doing. So after the first week he could see that I had some semblance of ability and that I knew how to light a set and I could get things prepped. There was a little chaos. Paul didn't know really how to run a set that well, so Francis would be riding Paul. Paul would get frustrated, and flustered, and he would start yelling at all the other grips, and Johnny Mazzoni was nowhere to be found, and they had an episode where Johnny had built himself a kitchen similar to the one he has over at *SVU*. He's in the kitchen making spaghetti sauce, and Paul is yelling and screaming, and he's being yelled at by Francis, and Paul runs into the room and he's yelling at Johnny and saying, "You're not answering. I've got to get this," and Mazzoni is saying, "I can't leave. The sauce is on. I've got to get the sauce."

It was a lot more of the antics, laughing, and watching the grip department be like Keystone Kops. It was six episodes and then it went away, but it was a lot more fun watching. I was off the hook. Francis Kenny had his target, and it was the grip department.

ALEC HIRSCHFELD: I got back to *Law and Order* on season 17. Because the B-cam operator stayed on until season 20, at which time it was canceled because their syndication deal was only for twenty years of episodes—so, after twenty seasons, they had no more syndication and NBC pulled the plug. Otherwise they may have kept going.

I finished my career working on *Law and Order,* and, as I said, it had already been there for seventeen years when I got on it, and it wasn't all that changed except for the cast, and so I was still doing a quintessentially New York show, and it still felt like that. I didn't even know a lot of different people that had gone through the doors. We still had a couple of people on the crew who had been there from the very beginning. So I don't think I experienced it in the same way.

INGRID PRICE: You get sucked into episodic television where you become one of Dick Wolf's people. It's a nice paycheck.

LARRY HOFF (SOUND MIXER, *CRIMINAL INTENT, SPECIAL VICTIMS UNIT*): Made a lot of money from them.

INGRID PRICE: The money is the golden handcuffs and we always called it that on the *Law and Order* series. It was always the golden handcuffs because it's such a grind. It is such a sausage-making process, cranking out episode after episode after episode, and yet you don't dare leave because this is your retirement fund and your health insurance and your bread and butter and your kid's college fund, and that's where the money is.

MARLENE ARVAN: Do you know that I still get residuals from that? I mean, not a lot—maybe forty cents or something, which is just amazing for me.

New Jack City

(1991)

New Jack City was a tough shoot. We were in New York, and it was my first feature and as you know, as a first time feature director—I had been directing Jump Streets *and* Wiseguys, *and working with Clint Eastwood on* Heartbreak Ridge. *Clint had taken me over to meet the Warner Brother hierarchy . . . Clint really was my connection in, and he was really cool. He was like, "Hey man, be all you can be." I thought to myself, "I got a chance to direct a gangster picture. I'm gonna put all the flavor in this."*[62]

—Mario Van Peebles, director of *New Jack City*

KEVIN LADSON (ASSISTANT PROP MASTER, *NEW JACK CITY*): That movie was crazy, and Mario Van Peebles directed. It was sort of a rebirth of his father's way of making movies, of gathering people to make a film up in Harlem as gritty as possible.

62 Joshua Harris, "The Road to *New Jack City*," Video 2005, https://youtu.be/Jz8W3qRlaWM, retrieved June 2, 2023.

MARLENE ARVAN (SECOND ASSISTANT DIRECTOR, *NEW JACK CITY*): That was a pretty big job. My first day of shooting was when we were on the 59th Street Bridge and somebody was getting thrown off the bridge.

AL CERULLO (HELICOPTER PILOT, *NEW JACK CITY*): That was a lot of exciting stuff—everything around the bridges and all of that. *New Jack City* was a lot of exciting flying.

MARLENE ARVAN: We weren't holding traffic on the bridge, but it still was fun to be doing a film shoot and there are cars inches away from you.

[Today] you wouldn't do it on the 59th Street Bridge. You'd do it on some bridge out in Staten Island where you could close the bridge. The mayor's office was incredibly helpful and pushed a lot of filming in New York and made it easy for producers.

STEVEN KIRSHOFF (SPECIAL EFFECTS, *NEW JACK CITY*): Oh, man, every day we were busy—bullet hits, rain, snow, fires—we had crashes. We just had a ton of stuff—a lot of people got shot, a lot of shootout stuff.

KEVIN LADSON: I think what shocked us was the amount of gunplay in that film, because it was really bringing a sort of realism from the streets to the [film] shooting.

OCTAVIO MOLINA (PROP MASTER, *NEW JACK CITY*): We used a lot of guns. Nobody got hurt. When I met Chris Rock, I was kind of reluctant to give him the gun because he was so nervous and had to jump over a fence.

KEVIN LADSON: We shot all through those buildings [the Graham Court Apartments in Harlem] and people thought we were crazy! And then we're shooting a movie about crack cocaine. I give Mario a lot of credit because he took no prisoners with that. He's like, "Okay, there'll be a shootout in this apartment," and all these people were looking at us like we were just nuts, and he had so much energy when we did that film.

MARLENE ARVAN: I mean, what was scary when they were in the club and all the people were there—I thought I was going to die that day because there were so many people. I was outside with all of them, and they were uncontrollable and it was like, "Help!" Joe Ray [second assistant director] had to come over and help me out—just make people, like, not be so nuts outside because they all wanted to get in and they all wanted to be in the movie.

STEVEN KIRSHOFF: I was stuck in this, like—they had this scene where they're in, like, a club and it's got—who's the guy with the big clock? Public Enemy?

MARLENE ARVAN: I forgot about Flavor Flav—holy smokes!

STEVEN KIRSHOFF: It was, like, three days in there and I was on a smoke machine, just miserable. That wasn't my favorite music at that time. I like a lot of it now, but I'm just sitting there. Even the director came over and says, "You're really not having fun now, are you?"

What I like about a lot of those Black movies is that they gave different people a chance to be in positions on a production.

FRANK STETTNER (SOUND MIXER, *NEW JACK CITY*): That's what we [the union] could do. That was before the mergers. I was going to bring Kevin Ladson up. He started as, I think, the third prop on *Do the Right Thing*, and by the time we got up to *New Jack City* he had learned his craft and he was running the department.

KEVIN LADSON: A lot of us from Spike's productions worked on *New Jack*. They infused hip-hop into it because, now that hip-hop was popular, they started using hip-hop actors and rappers. Ice-T was amazing. That was his first job, and it's interesting the way hip-hop came into feature films and television.

FRANK STETTNER: Here I was working with Ice-T, and then later I'm working with him again on *SVU*. There was a bunch of us at that time who seemed to be going from Black film to Black film.

KEVIN LADSON: *New Jack* had been one of the first feature films to do it [use hip-hop] on a big scale. There was *Wild Style* [1983] and there was *Krush Groove* [1985]. *Beat Street* [1984] was Hollywood calling Harry Belafonte, "We need to make a rap movie." It didn't seem real, authentic.

It took the Spike films and the Mario Van Peebles films and *Juice* [1992, directed by Ernest Dickerson] and even Robert Townsend on the West Coast to bring the culture into the storyline, rather than

Costume design for the character Nino Brown by Bernard Johnson for *New Jack City*. Photo courtesy of the Margaret Herrick Library, Academy of Motion Picture Arts and Sciences.

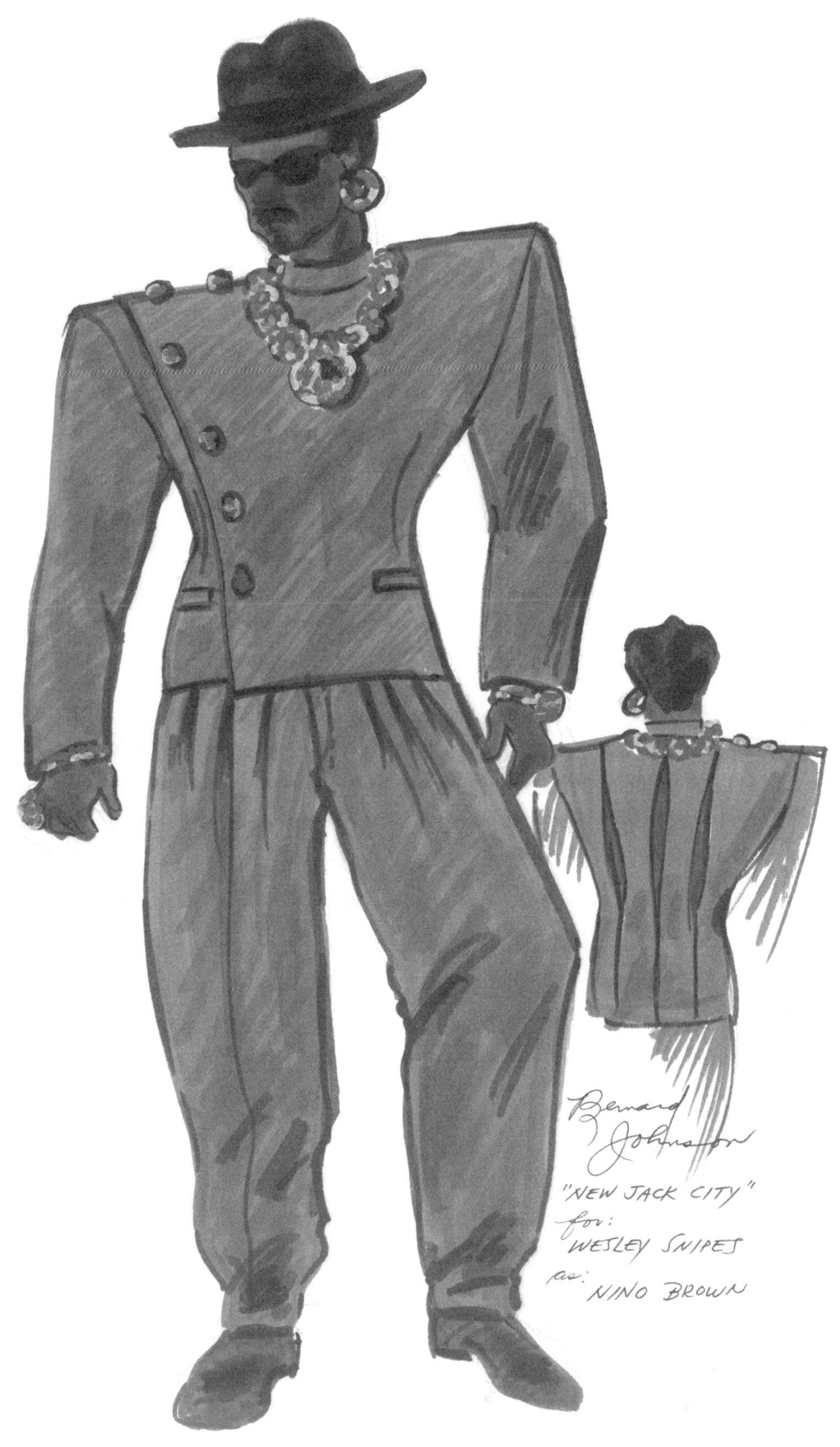
Bernard Johnston
"NEW JACK CITY"
for:
WESLEY SNIPES
as: NINO BROWN

Hollywood cashing in on a Black market. They had to bring the culture behind the scenes too, because if you look at *Beat Street*; *Beat Street* didn't have a lot of Black crew members on it. It's missing something. You're telling a story about Black culture, but the people who are designing the culture—it's not spot on. How I identify [if a film had Black crew members] is by looking for the picture of John F. Kennedy on a wall in the house interior, because it seemed like that was the go-to picture to put in "the Black home." I see that picture of John F. Kennedy on the wall and I'm like, "Okay they haven't been in too many Black homes."

JEFF GLAVE (CHARGE SCENIC ARTIST, *NEW JACK CITY*): One of the dopey things prop guys had to do was make about literally ten thousand crack vials. The crack vials consisted of Lifebuoy Soap. It was the right color, apparently. Lifebuoy Soap would be chipped up—you had to take X-Acto or matte knives and make little flakes to put into these stupid crack vials because they looked real.

We put a big bunch of crack vials in [scenic artist] Michelle Mayas's duffle bag with her work clothes and in our mind this will be funny because she'll go home and she'll find all the crack vials, and won't that be funny?

But of course she's on the subway going home and decides to pull her book out of her duffle bag and out with it come dozens of crack vials onto the subway floor. That backfired on us a little bit, because she described the horrified look she got.

OCTAVIO MOLINA: I still have like a whole crate full of crack vials filled with Safeguard soap, which is what we used to make the product. I just found them in my basement the other day. I've kept them so long I don't know what to do with them. Put them in a museum somewhere?

JEFF GLAVE: I remember taking crack vials, because at the time it was during the crack wave, and we had crackheads on our stoop all the time on my street. It's a tenement building with a new façade on it and it's all black stone and mortar. It was the perfect stoop because you could look up and down the street and not worry about getting surprised by cops or anything.

I started salting these fake crack vials onto our stoop so that the crackheads would take the soap and put it in the crack pipe and smoke it and ruin their crack pipe.

OCTAVIO MOLINA: They were kind of making it up as they went along. Halfway through we really thought it was not going to be a successful film because they started rewriting the script. There were a few days we showed up and we couldn't shoot because there was no script, or we were getting the pages in the morning, and what are you going to do? You can't do anything. You just sort of go to your truck and figure it out and see if you have anything like what they need, but it sort of took the pressure off the problem aspect, because you can always say, "Hey, well, what do you expect? I've tried to help you out."

MARLENE ARVAN: The shoots were definitely looser.

OCTAVIO MOLINA: It was a lot of locations.

JEFF GLAVE: We were in hellholes. We were trying to shoot in one of the old ballrooms. It was a real crackhouse. It was real. We didn't have to put shit in there, except for try to not get stuck by a needle and not touch anything. We had nightmare locations on that. It was terrible. But we were in worse locations on other movies.

BILL LOWRY, GRIP: There's a studio on 127th, I think it was—it was an empty supermarket, because if you had a certain amount of height you could do that work. We didn't have parking, so the crew was going to park all over the place and [get] their batteries ripped off.

JEFF GLAVE: Our shop was up on 126th Street where a big supermarket was made into a studio. It was called El Guapo. It's gone now, replaced by taller buildings.

OCTAVIO MOLINA: We had some sets at 126th and 2nd, right near the Triborough Bridge. What I remember is being outdoors a lot shooting mostly in Harlem, and we had a standing set at the old Filmways stages on 125th and 2nd avenue. They looked like airport hangars.

JEFF GLAVE: We had probably twenty-five big-size breakaway windows left over. We had set up all of these breakaway windows in a couple of jacked-up frames so that we, the scenic artists, could finally get the enjoyment of jumping through a breakaway window, and so we set it up with a mat on the backside of it and we all got to take turns, jumping through breakaway windows. Then we took all of our different aged, fake blood and we splattered them through all this breakaway glass—leave it for whoever came in later. We love pranks. Makes me think about pranking again because we don't do it now.

OCTAVIO MOLINA: Anyway, it was a very enjoyable experience to work on *New Jack City*. The producers were lovely people, very good to work with, and so was Mario. We had some fun. A lot of guns and a lot of great dialogue.

MARLENE ARVAN: I remember Wesley [Snipes] saying, "See ya, wouldn't want to be ya."

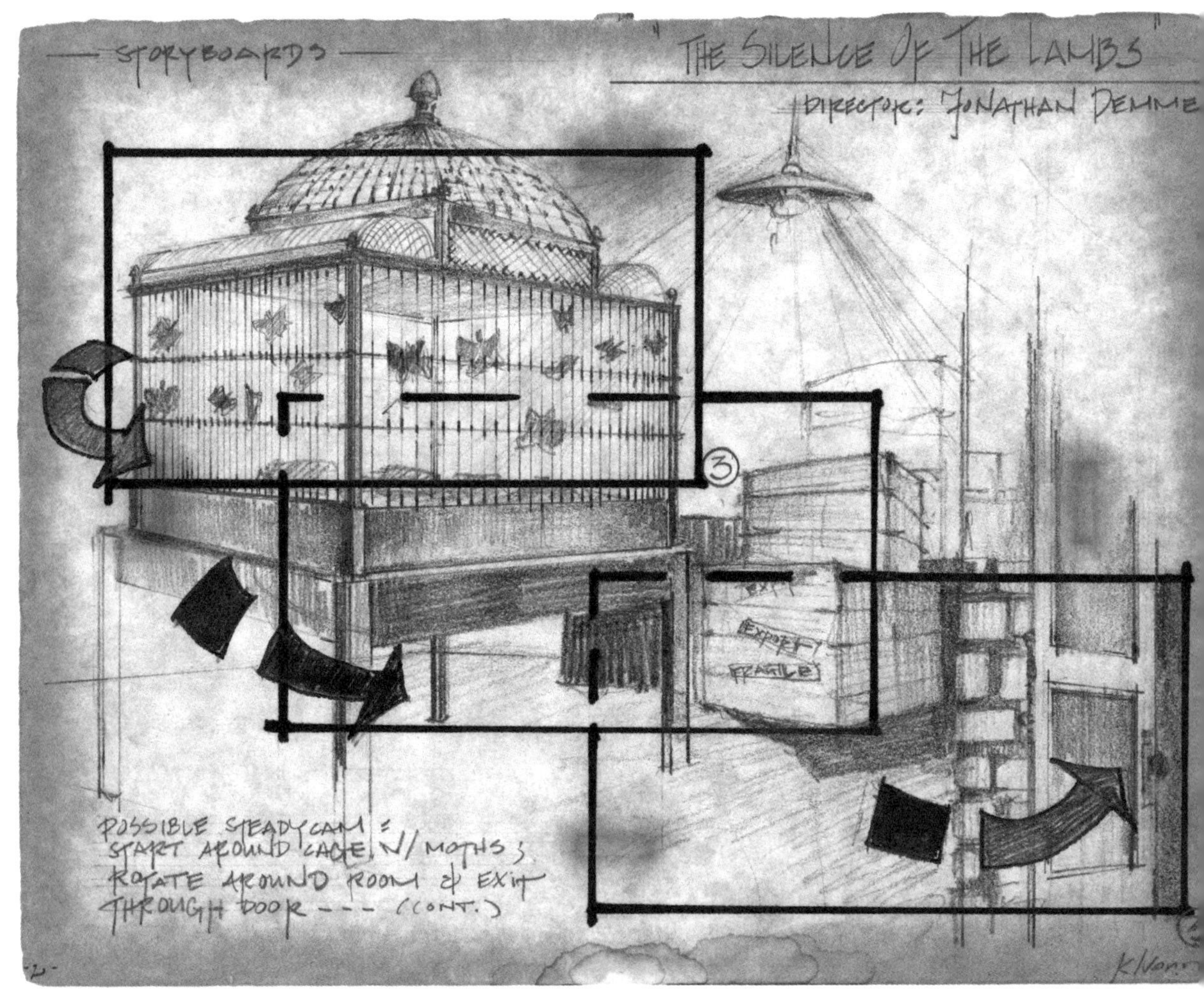

Storyboard for *The Silence of the Lambs* by Kalina Ivanov. Photo courtesy of the Margaret Herrick Library, Academy of Motion Picture Arts and Sciences.

The Silence of the Lambs

(1991)

MICHAEL F. BURKE (ELECTRICIAN, *THE SILENCE OF THE LAMBS*): *The Silence of the Lambs* was another great film. We did that in Pittsburgh and it was cold. Jonathan Demme is just wonderful. He really is. He's another one of those directors who are New York–oriented. I put him with [Paul] Mazursky and Woody Allen. He knows what he wants. He's got it well thought out. And he's very interested in music, culture, and the world. He would talk to you and get to know who you were.

IRA BRENNER (CAMERA OPERATOR): He was really loved by a lot of the crews, because he was a crew guy. I mean, he was someone that was approachable, and he lived around the corner, so I used to run into him all the time.

RUSSELL ENGELS (GAFFER, *THE SILENCE OF THE LAMBS*): One time I was walking down the street in New York and waiting to cross the street, and his car pulls up, screeching the brakes. "Hi, how are you doing?"

I said, "Holy Christ, it's Jonathan Demme!" All these years later. He is a very nice guy. Of course he knew exactly what he wanted to do, too. He was well prepared.

RAY MENDEZ (INSECT-WRANGLER, *THE SILENCE OF THE LAMBS*): People like Jonathan Demme were really ensemble directors, so their crews were their crews. When I did *Silence of the Lambs*, they said, "Well, tonight you're coming to dinner, we're going to do this, that, and the other thing." I forget what they did to me, but there was some activity where you are now part of the family. I mean, it was that formal.

MICHAEL F. BURKE: Rusty and Kenny and I decided not to stay in their housing, and we took money for a hotel. We rented the penthouse suite of the hotel, which was unoccupied. It was eighteen hundred dollars a month for this three-bedroom suite, and I think we were getting each twelve hundred dollars a week in per-diem. We had the penthouse. We had maid service. Rusty, Kenny, and I were all compatible, so we could live together with no problems. We had a good time.

RUSSELL ENGELS: Great picture. We were out in Pittsburgh for a length of time. That's where Mike wanted to get on the shelf with all the mannequins in the garage for one of his Christmas cards.[63] He wanted to get up there nude with all the dummies that were up on the shelf in the garage.

MICHAEL F. BURKE: The first time we see Anthony Hopkins is the scene when Jodie is walking through the cells, and then she sees Anthony in the straitjacket in his cell, and he does his soliloquy where he talks about the "fava beans and some chianti." Jonathan says, "Look. Before we figure out what we're going to do, let's just do a rehearsal and see how it feels."

The other cells were standard bar cells. Because they wanted to have the visibility, for Hopkins they did a plexiglass cell with him because they didn't want the bars to obstruct his performance.

As she walks in, the guy in the first cell is supposed to whip a handful of come and it hits her in the face, and she goes three or four cells and then she stands in front of the cell and Hopkins is facing away from her—then he turns and does his dialogue. I'm watching and he comes in and Jodie walks in and Anthony turns around and does his scene, and it is so fucking scary and good. It was the first time anybody's heard it. And Jonathan turns around and says, "Well, I think that's okay." We were thinking, "Fuck, that was incredible." That was just a moment in the show when we knew, "Wow, we've got an actor here."

63 Mike's yearly Christmas cards are a nude of him taken in some hilariously compromising position taken on set at some point throughout the year. I was around the year he had a colleague take nude snapshots of him being whipped on an S&M bondage set when we were on *Law and Order: Special Victims Unit.*

RAY MENDEZ: Between working on exhibits at the Museum [of Natural History], being an entomologist, and learning animal behavior, you start to think of "I'd like the animal to do X, and in order to get the animal to do X, I have to perform ABC," and you put those together. The other thing is a lot of people think that I arrive with a shopping cart full of crap, and we've just got the effects.

In the best of all situations as the guy who's coming in with the data, I would say, "No, we can't do this, but we can do this." I want to ensure success. I don't want to go on set and screw around for four hours and everybody having a coffee in the back going, "This wacko is in here doing who knows what." I would pre-do everything that was going to be done on set in a lab and that sometimes took months, but I wasn't on set. I had no pressure. There was no camera.

So, for *Silence of the Lambs,* we were looking for the death's head moth.[64] I met with Jonathan and the crew, and we got together, we laid all the shots out, and I said, "Now let me have a week to find out if this is even doable." I knew I could fly the moths, which is what they wanted them to do.

I found out that the one colony of death's head moth, that was in England, had gotten a virus and died out. There was no getting death's head moths. So now I had to try to figure out how to get a moth that was commercially available, the tomato hornworm.

For the death's head moth itself, I took fake nails and I painted the nails to look like the one that has the [Salvador Dalí photograph] on it, so to speak. They look very similar. You really can't tell. This is all part of the testing. I found out and I said, "Oh, [I can just] put it on with Krazy Glue. I just clean the back of the moth, put a costume on, and with a little bit of Krazy Glue and it's on.

64 A large dark hawk moth (*Acherontia atropos*), especially of Mediterranean regions, with markings resembling a human skull on the back of the thorax—an important plot point.

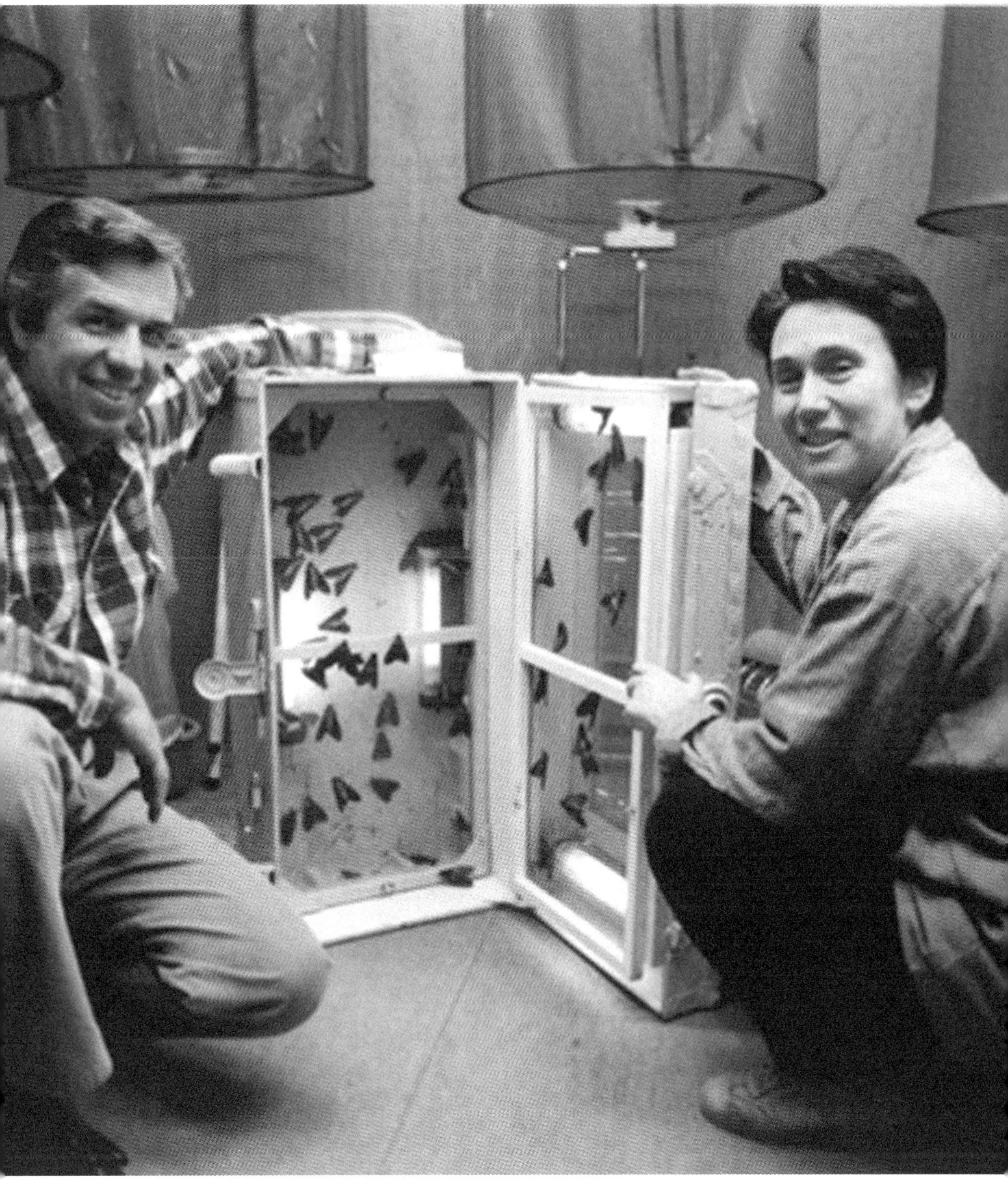

Ray Mendez and Leanore G. Drogin working on *Silence of the Lambs.* Photo courtesy of Ray Mendez.

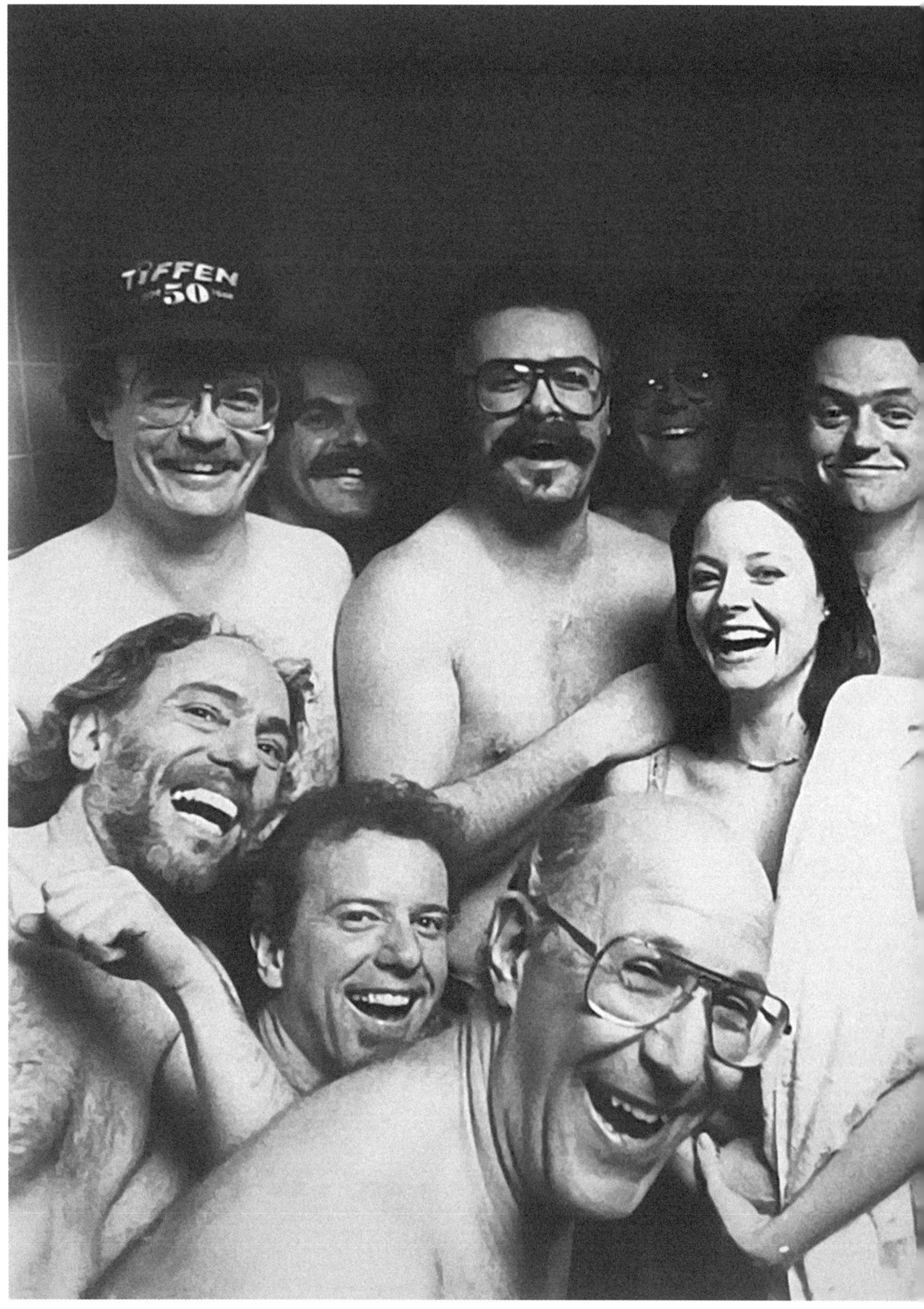
TIFFEN
50

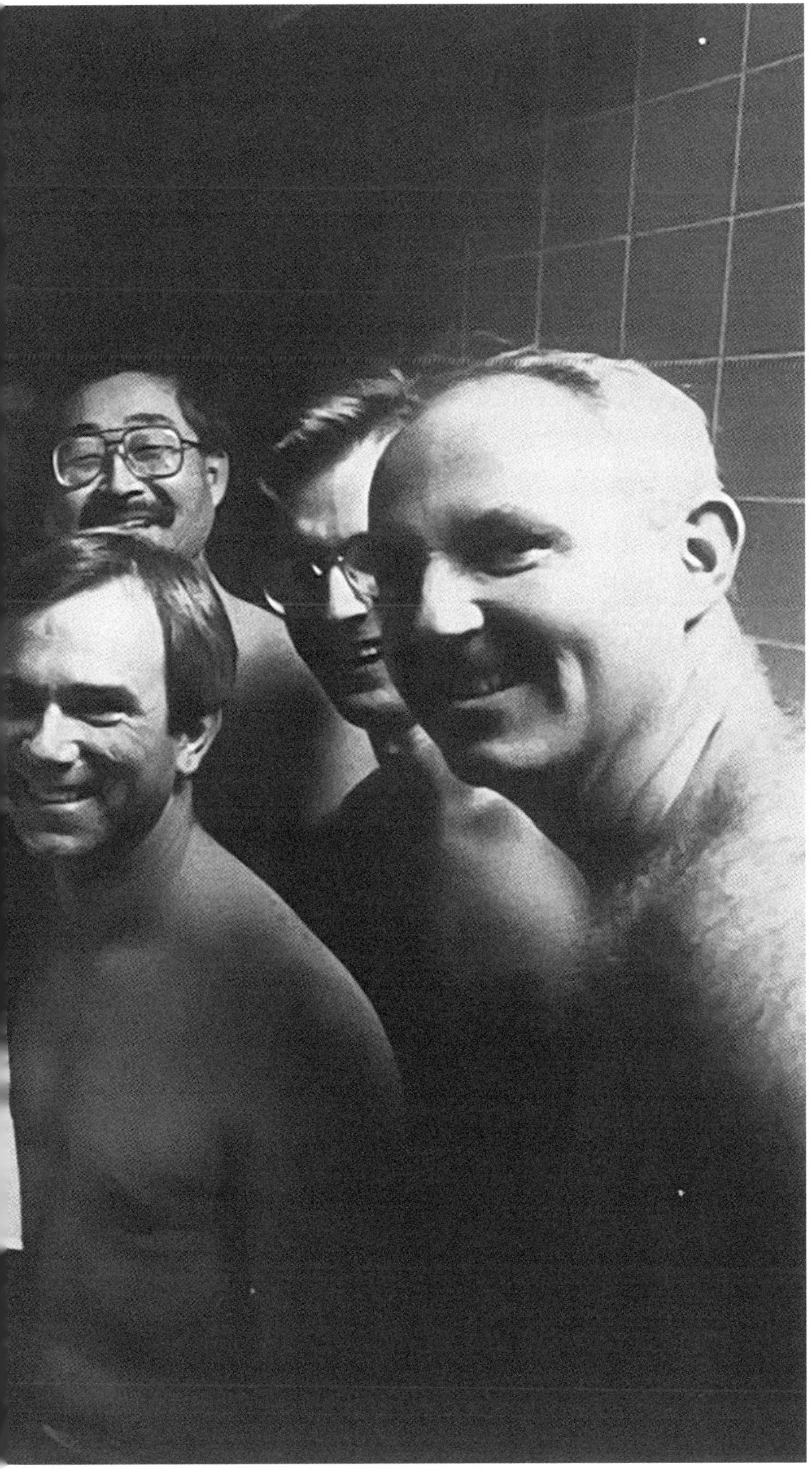

Jodie Foster and crew topless. Photo courtesy of Michael F. Burke.

AUTHOR: Does it have the fake nail on for the rest of its life?

RAY MENDEZ: No, that's on for life. It would be like you're wearing a beret for the rest of your life. It doesn't hurt you one way or the other. But the main thing was that when I glue the fake nail onto the back of the moth with the painting and I got everything done, I gassed them and took off the scales and made good contact and put it on and all that. So the moth now has got a costume on, looking good. I even have a flying harness on the costume so I can fly around. Once I've done that, I got the moth up to get it to fly, and the moth went poof and then froze because the exoskeleton flexes and the Krazy Glue wouldn't let that happen.

I had to call up Dow [Chemical] . I said, "Hey, look, let me talk to your chief scientist there, who works with Krazy Glue." And after telling him I was working on a science-fiction movie—and Stephen King—you mentioned a couple of names and people go, "Oh, cool." So I got to speak to the guy, and I told him my problem. I get one of these wonderful comments that—in life you just have to be ready for serendipity—and the comment was, "You know years ago when we were developing Krazy Glue, we had some Krazy Glue that flexed, but it wasn't any good because it wouldn't work for what we want. We want something that sticks and it's done. You know, we have a lab, and the lab is full of old experiments with the data that went with it, and I think we got a bottle of that stuff."

I asked, "Is there any chance I can either buy it or have you make me some new stuff?" He goes, "Nah, it's garbage. I mean, we just got it in the back in a library of chemical experiments." I say, "Mail it to me."

I put it [the moth costume] on with that rejected Krazy Glue and the butterfly wings moved, and it could fly. It stayed on. It was done.

Moths can only fly at a certain temperature. They won't fly below that temperature. What they do is they sit and they hum, and what they're doing is they're warming themselves up with their muscles to get up to an operating temperature and take off. But if you put them into a warm room, they'll fly. We did it in winter. It was bitter! Pittsburgh gets really cold. So what they had to do for me was they had to take whatever the shooting set was, and they had to put in the salamanders, like, three feet high for the set, whenever I was going to show.

I had a lab that I designed and they built for me on wheels that had heaters in it to keep the moths happy. It's a good-size room and I would hear [makes a thud sound]. Now, I had my daily shoot list, but you never know when they're going to do it. The one thing you learn, as you know, with movies—if you think it's going to happen at eight o'clock you better go have another cup of coffee, because it may not happen until eleven, and so I would sit in the mobile lab with my assistant Lea Drogin and we had a lot to do—we had to clean the animals, we had to put more costumes on, correspondence and all that—and the next thing you know, I would feel the room go plunk and we'd be driven away, and that meant we were going to go to the set and then we'd open up into the set, and the set was heated.

At one point the guys from the unions came over, and they said they wanted to talk to me, and, being my usual self, I was worried that I had done something wrong. They wanted me to represent them because they thought I had a lot of power with the director, because when I tell them to stop, that we were done for today with the moths, they thought that I could represent them, and I said, "Guys, I got no power at all. My power comes from the insects who say, 'We're not going to work.' What are you going to do, kill them? It doesn't matter. You can't get another one."

MICHAEL F. BURKE: The actor who played the killer [Ted Levine], he was a little strange bird. He was getting into the role of that killer. I remember he had a book on piercings and tattooing with photographs of people that would split their penises up the middle and all kinds of shit, different cuttings and stuff. He was just getting into that deviant role of a serial killer, so we were thinking "Oh my God, stay away from this guy." [laughs]

MICHAEL F. BURKE: We had to shoot a scene with Jodie. I don't know if she was nude or in the shower. She said that if she had to take her top off, then the whole crew had to take their tops off, so there were all of us: myself, Loren Levy, John Fundus, Jonathan—it was all guys, but we did one crew picture with everybody with our shirts off with Jodie. She was very cool about everything.

RUSSELL ENGELS: If you wanted to be on set when she had her top off, you had to take your shirt off.

MICHAEL F. BURKE: I didn't really get a sense of how good the movie was going to be because we're doing all this stuff, and when it was edited—we went to the screening of it. A lot of it is close-ups. When you're doing your movie, you do a master [shot], you've got your wide shots, you've got cuts, all your regular standard footage that you shoot, but the editing of it was so integral to the movie and the emotion of it.

Scenes from a Mall

(1991)

STEVE SAKLAD (ASSISTANT ART DIRECTOR, *SCENES FROM A MALL*): I drafted for a long time on *Scenes from a Mall*. That was also Stage E at Kaufman Astoria. We built two stories and sort of an entire quarter quadrant of the Beverly Center, a famous mall in L.A., on stage at the Kaufman Astoria, because the whole Paul Mazursky movie is set in this Los Angeles mall. I think there's maybe a couple of lead-in scenes and then there's the car in the garage and all the scenes in the mall, and that's the entire movie—Woody Allen and Bette Midler.

MICHAEL F. BURKE (ELECTRICIAN, *SCENES FROM A MALL*): Bette Midler and Woody Allen as a married couple—I forget if they were getting divorced or they were fighting.

STEVE SAKLAD: If you track the number-one employer of everybody who worked on *Scenes from A Mall*, it's probably a Woody Allen movie. So everybody in New York was beholden to him. They wanted the next yearly Woody Allen assignment like they'd been getting for all those years. I don't think anything could compete.

TOM PRIESTLEY, JR. (CAMERA OPERATOR): Woody lived between Canal Street and 125th Street. That was his whole life. I mean, for him to go to L.A., it was like an adventure. I mean, later on, after Gordon [Willis] left, he started to go to Europe a little bit more.

STEVE SAKLAD: Obviously, things have changed a lot because he's making movies in Spain and all over Europe for the last twenty years, but in 1990, I think he did give them two or three days of exteriors in Los Angeles at the very end, but the fifty days of shooting by and large was all done on stages at Kaufman Astoria.

STEVEN J. JORDAN (ART DIRECTOR, *SCENES FROM A MALL*): The company that owns the Beverly Center in California has many malls all over the country, and at the time they were all pretty much the same design, so we did a lot of interiors and escalator work at the Stamford Town Center—a huge mall in Connecticut that we worked at.

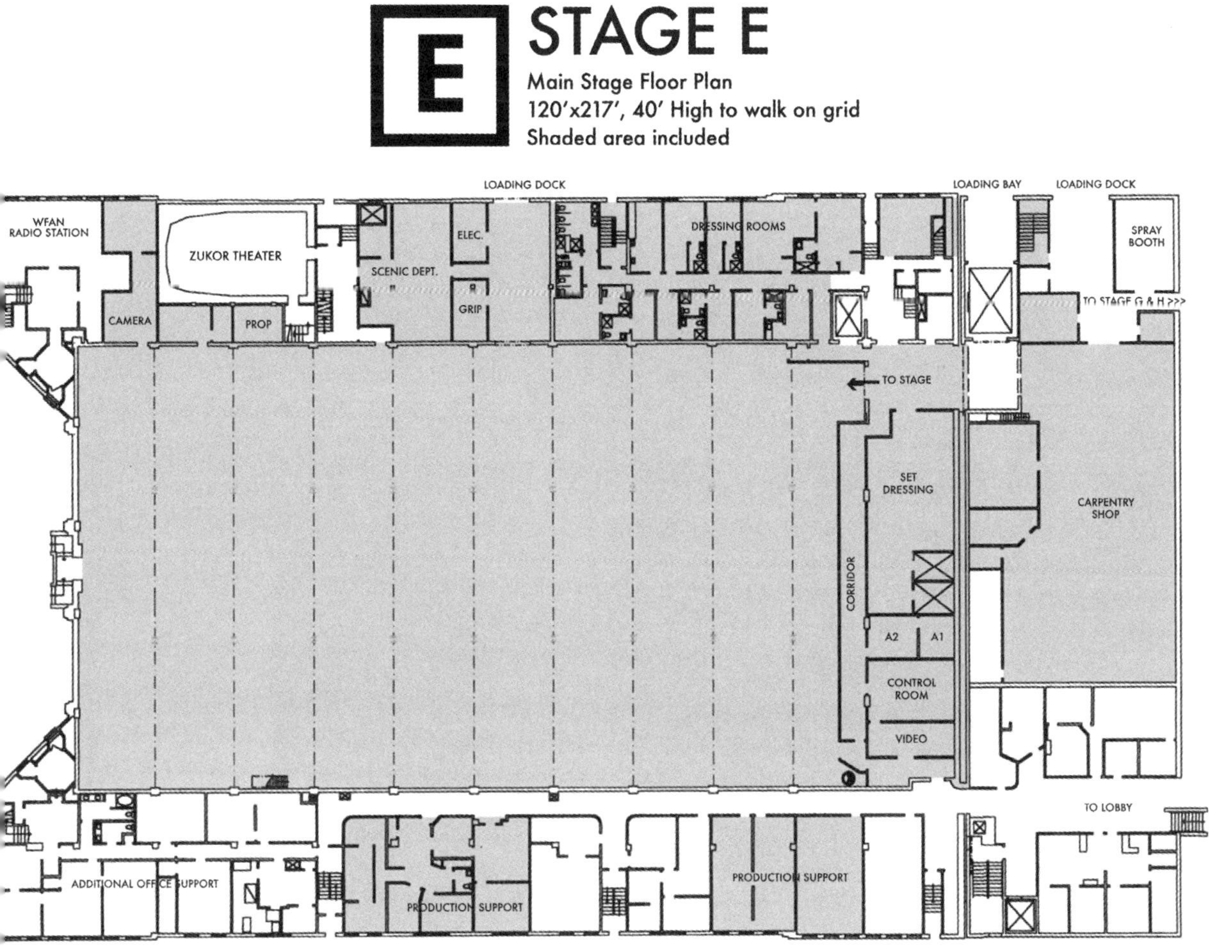

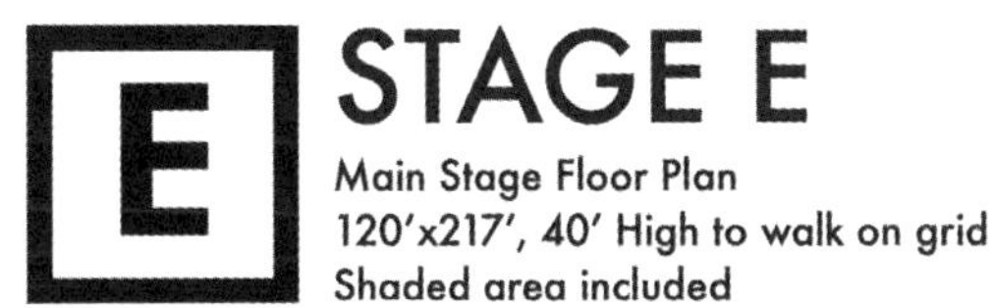

Stage E at Kaufman Astoria Studios, from their brochure.

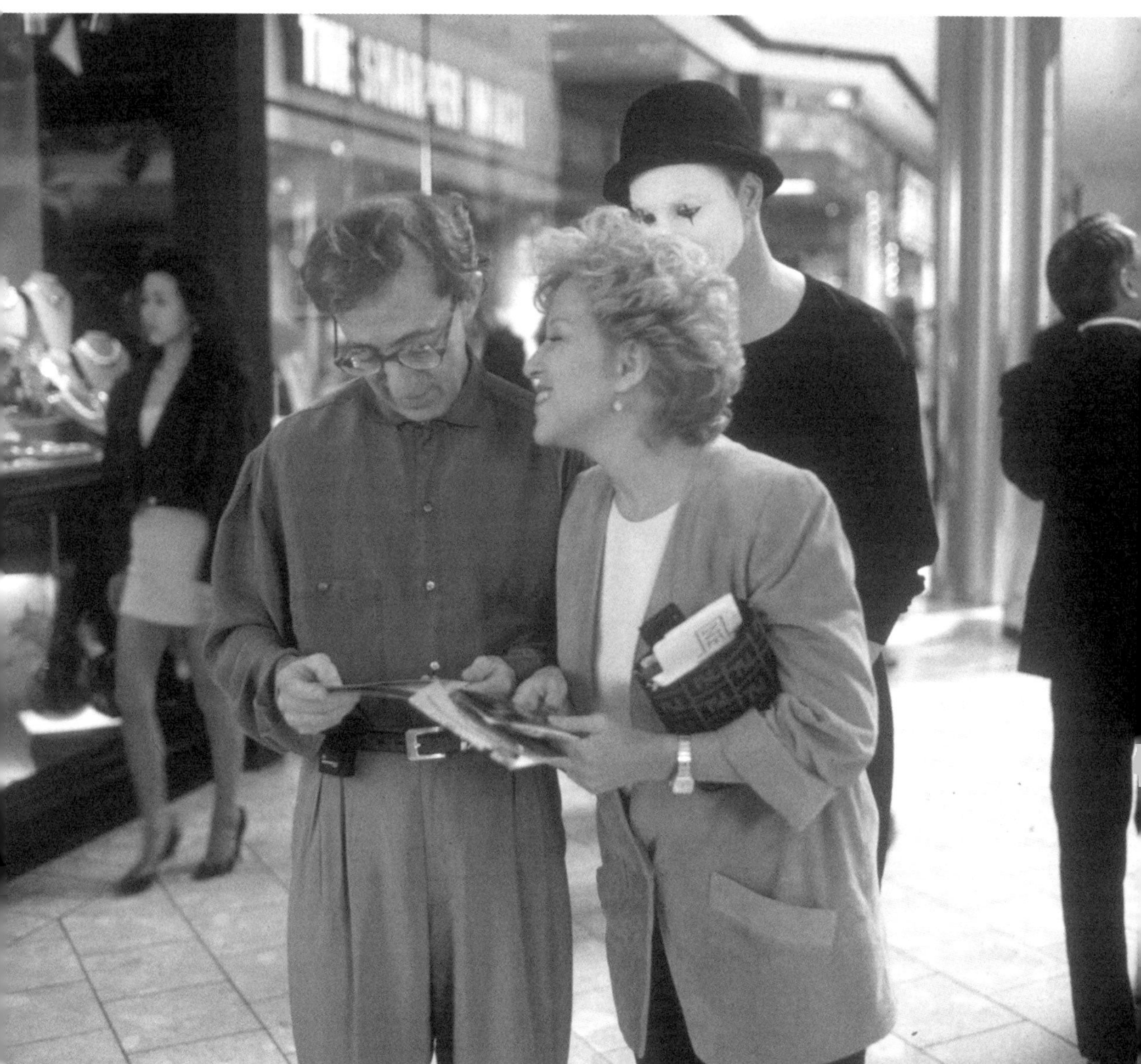

Pic shot exteriors at the Beverly Center and moved to a mall in Stamford, Conn, for two weeks of interior filming. For the remainder, a huge, two-story replica mall was constructed at Kaufman Astoria Studios, NY, and 2,600 New York extras were outfitted in LA garb.[65] —*Variety*, January 1, 1991

Woody Allen and Bette Midler in promotional image for *Scenes from a Mall*. Photo courtesy of the Margaret Herrick Library, Academy of Motion Picture Arts and Sciences.

STEVE SAKLAD: Steve Jordan was the art director on that one and it was just a wrangle, unbelievably complicated because they had to

65 "Scenes from a Mall," *Variety*, January 1, 1991.

get the permission of all the vendors that we were representing.

STEVEN J. JORDAN: [Production designer] Pato [Guzman] and I talked about *Scenes from a Mall* on *Enemies, a Love Story* [1989], and at the time the thinking was we'll probably go somewhere like Houston and get a closed-down mall and just take over, and then months later, when the show actually was green-lit, Woody was involved, and Disney was terrified when that decision was made because all of a sudden they were building probably one of the largest sets at the time that had gone into Kaufman. In terms of money, they were absolutely terrified.

I don't remember the exact number, but it was over a million dollars. And I remember Disney had sent an L.A. construction coordinator just to sort of sit around and keep an eye on everybody. It was kind of a weird situation. That was a big stage. We did *Arthur* [1981], too, on that stage.

STEVE SAKLAD: I remember I spent most of my time drafting the food court, which is fifteen different [restaurants]—California Pizza Kitchen and all the other sort of logoed things that all have to be recreated—and the legalities of it and the procuring of the actual graphics and procuring of the things to stock—all of these restaurants and stuff, all this storage—it was daunting.

STEVEN J. JORDAN: That was an absolutely massive set. And the amount of merchandising that went into it—I know Les Bloom and George [DeTitta], Jr., were the decorators and it was very tough keeping all the merchandise on set. Apparently at one point we had a Coach store on set, and somebody actually saw a Coach bag going through up to the grid [metal structure at the top of the stage to rig lights to]. Like, someone had a fishing rod.

MICHAEL F. BURKE: It was pretty funny because they built this whole mall out. They had all the stores in the mall, and the backs of the stores were all open, so the first weekend everything was stolen out of all the stores. Then they were putting video cameras up for security to make sure stuff wasn't stolen.

TONY GAMIELLO: When they left at night they put the shrink wrap around the clothes so stuff didn't disappear. I hate to say this, but things walk. People have sticky fingers. So you got to secure things as best you can.

Things walk. That's an ugly part of the Business.

Some stuff, they don't care. At the end of the movie, they are even giving stuff away, or selling stuff cheap because it costs money for them to ship it or store it. You want to wait until they finish with things and see what they get rid of, then you say, "All right, I'll take it," but just to take stuff while they're still shooting is to me not right, and it's not professional.

STEVEN J. JORDAN: Dick Ventre was the charge scenic on that, and the task of just laying the floor—the scenics had put up in their shop all these statistics, and apparently the amount of tile that was laid and put down was larger than the outfield at Shea Stadium.

Now mind you, what scenics had to do with those tiles was essentially with a magic marker, putting grout lines on every tile, because the mall that we were matching, we had to do a very faithful recreation.

STEVE SAKLAD: I probably didn't see the Beverly Center until years later. When the set was done, it was dazzling if you knew the work that went into it and completely unremarkable if you watched the movie, because it looked exactly like it.

Malcolm X

(1992)

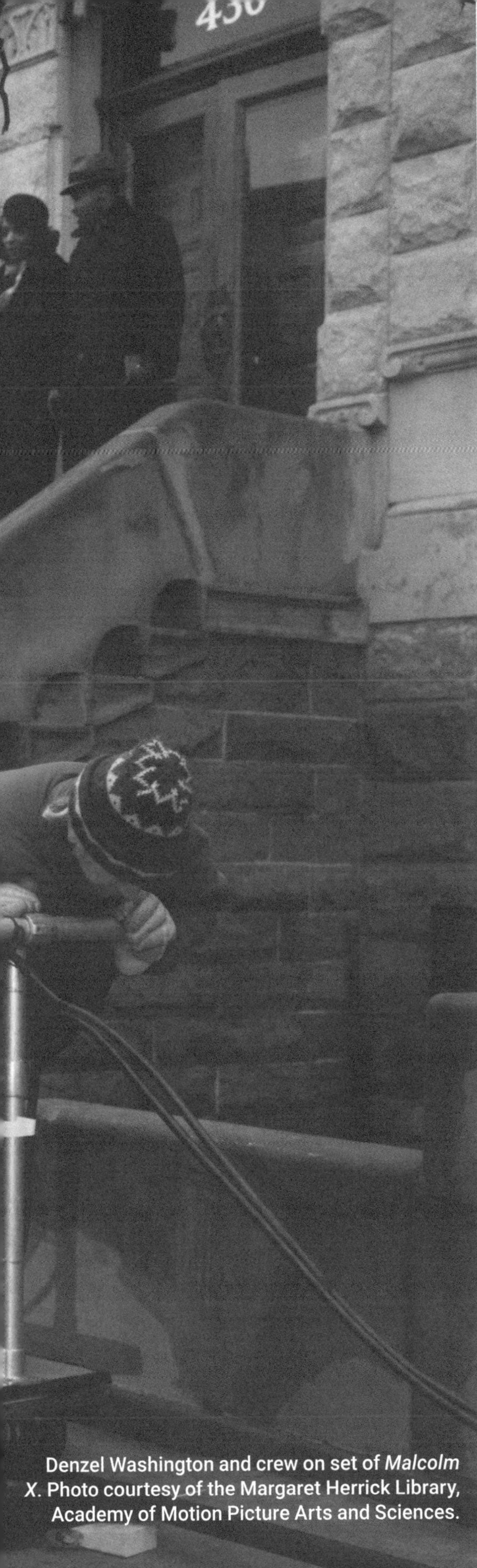
Denzel Washington and crew on set of *Malcolm X*. Photo courtesy of the Margaret Herrick Library, Academy of Motion Picture Arts and Sciences.

VAN HAYDEN (ASSISTANT DIRECTOR, *MALCOLM X*): I remember everything. I remember, before we even started filming the movie, we went up to Harlem and Spike passed out these posters to all these young kids because they wanted to get some buzz going about the pre-production period. And we were up on Lenox Avenue and we must have had three to four hundred kids with these posters. And they're all chanting towards the lens, "I am Malcolm X, I am Malcolm X, I am Malcolm X."

I think it's his most ambitious film. And the politics behind it—I don't think he's ever had an experience where he had to deal with the politics of making a movie that were as thick as that. Spike wasn't the initial director on that film. Originally, Norman Jewison was planning to direct the film and basically Spike obtained the okay to direct the film.

"I had problems with a white director directing this film," Lee said. "Unless you are black, you do not know what it means to be a black person in this country." He said that many of Malcolm X's friends and former associates would not have cooperated with white filmmakers on the project. "These people are very leery of opening up to white directors. . . . Most black people are suspicious of white people and their motives. That's just reality."

Lee recalled that at the time he was fighting to direct the film, "Warner Bros. was getting 100 letters a day protesting Norman Jewison directing the film." He said Jewison accused him of mounting the letter writing campaign although "I had nothing to do with it."

Lee said he finally met Jewison and afterward the noted director "was happy I got to do the film."[66]

—Spike Lee, *Los Angeles Times*, 1992

66 "Spike Lee Speaks Out on 'Malcolm X': Movies," *Los Angeles Times*, February 26, 1992.

VAN HAYDEN: Spike never disputed whether Norman Jewison could make a quality film. He just felt that the film that he would make would be a little more intuitive or definitely more of an African American perspective.

JEFF GLAVE (CHARGE SCENIC ARTIST, *MALCOLM X*): It was the greatest, from our point of view, because at the time we had been starved. California movie producers took work out of New York to bust up the unions and fuck us up, and it was very successful. There was a whole year with virtually no film work. And I was lucky because I did commercials, but other people—I mean, people were losing their houses. It was not good. It was a really tough time for people, and then Spike delivered *Malcolm X*.

DON NACE (SCENIC ARTIST, *MALCOLM X*): I was very lucky that I was hired by Jeff Glave, because the only movie that was done during that period was *Malcolm X,* because the contract had been signed and everything was all ready to go before Hollywood decided to pull a boycott.

JEFF GLAVE: It was 1990, and that was the days of the answering machine, and I needed a billion scenics, and I had everybody in the union calling up my answering machine. I would run out of my little tapes. They're ninety-minute tapes, and I'd run out because everybody was starving and dying for work.

VAN HAYDEN: It was amazing to work on that film because it was the first period film that I'd worked on, and just having to deal with—okay, if we look out a window, everything that we see outside of that window on the street has to be period-accurate. The production designer Wynn Thomas, the casting director Robbi Reed, and Ruth Carter, who had done all the costumes for Spike at that point since *School Daze* [1988]—all of the department had really made a tremendous effort to make sure that it was accurate.

The important thing to us was trying to recreate a little bit of the reality—streetlights, signage, trash cans, streetcars were all different then. We're just trying to recreate the time period.[67]

—Wynn Thomas, production designer

VAN HAYDEN: We shot [at] this armory up in—I guess it was in Upper Manhattan or the Bronx. It was this huge armory, and that's where Wynn Thomas built the big rally stage and they had four thousand extras. That was a lot.

BARBARA HAUSE (EXTRAS WARDROBE SUPERVISOR, *MALCOLM X*): We had an armory full of extras. I tell you, I would stand up on a table and scream for quiet and start giving instructions. I'd also let everyone know how long they were waiting and what's happening on set and what I knew, because of this massive group of backgrounds, who were practically just getting lunch for being there, once the union group [SAG-AFTRA] was hired.

VAN HAYDEN: You had the women of the Nation [of Islam] that had to be dressed in these very specific gowns with the hijabs.

To process four thousand extras—it was amazing. When you do that kind of thing and you have to hire the PAs [production assistants] and you have to organize that part of the staff, it was a big job. But, once you did, you gained incredible confidence and, "Okay, bring it on. What else you got for me?"

BARBARA HAUSE: We had the School of the Brotherhood—a perfect example of reusing clothes. We did tons of pre-fitting, but when people didn't show up you had a costume completely ready for them, so, when newbies came up, you had to check the measurements of the costumes that were dead that day and

67 From the documentary *By Any Means Necessary: The Making of Malcolm X* (2005).

get it to the other person. That means that that person comes again the next time, their clothes are off into another world. It was never consistent.

VAN HAYDEN: They all had to go through the hair and makeup process—at least have their hair checked. Maybe if their hair wasn't done, they had thirty barbers lined up to give haircuts. If they didn't get a haircut, maybe they could wear a cap and be deep in the background somewhere. But everyone on camera had to go through that process, and that process started, like, four in the morning the day that we shot that sequence, and we didn't get a single shot off until, I think, right before noon.

BARBARA HAUSE: What you just basically had to do was make everyone feel like they were a part of the project and just really make it worth their while that they gave this time to this project and how important it was to tell the story.

I think that the first step in this is basically costume design. But the next step is rental—if there's nothing that's going to happen to the clothes. The next step will be building it or buying it. If it's a period film, it's usually building it. There are lots of vintage stores all over the United States that you call and they'll memo clothes out to you, and for a certain percentage of money if you rent them. But if you send them back within a week, after you look through them, they will do that no problem for you.

For years after, I can't tell you how many years after that I get stopped on the street, "Oh, you're the supervisor on *Malcolm X*! Remember we were in this." I thought, "These people think I'm going to remember them? It's sweet they remember me."

VAN HAYDEN: That film hired a lot of people—not just extras, but a lot of craftsmen and technicians, and then that's just in the production side of it.

JEFF GLAVE: At the time, I think we had seventy-seven scenic [artists]. That was a big job. We had five separate shops, so there were four different foremen each running a shop in Brooklyn [and] three in Harlem. Jesus, it was killer. And we did really great work, and at the time we had spent a quarter of a million bucks on paint. So it was a pretty substantial film, and we absolutely had a ball.

The movies I had done up until then—I mean, *Do the Right Thing* had twelve scenic [artists] on it. We were full up with twelve people. That was a pretty standard-sized job. We did lots of signs there. We did whole building façades, that kind of thing. But we made it work with about twelve people. Then we had—I can't think of another one that was at that scale. I know there were other people that were charging that they did jobs that you'd have twenty, twenty-five people, I guess. But, yeah, it was pretty rare.

STEVEN KIRSHOFF (SPECIAL-EFFECTS SUPERVISOR, *MALCOLM X*): We had to do this propane-can thing from inside the room. There was no other way for me to fire it. I go to grab my Scott-Pak[68] and my fireproof hood and everything and the freaking camera guys had it. I say, "Wait a minute, that's my stuff!"

He goes, "Well, where's ours?"

I go, "Well, you get your own."

The bottom line is, I said F it and I just did it anyway. It was so hot in there for about three seconds, then I come running out of the room. My hair was smoking. I was fine—it wasn't like I got hurt—but it was just so funny. Spike Lee's cracking up, man.

JEFF GLAVE: You'd have a team on location. You'd have the sign-writers that were in the shop. That was our main shop, and I kept track of all the sign people, but we had people

68 The Scott Air-Pak SCBA is an open-circuit, self-contained breathing apparatus designed to meet the National Fire Protection Association Standard 1981. All components, excluding the air cylinder, were designed and manufactured by Scott Safety.

within the sign shop like Greg Sullivan, who was a fine sign-painter, fine organizer. He would keep things going for you. It was relying on people.

I think we had seventeen full time sign-writers, including, like, five of the real old-guard guys that still could just do show cards. They were from the real old-school sign-writing school, and, oh my God, I was so honored to have these guys on my crew. It was astonishing. They were so thrilled to be getting work. They were incredible.

It was the beginning of when computers were coming into play. We were doing a big couple of big Coca-Cola billboards and stuff, and it was hilarious because we had a guy calling up—I think he was a grip—but he was heavy into computers. He goes, "You guys, I could make you a big drawing of this. I could do it. It's full-size and it would"—blah, blah, blah, blah, blah—"It would only take this long to do it." He's describing making a drawing that we would then have to pounce [trace and paint]. And I listened to him, and his enthusiasm was wonderful, but I finally had to say, "I got to ask you, how long do you think it would take us to have this drawn?"

And he goes, "I don't know—a week." He's thinking he's going to save us time.

I said, "No, we're actually going to draw this in about six hours."

And he was like, "You're kidding." It's the other crew's understanding of how we work and what we were doing. But that was such a funny thing. We would have it drawn before he got the information put into his computer at the time.

We did fifteen hundred painted signs. We had to come up with a coding system to make a system for tracking signs. We printed up forms, and every step had to be initialed by somebody who completed the step. So, for instance, the sign would have a column and location would be the first part of the code, then it would be building number and then sign number at that building. So, it would say, like, "Third Avenue," and then it would say, "119 Third Avenue."

I mean, it could be fifty signs in a building, and the second-floor signs and above could all be vinyl letters—we didn't care because that's way up in the air—but everything below that had to be handmade. If you got the sign in the shop, the first thing that people had to initial was that it was filled, prepped, and primed. Then it would go to the next person and the background colors would be put in. Then somebody would be making a pounce for the lettering. Then somebody would put the lettering on. Then we had to age it. And there might even have been another column, but everybody had to initial each sign all the way through so we could track them all—because fifteen hundred hand painted signs from seventy-foot billboards to little show cards in a restaurant or a dry cleaner or a record shop . . .

VAN HAYDEN: I give Spike tremendous credit for changing the face—the access, the inclusion of folks other than white filmmakers in the industry, because he really campaigned and stuck his neck out for it. There's a legendary story—Tom O'Donnell, who was head of the New York Teamsters for twenty years, and in all that period, there'd never been an African American Teamster captain or a coordinator, and Spike said, "Look, I need a Black captain on this show," to Tom O'Donnell.

Spike Lee's busy getting "Jungle Fever" done for Cannes and doing preproduction on his Malcolm X biopic. He's also been busy clashing with Teamsters Local 817, which provides union drivers for all film, tv and theater projects in New York. Local 817 prexy Thomas O'Donnell, who says Spike called him "the biggest racist in the world" on a recent segment of "Donahue," is hopping mad. "I'm not a racist," said O'Donnell. "He's the racist." Lee said his TV comment was that 817 used "racist hiring practices. Two black people have gotten their book since 1960. I refuse to work with a union that has those kinds of racist hiring policies. I should be shot if I shoot 'Malcolm X' with a lily-white crew."[69]

—*Variety*, May 6, 1991

VAN HAYDEN: Spike's leverage was, "Look, we got here—here are fifteen thousand man-days. Do you guys want these days or not?" I wasn't involved anywhere—I wasn't even close to any of the negotiations—but from what I heard they were very, very nose-to-nose, toes-to-toes, and Spike didn't back down. That film was the first film in New York City history that had an African American Teamster coordinator and an African American Teamster captain—Ted Brown and Kenny Gaskin. It really showed that, if anyone had any doubts or any question about whether an African American captain and Teamster coordinator could pull that level of a project together in New York—it debunked all the stuff that had come before, because the guys did a great job.

MAGGIE RYAN (SCENIC ARTIST): Back in the 1950s, the unions, especially the Teamsters union, they have a very—I don't know if it was Mafia—but you just didn't mess with them, and if you were in the movie business they could stop the delivery of scenery. They could do all sorts of other things to the production office, like cause big stoppages. So they'd rather do what the unions wanted than risk any kind of disruption because the unions had a rough reputation.

BARBARA HAUSE: I couldn't have done *X* without the Teamsters. We sometimes had three trucks going in three different directions to set up. They really helped me through that and helped us load and offload. I mean, from the second I got into New York there was the rep that Teamsters had way back then, and I never found that. I never saw that.

VAN HAYDEN: I don't know if it cost Spike anything, but when you go to bat against very powerful industry executives who have had things a certain way for a long time and you start stepping on toes and you start insisting on some fairness and some balance and some diversity, they don't like that, because they haven't had to deal with that in the past, and their fears were, "Well, we've got our guys. They've done a great job. Why would you not want to have the best of the best? And that's what we're offering you.

They didn't look at it like, "Hey, is this a fair system? Is this a system where it's an even playing field for everyone to have an opportunity to work in those capacities and have those jobs?" Or it was just, "Hey, we're the best, take it or leave it, and we're not willing to really change."

I think for those old down-the-line unions and guilds—I think they were really intimidated, and they thought, "Who does this guy think he is?" and that, in the long run, I think probably hurt Spike in many cases because he kind of got branded this pushy, uppity guy who's trying to tell us how to run our business, and that creates a stigma under itself.

But, from my perspective, had Spike not done that, I wouldn't be on this conversation with you on this phone call tonight, because I would not have had the opportunity to go to Chicago, work as the first AD [assistant director] on these Nike commercials—a year or two later we did a national series of commercials for Levi's Button Your Fly campaign.

BARBARA HAUSE: I've just never found a bad New York Teamster in my life, and *Malcolm X* proved that again. These guys really covered me, helped me, advised me.

The *X* holding areas were three stories up. And we had twenty-five racks, thirty-eight

69 "Mo Union Blues," *Variety,* May 6, 1991.

million boxes. I mean, how do you get the shit up there with no elevator? It was suggested to me by locations that I hire a carting crew, which you're kind of used to being available whenever you need them, and there's a kind of a leader of that group, and if you at that time page him he'll grab up everybody, and I thought, "What a great idea," so I went to production and I asked, "Can I get a rack-moving crew?" I order a whole other crew that moves these fucking racks up the flights of stairs and in. "I also will need wardrobe people to be there, but not as many, and I just really don't think that this kind of heavy weight-fucking-lifting is a wardrobe person's forte." They approved it. And, of course, I got a call from the union on it.

When the union called me, I said, "You guys should look up how many people I've hired—how many day players, how many days I've given the union of work on this job—and then tell me that I'm doing the wrong thing here, and then if you still think I'm doing the wrong thing, then get me a group of [Local] 764 people that are willing to lift these racks, because these guys don't do it seven costumes at a time up three sets of stairs—they pick up the fucking racks and they go upstairs with them. Supply me with the crew, and I'll make sure that production hires them."

STEVEN KIRSHOFF: They had, like, two fire scenes—one where they burn down his house in Missouri. There were all these Klan guys outside doing all the action. Almost all of them were Black. I mean it was the New York stunt guys, and they put all the Black guys in with a few white guys, but it was pretty funny when they were taking off their hoods between scenes.

JEFF GLAVE: We were trying to shoot in some of the original ballrooms then, too. Renaissance Ballroom was one that we tried to shoot in, and it was impossible. They were going to shoot in the Audubon.[70] Somebody called the safety people about that one because of asbestos. We were in some pretty heinous places on all those jobs.

STEVEN KIRSHOFF: The assassination at the end, that was one of my favorite scenes. I built the podium out of balsa wood with the carpenter Martin Bernstein. We rigged it with charges, and, you know, the guys come up, shoot it, and then they shoot him, then he falls over. He's laying on the ground and they're shooting at him, and we had all the floorboards rigged with charges.

We didn't go overboard with blood. We just tried to make it kind of realistic. You'd have kind of free rein. Spike would just let us do what was good, pretty much.

BARBARA HAUSE: We went into a prison with *X*, and whenever you go into a prison you have to tell production who you're hiring for those days in the prison and their Social Security numbers and their addresses weeks ahead, and they get vetted, and they're allowed in, and once we're underway, or once the cutoff time happens, you can't hire anybody else. I'm in prison, with a great, big crew, and everybody is off either on set or doing this or doing that. Then Spike wanted seven more prison guards. We're hiring real people from the prisons, by the way. We hired real prisoners that were on good behavior. We hired real guards that were off work that day. Casting had these people standing by and I didn't have anyone to dress them.

But I had a male PA. I said to him, "Go in there and help these guys. You know the pieces. Help them in any way. Hang up their own clothes. Help them organize so they can get out of here quick."

It's uncomfortable for these guys to do this anyway. Somebody has to be in there with them, and it can't be a female, can't be me.

70 The actual ballroom where Malcolm X was assassinated.

One of my crew members called the union [Local 764]. They called me that day—I said, "I didn't have a choice about this. This is the best thing to do. I wasn't going to go in there with three people and get them naked in front of me." I said, "If you want to follow through on this, it's going to take time. It's going to take more of my time. So I'm going to quit the job. I'm going to quit the job in one hour. I'm going to call Preston [the production manager] and quit because of this. So call me back within an hour and tell me this is not happening, or find another supervisor for the job. Because I've had enough. I'm incredibly busy. I'm incredibly stressed. It's a nutcase job, and I'm outta here." They called me in, like, ten minutes and said, "Okay."

I lined them all up that night, before we got on the bus to be escorted out of the prison. I told them what happened. I told them my reaction, and I said, "If anyone else wants to challenge me, please, whoever did this please don't accept another day's work from me, because I can't take another challenge."

Like, I can't take people not getting what we're trying to do here. Of course, people came up to me and told me who called the union. I never hired that guy again.

JEFF GLAVE: [Spike Lee] was one of the best people to work for because he always—especially at this time—if you painted something that he spent money on to get in his film, you're going to see it. If it was in a shot, if it was painted by us for a location, he was going to make sure his camera caught that shit. *Malcolm X* is the first time where he ever had to cut things. He cut whole scenes that we had worked on. He left a lot of stuff on the cutting-room floor when he had to cut forty-five minutes out of his version of the movie.

STEVEN KIRSHOFF: When I did *BlacKKKlansmen* [2018] I figured this was the last thing I do, because I was about to retire. Spike said, "I just want to tell you guys I've been with this guy for thirty-five years." Spike Lee is a loyal guy. He hires the same people over and over again, even actors.

VAN HAYDEN: Those jobs not only kept me going, but they also helped me develop my craft. They helped me develop my skillset as a first AD that I count on today.

BARBARA HAUSE: When I finished that job, I decided that if I had done this job I can do anything. Every job scares me, and every job is a challenge, up till last year when I retired. Every single job. People look at my résumé—"Oh, you have this experience," and I say, "No, every job is different. Every job has been some new experience. I don't have experience on your particular job, because each one challenges me, and I'm up for the challenge, and each job that I did allows me to be more prepared."

VAN HAYDEN: Last March, we were all in Los Angeles for the Directors Guild of America annual awards, and it was so great to see Spike win the Lifetime Achievement Award and to have Ernest Dickerson, a fellow DGA director member, introduce him for the award, to see Spike's family there with him, and it was just this incredible overdue homecoming, really. And we had probably twenty-five, maybe thirty African American DGA members. We all took a big picture together, everyone from Mario Van Peebles to Ernest Dickerson to Spike. I was there. A bunch of other people were there and many of us had come up under Spike—him championing us to find work and to excel. It was just a beautiful event.

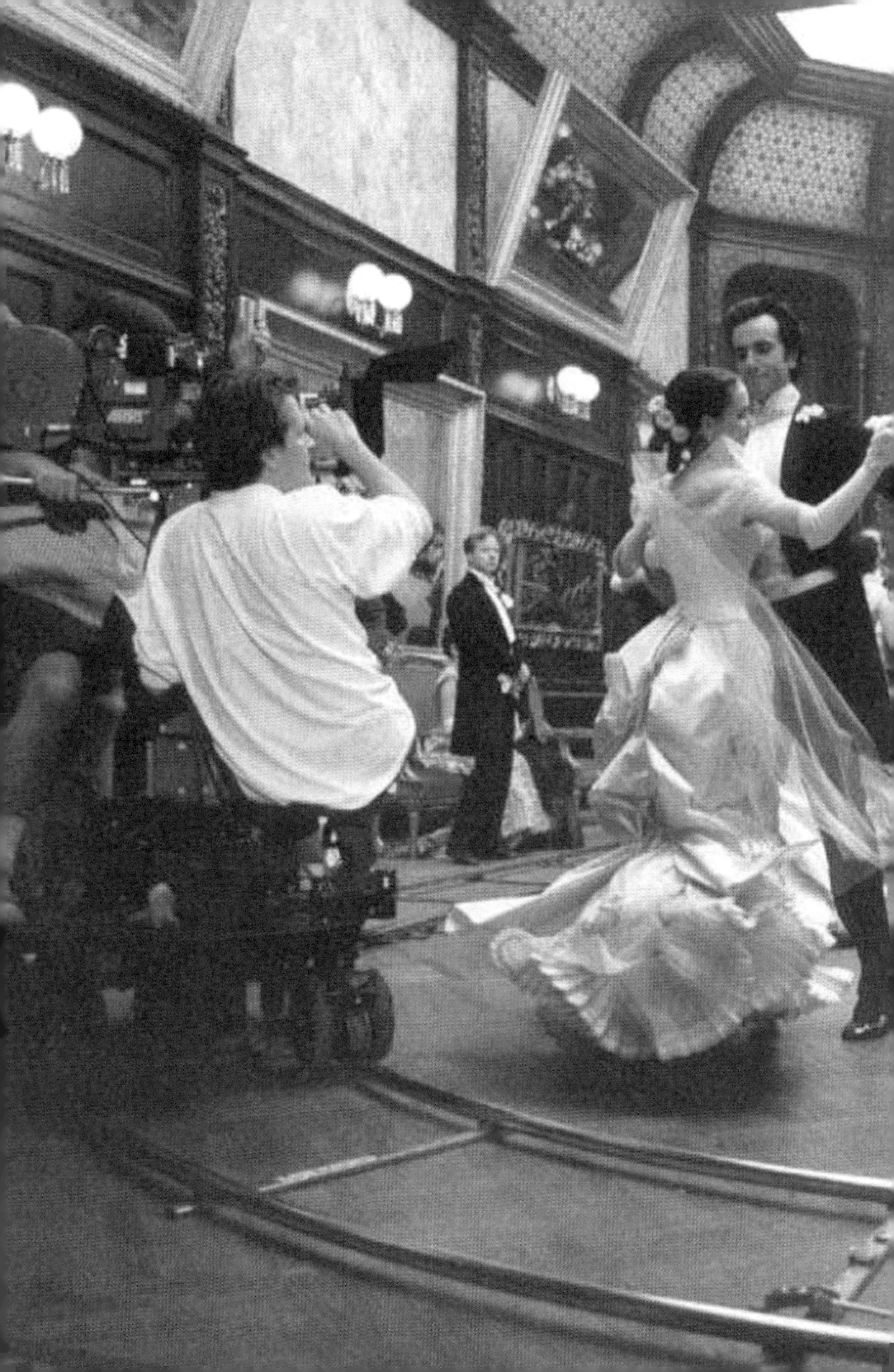

Age of Innocence

(1993)

JOHN MAZZONI: I was off for a little while. I took a little break, and Vinnie G. says to me, [Southern accent], "Come up to Troy [New York] and hang out with me. Give me seven days of your time." That's how he talks. He sounded like he was from the South, but he was from the South Bronx. So I take a ride to Troy. I go all the way up there and hang out, and we're going to build Times Square in 1879, which was on 23rd Street. Time Square wasn't on 42nd Street yet.

What's on the split of 23rd Street? The Flatiron Building. That's what made Time Square Times Square, but they're not allowed to shoot there. But in Troy, New York, [there's] a six-story Flatiron Building.

My job was to go to 23rd Street and make a plate. Plates are where you film the building. We made a plate of that building and we took it to Troy, and we Photostatted it in. We just matted it in. That's easy to do. You take your camera—you film the building. After you get parts of the building, you take another picture of the same-sized building, and they just make it.[71] Now we've got to change everything in Troy to 1879. We got to reface every building. We got to put gas lights in. We order five thousand cobblestones. We build all the things, me and Vinnie, and on the seventh day he goes, "Johnny-Boy, my best boy. You're the new best boy."

So I stayed with him not just seven days but seven weeks in Troy.

Everything's beautiful. We break our ass. You can't believe how hard we worked, and it was freezing, freezing, freezing! Next to the Troy Flatiron Building was a little club with all

71 The process of making a composite. In this case it's to add elements of the real Flatiron Building to the miniature one in Troy that looks . . . like the Flatiron.

Making Age of Innocence, 1992. Photo by Phillip Caruso. From the production files photograph collection and John Robert Lloyd production design material and courtesy of the Margaret Herrick Library, Academy of Motion Picture Arts and Sciences.

the Italians. They were real mobsters. I went in there. I talked to a Mr. Nero: "Hey, where are you from? Brooklyn?"

He says, "I know guys from Brooklyn. What's your name?"

"Johnny-Boy."

He shakes my hand. He's a big gangster. I introduced myself to all the gangsters there. "Listen, we are shooting the thing. I'm with my friend, Vinnie Guarriello."

"Anything you need." They gave us Italian bread. They were excellent to us. I became good friends with the mobster of Troy, Mr. Nero.

In the front of the Flatiron Building, where this thing was, was a big wooden cigar-store Indian—beautiful Indian, gorgeous. Martin Scorsese loved it. It was always chained up. I had a cup of coffee every morning with Mr. Nero and his gang. "Johnny-Boy, Bensonhurst Boy," he called me. He goes, "Hey, listen. Could you do me a little favor?"

And I said, "What is it, Mr. Nero?

He said, [gangster voice] "The wooden Indian. I like that."

"You like that?"

He said, "I don't like that. I love that. You think maybe I could purchase that?"

So, I go over to [leadman] David Weinman: "Johnny, we rented that thing. We can't sell it."

I said, "Really? The guys really want it. And they've really taken care of us here. Nothing has happened. They've been protecting us for the last three weeks."

He goes, "I can't."

He was busy. I went over to Mr. Nero. He said, "Oh, you can't do that for me? That's a shame. That's a shame, Johnny-Boy, but no problem." And he grabbed my hand like that, and he squeezed my hand and he looked at me.

The next day, the chains are gone and the Indian is gone. Martin Scorsese is coming in four hours to shoot. Production is panicking. "Johnny-Boy, you got to go over to the Italians and tell them. Maybe they know where the thing is. Maybe they know where the thing is. Please, oh my God. He's going to kill me. We're going to shoot. This is it." I am going to meet Mr. Nero.

He says, "Johnny-Boy, what happened? Oh, that's a shame. You know, it's dangerous around here. Nobody was here last night, then maybe something happened," he said, "but maybe I could find it for you. Maybe I could find it."

I said, "You've got to find it in four hours. Martin Scorsese's coming here."

"I said to my guys that maybe they'll find the thing. We find it and we will make a deal, no?"

I say, "Do whatever you can." I tell David. . . . We're all sitting there—he's coming—and two hours go by. All of a sudden, a big, giant Cadillac pulls up and this Indian is sticking out of the back window on its side. It's sticking out this way with the head.

And so he pulls up and he goes, "We found it, no problem. Tell your friend *Mr. Weinstein* we found it and maybe, just maybe, he takes care of me and I could have it." And sure enough, that's how we got it. Martin Scorsese came just in time, and we filmed that shot with the Indian in the film. So they all came over to me like I was a big gangster now because all I was doing was having coffee with the guy and he knew my family.

JOE BURNS: We learned in prep that as we were training the extras in etiquette, that the class of person that Daniel Lewis was

Making Age of Innocence, 1992. Photo by Phillip Caruso. From the production files photograph collection and John Robert Lloyd production design material and courtesy of the Margaret Herrick Library, Academy of Motion Picture Arts and Sciences.

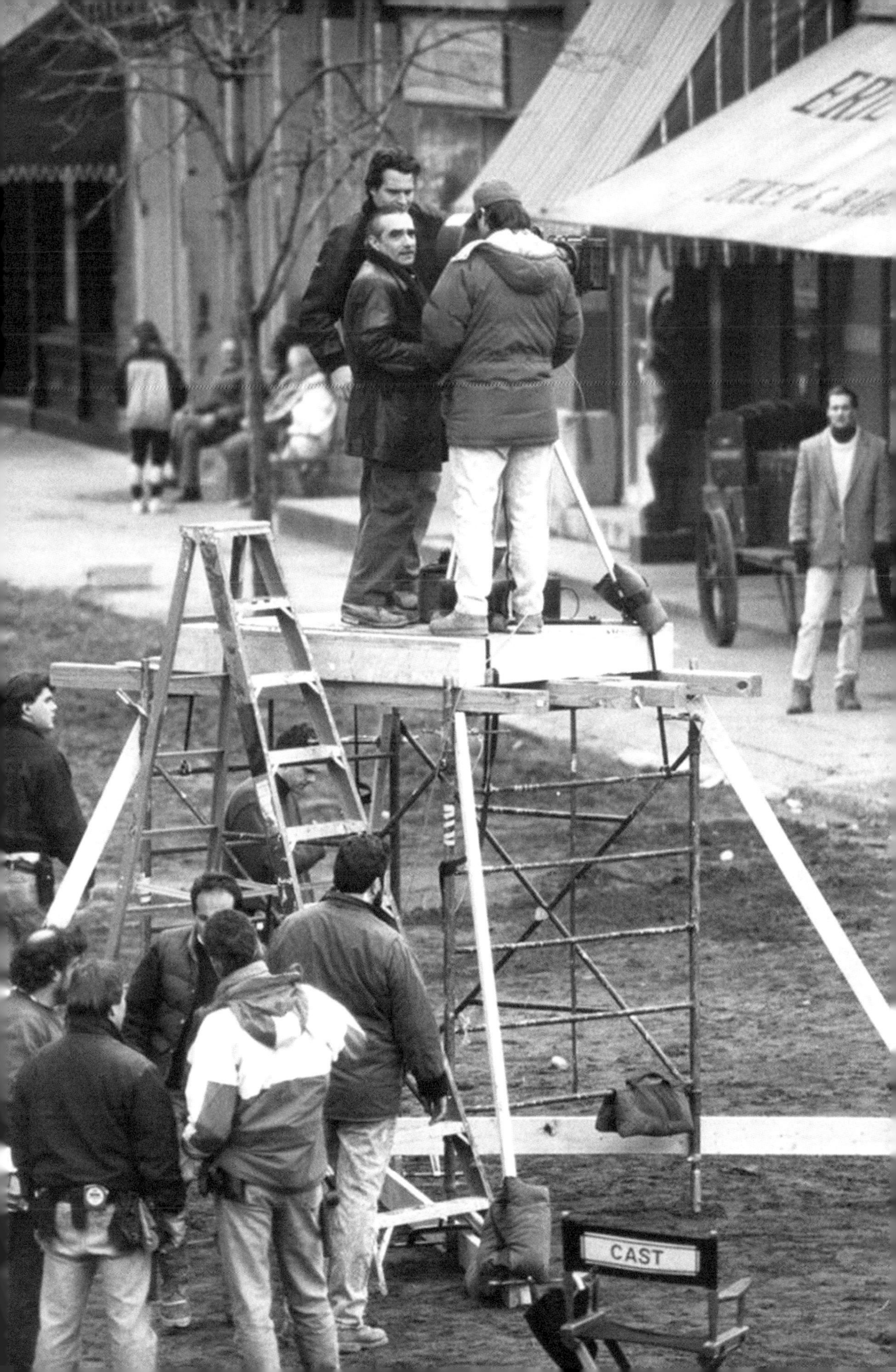
CAST

playing would never say anything to a servant. The food was put down in front of them. If somebody opened the door for them, they wouldn't say thank you. They would just walk by as if the person didn't exist, and so I figured out halfway through that when Daniel might say "hello" to me when he arrived. Once he was in costume, I was a servant, and he would just walk past, as if I did not exist.

On set he would talk to the director, and [first assistant director] Joe Reidy, and the director of photography [Michael Ballhaus], but everybody else is servants. He's not going to talk. So at the end of the shoot—we're in Paris, which was nice that I got to go to Paris with it—and we're shooting at this place where we see out a window, and we see the buildings outside the window, especially the building directly across the street, and we are not going to come back to this location. We are losing the light. I'm out at the camper, and the camper in Paris, it's like the West Village. There's no place to park, so we're parked very far away from where we're shooting, as far as the hair and makeup trailer goes. So I'm there. Daniel's almost—and he's got prosthetics. He's an old man at the end of the movie. So Daniel gets out of that trailer, and he starts walking like the old man—he's in character, he's not going to come out of character—and he's walking like an eighty-year-old man would walk, slowly hunched over, and he's got his cane, and Joe Reidy—I've got a thing in my head [walkie-talkie] and Joe's saying, "Where are you? We're losing the light." And I'm answering Joe loud enough for Daniel to hear me, without me having to say it to Daniel, because Daniel already knows. I've already told him we're losing the light.

"Yes, Joe, Daniel is aware we are losing the light. We are on the way. Couple minutes more, Joe."

"How far away are you?" "Yes, we're still on the way. Don't worry, Daniel knows." All of a sudden Daniel, who has not spoken to me the whole movie—three months of shooting when he is in costume—he turns and I'm walking behind him. He turns to me, puts his hand on my shoulder and says, "Joseph, no one ever got an award for doing it quickly," and turned around and walked just as slow as he could. We got there and we had to put a light across the street and made it look like daytime, and we got the shot.

Such a great line: "No one ever got an award for doing it quickly." And I think to myself, "Well, maybe not you, Daniel, but I get hired again for doing it quickly."

On the last day of shooting, he comes out of his camper and, saying goodbye, he says, "Joseph, I hope I wasn't too much of a pain in the ass."

I said, "No, Daniel, not at all."

JOHN MAZZONI: So, there's a big shot in Philadelphia in the theater. There's a big play. Michelle Pfeiffer was there. You'll see that big, beautiful theater scene. What we did was we put all fake people in with monocles. Don't forget, it's 1817. So we put fifteen hundred cardboards in the theater. Vinnie says, "Johnny-Boy. I want you to be the key grip in Philadelphia for three weeks and set up the theater. I've got a lot of rigging to do, and you're the guy." And I say, "All right, Vinnie, I'll do it."

I got a couple of guys from Philadelphia, and I take a couple of guys with me and we went. But before we go, Vinnie goes in to Marty because he knows Marty good: "Marty, how are you doing, man?"

"Vincent. How are you, Vincent?" And he loved Vincent Guarriello. He loved him. He says, "Vincent, listen. Vincent, are you going to do Philadelphia?"

And he says, "Well, I'm a little busy but I'm sending Johnny-Boy on it."

"Johnny-Boy? Johnny-Boy?"

"Yeah, I'm sending Johnny-Boy. You don't

have to worry about anything. He's a very good grip. His father is a fantastic man. You're going to love him. You could trust this guy. You don't worry about nothing, Marty."

Marty goes, "Okay, Vincent." Joe Valle was in the hallway while Vinnie was talking to Marty. As Vinnie walks out, Marty goes to his assistant Vern and says, "Who the fuck is Johnny-Boy?"

Vern says, "I don't know, but Vinnie says he's good. Don't worry about it," and that was it.

I go to Philadelphia, do my job in three weeks. Marty lands. We're all waiting for him. So we're going to do the first shot, the whole thing. We're looking down at the theater, walking up the stage. I'm all the way up on top in the back balcony with all the cardboards—I'm sitting there—but he's going to do the main shot. Marty walks in, he walks down those steps, but he doesn't sit in the seat. He sits on the steps, those little flat steps going to your seats all the way up on top. I'm standing up again and I've got my apron on, and I'm so excited to be the construction grip.

Marty don't know me. Jimmy Mazzola was the property master. Marty trusts him with everything and trusts him with his oxygen tank that I don't know anything about. He's got a hand-truck with an oxygen tank on it, a green giant oxygen tank . . .

So I looked at Jimmy and said, "Jimmy, what are you doing with this thing?" He says, "This is Marty's oxygen tank. He's very hypochondriac. He needs oxygen every once in a while. So he's going to be sitting down, but it's always next to him. That's my job today."

Then he goes, "I have to take a shit, so do me a favor, just hold . . ."

I said, "Where are you going, Jimmy? Where are you going?" He goes, "Listen, I've got to take a shit. If Marty raises his hand, you bring the hand truck all the way down the steps and turn it on 17 air and hand him the cup."

Marty passes me—he doesn't say a word to me. I've got my apron on. I'm standing there. I hear "Jimmy, Jimmy, Jimmy, Jimmy." That's me, right now: "I'm Jimmy, I'm Jimmy." I go down the steps and he's calling, "Jimmy, Jimmy." I shout, "I'm coming," then I pass the thing, and he looks at me. I turn the thing on 17. I gave it to him. He goes, "Who the fuck are you?" I go, "I'm Johnny-Boy."

He goes, "You're Johnny-Boy?" I go, "Yeah." He goes, "Oh, my God." He just put the thing on his head, and that was the end of it.

The Fisher King

(1991)

Home Alone 2: Alone in New York

(1992)

DEAN TAUCHER (PRODUCTION DESIGNER): Mel Bourne was the production designer on *Manhunter* [1986], and it was just immediately after *Manhunter* that I started designing *Miami Vice* [1984-1989]. I got hired again by Mel to do *Fatal Attraction* [1987], and I was the [scenic] chargeman, and the first week that I was hired I got asked to take over *Miami Vice* as the designer. Michael was my second. So I negotiated my rate—then, scared and wet behind the ears, went to Miami to do that, and left Michael with Mel. And so he ended up working with Mel a lot more than I did.

Did Michael tell you about working on *Fisher King*?

MICHAEL ZANSKY (CHARGE SCENIC ARTIST, *THE FISHER KING, HOME ALONE 2*): Let's go to *The Fisher King*. I'm doing this set in Lower Manhattan. It's a few blocks from Wall Street. The set is a tenement building that goes up, like, three or four stories high and there's a video record store on the first floor which they're going to use as the set. It's all fake above, but it's a trench and they have to build up platforms to raise the street level and then build the standing set on top of it. I'm working on this thing for a month, maybe a little longer than a month.

So it's Friday afternoon—traffic is going by. It's on one of the side streets, but it's

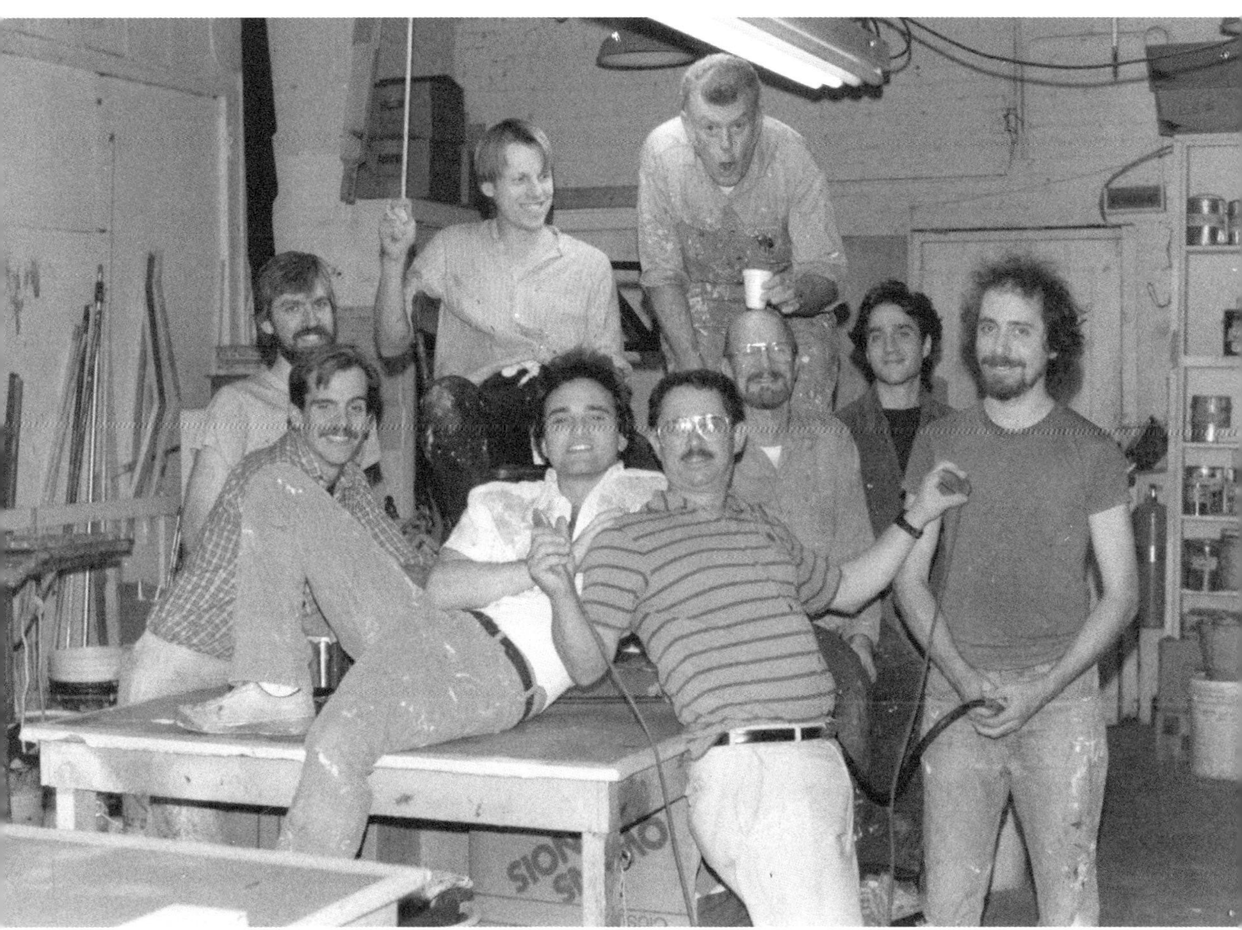

heavy traffic and I hear these two guys screaming at each other and I recognize one of them. It's Mel, and I don't know who the other guy is. I make my way across the street, and I'm just standing there listening to these two guys argue. One is screaming at the other. Mel is screaming at this other guy, then Mel turns around and looks at me.

He says, "Terry, this is Mike." I shake the hand. It's Terry Gilliam. "We got a problem," Mel says to me.

"What's the problem?"

"Terry doesn't like the set."

"What's wrong with the set?"

"Well, he doesn't like the building behind the set."

"What's wrong with the building behind the set?"

He says, "He doesn't like that whole brick wall that's behind the set that we're building."

I look and the building is forty or fifty stories high of brick with nothing on it—just brick. Mel says, "We have to come up with a solution. He doesn't like it."

I said, "Well, it's very easy."

He says, "It is?"

So now Terry's looking at me, and Mel is looking at me, and I say, "Yeah, we can have the carpenters work overtime and put

Back Row: Greg Sullivan, Dean Taucher, Bill Drake., Bill Moore (with cup on head), George Kousoulides,. Bottom Row: R. Lawrence Robinson, Benny Rappa, (white shirt), Fred Sammut, Michael Zansky (far right),. Undated photo and unknown photographer. Found by the author in a desk at *Law and Order SVU*.

up a thirty-story billboard on the roof of this tenement building."

Mel turns to Terry Gilliam, and says, "Pay no attention to this prick."

MICHAEL ZANSKY: Oh, god, I created a problem on *The Fisher King*. So we were shooting in the Plaza Hotel. At the time, I think it was owned by [Donald] Trump.

DEAN TAUCHER: Well, I got it second-hand, but I guess in *Fisher King* there was one set that they did this whole façade, and it looked like a tenement or a burned-out building. I'm not sure what it was. And this was when Trump was going through one of his series of being broke and there were headlines about Trump's financial problems. Trump also owned the Plaza Hotel at this point, which the movie had as a location. They were in negotiations to sign the contract for the Plaza Hotel.

Michael, in his inimitable way, takes some terrible brush and makes some crappy-looking sign. It has drips and hairy edges—and it says "Trump Plaza Casino"[72] or something like that—and tacks it up to the exterior of this building that looks like this burned-out tenement. It was very funny, except some photographer took a photo of it and it ended up on the cover of the *New York Post*.

Then Trump doubled the cost of the Plaza Hotel to the movie company so that the production manager gets a call asking, "Who did that sign? Where did that sign come from?" Mum's the word. Nobody says anything.

STEVEN J. JORDAN (ART DIRECTOR, *HOME ALONE 2*): One of the stipulations about him allowing us to film [*Home Alone 2*] there—he [Donald Trump] had to have an appearance in the film. That was a major sticking point: "I've gotta be in the film." So [director] Chris Columbus basically looked at it and said, "Okay, fine," and I remember standing in Video Village and Chris saying, "This is one of the easiest scenes I've ever done because I know it's not going to be in the movie."

Like most locations in New York City, you just pay a fee and you are allowed to shoot in that location. We approached the Plaza Hotel, which Trump owned at the time, because we wanted to shoot in the lobby. We couldn't rebuild the Plaza on a soundstage.

Trump said OK. We paid the fee, but he also said, "The only way you can use the Plaza is if I'm in the movie." So we agreed to put him in the movie, and when we screened it for the first time the oddest thing happened: people cheered when Trump showed up on-screen. So I said to my editor, "Leave him in the movie. It's a moment for the audience." But he did bully his way into the movie.[73]

—Chris Columbus, *Business Insider*, December 24, 2020

MICHAEL ZANSKY: Production managers with their nonsense. I sit down to make the deal for the crew and for what's going to happen. Then, for the umpteenth time, the production manager says, "Before we even start this conversation about salaries and everything, and kit rentals, there's really very little money in the budget."

I don't say a word. I just reach into my back pocket and pull out my checkbook and start to write in my checkbook. He says, "What are you doing?"

I say to him, "There's no money in the budget. Well, I'd like to contribute a couple of bucks to the budget of the movie." [laughs]

Oh, that was another job, actually, but it's always the same.

72 At the time of this writing, I can't find this. Man, did I look! If you find it send it over so we can include it in future editions of this book.

73 Jason Guerrasio, "'Home Alone' at 30: Director Chris Columbus Talks Trump 'Bullying His Way' into a Cameo and More Never-Before-Told Stories," *Insider*, December 24, 2020, www.insider.com/home-alone-30-anniversary-chris-columbus-trump-cameo-2020-11, retrieved August 31, 2023.

For *Home Alone 2*—this is another job that I remember—I said, "You don't have to worry about kit rental or any of that." He was giving me a hard time about kit rental. I said, "You'll have the best working plywood sets in the industry. Don't worry about it. No one is going to know the difference."

STEVEN J. JORDAN: I was the art director on that, and I hadn't worked with the designer, Sandy Veneziano. We had a mutual friend, and I met Sandy in L.A. and we had lunch, and one day out of the blue she calls—and Sandy grew up in Nebraska and she went to Hollywood—and she called me and said, [nasally voice] "Steven I got a show that's going in New York, and I don't want to go to New York."

Really, that was it. And I had a great time on that show, but it was crazy. They sent a plasterer in from L.A., a guy by the name of [Alexander] Scutti. He came from a long line of plasterers. I'm going back to his grandfather, and great-grandfather, and his kids and grandkids are now plasterers in L.A., but they flew Scutti to New York to go to Central Park and pull molds off the rock so they could build Central Park in Chicago.

My part of doing that was, basically, we took over the Plaza Hotel and we redid the registration, the check-in booth, which Zansky had a nightmare of a matching job with the marble, and I said, "Michael, I don't care what it takes. This match has to be dead on." And he said, "No problem."

And I think he would stop at the Plaza almost every day with a sample—sneak in, put it up against the wall, make notes, and come back, and he absolutely nailed it. The California crew could not believe just how good it was. I mean, they were stunned.

MICHAEL ZANSKY: They're shooting in the Plaza and I'm doing the standby.[74] I get to the set and it's a room on the second or fourth floor, whatever it is.

I had seen this young kid—I don't think I ever saw the movie, but I saw posters or something with the kid who plays the kid [Macaulay Culkin]—so they're setting up the shot and there's some touch-up behind the headboard in the room with the bed. Then there's the actor sitting on the bed. I'm, like, looking at this kid, and I'm thinking to myself, "My God, Hollywood could destroy somebody." I don't know what they did, but the kid is looking awful. He's small, tiny, a little kid, but he looks awful. The makeup looks horrible. Everything looks horrible.

I go out into the hall, and then I see the kid come out. Then this other kid comes by, and they shake hands—"How are you doing," blah, blah, blah, and the other person walks off. I turned to one of the guys standing there and I said, "What the hell's going on here? The kid looks awful."

He says, "Oh, no. That's a stunt dwarf." [laughing]

He was setting up the shot. I don't know what the fuck's going on. I just got there. I've been doing all of the set work. I was laughing and couldn't stop. A couple hours later, it's break time. There is a restaurant down there and there's this little dwarf sitting on the lap of a woman who has some of the biggest tits I've ever seen in my life. Jesus Christ, fame reaches at every level.

STEVEN J. JORDAN: One of the big things was there was a very pivotal scene where Macaulay Culkin does, like, a head-first slide into an elevator, and the whole lobby was carpeted, and I was talking to doormen who had been there for fifty years and said, "You know what's under these rugs?" Most of them didn't. And I finally found one guy who said, "Yeah, I think there's tile under there." We

74 A standby scenic artist or camera scenic artist works with the camera crew and takes care of any scenery-related problem or art project that happens on the set during actual filming. I've had this job for the last ten or so years until recently.

were able to arrange—I guess they negotiated with Trump to come in—and one night they agreed to pull up a little piece of carpet to see what was there.

Production got a room for me in the Plaza, and at midnight I went downstairs to the lobby, and they pulled up and revealed the most incredible mosaic floor you can imagine, so they ripped up all the carpeting, refinished the mosaic, and I don't think they ever put it [back] down.

This exquisite original mosaic-tile floor in the Lobby lay underneath wall-to-wall carpeting for many years. It was inadvertently discovered during the filming of Home Alone 2, when the carpeting was removed to allow Macaulay Culkin to slide across the floor into the elevator.

—Plaza Hotel Facebook post, August 29, 2012

STEVEN J. JORDAN: I remember shooting in Rockefeller at Christmas and, for one reason or another, there weren't enough Christmas trees in Rockefeller Center given their camera angles, so literally we basically bought dozens and dozens of Christmas trees for this one shot. It was like bringing coal to Newcastle.

ANGELO DIGIACOMO: We had to have snow and there was no snow, and so the weekend of the Super Bowl it snows. We had left equipment in the office, and they wanted me to come in to shoot the snow. And I'm like, "I live in Queens." I said, "It's going to take me hours." The DP [director of photography], Julio Macat, didn't want to wait. He went on his own, took whatever he wanted and went out and shot the snow and brought it all back. Either he didn't lock the door right or whatever, but all of the equipment was stolen.

It was a lot of my stuff. All of the equipment got stolen and they had to replace all of my stuff. They did the right thing, and they gave me a check for the entire amount.

STEVEN J JORDAN: The amount of snow that [special effects artist Al] Griswold had to make in Central Park, it was staggering, the scale. They were using what ski resorts used: snow-generating machines. All those shots with the pigeon lady in the park—that was all real man-made snow. It's so weather-dependent. You really can't do it unless it's 33, 34 degrees, and it takes a ton of water; water trucks were just going around the clock.

I must say that it was a rather enjoyable project, and I think for me personally it was enjoyable because I was pretty much able to run the art department as I saw. Because Sandy did not want to come to New York. She came once for a scout, and I never saw her again until years later. She did all the Chicago work. I don't dispute that, but for me I was just cutting my teeth as an art director, and it was fun.

Glengarry Glen Ross

(1992)

DANNY MICHAEL **(SOUND MIXER, *GLENGARRY GLEN ROSS*)**: That's a great movie. That's the one movie that I have to say, when a director that I'm working with finds out that I worked on—I promise you, at least a dozen circumstances where director says, "Oh my God, that's on my ten best movies of all time," and they go, "You worked on it?"

First of all, it was a very low-budget film because, like, who the hell wants to make a film of *Glengarry Glenn Ross*? From a commercial point of view this is not going to be a bang-them-up blockbuster.

JANE MUSKY **(PRODUCTION DESIGNER, *GLENGARRY GLEN ROSS*)**: I just remember the humility of all those actors working as an ensemble—and so gracious to each other. I mean, there was never any tension between them. I think Jack Lemmon kind of set the tone, sort of playing the piano in between takes off stage, and at lunchtime he would serenade everyone, and Jamie Foley was such a good director. He just worked so well with that gang. I think I did three or four pictures with Al [Pacino] after that. These are major actors and they're lifers too.

DANNY MICHAEL: We built a practical set. In other words, it had a roof on it. It looked like the real thing.

DANNY MICHAEL: It was just a challenge to get all of this overlapping dialogue and even off-camera dialogue that might be played. There wasn't a day when I wasn't on my feet thinking about what I had to do and how to do it. But that was great.

Jonathan Pryce was in it, and the first time he spoke I thought, "Oh shit, what is this about?" I hadn't worked with him before. I didn't know that he wasn't American, but he was supposed to be an American. The only problem is no one had bothered to give him a dialect coach. I realized that, unless I did something, he would be wrong, he'd have the

GLENGARRY GLEN ROSS

Screenplay by David Mamet

First Draft
ZUPNIK ENTERPRISES
9229 Sunset Blvd.
Suite 818
Los Angeles, CA 90069

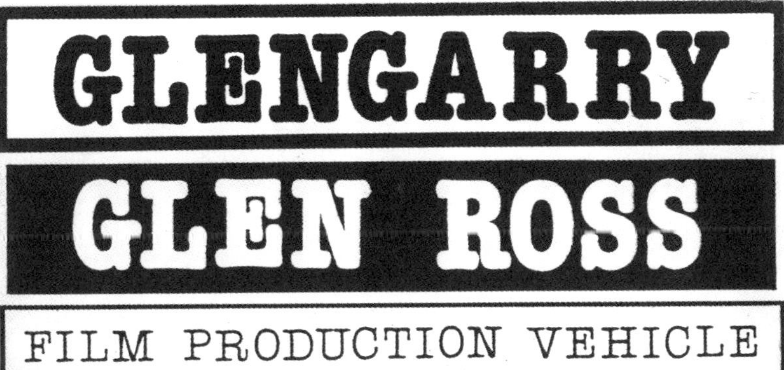

wrong dialect almost all the time. So the first time I heard the words come out of his mouth during a rehearsal, I had to figure out a subtle way of getting over to him and say, "Hey, I'm Danny, I'm the sound mixer. Did anyone offer you a dialect coach?"

He said, "No, I didn't get a dialect coach for this. Why? Is there a problem?"

And I said, "Well, every once in a while, I hear a little bit of the wrong phrasing, but it's something we could work with."

He says, "Oh, would you mind? That would be great."

So that's what happened. I became his de facto dialect coach but didn't draw attention to it because we didn't want to draw attention to the fact that he needed this done.

JANE MUSKY: That was all sets for walking across the street in the rain. So, you know, there was a lot of set-building.

DANNY MICHAEL: We built the set as a practical set. It had a roof on it. It looked like the real thing. It was very challenging for me to do because we constantly moved the camera on the dolly, and so the shots were orchestrated based on the blocking with the actors, but there were no marks put on the floor for the actors, or for the dolly, because you would see it. We had two boom people working all the time, and the dolly was moving all over the place—it was quite an ordeal. It's all overlapping dialogue. Everyone is talking over the other, and there are no pauses for someone to speak, and it was a challenge, but it was a challenge that I was up to.

It was a great accomplishment for me to have done it the way I had, and in fact it was a great accomplishment for the way it was shot. We just had an all-star cast, and then we even had Alec Baldwin who had just come from the TV world.

It was his first real movie, and he could not remember more than two lines without blowing it, and he had all these big speeches. He became a burden for the number of days that we had him. I guess it turned out fine, but Al really knew his lines. But you can't do *Glengarry Glen Ross* and not know your dialogue, and you can't when you're working with Jack Lemmon, who never missed a line.

Al didn't come in until ten in the morning, because he played poker at night at his place. Then he would drink double cappuccinos all day long. He was right on the mark. This was a time when we didn't do multiple cameras. We were using a camera that moved and had purpose to it, and so I played the room perspective. If someone was deep, I would let it play deep, or I would use a cheated microphone, like if Al was deep in the frame and a microphone couldn't get to him very well, I'd put a microphone on his desk and blend it in. It still sounded like he was far, but it would have a little sweetening to his voice, give it a little more body.

Everything I've talked about was done with the two-track recorder. We were using Nagras and people nowadays don't understand that this is a very big distinction. Now the sound-mixers are out there with recorders that can record sixteen tracks or more if they want to. There are shows where every actor is mic'd.

LARRY HOFF (SOUND MIXER): When I started, we did mono one-track, so, if you had five microphones, you had to mix them together onto one track. All they had for editing was that one track.

DANNY MICHAEL: Your mix was committed. If you missed something, it's gone, it's not there.

LARRY HOFF: Now every actor has their own track. The editors can manipulate the sound in ways that they couldn't even imagine forty years ago. Used to be, multi-track were these huge machines that were impractical because we had to shoot outside in the field, in the rain, or the snow. Now you can get a multi-track recorder that you can carry with one hand. The equipment has changed drastically, and, with that, the whole outlook and the expectation has changed drastically.

DANNY MICHAEL: It was a lot of pressure, not only to get all that dialogue but to also make it sound right for the shot, and that was all being done live. I could still have four or five microphones working, but I only had two tracks to go to.

For example, if we have two characters and one of them is by the camera but off camera and the other one is on camera, I mic'd both people and treat them as importantly as the person that was on camera. If they accidentally overlapped with each other and didn't mic the other person, then that overlap will not work because that person would be off mic when they did the overlap.

So why does this matter? Years later, I'm on *Glengarry Glen Ross,* and that's of course what I do all the time is I'm miking whoever is talking, whether they're on camera or not. We're doing a scene in what's supposed to be the Chinese restaurant which was actually a Chinese restaurant—not a set—and it's a scene between Ed Harris and Alan [Arkin]. They're just having a two-person dialogue at a bar, and then we come around, and do overs and then singles. I mic'd both people. I have two boom people. I have a mic on each of the characters and it's two tracks, so each one is going on an individual track. When Ed Harris is on camera, I'm miking Allan Arkin. This is, for me, normal procedure.

Two or three months later, I get a call from the post-production sound person. Jamie [Foley]'s sound person, and he says to me, "I want to thank you for doing all this off-camera miking," and I said, "What are you referring to?" He said, "Jamie and I both agreed that Alan was so nervous when he was on camera. He was so much better off camera, and we were able to use the dialogue you recorded that he did and save the scene, make it better."

There are some actors that will purposefully not do their dialogue well off camera. I think they're kind of trying to protect that [performance]. In their mind they're thinking, "I'm not going to give my all, because I don't want them to use this." But it's quite selfish, and I will occasionally come back to an actor like that, unless I know they're really ornery, and say, "I'm having that actor play up to you for your role. When you're on camera I'm having them really play the role, because it affects the pacing. If you guys overlap, it's usable that way. So, if you don't do it when we're on them, it won't be usable. It's not fair to that actor to not get what you are doing—what you are acting and supposed to be saying and supposed to be feeling—they're not getting that back. So that's kind of cheating them."

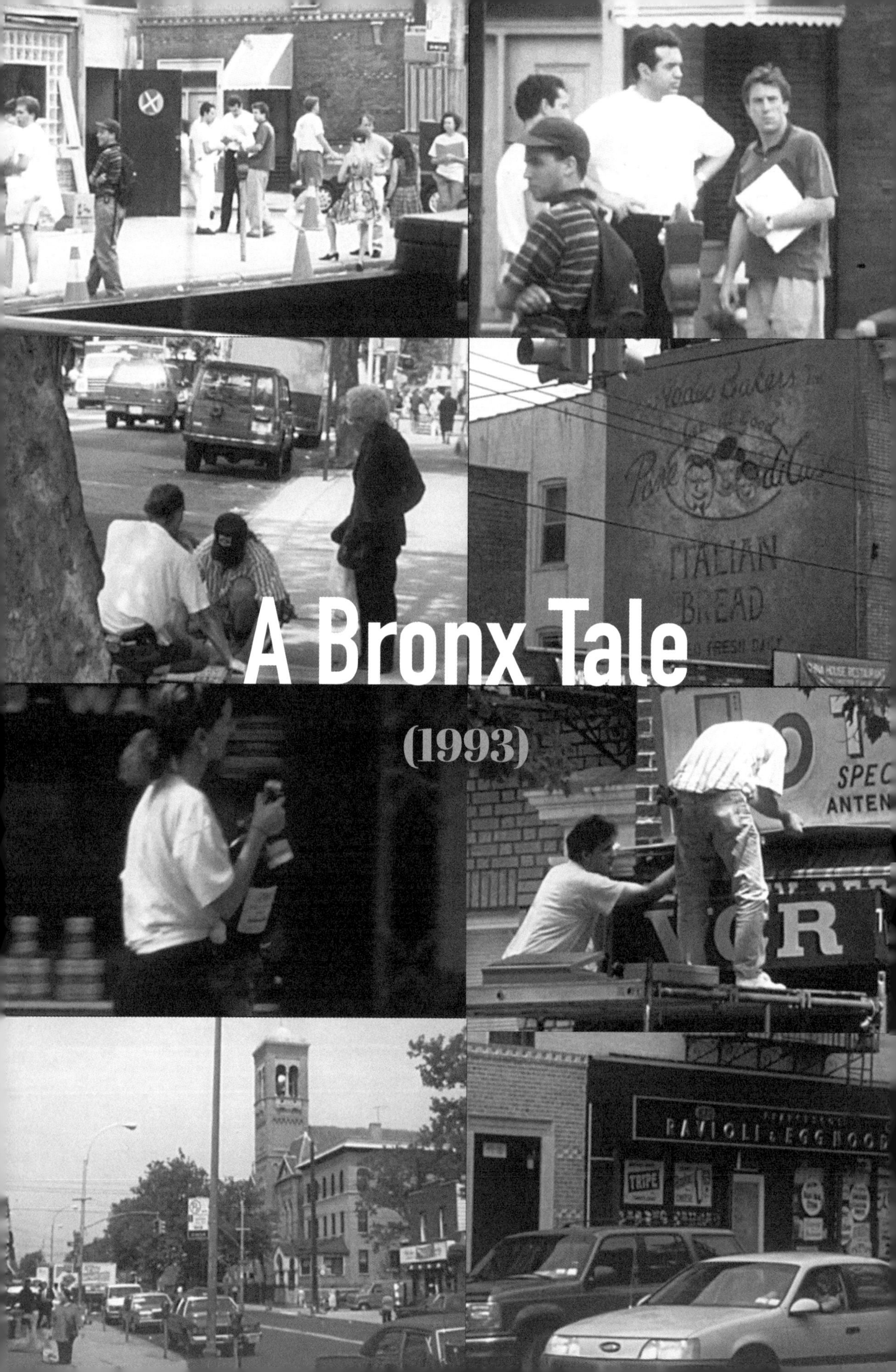
A Bronx Tale
(1993)
ITALIAN
BREAD
TRIPE

STEVEN KIRSHOFF (**SPECIAL EFFECTS, *A BRONX TALE***): De Niro was good to work with as usual. He was the director, so it was kind of nice working with him in that capacity.

JOE BURNS (**SECOND ASSISTANT DIRECTOR, *A BRONX TALE***): I did a couple of movies with him, but this was his first as a director. He didn't really like to talk to people, and it's because he's kind of shy. It's not like he doesn't like people or anything like that, but he's not real outgoing. So you'd give all the information to his assistant, the call time: "This is what we're doing." Then on *Bronx Tale* he had to talk to me—I'm the second AD [assistant director].

We were going to shoot in front of the bakery. Joe [Reidy, first AD] says, "Go ask Bob if he wants it busy here. How does he want the background in front of the bakery?"

I go over, and I knock on the door, "Hey, Bob, Joe's wondering, how do you want the extras in front of the bakery?"

He starts talking to me and I'm just seeing characters that he's done over the years. I'm seeing *The Godfather,* I'm seeing everything, and I'm having difficulty paying attention to what he's saying to me, and so I leave and Joe asks, "What did Bob say?"

"Oh, he said he doesn't want it too busy."

I couldn't really remember what specifically he was telling me, but I got over that. That was the beginning of shooting.

JOE REIDY (**FIRST ASSISTANT DIRECTOR**): Wynn Thomas was his production designer, and Wynn was just like him—wanted to get it right. And the neighborhood we were reproducing, which was meant to be the Bronx, we filmed in part of Astoria, Queens, and Wynn found a street that—let's say the bones of it were perfect for us to work with. A place that had a good place for a social club that was on a corner. Bob De Niro liked the idea. It had enough storefront that we could do other things with the storefronts. There was an apartment that was upstairs on the street that could be the family apartment, but it worked so beautifully in so many ways that we got this neighborhood that worked for us for much of the movie.

Wynn had a lot to do with our locations manager. Bob cared about everything, like the signs of the storefronts. He just wanted to make sure it was right. He'd check the artwork. He went over it. But Bob checked everyone, and it came to extras and casting extras for that neighborhood and the social club. Bob handpicked everybody. We did open calls. We went to the Tribeca Film Center where his office was, and we did extras in groups and individually for certain roles. We took photographs and then we started to make a chart, a diagram where these people would belong. We called people back, we had second looks, you know, things like that. This was not all done right away, no quick decisions. He took his time to get it right.

JEFF GLAVE (**CHARGE SCENIC ARTIST, *A BRONX TALE***): I just thought, "Man, he is going for it—he's a perfectionist and he's going for it," and to sit around and see how he shot—it was like a gift for me.

There are lines—he would do fifteen takes of himself reacting to something. It would be like—I don't remember any of the lines anymore—but he'd be like, "Are you kidding me? Are you kidding me? Are you kidding me? Are you kidding me? You're kidding me."

JOE BURNS: We went about seven weeks over schedule on that, and the main reason was that De Niro couldn't move on. He had to have every scene, every piece of coverage, perfect, and he was just shooting, shooting, shooting, to the point where nobody wanted to go to dailies because they'd be so long. He couldn't get out of scenes.

JEFF GLAVE: I thought he was really a good director. It was a pain for the shooting crew.

Behind the scenes of A Bronx Tale. Images courtesy of Alex Kuciw.

JOE BURNS: The wiseguys that were in the club scenes were all guys that he got from the clubs in Little Italy. I don't know if they still have those clubs today, but in those days they had social clubs, and De Niro would go there to cast people. Then SAG [the Screen Actors Guild] said, "Oh, you can't just use those people. You got to try to use our SAG people."

So he had an open call knowing that he wasn't going to pay any attention. He already had who he is going to have—the real wiseguys. Anytime they are on set, they're all playing cards. Really playing cards.

One day we don't finish the scene, and I tell everybody, "Okay, we're not finished with the scene. You got to come back on Monday," or whatever the next day was, "and you got to wear the exact same clothes that you have on now. All right, you got that, everybody? The same clothes—does everybody understand?"

Well, the next day the costume supervisor comes, says, "Joe, we got a problem. He's in the foreground, and he's got the wrong suit on."

The guy says, "This is a better suit."

I said, "It is a better suit, you're right. But where is the suit from the other day?"

"At home. You don't like this suit?"

I said, "No, we like your suit, but see, we need the other suit."

We ended up having to take him outta the foreground because it was going to stand out.

JOE BURNS: We had this guy, Clem. He played [Jimmy] Whispers in the show. He hung out with the wiseguys in Little Italy. So Bob made him sort of our technical advisor for the wiseguys. There was this older guy, Paulie somebody, comes to me and says, "Clem keeps putting me in the back. I want people to be able to see me. He keeps putting me in the back."

I said, "Well, I'm not really setting the background because Bob allowed him to set the background on this. I don't know if I can do anything about that."

Well, the next morning I come—everybody's out, hanging out in front of the Chez Bippy and this guy says, "Hey, we'll see what happens now."

I said, "What do you mean?"

He says, "My nephew just took Clem for a ride."

I said, "What do you mean?"

He said, "You'll see."

So about five minutes later, this car pulls up. Clem gets out of the car and says, "Okay, see you later. Thanks very much."

We go in. We're setting up a scene, and sure enough, this guy Paul is right up front in the foreground.

JEFF GLAVE: [Reynaldo] Villalobos was the DP [director of photography]. He was also known as the Prince of Darkness, because he likes stuff to be dark, dark, dark. I remember that there was a big meeting in the beginning because we had done the bar that was one of the main interiors. They did test shots. I remember seeing test shots in dailies.

They did test shots outdoors on the street. You couldn't tell what was what, and, I swear to you, I could only tell that there were traffic lights and streetlights with a little bit of an indication that they had some color in them, but you couldn't see anything in the exterior nighttime street scenes. We had to have a meeting because of it.

Then they showed some of the tests they did in our set, that was an interior bar, and it was so dark that Villabollos was blaming us for painting the wrong color. We already changed the color two to three times, and we were really trying to keep track of all of our money, on a big-expense job like this. We didn't want overages on set.

The tests kept showing everything being dark and greenish, and finally somebody had to yell out, "Look, everything's green. The faces are green, the costumes are green, everything's green. It's dark and green. You got the wrong film stock. For Christ's sake, can we change the film stock?"

Joe's Apartment

(1996)

RAY MENDEZ (ENTOMOLOGIST, INSECT-WRANGLER, *JOE'S APARTMENT*): When I did *Creepshow* [1982] they asked, "Okay, so was I going to be a bug-trainer? The roach-trainer?"

I said to them, "No, I'm more like the cowboys out west—wrangle cattle, you don't train cattle. So call me "the roach-wrangler."

The *Wall Street Journal* picked it up, and they said there's a new term in movies called the "roach-wrangler." And then it got picked up by the industry, and now it's a term.

BARBARA HAUSE (WARDROBE ASSISTANT, *JOE'S APARTMENT*): I did MTV's first movie. It was truly about roaches, and we had a roach-wrangler.

RAY MENDEZ: I was working at the American Museum of Natural History. I worked there as a taxonomist in entomology, and I was the "answer man," but in the process of being the answer man I got to be friends with the switchboard operators. We had an old-fashioned switchboard. They plugged in the cord and the whole routine, and so people would call and, being New Yorkers, they would call the museum and say, "I got something living in my house and it stopped paying rent, and so we're freaking out about it."

If it related to entomology, they would say, "Oh yeah, we got a young man you could talk to."

Somebody's got to answer it. The curators don't. [One] of my favorite conversations—a guy calls up and goes, "How much is an albino cockroach worth?"

"Well, sir, it's a cockroach that just shed its skin, and it'll get darker." He gave the typical New York response: "Oh, so you're trying to knock down the price, are you?" I realized I couldn't argue about something for which he was not willing to receive the data. I said, "Well, you got the roach?"

"Yes, I have the roach here in a jar."

I said, "Great. If it's still white tomorrow, call me."

Because, of course, the exoskeleton would harden and the conversation would be over. It was a shorthand on how to communicate without having to tell somebody they're wrong. And I fell in love with doing that. I did it for quite a while and came to the realization that removing fear was more important than almost everything else, because it wasn't about didactic information. You can always do that: "Oh, this is a so-and-so—this is a beetle that belongs to this group" blah, blah, blah. They didn't ask you for that. They ask you for information based on how they felt about the world. I made a decision that I would give them the gift of the removal of fear, and then if I could do that—you give somebody a gift for life.

BARBARA HAUSE: I had to get—the way you talk yourself into—if you're scared of heights, or if you're nervous about this—you just talk your way through the normality of it, and that it won't harm me. Why would I be scared of these things? It's not like they bite. This guy knows them better than I do.

RAY MENDEZ: If you were freaked out about them on Monday, by Tuesday you can see them and go, "Oh, that's really cool." You know about them. The act of storytelling is incredibly important amongst humans as a way of communicating information, be it fearful or not fearful. I tried to hone my voice and my information to remove fear. I then worked in the exhibits department because I realized that exhibits were a perfect place because what is an exhibit or a movie if not a storytelling venue.

BARBARA HAUSE: There was a gentleman—the star of *Man from U.N.C.L.E* [1964-1968] [Robert Vaughn]. What they wanted was the suit to basically have real roaches on it, and then they would CGI it to be more covered. The design showed his suit covered with roaches. Every three inches of the entire suit, a little roach was sewn onto it.

"Oh my god, how are you going to do that?" The roach-wrangler came to me and said, "You know, we have a way of doing this."

RAY MENDEZ: When we did *Joe's Apartment,* I got a book. Go look at the rules and regulations for the handling of live animals on set—it's biblical—and so I got the book, and I looked at it and I said, "This is nuts." So I called a woman who was the head at that time, many years ago, and I said, "Listen, I have to gas the roaches in order to put costumes on them because, as an insect, they have a biological switch, and they'll drop their legs. You don't want an animal with no legs running around on set. That's one of their escape mechanisms is they just lose a segment."

As we're talking, I say, "Yeah, I got a gas chamber, and I gas them and I do this and that," and I realized while she's freaking out, "No, you can't do that. No way."

I said to myself, "Wait a minute, okay, gas chamber seems to be not a good word," and I'm not saying that her last name was Schwartz or anything, but it just didn't go over well. I said to her, "Look, I have to do this in order to do the work I'm doing for the safety of the animals. Suppose I just rendered them unconscious." There was this sort of silence in the background and, "That's okay." So, for that movie, actually, they put me in charge of health for everything from the cat to the goldfish to the roaches that were in it.

BARBARA HAUSE: He put little harnesses on their necks that didn't harm them and didn't hurt them. But they were ready. This little harness could do all kinds of things with them. They put a little clip on the top of a stick, and they click it to their little harness, and then the stick would pull the rope up so that only his two back legs were on the ground, and then the stick would wait, and the little roach would dance. The live roach would dance because the stick is moving his body back and forth and his legs are floating, and his bottom legs are on the surface.

I mean, it's amazing. To sew the live roaches on the wardrobe, he would put him in a little Tupperware container and gas them with a safe gas, and that meant that they were going to be out for exactly—I forget the timing, but let's say one minute and thirty-seven seconds, or something like that.

We pick the roach up. We thread a thread and knot it into this little harness, and I have this thread already needled, and I go to suit—he'd be threading the next one—and I go to the suit, and the instruction was to give him three inches of play, then sew down the end of that small, see-through thread. So I'd be sewing and his antennas would start to move.

I thought, "Oh my god, he's coming out, he's coming out," and we did that all day. You know, I kind of got locked into it, and there are other things that I needed to do, but I was locked into this position of sewing. So this guy over here in his three-inch circle would be waking up when I'm doing the next three inches.

RAY MENDEZ: CO_2; it wasn't hurting the roaches. First of all, there's three segments—a head, thorax, and abdomen—and I'm behind the space between the head and thorax—when they're gassed, I'm putting them on the clothes and I'm sewing it underneath.

BARBARA HAUSE: We didn't do the shirt, just the jacket and pants. The more you covered the jacket and the pants, the more alive it would be while you're sewing. We just kept going. He couldn't gas them again. I mean, because he basically had to get them into that little Tupperware container with the tiny little hole sending gas.

RAY MENDEZ: Philosophically, I am a naturalist, and my training was that sort of incredibly organized way of looking at everything, because you can't be a taxonomist and deal with several million species and not know where shit it is, because you go crazy. So my way of looking at the world is to organize it. I'm also hyperactive and quite crazy, but that has nothing to do with it. In working on projects, it was always looking at, first of all, how to serve the project and, secondly, how to ensure the health and safety of the animals I was working with.

BARBARA HAUSE: In general, when we work with live roaches, they set up this huge fence, maybe only a foot, maybe a little taller, but only a foot high—they weren't going anywhere—but this netting that would be around the whole set that they couldn't go up, and the regulations were strong. This roach-wrangler, if he came in with one thousand roaches and four died, he documented that. He saved the bodies, and he had a little refrigerator of dead roaches, because it had to be documented.

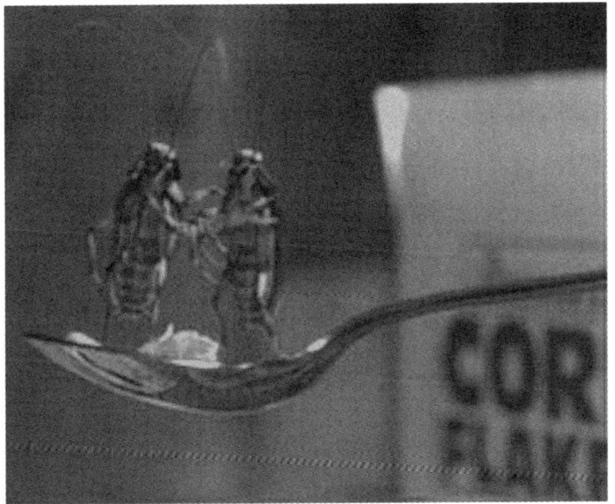

Captured still, closeup, of the Roaches starring in *Joe's Apartment*.

Oz

(1997-2003)

BILL REYNOLDS (PROP MASTER, SET DECORATOR, *OZ*): The Business [after the producer lockout] was called the best part-time employment a guy could get. But [when *Oz* began] it really started to get busy.

FRANK STETTNER (SOUND MIXER, *OZ*): In a sense, as a technician, you look at a situation, you make a decision quickly, you tell your crew, and they tell you what we can and can't do, you execute it—bang—and you move on. That is good training.

Then, after my time with *Oz* and a few of the other things that [producers] Levinson/Fontana did that I worked on—was on HBO. They weren't breathing down the producer's neck at the time. Now HBO has changed.

BILL REYNOLDS: Tom Fontana was just an amazing mind. I had a lot of interesting talks with Tom Fontana about religion. He had trained to be a Jesuit for a while and some of the stuff that came out in *Oz* . . .

I pretty much did everything there. I was there for the first year as prop master, then went away and came back decorating for a few years and I said to myself, "Okay, I'm coming back—I really should familiarize myself with this." I sat down and tried to watch a few episodes. I saw the first episode but, whatever one that was, I couldn't watch anymore. It could be really frigging dark.

CHRIS MARKUNAS (KEY CARPENTER, SHOP FOREMAN, *OZ*): I went and did *Oz* with Eddie Ferraro. That was my first job as a boss of any

Chris "Snaggletooth" Markunas. Photo by Henry Duys.

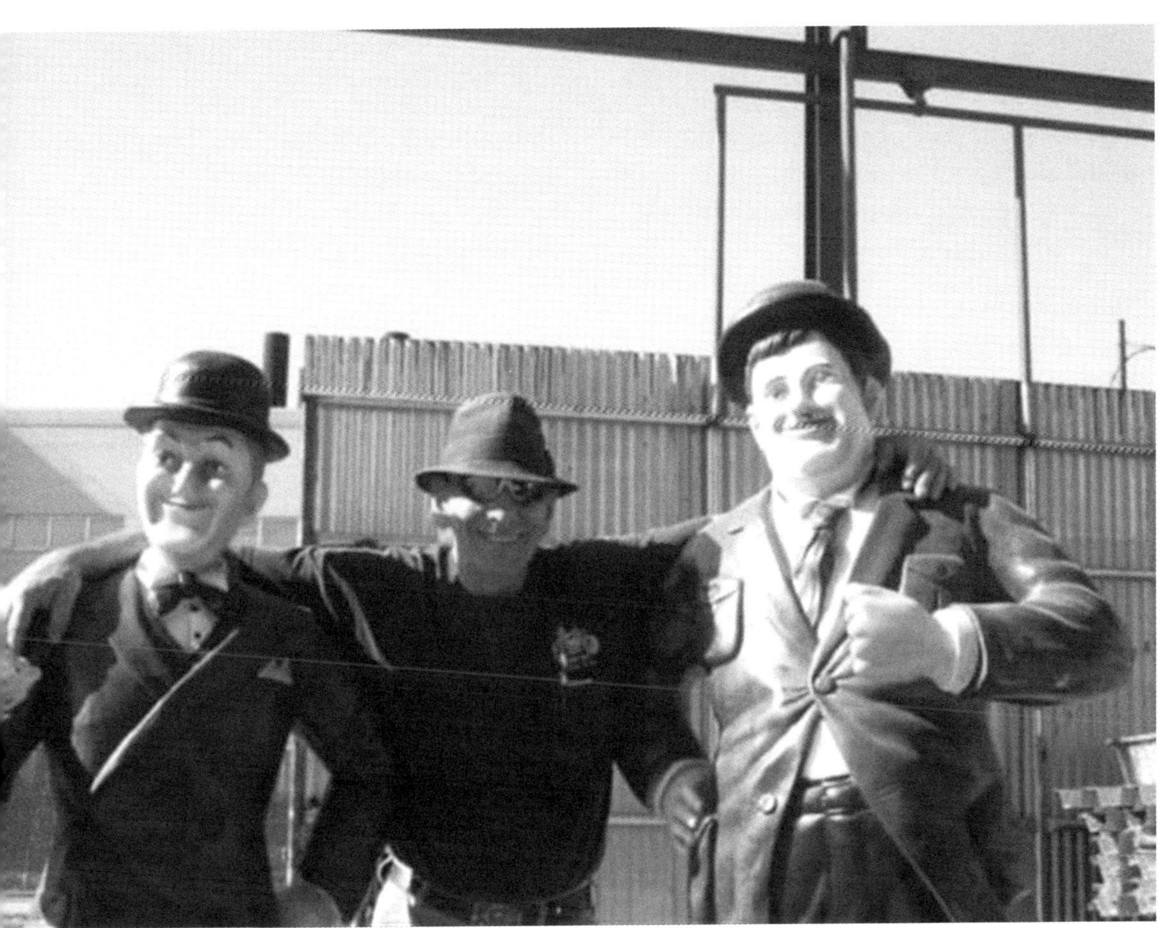

kind in Local 52. Man, I'm telling you, that's when I got introduced to cocaine on set. It used to snow, like you were on Kilimanjaro. Everybody had it. Everybody did it.

BILL REYNOLDS: I've got to say that I was never into drugs.

CHRIS MARKUNAS: It was sick. But we were doing sixteen-hour days. We built 120,000 square feet of prison scenery in the old Nabisco building, on 9th and 15th.

BILL REYNOLDS: Gary [Weist, production designer] shoehorned that set into that space. There wasn't any wasted space, given space on the floor was too small for the set, so, to make that happen, every inch had to be utilized.

CHRIS MARKUNAS: We did that in six weeks, soup to nuts. And we built the walls from the floor to the ceiling, thirty feet up with vaulted ceilings, and every wall was scribed into the ceilings. That was a sick job. There had to be fifty or sixty carpenters—probably thirty scenics, at least fifty grips all in that space—but we got it done. It was talent-ready in six weeks. What would happen is after ten hours, going on twelve hours, Eddie would call us into the office and say, "We've got to go late. Can you go late?"

"Okay. We can go late, Ed."

And he'd open his desk drawer and there was a piece of black plexiglass, and you pull that out and it had a fucking pile, at least an eight-ball on that plexiglass, and he said, "If you need it, use it."

We would all line up—literally line up—fucking hit rails and go out and go back to work.

BILL REYNOLDS: Also, when you'd break for lunch, I didn't want to eat—I would just crash, and we could crash in the jail cell. That became quite a thing.

CHRIS MARKUNAS: If we needed a recharge, we would go back and get the recharge. Eddie wasn't a coker. He did that for the guys. But Eddie was into scotch, and, man, we would drink. It was crazy. Morning coffee, I'm in Eddie's office pounding Johnny [Walker] Black. For lunch, we'd go down and there used to be a bar called the Red Rock West and pound there. Get back to the job, go up to the office, bump up our lines so we could work.

My first week on the job, I went to that bar. Eddie took me over to that bar for lunch, and I'm sitting there eating my lunch and the guy says to me, "Who the fuck are you?"

And I said, "I'm Chris Markunas."

"Where the fuck are you from?"

I said, "Well, I'm from Philadelphia."

He says, "Why don't you go back to Philadelphia? We don't fucking want you up here."

So, I said, "Really. Why don't you send me back to Philadelphia?"

When I left, he's waiting for me outside. We got into a big fight in the middle of 11th Avenue, which I won, and I can tell you who it was, but I don't want to embarrass anybody, and about four days later his brother came looking for me. We had another fight and I won that fight.

These kids today who whine because somebody was mean to them—what would they do if they walked out and there's fucking [name redacted] waiting to kick their fucking ass? Either you fight, or they pick on you for the rest of your fucking life. So I fought. And I'm pretty good. I'm a fucking Marine, plus I've been doing martial arts since I was, like, sixteen years old, so I didn't have many problems.

CHRIS QUILLES: He [Chris "Snaggletooth" Markunas] and Eddie Ferrara were a good team. And one of the things Eddie always told me—he hung out with Snaggle because Snaggle was a tough son of a bitch, bro. He was in Vietnam. He was one of the real-deal guys. He wasn't one of those guys that faked it, and Eddie always used to say, "He got a 'get out of jail free' card. I would ask, 'What are you talking about Eddie?'"

He would say "He's got some kind of a credential that it would take a lot to get him in trouble."

FRANK STETTNER: With Linson/Fontana, the producer was Jim Finnerty, who had spent years as a grip. He did *Saturday Night Fever*. He was really sharp. Jimmy said, "It's easy to say no, but the hard part about it is how to say yes to make the story happen."

On *Oz*, every department was given, "Good enough is not good enough. Reach for something better, make it so that it really is a compelling story," and it started with the scripts. The writing was great. So, if you got it on the page, every department right down the line would—was encouraged to do the best.

BILL REYNOLDS: Jim was a key grip that worked a lot with [Sidney] Lumet. Jimmy worked on the 1964 New York World's Fair with my father. That's how far back that goes and just an amazing human being.

TROY ADEE: Chuck Zito was the president of the Hell's Angels. He looks like he went through a meat-grinder. He's in the show. So we get there at five o'clock in the morning and we walk in [and] no one's there. It smells like someone smashed a bottle of cheap cologne in the fucking hall. I'm like—so it's me, my guy Vinnie Orofino, a couple other guys. We're walking and I'm like, "Who's wearing that cheap fucking guinea cologne? That's awful."

He literally turns the corner. I don't even know him at this point. He's like, "You got a problem with my cologne?"

I'm like, "That's your cologne?"

He's like, "Yeah."

I was like, "Oh, it's just—it's strong."

He just looks at me. I just walk away. And we walked down and Vinnie is like, "Dude, that's Chuck Zito."

So I'm like, "Who's that?"

He goes, "The leader of the Hell's Angels."

So I'm like, "Really?"

CHRIS MARKUNAS: Now, at that time, the baddest man in the union was Joe Valle, and Joe Valle was six-foot-two, and he was rock-solid. Chuck Zito was part of the cast because, in *Oz,* they went for realism. Ninety percent of the atmosphere players who were prisoners were actual ex-convicts. All of the bikers in the biker area of *Oz* were Hell's Angels from the New York City chapter of the Hell's Angels.

We built the Red Rock West Saloon—our crew, the *Oz* crew. We went in there a lot. We ordered materials as if they were going to *Oz* and snuck them off, like oak panels, the ceiling and the place—everything, man. We built that place and we considered it our bar. But IBEW [International Brotherhood of Electrical Workers] Local 3 started moving in, and they thought it was their bar, and there were more than a few fights between IA [IATSE, International Alliance of Theatrical Stage Employees] and IBEW. Brawls at the Red Rock West almost destroyed the place. Billy Egan and I were in there one day for lunch, and IBEW guys came in and started on us because of a trick Billy taught me. When you go to lunch, don't take your hammer belt off—leave it on. He says, "Because, if we're late, we can sneak back in, and then blend in. Whereas, if you've got to walk to your bench and pick up your hammer belt, somebody going to see you and say, "Where the fuck have you been?" But if you're already geared up for work, you walk in as if you're coming from the bathroom."

It worked! It worked all the time. So, Billy Egan and I, we've got our hammer belts on. These two yutzes started shit with us, and Billy takes a fucking Estwing sixteen-ounce, straight claw hammer, and he says, "We're going to bury our fucking hammers in your heads."

So they backed off and went back to work. And after work we always went to Red Rock. Everybody went. You didn't go right home. You went to the bar. So we go and there are these two IBEW guys with about twelve of their friends. I don't know whether they were graduating from class or what, but it was just me and Billy at the bar, and they're starting their shit with us. I call up Eddie, because he's still at the shop. I said, "Whoever's there, round them up and get over here because we're going to have a brouhaha."

Eddie and the boys show up. Red Rock called the police before it really got out of hand, but there were thirty guys out in the street on the corner, ready to go to war. There were a lot of fights, a lot of fights, and they all encouraged it.

BILL REYNOLDS: That is the one where there were secret rooms. Now I do remember that.

CHRIS MARKUNAS: When we built the shop for *Oz* on the third floor, we built offices for everybody. Joe Garzero had his office. I loved Joe. And then the grips had an office, the electrics had an office, and Eddie had an office. What I did was I staggered everything down four feet one way and then four feet the other way or three feet the other way. Then I put up the wall in the electric's office and I put up a wall in Eddie's office and there were seven sheets between the two walls. Then, when nobody else was there, Eddie and I removed one of the flags, a four-by-eight flag, and we hinged it and put it back, and then we put expandable racks on that entire wall, so, if you knew where to reach and move a couple of bottles of glue, there's a little panel—you slide it back and there was the doorknob.

TROY ADEE: I've known Eddie forever, and he's like, "What are you doing?" I said, "I'm on lunch. I'm going to go down, pick something up." He's like, "Yeah, pick me up a" blah, blah, blah. So I pick it up. I come back in there, and I drop it off. He's like, "Where are you eating?"

I said, "I gotta go back upstairs." And upstairs was the fucking jail. It sucked. So he goes, "Eat down here." He looks around, goes over to the wall, grabs a Skilsaw, and you push the Skilsaw down and it was a lever, like a gate lever. The whole shelving unit was a door that opened. There was a big room [with a] a pool table, a bed, a refrigerator, a bar. And I'm like, "What the fuck?"

He's like, "Yeah, I live here."

CHRIS MARKUNAS: We would disappear in there, because Eddie lived way out in Long Island, in Belmar. I lived in Philly, but at the time I was staying in Hoboken. We worked late hours. We'd get too drunk at the Red Rock to go home so we'd come back to the set because we had a place to crash.

HENRY DUYS: Snaggle has a million stories. Snaggle was on *Oz* and he brought these girls back to the shop. They were doing lines and partying. The girls were like, "We have to pee." He went "Okay, just go out there and the bathroom is at the corner of the shop." They go out of the secret hidden room that they were in. It was already six o'clock and the guys were already getting ready for work. They are having coffee and these girls walk out in their underwear. Eddie was really mad because Snaggle exposed their secret room.

CHRIS MARKUNAS: Well, that was it. The cat was out of the bag. Man, did we catch hell on that! They took it down. I'm pretty sure that's one of the reasons that Eddie wasn't asked back for a year and a half.

We thought we better drop in Big Jim's office. We said, "Well, we did it. What are you going to do, Jim? We live too far away. We needed a place to sleep over, that's all." We didn't get fired, but once the big build was over they were okay with getting rid of us.

TROY ADEE: Secret rooms are gone.

CHRIS MARKUNAS: I still do blow. Not as often—I just like it. I like cocaine. What can I tell you? Man, I can't tell you how much fucking . . . that's probably why I had my heart attack.

I assume if you've got stage-four cancer and they told you it's incurable, you kind of get to say, "Yeah. Who fucking cares?"

HENRY DUYS: He doesn't give a shit what people think of him. But now that he's dying, he really doesn't give a shit. He'll tell you anything.

CHRIS MARKUNAS: What do you have to lose? I don't know. I told the doctors, "I don't want to know how much longer I have. I want to be like everybody else." Nobody knows when their time's up, and I think it's working for me because I feel great.

The Sopranos

(1999-2007)

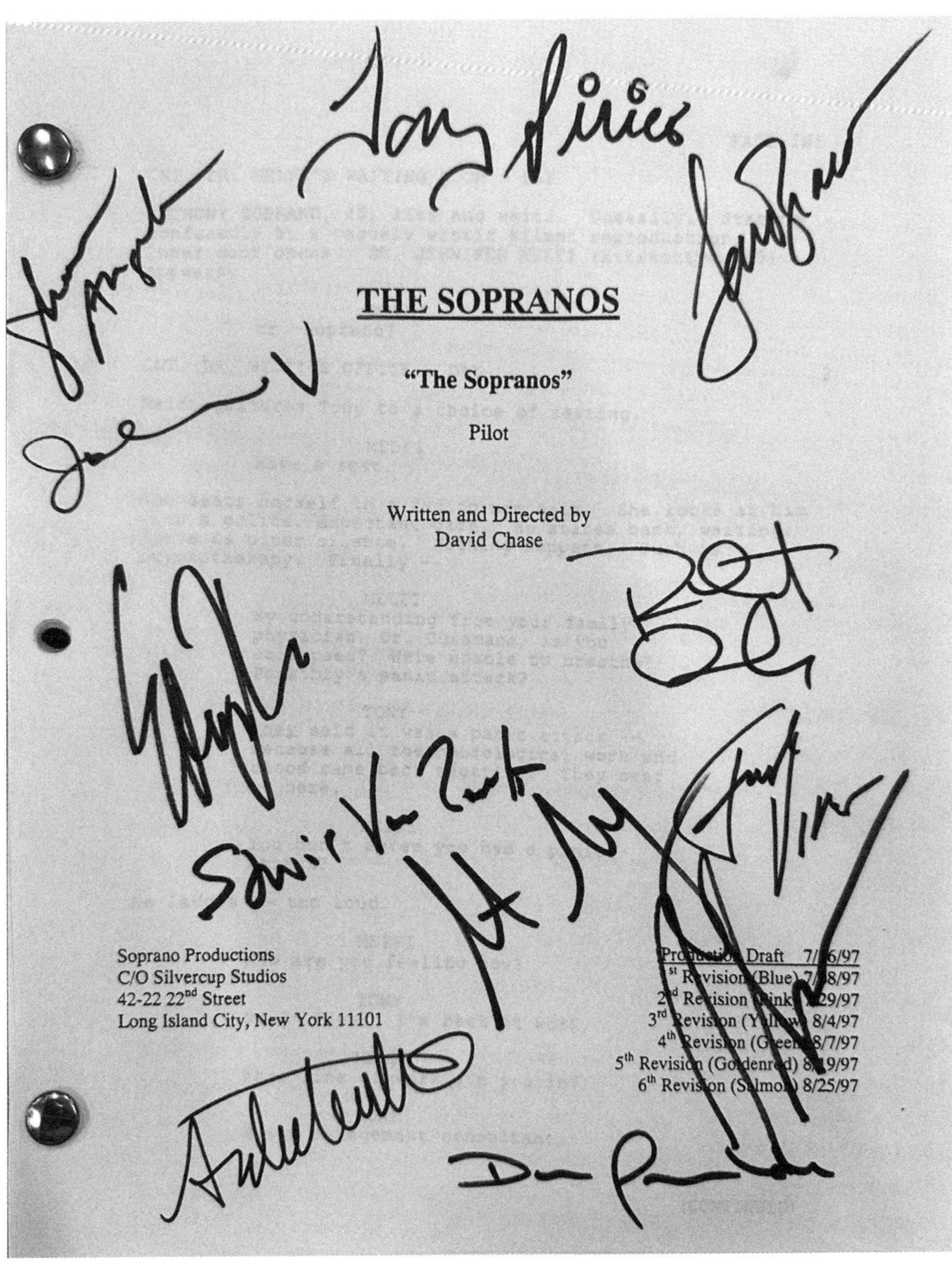

THE SOPRANOS

"The Sopranos"

Pilot

Written and Directed by
David Chase

Soprano Productions
C/O Silvercup Studios
42-22 22nd Street
Long Island City, New York 11101

Production Draft 7/[illegible]6/97
1st Revision (Blue) 7/[illegible]8/97
2nd Revision (Pink) [illegible]29/97
3rd Revision (Yellow) 8/4/97
4th Revision (Green) 8/7/97
5th Revision (Goldenrod) 8/[illegible]9/97
6th Revision (Salmon) 8/25/97

A signed *Sopranos* pilot script. Courtesy of Jimmy Archer.

TROY ADEE (SET DRESSER, *THE SOPRANOS*): The last job around here that was related to the old days was *The Sopranos*. I mean, it was fucking crazy.

BRADLEY RUBENSTEIN (SCENIC ARTIST, *THE SOPRANOS*): I think with *Sopranos* was where things changed.

MARK KAMINE: Early on, there's always feeling each other out and testing each other in a crew situation. I was a location manager, so I was not a pushover and I kind of knew the job.

MARK KAMINE: I remember scouting for a body-dump site, and there was a place that was an EPA Superfund site. I was walking out across this place and we all had this metallic taste in our mouth when we got back in the van.

We didn't film at that one, but all over the Meadowlands there are all kinds of places. I bet I can think of the place that Troy was talking about. There were these great, like, sort of underpasses of bridges and things around there that were great-looking sites, but they were scary—chemically scary—really polluted stuff.

JAMIE COVINGTON (SCENIC ARTIST, *THE SOPRANOS*): [Bad guy] Jackie Aprile gets his due, falling on a pile of snow beside a dog turd. The turd was one of a varied dozen I made, which were then packaged in a Krispy Kreme assortment box and brought to set for the director to make his choice. After much debate, a linear version won out over the other, more spiral configurations.

Another episode required bird shit on the windshield of a car. As the crew watched me do my magic, you wouldn't believe how now everybody becomes a fecal expert with an opinion on how it should look. I later saw a book on identifying birds from their droppings, lavishly illustrated. I could have broken that out and said, "Okay, what are we after here? Eastern seagull, North American wren, crow, pigeon?"

TROY ADEE: It was crazy. Like, when we went out of town it was like the old days. Gandolfini would be like, "You're not fucking staying in your fucking hotel room."

I'm like, "I got to get up at five, man. Take [set dresser] Tommy Heaps."

"Fuck you. Get down to the fucking bar and get some drinks." Gandolfini would show up and with a Dixie Cup full of Coke. Bang. "Come on."

It's six in the morning in August. It's, like, 120 degrees already. Can you imagine? You're doing that shit. You're going to die.

Another day, we're at Monmouth Racetrack. Gandolfini is like, "Tommy, let's go to a strip bar." I'm like, "I'm out, dude—I got to get up in the morning," and Gandolfini is like, "You fucking faggot. I'll fucking drag you down there."

They go and it's down in Monmouth [New Jersey]. The strippers look like fucking carpenters, you know what I mean. The girl is bitching at him because he's not tipping them. So Tommy throws a quarter at the girl, and now the girl's like, "Fuck you," and starts a big thing.

The cops come and they see Gandolfini, and they're like, "Holy shit, it's fucking Gandolfini," and they're bullshitting. They're like, "You guys want to go to a real strip bar?"

Gandolfini is like, "Yeah."

So now it's Tommy and Gandolfini in the police car.

I'm so glad I didn't fucking go. Just a nightmare of a night. So Gandolfini and Heaps are shooting the cop's gun out the cop car at stop signs. They get to the fucking strip bar and it's closed. So the cop calls the owner and says, "I got James Gandolfini in my police car."

And they're like, "Why?"

They're like, "Oh no, we just picked

them up from a strip bar. Come open the bar. Call the girls and open the bar up." So this has got to be by two o'clock in the morning, maybe one o'clock. It's Jersey. They heard Gandolfini was there. So the girls came down, the owner came down, opened it up. They're there the entire night.

We got a six-o'clock call [time] at the racetrack. Do you know in the show when he's fucking talking to the horse in the stall? So everyone's looking for him. Now they're coming to me. They said the last time that they saw him, he was with Tommy Heaps. And I'm like, "I don't know anything, dude. I don't know anything."

So I'm calling Tommy. It's just going to voicemail. A van pulls up. Tommy falls out of the van. I'm like, "What the fuck?"

He's like, "Dude, we just got back from the strip bar."

I'm like, "Really?"

He's like, "Yeah. It was closed. We were shooting the cop's guns out of the cop car."

I'm like, "Tommy, listen to me, I told you not to fucking do this. I told you."

And he's like, "I know, but whatever. I need something to eat."

I said, "You get in that stall and clean out all that horse shit."

He's like, "No. Please, dude, I'm fucking sick. I'm fucking drunk. I'm coked out. I can't."

Now, it's summertime. It's hot. There's a hot horse shit in there, and he's getting sick. So I throw him a shovel. He's like, "Adee, please don't."

"Get in there."

So Gandolfini is in his robe and he's just, like, standing there. He's like, "You're going to beat your friend up like that? That's fucked up, man, fucked up. What did you do last night?"

I said, "I slept."

And he's like, "Faggot."

So the producer is there, and he was a real asshole, and he's like "Tommy, you're getting fired."

And Tommy's like, "Why? What did I do? I'm here on time."

He's like, "You know what you did?"

And Tommy's like, "What? I went out. I'm allowed to go out."

He's fucking wasted. So I'm like, "Henry, I got it."

Gandolfini is sitting there and he's in way worse shape than Tommy. Tommy goes to the stall, and the whole crew is there. Now everyone is there. We're waiting to shoot, and Tommy's shoveling all this horse shit. And all of a sudden he, like, shovels it, brings it over there, throws it, takes a little shovel, looks over at the crew—he's like [vomiting sound]—"I told you, fucking Adee."

[He] got, like, string hanging from his mouth: "Ugghh, I told you!"

Director, DP, cast, and crew have done the first shots at the stables by lining up the camera over the shoulder of his stand-in, shooting coverage of the other actors saying their lines and reacting to the script supervisor's readings of Jim's lines. When Jim shows, we have two cameras ready for his medium and close shots, cameras that have been set for nearly an hour as we've run out of work without him, and after we accomplish those shots we drop back for wider coverage.

We get through the day with an extra hour and a half of shooting but without falling behind, Jim cursing his way through his half-learned lines, doing take after take, drinking coffees and bottles of water, alternately sheepish and churlish, the way he always is when he fucks up.

—Mark Kamine, *On Locations: Lessons Learned From My Life on Set with The Sopranos and in the Film Industry*

TONY STARBUCK, SET DRESSER: Ask him [Troy Adee] about Abel Ferrara. Maybe he already talked to you about this.

TROY ADEE: He [Gandolfini] hooked up with Abel Ferrara once and was gone for four days.

MARK KAMINE: I was on the other end of it—"He's not coming in today, and we can't find him."

TONY STARBUCK: David Chase [creator and showrunner] hired this life coach. This guy cleaned up—off drugs—they brought him out from L.A. to be Gandolfini's mentor and babysitter. Gandolfini turns the guy back into a fucking junkie.

They're shooting at a lake and the life coach guy stays in the trailer. Gandolfini's got a separate setup [trailer] where somehow they delivered him tons of coke. So they just give him this room and it's, like, ninety-five degrees out and he's just fucking doing massive amounts of coke and he's wearing a robe. It's crazy.

MICHAEL ZANSKY (CHARGE SCENIC ARTIST): People get carried away with the seriousness of the whole thing. That's their personality. They take it very seriously. I always found that, without the levity of the lunacy of what we do, it diminishes the experience. When I was doing *Sopranos* with this production designer Bob Shaw, who I didn't like at all, he was taking it all very personally, to a ridiculous level.

I'd go next door—it's *Sex in the City* [1998-2004] and they're working ten hours, twelve hours a day, and thinking to myself, "My god, he is putting the crew through this fucking nonsensical thing." [Set dresser] Jimmy Archer would come up to me every morning and say the same fucking thing: "Bob Shaw lost his mind." Shaw would stomp feet and have a temper tantrum, a real queen temper tantrum. It's like, what the fuck? Grow up!

BRADLEY RUBENSTEIN: Those guys came out of a New York theater, and the idea was that it was a huge show and there was so much money behind it.

The Sopranos was such a cultural phenomenon. How people behaved on that show—I saw the actors' behavior changed as they got more—it sort of coincided with, like, the very beginning of social media where what people did was publicly more visible. The idea that you would hang out with the cast disappeared. Those guys used to hang out at the bar across the street from my house every night after work, and that doesn't happen anymore.

There are so many layers of people now, where their whole job is to get between what the actors do, the publicity, and what things would be bad for the show. If you were fucked up in public, people weren't aware of it, and now it's on Twitter the next day.

You would get into a business where the psychology or the person who wants to be an actor, or who wants to be a director, or who wants to be a writer, is one where you're seeking the approval of strangers. That's the genius that produces the movie or the film or the book. I think it speaks to the corporatization of the industry, because when you take the personality defects or psychology of the creators out you lose something. No discredit to actors today, but you're not going to have a James Dean or a Marilyn Monroe when the business operates like a faceless corporation. The actor that's going to show up on time and do their bit and go home is not going to be the actor that delivers the same performance as James Dean or Brando.

A Different Industry

BILLY WARD (GAFFER): It was very loose. Somebody was saying one time that "You can't have fun anymore on the set."

And I looked back and said, "That wasn't fun. Some of the stuff was dangerous. They made laws against some of that stuff."

MITCHELL LILLIAN (KEY GRIP): It was different. We didn't have the regulations that we have now. There were no trucking regulations. Nobody said, "Oh, you couldn't do something," "Oh, you can't do this stunt in a populated neighborhood," or, "You can't blow up a car." We used to do crazy stuff.

BRADLEY RUBENSTEIN (SCENIC ARTIST): When millions of dollars, tens of millions of dollars have been put into a production, nobody wants to have a sexual-harassment charge.

CATHY NASCH (SCENIC ARTIST): Suddenly, the major harassment-training things would come in and you could not have a conversation with anyone about anything but work. It reminds me—when I first started at the [*Saturday Night Live*] shop, there was a party at the shop because they would throw a party at the end of the show or whatever, and there would be prostitutes dancing on the table, and that was just a part of the culture.

BRADLEY RUBENSTEIN: It's like anything else that is good and bad. You gain a lot, but you lose something. I would say, as an industry, it's better, but you do lose some aspect of—some element is gone when you lose the hedonism of the business.

CATHY NASCH: The biggest difference is what happened at *Saturday Night Live* [1975-present], actually. It's run by Comcast now. Before—you could feel the corporatization when it was run by GE. When they first took over it became another entity entirely, and they had fired—I believe it was a camera operator.

The poor guy came in earlier than his shift just to be in the building and everything. In a locker area or, like, a waiting-room area. He closed his eyes and was napping, and he was fired because Comcast takes different tours through the building, and if you are not there and working they don't want to see you napping because it's a bad image for the corporation.

Plus, after 9/11 you had these IDs and they'd track and look at when you go in and out, when people would smoke cigarettes—it became an issue for Comcast. They talked to one of the electrics at *SNL* because she was going out and smoking cigarettes because they were stressing her more and more. She was smoking more and more. But, "Oh, you're smoking too much. You should be upstairs doing it."

They would have efficiency experts come in, and just about every crew—they were trying to basically eradicate overtime in the NBC contract in that studio. They tried suggesting it to Mark [Rudolph, scenic charge], but they can't do it with a need for continuity, and they tried to do it with stagehands too. The lighting designer, Phil, put his foot down and said, "No, I need these stagehands."

We worked like a well-oiled machine. It's not going to work otherwise. They need to have within their knowledge-base exactly what happened, and they learn more experientially by doing the job and being here on Friday and Saturday to follow through. You have a live show here. It's kind of mind-blowing.

They have no idea that we are here to create a custom-made product. Yeah, it's a commodity, but it's a custom-made product. It's the writing, it's the artistry that has to go into it, it's the creativity that has to go into it, and they'll take it if it's good, but if it's not good, it doesn't matter.

JONATHAN HERRON (DIRECTOR OF PHOTOGRAPHY, DIRECTOR, CAMERA OPERATOR): It was sort of a gradual thing that happened throughout the nineties and continues going, where the business just got more and more corporatized.

CRAIG DIBONA (DIRECTOR OF PHOTOGRAPHY): I was at one of the ASC [American Society of Cinematographers] dinners and Francis [Ford Coppola] was sitting with us and I said, "How are you doing?"

He goes, "I'm depressed."

I said, "Really, why?"

He said, "Well, when the studios were all bought by offshore companies, when you were talking to a studio head, they weren't studio heads anymore. They were basically managers of a division. You're not going to see classic films made anymore." They'll make *Scary Movie 2, 3, 4, 5, 6, 7,* as long as it makes money, but they don't want to make *Godfather*s and movies like that anymore, you know what I'm saying?" And he said, "Unfortunately, a hundred years from now, when people want to look back and see how people lived back in our day, they're going to look at our films and they're going to look at some of these films and go, "This is the shit these people watched back then?"

BRADLEY RUBENSTEIN: I don't even think there's a difference between film culture and TV culture. I think it's all just content now.

TOM PRIESTLEY, JR. (DIRECTOR OF PHOTOGRAPHY): Every year TV became more pronounced. There was more work. In the beginning, the quality of the TV shows weren't up to par with the feature films for the obvious reasons, but as time went by the quality of TV shows was really good, and even to this day I think some of the more innovative stuff is being done on TV right now instead of on features.

MARK KAMINE (UNIT PRODUCTION MANAGER): I didn't do TV after *Sopranos* for a long time because I was sick of it, basically. Also, I liked the rhythm of the movies. because you prepped it and you finished prepping and then you shot it—and you weren't doing everything all at once, and you could be where the shooting was happening. In my position [then locations manager], there was obviously prepping and wrapping going on and there was office stuff, but it was way simpler for my mind to grasp a movie than an episodic TV show.

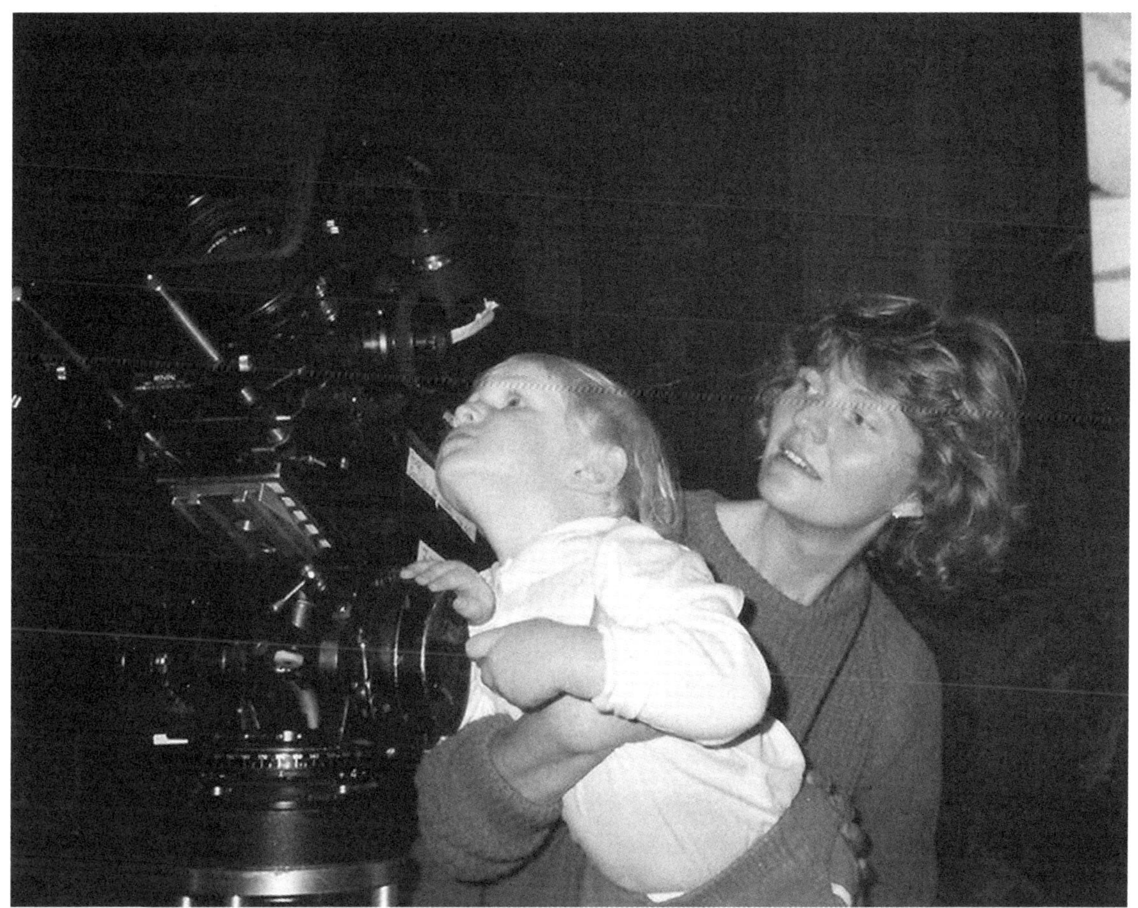

MITCHELL LILLIAN: Everything is a television series now. Now I guess it's more appropriate to say it's long-form. You do eight-hour movies now. I did that thing, *Mare of Easttown* [2021], that was seven or eight episodes. It's just like a long movie, a crazy, long movie.

The budgets on that are big. I mean, they're not the $200 million movies, but they're up there.

BEVERLY MILLER (FORMER PRESIDENT, LOCAL 829): There's less of a feeling that you're working for somebody who cares about you in production. It was smaller, so you had more of a social and humane kind of atmosphere. Clearly, everybody was there to make a viable product that was going to be profitable.

BRUNO ROBOTTI (CHARGE SCENIC ARTIST): It just got worse as time went on. There were accountants who came in and took over, so everything is about money. Some of the old production managers that I knew were all gone. They were replaced. They brought in these young people with numbers. They don't know what they're doing. They don't understand. They didn't understand the business. They only understood money.

BEVERLY MILLER: But I think what changed since the time I worked in movies and now is that the producers themselves have grown to the point where their accounting department dictates how things are. When I ran my last TV show, I didn't have to account for every

Martha Pinson with two year old Jack Carroll. Photo by David Dunlap.

gallon of paint—where it was used, and how long it took for somebody to use it—but now you have to do that.

BRUNO ROBOTTI: In those days we didn't know what the budget was. You got hired to do the job and that was it. It's not to say that the production manager wouldn't be aggressive and say, "Look, can we speed this up or whatever? What can we do?" Gradually it got a little worse.

BILL REYNOLDS (PROP MASTER): When we compare it to working high-steel construction workers, the guys that were at high steel used to make a lot of money—they've also come down some, too, but as an hourly rate, we were about the same as high steel—and now it's shit compared to what it was. At the end of the year, your W-2, your factory times will reflect it. You have to work a stupid amount of hours.

LARRY HOFF (SOUND MIXER): A production manager once said to me that if she does a ten-million film, the crew cost one and a half million. She does a hundred-million-dollar film, the crew costs a million and a half dollars. What costs money is not the crew. It's not the overtime. It's not the pension plan. It's not the health plan. It's the actors, the sets, the locations. That's what costs money. We're just like a drop in the bucket. Producers love coming after us.

MAGGIE RYAN (SCENIC ARTIST): *Stepford Wives* [2004], they spent thousands of thousands on a party scene where you had real orchids on the tables, and they had refrigerators in the carpenter shop, on the back of the stage or the big stage in the foyer. They had about sixteen refrigerators, all full of orchids. For each orchid, they charged thirty dollars, and they would change them out daily. They had chandeliers made out of orchids, hanging down for a shot that you don't really even see. You think, "Why aren't they using silk flowers?"

They covered the side of the building with ivy—bigger ivy at the bottom and smaller at the top. The producer Scott Rudin came, and he didn't like it. He wanted the ivy changed because it was too uniform. Nobody saw the ivy. Everything was on the faces.

They would buy these huge pear trees which cost a small fortune, and they put them down the drive of this big house in Connecticut, and they didn't shoot it, or they shot one scene and they were paying them some huge amounts of money to use their property and the time ran out. The homeowner got rid of it all: "I don't want them. Take them out." And then they wanted to reshoot it, so they had to come back and replant the trees, put them back, and pay them more money. These were bloody pear trees that were costing quite a bit of money laying on the side of the road because they were just very careless. They had so much money for set-dressing and things like this. At the end of the movie, you could go and buy beautiful pieces of furniture. It was very nice. They had wonderful sales.

GARY MARTONE (KEY GRIP): The accountant is not a CPA. The producers don't have business degrees. They're all BFAs. Maybe they didn't go to school—maybe there's nobody watching. Who's watching a multi-million-a-year company? Who has any idea of management, finance, accounting? Nobody. They're not even CPAs in the accounting office. Your head accountant, he's not a CPA. So things could be taken advantage of, as you can imagine—that money in inexperienced hands with nobody asking questions.

TOM PRIESTLEY, JR.: Everybody's trying to justify their job. They hire the best production managers, the best assistant directors. They give you a script—you break down the script. "We're going to shoot this in forty-five days."

"No, no you can't. You got to do it in forty-two days, but you can't take anything out of the script." So everybody starts jumping through hoops, and they tried to get it done in forty-two days and get it done in forty-three days, but the studios already gained two days of non-shooting. They saved all that money. They feel like they've won the battle. That's their favorite thing. They will do it all the time.

SUSAN KAUFMAN (SET DECORATOR): I have stepped back, because television for a set decorator or a designer is less about the creative aspect as it is about keeping up with the [location] scouts, keeping up with the notes, doing the budget.

MARLENE ARVAN (ASSISTANT DIRECTOR): I don't want to work in a business, like, just to feel like the little mouse in *Fantasia* [1940] that, like, just falls down and then everybody else just, like, walks over them.

I sure don't miss the 6-p.m. calls and working all night and coming home at, like, four in the morning, or when I had a dog before I met Frank [Stettner, sound mixer], and I'd have to go into the park at, like, three-thirty or four in the morning, walk the dog, and then leave the dog so I can get to work on time. People call Frank still for work and he's been out of the business for, like, eight years, but, I mean, working a twenty-two-hour day—like, what's the point?

JOE BURNS (ASSISTANT DIRECTOR): I don't miss the hours. I mean, I haven't been blamed for anything in eighteen years or however long it's been. As an AD, so many things can go wrong. You're always looking ahead trying to avoid what the problem is going to be, but you're always ready. I always felt like something bad has happened and nobody has told me about it yet.

JERRY DECARLO (HAIR DEPARTMENT HEAD): On the last TV show I got or had worked on, I received fifteen hundred emails. I think out of the fifteen hundred, maybe two hundred of them I needed to see, and the problem is that they get buried, so the important ones you can't find, and then if there's a chain, you can't find what you need in the chain. In the old days, when the call sheet came out, you didn't leave the show until the call sheet came out. They would [time] stamp it, and you would get it. Now, they'll let you go. I have not gotten that call sheet for an hour and a half. Now that's into my ten-hour turnaround, and I now have to get up and make six or seven phone calls to tell my people, who aren't getting call sheets, what time their call time is.

In the old days, if I had seven hairdressers to call to give call times, we handed the list over to ADs. They sat around and made the PAs make the phone calls and notify everyone. Now, we're not off the clock when we're off the clock.

Tom Whelan, producer: I was thinking about it the other day, about how things have changed over the last—I don't know—say, ten years—how the crew has grown so much and how the demands on the production are higher and the expectations of the crew have grown along with it, and as someone who got to spend the last several years as a production manager and producer, it's the growth of the business, not only in the amount of stuff that we're doing now but in the expectations from both producers and crew have grown—has been quite striking and quite amazing. What I mean by it is that the distributors and the producers of the stuff that we do expect a lot more from us, because the competition is so fierce. Everything has to look like a feature film.

MARK KAMINE: Netflix and Amazon and Apple—you got more and more shows. But once the streamers and things boomed, if there were, like, sixty-eight episodic shows shooting in New York, I would hear from people that means there's, like, sixty-eight or more gaffers or prop masters, and production managers and charge scenics. I don't know who was doing these shows. I mean, in some ways I guess it was great for crew members to move up.

TOM WHELAN: When streaming started really kicking in, it's when the crew base was reaching its limit to be able to have really good people working on every production. It started thinning out, and the crew members knew how much was being expected of them and so they said, "Well, if you want this, then we need to do that." Now, I'm not saying it's a bad thing. I'm just saying that professional crew people want to do a good job, and I think that drove an expectation that the production would support what they need to fulfill what the producer is asking for.

JERRY DECARLO: In the old days, as a hairdresser, they would let us go up to the camera and look through the lens to see if we saw anything, and we would fix what we would be able to. I think a lot of people in charge don't realize that was a thing that we did all the time to be able to make sure nothing was being seen. There's a thing that really pisses me off in the industry where they'll call "last looks"—you know, fifteen minutes before they shoot or while they're still blocking or doing stuff. Last looks is the last thing that happens before camera rolls. It has to do with wind, sweat, whatever, you know? And if you see the [wig] lace or anything, you're supposed to be able to fix something, because sometimes you can fix something and it's perishable—it'll only last five minutes—so you want to fix it and you want to shoot it. Then, when you go to do another take, you can fix it again.

TOM WHELAN: The high-resolution cameras also—the hair and makeup people can't get away with things that they used to get away with anymore. The costume people can't. The scenic art is not as forgiving. It has to be much more exacting and much more perfect. Then also the format of the frame changed as well, and now there's more frame to cover, and so that means more set-dressing, more scenic art, more decoration, more lighting, more background actors, more everything.

I don't know if people think about that as much either, as what has contributed to the growth of the crew, the equipment base. We could do with less. I think the crew could do with less. I think we could do with less everywhere, but there's things that are not in our favor. One is because of the relentlessness of our schedule; you almost need a couple of extra people on the crew and each department just to cover the intense schedule for the changes that need to be covered, whereas, before, the changes weren't there. Also, the crew members on the set are afraid not to have every single piece of equipment at their fingertips at all times. I really believe this comes from the pride of the crew. They don't want anyone waiting on them. As a producer, I say, "Guys, the stage is never more than ten miles from here. If we need something, we'll go get it."

But that's not acceptable to the crew, and I'm like, "Guys, I'm telling you, I'm the producer. I'm telling you, I'm willing to wait the hour that it's going to take to get that piece of equipment," and they're like, "Nope, we're not waiting. We're going to do a great job and you're not going to wait for us."

IRA BRENNER (CAMERA OPERATOR): I feel lucky that I've had a very wide range in experience. In documentaries you learn how to pitch in more than you do in the more structured environment of what Nester [Almendros] used to call fiction filmmaking, and I think there's a lot to be said for that, whereas if I was on a set and I did something that was, strictly speaking, something that the prop man should have cleaned up off the floor I would get chewed out.

Like, "Don't touch that. That's their job." I'm not taking away your job because I see a piece of gaffer tape sitting under the piano and nobody's around and I see it, so I get off the dolly and I pick it up. Is that such a horrible thing?

LELAND KRANE (CAMERA OPERATOR): Now there's this whole, like, cover-your-ass thing. Example: the first union show I operated on of any significance was a show called *Madam Secretary* [2014-2019], and the first day I got in there I was on a zoom lens— I was doing a rather complicated shot that had been rehearsed with the second team, the stand-ins—and when I framed up the end of my shot when we took a take, there were two booms in it, and so I just zoomed in, like, by reflex to try and save the shot.

And the DP came running over and said, "What the fuck are you doing?" and I said, "Well, I was trying to save the shot. There were booms in the shot. It's not usable."

And he goes, "No, no, no. If CBS sees you doing a weird zoom-in and getting a shot that's too tight, they're going to blame me and they're going to blame you, but if there are booms in the shot they're going to blame the boom operator, so you just leave the booms in the shot."

So now I'm in the world of, like, "Let's not make it good and save time" or whatever—"let's just cover our asses and do our jobs and then go home and make our money," and I get that too, but I've always been kind of torn between these two things because I feel like it's supposed to be a collaborative process.

TOD MAITLAND (SOUND MIXER): People were much more honest back then. I mean, I remember, like, DPs would scream at me from being a boom man and getting the mic in the shot—they would never do that anymore. They might get angry, but they're not going to scream at you like they did back then, and you just kind of took it. It was what it was. So the camera—there wasn't even a video assist; it was really up to the operator only. The operator would be the one that would scream at you, and then he would come yelling, and I was like, "Okay."

LELAND KRANE: *Blind Spot* [2015-2020]— that was one of the most toxic environments I've ever been in. It was just like, everyone was terrified of losing their jobs and the DP would yell at people and say, "You want your job tomorrow, you better do this." And I mean, it would be, like, really, really toxic to the point where everyone was terrified, and the quality of the work was not as good because people were not collaborating. There'd be sloppy stuff, because nobody wanted to take care of it, because it involved contacting another department, talking to somebody else, and nobody wanted to talk to anybody.

JERRY DECARLO: You can't fight every single battle. You have to choose the ones that are important, and you have to work around the system.

PETER ABRAHAM (CAMERA OPERATOR): For a bunch of years I was an emergency medical technician in addition to while I was shooting, and nothing rocks your head more than finishing a job where the director was screaming at the crew for some relatively minor reason, and then at two in the morning the next day you pick up a call and you're kneeling in broken glass next to a car that's flipped over on the side of the highway. Only one of those two situations is real life, and fortunately for all of us it's not the film set. People get hurt, and people get tired, and people pour their souls into these careers. It's only a horse race. It's only a baseball game. It's only *The View* [1997]. It's only a movie.

Dolly Grip	VINCE GUARRIELLO
Second Grip	STEVEN NALLAN
Grip	WILLIAM NALLAN
Property Master	JIMMY RAITT
Props	WILLIAM BISHOP ROBERT WILSON
Script Supervisor	RENEE BODNER
Camera Operators	RICHARD KRATINA DONALD SWEENEY
First Assistant Cameraman	HANK MULLER
Second Assistant Cameraman	GARY MULLER
Second Camera Operator	JON FAUER
Sound Mixer	JAMES J. SABAT
Sound Recordist	FRANK J. GRAZIADEI
Boom Man	LOUIS SABAT

RAY MURPHY
JEFF NAPARSTEK
JIM POWER
ERIC STEPPER
MITCH TOWSE
KEITH WALL
MICHAEL WEIGAND
WILLIAM WIGGINS
TRAVIS WRIGHT

Set Decoration Coordinator	JENNIFER MEISLE
Drapist	LEIGH KYLE
Property Master	KEVIN CURTIS LADSON
1st Assistant Props	ANTHONY BALDASARE
2nd Assistant Props	LAURA JEAN WEST

Gaffer DUSTY WALLACE
2nd Ass't Cameraman GARY MULLER
Sound Editor JANET DAVIDSON
Transportation RAYMOND HARTWICK
Electronic Music
Realised by SUZANNE CIANI
'LOCATIONS BY CINE MOBILE SYSTEMS'

script supervisor	Kay Chapin
camera operator	William Steiner
assistant cameramen	Hank Muller Gary Muller
second assistant cameraman	Bob Paone
stillman	Louis Goldman
sound mixer	James Sabat
boom men	Louis Sabat Frank Graziadei
art director	John Kasarda
set decorator	George DeTitta
scenic artists	Edward Garzero William Sohmer
prop master	Joseph Caracciolo, Jr.
props	John McDonnell
set dresser	David Weinman

Auditor SAM GOLDRICH

Matte Photography BILL TAYLOR, DENNIS GLOUNER
Camera Operator JIM CONTNER
Second Unit Photography JACK PRIESTLY
First Assistant Cameraman HANK MULLER

Sound Mixer JAMES T. SABAT
Rerecording Supervisor DICK VORISEK
Supervising Sound and Music Editor JACK FITZSTEPHENS
Sound Editors STAN BOCHNER MARC M. LAUB
HAL LEVINSOHN AL NAHMIAS RONALD ROOSE
Assistant Film Editors ANGELO CORRAO MARLAYNA FRANKLIN

Gaffer NORMAN LEIGH Key Grip KENNETH GOSS
Special Effects AL GRISWOLD Stunt Coordinator EVERETT CREACH
Property Master CONNIE BRINK Construction Chief WALTER WAY
Construction Grip GLEN ENGELS Carpenter CARLOS QUILES
Transportation Chief RAY HARTWICK

Second Unit Director	GEORGE FOLSEY JR.
Second Unit Cameraman	WARREN ROTHENBERGER
Second Unit Assistant Cameraman	JAMES HOVEY
Master Scenic Artist	GENE POWELL
Scenics	BRUNO ROBOTTI LESLIE SALTER-GRIFFIN WILLIAM CHAIKEN
Shop Craftsmen	RICHARD ALLEN HENRY BAUER BRUCE J. PAQUETTE RONALD PAQUETTE JR.
Construction Grips	PETER GRIPPALDI RICHARD GUINNESS RICHARD GUINNESS JR. MICHAEL GERRITY
Teamster Captain	TOM O'BRIEN
Teamsters	THOMAS REILLY CORNELIUS FORREST

Gretchen Rau	Set Decorator
Otto Jacoby	Set Builder
George Messaris	Set Builder
Elouise Meyer	Scenic Chargeperson
Steve Kerschoff	Prop Man
John Newby	Gaffer
Steve Baker	Key Grip
Crescenzo Notarile	Assistant Cameraman
Helen Butler	Costumer
Randy Coronato	Make-up/Hair
Jennifer Wyckoff	Production Secretary

Camera Operator	CRAIG DIBONA
Gaffer	MICHAEL J. DELANEY
Key Grip	BILLY MILLER
Property Master	BARBARA KASTNER
Assistant to Mr. De Niro	REBECCA WEYMOUTH
Production Office Coordinator	DENISE PINCKLEY
Location Manager	GINGER SLEDGE
Production Auditor	LYNDA "V" VAN DAMM
Construction Coordinator	MARTIN BERNSTEIN
Key Construction Grip	CARL PRINZI
Scenic Chargeman	JEFFREY L. GLAVE
Leadman	SCOTT ROSENSTOCK
Special Effects Coordinator	STEVE KIRSCHOFF
Stunt Coordinator	DOUG COLEMAN
Assistant Art Director	JEFFERSON SAGE

SOUND MIXER	JOHN BOLZ
SCRIPT SUPERVISOR	MARTHA PINSON
SET DECORATOR	RICHARD KANE
SET DRESSER	DEBORAH PRATE PANUCCIO
PROPERTY MASTER	WILLIAM REYNOLDS
SCENIC ARTIST	ROBERT TOPOL

Key Grip	Bob Ward
Set Grip	Ronald Burke
Construction Grip	Arne Olsen
Shop Craftsman	Tony Zappia

Glossary

2K LIGHTS 2,000-kilowatt tungsten lamps, often called blondes because of their yellow light.

10K LIGHTS 10,000-kilowatt tungsten lamps, often used to simulate daylight.

THE ABBY The penultimate shot of the night, named after Abby Singer, who was a production manager and assistant director who would say "this and one more." This shot is announced as a time-saving measure so people can start the packing-up process.

ADR Automated dialogue replacement. This means replacing actors' unusable dialogue with usable audio takes in postproduction.

APPLEBOX A wooden box used by every department for temporarily supporting or propping anything up. There are flatter ones called "pancakes."

BACK TO ONE or **BACK TO FIRST MARKS** Resetting a scene's actors or props from the beginning to do another take.

BLOCK SHOOTING Shooting all the day's scenes which take place on one side of the set to avoid using up time to relight that side.

BLOCKING Designating the position of each actor in a scene.

BOOM MICROPHONES or **BOOMS** Microphones at the ends of long poles placed over the set to pick up audio from actors.

BRUTE LIGHTS Large-scale carbon arc lamps used to simulate daylight. Today's brutes are far more energy-efficient and mean a few different kinds of lights.

CALL SHEET An information sheet with the next shooting day's schedule and call time, listed along with all the locations, props, costumes, etc.

CALL TIME The day's start time. Call times can be staggered as people are needed according to the day's scenes.

CANDY GLASS or **SUGAR GLASS** Fake, breakaway glass made of sugar. When I first started I saw someone bite into it.

COMPANY MOVE Packing up trucks and moving to another location, as opposed to pushing carts to a close location.

COOKIES and **CUTTERS** Shapes put in front of the lights to mold and bend the light.

DAILIES Screening of the previous day's filming when it comes back from the lab after processing.

EL Short for elevated train tracks.

EYELINES Where the actors eyes are looking in relation to the camera position.

FILL LIGHT One of three sources of light in a traditional three-point lighting set-up, generally placed to one side of the subject being filmed or photographed, opposite the back light and approximately perpendicular to the key light. The fill light is often used to reduce the contrast of a scene in order to match on the recording media the level of detail typically seen by the human eye in real-world lighting conditions.

FLAG A piece of black fabric on a frame used by the grip department to block light.

FLASH POT A container that holds pyrotechnic powder to do explosions.

FRATURDAYS When the Friday night shooting turns into Saturday morning.

FRENCH HOURS Shooting through lunch, but food is served all day instead.

GAG Any kind of special-effects trick is referred to in the Business as a gag.

GOBO ARM A metal extension pole for a c-stand (Century stand), which is a flexible, bent-arm stand. A gobo arm on a c-stand is usually used to hold a light or fabric to block light.

THE GRID, the ceiling structure built from I-beams or structural truss generally used to rig lights and walls.

HERO or **HERO PROP** An important prop that is featured on screen. It is often a plot point.

HONEYWAGON A bathroom trailer for the crew. In my experience in New York, there are usually about four or so stalls divided up as "Lucys" and "Desis."

KIT The tools needed by a department head, rented to the production.

LAST LOOKS The last moment hair and makeup get to touch the actors before cameras start rolling.

LOCK UP Securing the street so civilians don't walk through the shot.

LOOPED DIALOGUE see: ADR, automated dialogue replacement

MAGAZINE Within the camera, the unexposed film is housed in a totally dark chamber called the forward magazine. One or both edges of the film are lined with regularly-spaced perforations, or sprocket holes. Sprocket-driven gears grip these perforations, feeding the film into an enclosed exposure chamber. A mechanical claw pulls the film into position behind the shutter, locking the film momentarily in place. The shutter opens, exposes an image onto the film, and closes. Then the claw, with an automatic pulldown movement, advances the film for the next exposure

THE MARTINI The last shot of the night. It's based on Jack Priestley's line, "This next shot is through a glass." Like the Abby, it's used to tell the crew to pack up gear. Back in the day, it used to literally mean to pour drinks.

MARKS Designated spots on the set where actors need to stand or move to during a scene.

MATTE PAINTINGS Artwork executed on a relatively small scale (typically the size of a painting you might hang above your fireplace) and designed to be shot as a separate component to be composited with other elements (usually full scale) filmed elsewhere. Typically, matte paintings are used to create or enlarge an illusion.

MEAL PENALTIES A contractual obligation whereby the producer is financially motivated to provide a timely meal break after six hours or incur penalties, which vary from contract to contract.

PICTURE CARS Any vehicles that are in the production.

NAGRA The first portable sound recorder for capturing live sound on location.

NET A type of light-modifier used to reduce the intensity of light without altering its color temperature.

NINE LIGHTER A 9000-watt, 9 Light Par Bank for lighting large areas. The high-intensity output of this fixture permits a minimum number of lights for the required lighting level. It is for both television and film set use. A choice of bulbs is available for boosting the light output, with either 3200° or 5000° Kelvin color temperatures.

ON THE DAY An expression that indicates that whatever we're talking about will happen when we're actually rolling. You can even use this expression right before we shoot.

ONE-LINER An advanced schedule for the rest of the shoot in short single-line descriptions of the scenes.

OVER Short for an "over the shoulder" shot. Most commonly used in scenes with dialogue.

PIGEON BOX Open, cubby-like electrical distribution boxes on old film/TV stages, often carrying exposed AC and DC power.

PILOT TONE A single frequency transmitted over a communications system for reference purposes.

PLATE During the time we're discussing, a reel of motion-picture film which serves as the background image when a composite of any kind is being assembled. Occasionally, a still photograph in the form a transparency is made to serve the same purpose.

RABBI An older colleague who identifies someone's talent and guides them into the next phase of their career.

RAIN COVER or **COVER SET** Another set that's ready to shoot in case of inclement weather—or, in some cases, sunshine, for continuity or lighting reasons.

ROLLING A term that originated when it was common to run film through a camera. It means less today because we roll all the time, since data space is cheap and reusable.

RUN AND GUN Shooting fast in the streets, sometimes without permits.

SHAPING THE HALL or **THE SHAPE-UP** or **SHAPING** Looking for work (longshoreman's term—literally showing up to show you are in shape). Before most last-minute replacement work was routed through the union hall, men would show up to the theater with their tools, shaping the load in or out to look for work. "Shape the hall" means to go to the replacement room to wait for possible work.

SHOT, THE Whatever's inside the camera's frame. Sometimes interchangeable with "the scene."

SHOW, THE The production we're shooting or talking about shooting.

SHOW CARDS Hand-painted signs that were everywhere, on all businesses, before everything became computer-generated.

SIDES The day's scenes printed and distributed to the cast and crew at the start of the day.

SINGLE A shot that has only one person in the frame.

SQUIB A small pyrotechnic commonly used to simulate bullet impacts on actors or objects such as walls or cars. Often, squibs are coupled with fake-blood packets on actors to simulate bulletholes.

STEADICAM A handheld camera stabilizer mount that is rigged to the operator's upper body.

TURNAROUND The time between the wrap time and the following day's call time.

WILD WALLS Removable sections of the set, usually flats that allow you to get dolly tracks and large equipment in and out of a room.

UNIT PRODUCTION MANAGER (UPM) The producer in charge of the budget. The UPM is one of the most powerful people on the set because they are holding all the money. Nothing gets done without them signing off on it.

Roll Credits

In October of 2020, I set out on an ambitious two-year plan to interview and compose the first draft of this book you're holding. Being a terrible judge of time, space, and especially relativity it took me five years and an enormous amount of help. It'll be too late when I realize I omitted several key people who have helped me along the way. My apologies, but Christina rightfully says I gotta cut it off.

Thank you: Hope Ardizonne, Marisa Baldassaro, Matthew Balzarini, Alissa Bennett, Steven Bartilucci, Bob Baker, Shari Besanceney, Sam Bieber, Jenn Blum, Alex Brock, Sal Calcaterra, Jeff Crye, Jon Crystal, James Ellis Deakins, Izzy Decauwert, Mike Derrico, Heather Drain, Lena Dunham, Brian Durham, Jovita Dominguez at DGA, Dayson Engels, Kenny Engels, Ryan Freeborn, Peter Fonda, Naomi Fry, Ben Fulkman, Matthew Gamiello, Deirdre Kane, Lauren Kellett, Alex Kuciw, Matthew Danger Lippman, Christina Lynch, Kevin McCarthy, Ryan McGrath, Oliver Milman, Shannon Muchow at MGM, Nick Newman, Alex Nunez, Layton Price, Angelo Proscia, Joe Quirk, Joe Reidy, Bob Rosen, Michael Saccio, Sophie Saccio, Adrian Smith, Mark Sonderskov, John Torrani, Sharon White, the admins at Crew Stories Facebook Page, everyone at *Law and Order SVU* who helped me out in ways big and small, the union leaders who aren't compromised, and the credited and uncredited film workers who came before me.

Great interviews were done with Peter Allburn, Ben Bryant, Katie Bihr, Christine Domaniecki, Diane Rich, Monona Rossol, Mark Sonderskov, and Kjeld Tidemand who all did extraordinary and candid interviews, but the chapters they were featured in didn't really fit anywhere. I'm holding hope for a future expanded edition.

Special thanks to Gary Muller who became my New York movie rabbi, every conversation we had was film school. Marlene Arvan who was incredibly funny and generous with her time, stories, and contacts, Michael Goldsmith who gave me valuable advice at the outset when I was aimlessly trying to figure out what the hell to do with this thing, Jimmy Archer for loaning me the museum quality archive of materials he's held on to, (and for my daily ball busting)—a true friend since the day we met.

My continual gratitude to the phenomenal staff at The Academy of Motion Pictures Margaret Herrick Library: VP Matt Severson and his marvelous team, Elizabeth Cathcart, John Damer, Meg de Waal, Caroline Jorgenson, Genevieve Maxwell, and Elizabeth Youle. The week I spent there was like dying and going to cinema heaven.

Jim St. Clair, Jamie Covington, Dan Davis, and Feliks Parnell—It was an unbelievable stroke of luck that I had four of the best bosses a person could have during the writing and assembling of this book. Great friends who have taught me more than I could possibly absorb.

My crew in the scenery trenches, who have always had my back. We've been through a lot together. I'm the luckiest guy in the business. The A-Team: Millree Hughes, Aaqil Ka, Zenab Ka, Dan Kotler, Joe Kotler, Ajamu Kojo, Lauryn Pepe, Jake Scharbach, Nick Taucher, and Jeff Tedlis.

Everyone at Feral House—Jessica Parfrey, without whom we wouldn't be here, and Bloo Van Alst who passed me an important note I needed to hear during the final hours.

I cannot give enough credit to my editor, co-conspirator, confidant, hard truth-teller and close friend Christina Ward. She will deny this, but she sculpted what you are holding here out of a dense block of cinematic mush, into what I think is a pretty damn good book.

One tough week or so during the delivery of the first draft I lost my grandmother Shirley Nirenberg, and two of my closest friends Robert Catalfamo, and John Bjerklie—always with me, everyday.

Mom, Dad, Mary and Scott—I hope it's not too boring. Love you.

Of course, the highest thank you goes to my talented and beautiful wife Jessie who has patiently endured these stories over and over again and is kind enough to even laugh at them from time to time. Her patience with my antics, and low-grade anxiety was tested over the five years it took to get us here. Despite the stress of her own career. Can you imagine how intimidating it is to be an author married to the copy chief of *The New Yorker*? It's done, mami!

Oliver and Vivian, if you do end up in this wonderfully rotten business, run the other way. It's going to be done by robots when you're my age. The producers and accountants already take firmware updates. But if you must do this, insist on having fun at it. Love you!

• • •

Editor's Thanks: It takes a cast of thousands to create a book like *Cinematic Immunity*. Personal thanks to Christopher Roth for diligent copyediting and Bill Smith of designSimple for the beautiful design.

Thank you to Larry Karaszewski who kindly made a few significant introductions, Dennis Bartok for your incredible network, Heather Buckley of Black Mansions Productions for *reasons*, Alex Cox and Tod Davies for their invaluable support and kind words, and Sean Baker for the pre-order.

Columbia Pictures Industries, Inc.

"ISHTAR"
Columbia Pictures
110 West 57th Street
New York, NY 10019
(212) 399-1818
Astoria: (718) 706-5850

FINAL STAFF & CREW LIST

POSITION	NAME/ADDRESS	TEL
PRODUCTION		
PRODUCER	WARREN BEATTY c/o Columbia Pictures 110 West 57th Street New York, NY 10019	(212
WRITER/DIRECTOR	ELAINE MAY c/o Columbia Pictures 110 West 57th Street New York, NY 10019	(212
ASSOCIATE PRODUCER	DAVID L. MACLEOD c/o Columbia Pictures 110 West 57th Street New York, NY 10019	(212
ASSOCIATE PRODUCER	NIGEL WOOLL 18 Granard Avenue London SW15 England	(011 In N (212
PRODUCTION MANAGER	G. MAC BROWN 139 Alta Avenue Yonkers, NY 10705	(914
1ST ASSISTANT DIRECTOR	DON FRENCH 8911 Purgen Am Herrenberg 14 West Germany	(011 In N (212
1ST ASSISTANT DIRECTOR/NY	BOB GIROLAMI 28 Elm Street Valhalla, NY 10595	(914) (914)

ASST. DIR: KEN ORNSTEIN/DANNY IRON
CREW CALL: 5PM/5:30PM

CALL SHEET

SET DESCRIPTION	SCENE	CHARACTERS	PGS	LOCATION
INT. JOSH'S LOFT-N	96	1,3	3/8	AHARI Residence 83 Grand Street @Greene
INT. JOSH'S LOFT-N	97	1,3	2 4/8	N.Y.C. #431-1636

CAST	CHARACTER	PICK UP	REHEARSAL	M/U	SET
TOM HANKS	1-Josh	P/U @4:15PM	5PM	5:30PM	7PM
JARED RUSHTON	2-Billy	HOLD			
ELIZABETH PERKINS	3-Susan	P/U @4:30PM	5PM	5:30PM	7PM
DAVID MOSCOW	4-Young Josh	HOLD			

STANDINS AND EXTRAS
(2) Standins (#1,#3) Report LOC @5:30PM

PROPS AND SPECIAL INSTRUCTIONS
Board Game, Soda Can, Model Spaceship & Trampoline.
HAIR: Susan's hair comes loose.
SET: Inflatable Palm Trees & Flamingos Macaroni & Cheese, Pinball Machine, Coke Machine & Spaceship Fan.
DIRECTOR: HAVE A HAPPY BIRTHDAY!

DIRECTOR:	P/U @4:30PM	SOUND:	5:30PM	SCENIC:	5:30PM
ASST. DIR:	4:30PM	GRIPS:	5:30PM	MAKEUP:	5:30PM
SCRIPT:	5PM	PROPS:	5PM/5:30PM	HAIR:	5:30PM
CAMERA:	5PM/5:30PM	ELECT:	5:30PM	WARDROBE:	5:30PM
STILLS:	6PM	CARPS:	5:30PM	COFFEE &:	(70) @5PM
P.A.:	4:30PM	SET DRESSERS:	5:30PM	LUNCH:	(70) @11PM

ADVANCE SCHEDULE
FRIDAY, OCTOBER 16, 1987:
COMPLETE ABOVE IF NECESSARY, PLUS:
INT. JOSH'S LOFT/BEDROOM-N SC:98 (1,3) 6/8
INT. JOSH'S LOFT/BEDROOM-N SC:99 (1,3) 7/8
INT. JOSH'S LOFT-N SC:138 (-) 1/8
INT. JOSH'S LOFT-N SC:152 (1) 1/8
MONDAY, OCTOBER 19, 1987:
EXT. SEAPOINT PARK-D SC:182-184 (1,3,49)
TUESDAY, OCTOBER 20, 1987:
EXT. N.Y.C. LIBRARY STEPS-D SC:86pt. (1,2)
EXT. VIDEO PLACE-D SC:A52 (1,2)
EXT. KWIK STOP-D SC:161 (1,11,58) 3/8
EXT/INT. BUS/BRIDGE-D SC:170pt (2ND UNIT SHOT)
EXT. G.W. JUNIOR HIGH-D SC:160 (1,68) 2/8
EXT. BASEBALL FIELD-DUSK SC:162 (1) 3/8

TRANSPORTATION
P/U E. Perkins @4:30PM
P/U T. Hanks @4:15PM
P/U B. Sonnenfeld @4:30PM
P/U P. Marshall @4:30PM
All Other Transport As Per Pete

℅ Empire Hotel
44 West 63 Street
New York, NY 10023
(212) 245-7740

Toronto Production Office
Manitoulin Films
1177 Leslie Street
Don Mills, Ontario M3C 2J

"MOONSTRUCK"

CREW LIST - NEW YORK

PRODUCER/DIRECTOR	Norman Jewison
PRODUCER	Patrick Palmer
WRITER	John Patrick Shanle
ASSOCIATE PRODUCER	Bonnie Palef-Woolf 167 Glen Manor Way Thornhill, Ont. L4J
UNIT PRODUCTION MANAGER	Roger Paradiso
LOCATION MANAGER	Steve Schottenfeld 15 E. 94th St. New York, NY
ASST. LOCATION MANAGER	Jeff Flach 229 E. 67th St., #21 New York, NY
LOCATION ASSISTANT	Michael Fruhling 435 E. 76th Street New York, NY 10021
1ST ASSISTANT DIRECTOR	Lewis Gould 25 West 68th Street New York, NY 10023

"COOKIE"
LOCATION LIST

REVI

SCENE #S	LOCATION
STORE #1	Freedom Boutique 4701 Greenpoint Ave Queens
G/STAIRCASE	4705 Greenpoint Sunnyside, Queens
ENTRANCE	Mike's Place 4704 Queens Blvd Sunnyside, Queens
RTMENT 45-47,116,	Blackstar Garage 100 First Street Brooklyn, NY
UFACTURING 1,83-86	213 West 35th Street 12th Floor New York, NY
UFACTURING-TOR	213 West 35th Street 12th Floor New York, NY
GARAGE	100 First Str

THE THOMAS CROWN AFFAIR

CREW LIST
as of November 3, 1998-Green

NY Production Office
443 Greenwich Street
5th Fl.
New York, NY 10013
212/965-1883
212/625-9005 fax

CA United Artists Pictures Inc.
2500 Broadway Street
Santa Monica, CA 90404
310/449-3000
310/449-3078 fax

Yonkers Production Office
Art Department/Shop
291 Tuckahoe Road
Yonkers, NY 10710
914/395-3200
914/395-3771 fax

Yonkers Stage
285 Tuckahoe Road
Yonkers, NY 10710
914/395-3717
914/395-3718

Casting
McCorkle Casting
264 West 40th Street
9th Fl
New York, NY 10018
212/840-0992
212/840-1028 fax

Editing Facility
Magno Sound
729 7th Ave, 15th Fl.,Rm1507
(bet. 48th & 49th)
New York, NY 10019
212/302-2505 ext 1574
212/302-0025 fax
212/819-1282 fax

Extras Casting
Sylvia Fay Casting
71 Park Avenue
New York, NY 10016
212/889-2626
212/684-5939 fax

Trailer #1
Ken Nelson, Peter Betulis, Nicole DuCharme 914/395-3719 914/395-3723 fax

Trailer #2
Buddy McBride 914/395-3725
Ronnie Plant 914/395-3724

Trailer #3
Joe Garzero 914/395-0073
Adam Levine 914/395-3273

Wardrobe Space
United Artists Pictures Inc.
443 Greenwich Street
5th Fl.
New York, NY 10013
212/965-1883
212/625-9005 fax

917/716-7231- 1st Unit Cel Phone
917/301-8150- 1st Unit Fax
917/887-5676- Prod. Cel Phone
917/716-7229- 2nd Unit Cel Phone

DIRECTOR
Agent

John McTiernan
c/o CAA
9830 Wilshire Boulevard
Beverly Hills, CA 90212

310/288-4545-o
310/288-4800-f

DOMINION PRODUCTIONS, INC.

212-245-7740

℅ Empire Hotel
44 West 63 Street
New York, NY 10023
(212) 245-7740

Laird Inter
9336 W. W
Culver C
(213)

Empire 12th
971-0770
West 82
West 38

"MOONSTRUCK"

DIRECTOR:	NORMAN JEWISON
PRODUCERS:	PATRICK PALMER NORMAN JEWISON
ASSOCIATE PRODUCER:	BONNIE PALEF-WOOLF
PRODUCTION MANAGER:	ROGER PARADISO
ASSISTANT DIRECTOR:	LEWIS GOULD

SHOOTING SCHEDULE

November 21,

"JERK

1	EXT POLICE "SUSPECTS" EN				
2	INT POLICE WORZIC INTER				
A3	EXT QUEEN ESTABLISHING				
3	EXT JOHNN KAMAL MEETS				
4, 6	INT JOHNN JOHNNY TAKE				
A6	INT JOHNN JOHNNY'S SIDI				
5	INT WEIR "BUPER" CALL				
7, 7A, 7B	EXT JOHNN MRS. WEIR SPA				
7C, 8	INT JOHNN MRS. B SCREA				
9	INT JOHNN "WHAT'S UP F				
X10	INT JOHNN BOYS' SIDE OF				
10	INT HOSPIT "SOL" CALLS S				
11, 13	INT JOHNN MRS. B SAYS				
12	EXT CONST FOREMAN FIR				
14	EXT BURGE FAST FOOD FA				
X16	INT JOHNN BOY'S SIDE OF				
16	EXT TRUMP ESTABLISHING	D2			
16A	INT TRUMP'S OFFICE "DIRUCCI" CALLS DONALD TRUMP	D2	DAY	1 3/8 pgs	1D, 40
15	INT JOHNNY B'S APARTMENT MRS. B LEAVES/LOOKIN' FOR A JOB	D2	DAY	1 pgs	1, 2, 7
16B	INT JOHNNY B'S APARTMENT KAMAL CALLS EWING	D2	DAY	2/8 pgs	1, 2
16C	EXT MADISON SQUARE GARDEN ESTABLISHING	D2	DAY	1/8 pgs	
16D	INT MADISON SQ. LOCKER ROOM "EGYPTIAN" CALLS PATRICK EWING	D2	DAY	1 3/8 pgs	41
X16D	INT JOHNNY B'S APARTMENT BOYS' SIDE OF CALL TO EWING	D2	DAY	1 3/8 pgs	1, 2
17	INT JOHNNY B'S APARTMENT TIME TO HIT THE BAR	D2	DAY	2/8 pgs	1, 2
18	EXT JOHNNY B'S STREET BOYS WALK OUT OF HOUSE	D2	DAY	4/8 pgs	1, 2, 11
19	EXT JOHNNY B'S STREET/BUSINESS BOYS WALK TO THE BAR	D2	DAY	1/8 pgs	1, 2

"BULL... REET" - 7/11/86 page 2

DAY/DATE	SCENE	PGS	SET DESCRIPTION	CAST	EXTRAS/STANDINS	PROPS/VEHICLES/EFX/NOTES
DAY #12 & DAY #13 TUESDAY & WEDNESDAY 7/22/86 & 7/23/86 LOCATION: 65 Liberty Street Manhattan, New York	9	5-6/8	INT/D SENATE HEARING ROOM Byington, Salwen question Emily - she refuses records. Birthday party. CD: 3	1 EMILY 3 SALWEN 5 ALAN DWORKIN 7 SENATOR BYINGTON 11 A SENATOR 13 RANDLOPH SLOTE 37 MRS. BYINGTON 38 (2) CHILDREN 42 WOMAN (Liberty Watch)	2 standins, plus 2 from b.g. (for the day) 75 b.g.: 3 senators 10 aides (8 M, 2F) 1 M stenographer 61 audience (20 press - 16 reporters, 4 photographers) (10 lawyers) (10 defendants, including 4 b.g. from Sc. 7) (21 spectators - 2F w/secretary change)	PROPS: microphone Salwen's notes gavel briefcases photographer's equipment press materials birthday cake and candles EFX: smoke GRIP: tulip crane
	34	1/8	INT/D SENATE STAIRWAY Aide #1 gives Salwen file of photos of Emily. CD: 8	3 SALWEN 10 AIDE #1		PROPS: file folder photos of Emily
LOCATION: T.B.D.	27pt	1-4/8	INT/D T.V. STUDIO Byington interviewed on T.V. CD: 6	7 BYINGTON 26 INTERVIEWER		NOTE: To be shot on video.
END OF DAYS TWELVE AND THIRTEEN		7-3/8	total pages			

SHOOTING SCHEDULE

		SCENES-D/N	CHARACTERS	REQUIREM
		Sc. 57- DAY 1-4/8	Lyle Chuck Consulate Dark Skinned Man	Art Dept/SFX: Rig breakaway wal Props: souvenirs, forms
		Sc. 153 - DAY 3/8	Jim Harrison	Crowd: TBD Props: Harrison's gun/ho Radio equipment Technical Advisor
DAY 51	Medina. 114/133 Monitoring Chuck/Lyle in desert. STUDIO - STAGE H.	Scs. 81 - DAY 86 114 133 2-6/8	Jim Harrison CIA Agent #1-Glenn CIA Agent #2-Jeff (for scs 81,86) Jim Harrison CIA Agent #1-Glen CIA Agent #3-Rob (for scs 114,133)	Props: CIA Agents' guns/h Maps, speakers, cam Bandages Art Dept Electronic map and instruments. Tech. Advisor: Su Wardrobe: Slipper
WEDNESDAY JANUARY 22 DAY 52	INT. ISHTAR HOLIDAY INN Chuck pays porter / Maid "sterilizes" Harrison's appearance. STUDIO - STAGE H	Scs. 61 62 DAY/DUSK 1-4/8	Chuck Jim Harrison Maid Porter	Props: Chuck's luggage, cleaning materials Harrison's gun/ho Maid's "sterilized
(TO COMPLETE DURING STUDIO SHOOT. DATE: TBD)	EXT. BENI MALLAL/BEHIND BUILDING Close Shot - Lyle coverage STUDIO - STAGE H	Sc. 109 pt.- D	Lyle Shirra	Crowd: TBD Props: Beads